A NORTON CRITICAL EDITION

George Eliot

THE MILL ON THE FLOSS

AN AUTHORITATIVE TEXT

BACKGROUNDS AND

CONTEMPORARY REACTIONS

CRITICISM

Edited by

CAROL T. CHRIST

SMITH COLLEGE

W • W • NORTON & COMPANY • *New York* • *London*

This title is printed on permanent paper containing
30 percent post-consumer waste recycled fiber.

First Edition

The text of this book is composed in Electra
with the display set in Bernhard Modern.
Composition by PennSet, Inc.
Manufacturing by Courier.
Book design by A. Krass.

Library of Congress Cataloging-in-Publication Data
Eliot, George 1819–1880.
The mill on the Floss : an authoritatiave text, backgrounds and contemporary reactions, criticism / George Eliot; edited by Carol T. Christ.
p. cm.—(A Norton critical edition)
Includes bibliographical references.
1. Eliot, George, 1819–1880. Mill on the Floss. I. Christ, Carol T.
PR4661.A1 1994
823′.8—dc20 93-13151

ISBN 0-393-96332-2 (pa)

W. W. Norton & Company, Inc., 500 Fifth Avenue, New York, N.Y. 10110
W. W. Norton & Company Ltd., Castle House. 75/76 Wells Street,
London W1T 3QT

0

Contents

Preface

The Mill on the Floss was begun in 1859 and finished and sent to the publisher on March 21, 1860. It was published April 4, 1860 in three volumes. It went through four editions during George Eliot's life (two in 1860, a third in 1862, and a fourth in 1878).

Following Gordon Haight's example in the Clarendon *Mill on the Floss*, I have prepared this text from a stereotyped edition of the novel, which was set from the plates of the 1862 edition, the last for which Eliot made revisions. For a full account of the novel's textual history, see the Clarendon edition (Oxford University Press, 1980), edited by Gordon S. Haight. George Eliot's original manuscript is in the British Library.

I wish to thank my research assistants, William Cohen and Laura Green, for their help with this project. In preparing the notes, I am also indebted to the past editors of the novel—Gordon Haight, A. S. Byatt, who prepared the Penguin edition, and Sally Shuttleworth, who has prepared an edition for Routledge.

The Text of
THE MILL ON THE FLOSS

THE

MILL ON THE FLOSS

BY

GEORGE ELIOT

In their death they were not divided

STEREOTYPED EDITION

WILLIAM BLACKWOOD AND SONS
EDINBURGH AND LONDON

The Contents of *The Mill on the Floss*

Book First
Boy and Girl

Book Second
School-Time

Book Third

The Downfall

Book Fourth

The Valley of Humiliation

Book Fifth

Wheat and Tares

Book Sixth

The Great Temptation

Book Seventh

The Final Rescue

Book First

BOY AND GIRL

Chapter I

Outside Dorlcote Mill

A wide plain, where the broadening Floss hurries on between its green banks to the sea, and the loving tide, rushing to meet it, checks its passage with an impetuous embrace. On this mighty tide the black ships—laden with the fresh-scented fir-planks, with rounded sacks of oil-bearing seed, or with the dark glitter of coal—are borne along to the town of St Ogg's, which shows its aged, fluted red roofs and the broad gables of its wharves between the low wooded hill and the river brink, tinging the water with a soft purple hue under the transient glance of this February sun. Far away on each hand stretch the rich pastures, and the patches of dark earth, made ready for the seed of broad-leaved green crops, or touched already with the tint of the tender-bladed autumn-sown corn.[1] There is a remnant still of the last year's golden clusters of beehive ricks rising at intervals beyond the hedgerows; and everywhere the hedgerows are studded with trees: the distant ships seem to be lifting their masts and stretching their red-brown sails close among the branches of the spreading ash. Just by the red-roofed town the tributary Ripple flows with a lively current into the Floss. How lovely the little river is, with its dark, changing wavelets! It seems to me like a living companion while I wander along the bank and listen to its low placid voice, as to the voice of one who is deaf and loving. I remember those large dipping willows. I remember the stone bridge.

And this is Dorlcote Mill. I must stand a minute or two here on the bridge and look at it, though the clouds are threatening, and it is far on in the afternoon. Even in this leafless time of departing February it is pleasant to look at—perhaps the chill damp season adds a charm to the trimly-kept, comfortable dwelling-house, as old as the elms and chestnuts that shelter it from the northern blast. The stream is brimful now, and

1. Wheat.

lies high in this little withy[2] plantation, and half drowns the grassy fringe of the croft[3] in front of the house. As I look at the full stream, the vivid grass, the delicate bright-green powder softening the outline of the great trunks and branches that gleam from under the bare purple boughs, I am in love with moistness, and envy the white ducks that are dipping their heads far into the water here among the withes, unmindful of the awkward appearance they make in the drier world above.

The rush of the water, and the booming of the mill, bring a dreamy deafness, which seems to heighten the peacefulness of the scene. They are like a great curtain of sound, shutting one out from the world beyond. And now there is the thunder of the huge covered waggon coming home with sacks of grain. That honest waggoner is thinking of his dinner, getting sadly dry in the oven at this late hour; but he will not touch it till he has fed his horses,—the strong, submissive, meek-eyed beasts, who, I fancy, are looking mild reproach at him from between their blinkers, that he should crack his whip at them in that awful manner as if they needed that hint! See how they stretch their shoulders up the slope towards the bridge, with all the more energy because they are so near home. Look at their grand shaggy feet that seem to grasp the firm earth, at the patient strength of their necks, bowed under the heavy collar, at the mighty muscles of their struggling haunches! I should like well to hear them neigh over their hardly-earned feed of corn, and see them, with their moist necks freed from the harness, dipping their eager nostrils into the muddy pond. Now they are on the bridge, and down they go again at a swifter pace, and the arch of the covered waggon disappears at the turning behind the trees.

Now I can turn my eyes towards the mill again, and watch the unresting wheel sending out its diamond jets of water. That little girl is watching it too: she has been standing on just the same spot at the edge of the water ever since I paused on the bridge. And that queer white cur with the brown ear seems to be leaping and barking in ineffectual remonstrance with the wheel; perhaps he is jealous, because his playfellow in the beaver bonnet is so rapt in its movement. It is time the little playfellow went in, I think; and there is a very bright fire to tempt her: the red light shines out under the deepening grey of the sky. It is time, too, for me to leave off resting my arms on the cold stone of this bridge. . . .

Ah, my arms are really benumbed. I have been pressing my elbows on the arms of my chair, and dreaming that I was standing on the bridge in front of Dorlcote Mill, as it looked one February afternoon many years ago. Before I dozed off, I was going to tell you what Mr and Mrs Tulliver were talking about, as they sat by the bright fire in the left-hand parlour, on that very afternoon I have been dreaming of.

2. Willow.
3. A patch of farmland adjacent to a house or cottage.

Chapter II

Mr Tulliver, of Dorlcote Mill, Declares His Resolution About Tom

"What I want, you know," said Mr Tulliver—"what I want is to give Tom a good eddication; an eddication as'll be a bread to him.[1] That was what I was thinking of when I gave notice for him to leave the academy at Ladyday. I mean to put him to a downright good school at Midsummer.[2] The two years at th' academy 'ud ha' done well enough, if I'd meant to make a miller and farmer of him, for he's had a fine sight more schoolin' nor *I* ever got: all the learnin' *my* father ever paid for was a bit o' birch at one end and the alphabet at th' other. But I should like Tom to be a bit of a scholard, so as he might be up to the tricks o' these fellows as talk fine and write with a flourish. It 'ud be a help to me wi' these lawsuits, and arbitrations, and things. I wouldn't make a downright lawyer o' the lad—I should be sorry for him to be a raskill—but a sort o' engineer, or a surveyor, or an auctioneer and vallyer,[3] like Riley, or one o' them smartish businesses as are all profits and no outlay, only for a big watch-chain and a high stool.[4] They're pretty nigh all one, and they're not far off being even wi' the law, *I* believe; for Riley looks Lawyer Wakem i' the face as hard as one cat looks another. *He's* none frightened at him."

Mr Tulliver was speaking to his wife, a blond comely woman in a fan-shaped cap (I am afraid to think how long it is since fan-shaped caps were worn—they must be so near coming in again. At that time, when Mrs Tulliver was nearly forty, they were new at St Ogg's, and considered sweet things).

"Well, Mr Tulliver, you know best: *I've* no objections. But hadn't I better kill a couple o'fowl and have th' aunts and uncles to dinner next week, so as you may hear what sister Glegg and sister Pullet have got to say about it? There's a couple o' fowl *wants* killing!"

"You may kill every fowl i' the yard, if you like, Bessy; but I shall ask neither aunt nor uncle what I'm to do wi' my own lad," said Mr Tulliver, defiantly.

"Dear heart!" said Mrs Tulliver, shocked at this sanguinary rhetoric, "how can you talk so, Mr Tulliver? But it's your way to speak disrespectful o' my family; and sister Glegg throws all the blame upo' me, though I'm sure I'm as innocent as the babe unborn. For nobody's ever heard *me* say as it wasn't lucky for my children to have aunts and uncles as

1. There was no standardized system of secondary education at the time at which the novel is set. By removing Tom from his "academy" (day school) and sending him to a private boarding school, Mr Tulliver hopes to better his son's prospects.
2. Midsummer: June 24; Ladyday: March 25, the Feast of the Annunciation.
3. Valuer, appraiser.
4. Business men in the nineteenth century commonly sat on high stools in their offices in order to consult their ledgers.

can live independent. Howiver, if Tom's to go to a new school, I should like him to go where I can wash him and mend him; else he might as well have calico as linen, for they'd be one as yallow as th' other before they'd been washed half-a-dozen times. And then, when the box is goin' backards and forrards, I could send the lad a cake, or a pork-pie, or an apple; for he can do with an extry bit, bless him, whether they stint him at the meals or no. My children can eat as much victuals as most, thank God."

"Well, well, we won't send him out o' reach o' the carrier's cart, if other things fit in," said Mr Tulliver. "But you mustn't put a spoke i' the wheel about the washin', if we can't get a school near enough. That's the fault I have to find wi' you, Bessy; if you see a stick i' the road, you're allays thinkin' you can't step over it. You'd want me not to hire a good waggoner, 'cause he'd got a mole on his face."

"Dear heart!" said Mrs Tulliver, in mild surprise, "when did I iver make objections to a man because he'd got a mole on his face? I'm sure I'm rether fond o' the moles; for my brother, as is dead an' gone, had a mole on his brow. But I can't remember your iver offering to hire a waggoner with a mole, Mr Tulliver. There was John Gibbs hadn't a mole on his face no more nor you have, an' I was all for having you hire *him*; an' so you did hire him, an' if he hadn't died o' th' inflammation, as we paid Dr Turnbull for attending him, he'd very like ha' been driving the waggon now. He might have a mole somewhere out o' sight, but how was I to know that, Mr Tulliver?"

"No, no, Bessy; I didn't mean justly the mole; I meant it to stand for summat else; but niver mind—it's puzzling work, talking is. What I'm thinking on, is how to find the right sort o' school to send Tom to, for I might be ta'en in again, as I've been wi' th' academy. I'll have nothing to do wi' a 'cademy again: whativer school I send Tom to, it shan't be a 'cademy; it shall be a place where the lads spend their time i' summat else besides blacking the family's shoes, and getting up the potatoes. It's an uncommon puzzling thing to know what school to pick."

Mr Tulliver paused a minute or two, and dived with both hands into his breeches pockets as if he hoped to find some suggestion there. Apparently he was not disappointed, for he presently said, "I know what I'll do—I'll talk it over wi' Riley: he's coming to-morrow, t' arbitrate about the dam."

"Well, Mr Tulliver, I've put the sheets out for the best bed, and Kezia's got 'em hanging at the fire. They aren't the best sheets, but they're good enough for anybody to sleep in, be he who he will; for as for them best Holland sheets, I should repent buying 'em, only they'll do to lay us out in. An' if you was to die to-morrow, Mr Tulliver, they're mangled[5] beautiful, an' all ready, an' smell o' lavender as it 'ud be a

5. Pressed.

pleasure to lay 'em out; an' they lie at the left-hand corner o' the big oak linen-chest at the back: not as I should trust anybody to look 'em out but myself."

As Mrs Tulliver uttered the last sentence, she drew a bright bunch of keys from her pocket, and singled out one, rubbing her thumb and finger up and down it with a placid smile while she looked at the clear fire. If Mr Tulliver had been a susceptible man in his conjugal relation, he might have supposed that she drew out the key to aid her imagination in anticipating the moment when he would be in a state to justify the production of the best Holland sheets. Happily he was not so; he was only susceptible in respect of his right to water-power; moreover, he had the marital habit of not listening very closely, and since his mention of Mr Riley, had been apparently occupied in a tactile examination of his woollen stockings.

"I think I've hit it, Bessy," was his first remark after a short silence. "Riley's as likely a man as any to know o' some school; he's had schooling himself, an' goes about to all sorts o' places—arbitratin' and vallyin' and that. And we shall have time to talk it over to-morrow night when the business is done. I want Tom to be such a sort o' man as Riley, you know—as can talk pretty nigh as well as if it was all wrote out for him, and knows a good lot o' words as don't mean much, so as you can't lay hold of 'em i' law; and a good solid knowledge o' business too."

"Well," said Mrs Tulliver, "so far as talking proper, and knowing everything, and walking with a bend in his back, and setting his hair up, I shouldn't mind the lad being brought up to that. But them fine-talking men from the big towns mostly wear the false shirt-fronts; they wear a frill till it's all a mess, and then hide it with a bib; I know Riley does. And then, if Tom's to go and live at Mudport, like Riley, he'll have a house with a kitchen hardly big enough to turn in, an' niver get a fresh egg for his breakfast, an' sleep up three pair o' stairs—or four, for what I know—an' be burnt to death before he can get down."

"No, no," said Mr Tulliver, "I've no thoughts of his going to Mudport: I mean him to set up his office at St Ogg's, close by us, an' live at home. But," continued Mr Tulliver after a pause, "what I'm a bit afraid on is, as Tom hasn't got the right sort o' brains for a smart fellow. I doubt he's a bit slowish. He takes after your family, Bessy."

"Yes, that he does," said Mrs Tulliver, accepting the last proposition entirely on its own merits; "he's wonderful for liking a deal o' salt in his broth. That was my brother's way, and my father's before him."

"It seems a bit of a pity, though, said Mr Tulliver, "as the lad should take after the mother's side istead o' the little wench. That's the worst on't wi' the crossing o' breeds: you can never justly calkilate what'll come on't. The little un takes after my side, now: she's twice as 'cute[6] as Tom. Too 'cute for a woman, I'm afraid," continued Mr Tulliver, turning his head dubiously first on one side and then on the other. "It's no mischief much while she's a little un, but an over-'cute woman's no better nor a long-tailed sheep—she'll fetch none the bigger price for that."

"Yes it *is* a mischief while she's a little un, Mr Tulliver, for it all runs to naughtiness. How to keep her in a clean pinafore two hours together passes my cunning. An' now you put me i' mind," continued Mrs Tulliver, rising and going to the window, "I don't know where she is now, an' it's pretty nigh tea-time. Ah, I thought so—wanderin' up an' down by the water, like a wild thing: she'll tumble in some day."

Mrs Tulliver rapped the window sharply, beckoned, and shook her head,—a process which she repeated more than once before she returned to her chair.

"You talk o' 'cuteness, Mr Tulliver," she observed as she sat down, "but I'm sure the child's half an idiot i' some things; for if I send her up-stairs to fetch anything, she forgets what she's gone for, an' perhaps 'ull sit down on the floor i' the sunshine an' plait her hair an' sing to herself like a Bedlam creatur',[7] all the while I'm waiting for her down-stairs. That niver run i' my family, thank God, no more nor a brown skin as makes her look like a mulatter. I don't like to fly i' the face o' Providence, but it seems hard as I should have but one gell, an' her so comical."

"Pooh, nonsense!" said Mr Tulliver, "she's a straight black-eyed wench as anybody need wish to see. I don't know i' what she's behind other folks's children; and she can read almost as well as the parson."

"But her hair won't curl all I can do with it, and she's so franzy[8] about having it put i' paper, and I've such work as never was to make her stand and have it pinched with th' irons."

"Cut it off—cut it off short," said the father, rashly.

"How can you talk so, Mr Tulliver? She's too big a gell, gone nine, and tall of her age, to have her hair cut short; an' there's her cousin Lucy's got a row o' curls round her head, an' not a hair out o' place. It seems hard as my sister Deane should have that pretty child; I'm sure Lucy takes more after me nor my own child does. Maggie, Maggie," continued the mother, in a tone of half-coaxing fretfulness, as this small mistake of nature entered the room, "where's the use o' my telling you to keep away from the water? You'll tumble in and be drownded some day, an' then you'll be sorry you didn't do as mother told you."

Maggie's hair, as she threw off her bonnet, painfully confirmed her mother's accusation: Mrs Tulliver, desiring her daughter to have a curled

6. Acute, clever.
7. Inmate of Bedlam, popular name of a former lunatic asylum in London.
8. Frenzied.

crop, "like other folks's children," had had it cut too short in front to be pushed behind the ears; and as it was usually straight an hour after it had been taken out of paper, Maggie was incessantly tossing her head to keep the dark heavy locks out of her gleaming black eyes—an action which gave her very much the air of a small Shetland pony.

"O dear, O dear, Maggie, what are you thinkin' of, to throw your bonnet down there? Take it up-stairs, there's a good gell, an' let your hair be brushed, an' put your other pinafore on, an' change your shoes—do, for shame; an' come an' go on with your patch-work, like a little lady."

"O mother," said Maggie, in a vehemently cross tone, "I don't *want* to do my patchwork."

"What! not your pretty patchwork, to make a counterpane for your aunt Glegg?"

"It's foolish work," said Maggie, with a toss of her mane,—"tearing things to pieces to sew 'em together again. And I don't want to do anything for my aunt Glegg—I don't like her."

Exit Maggie, dragging her bonnet by the string, while Mr Tulliver laughs audibly.

"I wonder at you, as you'll laugh at her, Mr Tulliver," said the mother, with feeble fretfulness in her tone. "You encourage her i' naughtiness. An' her aunts will have it as it's me spoils her."

Mrs Tulliver was what is called a good-tempered person—never cried, when she was a baby, on any slighter ground than hunger and pins; and from the cradle upwards had been healthy, fair, plump, and dull-witted; in short, the flower of her family for beauty and amiability. But milk and mildness are not the best things for keeping, and when they turn only a little sour, they may disagree with young stomachs seriously. I have often wondered whether those early Madonnas of Raphael,[9] with the blond faces and somewhat stupid expression, kept their placidity undisturbed when their strong-limbed, strong-willed boys got a little too old to do without clothing. I think they must have been given to feeble remonstrance, getting more and more peevish as it became more and more ineffectual.

Chapter III

Mr Riley Gives His Advice Concerning a School for Tom

The gentleman in the ample white cravat and shirt-frill, taking his brandy-and-water so pleasantly with his good friend Tulliver, is Mr Riley, a gentleman with a waxen complexion and fat hands, rather highly

9. Italian Renaissance painter (1483–1520).

educated for an auctioneer and appraiser, but large-hearted enough to show a great deal of *bonhommie*[1] towards simple country acquaintances of hospitable habits. Mr Riley spoke of such acquaintances kindly as "people of the old school."

The conversation had come to a pause. Mr Tulliver, not without a particular reason, had abstained from a seventh recital of the cool retort by which Riley had shown himself too many for Dix, and how Wakem had had his comb cut[2] for once in his life, now the business of the dam had been settled by arbitration, and how there never would have been any dispute at all about the height of water if everybody was what they should be, and Old Harry[3] hadn't made the lawyers. Mr Tulliver was, on the whole, a man of safe traditional opinions; but on one or two points he had trusted to his unassisted intellect, and had arrived at several questionable conclusions; among the rest, that rats, weevils, and lawyers were created by Old Harry. Unhappily he had no one to tell him that this was rampant Manichæism,[4] else he might have seen his error. But to-day it was clear that the good principle was triumphant: this affair of the water-power had been a tangled business somehow, for all it seemed—look at it one way—as plain as water's water; but, big a puzzle as it was, it hadn't got the better of Riley. Mr Tulliver took his brandy-and-water a little stronger than usual, and, for a man who might be supposed to have a few hundreds lying idle at his banker's, was rather incautiously open in expressing his high estimate of his friend's business talents.

But the dam was a subject of conversation that would keep; it could always be taken up again at the same point, and exactly in the same condition; and there was another subject, as you know, on which Mr Tulliver was in pressing want of Mr Riley's advice. This was his particular reason for remaining silent for a short space after his last draught, and rubbing his knees in a meditative manner. He was not a man to make an abrupt transition. This was a puzzling world, as he often said, and if you drive your waggon in a hurry, you may light on an awkward corner. Mr Riley, meanwhile, was not impatient. Why should he be? Even Hotspur,[5] one would think, must have been patient in his slippers on a warm hearth, taking copious snuff, and sipping gratuitous brandy-and-water.

"There's a thing I've got i' my head," said Mr Tulliver at last, in rather a lower tone than usual, as he turned his head and looked steadfastly at his companion.

"Ah!" said Mr Riley, in a tone of mild interest. He was a man with

1. Affability.
2. Had been humiliated (like a rooster's having his comb cut off).
3. The devil.
4. Dualistic religious system, taught by Manes, third-century Persian prophet, which holds that God and Satan are coequal powers.
5. Nickname of Sir Henry Percy, noted for his hotheadedness in Shakespeare's *I Henry IV*.

heavy waxen eyelids and high-arched eyebrows, looking exactly the same under all circumstances. This immovability of face, and the habit of taking a pinch of snuff before he gave an answer, made him trebly oracular to Mr Tulliver.

"It's a very particular thing," he went on; "it's about my boy Tom."

At the sound of this name, Maggie, who was seated on a low stool close by the fire, with a large book open on her lap, shook her heavy hair back and looked up eagerly. There were few sounds that roused Maggie when she was dreaming over her book, but Tom's name served as well as the shrillest whistle: in an instant she was on the watch, with gleaming eyes, like a Skye terrier suspecting mischief, or at all events determined to fly at any one who threatened it towards Tom.

"You see, I want to put him to a new school at Midsummer," said Mr Tulliver; "he's comin' away from the 'cademy at Ladyday, an' I shall let him run loose for a quarter; but after that I want to send him to a downright good school, where they'll make a scholard of him."

"Well," said Mr Riley, "there's no greater advantage you can give him than a good education. Not," he added, with polite significance—"not that a man can't be an excellent miller and farmer, and a shrewd sensible fellow into the bargain, without much help from the schoolmaster."

"I believe you," said Mr Tulliver, winking, and turning his head on one side, "but that's where it is. I don't *mean* Tom to be a miller and farmer. I see no fun i' that: why, if I made him a miller an' farmer, he'd be expectin' to take to the mill an' the land, an' a-hinting at me as it was time for me to lay by an' think o' my latter end. Nay, nay, I've seen enough o' that wi' sons. I'll never pull my coat off before I go to bed. I shall give Tom an eddication an' put him to a business, as he may make a nest for himself, an' not want to push me out o' mine. Pretty well if he gets it when I'm dead an' gone. I shan't be put off wi' spoon-meat[6] afore I've lost my teeth."

This was evidently a point on which Mr Tulliver felt strongly, and the impetus which had given unusual rapidity and emphasis to his speech, showed itself still unexhausted for some minutes afterwards, in a defiant motion of the head from side to side, and an occasional "Nay, nay," like a subsiding growl.

These angry symptoms were keenly observed by Maggie, and cut her to the quick. Tom, it appeared, was supposed capable of turning his father out of doors, and of making the future in some way tragic by his wickedness. This was not to be borne; and Maggie jumped up from her stool, forgetting all about her heavy book, which fell with a bang within the fender; and going up between her father's knees, said, in a half-crying, half-indignant voice—

6. Soft foods for spoon-feeding invalids or infants.

"Father, Tom wouldn't be naughty to you ever; I know he wouldn't."

Mrs Tulliver was out of the room superintending a choice supper-dish, and Mr Tulliver's heart was touched; so Maggie was not scolded about the book. Mr Riley quietly picked it up and looked at it, while the father laughed with a certain tenderness in his hard-lined face, and patted his little girl on the back, and then held her hands and kept her between his knees.

"What! they mustn't say any harm o' Tom, eh?" said Mr Tulliver, looking at Maggie with a twinkling eye. Then, in a lower voice, turning to Mr Riley, as though Maggie couldn't hear, "She understands what one's talking about so as never was. And you should hear her read—straight off, as if she knowed it all beforehand. And allays at her book! But it's bad—it's bad," Mr Tulliver added, sadly, checking this blamable exultation; "a woman's no business wi' being so clever; it'll turn to trouble, I doubt. But, bless you!"—here the exultation was clearly recovering the mastery—"she'll read the books and understand 'em better nor half the folks as are growed up."

Maggie's cheeks began to flush with triumphant excitement: she thought Mr Riley would have a respect for her now; it had been evident that he thought nothing of her before.

Mr Riley was turning over the leaves of the book, and she could make nothing of his face, with its high-arched eyebrows; but he presently looked at her and said,

"Come, come and tell me something about this book; here are some pictures—I want to know what they mean."

Maggie with deepening colour went without hesitation to Mr Riley's elbow and looked over the book, eagerly seizing one corner, and tossing back her mane, while she said,

"O, I'll tell you what that means. It's a dreadful picture, isn't it? But I can't help looking at it. That old woman in the water's a witch—they've put her in to find out whether she's a witch or no, and if she swims she's a witch, and if she's drowned—and killed, you know—she's innocent, and not a witch, but only a poor silly old woman. But what good would it do her then, you know, when she was drowned? Only, I suppose, she'd go to heaven, and God would make it up to her. And this dreadful blacksmith with his arms akimbo, laughing—oh, isn't he ugly?—I'll tell you what he is. He's the devil *really*" (here Maggie's voice became louder and more emphatic), "and not a right blacksmith; for the devil takes the shape of wicked men, and walks about and sets people doing wicked things, and he's oftener in the shape of a bad man than any other, because, you know, if people saw he was the devil, and he roared at 'em, they'd run away, and he couldn't make 'em do what he pleased."

Mr Tulliver had listened to this exposition of Maggie's with petrifying wonder.

"Why, what book is it the wench has got hold on?" he burst out, at last.

" 'The History of the Devil,' by Daniel Defoe;[7] not quite the right book for a little girl," said Mr Riley. "How came it among your books, Tulliver?"

Maggie looked hurt and discouraged, while her father said,

"Why, it's one o' the books I bought at Partridge's sale. They was all bound alike—it's a good binding, you see—and I thought they'd be all good books. There's Jeremy Taylor's 'Holy Living and Dying'[8] among 'em; I read in it often of a Sunday" (Mr Tulliver felt somehow a familiarity with that great writer because his name was Jeremy); "and there's a lot more of 'em, sermons mostly, I think; but they've all got the same covers, and I thought they were all o' one sample, as you may say. But it seems one mustn't judge by th' outside. This is a puzzlin' world."

"Well," said Mr Riley, in an admonitory patronising tone, as he patted Maggie on the head, "I advise you to put by the 'History of the Devil,' and read some prettier book. Have you no prettier books?"

"O yes," said Maggie, reviving a little in the desire to vindicate the variety of her reading, "I know the reading in this book isn't pretty—but I like the pictures, and I make stories to the pictures out of my own head, you know. But I've got 'Æsop's Fables,' and a book about Kangaroos and things, and the 'Pilgrim's Progress.' "

. . . "Ah, a beautiful book," said Mr Riley; "you can't read a better."

"Well, but there's a great deal about the devil in that," said Maggie, triumphantly, "and I'll show you the picture of him in his true shape, as he fought with Christian."[9]

Maggie ran in an instant to the corner of the room, jumped on a chair, and reached down from the small bookcase a shabby old copy of Bunyan, which opened at once, without the least trouble of search, at the picture she wanted.

"Here he is," she said, running back to Mr Riley, "and Tom coloured him for me with his paints when he was at home last holidays—the body all black, you know, and the eyes red, like fire, because he's all fire inside, and it shines out at his eyes."

"Go, go!" said Mr Tulliver, peremptorily, beginning to feel rather uncomfortable at these free remarks on the personal appearance of a being powerful enough to create lawyers; "shut up the book, and let's hear no more o' such talk. It is as I thought—the child 'ull learn more mischief nor good wi' the books. Go, go and see after your mother."

Maggie shut up the book at once, with a sense of disgrace, but not being inclined to see after her mother, she compromised the matter by going into a dark corner behind her father's chair, and nursing her doll,

7. Religious polemic, first published in 1726.
8. Book of religious counsel (1650–51) by the chaplain to Charles I.
9. Protagonist of *Pilgrim's Progress* (1678, 1684) by John Bunyan (1628–88).

towards which she had an occasional fit of fondness in Tom's absence, neglecting its toilette, but lavishing so many warm kisses on it that the waxen cheeks had a wasted unhealthy appearance.

"Did you ever hear the like on't?" said Mr Tulliver, as Maggie retired. "It's a pity but what she'd been the lad—she'd ha' been a match for the lawyers, *she* would. It's the wonderful'st thing"—here he lowered his voice—"as I picked the mother because she wasn't o'er 'cute—bein' a good-looking woman too, an' come of a rare family for managing; but I picked her from her sisters o' purpose, 'cause she was a bit weak, like; for I wasn't agoin' to be told the rights o' things by my own fireside. But you see when a man's got brains himself, there's no knowing where they'll run to; an' a pleasant sort o' soft woman may go on breeding you stupid lads and 'cute wenches, till it's like as if the world was turned topsy-turvy. It's an uncommon puzzlin' thing."

Mr Riley's gravity gave way, and he shook a little under the application of his pinch of snuff, before he said—

"But your lad's not stupid, is he? I saw him, when I was here last, busy making fishing-tackle; he seemed quite up to it."

"Well, he isn't not to say stupid—he's got a notion o' things out o' door, an' a sort o' common-sense, as he'd lay hold o' things by the right handle. But he's slow with his tongue, you see, and he reads but poorly, and can't abide the books, and spells all wrong, they tell me, an' as shy as can be wi' strangers, an' you never hear him say 'cute things like the little wench. Now, what I want is to send him to a school where they'll make him a bit nimble with his tongue and his pen, and make a smart chap of him. I want my son to be even wi' these fellows as have got the start o' me with having better schooling. Not but what, if the world had been left as God made it, I could ha' seen my way, and held my own wi' the best of 'em; but things have got so twisted round and wrapped up i' unreasonable words, as aren't a bit like 'em, as I'm clean at fault, often an' often. Everything winds about so—the more straightforrard you are, the more you're puzzled."

Mr Tulliver took a draught, swallowed it slowly, and shook his head in a melancholy manner, conscious of exemplifying the truth that a perfectly sane intellect is hardly at home in this insane world.

"You're quite in the right of it Tulliver," observed Mr Riley. "Better spend an extra hundred or two on your son's education, than leave it him in your will. I know I should have tried to do so by a son of mine, if I'd had one, though, God knows, I haven't your ready-money to play with, Tulliver; and I have a houseful of daughters into the bargain."

"I daresay, now, you know of a school as 'ud be just the thing for Tom," said Mr Tulliver, not diverted from his purpose by any sympathy with Mr Riley's deficiency of ready cash.

Mr Riley took a pinch of snuff, and kept Mr Tulliver in suspence by a silence that seemed deliberative, before he said—

"I know of a very fine chance for any one that's got the necessary money, and that's what you have, Tulliver. The fact is, I wouldn't recommend any friend of mine to send a boy to a regular school, if he could afford to do better. But if any one wanted his boy to get superior instruction and training, where he would be the companion of his master, and that master a first-rate fellow—I know his man. I wouldn't mention the chance to everybody, because I don't think everybody would succeed in getting it, if he were to try; but I mention it to you, Tulliver—between ourselves."

The fixed inquiring glance with which Mr Tulliver had been watching his friend's oracular face became quite eager.

"Ay, now, let's hear," he said, adjusting himself in his chair with the complacency of a person who is thought worthy of important communications.

"He's an Oxford man," said Mr Riley, sententiously, shutting his mouth close, and looking at Mr Tulliver to observe the effect of this stimulating information.

"What! a parson?"[1] said Mr Tulliver, rather doubtfully.

"Yes, and an M.A. The bishop, I understand, thinks very highly of him: why, it was the bishop who got him his present curacy."

"Ah?" said Mr Tulliver, to whom one thing was as wonderful as another concerning these unfamiliar phenomena. "But what can he want wi' Tom, then?"

"Why, the fact is, he's fond of teaching, and wishes to keep up his studies, and a clergyman has but little opportunity for that in his parochial duties. He's willing to take one or two boys as pupils to fill up his time profitably. The boys would be quite of the family—the finest thing in the world for them; under Stelling's eye continually."

"But do you think they'd give the poor lad twice o' pudding?"[2] said Mrs Tulliver, who was now in her place again. "He's such a boy for pudding as never was; an' a growing boy like that—it's dreadful to think o' their stintin' him."

"And what money 'ud he want?" said Mr Tulliver, whose instinct told him that the services of this admirable M.A. would bear a high price.

"Why, I know of a clergyman who asks a hundred and fifty with his youngest pupils, and he's not to be mentioned with Stelling, the man I speak of. I know, on good authority, that one of the chief people at Oxford said, 'Stelling might get the highest honours if he chose.' But he didn't care about university honours. He's a quiet man—not noisy."

"Ah, a deal better—a deal better," said Mr Tulliver; "but a hundred

1. Many graduates of Oxford (and Cambridge) chose to become clergymen of the Church of England.
2. A second helping of dessert.

and fifty's an uncommon price. I never thought o' payin' so much as that."

"A good education, let me tell you, Tulliver—a good education is cheap at the money. But Stelling is moderate in his terms—he's not a grasping man. I've no doubt he'd take your boy at a hundred, and that's what you wouldn't get many other clergymen to do. I'll write to him about it, if you like."

Mr Tulliver rubbed his knees, and looked at the carpet in a meditative manner.

"But belike he's a bachelor," observed Mrs Tulliver in the interval, "an' I've no opinion o' housekeepers. There was my brother, as is dead an' gone, had a housekeeper once, an' she took half the feathers out o' the best bed, an' packed 'em up an' sent 'em away. An' it's unknown the linen she made away with—Stott her name was. It 'ud break my heart to send Tom where there's a housekeeper, an' I hope you won't think of it, Mr Tulliver."

"You may set your mind at rest on that score, Mrs Tulliver," said Mr Riley, "for Stelling is married to as nice a little woman as any man need wish for a wife. There isn't a kinder little soul in the world; I know her family well. She has very much your complexion—light curly hair. She comes of a good Mudport family, and it's not every offer that would have been acceptable in that quarter. But Stelling's not an everyday man. Rather a particular fellow as to the people he chooses to be connected with. But I *think* he would have no objection to take your son —I *think* he would not, on my representation."

"I don't know what he could have *against* the lad," said Mrs Tulliver, with a slight touch of motherly indignation, "a nice fresh-skinned lad as anybody need wish to see."

"But there's one thing I'm thinking on," said Mr Tulliver, turning his head on one side and looking at Mr Riley, after a long perusal of the carpet. "Wouldn't a parson be almost too high-learnt to bring up a lad to be a man o' business? My notion o' the parsons was as they'd got a sort o' learning as lay mostly out o' sight. And that isn't what I want for Tom. I want him to know figures, and write like print, and see into things quick, and know what folks mean, and how to wrap things up in words as aren't actionable.[3] It's an uncommon fine thing, that is," concluded Mr Tulliver, shaking his head, "when you can let a man know what you think of him without paying for it."

"O my dear Tulliver," said Mr Riley, "you're quite under a mistake about the clergy; all the best schoolmasters are of the clergy. The schoolmasters who are not clergymen, are a very low set of men generally". . . .

3. Expressions so contrived that the speaker could not be sued for libel.

"Ay, that Jacobs is, at the 'cademy," interposed Mr Tulliver.

"To be sure—men who have failed in other trades, most likely. Now a clergyman is a gentleman by profession and education; and besides that, he has the knowledge that will ground a boy, and prepare him for entering on any career with credit. There may be some clergymen who are mere book-men; but you may depend upon it, Stelling is not one of them—a man that's wide awake, let me tell you. Drop him a hint, and that's enough. You talk of figures, now; you have only to say to Stelling, 'I want my son to be a thorough arithmetician,' and you may leave the rest to him."

Mr Riley paused a moment, while Mr Tulliver, somewhat reassured as to clerical tutorship, was inwardly rehearsing to an imaginary Mr Stelling the statement, "I want my son to know 'rethmetic."

"You see, my dear Tulliver," Mr Riley continued, "when you get a thoroughly educated man, like Stelling, he's at no loss to take up any branch of instruction. When a workman knows the use of his tools, he can make a door as well as a window."

"Ay, that's true," said Mr Tulliver, almost convinced now that the clergy must be the best of schoolmasters.

"Well, I'll tell you what I'll do for you," said Mr Riley, "and I wouldn't do it for everybody. I'll see Stelling's father-in-law, or drop him a line when I get back to Mudport, to say that you wish to place your boy with his son-in-law, and I dare-say Stelling will write to you, and send you his terms."

"But there's no hurry, is there?" said Mrs Tulliver; "for I hope, Mr Tulliver, you won't let Tom begin at his new school before Midsummer. He began at the 'cademy at the Ladyday quarter, and you see what good's come of it."

"Ay, ay, Bessy, never brew wi' bad malt upo' Michaelmas day, else you'll have a poor tap," said Mr Tulliver, winking and smiling at Mr Riley with the natural pride of a man who has a buxom wife conspicuously his inferior in intellect. "But it's true there's no hurry—you've hit it there, Bessy."

"It might be as well not to defer the arrangement too long," said Mr Riley, quietly, "for Stelling may have propositions from other parties, and I know he would not take more than two or three boarders, if so many. If I were you, I think I would enter on the subject with Stelling at once: there's no necessity for sending the boy before Midsummer, but I would be on the safe side, and make sure that nobody forestalls you."

"Ay, there's summat in that," said Mr Tulliver.

"Father," broke in Maggie, who had stolen unperceived to her father's elbow again, listening with parted lips, while she held her doll topsy-turvy, and crushed its nose against the wood of the chair—"Father, is it a long way off where Tom is to go? shan't we ever go to see him?"

"I don't know, my wench," said the father, tenderly. "Ask Mr Riley; he knows."

Maggie came round promptly in front of Mr Riley, and said, "How far is it, please, sir."

"O, a long long way off," that gentleman answered, being of opinion that children, when they are not naughty, should always be spoken to jocosely. "You must borrow the seven-leagued boots to get to him."

"That's nonsense!" said Maggie, tossing her head haughtily, and turning away, with the tears springing in her eyes. She began to dislike Mr Riley: it was evident he thought her silly and of no consequence.

"Hush Maggie, for shame of you, asking questions and chattering," said her mother. "Come and sit down on your little stool and hold your tongue, do. But," added Mrs Tulliver, who had her own alarm awakened, "is it so far off as I couldn't wash him and mend him?"

"About fifteen miles, that's all," said Mr Riley. "You can drive there and back in a day quite comfortably. Or—Stelling is a hospitable, pleasant man—he'd be glad to have you stay."

"But it's too far off for the linen, I doubt," said Mrs Tulliver, sadly.

The entrance of supper opportunely adjourned this difficulty, and relieved Mr Riley from the labour of suggesting some solution or compromise—a labour which he would otherwise doubtless have undertaken; for, as you perceive, he was a man of very obliging manners. And he had really given himself the trouble of recommending Mr Stelling to his friend Tulliver without any positive expectation of a solid, definite advantage resulting to himself, notwithstanding the subtle indications to the contrary which might have misled a too sagacious observer. For there is nothing more widely misleading than sagacity if it happens to get on a wrong scent; and sagacity, persuaded that men usually act and speak from distinct motives, with a consciously proposed end in view, is certain to waste its energies on imaginary game. Plotting covetousness, and deliberate contrivance, in order to compass a selfish end, are nowhere abundant but in the world of the dramatist: they demand too intense a mental action for many of our fellow-parishioners to be guilty of them. It is easy enough to spoil the lives of our neighbours without taking so much trouble: we can do it by lazy acquiescence and lazy omission, by trivial falsities for which we hardly know a reason, by small frauds neutralised by small extravagancies, by maladroit flatteries, and clumsily improvised insinuations. We live from hand to mouth, most of us, with a small family of immediate desires—we do little else than snatch a morsel to satisfy the hungry brood, rarely thinking of seed-corn or the next year's crop.

Mr Riley was a man of business, and not cold towards his own interest, yet even he was more under the influence of small promptings than of far-sighted designs. He had no private understanding with the Rev.

Walter Stelling; on the contrary he knew very little of that M.A. and his acquirements—not quite enough perhaps to warrant so strong a recommendation of him as he had given to his friend Tulliver. But he believed Mr Stelling to be an excellent classic, for Gadsby had said so, and Gadsby's first cousin was an Oxford tutor; which was better ground for the belief even than his own immediate observation would have been, for though Mr Riley had received a tincture of the classics at the great Mudport Free School, and had a sense of understanding Latin generally, his comprehension of any particular Latin was not ready. Doubtless there remained a subtle aroma from his juvenile contact with the *De Senectute*[4] and the Fourth Book of the *Æneid*, but it had ceased to be distinctly recognisable as classical, and was only perceived in the higher finish and force of his auctioneering style. Then, Stelling was an Oxford man, and the Oxford men were always—no, no, it was the Cambridge men who were always good mathematicians. But a man who had had a university education could teach anything he liked; especially a man like Stelling who had made a speech at a Mudport dinner on a political occasion, and had acquitted himself so well that it was generally remarked, this son-in-law of Timpson's was a sharp fellow. It was to be expected of a Mudport man, from the parish of St Ursula, that he would not omit to do a good turn to a son-in-law of Timpson's, for Timpson was one of the most useful and influential men in the parish, and had a good deal of business, which he knew how to put into the right hands. Mr Riley liked such men, quite apart from any money which might be diverted, through their good judgment, from less worthy pockets into his own; and it would be a satisfaction to him to say to Timpson on his return home, "I've secured a good pupil for your son-in-law." Timpson had a large family of daughters; Mr Riley felt for him; besides, Louisa Timpson's face, with its light curls, had been a familiar object to him over the pew wainscot on a Sunday for nearly fifteen years: it was natural her husband should be a commendable tutor. Moreover, Mr Riley knew of no other schoolmaster whom he had any ground for recommending in preference: why then should he not recommend Stelling? His friend Tulliver had asked him for an opinion: it is always chilling in friendly intercourse, to say you have no opinion to give. And if you deliver an opinion at all, it is mere stupidity not to do it with an air of conviction and well-founded knowledge. You make it your own in uttering it, and naturally get fond of it. Thus, Mr Riley, knowing no harm of Stelling to begin with, and wishing him well, so far as he had any wishes at all concerning him, had no sooner recommended him than he began to think with admiration of a man recommended on such high authority, and would soon have gathered so warm an interest on the subject, that if Mr Tulliver had in the end declined to send Tom to Stelling, Mr

4. Book of moral philosophy on the subject of old age by the Roman statesman and orator Marcus Tullius Cicero (106–43 B.C.).

Riley would have thought his "friend of the old school" a thoroughly pig-headed fellow.

If you blame Mr Riley very severely for giving a recommendation on such slight grounds, I must say you are rather hard upon him. Why should an auctioneer and appraiser thirty years ago, who had as good as forgotten his free-school Latin, be expected to manifest a delicate scrupulosity which is not always exhibited by gentlemen of the learned professions, even in our present advanced stage of morality?

Besides, a man with the milk of human kindness in him can scarcely abstain from doing a good-natured action, and one cannot be good-natured all round. Nature herself occasionally quarters an inconvenient parasite on an animal towards whom she has otherwise no ill-will. What then? We admire her care for the parasite. If Mr Riley had shrunk from giving a recommendation that was not based on valid evidence, he would not have helped Mr Stelling to a paying pupil, and that would not have been so well for the reverend gentleman. Consider, too, that all the pleasant little dim ideas and complacencies—of standing well with Timpson, of dispensing advice when he was asked for it, of impressing his friend Tulliver with additional respect, of saying something, and saying it emphatically, with other inappreciably minute ingredients that went along with the warm hearth and the brandy-and-water to make up Mr Riley's consciousness on this occasion—would have been a mere blank.

Chapter IV

Tom Is Expected

It was a heavy disappointment to Maggie that she was not allowed to go with her father in the gig when he went to fetch Tom home from the academy; but the morning was too wet, Mrs Tulliver said, for a little girl to go out in her best bonnet. Maggie took the opposite view very strongly, and it was a direct consequence of this difference of opinion that when her mother was in the act of brushing out the reluctant black crop, Maggie suddenly rushed from under her hands and dipped her head in a basin of water standing near—in the vindictive determination that there should be no more chance of curls that day.

"Maggie, Maggie," exclaimed Mrs Tulliver, sitting stout and helpless with the brushes on her lap, "what is to become of you if you're so naughty? I'll tell your aunt Glegg and your aunt Pullet when they come next week, and they'll never love you any more. O dear, O dear! look at your clean pinafore, wet from top to bottom. Folks 'ull think it's a judgment on me as I've got such a child—they'll think I've done summat wicked."

Before this remonstrance was finished, Maggie was already out of hearing, making her way towards the great attic that ran under the old high-pitched roof, shaking the water from her black locks as she ran, like a Skye terrier escaped from his bath. This attic was Maggie's favourite retreat on a wet day, when the weather was not too cold; here she fretted out all her ill-humours, and talked aloud to the worm-eaten floors and the worm-eaten shelves, and the dark rafters festooned with cobwebs; and here she kept a Fetish which she punished for all her misfortunes. This was the trunk of a large wooden doll, which once stared with the roundest of eyes above the reddest of cheeks; but was now entirely defaced by a long career of vicarious suffering. Three nails driven into the head commemorated as many crises in Maggie's nine years of earthly struggle; that luxury of vengeance having been suggested to her by the picture of Jael destroying Sisera in the old Bible.[1] The last nail had been driven in with a fiercer stroke than usual, for the Fetish on that occasion represented aunt Glegg. But immediately afterwards Maggie had reflected that if she drove many nails in, she would not be so well able to fancy that the head was hurt when she knocked it against the wall, nor to comfort it, and make believe to poultice it, when her fury was abated; for even aunt Glegg would be pitiable when she had been hurt very much, and thoroughly humiliated, so as to beg her niece's pardon. Since then she had driven no more nails in, but had soothed herself by alternately grinding and beating the wooden head against the rough brick of the great chimneys that made two square pillars supporting the roof. That was what she did this morning on reaching the attic, sobbing all the while with a passion that expelled every other form of consciousness—even the memory of the grievance that had caused it. As at last the sobs were getting quieter, and the grinding less fierce, a sudden beam of sunshine, falling through the wire lattice across the worm-eaten shelves, made her throw away the Fetish and run to the window. The sun was really breaking out; the sound of the mill seemed cheerful again; the granary doors were open; and there was Yap, the queer white-and-brown terrier, with one ear turned back, trotting about and sniffing vaguely, as if he were in search of a companion. It was irresistible. Maggie tossed her hair back and ran downstairs, seized her bonnet without putting it on, peeped, and then dashed along the passage lest she should encounter her mother, and was quickly out in the yard, whirling round like a Pythoness,[2] and singing as she whirled, "Yap, Yap, Tom's coming home!" while Yap danced and barked round her, as much as to say, if there was any noise wanted he was the dog for it.

"Hegh, hegh, Miss, you'll make yourself giddy, an' tumble down i' the dirt," said Luke, the head miller, a tall broad-shouldered man of

1. See Judges 4:1–24; 5:24–31. Sisera, the leader of an invasion against Israel, was slain by a woman, Jael, who hammered a nail into his head.
2. Priestess or prophetess.

forty, black-eyed and black-haired, subdued by a general mealiness, like an auricula.[3]

Maggie paused in her whirling and said, staggering a little, "O no, it doesn't make me giddy, Luke; may I go into the mill with you?"

Maggie loved to linger in the great spaces of the mill, and often came out with her black hair powdered to a soft whiteness that made her dark eyes flash out with new fire. The resolute din, the unresting motion of the great stones, giving her a dim delicious awe as at the presence of an uncontrollable force—the meal for ever pouring, pouring—the fine white powder softening all surfaces, and making the very spider-nets look like a faery lace-work—the sweet pure scent of the meal—all helped to make Maggie feel that the mill was a little world apart from her outside everyday life. The spiders were especially a subject of speculation with her. She wondered if they had any relatives outside the mill, for in that case there must be a painful difficulty in their family intercourse—a fat and floury spider, accustomed to take his fly well dusted with meal, must suffer a little at a cousin's table where the fly was *au naturel*, and the lady-spiders must be mutually shocked at each other's appearance. But the part of the mill she liked best was the topmost story—the corn-hutch, where there were the great heaps of grain, which she could sit on and slide down continually. She was in the habit of taking this recreation as she conversed with Luke, to whom she was very communicative, wishing him to think well of her understanding, as her father did.

Perhaps she felt it necessary to recover her position with him on the present occasion, for, as she sat sliding on the heap of grain near which he was busying himself, she said, at that shrill pitch which was requisite in mill-society—

"I think you never read any book but the Bible—did you, Luke?"

"Nay, Miss—an' not much o' that," said Luke, with great frankness. "I'm no reader, I aren't."

"But if I lent you one of my books, Luke? I've not got any *very* pretty books that would be easy for you to read; but there's 'Pug's Tour of Europe'—that would tell you all about the different sorts of people in the world, and if you didn't understand the reading, the pictures would help you—they show the looks and ways of the people, and what they do. There are the Dutchmen, very fat, and smoking, you know—and one sitting on a barrel."[4]

"Nay, Miss, I'n no opinion o' Dutchmen. There ben't much good i' knowin' about *them*."

3. The powdery yellow flowers of a primrose, which he resembles because he is covered with dust from grinding grain in the mill.
4. An anonymous illustrated book of doggerel verse, published in 1824: *Pug's Tour through Europe: or the Travelled Monkey*. The monkey's final visit is to Holland.

"But they're our fellow-creatures, Luke—we ought to know about our fellow-creatures."

"Not much o' fellow-creaturs, I think, Miss; all I know—my old master, as war a knowin' man, used to say, says he, 'If e'er I sow my wheat wi'out brinin',[5] I'm a Dutchman,' says he; an' that war as much as to say as a Dutchman war a fool, or next door. Nay, nay, I aren't goin' to bother mysen about Dutchmen. There's fools enoo—an' rogues enoo—wi'out lookin' i' books for 'em."

"O, well," said Maggie, rather foiled by Luke's unexpectedly decided views about Dutchmen, "perhaps you would like 'Animated Nature'[6] better—that's not Dutchmen, you know, but elephants, and kangaroos, and the civet cat, and the sun-fish, and a bird sitting on its tail—I forget its name. There are countries full of those creatures, instead of horses and cows, you know. Shouldn't you like to know about them, Luke?"

"Nay, Miss, I'n got to keep count o' the flour an' corn—I can't do wi' knowin' so many things besides my work. That's what brings folks to the gallows—knowin' everything but what they'n got to get their bread by. An' they're mostly lies, I think, what's printed i' the books: them printed sheets are, anyhow, as the men cry i' the streets."

"Why, you're like my brother Tom, Luke," said Maggie, wishing to turn the conversation agreeably; "Tom's not fond of reading. I love Tom so dearly, Luke—better than anybody else in the world. When he grows up, I shall keep his house, and we shall always live together. I can tell him everything he doesn't know. But I think Tom's clever, for all he doesn't like books: he makes beautiful whipcord and rabbit-pens."

"Ah," said Luke, "but he'll be fine an' vexed, as the rabbits are all dead."

"Dead!" screamed Maggie, jumping up from her sliding seat on the corn. "O dear, Luke! What! the lop-eared one, and the spotted doe that Tom spent all his money to buy?"

"As dead as moles," said Luke, fetching his comparison from the unmistakable corpses nailed to the stable-wall.

"O dear, Luke," said Maggie, in a piteous tone, while the big tears rolled down her cheek; "Tom told me to take care of 'em, and I forgot. What *shall* I do?"

"Well, you see, Miss, they were in that far tool-house, an' it was nobody's business to see to 'em. I reckon Master Tom told Harry to feed 'em, but there's no countin' on Harry—*he's* an offal creatur as iver come about the primises, he is. He remembers nothing but his own inside—an' I wish it 'ud gripe him."

"O, Luke, Tom told me to be sure and remember the rabbits every day; but how could I, when they didn't come into my head, you know?

5. Burning.
6. Oliver Goldsmith's popular *History of Animated Nature* (1774).

O, he will be so angry with me, I know he will, and so sorry about his rabbits—and so am I sorry. O, what *shall* I do?"

"Don't you fret, Miss," said Luke, soothingly, "they're nash[7] things, them lop-eared rabbits—they'd happen ha' died, if they'd been fed. Things out o' natur niver thrive: God A'mighty doesn't like 'em. He made the rabbits' ears to lie back, an' it's nothin' but contrairiness to make 'em hing down like a mastiff dog's. Master Tom 'ull know better nor buy such things another time. Don't you fret, Miss. Will you come along home wi' me, and see my wife? I'm a-goin' this minute."

The invitation offered an agreeable distraction to Maggie's grief, and her tears gradually subsided as she trotted along by Luke's side to his pleasant cottage, which stood with its apple and pear trees, and with the added dignity of a lean-to pig-sty, at the other end of the Mill fields. Mrs Moggs, Luke's wife, was a decidedly agreeable acquaintance. She exhibited her hospitality in bread and treacle, and possessed various works of art. Maggie actually forgot that she had any special cause of sadness this morning, as she stood on a chair to look at a remarkable series of pictures representing the Prodigal Son in the costume of Sir Charles Grandison,[8] except that, as might have been expected from his defective moral character, he had not, like that accomplished hero, the taste and strength of mind to dispense with a wig. But the indefinable weight the dead rabbits had left on her mind caused her to feel more than usual pity for the career of this weak young man, particularly when she looked at the picture where he leaned against a tree with a flaccid appearance, his knee-breeches unbuttoned and his wig awry, while the swine, apparently of some foreign breed, seemed to insult him by their good spirits over their feast of husks.

"I'm very glad his father took him back again—aren't you, Luke?" she said. "For he was very sorry, you know, and wouldn't do wrong again."

"Eh, Miss," said Luke, "he'd be no great shakes, I doubt, let's feyther do what he would for him."

That was a painful thought to Maggie, and she wished much that the subsequent history of the young man had not been left a blank.

Chapter V

Tom Comes Home

Tom was to arrive early in the afternoon, and there was another fluttering heart besides Maggie's when it was late enough for the sound of the gig-

7. Soft, delicate.
8. The illustration of the story of the Prodigal Son (cf. Luke 15:11–32) features him wearing eighteenth-century costume such as had been worn by the extremely virtuous title character of Samuel Richardson's novel, *Sir Charles Grandison*.

wheels to be expected; for if Mrs Tulliver had a strong feeling, it was fondness for her boy. At last the sound came—that quick light bowling of the gig-wheels—and in spite of the wind, which was blowing the clouds about, and was not likely to respect Mrs Tulliver's curls and cap-strings, she came outside the door, and even held her hand on Maggie's offending head, forgetting all the griefs of the morning.

"There he is, my sweet lad! But, Lord ha' mercy! he's got never a collar on; it's been lost on the road, I'll be bound, and spoilt the set."

Mrs Tulliver stood with her arms open; Maggie jumped first on one leg and then on the other; while Tom descended from the gig, and said, with masculine reticence as to the tender emotions, "Hallo! Yap—what! are you there?"

Nevertheless he submitted to be kissed willingly enough, though Maggie hung on his neck in rather a strangling fashion, while his blue-grey eyes wandered towards the croft and the lambs and the river, where he promised himself that he would begin to fish the first thing to-morrow morning. He was one of those lads that grow everywhere in England, and, at twelve or thirteen years of age, look as much alike as goslings: —a lad with light-brown hair, cheeks of cream and roses, full lips, indeterminate nose and eyebrows—a physiognomy in which it seems impossible to discern anything but the generic character of boyhood; as different as possible from poor Maggie's phiz, which Nature seemed to have moulded and coloured with the most decided intention. But that same Nature has the deep cunning which hides itself under the appearance of openness, so that simple people think they can see through her quite well, and all the while she is secretly preparing a refutation of their confident prophecies. Under these average boyish physiognomies that she seems to turn off by the gross, she conceals some of her most rigid, inflexible purposes, some of her most unmodifiable characters; and the dark-eyed, demonstrative, rebellious girl may after all turn out to be a passive being compared with this pink-and-white bit of masculinity with the indeterminate features.

"Maggie," said Tom, confidentially, taking her into a corner, as soon as his mother was gone out to examine his box, and the warm parlour had taken off the chill he had felt from the long drive, "you don't know what I've got in *my* pockets," nodding his head up and down as a means of rousing her sense of mystery.

"No," said Maggie. "How stodgy they look, Tom! Is it marls (marbles) or cobnuts?" Maggie's heart sank a little, because Tom always said it was "no good" playing with *her* at those games—she played so badly.

"Marls! no; I've swopped all my marls with the little fellows, and cobnuts are no fun, you silly, only when the nuts are green. But see here!" He drew something half out of his right-hand pocket.

"What is it?" said Maggie, in a whisper. "I can see nothing but a bit of yellow."

"Why it's . . . a . . . new . . . guess, Maggie!"

"O, I *can't* guess, Tom," said Maggie, impatiently.

"Don't be a spitfire, else I won't tell you," said Tom, thrusting his hand back into his pocket, and looking determined.

"No, Tom," said Maggie, imploringly, laying hold of the arm that was held stiffly in the pocket. "I'm not cross, Tom; it was only because I can't bear guessing. *Please* be good to me."

Tom's arm slowly relaxed, and he said, "Well, then it's a new fish-line—two new uns—one for you, Maggie, all to yourself. I wouldn't go halves in the toffee and gingerbread on purpose to save the money; and Gibson and Spouncer fought with me because I wouldn't. And here's hooks; see here! . . . I say, *won't* we go and fish to-morrow down by the Round Pool? And you shall catch your own fish, Maggie, and put the worms on, and everything—won't it be fun?"

Maggie's answer was to throw her arms round Tom's neck and hug him, and hold her cheek against his without speaking, while he slowly unwound some of the line, saying, after a pause,

"Wasn't I a good brother, now, to buy you a line all to yourself? You know, I needn't have bought it, if I hadn't liked."

"Yes, very, very good. . . . I *do* love you, Tom."

Tom had put the line back in his pocket, and was looking at the hooks one by one, before he spoke again.

"And the fellows fought me, because I wouldn't give in about the toffee."

"O dear! I wish they wouldn't fight at your school, Tom. Didn't it hurt you?"

"Hurt me? no," said Tom, putting up the hooks again, taking out a large pocket-knife, and slowly opening the largest blade, which he looked at meditatively as he rubbed his finger along it. Then he added—

"I gave Spouncer a black eye, I know—that's what he got by wanting to leather *me*; I wasn't going to go halves because anybody leathered me."

"O how brave you are, Tom! I think you're like Samson.[1] If there came a lion roaring at me, I think you'd fight him—wouldn't you, Tom?"

"How can a lion come roaring at you, you silly thing? There's no lions, only in the shows."

"No; but if we were in the lion countries—I mean in Africa, where it's very hot—the lions eat people there. I can show it you in the book where I read it."

"Well, I should get a gun and shoot him."

"But if you hadn't got a gun—we might have gone out, you know, not thinking—just as we go fishing; and then a great lion might run

1. Legendary strong man in Judges 14–16.

towards us roaring, and we couldn't get away from him. What should you do, Tom?"

Tom paused, and at last turned away contemptuously, saying, "But the lion *isn't* coming. What's the use of talking?"

"But I like to fancy how it would be," said Maggie, following him. "Just think what you would do, Tom."

"O don't bother, Maggie! you're such a silly—I shall go and see my rabbits."

Maggie's heart began to flutter with fear. She dared not tell the sad truth at once, but she walked after Tom in trembling silence as he went out, thinking how she could tell him the news so as to soften at once his sorrow and his anger; for Maggie dreaded Tom's anger of all things—it was quite a different anger from her own.

"Tom," she said, timidly, when they were out of doors, "how much money did you give for your rabbits?"

"Two half-crowns and a sixpence," said Tom, promptly.

"I think I've got a great deal more than that in my steel purse upstairs. I'll ask mother to give it you."

"What for?" said Tom. "I don't want *your* money, you silly thing. I've got a great deal more money than you, because I'm a boy. I always have half-sovereigns and sovereigns for my Christmas boxes, because I shall be a man, and you only have five-shilling pieces, because you're only a girl."

"Well, but, Tom—if mother would let me give you two half-crowns and a sixpence out of my purse to put into your pocket and spend, you know; and buy some more rabbits with it?"

"More rabbits? I don't want any more."

"O, but, Tom, they're all dead."

Tom stopped immediately in his walk and turned round towards Maggie. "You forgot to feed 'em, then, and Harry forgot?" he said, his colour heightening for a moment, but soon subsiding. "I'll pitch into Harry—I'll have him turned away. And I don't love you, Maggie. You shan't go fishing with me to-morrow. I told you to go and see the rabbits every day." He walked on again.

"Yes, but I forgot—and I couldn't help it, indeed, Tom. I'm so very sorry," said Maggie, while the tears rushed fast.

"You're a naughty girl," said Tom, severely, "and I'm sorry I bought you the fish-line. I don't love you."

"O, Tom, it's very cruel," sobbed Maggie. "I'd forgive you, if *you* forgot anything—I wouldn't mind what you did—I'd forgive you and love you."

"Yes, you're a silly—but I never *do* forget things—*I* don't."

"O, please forgive me, Tom; my heart will break," said Maggie, shaking with sobs, clinging to Tom's arm, and laying her wet cheek on his shoulder.

Tom shook her off, and stopped again, saying in a peremptory tone, "Now, Maggie, you just listen. Aren't I a good brother to you?"

"Ye-ye-es," sobbed Maggie, her chin rising and falling convulsedly.

"Didn't I think about your fish-line all this quarter, and mean to buy it, and saved my money o' purpose, and wouldn't go halves in the toffee, and Spouncer fought me because I wouldn't?"

"Ye-ye-es . . . and I . . . lo-lo-love you so, Tom."

"But you're a naughty girl. Last holidays you licked the paint off my lozenge box, and the holidays before that you let the boat drag my fish-line down when I'd set you to watch it and you pushed your head through my kite, all for nothing."

"But I didn't mean," said Maggie; "I couldn't help it."

"Yes, you could," said Tom, "if you'd minded what you were doing. And you're a naughty girl, and you shan't go fishing with me to-morrow."

With this terrible conclusion, Tom ran away from Maggie towards the mill, meaning to greet Luke there, and complain to him of Harry.

Maggie stood motionless, except from her sobs, for a minute or two; then she turned round and ran into the house, and up to her attic, where she sat on the floor, and laid her head against the worm-eaten shelf, with a crushing sense of misery. Tom was come home, and she had thought how happy she should be—and now he was cruel to her. What use was anything, if Tom didn't love her? O, he was very cruel! Hadn't she wanted to give him the money, and said how very sorry she was? She knew she was naughty to her mother, but she had never been naughty to Tom—had never *meant* to be naughty to him.

"O, he is cruel!" Maggie sobbed aloud, finding a wretched pleasure in the hollow resonance that came through the long empty space of the attic. She never thought of beating or grinding her Fetish; she was too miserable to be angry.

These bitter sorrows of childhood! when sorrow is all new and strange, when hope has not yet got wings to fly beyond the days and weeks, and the space from summer to summer seems measureless.

Maggie soon thought she had been hours in the attic, and it must be tea-time, and they were all having their tea, and not thinking of her. Well, then, she would stay up there and starve herself—hide herself behind the tub, and stay there all night; and then they would all be frightened, and Tom would be sorry. Thus Maggie thought in the pride of her heart, as she crept behind the tub; but presently she began to cry again at the idea that they didn't mind her being there. If she went down again to Tom now—would he forgive her?—perhaps her father would be there, and he would take her part. But, then, she wanted Tom to forgive her because he loved her, not because his father told him. No, she would never go down if Tom didn't come to fetch her. This resolution lasted in great intensity for five dark minutes behind the tub; but then the need of being loved, the strongest need in poor Maggie's nature, began to wrestle with her pride, and soon threw it. She crept from behind her tub into the twilight of the long attic, but just then she heard a quick footstep on the stairs.

Tom had been too much interested in his talk with Luke, in going the round of the premises, walking in and out where he pleased, and whittling sticks without any particular reason, except that he didn't whittle sticks at school, to think of Maggie and the effect his anger had produced on her. He meant to punish her, and that business having been performed, he occupied himself with other matters, like a practical person. But when he had been called in to tea, his father said, "Why, where's the little wench?" and Mrs Tulliver, almost at the same moment, said, "Where's your little sister?"—both of them having supposed that Maggie and Tom had been together all the afternoon.

"I don't know," said Tom. He didn't want to "tell" of Maggie, though he was angry with her; for Tom Tulliver was a lad of honour.

"What! hasn't she been playing with you all this while?" said the father. "She'd been thinking o' nothing but your coming home."

"I haven't seen her this two hours," says Tom, commencing on the plumcake.

"Goodness heart! she's got drownded," exclaimed Mrs Tulliver, rising from her seat and running to the window. "How could you let her do so?" she added, as became a fearful woman, accusing she didn't know whom of she didn't know what.

"Nay, nay, she's none drownded," said Mr Tulliver. "You've been naughty to her, I doubt, Tom?"

"I'm sure I haven't, father," said Tom, indignantly. "I think she's in the house."

"Perhaps up in that attic," said Mrs Tulliver, "a-singing and talking to herself, and forgetting all about meal-times."

"You go and fetch her down, Tom," said Mr Tulliver, rather sharply, his perspicacity or his fatherly fondness for Maggie making him suspect that the lad had been hard upon "the little un," else she would never have left his side. "And be good to her, do you hear? Else I'll let you know better."

Tom never disobeyed his father, for Mr Tulliver was a peremptory man, and, as he said, would never let anybody get hold of his whip-hand; but he went out rather sullenly, carrying his piece of plumcake, and not intending to reprieve Maggie's punishment, which was no more than she deserved. Tom was only thirteen, and had no decided views in grammar and arithmetic, regarding them for the most part as open questions, but he was particularly clear and positive on one point—namely, that he would punish everybody who deserved it: why, he wouldn't have minded being punished himself, if he deserved it; but, then, he never *did* deserve it.

It was Tom's step, then, that Maggie heard on the stairs, when her need of love had triumphed over her pride, and she was going down with her swollen eyes and dishevelled hair to beg for pity. At least her father would stroke her head and say, "Never mind, my wench." It is a wonderful subduer, this need of love—this hunger of the heart—as peremptory as that other hunger by which Nature forces us to submit to the yoke, and change the face of the world.

But she knew Tom's step, and her heart began to beat violently with the sudden shock of hope. He only stood still at the top of the stairs and said, "Maggie, you're to come down." But she rushed to him and clung round his neck, sobbing, "O Tom, please forgive me—I can't bear it —I will always be good—always remember things—do love me—please, dear Tom!"

We learn to restrain ourselves as we get older. We keep apart when we have quarrelled, express ourselves in well-bred phrases, and in this way preserve a dignified alienation, showing much firmness on one side, and swallowing much grief on the other. We no longer approximate in our behaviour to the mere impulsiveness of the lower animals, but conduct ourselves in every respect like members of a highly civilised society. Maggie and Tom were still very much like young animals, and so she could rub her cheek against his, and kiss his ear in a random, sobbing way; and there were tender fibres in the lad that had been used to answer to Maggie's fondling; so that he behaved with a weakness quite inconsistent with his resolution to punish her as much as she deserved: he actually began to kiss her in return, and say—

"Don't cry, then, Magsie—here, eat a bit o' cake."

Maggie's sobs began to subside, and she put out her mouth for the cake and bit a piece: and then Tom bit a piece, just for company, and they ate together and rubbed each other's cheeks and brows and noses together, while they ate, with a humiliating resemblance to two friendly ponies.

"Come along, Magsie, and have tea," said Tom at last, when there was no more cake except what was down-stairs.

So ended the sorrows of this day, and the next morning Maggie was trotting with her own fishing-rod in one hand and a handle of the basket in the other, stepping always, by a peculiar gift, in the muddiest places, and looking darkly radiant from under her beaver-bonnet because Tom was good to her. She had told Tom, however, that she should like him to put the worms on the hook for her, although she accepted his word when he assured her that worms couldn't feel (it was Tom's private opinion that it didn't much matter if they did). He knew all about worms, and fish, and those things; and what birds were mischievous, and how padlocks opened, and which way the handles of the gates were to be lifted. Maggie thought this sort of knowledge was very wonderful—much more difficult than remembering what was in the books; and she was rather in awe of Tom's superiority, for he was the only person who called her knowledge "stuff," and did not feel surprised at her cleverness. Tom, indeed, was of opinion that Maggie was a silly little thing; all girls were silly—they couldn't throw a stone so as to hit anything, couldn't do anything with a pocket-knife, and were frightened at frogs. Still he was very fond of his sister, and meant always to take care of her, make her his housekeeper, and punish her when she did wrong.

They were on their way to the Round Pool—that wonderful pool, which the floods had made a long while ago: no one knew how deep it was; and it was mysterious, too, that it should be almost a perfect round, framed in with willows and tall reeds, so that the water was only to be seen when you got close to the brink. The sight of the old favourite spot always heightened Tom's good-humour, and he spoke to Maggie in the most amicable whispers, as he opened the precious basket, and prepared their tackle. He threw her line for her, and put the rod into her hand. Maggie thought it probable that the small fish would come to her hook, and the large ones to Tom's. But she had forgotten all about the fish, and was looking dreamily at the glassy water, when Tom said, in a loud whisper, "Look, look, Maggie!" and came running to prevent her from snatching her line away.

Maggie was frightened lest she had been doing something wrong, as usual, but presently Tom drew out her line and brought a large tench bouncing on the grass.

Tom was excited.

"O Magsie! you little duck! Empty the basket."

Maggie was not conscious of unusual merit, but it was enough that Tom called her Magsie, and was pleased with her. There was nothing to mar her delight in the whispers and the dreamy silences, when she listened to the light dipping sounds of the rising fish, and the gentle rustling, as if the willows and the reeds and the water had their happy whisperings also. Maggie thought it would make a very nice heaven to sit by the pool in that way, and never be scolded. She never knew she had a bite till Tom told her; but she liked fishing very much.

It was one of their happy mornings. They trotted along and sat down together, with no thought that life would ever change much for them: they would only get bigger and not go to school, and it would always be like the holidays; they would always live together and be fond of each other. And the mill with its booming—the great chestnut-tree under which they played at houses—their own little river, the Ripple, where the banks seemed like home, and Tom was always seeing the water-rats, while Maggie gathered the purple plumy tops of the reeds, which she forgot and dropped afterwards—above all, the great Floss, along which they wandered with a sense of travel, to see the rushing spring-tide, the awful Eagre,[2] come up like a hungry monster, or to see the

2. A tidal wave of unusual height, caused by the rushing of the tide up a narrow estuary.

Great Ash which had once wailed and groaned like a man—these things would always be just the same to them. Tom thought people were at a disadvantage who lived on any other spot of the globe; and Maggie, when she read about Christiana[3] passing "the river over which there is no bridge," always saw the Floss between the green pastures by the Great Ash.

Life did change for Tom and Maggie; and yet they were not wrong in believing that the thoughts and loves of these first years would always make part of their lives. We could never have loved the earth so well if we had had no childhood in it,—if it were not the earth where the same flowers come up again every spring that we used to gather with our tiny fingers as we sat lisping to ourselves on the grass—the same hips and haws on the autumn hedgerows—the same redbreasts that we used to call "God's birds," because they did no harm to the precious crops. What novelty is worth that sweet monotony where everything is known, and *loved* because it is known?

The wood I walk in on this mild May day, with the young yellow-brown foliage of the oaks between me and the blue sky, the white star-flowers and the blue-eyed speedwell and the ground ivy at my feet—what grove of tropic palms, what strange ferns or splendid broad-petalled blossoms, could ever thrill such deep and delicate fibres within me as this home-scene? These familiar flowers, these well-remembered bird-notes, this sky, with its fitful brightness, these furrowed and grassy fields, each with a sort of personality given to it by the capricious hedgerows—such things as these are the mother tongue of our imagination, the language that is laden with all the subtle inextricable associations the fleeting hours of our childhood left behind them. Our delight in the sunshine on the deep-bladed grass to-day, might be no more than the faint perception of wearied souls, if it were not for the sunshine and the grass in the far-off years which still live in us, and transform our perception into love.

Chapter VI

The Aunts and Uncles Are Coming

It was Easter week, and Mrs Tulliver's cheese-cakes were more exquisitely light than usual: "a puff o' wind 'ud make 'em blow about like feathers," Kezia the housemaid said,—feeling proud to live under a mistress who could make such pastry; so that no season or circumstances could have been more propitious for a family party, even if it had not

3. Protagonist of the second part of *Pilgrim's Progress*: "the river over which there is no bridge" is Bunyan's river of death.

been advisable to consult sister Glegg and sister Pullet about Tom's going to school.

"I'd as lief not invite sister Deane this time," said Mrs Tulliver, "for she's as jealous and having as can be, and 's allays trying to make the worst o' my poor children to their aunts and uncles."

"Yes, yes," said Mr Tulliver, "ask her to come. I never hardly get a bit o' talk with Deane now: we haven't had him this six months. What's it matter what she says?—my children need be beholding to nobody."

"That's what you allays say, Mr Tulliver; but I'm sure there's nobody o' your side, neither aunt nor uncle, to leave 'em so much as a five-pound note for a leggicy. And there's sister Glegg, and sister Pullet too, saving money unknown—for they put by all their own interest and butter-money too; their husbands buy 'em everything." Mrs Tulliver was a mild woman, but even a sheep will face about a little when she has lambs.

"Tchuh!" said Mr Tulliver. "It takes a big loaf when there's many to breakfast. What signifies your sisters' bits o' money when they've got half-a-dozen nevvies and nieces to divide it among? And your sister Deane won't get 'em to leave all to one, I reckon, and make the country cry shame on 'em when they are dead?"

"I don't know what she won't get 'em to do," said Mrs Tulliver, "for my children are so awk'ard wi' their aunts and uncles. Maggie's ten times naughtier when they come than she is other days, and Tom doesn't like 'em, bless him—though it's more nat'ral in a boy than a gell. And there's Lucy Deane's such a good child—you may set her on a stool, and there she'll sit for an hour together, and never offer to get off. I can't help loving the child as if she was my own; and I'm sure she's more like *my* child than sister Deane's, for she'd allays a very poor colour for one of our family, sister Deane had."

"Well, well, if you're fond o' the child, ask her father and mother to bring her with 'em. And won't you ask their aunt and uncle Moss too? and some o' *their* children?"

"O dear, Mr Tulliver, why, there'd be eight people besides the children, and I must put two more leaves i' the table, besides reaching down more o' the dinner-service; and you know as well as I do, as *my* sisters and *your* sister don't suit well together."

"Well, well, do as you like, Bessy," said Mr Tulliver, taking up his hat and walking out to the mill. Few wives were more submissive than Mrs Tulliver on all points unconnected with her family relations; but she had been a Miss Dodson, and the Dodsons were a very respectable family indeed—as much looked up to as any in their own parish, or the next to it. The Miss Dodsons had always been thought to hold up their heads very high, and no one was surprised the two eldest had married so well—not at an early age, for that was not the practice of the Dodson family. There were particular ways of doing everything in that family: particular ways of bleaching the linen, of making the cowslip wine, curing the hams, and keeping the bottled gooseberries; so that no daughter of that house could be indifferent to the privilege of having been born a Dodson, rather than a Gibson or a Watson. Funerals were always conducted with peculiar propriety in the Dodson family: the hat-bands were never of a blue shade, the gloves never split at the thumb, everybody was a mourner who ought to be, and there were always scarfs for the bearers. When one of the family was in trouble or sickness, all the rest went to visit the unfortunate member, usually at the same time, and did not shrink from uttering the most disagreeable truths that correct family feeling dictated: if the illness or trouble was the sufferer's own fault, it was not in the practice of the Dodson family to shrink from saying so. In short, there was in this family a peculiar tradition as to what was the right thing in household management and social de-meanour, and the only bitter circumstance attending this superiority was a painful inability to approve the condiments or the conduct of families ungoverned by the Dodson tradition. A female Dodson, when in "strange houses," always ate dry bread with her tea, and declined any sort of preserves, having no confidence in the butter, and thinking that the preserves had probably begun to ferment from want of due sugar and boiling. There were some Dodsons less like the family than others—that was admitted; but in so far as they were "kin," they were of necessity better than those who were "no kin." And it is remarkable that while no individual Dodson was satisfied with any other individual Dodson, each was satisfied, not only with him or her self, but with the Dodsons collectively. The feeblest member of a family—the one who has the least character—is often the merest[1] epitome of the family habits and traditions; and Mrs Tulliver was a thorough Dodson, though a mild one, as small-beer, so long as it is anything, is only describable as very weak ale: and though she had groaned a little in her youth under the yoke of her elder sisters, and still shed occasional tears at their sisterly reproaches, it was not in Mrs Tulliver to be an innovator on the family ideas. She was thankful to have been a Dodson, and to have one child who took after her own family, at least in his features and complexion, in liking salt and in eating beans, which a Tulliver never did.

In other respects the true Dodson was partly latent in Tom, and he was as far from appreciating his "kin" on the mother's side as Maggie herself; generally absconding for the day with a large supply of the most portable food, when he received timely warning that his aunts and uncles were coming; a moral symptom from which his aunt Glegg deduced the gloomiest views of his future. It was rather hard on Maggie that Tom always absconded without letting her into the secret, but the

1. Most complete.

weaker sex are acknowledged to be serious *impedimenta* in cases of flight.

On Wednesday, the day before the aunts and uncles were coming, there were such various and suggestive scents, as of plumcakes in the oven and jellies in the hot state, mingled with the aroma of gravy, that it was impossible to feel altogether gloomy: there was hope in the air. Tom and Maggie made several inroads into the kitchen, and, like other marauders, were induced to keep aloof for a time only by being allowed to carry away a sufficient load of booty.

"Tom," said Maggie, as they sat on the boughs of the elder-tree, eating their jam puffs, "shall you run away to-morrow?"

"No," said Tom, slowly, when he had finished his puff, and was eyeing the third, which was to be divided between them—"No, I shan't."

"Why, Tom? Because Lucy's coming?"

"No," said Tom, opening his pocket-knife and holding it over the puff, with his head on one side in a dubitative manner. (It was a difficult problem to divide that very irregular polygon into two equal parts.) "What do *I* care about Lucy? She's only a girl—*she* can't play at bandy."[2]

"Is it the tipsy-cake, then?" said Maggie, exerting her hypothetic powers, while she leaned forward towards Tom with her eyes fixed on the hovering knife.

"No, you silly, that'll be good the day after. It's the pudden. I know what the pudden's to be—apricot roll-up—O my buttons!"

With this interjection, the knife descended on the puff and it was in two, but the result was not satisfactory to Tom, for he still eyed the halves doubtfully. At last he said—

"Shut your eyes, Maggie."

"What for?"

"You never mind what for. Shut 'em, when I tell you."

Maggie obeyed.

"Now, which'll you have, Maggie—right hand or left?"

"I'll have that with the jam run out," said Maggie, keeping her eyes shut to please Tom.

"Why, you don't like that, you silly. You may have it if it comes to you fair, but I shan't give it you without. Right or left—you choose, now. Ha-a-a!" said Tom, in a tone of exasperation, as Maggie peeped. "You keep your eyes shut, now, else you shan't have any."

Maggie's power of sacrifice did not extend so far; indeed, I fear she cared less that Tom should enjoy the utmost possible amount of puff, than that he should be pleased with her for giving him the best bit. So she shut her eyes quite close, till Tom told her to "say which," and then she said, "Left-hand."

"You've got it," said Tom, in rather a bitter tone.

2. A game similar to hockey.

"What! the bit with the jam run out?"

"No; here, take it," said Tom, firmly, handing decidedly the best piece to Maggie.

"O, please, Tom, have it: I don't mind—I like the other: please take this."

"No, I shan't," said Tom, almost crossly, beginning on his own inferior piece.

Maggie, thinking it was no use to contend further, began too, and ate up her half puff with considerable relish as well as rapidity. But Tom had finished first, and had to look on while Maggie ate her last morsel or two, feeling in himself a capacity for more. Maggie didn't know Tom was looking at her; she was seesawing on the elder bough, lost to almost everything but a vague sense of jam and idleness.

"O, you greedy thing!" said Tom, when she had swallowed the last morsel. He was conscious of having acted very fairly, and thought she ought to have considered this, and made up to him for it. He would have refused a bit of hers beforehand, but one is naturally at a different point of view before and after one's own share of puff is swallowed.

Maggie turned quite pale. "O, Tom, why didn't you ask me?"

"*I* wasn't going to ask you for a bit, you greedy. You might have thought of it without, when you knew I gave you the best bit."

"But I wanted you to have it—you know I did," said Maggie, in an injured tone.

"Yes, but I wasn't going to do what wasn't fair, like Spouncer. He always takes the best bit, if you don't punch him for it; and if you choose the best with your eyes shut, he changes his hands. But if I go halves, I'll go 'em fair—only I wouldn't be a greedy."

With this cutting innuendo, Tom jumped down from his bough, and threw a stone with a "hoigh!" as a friendly attention to Yap, who had also been looking on while the eatables vanished, with an agitation of his ears and feelings which could hardly have been without bitterness. Yet the excellent dog accepted Tom's attention with as much alacrity as if he had been treated quite generously.

But Maggie, gifted with that superior power of misery which distinguishes the human being, and places him at a proud distance from the most melancholy chimpanzee, sat still on her bough, and gave herself up to the keen sense of unmerited reproach. She would have given the world not to have eaten all her puff, and to have saved some of it for Tom. Not but that the puff was very nice, for Maggie's palate was not at all obtuse, but she would have gone without it many times over, sooner than Tom should call her greedy and be cross with her. And he had said he wouldn't have it—and she ate it without thinking—how could she help it? The tears flowed so plentifully that Maggie saw nothing around her for the next ten minutes; but by that time resentment began to give way to the desire of reconciliation, and she jumped from her bough to look for Tom. He was no longer in the paddock behind the rickyard—where was he likely to be gone, and Yap with him? Maggie ran to the high bank against the great holly-tree, where she could see far away towards the Floss. There was Tom; but her heart sank again as she saw how far off he was on his way to the great river, and that he had another companion besides Yap—naughty Bob Jakin, whose official, if not natural function, of frightening the birds, was just now at a standstill. Maggie felt sure that Bob was wicked, without very distinctly knowing why; unless it was because Bob's mother was a dreadfully large fat woman, who lived at a queer round house down the river; and once, when Maggie and Tom had wandered thither, there rushed out a brindled[3] dog that wouldn't stop barking; and when Bob's mother came out after it, and screamed above the barking to tell them not to be frightened, Maggie thought she was scolding them fiercely, and her heart beat with terror. Maggie thought it very likely that the round house had snakes on the floor, and bats in the bed-room: for she had seen Bob take off his cap to show Tom a little snake that was inside it, and another time he had a handful of young bats: altogether, he was an irregular character, perhaps even slightly diabolical, judging from his intimacy with snakes and bats; and to crown all, when Tom had Bob for a companion, he didn't mind about Maggie, and would never let her go with him.

It must be owned that Tom was fond of Bob's company. How could it be otherwise? Bob knew, directly he saw a bird's egg, whether it was a swallow's, or a tomtit's, or a yellow-hammer's; he found out all the wasps' nests, and could set all sorts of traps; he could climb the trees like a squirrel, and had quite a magical power of detecting hedgehogs and stoats; and he had courage to do things that were rather naughty, such as making gaps in the hedgerows, throwing stones after the sheep, and killing a cat that was wandering *incognito*. Such qualities in an inferior, who could always be treated with authority in spite of his superior knowingness, had necessarily a fatal fascination for Tom; and every holiday-time Maggie was sure to have days of grief because he had gone off with Bob.

Well! there was no hope for it: he was gone now, and Maggie could think of no comfort but to sit down by the holly, or wander by the hedgerow, and fancy it was all different, refashioning her little world into just what she should like it to be.

Maggie's was a troublous life, and this was the form in which she took her opium.

Meanwhile Tom, forgetting all about Maggie and the sting of reproach which he had left in her heart, was hurrying along with Bob, whom he had met accidentally, to the scene of a great rat-catching in a neigh-

3. Having dark streaks or flecks.

bouring barn. Bob knew all about this particular affair, and spoke of the sport with an enthusiasm which no one who is not either divested of all manly feeling, or pitiably ignorant of rat-catching, can fail to imagine. For a person suspected of preternatural wickedness, Bob was really not so very villanous-looking; there was even something agreeable in his snub-nosed face, with its close-curled border of red hair. But then his trousers were always rolled up at the knee, for the convenience of wading on the slightest notice; and his virtue, supposing it to exist, was undeniably "virtue in rags,"[4] which, on the authority even of bilious philosophers, who think all well-dressed merit over-paid, is notoriously likely to remain unrecognised (perhaps because it is seen so seldom).

"I know the chap as owns the ferrets," said Bob, in a hoarse treble voice, as he shuffled along, keeping his blue eyes fixed on the river, like an amphibious animal who foresaw occasion for darting in. "He lives up the Kennel Yard at Sut Ogg's—he does. He's the biggest rot-catcher anywhere—he is. I'd sooner be a rot-catcher nor anything—I would. The moles is nothing to the rots. But Lors! you mun ha' ferrets. Dogs is no good. Why, there's that dog, now!" Bob continued, pointing with an air of disgust towards Yap, "he's no more good wi' a rot nor nothin'. I see it myself—I did—at the rot-catchin' i' your feyther's barn."

Yap, feeling the withering influence of this scorn, tucked his tail in and shrank close to Tom's leg, who felt a little hurt for him, but had not the superhuman courage to seem behindhand with Bob in contempt for a dog who made so poor a figure.

"No, no," he said, "Yap's no good at sport. I'll have regular good dogs for rats and everything, when I've done school."

"Hev ferrets, Measter Tom," said Bob, eagerly,—"them white ferrets wi' pink eyes; Lors, you might catch your own rots, an' you might put a rot in a cage wi' a ferret, an' see 'em fight—you might. That's what I'd do, I know, an' it 'ud be better fun a'most nor seein' two chaps fight—if it wasn't them chaps as sold cakes an' oranges at the Fair, as the things flew out o' their baskets, an' some o' the cakes was smashed. . . . But they tasted just as good," added Bob, by way of note or addendum, after a moment's pause.

"But, I say, Bob," said Tom, in a tone of deliberation, "ferrets are nasty biting things—they'll bite a fellow without being set on."

"Lors! why, that's the beauty on 'em. If a chap lays hold o' your ferret, he won't be long before he hollows out a good un—*he* won't."

At this moment a striking incident made the boys pause suddenly in their walk. It was the plunging of some small body in the water from among the neighbouring bulrushes: if it was not a water-rat, Bob intimated that he was ready to undergo the most unpleasant consequences.

"Hoigh! Yap—hoigh! there he is," said Tom, clapping his hands, as

4. From Horace's *Odes*, 3.29.55–56 (Dryden's translation).

the little black snout made its arrowy course to the opposite bank. "Seize him, lad, seize him!"

Yap agitated his ears and wrinkled his brows, but declined to plunge, trying whether barking would not answer the purpose just as well.

"Ugh! you coward!" said Tom, and kicked him over, feeling humiliated as a sportsman to possess so poor-spirited an animal. Bob abstained from remark and passed on, choosing, however, to walk in the shallow edge of the overflowing river by way of change.

"He's none so full now, the Floss isn't," said Bob, as he kicked the water up before him, with an agreeable sense of being insolent to it. "Why, last 'ear, the meadows was all one sheet o' water, they was."

"Ay, but," said Tom, whose mind was prone to see an opposition between statements that were really quite accordant—"but there was a big flood once, when the Round Pool was made. *I* know there was, 'cause father says so. And the sheep and cows were all drowned, and the boats went all over the fields ever such a way."

"*I* don't care about a flood comin'," said Bob; "I don't mind the water, no more nor the land. I'd swim—*I* would."

"Ah, but if you got nothing to eat for ever so long?" said Tom, his imagination becoming quite active under the stimulus of that dread. "When I'm a man, I shall make a boat with a wooden house on the top of it, like Noah's ark, and keep plenty to eat in it—rabbits and things—all ready. And then if the flood came, you know, Bob, I shouldn't mind. . . . And I'd take you in, if I saw you swimming," he added, in the tone of a benevolent patron.

"I aren't frighted," said Bob, to whom hunger did not appear so appalling. "But I'd get in an' knock the rabbits on the' head when you wanted to eat 'em."

"Ah, and I should have halfpence, and we'd play at heads-and-tails," said Tom, not contemplating the possibility that this recreation might have fewer charms for his mature age. "I'd divide fair to begin with, and then we'd see who'd win."

"I've got a halfpenny o' my own," said Bob, proudly, coming out of the water and tossing his halfpenny in the air. "Yeads or tails?"

"Tails," said Tom, instantly fired with the desire to win.

"It's yeads," said Bob, hastily, snatching up the halfpenny as it fell.

"It wasn't," said Tom, loudly and peremptorily. "You give me the halfpenny—I've won it fair."

"I shan't," said Bob, holding it tight in his pocket.

"Then I'll make you—see if I don't," said Tom.

"You can't make me do nothing, you can't," said Bob.

"Yes, I can."

"No, you can't."

"I'm master."

"I don't care for you."

"But I'll make you care, you cheat," said Tom, collaring Bob and shaking him.

"You get out wi' you," said Bob, giving Tom a kick.

Tom's blood was thoroughly up: he went at Bob with a lunge and threw him down, but Bob seized hold and kept it like a cat, and pulled Tom down after him. They struggled fiercely on the ground for a moment or two, till Tom, pinning Bob down by the shoulders, thought he had the mastery.

"*You* say you'll give me the halfpenny now," he said, with difficulty, while he exerted himself to keep the command of Bob's arms.

But at this moment, Yap, who had been running on before, returned barking to the scene of action, and saw a favourable opportunity for biting Bob's bare leg not only with impunity but with honour. The pain from Yap's teeth, instead of surprising Bob into a relaxation of his hold, gave it a fiercer tenacity, and, with a new exertion of his force, he pushed Tom backward and got uppermost. But now Yap, who could get no sufficient purchase before, set his teeth in a new place, so that Bob, harassed in this way, let go his hold of Tom, and, almost throttling Yap, flung him into the river. By this time Tom was up again, and before Bob had quite recovered his balance after the act of swinging Yap, Tom fell upon him, threw him down, and got his knees firmly on on Bob's chest.

"You give me the halfpenny now," said Tom.

"Take it," said Bob, sulkily.

"No, I shan't take it; you give it me."

Bob took the halfpenny out of his pocket, and threw it away from him on the ground.

Tom loosed his hold, and left Bob to rise.

"There the halfpenny lies," he said. "I don't want your halfpenny; I wouldn't have kept it. But you wanted to cheat: I hate a cheat. I shan't go along with you any more," he added, turning round homeward, not without casting a regret towards the rat-catching and other pleasures which he must relinquish along with Bob's society.

"You may let it alone, then," Bob called out after him. "I shall cheat if I like; there's no fun i' playing else; and I know where there's a goldfinch's nest, but I'll take care *you* don't. . . . An' you're a nasty fightin' turkey-cock, you are. . . ."

Tom walked on without looking round, and Yap followed his example, the cold bath having moderated his passions.

"Go along wi' you, then, wi' your drownded dog; I wouldn't own such a dog—*I* wouldn't," said Bob, getting louder, in a last effort to sustain his defiance. But Tom was not to be provoked into turning round, and Bob's voice began to falter a little as he said,

"An' I'n gi'en you everything, an' showed you everything, an' niver wanted nothin' from you. . . . An' there's your horn-handed knife, then, as you gi'en me". . . . Here Bob flung the knife as far as he could after Tom's retreating footsteps. But it produced no effect, except the sense in Bob's mind that there was a terrible void in his lot, now that knife was gone.

He stood still till Tom had passed through the gate and disappeared behind the hedge. The knife would do no good on the ground there—it wouldn't vex Tom, and pride or resentment was a feeble passion in Bob's mind compared with the love of a pocket-knife. His very fingers sent entreating thrills that he would go and clutch that familiar rough buck's-horn handle, which they had so often grasped for mere affection as it lay idle in his pocket. And there were two blades, and they had just been sharpened! What is life without a pocket-knife to him who has once tasted a higher existence? No: to throw the handle after the hatchet is a comprehensible act of desperation, but to throw one's pocket-knife after an implacable friend is clearly in every sense a hyperbole, or throwing beyond the mark. So Bob shuffled back to the spot where the beloved knife lay in the dirt, and felt quite a new pleasure in clutching it again after the temporary separation, in opening one blade after the other, and feeling their edge with his well-hardened thumb. Poor Bob! he was not sensitive on the point of honour—not a chivalrous character. That fine moral aroma would not have been thought much of by the public opinion of Kennel Yard, which was the very focus or heart of Bob's world, even if it could have made itself perceptible there; yet, for all that, he was not utterly a sneak and a thief, as our friend Tom had hastily decided.

But Tom, you perceive, was rather a Rhadamanthine[5] personage, having more than the usual share of boy's justice in him—the justice that desires to hurt culprits as much as they deserve to be hurt, and is troubled with no doubts concerning the exact amount of their deserts. Maggie saw a cloud on his brow when he came home, which checked her joy at his coming so much sooner than she had expected, and she dared hardly speak to him as he stood silently throwing the small gravel-stones into the mill-dam. It is not pleasant to give up a rat-catching when you have set your mind on it. But if Tom had told his strongest feeling at that moment, he would have said, "I'd do just the same again." That was his usual mode of viewing his past actions; whereas Maggie was always wishing she had done something different.

5. Inflexibly just; Rhadamanthus, son of the Greek God Zeus and Europa, became ruler and judge of the dead in Elysium as a reward for his just life on earth.

Chapter VII

Enter the Aunts and Uncles

The Dodsons were certainly a handsome family, and Mrs Glegg was not the least handsome of the sisters. As she sat in Mrs Tulliver's arm-chair, no impartial observer could have denied that for a woman of fifty she had a very comely face and figure, though Tom and Maggie considered their aunt Glegg as the type of ugliness. It is true she despised the advantages of costume, for though, as she often observed, no woman had better clothes, it was not her way to wear her new things out before her old ones. Other women, if they liked, might have their best thread-lace in every wash; but when Mrs Glegg died, it would be found that she had better lace laid by in the right-hand drawer of her wardrobe, in the Spotted Chamber, than ever Mrs Wooll of St Ogg's had bought in her life, although Mrs Wooll wore her lace before it was paid for. So of her curled fronts:[1] Mrs Glegg had doubtless the glossiest and crispest brown curls in her drawers, as well as curls in various degrees of fuzzy laxness; but to look out on the week-day world from under a crisp and glossy front, would be to introduce a most dreamlike and unpleasant confusion between the sacred and the secular. Occasionally, indeed, Mrs Glegg wore one of her third-best fronts on a week-day visit, but not at a sister's house; especially not at Mrs Tulliver's, who, since her marriage, had hurt her sisters' feelings greatly by wearing her own hair, though, as Mrs Glegg observed to Mrs Deane, a mother of a family, like Bessy, with a husband always going to law, might have been expected to know better. But Bessy was always weak!

So if Mrs Glegg's front to-day was more fuzzy and lax than usual, she had a design under it: she intended the most pointed and cutting allusion to Mrs Tulliver's bunches of blond curls, separated from each other by a due wave of smoothness on each side of the parting. Mrs Tulliver had shed tears several times at sister Glegg's unkindness on the subject of these unmatronly curls, but the consciousness of looking the handsomer for them, naturally administered support. Mrs Glegg chose to wear her bonnet in the house to-day—untied and tilted slightly, of course—a frequent practice of hers when she was on a visit, and happened to be in a severe humour: she didn't know what draughts there might be in strange houses. For the same reason she wore a small sable tippet,[2] which reached just to her shoulders, and was very far from meeting across her well-formed chest, while her long neck was protected by a *chevaux-de-frise*[3] of miscellaneous frilling. One would need to be

1. Hairpieces.
2. A small cape.
3. A protecting line of spikes.

learned in the fashions of those times to know how far in the rear of them Mrs Glegg's slate-coloured silk-gown must have been; but from certain constellations of small yellow spots upon it, and a mouldy odour about it suggestive of a damp clothes-chest, it was probable that it belonged to a stratum of garments just old enough to have come recently into wear.

Mrs Glegg held her large gold watch in her hand with the many-doubled chain round her fingers, and observed to Mrs Tulliver, who had just returned from a visit to the kitchen, that whatever it might be by other people's clocks and watches, it was gone half-past twelve by hers.

"I don't know what ails sister Pullet," she continued. "It used to be the way in our family for one to be as early as another,—I'm sure it was so in my poor father's time—and not for one sister to sit half an hour before the others came. But if the ways o' the family are altered, it shan't be *my* fault—*I'll* never be the one to come into a house when all the rest are going away. I wonder *at* sister Deane—she used to be more like me. But if you'll take my advice, Bessy, you'll put the dinner forrard a bit, sooner than put it back, because folks are late as ought to ha' known better."

"O dear, there's no fear but what they'll be all here in time, sister," said Mrs Tulliver, in her mild-peevish tone. "The dinner won't be ready till half-past one. But if it's long for you to wait, let me fetch you a cheese-cake and a glass o' wine."

"Well, Bessy!" said Mrs Glegg, with a bitter smile, and a scarcely perceptible toss of her head, "I should ha' thought you'd known your own sister better. I never *did* eat between meals, and I'm not going to begin. Not but what I hate that nonsense of having your dinner at half-past one, when you might have it at one. You was never brought up in that way, Bessy."

"Why, Jane, what can I do? Mr Tulliver doesn't like his dinner before two o'clock, but I put it half an hour earlier because o' you."

"Yes, yes, I know how it is with husbands—they're for putting everything off—they'll put the dinner off till after tea, if they've got wives as are weak enough to give in to such work; but it's a pity for you, Bessy, as you haven't got more strength o' mind. It'll be well if your children don't suffer for it. And I hope you've not gone and got a great dinner for us—going to expense for your sisters, as 'ud sooner eat a crust o' dry bread nor help to ruin you with extravagance. I wonder you don't take pattern by your sister Deane—she's far more sensible. And here you've got two children to provide for, and your husband's spent your fortin i' going to law, and's likely to spend his own too. A boiled joint, as you could make broth of for the kitchen," Mrs Glegg added, in a tone of emphatic protest, "and a plain pudding, with a spoonful o' sugar, and no spice, 'ud be far more becoming."

With sister Glegg in this humour, there was a cheerful prospect for the day. Mrs Tulliver never went the length of quarrelling with her, any more than a waterfowl that puts out its leg in a deprecating manner can be said to quarrel with a boy who throws stones. But this point of the dinner was a tender one, and not at all new, so that Mrs Tulliver could make the same answer she had often made before.

"Mr Tulliver says he always *will* have a good dinner for his friends while he can pay for it," she said, "and he's a right to do as he likes in his own house, sister."

"Well, Bessy, *I* can't leave your children enough out o' my savings, to keep 'em from ruin. And you mustn't look to having any o' Mr Glegg's money, for it's well if I don't go first—he comes of a long-lived family; and if he was to die and leave me well for my life, he'd tie all the money up to go back to his own kin."

The sound of wheels while Mrs Glegg was speaking was an interruption highly welcome to Mrs Tulliver, who hastened out to receive sister Pullet—it must be sister Pullet, because the sound was that of a four-wheel.[4]

Mrs Glegg tossed her head and looked rather sour about the mouth at the thought of the "four-wheel." She had a strong opinion on that subject.

Sister Pullet was in tears when the one-horse chaise stopped before Mrs Tulliver's door, and it was apparently requisite that she should shed a few more before getting out, for though her husband and Mrs Tulliver stood ready to support her, she sat still and shook her head sadly, as she looked through her tears at the vague distance.

"Why, whativer is the matter, sister?" said Mrs Tulliver. She was not an imaginative woman, but it occurred to her that the large toilet-glass in sister Pullet's best bedroom was possibly broken for the second time.

There was no reply but a further shake of the head, as Mrs Pullet slowly rose and got down from the chaise, not without casting a glance at Mr Pullet to see that he was guarding her handsome silk dress from injury. Mr Pullet was a small man with a high nose, small twinkling eyes, and thin lips, in a fresh-looking suit of black and a white cravat, that seemed to have been tied very tight on some higher principle than that of mere personal ease. He bore about the same relation to his tall, good-looking wife, with her balloon sleeves, abundant mantle, and large be-feathered and be-ribboned bonnet, as a small fishing-smack bears to a brig with all its sails spread.

It is a pathetic sight and a striking example of the complexity introduced into the emotions by a high state of civilisation—the sight of a fashionably drest female in grief. From the sorrow of a Hottentot[5] to

4. Chair-backed horse-drawn carriage with four wheels.
5. Member of a south African people who symbolized primitive culture to the Victorians.

that of a woman in large buckram[6] sleeves, with several bracelets on each arm, an architectural bonnet, and delicate ribbon-strings—what a long series of gradations! In the enlightened child of civilisation the abandonment characteristic of grief is checked and varied in the subtlest manner, so as to present an interesting problem to the analytic mind. If, with a crushed heart and eyes half-blinded by the mist of tears, she were to walk with a too devious step through a door-place, she might crush her buckram sleeves too, and the deep consciousness of this possibility produces a composition of forces by which she takes a line that just clears the doorpost. Perceiving that the tears are hurrying fast, she unpins her strings and throws them languidly backward—a touching gesture, indicative, even in the deepest gloom, of the hope in future dry moments when cap-strings will once more have a charm. As the tears subside a little, and with her head leaning backward at the angle that will not injure her bonnet, she endures that terrible moment when grief, which has made all things else a weariness, has itself become weary; she looks down pensively at her bracelets, and adjusts their clasps with that pretty studied fortuity which would be gratifying to her mind if it were once more in a calm and healthy state.

Mrs Pullet brushed each doorpost with great nicety, about the latitude of her shoulders (at that period a woman was truly ridiculous to an instructed eye if she did not measure a yard and a half across the shoulders), and having done that, sent the muscles of her face in quest of fresh tears as she advanced into the parlour where Mrs Glegg was seated.

"Well, sister, you're late; what's the matter?" said Mrs Glegg, rather sharply, as they shook hands.

Mrs Pullet sat down—lifting up her mantle carefully behind, before she answered,—

"She's gone," unconsciously using an impressive figure of rhetoric.

"It isn't the glass this time, then," thought Mrs Tulliver.

"Died the day before yesterday," continued Mrs Pullet; "an' her legs was as thick as my body," she added, with deep sadness, after a pause. "They'd tapped[7] her no end o' times, and the water—they say you might ha' swum in it, if you'd liked."

"Well, Sophy, it's a mercy she's gone, then, whoever she may be," said Mrs Glegg, with the promptitude and emphasis of a mind naturally clear and decided; "but I can't think who you're talking of, for my part."

"But *I* know," said Mrs Pullet, sighing and shaking her head; "and there isn't another such a dropsy in the parish. *I* know as it's old Mrs Sutton o' the Twentylands."

"Well, she's no kin o' yours, nor much acquaintance as I've ever heard of," said Mrs Glegg, who always cried just as much as was proper

6. Fine linen or cotton.
7. Drained fluid from.

when anything happened to her own "kin," but not on other occasions.

"She's so much acquaintance as I've seen her legs when they was like bladders. . . . And an old lady as had doubled her money over and over again, and kept it all in her own management to the last, and had her pocket with her keys in under her pillow constant. There isn't many old *par*ish'ners like her, I doubt."[8]

"And they say she'd took as much physic as 'ud fill a waggon," observed Mr Pullet.

"Ah," sighed Mrs Pullet, "she'd another complaint ever so many years before she had the dropsy, and the doctors couldn't make out what it was. And she said to me, when I went to see her last Christmas, she said, 'Mrs Pullet, if ever you have the dropsy, you'll think o' me.' She *did* say so," added Mrs Pullet, beginning to cry bitterly again; "those were her very words. And she's to be buried o' Saturday, and Pullet's bid to the funeral."

"Sophy," said Mrs Glegg, unable any longer to contain her spirit of rational remonstrance—"Sophy, I wonder *at* you, fretting and injuring your health about people as don't belong to you. Your poor father never did so, nor your aunt Frances neither, nor any o' the family as I ever heard of. You couldn't fret no more than this, if we'd heared as our cousin Abbott had died sudden without making his will."

Mrs Pullet was silent, having to finish her crying, and rather flattered than indignant at being upbraided for crying too much. It was not everybody who could afford to cry so much about their neighbours who had left them nothing; but Mrs Pullet had married a gentleman farmer, and had leisure and money to carry her crying and everything else to the highest pitch of respectability.

"Mrs Sutton didn't die without making her will, though," said Mr Pullet, with a confused sense that he was saying something to sanction his wife's tears; "ours is a rich parish, but they say there's nobody else to leave as many thousands behind 'em as Mrs Sutton. And she's left no leggicies, to speak on—left it all in a lump to her husband's nevvy."

"There wasn't much good i' being so rich, then," said Mrs Glegg, "if she'd got none but husband's kin to leave it to. It's poor work when that's all you've got to pinch yourself for;—not as I'm one o' those as 'ud like to die without leaving more money out at interest than other folks had reckoned. But it's a poor tale when it must go out o' your own family."

"I'm sure, sister," said Mrs Pullet, who had recovered sufficiently to take off her veil and fold it carefully, "it's a nice sort o' man as Mrs Sutton has left her money to, for he's troubled with the asthmy, and goes to bed every night at eight o'clock. He told me about it himself—as free as could be—one Sunday when he came to our church. He

8. Suspect.

wears a hare-skin on his chest, and has a trembling in his talk—quite a gentleman sort o' man. I told him there wasn't many months in the year as I wasn't under the doctor's hands. And he said, 'Mrs Pullet, I can feel for you.' That was what he said—the very words. Ah!" sighed Mrs Pullet, shaking her head at the idea that there were but few who could enter fully into her experiences in pink mixture and white mixture, strong stuff in small bottles, and weak stuff in large bottles, damp boluses[9] at a shilling, and draughts at eighteenpence. "Sister, I may as well go and take my bonnet off now. Did you see as the cap-box was put out?" she added, turning to her husband.

Mr Pullet, by an unaccountable lapse of memory, had forgotten it, and hastened out, with a stricken conscience, to remedy the omission.

"They'll bring it up-stairs, sister," said Mrs Tulliver, wishing to go at once, lest Mrs Glegg should begin to explain her feelings about Sophy's being the first Dodson who ever ruined her constitution with doctor's stuff.

Mrs Tulliver was fond of going up-stairs with her sister Pullet, and looking thoroughly at her cap before she put it on her head, and discussing millinery in general. This was part of Bessy's weakness, that stirred Mrs Glegg's sisterly compassion: Bessy went far too well drest, considering; and she was too proud to dress her child in the good clothing her sister Glegg gave her from the primeval strata of her wardrobe; it was a sin and a shame to buy anything to dress that child, if it wasn't a pair of shoes. In this particular, however, Mrs Glegg did her sister Bessy some injustice, for Mrs Tulliver had really made great efforts to induce Maggie to wear a leghorn bonnet[1] and a dyed silk frock made out of her aunt Glegg's, but the results had been such that Mrs Tulliver was obliged to bury them in her maternal bosom; for Maggie, declaring that the frock smelt of nasty dye, had taken an opportunity of basting it together with the roast-beef the first Sunday she wore it, and, finding this scheme answer, she had subsequently pumped on the bonnet with its green ribbons, so as to give it a general resemblance to a sage cheese garnished with withered lettuces. I must urge in excuse for Maggie, that Tom had laughed at her in the bonnet, and said she looked like an old Judy.[2] Aunt Pullet, too, made presents of clothes, but these were always pretty enough to please Maggie as well as her mother. Of all her sisters, Mrs Tulliver certainly preferred her sister Pullet, not without a return of preference; but Mrs Pullet was sorry Bessy had those naughty awkward children; she would do the best she could by them, but it was a pity they weren't as good and as pretty as sister Deane's child. Maggie and Tom, on their part, thought their aunt Pullet tolerable, chiefly because she was not their aunt Glegg. Tom always declined to go more than

9. Large pills.
1. Italian straw bonnet.
2. The shabby wife in the Punch and Judy puppet shows.

once, during his holidays, to see either of them: both his uncles tipped him that once, of course; but at his aunt Pullet's there was a great many toads to pelt in the cellar-area, so that he preferred the visit to her. Maggie shuddered at the toads, and dreamed of them horribly, but she liked her uncle Pullet's musical snuff-box. Still, it was agreed by the sisters, in Mrs Tulliver's absence, that the Tulliver blood did not mix well with the Dodson blood; that, in fact, poor Bessy's children were Tullivers, and that Tom, notwithstanding he had the Dodson complexion, was likely to be as "contrairy" as his father. As for Maggie, she was the picture of her aunt Moss, Mr Tulliver's sister,—a large-boned woman, who had married as poorly as could be; had no china, and had a husband who had much ado to pay his rent. But when Mrs Pullet was alone with Mrs Tulliver up-stairs, the remarks were naturally to the disadvantage of Mrs Glegg, and they agreed, in confidence, that there was no knowing what sort of fright sister Jane would come out next. But their *tête-ù-tête* was curtailed by the appearance of Mrs Deane with little Lucy; and Mrs Tulliver had to look on with a silent pang while Lucy's blond curls were adjusted. It was quite unaccountable that Mrs Deane, the thinnest and sallowest of all the Miss Dodsons, should have had this child, who might have been taken for Mrs Tulliver's any day. And Maggie always looked twice as dark as usual when she was by the side of Lucy.

She did to-day, when she and Tom came in from the garden with their father and their uncle Glegg. Maggie had thrown her bonnet off very carelessly, and, coming in with her hair rough as well as out of curl, rushed at once to Lucy, who was standing by her mother's knee. Certainly the contrast between the cousins was conspicuous, and, to superficial eyes, was very much to the disadvantage of Maggie, though a connoisseur might have seen "points" in her which had a higher promise for maturity than Lucy's natty completeness. It was like the contrast between a rough, dark, overgrown puppy and a white kitten. Lucy put up the neatest little rosebud mouth to be kissed: everything about her was neat—her little round neck, with the row of coral beads; her little straight nose, not at all snubby; her little clear eyebrows, rather darker than her curls, to match her hazel eyes, which looked up with shy pleasure at Maggie, taller by the head, though scarcely a year older. Maggie always looked at Lucy with delight. She was fond of fancying a world where the people never got any larger than children of their own age, and she made the queen of it just like Lucy, with a little crown on her head, and a little sceptre in her hand . . . only the queen was Maggie herself in Lucy's form.

"O Lucy," she burst out, after kissing her, "you'll stay with Tom and me, won't you? O kiss her, Tom."

Tom, too, had come up to Lucy, but he was not going to kiss her—no; he came up to her with Maggie, because it seemed easier, on the whole, than saying, "How do you do?" to all those aunts and uncles: he stood looking at nothing in particular, with the blushing, awkward air and semi-smile which are common to shy boys when in company —very much as if they had come into the world by mistake, and found it in a degree of undress that was quite embarrassing.

"Heyday!" said aunt Glegg, with loud emphasis. "Do little boys and gells come into a room without taking notice o' their uncles and aunts? That wasn't the way when *I* was a little gell."

"Go and speak to your aunts and uncles, my dears," said Mrs Tulliver, looking anxious and melancholy. She wanted to whisper to Maggie a command to go and have her hair brushed.

"Well, and how do you do? And I hope you're good children, are you?" said aunt Glegg, in the same loud emphatic way, as she took their hands, hurting them with her large rings, and kissing their cheeks much against their desire. "Look up, Tom, look up. Boys as go to boarding-schools should hold their heads up. Look at me now." Tom declined that pleasure apparently, for he tried to draw his hand away. "Put your hair behind your ears, Maggie, and keep your frock on your shoulder."

Aunt Glegg always spoke to them in this loud emphatic way, as if she considered them deaf, or perhaps rather idiotic: it was a means, she thought, of making them feel that they were accountable creatures, and might be a salutary check on naughty tendencies. Bessy's children were so spoiled—they'd need have somebody to make them feel their duty.

"Well, my dears," said aunt Pullet, in a compassionate voice, "you grow wonderful fast. I doubt they'll outgrow their strength," she added, looking over their heads with a melancholy expression, at their mother. "I think the gell has too much hair. I'd have it thinned and cut shorter, sister, if I was you: it isn't good for her health. It's that as makes her skin so brown. I shouldn't wonder. Don't you think so, sister Deane?"

"I can't say, I'm sure, sister," said Mrs Deane, shutting her lips close again, and looking at Maggie with a critical eye.

"No, no," said Mr Tulliver, "the child's healthy enough—there's nothing ails her. There's red wheat as well as white, for that matter, and some like the dark grain best. But it 'ud be as well if Bessy 'ud have the child's hair cut, so as it 'ud lie smooth."

A dreadful resolve was gathering in Maggie's breast, but it was arrested by the desire to know from her aunt Deane whether she would leave Lucy behind: aunt Deane would hardly ever let Lucy come to see them. After various reasons for refusal, Mrs Deane appealed to Lucy herself.

"You wouldn't like to stay behind without mother, should you, Lucy?"

"Yes, please, mother," said Lucy, timidly, blushing very pink all over her little neck.

"Well done, Lucy! Let her stay, Mrs Deane, let her stay," said Mr Deane, a large but alert-looking man, with a type of physique to be seen in all ranks of English society—bald crown, red whiskers, full forehead, and general solidity without heaviness. You may see noblemen like Mr Deane, and you may see grocers or day-labourers like him; but the keenness of his brown eyes was less common than his contour. He held a silver snuff-box very tightly in his hand, and now and then exchanged a pinch with Mr Tulliver, whose box was only silver-mounted, so that it was naturally a joke between them that Mr Tulliver wanted to exchange snuff-boxes also. Mr Deane's box had been given him by the superior partners in the firm to which he belonged, at the same time that they gave him a share in the business, in acknowledgment of his valuable services as manager. No man was thought more highly of in St Ogg's than Mr Deane, and some persons were even of opinion that Miss Susan Dodson, who was once held to have made the worst match of all the Dodson sisters, might one day ride in a better carriage, and live in a better house, even than her sister Pullet. There was no knowing where a man would stop, who had got his foot into a great mill-owning, ship-owning business like that of Guest & Co., with a banking concern attached. And Mrs Deane, as her intimate female friends observed, was proud and "having" enough: *she* wouldn't let her husband stand still in the world for want of spurring.

"Maggie," said Mrs Tulliver, beckoning Maggie to her, and whispering in her ear, as soon as this point of Lucy's staying was settled, "go and get your hair brushed—do, for shame. I told you not to come in without going to Martha first; you know I did."

"Tom, come out with me," whispered Maggie, pulling his sleeve as she passed him; and Tom followed willingly enough.

"Come up-stairs with me, Tom," she whispered, when they were outside the door. "There's something I want to do before dinner."

"There's no time to play at anything before dinner," said Tom, whose imagination was impatient of any intermediate prospect.

"O, yes, there is time for this—*do* come, Tom."

Tom followed Maggie up-stairs into her mother's room, and saw her go at once to a drawer, from which she took out a large pair of scissors.

"What are they for, Maggie?" said Tom, feeling his curiosity awakened.

Maggie answered by seizing her front locks and cutting them straight across the middle of her forehead.

"O, my buttons, Maggie, you'll catch it!" exclaimed Tom; "you'd better not cut any more off."

Snip! went the great scissors again while Tom was speaking; and he couldn't help feeling it was rather good fun: Maggie would look so queer.

"Here, Tom, cut it behind for me," said Maggie, excited by her own daring, and anxious to finish the deed.

"You'll catch it, you know," said Tom, nodding his head in an admonitory manner, and hesitating a little as he took the scissors.

"Never mind—make haste!" said Maggie, giving a little stamp with her foot. Her cheeks were quite flushed.

The black locks were so thick—nothing could be more tempting to a lad who had already tasted the forbidden pleasure of cutting the pony's mane. I speak to those who know the satisfaction of making a pair of shears meet through a duly resisting mass of hair. One delicious grinding snip, and then another and another, and the hinder-locks fell heavily on the floor, and Maggie stood cropped in a jagged, uneven manner, but with a sense of clearness and freedom, as if she had emerged from a wood into the open plain.

"O, Maggie," said Tom, jumping round her, and slapping his knees as he laughed, "O, my buttons, what a queer thing you look! Look at yourself in the glass—you look like the idiot we throw our nut-shells to at school."

Maggie felt an unexpected pang. She had thought before-hand chiefly of her own deliverance from her teasing hair and teasing remarks about it, and something also of the triumph she should have over her mother and her aunts by this very decided course of action: she didn't want her hair to look pretty—that was out of the question—she only wanted people to think her a clever little girl, and not to find fault with her. But now, when Tom began to laugh at her, and say she was like the idiot, the affair had quite a new aspect. She looked in the glass, and still Tom laughed and clapped his hands, and Maggie's flushed cheeks began to pale, and her lips to tremble a little.

"O Maggie, you'll have to go down to dinner directly," said Tom. "O my!"

"Don't laugh at me, Tom," said Maggie, in a passionate tone, with an outburst of angry tears, stamping, and giving him a push.

"Now, then, spitfire!" said Tom. "What did you cut it off for, then? I shall go down: I can smell the dinner going in."

He hurried down-stairs and left poor Maggie to that bitter sense of the irrevocable which was almost an everyday experience of her small soul. She could see clearly enough, now the thing was done, that it was very foolish, and that she should have to hear and think more about her hair than ever; for Maggie rushed to her deeds with passionate impulse, and then saw not only their consequences, but what would have happened if they had not been done, with all the detail and exaggerated circumstance of an active imagination. Tom never did the same sort of foolish things as Maggie, having a wonderful instinctive discernment of what would turn to his advantage or disadvantage; and so it happened, that though he was much more wilful and inflexible than Maggie, his mother hardly ever called him naughty. But if Tom did make a mistake of that sort, he espoused it, and stood by it: he "didn't mind." If he broke the lash of his father's gig-whip by lashing the gate, he couldn't help it—the whip shouldn't have got caught in the hinge. If Tom Tulliver whipped a gate, he was convinced, not that the whipping of gates by all boys was a justifiable act, but that he, Tom Tulliver, was justifiable in whipping that particular gate, and he wasn't going to be sorry. But Maggie, as she stood crying before the glass, felt it impossible that she should go down to dinner and endure the severe eyes and severe words of her aunts, while Tom, and Lucy, and Martha, who waited at table, and perhaps her father and her uncles, would laugh at her,—for if Tom had laughed at her, of course every one else would; and if she had only let her hair alone, she could have sat with Tom and Lucy, and had the apricot pudding and the custard! What could she do but sob? She sat as helpless and despairing among her black locks as Ajax among the slaughtered sheep.[3] Very trivial, perhaps, this anguish seems to weather-worn mortals who have to think of Christmas bills, dead loves, and broken friendships; but it was not less bitter to Maggie —perhaps it was even more bitter—than what we are fond of calling antithetically the real troubles of mature life. "Ah, my child, you will have real troubles to fret about by-and-by," is the consolation we have almost all of us had administered to us in our childhood, and have repeated to other children since we have been grown up. We have all of us sobbed so piteously, standing with tiny bare legs above our little socks, when we lost sight of our mother or nurse in some strange place; but we can no longer recall the poignancy of that moment and weep over it, as we do over the remembered sufferings of five or ten years ago. Every one of those keen moments has left its trace, and lives in us still, but such traces have blent themselves irrecoverably with the firmer texture of our youth and manhood; and so it comes that we can look on at the troubles of our children with a smiling disbelief in the reality of their pain. Is there any one who can recover the experience of his childhood, not merely with a memory of what he did and what happened to him, of what he liked and disliked when he was in frock and trousers, but with an intimate penetration, a revived consciousness of what he felt then—when it was so long from one Midsummer to another? what he felt when his schoolfellows shut him out of their game because he would pitch the ball wrong out of mere wilfulness; or on a rainy day in the holidays, when he didn't know how to amuse himself, and fell from idleness into mischief, from mischief into defiance, and from defiance into sulkiness; or when his mother absolutely refused to let him have a tailed coat that "half,"[4] although every other boy of his age had gone into tails already? Surely if we could recall that early bitterness, and the dim guesses, the strangely perspectiveless conception of life that gave

3. In Sophocles' play *Ajax*, the title character, in a moment of madness, slaughters a flock of sheep whom he has mistaken for enemy soldiers.
4. Half-term.

the bitterness its intensity, we should not pooh-pooh the griefs of our children.

"Miss Maggie, you're to come down this minute," said Kezia, entering the room hurriedly. "Lawks! what have you been a-doing? I niver *see* such a fright."

"Don't Kezia," said Maggie, angrily. "Go away!"

"But I tell you, you're to come down, Miss, this minute: your mother says so," said Kezia, going up to Maggie and taking her by the hand to raise her from the floor.

"Get away, Kezia; I don't want any dinner," said Maggie, resisting Kezia's arm. "I shan't come."

"O, well, I can't stay. I've got to wait at dinner," said Kezia, going out again.

"Maggie, you little silly," said Tom, peeping into the room ten minutes after, "why don't you come and have your dinner? There's lots o' goodies, and mother says you're to come. What are you crying for, you little spooney?"[5]

O, it was dreadful! Tom was so hard and unconcerned; if *he* had been crying on the floor, Maggie would have cried too. And there was the dinner, so nice; and she was *so* hungry. It was very bitter.

But Tom was not altogether hard. He was not inclined to cry, and did not feel that Maggie's grief spoiled his prospect of the sweets; but he went and put his head near her, and said in a lower, comforting tone—

"Won't you come, then, Maggie? Shall I bring you a bit o' pudding when I've had mine? . . . and a custard and things?"

"Ye-e-es," said Maggie, beginning to feel life a little more tolerable.

"Very well," said Tom, going away. But he turned again at the door and said, "But you'd better come, you know. There's the dessert—nuts, you know—and cowslip wine."[6]

Maggie's tears had ceased, and she looked reflective as Tom left her. His good nature had taken off the keenest edge of her suffering, and nuts with cowslip wine began to assert their legitimate influence.

Slowly she rose from amongst her scattered locks, and slowly she made her way down-stairs. Then she stood leaning with one shoulder against the frame of the dining-parlour door, peeping in when it was ajar. She saw Tom and Lucy with an empty chair between them, and there were the custards on a side-table—it was too much. She slipped in and went towards the empty chair. But she had no sooner sat down than she repented, and wished herself back again.

Mrs Tulliver gave a litle scream as she saw her, and felt such a "turn" that she dropt the large gravy-spoon into the dish with the most serious

5. Crybaby.
6. Homemade wine, from primroses.

results to the table-cloth. For Kezia had not betrayed the reason of Maggie's refusal to come down, not liking to give her mistress a shock in the moment of carving, and Mrs Tulliver thought there was nothing worse in question than a fit of perverseness, which was inflicting its own punishment by depriving Maggie of half her dinner.

Mrs Tulliver's scream made all eyes turn towards the same point as her own, and Maggie's cheeks and ears began to burn, while uncle Glegg, a kind-looking, white-haired old gentleman, said—

"Heyday! what little gell's this—why, I don't know her. Is it some little gell you've picked up in the road, Kezia?"

"Why, she's gone and cut her hair herself," said Mr Tulliver in an under-tone to Mr Deane, laughing with much enjoyment. "Did you ever know such a little hussy as it is?"

"Why, little miss, you've made yourself look very funny," said uncle Pullet, and perhaps he never in his life made an observation which was felt to be so lacerating.

"Fie, for shame!" said aunt Glegg, in her loudest, severest tone of reproof. "Little gells as cut their own hair should be whipped and fed on bread-and-water—not come and sit down with their aunts and uncles."

"Ay, ay," said uncle Glegg, meaning to give a playful turn to this denunciation, "she must be sent to jail, I think, and they'll cut the rest of her hair off there, and make it all even."

"She's more like a gypsy nor ever," said aunt Pullet, in a pitying tone; "its very bad luck, sister, as the gell should be so brown—the boy's fair enough. I doubt it'll stand in her way i' life to be so brown."

"She's a naughty child, as'll break her mother's heart," said Mrs Tulliver, with the tears in her eyes.

Maggie seemed to be listening to a chorus of reproach and derision. Her first flush came from anger, which gave her a transient power of defiance, and Tom thought she was braving it out, supported by the recent appearance of the pudding and custard. Under this impression, he whispered, "O my! Maggie, I told you you'd catch it." He meant to be friendly, but Maggie felt convinced that Tom was rejoicing in her ignominy. Her feeble power of defiance left her in an instant, her heart swelled, and, getting up from her chair, she ran to her father, hid her face on his shoulder, and burst out into loud sobbing.

"Come, come, my wench," said her father soothingly, putting his arm round her, "never mind; you was i' the right to cut it off if it plagued you; give over crying: father'll take your part."

Delicious words of tenderness! Maggie never forgot any of these moments when her father "took her part;" she kept them in her heart, and thought of them long years after, when every one else said that her father had done very ill by his children.

"How your husband does spoil that child, Bessy!" said Mrs Glegg, in a loud "aside," to Mrs Tulliver. "It'll be the ruin of her, if you don't take care. *My* father niver brought his children up so, else we should ha' been a different sort o' family to what we are."

Mrs Tulliver's domestic sorrows seemed at this moment to have reached the point at which insensibility begins. She took no notice of her sister's remark, but threw back her cap-strings and dispensed the pudding, in mute resignation.

With the dessert there came entire deliverance for Maggie, for the children were told they might have their nuts and wine in the summer-house, since the day was so mild, and they scampered out among the budding bushes of the garden with the alacrity of small animals getting from under a burning glass.

Mrs Tulliver had her special reason for this permission: now the dinner was despatched, and every one's mind disengaged, it was the right moment to communicate Mr Tulliver's intention concerning Tom, and it would be as well for Tom himself to be absent. The children were used to hear themselves talked of as freely as if they were birds, and could understand nothing, however they might stretch their necks and listen; but on this occasion Mrs Tulliver manifested an unusual discretion, because she had recently had evidence that the going to school to a clergyman was a sore point with Tom, who looked at it as very much on a par with going to school to a constable. Mrs Tulliver had a sighing sense that her husband would do as he liked, whatever sister Glegg said, or sister Pullet either, but at least they would not be able to say, if the thing turned out ill, that Bessy had fallen in with her husband's folly without letting her own friends know a word about it.

"Mr Tulliver," she said, interrupting her husband in his talk with Mr Deane, "it's time now to tell the children's aunts and uncles what you're thinking of doing with Tom, isn't it?"

"Very well," said Mr Tulliver, rather sharply, "I've no objections to tell anybody what I mean to do with him. I've settled," he added, looking towards Mr Glegg and Mr Deane—"I've settled to send him to a Mr Stelling, a parson, down at King's Lorton, there—an uncommon clever fellow, I understand—as'll put him up to most things."

There was a rustling demonstration of surprise in the company, such as you may have observed in a country congregation when they hear an allusion to their week-day affairs from the pulpit. It was equally astonishing to the aunts and uncles to find a parson introduced into Mr Tulliver's family arrangements. As for uncle Pullet, he could hardly have been more thoroughly obfuscated if Mr Tulliver had said that he was going to send Tom to the Lord Chancellor: for uncle Pullet belonged to that extinct class of British yeomen who, dressed in good broadcloth, paid high rates and taxes, went to church, and ate a particularly good dinner on Sunday, without dreaming that the British constitution in Church and State had a traceable origin any more than the solar system and the fixed stars. It is melancholy, but true, that Mr Pullet had the most confused idea of a bishop as a sort of a baronet, who might or might not be a clergyman; and as the rector of his own parish was a man of high family and fortune, the idea that a clergyman could be a schoolmaster was too remote from Mr Pullet's experience to be readily conceivable. I know it is difficult for people in these instructed times to believe in uncle Pullet's ignorance; but let them reflect on the remarkable results of a great natural faculty under favouring circumstances. And uncle Pullet had a great natural faculty for ignorance. He was the first to give utterance to his astonishment.

"Why, what can you be going to send him to a parson for?" he said, with an amazed twinkling in his eyes, looking at Mr Glegg and Mr Deane, to see if they showed any signs of comprehension.

"Why, because the parsons are the best schoolmasters, by what I can make out," said poor Mr Tulliver, who, in the maze of this puzzling world, laid hold of any clue with great readiness and tenacity. "Jacobs at th' academy's no parson, and he's done very bad by the boy; and I made up my mind, if I sent him to school again, it should be to somebody different to Jacobs. And this Mr Stelling, by what I can make out, is the sort o' man I want. And I mean my boy to go to him at Midsummer," he concluded, in a tone of decision, tapping his snuff-box and taking a pinch.

"You'll have to pay a swinging half-yearly bill, then, eh, Tulliver? The clergymen have highish notions, in general," said Mr Deane, taking snuff vigorously, as he always did when wishing to maintain a neutral position.

"What! do you think the parson'll teach him to know a good sample o' wheat when he sees it, neighbour Tulliver?" said Mr Glegg, who was fond of his jest; and, having retired from business, felt that it was not only allowable but becoming in him to take a playful view of things.

"Why, you see, I've got a plan i' my head about Tom," said Mr Tulliver, pausing after that statement and lifting up his glass.

"Well, if I may be allowed to speak, and it's seldom as I am," said Mrs Glegg, with a tone of bitter meaning, "I should like to know what good is to come to the boy, by bringin' him up above his fortin."

"Why," said Mr Tulliver, not looking at Mrs Glegg, but at the male part of his audience, "you see, I've made up my mind not to bring Tom up to my own business. I've had my thoughts about it all along, and I made up my mind by what I saw with Garnett and *his* son. I mean to put him to some business, as he can go into without capital, and I want to give him an eddication as he'll be even wi' the lawyers and folks, and put me up to a notion now an' then."

Mrs Glegg emitted a long sort of guttural sound with closed lips, that smiled in mingled pity and scorn.

"It 'ud be a fine deal better for some people," she said, after that introductory note, "if they'd let the lawyers alone."

"Is he at the head of a grammar school, then, this clergyman—such as that at Market Bewley?" said Mr Deane.

"No—nothing o' that," said Mr Tulliver. "He won't take more than two or three pupils—and so he'll have the more time to attend to 'em, you know."

"Ah, and get his eddication done the sooner: they can't learn much at a time when there's so many of 'em," said uncle Pullet, feeling that he was getting quite an insight into this difficult matter.

"But he'll want the more pay, I doubt," said Mr Glegg.

"Ay, ay, a cool hundred a-year—that's all," said Mr Tulliver, with some pride at his own spirited course. "But then, you know, it's an investment; Tom's eddication 'ull be so much capital to him."

"Ay, there's something in that," said Mr Glegg. "Well, well, neighbour Tulliver, you may be right, you may be right:

'When land is gone and money's spent,
Then learning is most excellent.'[7]

I remember seeing those two lines wrote on a window at Buxton. But us that have got no learning had better keep our money, eh, neighbour Pullet?" Mr Glegg rubbed his knees and looked very pleasant.

"Mr Glegg, I wonder *at* you," said his wife. "It's very unbecoming in a man o' your age and belongings."

"What's unbecoming, Mrs G.?" said Mr Glegg, winking pleasantly at the company. "My new blue coat as I've got on?"

"I pity your weakness, Mr Glegg. I say it's unbecoming to be making a joke when you see your own kin going headlongs to ruin."

"If you mean me by that," said Mr Tulliver, considerably nettled, "you needn't trouble yourself to fret about me. I can manage my own affairs without troubling other folks."

"Bless me," said Mr Deane, judiciously introducing a new idea, "why, now I come to think of it, somebody said Wakem was going to send *his* son—the deformed lad—to a clergyman, didn't they, Susan?" (appealing to his wife).

"I can give no account of it, I'm sure," said Mrs Deane, closing her lips very tightly again. Mrs Deane was not a woman to take part in a scene where missiles were flying.

"Well," said Mr Tulliver, speaking all the more cheerfully, that Mrs Glegg might see he didn't mind her, "if Wakem thinks o' sending his son to a clergyman, depend on it I shall make no mistake i' sending Tom to one. Wakem's as big a scoundrel as Old Harry ever made, but

7. From Samuel Foote's *Taste*, I.1–2 (1752).

he knows the length of every man's foot he's got to deal with. Ay, ay, tell me who's Wakem's butcher, and I'll tell you where to get your meat."

"But lawyer Wakem's son's got a hump-back," said Mrs Pullet, who felt as if the whole business had a funereal aspect; "it's more nat'ral to send *him* to a clergyman."

"Yes," said Mr Glegg, interpreting Mrs Pullet's observation with erroneous plausibility, "you must consider that, neighbour Tulliver; Wakem's son isn't likely to follow any business. Wakem 'ull make a gentleman of him, poor fellow."

"Mr Glegg," said Mrs G., in a tone which implied that her indignation would fizz and ooze a little, though she was determined to keep it corked up, "you'd far better hold your tongue. Mr Tulliver doesn't want to know your opinion nor mine neither. There's folks in the world as know better than everybody else."

"Why, I should think that's you, if we're to trust your own tale," said Mr Tulliver, beginning to boil up again.

"O, *I* say nothing," said Mrs Glegg, sarcastically. "My advice has never been asked, and I don't give it."

"It'll be the first time, then," said Mr Tulliver. "It's the only thing you're over-ready at giving."

"I've been over-ready at lending, then, if I haven't been over-ready at giving," said Mrs Glegg. "There's folk I've lent money to, as perhaps I shall repent o' lending money to kin."

"Come, come, come," said Mr Glegg, soothingly. But Mr Tulliver was not to be hindered of his retort.

"You've got a bond for it, I reckon," he said; "and you've had your five per cent, kin or no kin."

"Sister," said Mrs Tulliver, pleadingly, "drink your wine, and let me give you some almonds and raisins."

"Bessy, I'm sorry for you," said Mrs Glegg, very much with the feeling of a cur that seizes the opportunity of diverting his bark towards the man who carries no stick. "It's poor work, talking o' almonds and raisins."

"Lors, sister Glegg, don't be so quarrelsome," said Mrs Pullet, beginning to cry a little. "You may be struck with a fit, getting so red in the face after dinner, and we are but just out o' mourning, all of us—and all wi' gowns craped alike and just put by—its very bad among sisters."

"I should think it *is* bad," said Mrs Glegg. "Things are come to a fine pass when one sister invites the other to her house o' purpose to quarrel with her and abuse her."

"Softly, softly, Jane—be reasonable—be reasonable," said Mr Glegg.

But while he was speaking, Mr Tulliver, who had by no means said enough to satisfy his anger, burst out again,

"Who wants to quarrel with you?" he said. "It's you as can't let people alone, but must be gnawing at 'em for ever. *I* should never want to quarrel with any woman, if she kept her place."

"My place indeed!" said Mrs Glegg, getting rather more shrill. "There's your betters, Mr Tulliver, as are dead and in their grave, treated me with a different sort o' respect to what you do—*though* I've got a husband as'll sit by and see me abused by them as 'ud never ha' had the chance if there hadn't been them in our family as married worse than they might ha' done."

"If you talk o' that," said Mr Tulliver, "my family's as good as yours—and better, for it hasn't got a damned ill-tempered woman in it."

"Well!" said Mrs Glegg, rising from her chair, "I don't know whether you think it's a fine thing to sit by and hear me swore at, Mr Glegg; but I'm not going to stay a minute longer in this house. You can stay behind, and come home with the gig—and I'll walk home."

"Dear heart, dear heart!" said Mr Glegg in a melancholy tone, as he followed his wife out of the room.

"Mr Tulliver, how could you talk so?" said Mrs Tulliver, with the tears in her eyes.

"Let her go," said Mr Tulliver, too hot to be damped by any amount of tears. "Let her go, and the sooner the better: she won't be trying to domineer over *me* again in a hurry."

"Sister Pullet," said Mrs Tulliver helplessly, "do you think it 'ud be any use for you to go after her and try to pacify her?"

"Better not, better not," said Mr Deane. "You'll make it up another day."

"Then, sisters, shall we go and look at the children?" said Mrs Tulliver, drying her eyes.

No proposition could have been more seasonable. Mr Tulliver felt very much as if the air had been cleared of obtrusive flies now the women were out of the room. There were few things he liked better than a chat with Mr Deane, whose close application to business allowed the pleasure very rarely. Mr Deane, he considered, was the "knowingest" man of his acquaintance, and he had besides a ready causticity of tongue that made an agreeable supplement to Mr Tulliver's own tendency that way, which had remained in rather an inarticulate condition. And now the women were gone, they could carry on their serious talk without frivolous interruption. They could exchange their views concerning the Duke of Wellington, whose conduct in the Catholic Question had thrown such an entirely new light on his character[8] and speak slightingly of his conduct at the battle of Waterloo, which he would never have

8. The Duke of Wellington, who defeated Napoleon at Waterloo in 1815, became prime minister in 1828 and passed the Act of Catholic Emancipation in 1829.

won if there hadn't been a great many Englishmen at his back, not to speak of Blucher[9] and the Prussians, who, as Mr Tulliver had heard from a person of particular knowledge in that matter, had come up in the very nick of time; though here there was a slight dissidence, Mr Deane remarking that he was not disposed to give much credit to the Prussians,—the build of their vessels, together with the unsatisfactory character of transactions in Dantzic[1] beer, inclining him to form rather a low view of Prussian pluck generally. Rather beaten on this ground, Mr Tulliver proceeded to express his fears that the country could never again be what it used to be; but Mr Deane, attached to a firm of which the returns were on the increase, naturally took a more lively view of the present; and had some details to give concerning the state of the imports, especially in hides and spelter,[2] which soothed Mr Tulliver's imagination by throwing into more distant perspective the period when the country would become utterly the prey of Papists and Radicals, and there would be no more chance for honest men.

Uncle Pullet sat by and listened with twinkling eyes to these high matters. He didn't understand politics himself—thought they were a natural gift—but by what he could make out, this Duke of Wellington was no better than he should be.

Chapter VIII

Mr Tulliver Shows His Weaker Side

"Suppose sister Glegg should call her money in—it 'ud be very awkward for you to have to raise five hundred pounds now," said Mrs Tulliver to her husband that evening, as she took a plaintive review of the day.

Mrs Tulliver had lived thirteen years with her husband, yet she retained in all the freshness of her early married life a facility of saying things which drove him in the opposite direction to the one she desired. Some minds are wonderful for keeping their bloom in this way, as a patriarchal gold-fish apparently retains to the last its youthful illusion that it can swim in a straight line beyond the encircling glass. Mrs Tulliver was an amiable fish of this kind, and, after running her head against the same resisting medium for thirteen years, would go at it again to-day with undulled alacrity.

This observation of hers tended directly to convince Mr Tulliver that it would not be at all awkward for him to raise five hundred pounds; and when Mrs Tulliver became rather pressing to know *how* he would raise it without mortgaging the mill and the house which he had said

9. Prussian field-marshal.
1. From Danzig, a city in what is now northern Poland.
2. Zinc.

he never *would* mortgage, since nowadays people were none so ready to lend money without security, Mr Tulliver, getting warm, declared that Mrs Glegg might do as she liked about calling in her money—he should pay it in, whether or not. He was not going to be beholden to his wife's sisters. When a man had married into a family where there was a whole litter of women, he might have plenty to put up with if he chose. But Mr Tulliver did *not* choose.

Mrs Tulliver cried a little in a trickling quiet way as she put on her nightcap; but presently sank into a comfortable sleep, lulled by the thought that she would talk everything over with her sister Pullet to-morrow, when she was to take the children to Garum Firs to tea. Not that she looked forward to any distinct issue from that talk; but it seemed impossible that past events should be so obstinate as to remain unmodified when they were complained against.

Her husband lay awake rather longer, for he too was thinking of a visit he would pay on the morrow; and his ideas on the subject were not of so vague and soothing a kind as those of his amiable partner.

Mr Tulliver, when under the influence of a strong feeling, had a promptitude in action that may seem inconsistent with that painful sense of the complicated puzzling nature of human affairs under which his more dispassionate deliberations were conducted; but it is really not improbable that there was a direct relation between these apparently contradictory phenomena, since I have observed that for getting a strong impression that a skein is tangled, there is nothing like snatching hastily at a single thread. It was owing to this promptitude that Mr Tulliver was on horseback soon after dinner the next day (he was not dyspeptic) on his way to Basset to see his sister Moss and her husband. For having made up his mind irrevocably that he would pay Mrs Glegg her loan of five hundred pounds, it naturally occurred to him that he had a promissory note for three hundred pounds lent to his brother-in-law Moss, and if the said brother-in-law could manage to pay in the money within a given time, it would go far to lessen the fallacious air of inconvenience which Mr Tulliver's spirited step might have worn in the eyes of weak people who require to know precisely *how* a thing is to be done before they are strongly confident that it will be easy.

For Mr Tulliver was in a position neither new nor striking, but, like other everyday things, sure to have a cumulative effect that will be felt in the long run: he was held to be a much more substantial man than he really was. And as we are all apt to believe what the world believes about us, it was his habit to think of failure and ruin with the same sort of remote pity with which a spare long-necked man hears that his plethoric short-necked neighbour is stricken with apoplexy. He had been always used to hear pleasant jokes about his advantages as a man who worked his own mill, and owned a pretty bit of land; and these jokes naturally kept up his sense that he was a man of considerable substance.

They gave a pleasant flavour to his glass on a market-day, and if it had not been for the recurrence of half-yearly payments, Mr Tulliver would really have forgotten that there was a mortgage of two thousand pounds on his very desirable freehold. That was not altogether his own fault, since one of the thousand pounds was his sister's fortune, which he had to pay on her marriage; and a man who has neighbours that *will* go to law with him, is not likely to pay off his mortgages, especially if he enjoys the good opinion of acquaintances who want to borrow a hundred pounds on security too lofty to be represented by parchment. Our friend Mr Tulliver had a good-natured fibre in him, and did not like to give harsh refusals even to a sister, who had not only come into the world in that superfluous way characteristic of sisters, creating a necessity for mortgages, but had quite thrown herself away in marriage, and had crowned her mistakes by having an eighth baby. On this point Mr Tulliver was conscious of being a little weak; but he apologised to himself by saying that poor Gritty had been a good-looking wench before she married Moss—he would sometimes say this even with a slight tremulousness in his voice. But this morning he was in a mood more becoming a man of business, and in the course of his ride along the Basset lanes, with their deep ruts,—lying so far away from a market-town that the labour of drawing produce and manure was enough to take away the best part of the profits on such poor land as that parish was made of,—he got up a due amount of irritation against Moss as a man without capital, who, if murrain and blight[1] were abroad, was sure to have his share of them, and who, the more you tried to help him out of the mud, would sink the further in. It would do him good rather than harm, now, if he were obliged to raise this three hundred pounds: it would make him look about him better, and not act so foolishly about his wool this year as he did the last: in fact, Mr Tulliver had been too easy with his brother-in-law, and because he had let the interest run on for two years, Moss was likely enough to think that he should never be troubled about the principal. But Mr Tulliver was determined not to encourage such shuffling people any longer; and a ride along the Basset lanes was not likely to enervate a man's resolution by softening his temper. The deep-trodden hoof-marks, made in the muddiest days of winter, gave him a shake now and then which suggested a rash but stimulating snarl at the father of lawyers, who, whether by means of his hoof or otherwise, had doubtless something to do with this state of the roads; and the abundance of foul land and neglected fences that met his eye, though they made no part of his brother Moss's farm, strongly contributed to his dissatisfaction with that unlucky agriculturist. If this wasn't Moss's fallow, it might have been: Basset was all alike; it was a beggarly parish in Mr Tulliver's opinion, and his opinion was certainly not groundless.

1. Cattle and crop pestilences.

Basset had a poor soil, poor roads, a poor non-resident landlord, a poor non-resident vicar, and rather less than half a curate,[2] also poor. If any one strongly impressed with the power of the human mind to triumph over circumstances, will contend that the parishioners of Basset might nevertheless have been a very superior class of people, I have nothing to urge against that abstract proposition; I only know that, in point of fact, the Basset mind was in strict keeping with its circumstances. The muddy lanes, green or clayey, that seemed to the unaccustomed eye to lead nowhere but into each other, did really lead, with patience, to a distant high-road; but there were many feet in Basset which they led more frequently to a centre of dissipation, spoken of formally as the "Markis o' Granby," but among intimates as "Dickison's." A large low room with a sanded floor, a cold scent of tobacco, modified by undetected beer-dregs, Mr Dickison leaning against the doorpost with a melancholy pimpled face, looking as irrelevant to the daylight as a last night's guttered candle—all this may not seem a very seductive form of temptation; but the majority of men in Basset found it fatally alluring when encountered on their road towards four o'clock on a wintry afternoon; and if any wife in Basset wished to indicate that her husband was not a pleasure-seeking man, she could hardly do it more emphatically than by saying that he didn't spend a shilling at Dickison's from one Whitsuntide[3] to another. Mrs Moss had said so of *her* husband more than once, when her brother was in a mood to find fault with him, as he certainly was to-day. And nothing could be less pacifying to Mr Tulliver than the behaviour of the farmyard gate, which he no sooner attempted to push open with his riding-stick, than it acted as gates without the upper hinge are known to do, to the peril of shins, whether equine or human. He was about to get down and lead his horse through the damp dirt of the hollow farmyard, shadowed drearily by the large half-timbered buildings, up to the long line of tumble-down dwelling-house standing on a raised causeway; but the timely appearance of a cowboy saved him that frustration of a plan he had determined on—namely, not to get down from his horse during this visit. If a man means to be hard, let him keep in his saddle and speak from that height, above the level of pleading eyes, and with the command of a distant horizon. Mrs Moss heard the sound of the horse's feet, and, when her brother rode up, was already outside the kitchen door, with a half-weary smile on her face, and a black-eyed baby in her arms. Mrs Moss's face bore a faded resemblance to her brother's; baby's little fat hand, pressed against her cheek, seemed to show more strikingly that the cheek was faded.

"Brother, I'm glad to see you," she said, in an affectionate tone. "I didn't look for you to-day. How do you do?"

"Oh, . . . pretty well, Mrs Moss . . . pretty well," answered the

2. Vicar: priest of a parish; curate: clergyman who is the vicar's assistant.
3. Week beginning with Pentecost (the seventh Sunday after Easter).

brother, with cool deliberation, as if it were rather too forward of her to ask that question. She knew at once that her brother was not in a good humour: he never called her Mrs Moss except when he was angry, and when they were in company. But she thought it was in the order of nature that people who were poorly off should be snubbed. Mrs Moss did not take her stand on the equality of the human race: she was a patient, prolific, loving-hearted woman.[4]

"Your husband isn't in the house, I suppose?" added Mr Tulliver, after a grave pause, during which four children had run out, like chickens whose mother has been suddenly in eclipse behind the hencoop.

"No," said Mrs Moss, "but he's only in the potato-field yonders. Georgy, run to the Far Close in a minute, and tell father your uncle's come. You'll get down, brother, won't you, and take something?"

"No, no; I can't get down. I must be going home again directly," said Mr Tulliver, looking at the distance.

"And how's Mrs Tulliver and the children?" said Mrs Moss, humbly, not daring to press her invitation.

"Oh . . . pretty well. Tom's going to a new school at Midsummer—a deal of expense to me. It's bad work for me, lying out o' my money."

"I wish you'd be so good as let the children come and see their cousins some day. My little uns want to see their cousin Maggie, so as never was. And me her god-mother, and so fond of her—there's nobody 'ud make a bigger fuss with her, according to what they've got. And I know she likes to come, for she's a loving child, and how quick and clever she is, to be sure!"

If Mrs Moss had been one of the most astute women in the world, instead of being one of the simplest, she could have thought of nothing more likely to propitiate her brother than this praise of Maggie. He seldom found any one volunteering praise of "the little wench": it was usually left entirely to himself to insist on her merits. But Maggie always appeared in the most amiable light at her aunt Moss's: it was her Alsatia,[5] where she was out of the reach of law—if she upset anything, dirtied her shoes, or tore her frock, these things were matters of course at her aunt Moss's. In spite of himself, Mr Tulliver's eyes got milder, and he did not look away from his sister, as he said,

"Ay: she's fonder o' you than o' the other aunts, I think. She takes after our family: not a bit of her mother's in her."

"Moss says she's just like what I used to be," said Mrs Moss, "though I was never so quick and fond o' the books. But I think my Lizzy's like her—*she's* sharp. Come here, Lizzy, my dear, and let your uncle see you: he hardly knows you; you grow so fast."

4. Eliot's manuscript reads: "patient, loosely-hung, child-producing woman." The wording was changed by Eliot at her publisher's request.
5. An outlaw's sanctuary in Sir Walter Scott's *The Fortunes of Nigel* (1822).

Lizzy, a black-eyed child of seven, looked very shy when her mother drew her forward, for the small Mosses were much in awe of their uncle from Dorlcote Mill. She was inferior enough to Maggie in fire and strength of expression, to make the resemblance between the two entirely flattering to Mr Tulliver's fatherly love.

"Ay, they're a bit alike," he said, looking kindly at the little figure in the soiled pinafore. "They both take after our mother. You've got enough o' gells, Gritty," he added, in a tone half compassionate, half reproachful.

"Four of 'em, bless 'em," said Mrs Moss, with a sigh, stroking Lizzy's hair on each side of her forehead; "as many as there's boys. They've got a brother a-piece."

"Ah, but they must turn out and fend for themselves," said Mr Tulliver, feeling that his severity was relaxing, and trying to brace it by throwing out a wholesome hint. "They mustn't look to hanging on their brothers."

"No: but I hope their brothers 'ull love the poor things, and remember they came o' one father and mother: the lads 'ull never be the poorer for that," said Mrs Moss, flashing out with hurried timidity, like a half-smothered fire.

Mr Tulliver gave his horse a little stroke on the flank, then checked it, and said, angrily, "Stand still with you!" much to the astonishment of that innocent animal.

"And the more there is of 'em, the more they must love one another," Mrs Moss went on, looking at her children with a didactic purpose. But she turned towards her brother again to say, "Not but what I hope your boy 'ull allays be good to his sister, though there's but two of 'em, like you and me, brother."

That arrow went straight to Mr Tulliver's heart. He had not a rapid imagination, but the thought of Maggie was very near to him, and he was not long in seeing his relation to his own sister side by side with Tom's relation to Maggie. Would the little wench ever be poorly off, and Tom rather hard upon her?

"Ay, ay, Gritty," said the miller, with a new softness in his tone; "but I've allays done what I could for you," he added, as if vindicating himself from a reproach.

"I'm not denying that, brother, and I'm noways ungrateful," said poor Mrs Moss, too fagged by toil and children to have strength left for any pride. "But here's the father. What a while you've been, Moss!"

"While, do you call it?" said Mr Moss, feeling out of breath and injured. "I've been running all the way. Won't you 'light, Mr Tulliver?"

"Well, I'll just get down and have a bit o' talk with you in the garden," said Mr Tulliver, thinking that he should be more likely to show a due spirit of resolve if his sister were not present.

He got down, and passed with Mr Moss into the garden, towards an old yew-tree arbour, while his sister stood tapping her baby on the back, and looking wistfully after them.

Their entrance into the yew-tree arbour surprised several fowls that were recreating themselves by scratching deep holes in the dusty ground, and at once took flight with much pother and cackling. Mr Tulliver sat down on the bench, and tapping the ground curiously here and there with his stick, as if he suspected some hollowness, opened the conversation by observing, with something like a snarl in his tone—

"Why, you've got wheat again in that Corner Close, I see; and never a bit o' dressing on it. You'll do no good with it this year."

Mr Moss, who, when he married Miss Tulliver, had been regarded as the buck of Basset, now wore a beard nearly a week old, and had the depressed, unexpectant air of a machine-horse. He answered in a patient-grumbling tone, "Why, poor farmers like me must do as they can: they must leave it to them as have got money to play with, to put half as much into the ground as they mean to get out of it."

"I don't know who should have money to play with, if it isn't them as can borrow money without paying interest," said Mr Tulliver, who wished to get into a slight quarrel; it was the most natural and easy introduction to calling in money.

"I know I'm behind with the interest," said Mr Moss, "but I was so unlucky wi' the wool last year; and what with the Missis being laid up so, things have gone awk'arder nor usual."

"Ay," snarled Mr Tulliver, "there's folks as things 'ull allays go awk'ard with: empty sacks 'ull never stand upright."

"Well, I don't know what fault you've got to find wi' me, Mr Tulliver," said Mr Moss, deprecatingly; "I know there isn't a day-labourer works harder."

"What's the use o' that," said Mr Tulliver, sharply, "when a man marries, and 's got no capital to work his farm but his wife's bit o' fortin? I was against it from the first; but you'd neither of you listen to me. And I can't lie out o' my money any longer, for I've got to pay five hundred o' Mrs Glegg's, and there'll be Tom an expense to me—I should find myself short, even saying I'd got back all as is my own. You must look about and see how you can pay me the three hundred pound."

"Well, if that's what you mean," said Mr Moss, looking blankly before him, "we'd better be sold up, and ha' done with it; I must part wi' every head o' stock I've got, to pay you and the landlord too."

Poor relations are undeniably irritating—their existence is so entirely uncalled for on our part, and they are almost always very faulty people. Mr Tulliver had succeeded in getting quite as much irritated with Mr Moss as he had desired, and he was able to say angrily, rising from his seat—

"Well, you must do as you can. *I* can't find money for everybody else as well as myself. I must look to my own business and my own family. I can't lie out o' my money any longer. You must raise it as quick as you can."

Mr Tulliver walked abruptly out of the arbour as he uttered the last sentence, and, without looking round at Mr Moss, went on to the kitchen door, where the eldest boy was holding his horse, and his sister was waiting in a state of wondering alarm, which was not without its alleviations, for baby was making pleasant gurgling sounds, and performing a great deal of finger practice on the faded face. Mrs Moss had eight children, but could never overcome her regret that the twins had not lived. Mr Moss thought their removal was not without its consolations. "Won't you come in, brother?" she said, looking anxiously at her husband, who was walking slowly up, while Mr Tulliver had his foot already in the stirrup.

"No, no; good-bye," said he, turning his horse's head, and riding away.

No man could feel more resolute till he got outside the yard-gate, and a little way along the deep-rutted lane; but before he reached the next turning, which would take him out of sight of the dilapidated farm-buildings, he appeared to be smitten by some sudden thought. He checked his horse, and made it stand still in the same spot for two or three minutes, during which he turned his head from side to side in a melancholy way, as if he were looking at some painful object on more sides than one. Evidently, after his fit of promptitude, Mr Tulliver was relapsing into the sense that this is a puzzling world. He turned his horse, and rode slowly back, giving vent to the climax of feeling which had determined this movement by saying aloud, as he struck his horse, "Poor little wench! she'll have nobody but Tom, belike, when I'm gone."

Mr Tulliver's return into the yard was descried by several young Mosses, who immediately ran in with the exciting news to their mother, so that Mrs Moss was again on the door-step when her brother rode up. She had been crying, but was rocking baby to sleep in her arms now, and made no ostentatious show of sorrow as her brother looked at her, but merely said—

"The father's gone to the field again, if you want him, brother."

"No, Gritty, no," said Mr Tulliver, in a gentle tone. "Don't you fret—that's all—I'll make a shift without the money a bit—only you must be as clever and contriving as you can."

Mrs Moss's tears came again at this unexpected kindness, and she could say nothing.

"Come, come!—the little wench shall come and see you. I'll bring her and Tom some day before he goes to school. You mustn't fret . . . I'll allays be a good brother to you."

"Thank you for that word, brother," said Mrs Moss, drying her tears; then turning to Lizzy, she said, "Run now, and fetch the coloured egg for cousin Maggie." Lizzy ran in, and quickly reappeared with a small paper parcel.

"It's boiled hard, brother, and coloured with thrums[6]—very pretty: it was done o' purpose for Maggie. Will you please to carry it in your pocket?"

"Ay, ay," said Mr Tulliver, putting it carefully in his side-pocket. "Good-bye."

And so the respectable miller returned along the Basset lanes rather more puzzled than before as to ways and means, but still with the sense of a danger escaped. It had come across his mind that if he were hard upon his sister, it might somehow tend to make Tom hard upon Maggie at some distant day, when her father was no longer there to take her part; for simple people, like our friend Mr Tulliver, are apt to clothe unimpeachable feelings in erroneous ideas, and this was his confused way of explaining to himself that his love and anxiety for "the little wench" had given him a new sensibility towards his sister.

Chapter IX

To Garum Firs

While the possible troubles of Maggie's future were occupying her father's mind, she herself was tasting only the bitterness of the present. Childhood has no forebodings; but then, it is soothed by no memories of outlived sorrow.

The fact was, the day had begun ill with Maggie. The pleasure of having Lucy to look at, and the prospect of the afternoon visit to Garum Firs, where she would hear uncle Pullet's musical box, had been marred as early as eleven o'clock by the advent of the hairdresser from St Ogg's, who had spoken in the severest terms of the condition in which he had found her hair, holding up one jagged lock after another and saying, "See here! tut-tut-tut!" in a tone of mingled disgust and pity, which to Maggie's imagination was equivalent to the strongest expression of public opinion. Mr Rappit, the hairdresser, with his well-anointed coronal locks tending wavily upward, like the simulated pyramid of flame on a monumental urn, seemed to her at that moment the most formidable of her contemporaries, into whose street at St Ogg's she would carefully refrain from entering through the rest of her life.

Moreover, the preparation for a visit being always a serious affair in the Dodson family, Martha was enjoined to have Mrs Tulliver's room ready an hour earlier than usual, that the laying-out of the best clothes might not be deferred till the last moment, as was sometimes the case in families of lax views, where the ribbon-strings were never rolled up,

6. Bits of waste yarn.

where there was little or no wrapping in silver paper, and where the sense that the Sunday clothes could be got at quite easily produced no shock to the mind. Already, at twelve o'clock, Mrs Tulliver had on her visiting costume, with a protective apparatus of brown holland,[1] as if she had been a piece of satin furniture in danger of flies; Maggie was frowning and twisting her shoulders, that she might if possible shrink away from the prickliest of tuckers,[2] while her mother was remonstrating, "Don't, Maggie, my dear—don't make yourself so ugly!" and Tom's cheeks were looking particularly brilliant as a relief to his best blue suit, which he wore with becoming calmness; having, after a little wrangling, effected what was always the one point of interest to him in his toilette—he had transferred all the contents of his everyday pockets to those actually in wear.

As for Lucy, she was just as pretty and neat as she had been yesterday: no accidents ever happened to her clothes, and she was never uncomfortable in them, so that she looked with wondering pity at Maggie pouting and writhing under the exasperating tucker. Maggie would certainly have torn it off, if she had not been checked by the remembrance of her recent humiliation about her hair: as it was, she confined herself to fretting and twisting, and behaving peevishly about the card-houses which they were allowed to build till dinner, as a suitable amusement for boys and girls in their best clothes. Tom could build perfect pyramids of houses; but Maggie's would never bear the laying on of the roof:—it was always so with the things that Maggie made; and Tom had deduced the conclusion that no girls could ever make anything. But it happened that Lucy proved wonderfully clever at building: she handled the cards so lightly, and moved so gently, that Tom condescended to admire her houses as well as his own, the more readily because she had asked him to teach her. Maggie, too, would have admired Lucy's houses, and would have given up her own unsuccessful building to contemplate them, without ill-temper, if her tucker had not made her peevish and if Tom had not inconsiderately laughed when her houses fell, and told her she was "a stupid."

"Don't laugh at me, Tom!" she burst out, angrily; "I'm not a stupid. I know a great many things you don't."

"O, I daresay, Miss Spitfire! I'd never be such a cross thing as you—making faces like that. Lucy doesn't do so. I like Lucy better than you: *I* wish Lucy was *my* sister."

"Then it's very wicked and cruel of you to wish so," said Maggie, starting up hurriedly from her place on the floor, and upsetting Tom's wonderful pagoda. She really did not mean it, but the circumstantial evidence was against her, and Tom turned white with anger, but said nothing: he would have struck her, only he knew it was cowardly to

1. Starched cotton or linen fabric.
2. Lace collar-lining.

strike a girl, and Tom Tulliver was quite determined he would never do anything cowardly.

Maggie stood in dismay and terror, while Tom got up from the floor and walked away, pale, from the scattered ruins of his pagoda, and Lucy looked on mutely, like a kitten pausing from its lapping.

"O Tom," said Maggie, at last, going half-way towards him, "I didn't mean to knock it down—indeed, indeed I didn't."

Tom took no notice of her, but took, instead, two or three hard peas out of his pocket, and shot them with his thumb-nail against the window—vaguely at first, but presently with the distinct aim of hitting a superannuated blue-bottle which was exposing its imbecility in the spring sunshine, clearly against the views of Nature, who had provided Tom and the peas for the speedy destruction of this weak individual.

Thus the morning had been made heavy to Maggie, and Tom's persistent coldness to her all through their walk spoiled the fresh air and sunshine for her. He called Lucy to look at the half-built bird's nest without caring to show it Maggie, and peeled a willow switch for Lucy and himself, without offering one to Maggie. Lucy had said, "Maggie, shouldn't *you* like one?" but Tom was deaf.

Still the sight of the peacock opportunely spreading his tail on the stackyard wall, just as they reached Garum Firs, was enough to divert the mind temporarily from personal grievances. And this was only the beginning of beautiful sights at Garum Firs. All the farmyard life was wonderful there—bantams, speckled and top-knotted; Friesland hens, with their feathers all turned the wrong way; Guinea-fowls that flew and screamed and dropped their pretty-spotted feathers; pouter-pigeons and a tame magpie; nay, a goat, and a wonderful brindled dog, half mastiff half bull-dog, as large as a lion. Then there were white railings and white gates all about, and glittering weathercocks of various design, and garden-walks paved with pebbles in beautiful patterns—nothing was quite common at Garum Firs: and Tom thought that the unusual size of the toads there was simply due to the general unusualness which characterised uncle Pullet's possessions as a gentleman farmer. Toads who paid rent were naturally leaner. As for the house, it was not less remarkable: it had a receding centre, and two wings with battlemented turrets, and was covered with glittering white stucco.

Uncle Pullet had seen the expected party approaching from the window, and made haste to unbar and unchain the front door, kept always in this fortified condition from fear of tramps, who might be supposed to know of the glass-case of stuffed birds in the hall, and to contemplate rushing in and carrying it away on their heads. Aunt Pullet, too, appeared at the doorway, and as soon as her sister was within hearing said, "Stop the children, for God's sake, Bessy—don't let 'em come up the door-steps: Sally's bringing the old mat and the duster, to rub their shoes."

Mrs Pullet's front-door mats were by no means intended to wipe shoes on: the very scraper had a deputy to do its dirty work. Tom rebelled particularly against this shoe-wiping, which he always considered in the light of an indignity to his sex. He felt it as the beginning of the disagreeables incident to a visit at aunt Pullet's, where he had once been compelled to sit with towels wrapped round his boots; a fact which may serve to correct the too hasty conclusion that a visit to Garum Firs must have been a great treat to a young gentleman fond of animals—fond, that is, of throwing stones at them.

The next disagreeable was confined to his feminine companions: it was the mounting of the polished oak stairs, which had very handsome carpets rolled up and laid by in a spare bedroom, so that the ascent of these glossy steps might have served, in barbarous times, as a trial by ordeal from which none but the most spotless virtue could have come off with unbroken limbs. Sophy's weakness about these polished stairs was always a subject of bitter remonstrance on Mrs Glegg's part; but Mrs Tulliver ventured on no comment, only thinking to herself it was a mercy when she and the children were safe on the landing.

"Mrs Gray has sent home my new bonnet, Bessy," said Mrs Pullet, in a pathetic tone, as Mrs Tulliver adjusted her cap.

"Has she, sister?" said Mrs Tulliver, with an air of much interest. "And how do you like it?"

"It's apt to make a mess with clothes, taking 'em out and putting 'em in again," said Mrs Pullet, drawing a bunch of keys from her pocket and looking at them earnestly, "but it 'ud be a pity for you to go away without seeing it. There's no knowing what may happen."

Mrs Pullet shook her head slowly at this last serious consideration, which determined her to single out a particular key.

"I'm afraid it'll be troublesome to you getting it out, sister," said Mrs Tulliver, "but I *should* like to see what sort of a crown she's made you."

Mrs Pullet rose with a melancholy air and unlocked one wing of a very bright wardrobe, where you may have hastily supposed she would find the new bonnet. Not at all. Such a supposition could only have arisen from a too superficial acquaintance with the habits of the Dodson family. In this wardrobe Mrs Pullet was seeking something small enough to be hidden among layers of linen—it was a door-key.

"You must come with me into the best room," said Mrs Pullet.

"May the children come too, sister?" inquired Mrs Tulliver, who saw that Maggie and Lucy were looking rather eager.

"Well," said aunt Pullet, reflectively "it'll perhaps be safer for 'em to come—they'll be touching something if we leave 'em behind."

So they went in procession along the bright and slippery corridor, dimly lighted by the semi-lunar top of the window which rose above the closed shutter: it was really quite solemn. Aunt Pullet paused and unlocked a door which opened on something still more solemn than the passage: a darkened room, in which the outer light, entering feebly, showed what looked like the corpses of furniture in white shrouds. Everything that was not shrouded stood with its legs upwards. Lucy laid hold of Maggie's frock, and Maggie's heart beat rapidly.

Aunt Pullet half-opened the shutter and then unlocked the wardrobe, with a melancholy deliberateness which was quite in keeping with the funereal solemnity of the scene. The delicious scent of rose-leaves that issued from the wardrobe, made the process of taking out sheet after sheet of silver paper quite pleasant to assist at, though the sight of the bonnet at last was an anticlimax to Maggie, who would have preferred something more strikingly preternatural. But few things could have been more impressive to Mrs Tulliver. She looked all round it in silence for some moments, and then said emphatically, "Well, sister, I'll never speak against the full crowns again!"

It was a great concession, and Mrs Pullet felt it: she felt something was due to it.

"You'd like to see it on, sister?" she said, sadly. "I'll open the shutter a bit further."

"Well, if you don't mind taking off your cap, sister," said Mrs Tulliver.

Mrs Pullet took off her cap, displaying the brown silk scalp[3] with a jutting promontory of curls which was common to the more mature and judicious women of those times, and, placing the bonnet on her head, turned slowly round, like a draper's lay-figure,[4] that Mrs Tulliver might miss no point of view.

"I've sometimes thought there's a loop too much o' ribbon on this left side, sister; what do you think?" said Mrs Pullet.

Mrs Tulliver looked earnestly at the point indicated, and turned her head on one side. "Well, I think it's best as it is; if you meddled with it, sister, you might repent."

"That's true," said aunt Pullet, taking off the bonnet and looking at it contemplatively.

"How much might she charge you for that bonnet, sister?" said Mrs Tulliver, whose mind was actively engaged on the possibility of getting a humble imitation of this *chef-d'œuvre*[5] made from a piece of silk she had at home.

Mrs Pullet screwed up her mouth and shook her head, and then whispered, "Pullet pays for it; he said I was to have the best bonnet at Garum Church, let the next best be whose it would."

She began slowly to adjust the trimmings in preparation for returning it to its place in the wardrobe, and her thoughts seemed to have taken a melancholy turn, for she shook her head.

3. The base to which the curls of a hair piece are attached.
4. Dressmaker's form.
5. Masterpiece.

"Ah," she said at last, "I may never wear it twice, sister: who knows?"

"Don't talk o' that, sister," answered Mrs Tulliver. "I hope you'll have your health this summer."

"Ah! but there may come a death in the family, as there did soon after I had my green satin bonnet. Cousin Abbott may go, and we can't think o' wearing crape less nor half a year for him."

"That *would* be unlucky," said Mrs Tulliver, entering thoroughly into the possibility of an inopportune decease. "There's never so much pleasure i' wearing a bonnet the second year, especially when the crowns are so chancy—never two summers alike."

"Ah, it's the way i' this world," said Mrs Pullet, returning the bonnet to the wardrobe and locking it up. She maintained a silence characterised by head-shaking, until they had all issued from the solemn chamber and were in her own room again. Then, beginning to cry, she said, "Sister, if you should never see that bonnet again till I'm dead and gone, you'll remember I showed it you this day."

Mrs Tulliver felt that she ought to be affected, but she was a woman of sparse tears, stout and healthy—she couldn't cry so much as her sister Pullet did, and had often felt her deficiency at funerals. Her effort to bring tears into her eyes issued in an odd contraction of her face. Maggie, looking on attentively, felt that there was some painful mystery about her aunt's bonnet which she was considered too young to understand; indignantly conscious, all the while, that she could have understood that, as well as everything else, if she had been taken into confidence.

When they went down, uncle Pullet observed with some acumen, that he reckoned the missis had been showing her bonnet—that was what had made them so long up-stairs. With Tom the interval had seemed still longer, for he had been seated in irksome constraint on the edge of a sofa directly opposite his uncle Pullet, who regarded him with twinkling grey eyes, and occasionally addressed him as "Young sir."

"Well, young sir, what do you learn at school?" was a standing question with uncle Pullet; whereupon Tom always looked sheepish, rubbed his hands across his face and answered, "I don't know." It was altogether so embarrassing to be seated *tête-à-tête* with uncle Pullet, that Tom could not even look at the prints on the walls, or the fly-cages, or the wonderful flowerpots; he saw nothing but his uncle's gaiters. Not that Tom was in awe of his uncle's mental superiority; indeed, he had made up his mind that he didn't want to be a gentleman farmer, because he shouldn't like to be such a thin-legged silly fellow as his uncle Pullet—a mollycoddle, in fact. A boy's sheepishness is by no means a sign of overmastering reverence; and while you are making encouraging advances to him under the idea that he is overwhelmed by a sense of your age and wisdom, ten to one he is thinking you extremely queer. The only consolation I can suggest to you is, that the Greek boys probably thought the same of Aristotle. It is only when you have mastered a restive horse, or thrashed a drayman,[6] or have got a gun in your hand, that these shy juniors feel you to be a truly admirable and enviable character. At least, I am quite sure of Tom Tulliver's sentiments on these points. In very tender years, when he still wore a lace border under his outdoor cap, he was often observed peeping through the bars of a gate and making minatory gestures with his small fore-finger while he scolded the sheep with an inarticulate burr, intended to strike terror into their astonished minds; indicating thus early that desire for mastery over the inferior animals, wild and domestic, including cockchafers,[7] neighbours' dogs, and small sisters, which in all ages has been an attribute of so much promise for the fortunes of our race. Now Mr Pullet never rode anything taller than a low pony, and was the least predatory of men, considering fire-arms dangerous, as apt to go off of themselves by nobody's particular desire. So that Tom was not without strong reasons when, in confidential talk with a chum, he had described uncle Pullet as a nincompoop, taking care at the same time to observe that he was a very "rich fellow."

The only alleviating circumstance in a *tête-à-tête* with uncle Pullet was that he kept a variety of lozenges and peppermint drops about his person, and when at a loss for conversation, he filled up the void by proposing a mutual solace of this kind.

"Do you like peppermints, young sir?" required only a tacit answer when it was accompanied by a presentation of the article in question.

The appearance of the little girls suggested to uncle Pullet the further solace of small sweet-cakes, of which he also kept a stock under lock and key for his own private eating on wet days; but the three children had no sooner got the tempting delicacy between their fingers, than aunt Pullet desired them to abstain from eating it till the tray and the plates came, since with those crisp cakes they would make the floor "all over" crumbs. Lucy didn't mind that much, for the cake was so pretty, she thought it was rather a pity to eat it; but Tom, watching his opportunity while the elders were talking, hastily stowed it in his mouth at two bites, and chewed it furtively. As for Maggie, becoming fascinated, as usual, by a print of Ulysses and Nausicaa,[8] which uncle Pullet had bought as a "pretty Scripture thing," she presently let fall her cake, and in an unlucky movement crushed it beneath her foot—a source of so much agitation to aunt Pullet and conscious disgrace to Maggie, that she began to despair of hearing the musical snuff-box to-day, till, after some reflection, it occurred to her that Lucy was in high favour enough to venture on asking for a tune. So she whispered to Lucy, and Lucy, who always did what she was desired to do, went up quietly to her uncle's

6. Hauler.
7. Beetles.
8. The shipwrecked Odysseus (Ulysses) steps naked onto the shore where Nausicaa, daughter of the Phaecian king, is playing ball with her maids (from Homer's *Odyssey*, 6.15 ff.).

knee, and, blushing all over her neck while she fingered her necklace, said, "Will you please play us a tune, uncle?"

Lucy thought it was by reason of some exceptional talent in uncle Pullet that the snuff-box played such beautiful tunes, and indeed the thing was viewed in that light by the majority of his neighbours in Garum. Mr Pullet had *bought* the box, to begin with, and he understood winding it up, and knew which tune it was going to play beforehand; altogether, the possession of this unique "piece of music" was a proof that Mr Pullet's character was not of that entire nullity which might otherwise have been attributed to it. But uncle Pullet, when entreated to exhibit his accomplishment, never depreciated it by a too ready consent. "We'll see about it," was the answer he always gave, carefully abstaining from any sign of compliance till a suitable number of minutes had passed. Uncle Pullet had a programme for all great social occasions, and in this way fenced himself in from much painful confusion and perplexing freedom of will.

Perhaps the suspense did heighten Maggie's enjoyment when the fairy tune began: for the first time she quite forgot that she had a load on her mind—that Tom was angry with her; and by the time "Hush, ye pretty warbling choir,"[9] had been played, her face wore that bright look of happiness, while she sat immovable with her hands clasped, which sometimes comforted her mother with the sense that Maggie could look pretty now and then, in spite of her brown skin. But when the magic music ceased, she jumped up, and, running towards Tom, put her arm round his neck and said, "O, Tom, isn't it pretty?"

Lest you should think it showed a revolting insensibility in Tom that he felt any new anger towards Maggie for this uncalled-for and, to him, inexplicable caress, I must tell you that he had his glass of cowslip wine in his hand, and that she jerked him so as to make him spill half of it. He must have been an extreme milksop not to say angrily, "Look there now!" especially when his resentment was sanctioned, as it was, by general disapprobation of Maggie's behaviour.

"Why don't you sit still, Maggie?" her mother said, peevishly.

"Little gells mustn't come to see me if they behave in that way," said aunt Pullet.

"Why, you're too rough, little miss," said uncle Pullet.

Poor Maggie sat down again, with the music all chased out of her soul, and the seven small demons[1] all in again.

Mrs Tulliver, foreseeing nothing but misbehaviour while the children remained in-doors, took an early opportunity of suggesting that, now they were rested after their walk, they might go and play out of doors; and aunt Pullet gave permission, only enjoining them not to go off the paved walks in the garden, and if they wanted to see the poultry fed, to

9. Song from Handel's dramatic cantata *Acis and Galatea* (1732), with lyrics by John Gay.
1. A reference to the seven devils Christ cast out of Mary Magdalene (Mark 16.9).

view them from a distance on the horse-block; a restriction which had been imposed ever since Tom had been found guilty of running after the peacock, with an illusory idea that fright would make one of its feathers drop off.

Mrs Tulliver's thoughts had been temporarily diverted from the quarrel with Mrs Glegg by millinery and maternal cares, but now the great theme of the bonnet was thrown into perspective, and the children were out of the way, yesterday's anxieties recurred.

"It weighs on my mind so as never was," she said, by way of opening the subject, "sister Glegg's leaving the house in that way. I'm sure I'd no wish t' offend a sister."

"Ah," said aunt Pullet, "there's no accounting for what Jane 'ull do. I wouldn't speak of it out o' the family—if it wasn't to Dr Turnbull; but it's my belief Jane lives too low. I've said so to Pullet often and often, and he knows it."

"Why, you said so last Monday was a week, when we came away from drinking tea with 'em," said Mr Pullet, beginning to nurse his knee and shelter it with his pocket-handkerchief, as was his way when the conversation took an interesting turn.

"Very like I did," said Mrs Pullet, "for you remember when I said things, better than I can remember myself. He's got a wonderful memory, Pullet has," she continued, looking pathetically at her sister. "I should be poorly off if he was to have a stroke, for he always remembers when I've got to take my doctor's stuff—and I'm taking three sorts now."

"There's the 'pills as before' every other night, and the new drops at eleven and four, and the 'fervescing mixture 'when agreeable,' " rehearsed Mr Pullet, with a punctuation determined by a lozenge on his tongue.

"Ah, perhaps it 'ud be better for sister Glegg, if *she*'d go to the doctor sometimes, instead o' chewing Turkey rhubarb[2] whenever there's anything the matter with her," said Mrs Tulliver, who naturally saw the wide subject of medicine chiefly in relation to Mrs Glegg.

"It's dreadful to think on," said aunt Pullet, raising her hands and letting them fall again, "people playing with their own insides in that way! And it's flying i' the face o' Providence; for what are the doctors for, if we aren't to call 'em in? And when folks have got the money to pay for a doctor, it isn't respectable, as I've told Jane many a time. I'm ashamed of acquaintance knowing it."

"Well, *we*'ve no call to be ashamed," said Mr Pullet, "for Doctor Turnbull hasn't got such another patient as you i' this parish, now old Mrs Sutton's gone."

"Pullet keeps all my physic-bottles—did you know, Bessy?" said Mrs Pullet. "He won't have one sold. He says it's nothing but right folks

2. Dried Chinese medicinal herb, imported from Turkey.

should see 'em when I'm gone. They fill two o' the long store-room shelves a'ready—but," she added, beginning to cry a little, "it's well if they ever fill three. I may go before I've made up the dozen o' these last sizes. The pill-boxes are in the closet in my room—you'll remember that, sister—but there's nothing to show for the boluses, if it isn't the bills."

"Don't talk o' your going, sister," said Mrs Tulliver: "I should have nobody to stand between me and sister Glegg if you was gone. And there's nobody but you can get her to make it up with Mr Tulliver, for sister Deane's never o' my side, and if she was, it's not to be looked for as she can speak like them as have got an independent fortin."

"Well, your husband *is* awk'ard, you know, Bessy," said Mrs Pullet, good-naturedly ready to use her deep depression on her sister's account as well as her own. "He's never behaved quite so pretty to our family as he should do, and the children take after him—the boy's very mischievous, and runs away from his aunts and uncles, and the gell's rude and brown. It's your bad-luck, and I'm sorry for you, Bessy; for you was allays my favourite sister, and we allays liked the same patterns."

"I know Tulliver's hasty, and says odd things," said Mrs Tulliver, wiping away one small tear from the corner of her eye, "but I'm sure he's never been the man, since he married me, to object to my making the friends o' my side o' the family welcome to the house."

"*I* don't want to make the worst of you, Bessy," said Mrs Pullet, compassionately, "for I doubt you'll have trouble enough without that; and your husband's got that poor sister and her children hanging on him,—and so given to lawing, they say. I doubt he'll leave you poorly off when he dies. Not as I'd have it said out o' the family."

This view of her position was naturally far from cheering to Mrs Tulliver. Her imagination was not easily acted on, but she could not help thinking that her case was a hard one, since it appeared that other people thought it hard.

"I'm sure, sister, I can't help myself," she said, urged by the fear lest her anticipated misfortunes might be held retributive, to take a comprehensive review of her past conduct. "There's no woman strives more for her children; and I'm sure, at scouring-time this Ladyday as I've had all the bed-hangings taken down, I did as much as the two gells put together; and there's this last elder-flower wine I've made—beautiful! I allays offer it along with the sherry, though sister Glegg will have it I'm so extravagant; and as for liking to have my clothes tidy, and not go a fright about the house, there's nobody in the parish can say anything against me in respect o' backbiting and making mischief, for I don't wish anybody any harm; and nobody loses by sending me a pork-pie, for my pies are fit to show with the best o' my neighbours'; and the linen's so in order, as if I was to die to-morrow I shouldn't be ashamed. A woman can do no more nor she can."

"But it's all o' no use, you know, Bessy," said Mrs Pullet, holding her head on one side, and fixing her eyes pathetically on her sister, "if your husband makes away with his money. Not but what if you was sold up, and other folks bought your furniture, it's a comfort to think as you've kept it well rubbed. And there's the linen, with your maiden mark on, might go all over the country. It 'ud be a sad pity for our family." Mrs Pullet shook her head slowly.

"But what can I do, sister?" said Mrs Tulliver. "Mr Tulliver's not a man to be dictated to—not if I was to go to the parson, and get by heart what I should tell my husband for the best. And I'm sure I don't pretend to know anything about putting out money and all that. I could never see into men's business as sister Glegg does."

"Well, you're like me in that, Bessy," said Mrs Pullet; "and I think it 'ud be a deal more becoming o' Jane if she'd have that pier-glass[3] rubbed oftener—there was ever so many spots on it last week—instead o' dictating to folks as have more comings in than she ever had, and telling 'em what they've to do with their money. But Jane and me were allays contrairy: she *would* have striped things, and I like spots. You like a spot too, Bessy: we allays hung together i' that."

"Yes, Sophy," said Mrs Tulliver, "I remember our having a blue ground with a white spot both alike—I've got a bit in a bed-quilt now; and if you would but go and see sister Glegg, and persuade her to make it up with Tulliver, I should take it very kind of you. You was allays a good sister to me."

"But the right thing 'ud be for Tulliver to go and make it up with her himself, and say he was sorry for speaking so rash. If he's borrowed money of her, he shouldn't be above that," said Mrs Pullet, whose partiality did not blind her to principles: she did not forget what was due to people of independent fortune.

"It's no use talking o' that," said poor Mrs Tulliver, almost peevishly. "If I was to go down on my bare knees on the gravel to Tulliver, he'd never humble himself."

"Well, you can't expect me to persuade *Jane* to beg pardon," said Mrs Pullet. "Her temper's beyond everything; it's well if it doesn't carry her off her mind, though there never *was* any of our family went to a madhouse."

"I'm not thinking of her begging pardon," said Mrs Tulliver. "But if she'd just take no notice, and not call her money in; as it's not so much for one sister to ask of another; time 'ud mend things, and Tulliver 'ud forget all about it, and they'd be friends again."

Mrs Tulliver, you perceive, was not aware of her husband's irrevocable determination to pay in the five hundred pounds; at least such a determination exceeded her powers of belief.

3. Large, high mirror.

"Well, Bessy," said Mrs Pullet, mournfully, "*I* don't want to help you on to ruin. I won't be behindhand i' doing you a good turn, if it is to be done. And I don't like it said among acquaintance as we've got quarrels in the family. I shall tell Jane that; and I don't mind driving to Jane's to-morrow, if Pullet doesn't mind. What do you say, Mr Pullet?"

"I've no objections," said Mr Pullet, who was perfectly contented with any course the quarrel might take, so that Mr Tulliver did not apply to *him* for money. Mr Pullet was nervous about his investments, and did not see how a man could have any security for his money unless he turned it into land.

After a little further discussion as to whether it would not be better for Mrs Tulliver to accompany them on a visit to sister Glegg, Mrs Pullet, observing that it was tea-time, turned to reach from a drawer a delicate damask napkin, which she pinned before her in the fashion of an apron. The door did, in fact, soon open, but instead of the tea-tray, Sally introduced an object so startling that both Mrs Pullet and Mrs Tulliver gave a scream, causing uncle Pullet to swallow his lozenge—for the fifth time in his life, as he afterwards noted.

Chapter X

Maggie Behaves Worse Than She Expected

The startling object which thus made an epoch for uncle Pullet was no other than little Lucy, with one side of her person, from her small foot to her bonnet-crown, wet and discoloured with mud, holding out two tiny blackened hands, and making a very piteous face. To account for this unprecedented apparition in aunt Pullet's parlour, we must return to the moment when the three children went to play out of doors, and the small demons who had taken possession of Maggie's soul at an early period of the day had returned in all the greater force after a temporary absence. All the disagreeable recollections of the morning were thick upon her, when Tom, whose displeasure towards her had been considerably refreshed by her foolish trick of causing him to upset his cowslip wine, said, "Here, Lucy, you come along with me," and walked off to the area where the toads were, as if there were no Maggie in existence. Seeing this, Maggie lingered at a distance, looking like a small Medusa[1] with her snakes cropped. Lucy was naturally pleased that cousin Tom was so good to her, and it was very amusing to see him tickling a fat toad with a piece of string when the toad was safe down the area, with an iron grating over him. Still Lucy wished Maggie to enjoy the spectacle also, especially as she would doubtless find a name for the toad, and

1. In Greek mythology, one of three Gorgons with snakes for hair, the sight of whom turns men to stone.

say what had been his past history; for Lucy had a delighted semi-belief in Maggie's stories about the live things they came upon by accident—how Mrs Earwig had a wash at home, and one of her children had fallen into the hot copper, for which reason she was running so fast to fetch the doctor. Tom had a profound contempt for this nonsense of Maggie's, smashing the earwig at once as a superfluous yet easy means of proving the entire unreality of such a story; but Lucy, for the life of her, could not help fancying there was something in it, and at all events thought it was very pretty make-believe. So now the desire to know the history of a very portly toad, added to her habitual affectionateness, made her run back to Maggie and say, "O, there is such a big, funny toad, Maggie! Do come and see."

Maggie said nothing, but turned away from her with a deeper frown. As long as Tom seemed to prefer Lucy to her, Lucy made part of his unkindness. Maggie would have thought a little while ago that she could never be cross with pretty little Lucy, any more than she could be cruel to a little white mouse; but then, Tom had always been quite indifferent to Lucy before, and it had been left to Maggie to pet and make much of her. As it was, she was actually beginning to think that she should like to make Lucy cry, by slapping or pinching her, especially as it might vex Tom, whom it was of no use to slap, even if she dared, because he didn't mind it. And if Lucy hadn't been there, Maggie was sure he would have got friends with her sooner.

Tickling a fat toad who is not highly sensitive, is an amusement that it is possible to exhaust, and Tom by-and-by began to look round for some other mode of passing the time. But in so prim a garden, where they were not to go off the paved walks, there was not a great choice of sport. The only great pleasure such a restriction suggested was the pleasure of breaking it, and Tom began to meditate an insurrectionary visit to the pond, about a field's length beyond the garden.

"I say, Lucy," he began, nodding his head up and down with great significance, as he coiled up his string again, "what do you think I mean to do?"

"What, Tom?" said Lucy, with curiosity.

"I mean to go to the pond, and look at the pike. You may go with me if you like," said the young sultan.

"O Tom, *dare* you?" said Lucy. "Aunt said we mustn't go out of the garden."

"O, I shall go out at the other end of the garden," said Tom. "Nobody 'ull see us. Besides, I don't care if they do—I'll run off home."

"But *I* couldn't run," said Lucy, who had never before been exposed to such severe temptation.

"O, never mind—they won't be cross with *you*," said Tom. "You say I took you."

Tom walked along, and Lucy trotted by his side, timidly enjoying the rare treat of doing something naughty—excited also by the mention of that celebrity, the pike, about which she was quite uncertain whether it was a fish or a fowl. Maggie saw them leaving the garden, and could not resist the impulse to follow. Anger and jealousy can no more bear to lose sight of their objects than love, and that Tom and Lucy should do or see anything of which she was ignorant would have been an intolerable idea to Maggie. So she kept a few yards behind them, unobserved by Tom, who was presently absorbed in watching for the pike—a highly interesting monster; he was said to be so very old, so very large, and to have such a remarkable appetite. The pike, like other celebrities, did not show when he was watched for, but Tom caught sight of something in rapid movement in the water, which attracted him to another spot on the brink of the pond.

"Here, Lucy!" he said in a loud whisper, "come here! take care! keep on the grass—don't step where the cows have been!" he added, pointing to a peninsula of dry grass, with trodden mud on each side of it; for Tom's contemptuous conception of a girl included the attribute of being unfit to walk in dirty places.

Lucy came carefully as she was bidden, and bent down to look at what seemed a golden arrow-head darting through the water. It was a water-snake, Tom told her, and Lucy at last could see the serpentine wave of its body, very much wondering that a snake could swim. Maggie had drawn nearer and nearer—she *must* see it too, though it was bitter to her like everything else, since Tom did not care about her seeing it. At last, she was close by Lucy, and Tom, who had been aware of her approach, but would not notice it till he was obliged, turned round and said—

"Now, get away, Maggie; there's no room for you on the grass here. Nobody asked *you* to come."

There were passions at war in Maggie at that moment to have made a tragedy, if tragedies were made by passion only; but the essential τι μέγεθος[2] which was present in the passion was wanting to the action: the utmost Maggie could do, with a fierce thrust of her small brown arm, was to push poor little pink-and-white Lucy into the cow-trodden mud.

Then Tom could not restrain himself, and gave Maggie two smart slaps on the arm as he ran to pick up Lucy, who lay crying helplessly. Maggie retreated to the roots of a tree a few yards off, and looked on impenitently. Usually her repentance came quickly after one rash deed, but now Tom and Lucy had made her so miserable, she was glad to

2. Of a certain magnitude: George Eliot quotes the Greek for this phrase (set italic below) in Aristotle's definition of tragedy, "the representation of an action that is heroic, complete and *of a certain magnitude*" (From *Poetics* 6.2, trans. W. Hamilton Fyfe).

spoil their happiness—glad to make everybody uncomfortable. Why should she be sorry? Tom was very slow to forgive *her*, however sorry she might have been.

"I shall tell mother, you know, Miss Mag," said Tom, loudly and emphatically, as soon as Lucy was up and ready to walk away. It was not Tom's practice to "tell," but here justice clearly demanded that Maggie should be visited with the utmost punishment: not that Tom had learnt to put his views in that abstract form; he never mentioned "justice," and had no idea that his desire to punish might be called by that fine name. Lucy was too entirely absorbed by the evil that had befallen her—the spoiling of her pretty best clothes, and the discomfort of being wet and dirty—to think much of the cause, which was entirely mysterious to her. She could never have guessed what she had done to make Maggie angry with her; but she felt that Maggie was very unkind and disagreeable, and made no magnanimous entreaties to Tom that he would not "tell," only running along by his side and crying piteously, while Maggie sat on the roots of the tree and looked after them with her small Medusa face.

"Sally," said Tom, when they reached the kitchen door, and Sally looked at them in speechless amaze, with a piece of bread-and-butter in her mouth and a toasting-fork in her hand—"Sally, tell mother it was Maggie pushed Lucy into the mud."

"But Lors ha' massy, how did you get near such mud as that?" said Sally, making a wry face, as she stooped down and examined the *corpus delicti*.[3]

Tom's imagination had not been rapid and capacious enough to include this question among the foreseen consequences, but it was no sooner put than he foresaw whither it tended, and that Maggie would not be considered the only culprit in the case. He walked quietly away from the kitchen door, leaving Sally to that pleasure of guessing which active minds notoriously prefer to ready-made knowledge.

Sally, as you are aware, lost no time in presenting Lucy at the parlour door, for to have so dirty an object introduced into the house at Garum Firs was too great a weight to be sustained by a single mind.

"Goodness gracious!" aunt Pullet exclaimed, after preluding by an inarticulate scream; "keep her at the door, Sally! Don't bring her off the oil-cloth, whatever you do."

"Why, she's tumbled into some nasty mud," said Mrs Tulliver, going up to Lucy to examine into the amount of damage to clothes for which she felt herself responsible to her sister Deane.

"If you please, 'um, it was Miss Maggie as pushed her in," said Sally; "Master Tom's been and said so, and they must ha' been to the pond, for it's only there they could ha' got into such dirt."

3. The fundamental facts necessary to prove that a crime has been committed (lit. "body of the crime").

"There it is, Bessy; it's what I've been telling you," said Mrs Pullet, in a tone of prophetic sadness: "it's your children—there's no knowing what they'll come to."

Mrs Tulliver was mute, feeling herself a truly wretched mother. As usual, the thought pressed upon her that people would think she had done something wicked to deserve her maternal troubles, while Mrs Pullet began to give elaborate directions to Sally how to guard the premises from serious injury in the course of removing the dirt. Meantime tea was to be brought in by the cook, and the two naughty children were to have theirs in an ignominious manner in the kitchen. Mrs Tulliver went out to speak to these naughty children, supposing them to be close at hand; but it was not until after some search that she found Tom leaning with rather a hardened careless air against the white paling[4] of the poultry-yard, and lowering his piece of string on the other side as a means of exasperating the turkey-cock.

"Tom, you naughty boy, where's your sister?" said Mrs Tulliver, in a distressed voice.

"I don't know," said Tom; his eagerness for justice on Maggie had diminished since he had seen clearly that it could hardly be brought about without the injustice of some blame on his own conduct.

"Why, where did you leave her?" said his mother, looking round.

"Sitting under the tree against the pond," said Tom, apparently indifferent to everything but the string and the turkey-cock.

"Then go and fetch her in this minute, you naughty boy. And how could you think o' going to the pond, and taking your sister where there was dirt? You know she'll do mischief, if there's mischief to be done."

It was Mrs Tulliver's way, if she blamed Tom, to refer his misdemeanour, somehow or other, to Maggie.

The idea of Maggie sitting alone by the pond, roused an habitual fear in Mrs Tulliver's mind, and she mounted the horse-block to satisfy herself by a sight of that fatal child, while Tom walked—not very quickly—on his way towards her.

"They're such children for the water, mine are," she said aloud, without reflecting that there was no one to hear her; "they'll be brought in dead and drownded some day. I wish that river was far enough."

But when she not only failed to discern Maggie, but presently saw Tom returning from the pool alone, this hovering fear entered and took complete possession of her, and she hurried to meet him.

"Maggie's nowhere about the pond, mother," said Tom; "she's gone away."

You may conceive the terrified search for Maggie, and the difficulty of convincing her mother that she was not in the pond. Mrs Pullet

4. Picket fence.

observed that the child might come to a worse end if she lived—there was no knowing; and Mr Pullet, confused and overwhelmed by this revolutionary aspect of things—the tea deferred and the poultry alarmed by the unusual running to and fro—took up his spud[5] as an instrument of search, and reached down a key to unlock the goose-pen, as a likely place for Maggie to lie concealed in.

Tom, after a while, started the idea that Maggie was gone home (without thinking it necessary to state that it was what he should have done himself under the circumstances), and the suggestion was seized as a comfort by his mother.

"Sister, for goodness' sake let 'em put the horse in the carriage and take me home—we shall perhaps find her on the road. Lucy can't walk in her dirty clothes," she said, looking at that innocent victim, who was wrapped up in a shawl, and sitting with naked feet on the sofa.

Aunt Pullet was quite willing to take the shortest means of restoring her premises to order and quiet, and it was not long before Mrs Tulliver was in the chaise looking anxiously at the most distant point before her. What the father would say if Maggie was lost? was a question that predominated over every other.

Chapter XI

Maggie Tries to Run Away from Her Shadow

Maggie's intentions, as usual, were on a larger scale than Tom had imagined. The resolution that gathered in her mind, after Tom and Lucy had walked away, was not so simple as that of going home. No! she would run away and go to the gypsies, and Tom should never see her any more. That was by no means a new idea to Maggie; she had been so often told she was like a gypsy, and "half wild," that when she was miserable it seemed to her the only way of escaping opprobrium, and being entirely in harmony with circumstances would be to live in a little brown tent on the commons:[1] the gypsies, she considered, would gladly receive her, and pay her much respect on account of her superior knowledge. She had once mentioned her views on this point to Tom, and suggested that he should stain his face brown, and they should run away together; but Tom rejected the scheme with contempt, observing that gypsies were thieves, and hardly got anything to eat, and had nothing to drive but a donkey. To-day, however, Maggie thought her misery had reached a pitch at which gypsydom was her only refuge, and she rose from her seat on the roots of the tree with the sense that this was a great crisis in her life; she would run straight away till she came to

5. Spade.
1. Public land.

Dunlow Common, where there would certainly be gypsies; and cruel Tom, and the rest of her relations who found fault with her, should never see her any more. She thought of her father as she ran along, but she reconciled herself to the idea of parting with him, by determining that she would secretly send him a letter by a small gypsy, who would run away without telling where she was, and just let him know that she was well and happy, and always loved him very much.

Maggie soon got out of breath with running, but by the time Tom got to the pond again, she was at the distance of three long fields, and was on the edge of the lane leading to the high-road. She stopped to pant a little, reflecting that running away was not a pleasant thing until one had got quite to the common where the gypsies were, but her resolution had not abated: she presently passed through the gate into the lane, not knowing where it would lead her, for it was not this way that they came from Dorlcote Mill to Garum Firs, and she felt all the safer for that, because there was no chance of her being overtaken. But she was soon aware, not without trembling, that there were two men coming along the lane in front of her: she had not thought of meeting strangers—she had been too much occupied with the idea of her friends coming after her. The formidable strangers were two shabby-looking men with flushed faces, one of them carrying a bundle on a stick over his shoulder: but to her surprise, while she was dreading their disapprobation as a runaway, the man with the bundle stopped, and in a half-whining half-coaxing tone asked her if she had a copper to give a poor man. Maggie had a sixpence in her pocket—her uncle Glegg's present—which she immediately drew out and gave this poor man with a polite smile, hoping he would feel very kindly towards her as a generous person. "That's the only money I've got," she said, apologetically. "Thank you, little miss," said the man in a less respectful and grateful tone than Maggie anticipated, and she even observed that he smiled and winked at his companion. She walked on hurriedly, but was aware that the two men were standing still, probably to look after her, and she presently heard them laughing loudly. Suddenly it occurred to her that they might think she was an idiot: Tom had said that her cropped hair made her look like an idiot, and it was too painful an idea to be readily forgotten. Besides, she had no sleeves on—only a cape and a bonnet. It was clear that she was not likely to make a favourable impression on passengers, and she thought she would turn into the fields again; but not on the same side of the lane as before, lest they should still be uncle Pullet's fields. She turned through the first gate that was not locked, and felt a delightful sense of privacy in creeping along by the hedgerows, after her recent humiliating encounter. She was used to wandering about the fields by herself, and was less timid there than on the high-road. Sometimes she had to climb over high gates, but that was a small evil; she was getting out of reach very fast, and she should probably soon come within sight of Dunlow Common, or at least of some other common, for she had heard her father say that you couldn't go very far without coming to a common. She hoped so, for she was getting rather tired and hungry, and until she reached the gypsies there was no definite prospect of bread-and-butter. It was still broad daylight, for aunt Pullet, retaining the early habits of the Dodson family, took tea at half-past four by the sun, and at five by the kitchen clock; so, though it was nearly an hour since Maggie started, there was no gathering gloom on the fields to remind her that the night would come. Still, it seemed to her that she had been walking a very great distance indeed, and it was really surprising that the common did not come within sight. Hitherto she had been in the rich parish of Garum, where there was a great deal of pasture-land, and she had only seen one labourer at a distance. That was fortunate in some respects, as labourers might be too ignorant to understand the propriety of her wanting to go to Dunlow Common; yet it would have been better if she could have met some one who would tell her the way without wanting to know anything about her private business. At last, however, the green fields came to an end, and Maggie found herself looking through the bars of a gate into a lane with a wide margin of grass on each side of it. She had never seen such a wide lane before, and, without her knowing why, it gave her the impression that the common could not be far off; perhaps it was because she saw a donkey with a log to his foot feeding on the grassy margin, for she had seen a donkey with that pitiable encumbrance on Dunlow Common when she had been across it in her father's gig.[2] She crept through the bars of the gate and walked on with new spirit, though not without haunting images of Apollyon,[3] and a highwayman with a pistol, and a blinking dwarf in yellow, with a mouth from ear to ear, and other miscellaneous dangers. For poor little Maggie had at once the timidity of an active imagination and the daring that comes from overmastering impulse. She had rushed into the adventure of seeking her unknown kindred, the gypsies; and now she was in this strange lane, she hardly dared look on one side of her, lest she should see the diabolical blacksmith in his leathern apron grinning at her with arms akimbo. It was not without a leaping of the heart that she caught sight of a small pair of bare legs sticking up, feet uppermost, by the side of a hillock;[4] they seemed something hideously preternatural—a diabolical kind of fungus; for she was too much agitated at the first glance to see the ragged clothes and the dark shaggy head attached to them. It was a boy asleep, and Maggie trotted along faster and more lightly, lest she should wake him: it did not occur to her that he was one of her friends the gypsies, who in all probability would have very genial manners. But the fact was so,

2. Light carriage.
3. The "foul fiend" fought by Christian in the Valley of Humiliation in *Pilgrim's Progress*.
4. Small hill.

for at the next bend in the lane, Maggie actually saw the little semicircular black tent with the blue smoke rising before it, which was to be her refuge from all the blighting obloquy that had pursued her in civilised life. She even saw a tall female figure by the column of smoke—doubtless the gypsy-mother, who provided the tea and other groceries; it was astonishing to herself that she did not feel more delighted. But it was startling to find the gypsies in a lane, after all, and not on a common; indeed, it was rather disappointing; for a mysterious illimitable common, where there were sand-pits to hide in, and one was out of everybody's reach, had always made part of Maggie's picture of gypsy life. She went on, however, and thought with some comfort that gypsies most likely knew nothing about idiots, so there was no danger of their falling into the mistake of setting her down at the first glance as an idiot. It was plain she had attracted attention; for the tall figure, who proved to be a young woman with a baby on her arm, walked slowly to meet her. Maggie looked up in the new face rather tremblingly as it approached, and was reassured by the thought that her aunt Pullet and the rest were right when they called her a gypsy, for this face, with the bright dark eyes and the long hair, was really something like what she used to see in the glass before she cut her hair off.

"My little lady, where are you going to?" the gypsy said, in a tone of coaxing deference.

It was delightful, and just what Maggie expected: the gypsies saw at once that she was a little lady, and were prepared to treat her accordingly.

"Not any farther," said Maggie, feeling as if she were saying what she had rehearsed in a dream. "I'm come to stay with *you*, please."

"That's pretty; come, then. Why, what a nice little lady you are, to be sure," said the gypsy, taking her by the hand. Maggie thought her very agreeable, but wished she had not been so dirty.

There was quite a group round the fire when they reached it. An old gypsy woman was seated on the ground nursing her knees, and occasionally poking a skewer into the round kettle that sent forth an odorous steam: two small shock-headed children were lying prone and resting on their elbows something like small sphinxes; and a placid donkey was bending his head over a tall girl, who, lying on her back, was scratching his nose and indulging him with a bite of excellent stolen hay. The slanting sunlight fell kindly upon them, and the scene was really very pretty and comfortable, Maggie thought, only she hoped they would soon set out the tea-cups. Everything would be quite charming when she had taught the gypsies to use a washing-basin, and to feel an interest in books. It was a little confusing, though, that the young woman began to speak to the old one in a language which Maggie did not understand, while the tall girl, who was feeding the donkey, sat up and stared at her without offering any salutation. At last the old woman said—

"What, my pretty lady, are you come to stay with us? Sit ye down and tell us where ye come from."

It was just like a story: Maggie liked to be called pretty lady and treated in this way. She sat down and said—

"I'm come from home because I'm unhappy, and I mean to be a gypsy. I'll live with you if you like, and I can teach you a great many things."

"Such a clever little lady," said the woman with the baby, sitting down by Maggie, and allowing baby to crawl; "and such a pretty bonnet and frock," she added, taking off Maggie's bonnet and looking at it while she made an observation to the old woman, in the unknown language. The tall girl snatched the bonnet and put it on her own head hind-foremost with a grin; but Maggie was determined not to show any weakness on this subject, as if she were susceptible about her bonnet.

"I don't want to wear a bonnet," she said, "I'd rather wear a red handkerchief, like yours" (looking at her friend by her side); "my hair was quite long till yesterday, when I cut it off: but I daresay it will grow again very soon," she added apologetically, thinking it probable the gypsies had a strong prejudice in favour of long hair. And Maggie had forgotten even her hunger at that moment in the desire to conciliate gypsy opinion.

"O what a nice little lady!—and rich, I'm sure," said the old woman. "Didn't you live in a beautiful house at home?"

"Yes, my home is pretty, and I'm very fond of the river, where we go fishing—but I'm often very unhappy. I should have liked to bring my books with me, but I came away in a hurry, you know. But I can tell you almost everything there is in my books, I've read them so many times—and that will amuse you. And I can tell you something about Geography too—that's about the world we live in—very useful and interesting. Did you ever hear about Columbus?"

Maggie's eyes had begun to sparkle and her cheeks to flush—she was really beginning to instruct the gypsies, and gaining great influence over them. The gypsies themselves were not without amazement at this talk, though their attention was divided by the contents of Maggie's pocket, which the friend at her right hand had by this time emptied without attracting her notice.

"Is that where you live, my little lady?" said the old woman, at the mention of Columbus.

"O no!" said Maggie, with some pity; "Columbus was a very wonderful man, who found out half the world, and they put chains on him and treated him very badly, you know—it's in my Catechism of Geography[5]—but perhaps it's rather too long to tell before tea . . . *I want my tea so.*"

5. Probably one of William Pinnock's *Catechisms*, produced during the 1820s and 1830s. These lists of questions and answers were popular teaching aids.

The last words burst from Maggie, in spite of herself, with a sudden drop from patronising instruction to simple peevishness.

"Why, she's hungry, poor little lady," said the younger woman. "Give her some o' the cold victual. You've been walking a good way, I'll be bound, my dear. Where's your home?"

"It's Dorlcote Mill, a good way off," said Maggie. "My father is Mr Tulliver, but we mustn't let him know where I am, else he'll fetch me home again. Where does the queen of the gypsies live?"

"What! do you want to go to her, my little lady?" said the younger woman. The tall girl meanwhile was constantly staring at Maggie and grinning. Her manners were certainly not agreeable.

"No," said Maggie, "I'm only thinking that if she isn't a very good queen you might be glad when she died, and you could choose another. If I was a queen, I'd be a very good queen, and kind to everybody."

"Here's a bit o' nice victual, then," said the old woman, handing to Maggie a lump of dry bread, which she had taken from a bag of scraps, and a piece of cold bacon.

"Thank you," said Maggie, looking at the food without taking it; "but will you give me some bread-and-butter and tea instead? I don't like bacon."

"We've got no tea nor butter," said the old woman with something like a scowl, as if she were getting tired of coaxing.

"O, a little bread and treacle would do," said Maggie.

"We han't got no treacle," said the old woman crossly, whereupon there followed a sharp dialogue between the two women in their unknown tongue, and one of the small sphinxes snatched at the bread-and-bacon, and began to eat it. At this moment the tall girl, who had gone a few yards off, came back, and said something which produced a strong effect. The old woman, seeming to forget Maggie's hunger, poked the skewer into the pot with new vigour, and the younger crept under the tent, and reached out some platters and spoons. Maggie trembled a little, and was afraid the tears would come into her eyes. Meanwhile the tall girl gave a shrill cry, and presently came running up the boy whom Maggie had passed as he was sleeping—a rough urchin about the age of Tom. He stared at Maggie, and there ensued much incomprehensible chattering. She felt very lonely, and was quite sure she should begin to cry before long: the gypsies didn't seem to mind her at all, and she felt quite weak among them. But the springing tears were checked by new terror, when two men came up, whose approach had been the cause of the sudden excitement. The elder of the two carried a bag, which he flung down, addressing the women in a loud and scolding tone, which they answered by a shower of treble sauciness; while a black cur ran barking up to Maggie, and threw her into a tremor that only found a new cause in the curses with which the younger man called the dog off, and gave him a rap with a great stick he held in his hand.

Maggie felt that it was impossible she should ever be queen of these people, or even communicate to them amusing and useful knowledge.

Both the men now seemed to be inquiring about Maggie, for they looked at her, and the tone of the conversation became of that pacific kind which implies curiosity on one side and the power of satisfying it on the other. At last the younger woman said in her previous deferential coaxing tone—

"This nice little lady's come to live with us: aren't you glad?"

"Ay, very glad," said the younger man, who was looking at Maggie's silver thimble and other small matters that had been taken from her pocket. He returned them all except the thimble to the younger woman, with some observation, and she immediately restored them to Maggie's pocket, while the men seated themselves, and began to attack the contents of the kettle—a stew of meat and potatoes—which had been taken off the fire and turned out into a yellow platter.

Maggie began to think that Tom must be right about the gypsies—they must certainly be thieves, unless the man meant to return her thimble by-and-by. She would willingly have given it to him, for she was not at all attached to her thimble; but the idea that she was among thieves prevented her from feeling any comfort in the revival of deference and attention towards her—all thieves, except Robin Hood, were wicked people. The women saw she was frightened.

"We've got nothing nice for a lady to eat," said the old woman, in her coaxing tone. "And she's so hungry, sweet little lady."

"Here, my dear, try if you can eat a bit o' this," said the younger woman, handing some of the stew on a brown dish with an iron spoon to Maggie, who, remembering that the old woman had seemed angry with her for not liking the bread-and-bacon, dared not refuse the stew, though fear had chased away her appetite. If her father would but come by in the gig and take her up! Or even if Jack the Giantkiller, or Mr Greatheart, or St George who slew the dragon on the halfpennies,[6] would happen to pass that way! But Maggie thought with a sinking heart that these heroes were never seen in the neighbourhood of St Ogg's—nothing very wonderful ever came there.

Maggie Tulliver, you perceive, was by no means that well-trained, well-informed young person that a small female of eight or nine necessarily is in these days: she had only been to school a year at St Ogg's, and had so few books that she sometimes read the dictionary; so that in travelling over her small mind you would have found the most unexpected ignorance as well as unexpected knowledge. She could have

6. Mr. Greatheart: a giant-killer, guide, and protector of Christiana in part two of *Pilgrim's Progress* (1684); St. George: dragon-slayer and patron saint of England.

informed you that there was such a word as "polygamy," and being also acquainted with "polysyllable," she had deduced the conclusion that "poly" meant "many;" but she had had no idea that gypsies were not well supplied with groceries, and her thoughts generally were the oddest mixture of clear-eyed acumen and blind dreams.

Her ideas about the gypsies had undergone a rapid modification in the last five minutes. From having considered them very respectful companions, amenable to instruction, she had begun to think that they meant perhaps to kill her as soon as it was dark, and cut up her body for gradual cooking: the suspicion crossed her that the fierce-eyed old man was in fact the devil, who might drop that transparent disguise at any moment, and turn either into the grinning blacksmith or else a fiery-eyed monster with dragon's wings. It was no use trying to eat the stew, and yet the thing she most dreaded was to offend the gypsies, by betraying her extremely unfavourable opinion of them, and she wondered, with a keenness of interest that no theologian could have exceeded, whether, if the devil were really present, he would know her thoughts.

"What! you don't like the smell of it, my dear," said the young woman, observing that Maggie did not even take a spoonful of the stew. "Try a bit—come."

"No, thank you," said Maggie, summoning all her force for a desperate effort, and trying to smile in a friendly way. "I haven't time, I think—it seems getting darker. I think I must go home now, and come again another day, and then I can bring you a basket with some jam-tarts and things."

Maggie rose from her seat as she threw out this illusory prospect, devoutly hoping that Apollyon was gullible; but her hope sank when the old gypsy-woman said, "Stop a bit, stop a bit, little lady—we'll take you home, all safe, when we've done supper: you shall ride home, like a lady."

Maggie sat down again, with little faith in this promise, though she presently saw the tall girl putting a bridle on the donkey, and throwing a couple of bags on his back.

"Now, then, little missis," said the younger man, rising, and leading the donkey forward, "tell us where you live—what's the name o' the place?"

"Dorlcote Mill is my home," said Maggie, eagerly. "My father is Mr Tulliver—he lives there."

"What! a big mill a little way this side o' St Ogg's?"

"Yes," said Maggie. "Is it far off? I think I should like to walk there, if you please."

"No, no, it'll be getting dark, we must make haste. And the donkey'll carry you as nice as can be—you'll see."

He lifted Maggie as he spoke, and set her on the donkey. She felt relieved that it was not the old man who seemed to be going with her, but she had only a trembling hope that she was really going home.

"Here's your pretty bonnet," said the younger woman, putting that recently-despised but now welcome article of costume on Maggie's head; "and you'll say we've been very good to you, won't you? and what a nice little lady we said you was."

"O, yes, thank you," said Maggie, "I'm very much obliged to you. But I wish you'd go with me too." She thought anything was better than going with one of the dreadful men alone: it would be more cheerful to be murdered by a larger party.

"Ah, you're fondest o' *me*, aren't you?" said the woman. "But I can't go—you'll go too fast for me."

It now appeared that the man also was to be seated on the donkey, holding Maggie before him, and she was as incapable of remonstrating against this arrangement as the donkey himself, though no nightmare had ever seemed to her more horrible. When the woman had patted her on the back, and said "Good-bye," the donkey, at a strong hint from the man's stick, set off at a rapid walk along the lane towards the point Maggie had come from an hour ago, while the tall girl and the rough urchin, also furnished with sticks, obligingly escorted them for the first hundred yards, with much screaming and thwacking.

Not Leonore,[7] in that preternatural midnight excursion with her phantom lover, was more terrified than poor Maggie in this entirely natural ride on a short-paced donkey, with a gypsy behind her, who considered that he was earning half-a-crown. The red light of the setting sun seemed to have a portentous meaning, with which the alarming bray of the second donkey with the log on its foot must surely have some connection. Two low thatched cottages—the only houses they passed in this lane—seemed to add to its dreariness: they had no windows to speak of, and the doors were closed: it was probable that they were inhabited by witches, and it was a relief to find that the donkey did not stop there.

At last—O, sight of joy!—this lane, the longest in the world was coming to an end, was opening on a broad high-road, where there was actually a coach passing! And there was a finger-post at the corner: she had surely seen that finger-post before—"To St Ogg's, 2 miles." The gypsy really meant to take her home, then: he was probably a good man, after all, and might have been rather hurt at the thought that she didn't like coming with him alone. This idea became stronger as she felt more and more certain that she knew the road quite well, and she was considering how she might open a conversation with the injured gypsy, and not only gratify his feelings but efface the impression of her cowardice,

7. Heroine of Gottfried August Bürger's ballad of the same name (1774).

when, as they reached a cross-road, Maggie caught sight of some one coming on a white-faced horse.

"O, stop, stop!" she cried out. "There's my father! O, father, father!"

The sudden joy was almost painful, and before her father reached her, she was sobbing. Great was Mr Tulliver's wonder, for he had made a round from Basset, and had not yet been home.

"Why, what's the meaning o' this?" he said, checking his horse, while Maggie slipped from the donkey and ran to her father's stirrup.

"The little miss lost herself, I reckon," said the gypsy. "She'd come to our tent at the far end o' Dudlow Lane, and I was bringing her where she said her home was. It's a good way to come arter being on the tramp all day."

"O, yes, father, he's been very good to bring me home," said Maggie. "A very kind, good man!"

"Here, then, my man," said Mr Tulliver, taking out five shillings. "It's the best day's work *you* ever did. I couldn't afford to lose the little wench; here, lift her up before me."

"Why, Maggie, how's this, how's this?" he said, as they rode along, while she laid her head against her father, and sobbed. "How came you to be rambling about and lose yourself?"

"O, father," sobbed Maggie, "I ran away because I was so unhappy —Tom was so angry with me. I couldn't bear it."

"Pooh, pooh," said Mr Tulliver, soothingly, "you mustn't think o' running away from father. What 'ud father do without his little wench?"

"O no, I never will again, father—never."

Mr Tulliver spoke his mind very strongly when he reached home that evening, and the effect was seen in the remarkable fact, that Maggie never heard one reproach from her mother, or one taunt from Tom, about this foolish business of her running away to the gypsies. Maggie was rather awe-stricken by this unusual treatment, and sometimes thought that her conduct had been too wicked to be alluded to.

Chapter XII

Mr and Mrs Glegg at Home

In order to see Mr and Mrs Glegg at home, we must enter the town of St Ogg's—that venerable town with the red-fluted roofs and the broad warehouse gables, where the black ships unlade themselves of their burthens from the far north, and carry away, in exchange, the precious inland products, the well-crushed cheese and the soft fleeces, which my refined readers have doubtless become acquainted with through the medium of the best classic pastorals.

It is one of those old, old towns which impress one as a continuation and outgrowth of nature, as much as the nests of the bower-birds or the winding galleries of the white ants: a town which carries the traces of its long growth and history like a millennial tree, and has sprung up and developed in the same spot between the river and the low hill from the time when the Roman legions turned their backs on it from the camp on the hill-side, and the long-haired sea-kings came up the river and looked with fierce eager eyes at the fatness of the land. It is a town "familiar with forgotten years."[1] The shadow of the Saxon hero-king still walks there fitfully, reviewing the scenes of his youth and lovetime, and is met by the gloomier shadow of the dreadful heathen Dane, who was stabbed in the midst of his warriors by the sword of an invisible avenger, and who rises on autumn evenings like a white mist from his tumulus[2] on the hill, and hovers in the court of the old hall by the river-side—the spot where he was thus miraculously slain in the days before the old hall was built. It was the Normans who began to build that fine old hall, which is like the town, telling of the thoughts and hands of widely-sundered generations; but it is all so old that we look with loving pardon at its inconsistencies, and are well content that they who built the stone oriel, and they who built the Gothic façade and towers of finest small brickwork with the trefoil ornament,[3] and the windows and battlements defined with stone, did not sacrilegiously pull down the ancient half-timbered body with its oak-roofed banqueting-hall.

But older even than this old hall is perhaps the bit of wall now built into the belfry of the parish church, and said to be a remnant of the original chapel dedicated to St Ogg, the patron saint of this ancient town, of whose history I possess several manuscript versions. I incline to the briefest, since, if it should not be wholly true, it is at least likely to contain the least falsehood. "Ogg the son of Beorl," says my private hagiographer, "was a boatman who gained a scanty living by ferrying passengers across the river Floss. And it came to pass, one evening when the winds were high, that there sat moaning by the brink of the river a woman with a child in her arms; and she was clad in rags, and had a worn and withered look, and she craved to be rowed across the river. And the men there about questioned her, and said, 'Wherefore dost thou desire to cross the river? Tarry till the morning, and take shelter here for the night: so shalt thou be wise, and not foolish.' Still she went on to mourn and crave. But Ogg the son of Beorl came up and said, 'I will ferry thee across: it is enough that thy heart needs it.' And he ferried her across. And it came to pass, when she stepped ashore, that her rags were turned into robes of flowing white, and her face became bright

1. Line 276 from book 1 of Wordsworth's *The Excursion*.
2. Ancient grave-mound.
3. Oriel: large bay window; trefoil: ornamental foliage with three leaves.

with exceeding beauty, and there was a glory around it, so that she shed a light on the water like the moon in its brightness. And she said—Ogg the son of Beorl, thou art blessed in that thou didst not question and wrangle with the heart's need, but wast smitten with pity, and didst straightway relieve the same. And from henceforth whoso steps into thy boat shall be in no peril from the storm; and whenever it puts forth to the rescue, it shall save the lives both of men and beasts.' And when the floods came, many were saved by reason of that blessing on the boat. But when Ogg the son of Beorl died, behold, in the parting of his soul, the boat loosed itself from its moorings, and was floated with the ebbing tide in great swiftness to the ocean, and was seen no more. Yet it was witnessed in the floods of aftertime, that at the coming on of eventide, Ogg the son of Beorl was always seen with his boat upon the wide-spreading waters, and the Blessed Virgin sat in the prow, shedding a light around as of the moon in its brightness, so that the rowers in the gathering darkness took heart and pulled anew."

This legend, one sees, reflects from a far-off time the visitation of the floods, which, even when they left human life untouched, were widely fatal to the helpless cattle, and swept as sudden death over all smaller living things. But the town knew worse troubles even than the floods—troubles of the civil wars, when it was a continual fighting-place, where first Puritans thanked God for the blood of the Loyalists,[4] and then Loyalists thanked God for the blood of the Puritans. Many honest citizens lost all their possessions for conscience' sake in those times, and went forth beggared from their native town. Doubtless there are many houses standing now on which those honest citizens turned their backs in sorrow: quaint-gabled houses looking on the river, jammed between newer warehouses, and penetrated by surprising passages, which turn and turn at sharp angles till they lead you out on a muddy strand overflowed continually by the rushing tide. Everywhere the brick houses have a mellow look, and in Mrs Glegg's day there was no incongruous new-fashioned smartness, no plate-glass in shop windows, no fresh stucco-facing or other fallacious attempt to make fine old red St Ogg's wear the air of a town that sprang up yesterday. The shop windows were small and unpretending; for the farmers' wives and daughters who came to do their shopping on market-days were not to be withdrawn from their regular, well-known shops; and the tradesmen had no wares intended for customers who would go on their way and be seen no more. Ah! even Mrs Glegg's day seems far back in the past now, separated from us by changes that widen the years. War and the rumour of war had then died out from the minds of men, and if they were ever thought of by the farmers in drab great-coats, who shook the grain out of their sample-bags and buzzed over it in the full market-place, it was as a state of things that

4. Puritans: revolutionary sixteenth-century Protestants, who fought the king and church under Oliver Cromwell; Loyalists: those who supported the king and opposed the Puritans.

belonged to a past golden age, when prices were high. Surely the time was gone for ever when the broad river could bring up unwelcome ships: Russia was only the place where the linseed came from—the more the better—making grist for the great vertical millstones with their scythe-like arms, roaring and grinding and carefully sweeping as if an informing soul were in them. The Catholics, bad harvests, and the mysterious fluctuations of trade, were the three evils mankind had to fear: even the floods had not been great of late years. The mind of St Ogg's did not look extensively before or after. It inherited a long past without thinking of it, and had no eyes for the spirits that walk the streets. Since the centuries when St Ogg with his boat and the Virgin Mother at the prow had been seen on the wide water, so many memories had been left behind, and had gradually vanished like the receding hill-tops! And the present time was like the level plain where men lose their belief in volcanoes and earthquakes, thinking to-morrow will be as yesterday, and the giant forces that used to shake the earth are for ever laid to sleep. The days were gone when people could be greatly wrought upon by their faith, still less change it: the Catholics were formidable because they would lay hold of government and property, and burn men alive; not because any sane and honest parishioner of St Ogg's could be brought to believe in the Pope. One aged person remembered how a rude multitude had been swayed when John Wesley[5] preached in the cattle-market; but for a long while it had not been expected of preachers that they should shake the souls of men. An occasional burst of fervour, in Dissenting pulpits,[6] on the subject of infant baptism, was the only symptom of a zeal unsuited to sober times when men had done with change. Protestantism sat at ease, unmindful of schisms, careless of proselytism: Dissent was an inheritance along with a superior pew and a business connection; and Churchmanship only wondered contemptuously at Dissent as a foolish habit that clung greatly to families in the grocery and chandlering[7] lines, though not incompatible with prosperous wholesale dealing. But with the Catholic Question[8] had come a slight wind of controversy to break the calm: the elderly rector had become occasionally historical and argumentative, and Mr Spray, the Independent minister, had begun to preach political sermons, in which he distinguished with much subtlety between his fervent belief in the right of the Catholics to the franchise and his fervent belief in their eternal perdition. Most of Mr Spray's hearers, however, were incapable of following his subtleties, and many old-fashioned Dissenters were much pained by his "siding with the Catholics;" while others thought he had better let politics alone. Public spirit was not held in high esteem at St Ogg's, and men who

5. Eighteenth-century evangelist, founder of Methodism.
6. Churches of Protestant denominations outside the Church of England.
7. Retailing.
8. Controversy over the granting of full civil rights to Catholics, resulting in passage of the Act of Catholic Emancipation in 1829.

busied themselves with political questions were regarded with some suspicion, as dangerous characters: they were usually persons who had little or no business of their own to manage, or, if they had, were likely enough to become insolvent.

This was the general aspect of things at St Ogg's in Mrs Glegg's day, and at that particular period in her family history when she had had her quarrel with Mr Tulliver. It was a time when ignorance was much more comfortable than at present, and was received with all the honours in very good society, without being obliged to dress itself in an elaborate costume of knowledge; a time when cheap periodicals were not, and when country surgeons never thought of asking their female patients if they were fond of reading, but simply took it for granted that they preferred gossip; a time when ladies in rich silk gowns wore large pockets, in which they carried a mutton-bone to secure them against cramp. Mrs Glegg carried such a bone, which she had inherited from her grandmother with a brocaded gown that would stand up empty, like a suit of armour, and a silver-headed walking-stick; for the Dodson family had been respectable for many generations.

Mrs Glegg had both a front and a back parlour in her excellent house at St Ogg's, so that she had two points of view from which she could observe the weakness of her fellow-beings, and reinforce her thankfulness for her own exceptional strength of mind. From her front windows she could look down the Tofton Road, leading out of St Ogg's, and note the growing tendency to "gadding about" in the wives of men not retired from business, together with a practice of wearing woven cotton stockings, which opened a dreary prospect for the coming generation; and from her back windows she could look down the pleasant garden and orchard which stretched to the river, and observe the folly of Mr Glegg in spending his time among "them flowers and vegetables." For Mr Glegg, having retired from active business as a wool-stapler,[9] for the purpose of enjoying himself through the rest of his life, had found this last occupation so much more severe than his business, that he had been driven into amateur hard labour as a dissipation, and habitually relaxed by doing the work of two ordinary gardeners. The economising of a gardener's wages might perhaps have induced Mrs Glegg to wink at this folly, if it were possible for a healthy female mind even to simulate respect for a husband's hobby. But it is well known that this conjugal complacency belongs only to the weaker portion of the sex, who are scarcely alive to the responsibilities of a wife as a constituted check on her husband's pleasures, which are hardly ever of a rational or commendable kind.

Mr Glegg on his side, too, had a double source of mental occupation, which gave every promise of being inexhaustible. On the one hand, he

9. Dealer in wool.

surprised himself by his discoveries in natural history, finding that his piece of garden-ground contained wonderful caterpillars, slugs, and insects, which, so far as he had heard, had never before attracted human observation; and he noticed remarkable coincidences between these zoological phenomena and the great events of that time,—as, for example, that before the burning of York Minster[1] there had been mysterious serpentine marks on the leaves of the rose-trees, together with an unusual prevalence of slugs, which he had been puzzled to know the meaning of, until it flashed upon him with this melancholy conflagration. (Mr Glegg had an unusual amount of mental activity, which, when disengaged from the wool business, naturally made itself a pathway in other directions.) And his second subject of meditation was the "contrairiness" of the female mind, as typically exhibited in Mrs Glegg. That a creature made—in a genealogical sense—out of a man's rib, and in this particular case maintained in the highest respectability without any trouble of her own, should be normally in a state of contradiction to the blandest propositions and even to the most accommodating concessions, was a mystery in the scheme of things to which he had often in vain sought a clue in the early chapters of Genesis. Mr Glegg had chosen the eldest Miss Dodson as a handsome embodiment of female prudence and thrift, and being himself of a money-getting, money-keeping turn, had calculated on much conjugal harmony. But in that curious compound, the feminine character, it may easily happen that the flavour is unpleasant in spite of excellent ingredients; and a fine systematic stinginess may be accompanied with a seasoning that quite spoils its relish. Now, good Mr Glegg himself was stingy in the most amiable manner: his neighbours called him "near," which always means that the person in question is a lovable skinflint. If you expressed a preference for cheese-parings, Mr Glegg would remember to save them for you, with a good-natured delight in gratifying your palate, and he was given to pet all animals which required no appreciable keep. There was no humbug or hypocrisy about Mr Glegg: his eyes would have watered with true feeling over the sale of a widow's furniture, which a five-pound note from his side-pocket would have prevented; but a donation of five pounds to a person "in a small way of life" would have seemed to him a mad kind of lavishness rather than "charity," which had always presented itself to him as a contribution of small aids, not a neutralising of misfortune. And Mr Glegg was just as fond of saving other people's money as his own: he would have ridden as far round to avoid a turnpike when his expenses were to be paid for him, as when they were to come out of his own pocket, and was quite zealous in trying to induce indifferent acquaintances to adopt a cheap substitute for blacking. This inalienable habit of saving, as an end in itself, belonged to the industrious men of

1. Fire set by a lunatic in 1829.

business of a former generation, who made their fortunes slowly, almost as the tracking of the fox belongs to the harrier[2]—it constituted them a "race," which is nearly lost in these days of rapid money-getting, when lavishness comes close on the back of want. In old-fashioned times, an "independence" was hardly ever made without a little miserliness as a condition, and you would have found that quality in every provincial district, combined with characters as various as the fruits from which we can extract acid. The true Harpagons[3] were always marked and exceptional characters: not so the worthy tax-payers, who, having once pinched from real necessity, retained even in the midst of their comfortable retirement, with their wall-fruit and wine-bins, the habit of regarding life as an ingenious process of nibbling out one's livelihood without leaving any perceptible deficit, and who would have been as immediately prompted to give up a newly-taxed luxury when they had their clear five hundred a-year, as when they had only five hundred pounds of capital. Mr Glegg was one of these men, found so impracticable by chancellors of the exchequer; and knowing this, you will be the better able to understand why he had not swerved from the conviction that he had made an eligible marriage, in spite of the too pungent seasoning that nature had given to the eldest Miss Dodson's virtues. A man with an affectionate disposition, who finds a wife to concur with his fundamental idea of life, easily comes to persuade himself that no other woman would have suited him so well, and does a little daily snapping and quarrelling without any sense of alienation. Mr Glegg, being of a reflective turn, and no longer occupied with wool, had much wondering meditation on the peculiar constitution of the female mind as unfolded to him in his domestic life; and yet he thought Mrs Glegg's household ways a model for her sex: it struck him as a pitiable irregularity in other women if they did not roll up their table-napkins with the same tightness and emphasis as Mrs Glegg did, if their pastry had a less leathery consistence, and their damson cheese a less venerable hardness than hers: nay, even the peculiar combination of grocery and drug-like odours in Mrs Glegg's private cupboard impressed him as the only right thing in the way of cupboard smells. I am not sure that he would not have longed for the quarrelling again, if it had ceased for an entire week; and it is certain that an acquiescent mild wife would have left his meditations comparatively jejune and barren of mystery.

Mr Glegg's unmistakeable kind-heartedness was shown in this, that it pained him more to see his wife at variance with others—even with Dolly, the servant—than to be in a state of cavil with her himself; and the quarrel between her and Mr Tulliver vexed him so much that it quite nullified the pleasure he would otherwise have had in the state of his early cabbages, as he walked in his garden before breakfast the next

2. Dogs used to hunt hares.
3. Misers, after the character Harpagon in Molière's play *L'Avare* (The miser) (1668).

morning. Still he went into breakfast with some slight hope that, now Mrs Glegg had "slept upon it," her anger might be subdued enough to give way to her usually strong sense of family decorum. She had been used to boast that there had never been any of those deadly quarrels among the Dodsons which had disgraced other families; that no Dodson had ever been "cut off with a shilling," and no cousin of the Dodsons disowned; as, indeed, why should they be? for they had no cousins who had not money out at use, or some houses of their own, at the very least.

There was one evening-cloud which had always disappeared from Mrs Glegg's brow when she sat at the breakfast-table: it was her fuzzy front of curls; for as she occupied herself in household matters in the morning, it would have been a mere extravagance to put on anything so superfluous to the making of leathery pastry as a fuzzy curled front. By half-past ten decorum demanded the front: until then Mrs Glegg could economise it, and society would never be any the wiser. But the absence of that cloud only left it more apparent that the cloud of severity remained; and Mr Glegg, perceiving this, as he sat down to his milk-porridge, which it was his old frugal habit to stem his morning hunger with, prudently resolved to leave the first remark to Mrs Glegg, lest, to so delicate an article as a lady's temper, the slightest touch should do mischief. People who seem to enjoy their ill-temper have a way of keeping it in fine condition by inflicting privations on themselves. That was Mrs Glegg's way: she made her tea weaker than usual this morning, and declined butter. It was a hard case that a vigorous mood for quarrelling, so highly capable of using any opportunity, should not meet with a single remark from Mr Glegg on which to exercise itself. But by-and-by it appeared that his silence would answer the purpose, for he heard himself apostrophised at last in that tone peculiar to the wife of one's bosom.

"Well, Mr Glegg! it's a poor return I get for making you the wife I've made you all these years. If this is the way I'm to be treated, I'd better ha' known it before my poor father died, and then, when I'd wanted a home, I should ha' gone elsewhere—as the choice was offered me."

Mr Glegg paused from his porridge and looked up—not with any new amazement, but simply with that quiet, habitual wonder with which we regard constant mysteries.

"Why, Mrs G., what have I done now?"

"Done now, Mr Glegg? *done now?* . . . I'm sorry for you."

Not seeing his way to any pertinent answer, Mr Glegg reverted to his porridge.

"There's husbands in the world," continued Mrs Glegg, after a pause, "as 'ud have known how to do something different to siding with everybody else against their own wives. Perhaps I'm wrong, and you can teach me better. But I've allays heard as it's the husband's place to stand by the wife, instead o' rejoicing and triumphing when folks insult her."

"Now, what call have you to say that?" said Mr Glegg, rather warmly, for though a kind man, he was not as meek as Moses.[4] "When did I rejoice or triumph over you?"

"There's ways o' doing things worse than speaking out plain, Mr Glegg. I'd sooner you'd tell me to my face as you make light of me, than try to make out as everybody's in the right but me, and come to your breakfast in the morning, as I've hardly slept an hour this night, and sulk at me as if I was the dirt under your feet."

"Sulk at you?" said Mr Glegg, in a tone of angry facetiousness. "You're like a tipsy man as thinks everybody's had too much but himself."

"Don't lower yourself with using coarse language to *me*, Mr Glegg! It makes you look very small, though you can't see yourself," said Mrs Glegg, in a tone of energetic compassion. "A man in your place should set an example, and talk more sensible."

"Yes; but will you listen to sense?" retorted Mr Glegg, sharply. "The best sense I can talk to you is what I said last night—as you're i' the wrong to think o' calling in your money, when it's safe enough if you'd let it alone, all because of a bit of a tiff, and I was in hopes you'd ha' altered your mind this morning. But if you'd like to call it in, don't do it in a hurry now, and breed more enmity in the family—but wait till there's a pretty mortgage to be had without any trouble. You'd have to set the lawyer to work now to find an investment, and make no end o' expense."

Mrs Glegg felt there was really something in this, but she tossed her head and emitted a guttural interjection to indicate that her silence was only an armistice, not a peace. And, in fact, hostilities soon broke out again.

"I'll thank you for my cup o' tea, now, Mrs G.," said Mr Glegg, seeing that she did not proceed to give it him as usual, when he had finished his porridge. She lifted the teapot with a slight toss of the head, and said,

"I'm glad to hear you'll *thank* me, Mr Glegg. It's little thanks *I* get for what I do for folks i' this world. Though there's never a woman o' *your* side o' the family, Mr Glegg, as is fit to stand up with me, and I'd say it if I was on my dying bed. Not but what I've allays conducted myself civil to your kin, and there isn't one of 'em can say the contrary, though my equils they aren't, and nobody shall make me say it."

"You'd better leave finding fault wi' my kin till you've left off quarrelling with your own, Mrs G.," said Mr Glegg, with angry sarcasm. "I'll trouble you for the milk-jug."

"That's as false a word as ever you spoke, Mr Glegg," said the lady, pouring out the milk with unusual profuseness, as much as to say, if he wanted milk he should have it with a vengeance. "And you know

4. From Numbers 12:3.

it's false. I'm not the woman to quarrel with my own kin: *you* may, for I've known you do it."

"Why, what did you call it yesterday, then, leaving your sister's house in a tantrum?"

"I'd no quarrel wi' my sister, Mr Glegg, and it's false to say it. Mr Tulliver's none o' my blood, and it was him quarrelled with me, and drove me out o' the house. But perhaps you'd have had me stay and be swore at, Mr Glegg; perhaps you was vexed not to hear more abuse and foul language poured out upo' your own wife. But, let me tell you, it's *your* disgrace."

"Did ever anybody hear the like i' this parish?" said Mr Glegg, getting hot. "A woman, with everything provided for her, and allowed to keep her own money the same as if it was settled on her, and with a gig new stuffed and lined at no end o' expense, and provided for when I die beyond anything she could expect . . . to go on i' this way, biting and snapping like a mad dog! It's beyond everything, as God A'mighty should ha' made women *so*." (These last words were uttered in a tone of sorrowful agitation. Mr Glegg pushed his tea from him, and tapped the table with both his hands.)

"Well, Mr Glegg! if those are your feelings, it's best they should be known," said Mrs Glegg, taking off her napkin, and folding it in an excited manner. "But if you talk o' my being provided for beyond what I could expect, I beg leave to tell you as I'd a right to expect a many things as I don't find. And as to my being like a mad dog, it's well if you're not cried shame on by the county for your treatment of me, for it's what I can't bear, and I won't bear". . . .

Here Mrs Glegg's voice intimated that she was going to cry, and, breaking off from speech, she rang the bell violently.

"Sally," she said, rising from her chair, and speaking in rather a choked voice, "light a fire up-stairs, and put the blinds down. Mr Glegg, you'll please to order what you'd like for dinner. I shall have gruel."

Mrs Glegg walked across the room to the small book-case, and took down Baxter's "Saints' Everlasting Rest,"[5] which she carried with her up-stairs. It was the book she was accustomed to lay open before her on special occasions: on wet Sunday mornings, or when she heard of a death in the family, or when, as in this case, her quarrel with Mr Glegg had been set an octave higher than usual.

But Mrs Glegg carried something else up-stairs with her, which, together with the "Saints' Rest" and the gruel, may have had some influence in gradually calming her feelings, and making it possible for her to endure existence on the ground-floor shortly before tea-time. This was, partly, Mr Glegg's suggestion, that she would do well to let her five hundred lie still until a good investment turned up; and, further,

5. Popular devotional work by Richard Baxter, first published in 1650.

his parenthetic hint at his handsome provision for her in case of his death. Mr Glegg, like all men of his stamp, was extremely reticent about his will; and Mrs Glegg, in her gloomier moments, had forebodings that, like other husbands of whom she had heard, he might cherish the mean project of heightening her grief at his death by leaving her poorly off, in which case she was firmly resolved that she would have scarcely any weeper on her bonnet, and would cry no more than if he had been a second husband. But if he had really shown her any testamentary tenderness, it would be affecting to think of him, poor man, when he was gone; and even his foolish fuss about the flowers and garden-stuff, and his insistance on the subject of snails, would be touching when it was once fairly at an end. To survive Mr Glegg, and talk eulogistically of him as a man who might have his weaknesses, but who had done the right thing by her, notwithstanding his numerous poor relations—to have sums of interest coming in more frequently, and secrete it in various corners, baffling to the most ingenious of thieves (for, to Mrs Glegg's mind, banks and strong-boxes would have nullified the pleasure of property—she might as well have taken her food in capsules)—finally, to be looked up to by her own family and the neighbourhood, so as no woman can ever hope to be who has not the præterite and present dignity comprised in being a "widow well left,"—all this made a flattering and conciliatory view of the future. So that when good Mr Glegg, restored to good-humour by much hoeing, and moved by the sight of his wife's empty chair, with her knitting rolled up in the corner, went up-stairs to her, and observed that the bell had been tolling for poor Mr Morton, Mrs Glegg answered magnanimously, quite as if she had been an uninjured woman, "Ah! then, there'll be a good business for somebody to take to."

Baxter had been open at least eight hours by this time, for it was nearly five o'clock; and if people are to quarrel often, it follows as a corollary that their quarrels cannot be protracted beyond certain limits.

Mr and Mrs Glegg talked quite amicably about the Tullivers that evening. Mr Glegg went the length of admitting that Tulliver was a sad man for getting into hot water, and was like enough to run through his property; and Mrs Glegg, meeting this acknowledgment half-way, declared that it was beneath her to take notice of such a man's conduct, and that, for her sister's sake, she would let him keep the five hundred a while longer, for when she put it out on a mortgage she should only get four per cent.

Chapter XIII

Mr Tulliver Further Entangles the Skein of Life

Owing to this new adjustment of Mrs Glegg's thoughts, Mrs Pullet found her task of mediation the next day surprisingly easy. Mrs Glegg, indeed, checked her rather sharply for thinking it would be necessary to tell her eldest sister what was the right mode of behaviour in family matters. Mrs Pullet's argument, that it would look ill in the neighbourhood if people should have it in their power to say that there was a quarrel in the family, was particularly offensive. If the family name never suffered except through Mrs Glegg, Mrs Pullet might lay her head on her pillow in perfect confidence.

"It's not to be expected, I suppose," observed Mrs Glegg, by way of winding up the subject, "as I shall go to the mill again before Bessy comes to see me, or as I shall go and fall down o' my knees to Mr Tulliver, and ask his pardon for showing him favours; but I shall bear no malice, and when Mr Tulliver speaks civil to me, I'll speak civil to him. Nobody has any call to tell me what's becoming."

Finding it unnecessary to plead for the Tullivers, it was natural that aunt Pullet should relax a little in her anxiety for them, and recur to the annoyance she had suffered yesterday from the offspring of that apparently ill-fated house. Mrs Glegg heard a circumstantial narrative, to which Mr Pullet's remarkable memory furnished some items; and while aunt Pullet pitied poor Bessy's bad-luck with her children, and expressed a half-formed project of paying for Maggie's being sent to a distant boarding-school, which would not prevent her being so brown, but might tend to subdue some other vices in her, aunt Glegg blamed Bessy for her weakness, and appealed to all witnesses who should be living when the Tulliver children had turned out ill, that she, Mrs Glegg, had always said how it would be from the very first, observing that it was wonderful to herself how all her words came true.

"Then I may call and tell Bessy you'll bear no malice, and everything be as it was before?" Mrs Pullet said, just before parting.

"Yes, you may, Sophy," said Mrs Glegg; "you may tell Mr Tulliver, and Bessy too, as I'm not going to behave ill because folks behave ill to me: I know it's my place, as the eldest, to set an example in every respect, and I do it. Nobody can say different of me, if they'll keep to the truth."

Mrs Glegg being in this state of satisfaction in her own lofty magnanimity, I leave you to judge what effect was produced on her by the reception of a short letter from Mr Tulliver, that very evening, after Mrs Pullet's departure, informing her that she needn't trouble her mind about her five hundred pounds, for it should be paid back to her in the course of the next month at farthest, together with the interest due thereon until the time of payment. And furthermore, that Mr Tulliver had no wish to behave uncivilly to Mrs Glegg, and she was welcome to his house whenever she liked to come, but he desired no favours from her, either for himself or his children.

It was poor Mrs Tulliver who had hastened this catastrophe, entirely through that irrepressible hopefulness of hers which led her to expect that similar causes may at any time produce different results. It had very often occurred in her experience that Mr Tulliver had done something because other people had said he was not able to do it, or had pitied him for his supposed inability, or in any other way piqued his pride; still, she thought to-day, if she told him when he came in to tea that sister Pullet was gone to try and make everything up with sister Glegg, so that he needn't think about paying in the money, it would give a cheerful effect to the meal. Mr Tulliver had never slackened in his resolve to raise the money, but now he at once determined to write a letter to Mrs Glegg which should cut off all possibility of mistake. Mrs Pullet gone to beg and pray for *him* indeed! Mr Tulliver did not willingly write a letter, and found the relation between spoken and written language, briefly known as spelling, one of the most puzzling things in this puzzling world. Nevertheless, like all fervid writing, the task was done in less time than usual, and if the spelling differed from Mrs Glegg's—why she belonged, like himself, to a generation with whom spelling was a matter of private judgment.

Mrs Glegg did not alter her will in consequence of this letter, and cut off the Tulliver children from their sixth and seventh share in her thousand pounds; for she had her principles. No one must be able to say of her when she was dead that she had not divided her money with perfect fairness among her own kin: in the matter of wills, personal qualities were subordinate to the great fundamental fact of blood; and to be determined in the distribution of your property by caprice, and not make your legacies bear a direct ratio to degrees of kinship, was a prospective disgrace that would have embittered her life. This had always been a principle in the Dodson family; it was one form of that sense of honour and rectitude which was a proud tradition in such families—a tradition which has been the salt of our provincial society.

But though the letter could not shake Mrs Glegg's principles, it made the family breach much more difficult to mend; and as to the effect it produced on Mrs Glegg's opinion of Mr Tulliver—she begged to be understood from that time forth that she had nothing whatever to say about him: his state of mind, apparently, was too corrupt for her to contemplate it for a moment. It was not until the evening before Tom went to school, at the beginning of August, that Mrs Glegg paid a visit to her sister Tulliver, sitting in her gig all the while, and showing her displeasure by markedly abstaining from all advice and criticism, for, as she observed to her sister Deane, "Bessy must bear the consequence o' having such a husband, though I'm sorry for her," and Mrs Deane agreed that Bessy was pitiable.

That evening Tom observed to Maggie, "O my! Maggie, aunt Glegg's beginning to come again; I'm glad I'm going to school. *You'll* catch it all now!"

Maggie was already so full of sorrow at the thought of Tom's going away from her, that this playful exultation of his seemed very unkind, and she cried herself to sleep that night.

Mr Tulliver's prompt procedure entailed on him further promptitude in finding the convenient person who was desirous of lending five hundred pounds on bond. "It must be no client of Wakem's," he said to himself; and yet at the end of a fortnight it turned out to the contrary; not because Mr Tulliver's will was feeble, but because external fact was stronger. Wakem's client was the only convenient person to be found. Mr Tulliver had a destiny as well as Œdipus, and in this case he might plead, like Œdipus, that his deed was inflicted on him rather than committed by him.

Book Second

SCHOOL-TIME

Chapter I

Tom's "First Half"

Tom Tulliver's sufferings during the first quarter he was at King's Lorton, under the distinguished care of the Rev. Walter Stelling, were rather severe. At Mr Jacobs' academy, life had not presented itself to him as a difficult problem: there were plenty of fellows to play with, and Tom being good at all active games—fighting especially—had that precedence among them which appeared to him inseparable from the personality of Tom Tulliver. Mr Jacobs himself, familiarly known as Old Goggles, from his habit of wearing spectacles, imposed no painful awe; and if it was the property of snuffy old hypocrites like him to write like copperplate and surround their signatures with arabesques, to spell without forethought, and to spout "My name is Norval"[1] without bungling, Tom, for his part, was rather glad he was not in danger of those mean accomplishments. He was not going to be a snuffy schoolmaster—he; but a substantial man, like his father, who used to go hunting when he was younger, and rode a capital black mare—as pretty a bit of horse-flesh as ever you saw: Tom had heard what her points were a hundred times. *He* meant to go hunting too, and to be generally respected. When people were grown up, he considered, nobody inquired about their writing and spelling: when he was a man, he should be master of everything, and do just as he liked. It had been very difficult for him to reconcile himself to the idea that his school-time was to be prolonged, and that he was not to be brought up to his father's business, which he had always thought extremely pleasant, for it was nothing but riding about, giving orders, and going to market; and he thought that a clergyman would give him a great many Scripture lessons, and probably make him learn the Gospel and Epistle on a Sunday as well as the Collect.[2] But in the absence of

1. Write like copperplate: i.e., with machinelike regularity; "my name is Norval": from John Home's *Douglas: A Tragedy* (1757).
2. Gospel and Epistle: reading from the New Testament; Collect: short daily prayer.

specific information, it was impossible for him to imagine that school and a schoolmaster would be something entirely different from the academy of Mr Jacobs. So, not to be at a deficiency, in case of his finding genial companions, he had taken care to carry with him a small box of percussion-caps; not that there was anything particular to be done with them, but they would serve to impress strange boys with a sense of his familiarity with guns. Thus poor Tom, though he saw very clearly through Maggie's illusions, was not without illusions of his own, which were to be cruelly dissipated by his enlarged experience at King's Lorton.

He had not been there a fortnight before it was evident to him that life, complicated not only with the Latin grammar but with a new standard of English pronunciation, was a very difficult business, made all the more obscure by a thick mist of bashfulness. Tom, as you have observed, was never an exception among boys for ease of address; but the difficulty of enunciating a monosyllable in reply to Mr or Mrs Stelling was so great, that he even dreaded to be asked at table whether he would have more pudding. As to the percussion-caps, he had almost resolved, in the bitterness of his heart, that he would throw them into a neighbouring pond; for not only was he the solitary pupil, but he began even to have a certain scepticism about guns, and a general sense that his theory of life was undermined. For Mr Stelling thought nothing of guns, or horses either, apparently; and yet it was impossible for Tom to despise Mr St[illegible]g as he had despised Old Goggles. If there were anything that [illegible]oroughly genuine about Mr Stelling, it lay quite beyond Tom's [illegible]etect it: it is only by a wide comparison of facts that the wisest [illegible] man can distinguish well-rolled barrels from more supernal thunder.

Mr Stelling was a well-sized, broad-chested man, not yet thirty, with flaxen hair standing erect, and large lightish-grey eyes, which were always very wide open; he had a sonorous bass voice, and an air of defiant self-confidence inclining to brazenness. He had entered on his career with great vigour, and intended to make a considerable impression on his fellow-men. The Rev. Walter Stelling was not a man who would remain among the "inferior clergy" all his life. He had a true British determination to push his way in the world. As a schoolmaster, in the first place; for there were capital masterships of grammar-schools to be had, and Mr Stelling meant to have one of them. But as a preacher also, for he meant always to preach in a striking manner, so as to have his congregation swelled by admirers from neighbouring parishes, and to produce a great sensation whenever he took occasional duty for a brother clergyman of minor gifts. The style of preaching he had chosen was the extemporaneous, which was held little short of the miraculous in rural parishes like King's Lorton. Some passages of Massillon and Bourdaloue,[3] which he knew by heart, were really very effective when rolled out in Mr Stelling's deepest tones; but as comparatively feeble appeals of his own were delivered in the same loud and impressive manner, they were often thought quite as striking by his hearers. Mr Stelling's doctrine was of no particular school; if anything, it had a tinge of evangelicalism, for that was "the telling thing" just then in the diocese to which King's Lorton belonged. In short, Mr Stelling was a man who meant to rise in his profession, and to rise by merit, clearly, since he had no interest beyond what might be promised by a problematic relationship to a great lawyer who had not yet become Lord Chancellor. A clergyman who has such vigorous intentions naturally gets a little into debt at starting; it is not to be expected that he will live in the meagre style of a man who means to be a poor curate all his life, and if the few hundreds Mr Timpson advanced towards his daughter's fortune did not suffice for the purchase of handsome furniture, together with a stock of wine, a grand piano, and the laying-out of a superior flower-garden, it followed in the most rigorous manner, either that these things must be procured by some other means, or else that the Rev. Mr Stelling must go without them—which last alternative would be an absurd procrastination of the fruits of success, where success was certain. Mr Stelling was so broad-chested and resolute that he felt equal to anything; he would become celebrated by shaking the consciences of his hearers, and he would by-and-by edit a Greek play, and invent several new readings. He had not yet selected the play, for having been married little more than two years, his leisure time had been much occupied with attentions to Mrs Stelling; but he had told that fine woman what he meant to do some day, and she felt great confidence in her husband, as a man who understood everything of that sort.

But the immediate step to future success was to bring on Tom Tulliver during this first half-year; for, by a singular coincidence, there had been some negotiation concerning another pupil from the same neighbourhood, and it might further a decision in Mr Stelling's favour, if it were understood that young Tulliver, who, Mr Stelling observed in conjugal privacy, was rather a rough cub, had made prodigious progress in a short time. It was on this ground that he was severe with Tom about his lessons: he was clearly a boy whose powers would never be developed through the medium of the Latin grammar, without the application of some sternness. Not that Mr Stelling was a harsh-tempered or unkind man—quite the contrary: he was jocose with Tom at table, and corrected his provincialisms and his deportment in the most playful manner; but poor Tom was only the more cowed and confused by this double novelty, for he had never been used to jokes at all like Mr Stelling's; and for the first time in his life he had a painful sense that he was all wrong somehow.

3. French preachers of the late seventeenth and early eighteenth centuries.

When Mr Stelling said, as the roast-beef was being uncovered, "Now, Tulliver! which would you rather decline, roast-beef or the Latin for it?"[4]—Tom, to whom in his coolest moments a pun would have been a hard nut, was thrown into a state of embarrassed alarm that made everything dim to him except the feeling that he would rather not have anything to do with Latin: of course he answered, "Roast-beef," whereupon there followed much laughter and some practical joking with the plates, from which Tom gathered that he had in some mysterious way refused beef, and, in fact, made himself appear "a silly." If he could have seen a fellow-pupil undergo these painful operations and survive them in good spirits, he might sooner have taken them as a matter of course. But there are two expensive forms of education, either of which a parent may procure for his son by sending him as solitary pupil to a clergyman: one is, the enjoyment of the reverend gentleman's undivided neglect; the other is, the endurance of the reverend gentleman's undivided attention. It was the latter privilege for which Mr Tulliver paid a high price in Tom's initiatory months at King's Lorton.

That respectable miller and maltster had left Tom behind, and driven homeward in a state of great mental satisfaction. He considered that it was a happy moment for him when he had thought of asking Riley's advice about a tutor for Tom. Mr Stelling's eyes were so wide open, and he talked in such an off-hand, matter-of-fact way—answering every difficult slow remark of Mr Tulliver's with, "I see, my good sir, I see;" "To be sure, to be sure;" "You want your son to be a man who will make his way in the world,"—that Mr Tulliver was delighted to find in him a clergyman whose knowledge was so applicable to the everyday affairs of this life. Except Counsellor Wylde, whom he had heard at the last sessions, Mr Tulliver thought the Rev. Mr Stelling was the shrewdest fellow he had ever met with—not unlike Wylde, in fact: he had the same way of sticking his thumbs in the armholes of his waistcoat. Mr Tulliver was not by any means an exception in mistaking brazenness for shrewdness: most laymen thought Stelling shrewd, and a man of remarkable powers generally: it was chiefly by his clerical brethren that he was considered rather a dull fellow. But he told Mr Tulliver several stories about "Swing" and incendiarism,[5] and asked his advice about feeding pigs in so thoroughly secular and judicious a manner, with so much polished glibness of tongue, that the miller thought, here was the very thing he wanted for Tom. He had no doubt this first-rate man was acquainted with every branch of information, and knew exactly what Tom must learn in order to become a match for the lawyers—which poor Mr Tulliver himself did *not* know, and so was necessarily thrown

4. Mr. Stelling uses the term "decline" in the sense of both "turn down" and "list the forms of a noun or adjective."
5. Unemployed farm laborers in the 1830s set fire to hayricks and sent threatening letters, signed "Captain Swing," to owners of threshing machines.

for self-direction on this wide kind of inference. It is hardly fair to laugh at him, for I have known much more highly-instructed persons than he make inferences quite as wide, and not at all wiser.

As for Mrs Tulliver—finding that Mrs Stelling's views as to the airing of linen and the frequent recurrence of hunger in a growing boy, entirely coincided with her own; moreover, that Mrs Stelling, though so young a woman, and only anticipating her second confinement, had gone through very nearly the same experience as herself with regard to the behaviour and fundamental character of the monthly nurse[6]—she expressed great contentment to her husband, when they drove away, at leaving Tom with a woman who, in spite of her youth, seemed quite sensible and motherly, and asked advice as prettily as could be.

"They must be very well off, though," said Mrs Tulliver, "for everything's as nice as can be all over the house, and that watered-silk she had on cost a pretty penny. Sister Pullet has got one like it."

"Ah," said Mr Tulliver, "he's got some income besides the curacy, I reckon. Perhaps her father allows 'em something. There's Tom 'ull be another hundred to him, and not much trouble either, by his own account: he says teaching comes natural to him. That's wonderful, now," added Mr Tulliver, turning his head on one side, and giving his horse a meditative tickling on the flank.

Perhaps it was because teaching came naturally to Mr Stelling, that he set about it with that uniformity of method and independence of circumstances, which distinguish the actions of animals understood to be under the immediate teaching of nature. Mr Broderip's amiable beaver,[7] as that charming naturalist tells us, busied himself as earnestly in constructing a dam, in a room up three pair of stairs in London, as if he had been laying his foundation in a stream or lake in Upper Canada. It was "Binny's" function to build: the absence of water or of possible progeny was an accident for which he was not accountable. With the same unerring instinct Mr Stelling set to work at his natural method of instilling the Eton Grammar and Euclid[8] into the mind of Tom Tulliver. This, he considered, was the only basis of solid instruction: all other means of education were mere charlatanism, and could produce nothing better than smatterers. Fixed on this firm basis, a man might observe the display of various or special knowledge made by irregularly educated people with a pitying smile: all that sort of thing was very well, but it was impossible these people could form sound opinions. In holding this conviction Mr Stelling was not biassed, as some tutors have been, by the excessive accuracy or extent of his own scholarship; and as to his views about Euclid, no opinion could have been freer from personal

6. Nurse hired to tend a child for the first month after birth.
7. Discussed in W. J. Broderip's *Leaves from the Note Book of a Naturalist* (1852).
8. Eton Grammar: Latin grammar book, edited by T. W. C. Edwards, popular in the early nineteenth century; Euclid: i.e., geometry.

partiality. Mr Stelling was very far from being led astray by enthusiasm, either religious or intellectual; on the other hand, he had no secret belief that everything was humbug. He thought religion was a very excellent thing, and Aristotle a great authority, and deaneries and prebends[9] useful institutions, and Great Britain the providential bulwark of Protestantism, and faith in the unseen a great support to afflicted minds: he believed in all these things, as a Swiss hotel-keeper believes in the beauty of the scenery around him, and in the pleasure it gives to artistic visitors. And in the same way Mr Stelling believed in his method of education: he had no doubt that he was doing the very best thing for Mr Tulliver's boy. Of course, when the miller talked of "mapping" and "summing" in a vague and diffident manner, Mr Stelling had set his mind at rest by an assurance that he understood what was wanted; for how was it possible the good man could form any reasonable judgment about the matter? Mr Stelling's duty was to teach the lad in the only right way—indeed, he knew no other: he had not wasted his time in the acquirement of anything abnormal.

He very soon set down poor Tom as a thoroughly stupid lad; for though by hard labour he could get particular declensions into his brain, anything so abstract as the relation between cases and terminations could by no means get such a lodgment there as to enable him to recognise a chance genitive or dative. This struck Mr Stelling as something more than natural stupidity: he suspected obstinacy, or at any rate, indifference; and lectured Tom severely on his want of thorough application. "You feel no interest in what you're doing, sir," Mr Stelling would say, and the reproach was painfully true. Tom had never found any difficulty in discerning a pointer from a setter, when once he had been told the distinction, and his perceptive powers were not at all deficient. I fancy they were quite as strong as those of the Rev. Mr Stelling; for Tom could predict with accuracy what number of horses were cantering behind him, he could throw a stone right into the centre of a given ripple, he could guess to a fraction how many lengths of his stick it would take to reach across the playground, and could draw almost perfect squares on his slate without any measurement. But Mr Stelling took no note of these things: he only observed that Tom's faculties failed him before the abstractions hideously symbolised to him in the pages of the Eton Grammar, and that he was in a state bordering on idiocy with regard to the demonstration that two given triangles must be equal—though he could discern with great promptitude and certainty the fact that they *were* equal. Whence Mr Stelling concluded that Tom's brain being peculiarly impervious to etymology and demonstrations, was peculiarly in need of being ploughed and harrowed by these patent implements: it was his favourite metaphor, that the classics and geometry constituted that cul-

9. Offices and stipends of clergymen.

ture of the mind which prepared it for the reception of any subsequent crop. I say nothing against Mr Stelling's theory: if we are to have one regimen for all minds, his seems to me as good as any other. I only know it turned out as uncomfortably for Tom Tulliver as if he had been plied with cheese in order to remedy a gastric weakness which prevented him from digesting it. It is astonishing what a different result one gets by changing the metaphor! Once call the brain an intellectual stomach, and one's ingenious conception of the classics and geometry as ploughs and harrows seems to settle nothing. But then it is open to some one else to follow great authorities, and call the mind a sheet of white paper or a mirror, in which case one's knowledge of the digestive process becomes quite irrelevant. It was doubtless an ingenious idea to call the camel the ship of the desert, but it would hardly lead one far in training that useful beast. O Aristotle! if you had had the advantage of being "the freshest modern" instead of the greatest ancient, would you not have mingled your praise of metaphorical speech, as a sign of high intelligence, with a lamentation that intelligence so rarely shows itself in speech without metaphor,—that we can so seldom declare what a thing is, except by saying it is something else?[1]

Tom Tulliver, being abundant in no form of speech, did not use any metaphor to declare his views as to the nature of Latin: he never called it an instrument of torture; and it was not until he had got on some way in the next half-year, and in the Delectus,[2] that he was advanced enough to call it a "bore" and "beastly stuff." At present, in relation to this demand that he should learn Latin declensions and conjugations, Tom was in a state of as blank unimaginativeness concerning the cause and tendency of his sufferings, as if he had been an innocent shrew-mouse imprisoned in the split trunk of an ash-tree in order to cure lameness in cattle. It is doubtless almost incredible to instructed minds of the present day that a boy of twelve, not belonging strictly to "the masses," who are now understood to have the monopoly of mental darkness, should have had no distinct idea how there came to be such a thing as Latin on this earth: yet so it was with Tom. It would have taken a long while to make conceivable to him that there ever existed a people who bought and sold sheep and oxen, and transacted the everyday affairs of life, through the medium of this language, and still longer to make him understand why he should be called upon to learn it, when its connection with those affairs had become entirely latent. So far as Tom had gained any acquaintance with the Romans at Mr Jacobs' academy, his knowledge was strictly correct, but it went no farther than the fact that they were "in the New Testament;" and Mr Stelling was not the man to enfeeble and emasculate his pupil's mind by simplifying and explaining,

1. From the *Poetics* 22, where Aristotle celebrates the use of metaphor; the phrase "the freshest modern" comes from Jonathan Swift's A *Tale of a Tub* (1704).
2. T. W. C. Edwards's Latin primer.

or to reduce the tonic effect of etymology by mixing it with smattering, extraneous information, such as is given to girls.

Yet, strange to say, under this vigorous treatment Tom became more like a girl than he had ever been in his life before. He had a large share of pride, which had hitherto found itself very comfortable in the world, despising old Goggles, and reposing in the sense of unquestioned rights; but now this same pride met with nothing but bruises and crushings. Tom was too clear-sighted not to be aware that Mr Stelling's standard of things was quite different, was certainly something higher in the eyes of the world than that of the people he had been living amongst, and that, brought in contact with it, he, Tom Tulliver, appeared uncouth and stupid: he was by no means indifferent to this, and his pride got into an uneasy condition which quite nullified his boyish self-satisfaction, and gave him something of the girl's susceptibility. He was of a very firm, not to say obstinate disposition, but there was no brute-like rebellion and recklessness in his nature: the human sensibilities predominated, and if it had occurred to him that he could enable himself to show some quickness at his lessons, and so acquire Mr Stelling's approbation, by standing on one leg for an inconvenient length of time, or rapping his head moderately against the wall, or any voluntary action of that sort, he would certainly have tried it. But no—Tom had never heard that these measures would brighten the understanding, or strengthen the verbal memory; and he was not given to hypothesis and experiment. It did occur to him that he could perhaps get some help by praying for it; but as the prayers he said every evening were forms learned by heart, he rather shrank from the novelty and irregularity of introducing an extempore passage on a topic of petition for which he was not aware of any precedent. But one day when he had broken down, for the fifth time, in the supines[3] of the third conjugation, and Mr Stelling, convinced that this must be carelessness, since it transcended the bounds of possible stupidity, had lectured him very seriously, pointing out that if he failed to seize the present golden opportunity of learning supines, he would have to regret it when he became a man,—Tom, more miserable than usual, determined to try his sole resource; and that evening, after his usual form of prayer for his parents and "little sister" (he had begun to pray for Maggie when she was a baby), and that he might be able always to keep God's commandments, he added, in the same low whisper, "and please to make me always remember my Latin." He paused a little to consider how he should pray about Euclid—whether he should ask to see what it meant, or whether there was any other mental state which would be more applicable to the case. But at last he added—"And make Mr Stelling say I shan't do Euclid any more. Amen."

3. A type of verbal noun in Latin.

The fact that he got through his supines without mistake the next day, encouraged him to persevere in this appendix to his prayers, and neutralised any scepticism that might have arisen from Mr Stelling's continued demand for Euclid. But his faith broke down under the apparent absence of all help when he got into the irregular verbs. It seemed clear that Tom's despair under the caprices of the present tense did not constitute a *nodus*[4] worthy of interference, and since this was the climax of his difficulties, where was the use of praying for help any longer? He made up his mind to this conclusion in one of his dull, lonely evenings, which he spent in the study, preparing his lessons for the morrow. His eyes were apt to get dim over the page—though he hated crying, and was ashamed of it: he couldn't help thinking with some affection even of Spouncer, whom he used to fight and quarrel with; he would have felt at home with Spouncer, and in a condition of superiority. And then the mill, and the river, and Yap pricking up his ears, ready to obey the least sign when Tom said "Hoigh!" would all come before him in a sort of calenture,[5] when his fingers played absently in his pocket with his great knife and his coil of whip-cord, and other relics of the past. Tom, as I said, had never been so much like a girl in his life before, and at that epoch of irregular verbs his spirit was further depressed by a new means of mental development, which had been thought of for him out of school hours. Mrs Stelling had lately had her second baby, and as nothing could be more salutary for a boy than to feel himself useful, Mrs Stelling considered she was doing Tom a service by setting him to watch the little cherub Laura while the nurse was occupied with the sickly baby. It was quite a pretty employment for Tom to take little Laura out in the sunniest hour of the autumn day—it would help to make him feel that Lorton Parsonage was a home for him, and that he was one of the family. The little cherub Laura, not being an accomplished walker at present, had a ribbon fastened round her waist, by which Tom held her as if she had been a little dog during the minutes in which she chose to walk; but as these were rare, he was for the most part carrying this fine child round and round the garden, within sight of Mrs Stelling's window—according to orders. If any one considers this unfair and even oppressive towards Tom, I beg him to consider that there are feminine virtues which are with difficulty combined, even if they are not incompatible. When the wife of a poor curate contrives, under all her disadvantages, to dress extremely well, and to have a style of coiffure which requires that her nurse shall occasionally officiate as lady's-maid,—when, moreover, her dinner-parties and her drawing-room show that effort at elegance and completeness of appointment to which ordinary women might imagine a large income necessary, it would be unreasonable to expect of her that she should employ a second nurse,

4. Difficulty.
5. Fever characterized by delirium.

or even act as a nurse herself. Mr Stelling knew better: he saw that his wife did wonders already, and was proud of her: it was certainly not the best thing in the world for young Tulliver's gait to carry a heavy child, but he had plenty of exercise in long walks with himself, and next half-year Mr Stelling would see about having a drilling-master. Among the many means whereby Mr Stelling intended to be more fortunate than the bulk of his fellow-men, he had entirely given up that of having his own way in his own house. What then? he had married "as kind a little soul as ever breathed," according to Mr Riley, who had been acquainted with Mrs Stelling's blond ringlets and smiling demeanour throughout her maiden life, and on the strength of that knowledge would have been ready any day to pronounce that whatever domestic differences might arise in her married life must be entirely Mr Stelling's fault.

If Tom had had a worse disposition, he would certainly have hated the little cherub Laura, but he was too kind-hearted a lad for that—there was too much in him of the fibre that turns to true manliness, and to protecting pity for the weak. I am afraid he hated Mrs Stelling, and contracted a lasting dislike to pale blond ringlets and broad plaits, as directly associated with haughtiness of manner, and a frequent reference to other people's "duty." But he couldn't help playing with little Laura, and liking to amuse her: he even sacrificed his percussion-caps for her sake, in despair of their ever serving a greater purpose—thinking the small flash and bang would delight her, and thereby drawing down on himself a rebuke from Mrs Stelling for teaching her child to play with fire. Laura was a sort of playfellow—and O how Tom longed for playfellows! In his secret heart he yearned to have Maggie with him, and was almost ready to dote on her exasperating acts of forgetfulness; though, when he was at home, he always represented it as a great favour on his part to let Maggie trot by his side on his pleasure excursions.

And before this dreary half-year was ended, Maggie actually came. Mrs Stelling had given a general invitation for the little girl to come and stay with her brother: so when Mr Tulliver drove over to King's Lorton late in October, Maggie came too, with the sense that she was taking a great journey, and beginning to see the world. It was Mr Tulliver's first visit to see Tom, for the lad must learn not to think too much about home.

"Well, my lad," he said to Tom, when Mr Stelling had left the room to announce the arrival to his wife, and Maggie had begun to kiss Tom freely, "you look rarely! School agrees with you."

Tom wished he had looked rather ill.

"I don't think I *am* well, father," said Tom; "I wish you'd ask Mr Stelling not to let me do Euclid—it brings on the toothache, I think."

(The toothache was the only malady to which Tom had ever been subject.)

"Euclid, my lad—why, what's that?" said Mr Tulliver.

"O, I don't know: it's definitions, and axioms, and triangles, and things. It's a book I've got to learn in—there's no sense in it."

"Go, go!" said Mr Tulliver, reprovingly, "you mustn't say so. You must learn what your master tells you. He knows what it's right for you to learn."

"*I'll* help you now, Tom," said Maggie, with a little air of patronising consolation. "I'm come to stay ever so long, if Mrs Stelling asks me. I've brought my box and my pinafores, haven't I, father?"

"*You* help me, you silly little thing!" said Tom, in such high spirits at this announcement that he quite enjoyed the idea of confounding Maggie by showing her a page of Euclid. "I should like to see you doing one of *my* lessons! Why, I learn Latin too! Girls never learn such things. They're too silly."

"I know what Latin is very well," said Maggie, confidently. "Latin's a language. There are Latin words in the Dictionary. There's bonus, a gift."

"Now, you're just wrong there, Miss Maggie!" said Tom, secretly astonished. "You think you're very wise! But 'bonus' means 'good,' as it happens—bonus, bona, bonum."

"Well, that's no reason why it shouldn't mean 'gift,' " said Maggie, stoutly. "It may mean several things—almost every word does. There's 'lawn,'—it means the grass-plot, as well as the stuff pocket-handkerchiefs are made of."

"Well done, little 'un," said Mr Tulliver, laughing, while Tom felt rather disgusted with Maggie's knowingness, though beyond measure cheerful at the thought that she was going to stay with him. Her conceit would soon be overawed by the actual inspection of his books.

Mrs Stelling, in her pressing invitation, did not mention a longer time than a week for Maggie's stay; but Mr Stelling, who took her between his knees, and asked her where she stole her dark eyes from, insisted that she must stay a fortnight. Maggie thought Mr Stelling was a charming man, and Mr Tulliver was quite proud to leave his little wench where she would have an opportunity of showing her cleverness to appreciating strangers. So it was agreed that she should not be fetched home till the end of the fortnight.

"Now, then, come with me into the study, Maggie," said Tom, as their father drove away. "What do you shake and toss your head now for, you silly?" he continued; for though her hair was now under a new dispensation, and was brushed smoothly behind her ears, she seemed still in imagination to be tossing it out of her eyes. "It makes you look as if you were crazy."

"O, I can't help it," said Maggie, impatiently. "Don't tease me, Tom. O, what books!" she exclaimed, as she saw the bookcases in the study. "How I should like to have as many books as that!"

"Why, you couldn't read one of 'em," said Tom, triumphantly. "They're all Latin."

"No, they aren't," said Maggie. "I can read the back of this . . . History of the Decline and Fall of the Roman Empire."[6]

"Well, what does that mean? *You* don't know," said Tom, wagging his head.

"But I could soon find out," said Maggie, scornfully.

"Why, how?"

"I should look inside, and see what it was about."

"You'd better not, Miss Maggie," said Tom, seeing her hand on the volume. "Mr Stelling lets nobody touch his books without leave, and *I* shall catch it, if you take it out."

"O, very well! Let me see all *your* books, then," said Maggie, turning to throw her arms round Tom's neck, and rub his cheek with her small round nose.

Tom, in the gladness of his heart at having dear old Maggie to dispute with and crow over again, seized her round the waist, and began to jump with her round the large library table. Away they jumped with more and more vigour, till Maggie's hair flew from behind her ears, and twirled about like an animated mop. But the revolutions round the table became more and more irregular in their sweep, till at last reaching Mr Stelling's reading-stand, they sent it thundering down with its heavy lexicons to the floor. Happily it was the ground-floor, and the study was a one-storied wing to the house, so that the downfall made no alarming resonance, though Tom stood dizzy and aghast for a few minutes, dreading the appearance of Mr or Mrs Stelling.

"O, I say, Maggie," said Tom at last, lifting up the stand, "we must keep quiet here, you know. If we break anything, Mrs Stelling'll make us cry peccavi."[7]

"What's that?" said Maggie.

"O, it's the Latin for a good scolding," said Tom, not without some pride in his knowledge.

"Is she a cross woman?" said Maggie.

"I believe you!" said Tom, with an emphatic nod.

"I think all women are crosser than men," said Maggie. "Aunt Glegg's a great deal crosser that Uncle Glegg, and mother scolds me more than father does."

"Well, *you'll* be a woman some day," said Tom, "so *you* needn't talk."

"But I shall be a *clever* woman," said Maggie, with a toss.

"O, I daresay, and a nasty conceited thing. Everybody'll hate you."

6. Influential work (1776–88) by Edward Gibbon.
7. "I have sinned."

"But you oughtn't to hate me, Tom: it'll be very wicked of you, for I shall be your sister."

"Yes, but if you're a nasty disagreeable thing, I *shall* hate you."

"O but, Tom, you won't! I shan't be disagreeable. I shall be very good to you—and I shall be good to everybody. You won't hate me really, will you, Tom?"

"O, bother! never mind! Come, it's time for me to learn my lessons. See here! what I've got to do," said Tom, drawing Maggie towards him and showing her his theorem, while she pushed her hair behind her ears, and prepared herself to prove her capability of helping him in Euclid. She began to read with full confidence in her own powers, but presently, becoming quite bewildered, her face flushed with irritation. It was unavoidable—she must confess her incompetency, and she was not fond of humiliation.

"It's nonsense!" she said, "and very ugly stuff—nobody need want to make it out."

"Ah, there now, Miss Maggie!" said Tom, drawing the book away, and wagging his head at her, "you see you're not so clever as you thought you were."

"O," said Maggie, pouting, "I daresay I could make it out, if I'd learned what goes before, as you have."

"But that's what you just couldn't, Miss Wisdom," said Tom. "For it's all the harder when you know what goes before: for then you've got to say what definition 3. is and what axiom V. is. But get along with you now: I must go on with this. Here's the Latin Grammar. See what you can make of that."

Maggie found the Latin Grammar quite soothing after her mathematical mortification; for she delighted in new words, and quickly found that there was an English Key at the end, which would make her very wise about Latin, at slight expense. She presently made up her mind to skip the rules in the Syntax—the examples became so absorbing. These mysterious sentences, snatched from an unknown context,—like strange horns of beasts, and leaves of unknown plants, brought from some far-off region,—gave boundless scope to her imagination, and were all the more fascinating because they were in a peculiar tongue of their own, which she could learn to interpret. It was really very interesting—the Latin Grammar that Tom had said no girls could learn: and she was proud because she found it interesting. The most fragmentary examples were her favourites. *Mors omnibus est communis*[8] would have been jejune, only she liked to know the Latin; but the fortunate gentleman whom every one congratulated because he had a son "endowed with *such* a disposition" afforded her a great deal of pleasant conjecture, and

8. "Death is common to all" (Cicero); this and the following Latin phrases, from Terrence and Statius respectively, come from the *Eton Grammar*.

she was quite lost in the "thick grove penetrable by no star," when Tom called out,

"Now, then, Magsie, give us the Grammar!"

"O, Tom, it's such a pretty book!" she said, as she jumped out of the large arm-chair to give it him; "it's much prettier than the Dictionary. I could learn Latin very soon. I don't think it's at all hard."

"O, I know what you've been doing," said Tom; "you've been reading the English at the end. Any donkey can do that."

Tom seized the book and opened it with a determined and business-like air, as much as to say that he had a lesson to learn which no donkeys would find themselves equal to. Maggie, rather piqued, turned to the bookcases to amuse herself with puzzling out the titles.

Presently Tom called to her: "Here, Magsie, come and hear if I can say this. Stand at that end of the table, where Mr Stelling sits when he hears me."

Maggie obeyed, and took the open book.

"Where do you begin, Tom?"

"O, I begin at '*Appellativa arborum*,'[9] because I say all over again what I've been learning this week."

Tom sailed along pretty well for three lines; and Maggie was beginning to forget her office of prompter in speculating as to what *mas* could mean, which came twice over, when he stuck fast at *Sunt etiam volucrum*.

"Don't tell me, Maggie; *Sunt etiam volucrum . . . Sunt etiam volucrum . . . ut ostrea, cetus . . .*"

"No," said Maggie, opening her mouth and shaking her head.

"*Sunt etiam volucrum*," said Tom, very slowly, as if the next words might be expected to come sooner when he gave them this strong hint that they were waited for.

"C, e, u," said Maggie, getting impatient.

"O, I know—hold your tongue," said Tom. "*Ceu passer, hirundo; Ferarum . . . ferarum . . .*" Tom took his pencil and made several hard dots with it on his book-cover . . . "*ferarum. . . .*"

"O dear, O dear, Tom," said Maggie, "what a time you are! *Ut. . . .*"

"*Ut, ostrea . . .*"

"No, no," said Maggie, "*ut, tigris. . . .*"

"O yes, now I can do," said Tom; "it was *tigris, vulpes*, I'd forgotten: *ut tigris, vulpes; et Piscium*."

9. Tom is stumbling through a passage from "Rules for the Genders of Nouns." "*Appellativa arborum*": the names of trees; *mas*, masculine; "*Sunt etiam volucrum*": there are also names of birds; "*ut ostrea, cetus*": such as oyster, whale; "*Ceu passer, hirundo*": such as sparrow and swallow; "*Ferarum*": of wild beasts; "*ut tigris, vulpes; et Piscium*": such as tiger, fox; and of fishes; "*Mascula nomina in a*": masculine nouns [ending] in -a; "*creskeus genittivo*": a noun not increasing in the genitive; "false quantity": incorrect pronunciation of a syllable.

With some further stammering and repetition, Tom got through the next few lines.

"Now, then," he said, "the next is what I've just learnt for to-morrow. Give me hold of the book a minute."

After some whispered gabbling, assisted by the beating of his fist on the table, Tom returned the book.

"*Mascula nomina in a*," he began.

"No, Tom," said Maggie, "that doesn't come next. It's *Nomen non creskens genīttivo*. . . ."

"*Creskens genittivo*," exclaimed Tom, with a derisive laugh, for Tom had learned this omitted passage for his yesterday's lesson, and a young gentleman does not require an intimate or extensive acquaintance with Latin before he can feel the pitiable absurdity of a false quantity. "*Creskens genittivo*! What a little silly you are, Maggie!"

"Well, you needn't laugh, Tom, for you didn't remember it at all. I'm sure it's spelt so; how was I to know?"

"Phee-e-e-h! I told you girls couldn't learn Latin. It's *Nomen non crescens genitivo*."

"Very well, then," said Maggie, pouting. "I can say that as well as you can. And you don't mind your stops. For you ought to stop twice as long at a semicolon as you do at a comma, and you make the longest stops where there ought to be no stop at all."

"O, well, don't chatter. Let me go on."

They were presently fetched to spend the rest of the evening in the drawing-room, and Maggie became so animated with Mr Stelling, who, she felt sure, admired her cleverness, that Tom was rather amazed and alarmed at her audacity. But she was suddenly subdued by Mr Stelling's alluding to a little girl of whom he had heard that she once ran away to the gypsies.

"What a very odd little girl that must be!" said Mrs Stelling, meaning to be playful—but a playfulness that turned on her supposed oddity was not at all to Maggie's taste. She feared that Mr Stelling, after all, did not think much of her, and went to bed in rather low spirits. Mrs Stelling, she felt, looked at her as if she thought her hair was very ugly because it hung down straight behind.

Nevertheless it was a very happy fortnight to Maggie, this visit to Tom. She was allowed to be in the study while he had his lessons, and in her various readings got very deep into the examples in the Latin Grammar. The astronomer who hated women generally, caused her so much puzzling speculation that she one day asked Mr Stelling if all astronomers hated women, or whether it was only this particular astronomer. But, forestalling his answer, she said,

"I suppose it's all astronomers: because, you know, they live up in high towers, and if the women came there, they might talk and hinder them from looking at the stars."

Mr Stelling liked her prattle immensely, and they were on the best terms. She told Tom she should like to go to school to Mr Stelling, as he did, and learn just the same things. She knew she could do Euclid, for she had looked into it again, and she saw what A B C meant: they were the names of the lines.

"I'm sure you couldn't do it, now," said Tom; "and I'll just ask Mr Stelling if you could."

"I don't mind," said the little conceited minx. "I'll ask him myself."

"Mr Stelling," she said, that same evening when they were in the drawing-room, "couldn't I do Euclid, and all Tom's lessons, if you were to teach me instead of him?"

"No; you couldn't," said Tom, indignantly. "Girls can't do Euclid: can they, sir?"

"They can pick up a little of everything, I daresay," said Mr Stelling. "They've a great deal of superficial cleverness; but they couldn't go far into anything. They're quick and shallow."

Tom, delighted with this verdict, telegraphed his triumph by wagging his head at Maggie behind Mr Stelling's chair. As for Maggie, she had hardly ever been so mortified. She had been so proud to be called "quick" all her little life, and now it appeared that this quickness was the brand of inferiority. It would have been better to be slow, like Tom.

"Ha, ha! Miss Maggie!" said Tom, when they were alone; "you see it's not such a fine thing to be quick. You'll never go far into anything, you know."

And Maggie was so oppressed by this dreadful destiny that she had no spirit for a retort.

But when this small apparatus of shallow quickness was fetched away in the gig by Luke, and the study was once more quite lonely for Tom, he missed her grievously. He had really been brighter, and had got through his lessons better, since she had been there; and she had asked Mr Stelling so many questions about the Roman empire, and whether there really ever was a man who said, in Latin, "I would not buy it for a farthing or a rotten nut," or whether that had only been turned into Latin, that Tom had actually come to a dim understanding of the fact that there had once been people upon the earth who were so fortunate as to know Latin without learning it through the medium of the Eton Grammar. This luminous idea was a great addition to his historical acquirements during this half-year, which were otherwise confined to an epitomised history of the Jews.

But the dreary half-year *did* come to an end. How glad Tom was to see the last yellow leaves fluttering before the cold wind! The dark afternoons, and the first December snow, seemed to him far livelier than the August sunshine; and that he might make himself the surer about the flight of the days that were carrying him homeward, he stuck twenty-one sticks deep in a corner of the garden, when he was three weeks from the holidays, and pulled one up every day with a great wrench, throwing it to a distance with a vigour of will which would have carried it to limbo, if it had been in the nature of sticks to travel so far.

But it was worth purchasing, even at the heavy price of the Latin Grammar—the happiness of seeing the bright light in the parlour at home, as the gig passed noiselessly over the snow-covered bridge: the happiness of passing from the cold air to the warmth and the kisses and the smiles of that familiar hearth, where the pattern of the rug and the grate and the fire-irons were "first ideas" that it was no more possible to criticise than the solidity and extension of matter. There is no sense of ease like the ease we felt in those scenes where we were born, where objects became dear to us before we had known the labour of choice, and where the outer world seemed only an extension of our own personality: we accepted and loved it as we accepted our own sense of existence and our own limbs. Very commonplace, even ugly, that furniture of our early home might look if it were put up to auction; an improved taste in upholstery scorns it; and is not the striving after something better and better in our surroundings, the grand characteristic that distinguishes man from the brute—or, to satisfy a scrupulous accuracy of definition, that distinguishes the British man from the foreign brute? But heaven knows where that striving might lead us, if our affections had not a trick of twining round those old inferior things—if the loves and sanctities of our life had no deep immovable roots in memory. One's delight in an elderberry bush overhanging the confused leafage of a hedgerow bank, as a more gladdening sight than the finest cistus or fuchsia spreading itself on the softest undulating turf, is an entirely unjustifiable preference to a nursery-gardener, or to any of those severely regulated minds who are free from the weakness of any attachment that does not rest on a demonstrable superiority of qualities. And there is no better reason for preferring this elderberry bush than that it stirs an early memory—that it is no novelty in my life, speaking to me merely through my present sensibilities to form and colour, but the long companion of my existence, that wove itself into my joys when joys were vivid.

Chapter II

The Christmas Holidays

Fine old Christmas, with the snowy hair and ruddy face, had done his duty that year in the noblest fashion, and had set off his rich gifts of warmth and colour with all the heightening contrast of frost and snow.

Snow lay on the croft and river-bank in undulations softer than the limbs of infancy; it lay with the neatliest finished border on every sloping roof, making the dark-red gables stand out with a new depth of colour; it weighed heavily on the laurels and fir-trees, till it fell from them with a shuddering sound; it clothed the rough turnip-field with whiteness, and made the sheep look like dark blotches; the gates were all blocked up with the sloping drifts, and here and there a disregarded four-footed beast stood as if petrified "in unrecumbent sadness;"[1] there was no gleam, no shadow, for the heavens, too, were one still, pale cloud—no sound or motion in anything but the dark river that flowed and moaned like an unresting sorrow. But old Christmas smiled as he laid this cruel-seeming spell on the out-door world, for he meant to light up home with new brightness, to deepen all the richness of in-door colour, and give a keener edge of delight to the warm fragrance of food: he meant to prepare a sweet imprisonment that would strengthen the primitive fellowship of kindred, and make the sunshine of familiar human faces as welcome as the hidden day-star. His kindness fell but hardly on the homeless—fell but hardly on the homes where the hearth was not very warm, and where the food had little fragrance; where the human faces had no sunshine in them, but rather the leaden, blank-eyed gaze of unexpectant want. But the fine old season meant well; and if he has not learnt the secret how to bless men impartially, it is because his father Time, with ever-unrelenting purpose, still hides that secret in his own mighty, slow-beating heart.

And yet this Christmas day, in spite of Tom's fresh delight in home, was not, he thought, somehow or other, quite so happy as it had always been before. The red berries were just as abundant on the holly, and he and Maggie had dressed all the windows and mantelpieces and picture-frames on Christmas eve with as much taste as ever, wedding the thick-set scarlet clusters with branches of the black-berried ivy. There had been singing under the windows after midnight—supernatural singing, Maggie always felt, in spite of Tom's contemptuous insistence that the singers were old Patch, the parish clerk, and the rest of the church choir: she trembled with awe when their caroling broke in upon her dreams, and the image of men in fustian clothes was always thrust away by the vision of angels resting on the parted cloud. The midnight chant had helped as usual to lift the morning above the level of common days; and then there was the smell of hot toast and ale from the kitchen, at the breakfast hour; the favourite anthem, the green boughs, and the short sermon, gave the appropriate festal character to the church-going; and aunt and uncle Moss, with all their seven children, were looking like so many reflectors of the bright parlour-fire, when the church-goers

1. Line 29 from book 5 of William Cowper's *The Task* (1785).

came back, stamping the snow from their feet. The plum-pudding was of the same handsome roundness as ever, and came in with the symbolic blue flames around it, as if it had been heroically snatched from the nether fires into which it had been thrown by dyspeptic Puritans; the dessert was as splendid as ever, with its golden oranges, brown nuts, and the crystalline light and dark of apple jelly and damson cheese: in all these things Christmas was as it had always been since Tom could remember; it was only distinguished, if by anything, by superior sliding and snowballs.

Christmas was cheery, but not so Mr Tulliver. He was irate and defiant, and Tom, though he espoused his father's quarrels and shared his father's sense of injury, was not without some of the feeling that oppressed Maggie when Mr Tulliver got louder and more angry in narration and assertion with the increased leisure of dessert. The attention that Tom might have concentrated on his nuts and wine was distracted by a sense that there were rascally enemies in the world, and that the business of grown-up life could hardly be conducted without a good deal of quarrelling. Now Tom was not fond of quarrelling, unless it could soon be put an end to by a fair stand-up fight with an adversary whom he had every chance of thrashing; and his father's irritable talk made him uncomfortable, though he never accounted to himself for the feeling, or conceived the notion that his father was faulty in this respect.

The particular embodiment of the evil principle now exciting Mr Tulliver's determined resistance was Mr Pivart, who, having lands higher up the Ripple, was taking measures for their irrigation, which either were, or would be, or were bound to be (on the principle that water was water), an infringement on Mr Tulliver's legitimate share of water-power. Dix, who had a mill on the stream, was a feeble auxiliary of Old Harry compared with Pivart. Dix had been brought to his senses by arbitration, and Wakem's advice had not carried *him* far; no: Dix, Mr Tulliver considered, had been as good as nowhere in point of law; and in the intensity of his indignation against Pivart, his contempt for a baffled adversary like Dix began to wear the air of a friendly attachment. He had no male audience to-day except Mr Moss, who knew nothing, as he said, of the "natur' o' mills," and could only assent to Mr Tulliver's arguments on the *a priori* ground of family relationship and monetary obligation; but Mr Tulliver did not talk with the futile intention of convincing his audience—he talked to relieve himself; while good Mr Moss made strong efforts to keep his eyes wide open, in spite of the sleepiness which an unusually good dinner produced in his hard-worked frame. Mrs Moss, more alive to the subject, and interested in everything that affected her brother, listened and put in a word as often as maternal preoccupations allowed.

"Why, Pivart's a new name hereabout, brother, isn't it?" she said: "he didn't own the land in father's time, nor yours either, before I was married."

"New name? Yes—I should think it *is* a new name," said Mr Tulliver, with angry emphasis. "Dorlcote Mill's been in our family a hundred year and better, and nobody ever heard of a Pivart meddling with the river, till this fellow came and bought Bincome's farm out of hand, before anybody else could so much as say 'snap.' But I'll *Pivart* him!" added Mr Tulliver, lifting his glass with a sense that he had defined his resolution in an unmistakeable manner.

"You won't be forced to go to law with him, I hope, brother?" said Mrs Moss, with some anxiety.

"I don't know what I shall be forced to; but I know what I shall force *him* to, with his dykes and erigations, if there's any law to be brought to bear o' the right side. I know well enough who's at the bottom of it; he's got Wakem to back him and egg him on. I know Wakem tells him the law can't touch him for it, but there's folks can handle the law besides Wakem. It takes a big raskil to beat him; but there's bigger to be found, as know more o' th' ins and outs o' the law, else how came Wakem to lose Brumley's suit for him?"

Mr Tulliver was a strictly honest man, and proud of being honest, but he considered that in law the ends of justice could only be achieved by employing a stronger knave to frustrate a weaker. Law was a sort of cock-fight, in which it was the business of injured honesty to get a game bird with the best pluck and the strongest spurs.

"Gore's no fool—you needn't tell me that," he observed presently, in a pugnacious tone, as if poor Gritty had been urging that lawyer's capabilities; "but, you see, he isn't up to the law as Wakem is. And water's a very particular thing—you can't pick it up with a pitchfork. That's why it's been nuts to Old Harry and the lawyers. It's plain enough what's the rights and the wrongs of water, if you look at it straightforrard; for a river's a river, and if you've got a mill, you must have water to turn it; and it's no use telling me, Pivart's erigation and nonsense won't stop my wheel; I know what belongs to water better than that. Talk to me o' what th' engineers say! I say it's common sense, as Pivart's dykes must do me an injury. But if that's their engineering, I'll put Tom to it by-and-by, and he shall see if he can't find a bit more sense in th' engineering business than what *that* comes to."

Tom, looking round with some anxiety at this announcement of his prospects, unthinkingly withdrew a small rattle he was amusing Baby Moss with, whereupon she, being a baby that knew her own mind with remarkable clearness, instantaneously expressed her sentiments in a piercing yell, and was not to be appeased even by the restoration of the rattle, feeling apparently that the original wrong of having it taken from her remained in all its force. Mrs Moss hurried away with her into another room, and expressed to Mrs Tulliver, who accompanied her, the conviction that the dear child had good reasons for crying; implying that if it was supposed to be the rattle that baby clamoured for, she was a misunderstood baby. The thoroughly justifiable yell being quieted, Mrs Moss looked at her sister-in-law and said—

"I'm sorry to see brother so put out about this water work."

"It's your brother's way, Mrs Moss; I'd never anything o' that sort before I was married," said Mrs Tulliver, with a half-implied reproach. She always spoke of her husband as "your brother" to Mrs Moss in any case when his line of conduct was not matter of pure admiration. Amiable Mrs Tulliver, who was never angry in her life, had yet her mild share of that spirit without which she could hardly have been at once a Dodson and a woman. Being always on the defensive towards her own sisters, it was natural that she should be keenly conscious of her superiority, even as the weakest Dodson, over a husband's sister, who, besides being poorly off, and inclined to "hang on" her brother, had the good-natured submissiveness of a large, easy-tempered, untidy, prolific woman, with affection enough in her not only for her own husband and abundant children, but for any number of collateral relations.

"I hope and pray he won't go to law," said Mrs Moss, "for there's never any knowing where that'll end. And the right doesn't allays win. This Mr Pivart's a rich man, by what I can make out, and the rich mostly get things their own way."

"As to that," said Mrs Tulliver, stroking her dress down, "I've seen what riches are in my own family; for my sisters have got husbands as can afford to do pretty much what they like. But I think sometimes I shall be drove off my head with the talk about this law and erigation; and my sisters lay all the fault to me, for they don't know what it is to marry a man like your brother—how should they? Sister Pullet has her own way from morning till night."

"Well," said Mrs Moss, "I don't think I should like my husband if he hadn't got any wits of his own, and I had to find head-piece for him. It's a deal easier to do what pleases one's husband, than to be puzzling what else one should do."

"If people come to talk o' doing what pleases their husbands," said Mrs Tulliver, with a faint imitation of her sister Glegg, "I'm sure your brother might have waited a long while before he'd have found a wife that 'ud have let him have his say in everything, as I do. It's nothing but law and erigation now, from when we first get up in the morning till we go to bed at night; and I never contradict him; I only say—'Well, Mr Tulliver, do as you like; but whativer you do, don't go to law.' "

Mrs Tulliver, as we have seen, was not without influence over her husband. No woman is; she can always incline him to do either what she wishes, or the reverse; and on the composite impulses that were threatening to hurry Mr Tulliver into "law," Mrs Tulliver's monotonous pleading had doubtless its share of force; it might even be comparable to that proverbial feather which has the credit or discredit of breaking the camel's back; though, on a strictly impartial view, the blame ought rather to lie with the previous weight of feathers which had already placed the back in such imminent peril, that an otherwise innocent feather could not settle on it without mischief. Not that Mrs Tulliver's feeble beseeching could have had this feather's weight in virtue of her single personality; but whenever she departed from entire assent to her husband, he saw in her the representative of the Dodson family; and it was a guiding principle with Mr Tulliver, to let the Dodsons know that they were not to domineer over *him*, or—more specifically—that a male Tulliver was far more than equal to four female Dodsons, even though one of them was Mrs Glegg.

But not even a direct argument from that typical Dodson female herself against his going to law, could have heightened his disposition towards it so much as the mere thought of Wakem, continually freshened by the sight of the too able attorney on market-days. Wakem, to his certain knowledge, was (metaphorically speaking) at the bottom of Pivart's irrigation: Wakem had tried to make Dix stand out, and go to law about the dam: it was unquestionably Wakem who had caused Mr Tulliver to lose the suit about the right of road and the bridge that made a thoroughfare of his land for every vagabond who preferred an opportunity of damaging private property to walking like an honest man along the high-road: all lawyers were more or less rascals, but Wakem's rascality was of that peculiarly aggravated kind which placed itself in opposition to that form of right embodied in Mr Tulliver's interests and opinions. And as an extra touch of bitterness, the injured miller had recently, in borrowing the five hundred pounds, been obliged to carry a little business to Wakem's office on his own account. A hook-nosed glib fellow! as cool as a cucumber—always looking so sure of his game! And it was vexatious that Lawyer Gore was not more like him, but was a bald, round-featured man, with bland manners and fat hands; a game-cock that you would be rash to bet upon against Wakem. Gore was a sly fellow; his weakness did not lie on the side of scrupulosity: but the largest amount of winking, however significant, is not equivalent to seeing through a stone wall; and confident as Mr Tulliver was in his principle that water was water, and in the direct inference that Pivart had not a leg to stand on in this affair of irrigation, he had an uncomfortable suspicion that Wakem had more law to show against this (rationally) irrefragable inference, than Gore could show for it. But then, if they went to law, there was a chance for Mr Tulliver to employ Counsellor Wylde on his side, instead of having that admirable bully against him; and the prospect of seeing a witness of Wakem's made to perspire and become confounded, as Mr Tulliver's witness had once been, was alluring to the love of retributive justice.

Much rumination had Mr Tulliver on these puzzling subjects during his rides on the grey horse—much turning of the head from side to side, as the scales dipped alternately; but the probable result was still out of sight, only to be reached through much hot argument and iteration in domestic and social life. That initial stage of the dispute which consisted in the narration of the case and the enforcement of Mr Tulliver's views concerning it throughout the entire circle of his connections would necessarily take time, and at the beginning of February, when Tom was going to school again, there were scarcely any new items to be detected in his father's statement of the case against Pivart, or any more specific indication of the measures he was bent on taking against that rash contravener of the principle that water was water. Iteration, like friction, is likely to generate heat instead of progress, and Mr Tulliver's heat was certainly more and more palpable. If there had been no new evidence on any other point, there had been new evidence that Pivart was as "thick as mud" with Wakem.

"Father," said Tom, one evening near the end of the holidays, "uncle Glegg says Lawyer Wakem *is* going to send his son to Mr Stelling. It isn't true—what they said about his going to be sent to France. You won't like me to go to school with Wakem's son, shall you?"

"It's no matter for that, my boy," said Mr Tulliver; "don't you learn anything bad of him, that's all. The lad's a poor deformed creatur, and takes after his mother in the face: I think there isn't much of his father in him. It's a sign Wakem thinks high o' Mr Stelling, as he sends his son to him, and Wakem knows meal from bran."

Mr Tulliver in his heart was rather proud of the fact that his son was to have the same advantages as Wakem's: but Tom was not at all easy on the point; it would have been much clearer if the lawyer's son had not been deformed, for then Tom would have had the prospect of pitching into him with all that freedom which is derived from a high moral sanction.

Chapter III

The New Schoolfellow

It was a cold, wet January day on which Tom went back to school; a day quite in keeping with this severe phase of his destiny. If he had not carried in his pocket a parcel of sugar-candy and a small Dutch doll for little Laura, there would have been no ray of expected pleasure to enliven the general gloom. But he liked to think how Laura would put out her lips and her tiny hands for the bits of sugar-candy; and, to give the greater keenness to these pleasures of imagination, he took out the parcel, made a small hole in the paper, and bit off a crystal or two, which had so solacing an effect under the confined prospect and damp odours of the gig-umbrella, that he repeated the process more than once on his way.

"Well, Tulliver, we're glad to see you again," said Mr Stelling, heartily. "Take off your wrappings and come into the study till dinner. You'll find a bright fire there, and a new companion."

Tom felt in an uncomfortable flutter as he took off his woollen comforter and other wrappings. He had seen Philip Wakem at St Ogg's, but had always turned his eyes away from him as quickly as possible. He would have disliked having a deformed boy for his companion, even if Philip had not been the son of a bad man. And Tom did not see how a bad man's son could be very good. His own father was a good man, and he would readily have fought any one who said the contrary. He was in a state of mingled embarrassment and defiance as he followed Mr Stelling to the study.

"Here is a new companion for you to shake hands with, Tulliver," said that gentleman on entering the study—"Master Philip Wakem. I shall leave you to make acquaintance by yourselves. You already know something of each other, I imagine; for you are neighbours at home."

Tom looked confused and awkward, while Philip rose and glanced at him timidly. Tom did not like to go up and put out his hand, and he was not prepared to say, "How do you do?" on so short a notice.

Mr Stelling wisely turned away, and closed the door behind him: boys' shyness only wears off in the absence of their elders.

Philip was at once too proud and too timid to walk towards Tom. He thought, or rather felt, that Tom had an aversion to looking at him: every one, almost, disliked looking at him; and his deformity was more conspicuous when he walked. So they remained without shaking hands or even speaking, while Tom went to the fire and warmed himself, every now and then casting furtive glances at Philip, who seemed to be drawing absently first one object and then another on a piece of paper he had before him. He had seated himself again, and as he drew, was thinking what he could say to Tom, and trying to overcome his own repugnance to making the first advances.

Tom began to look oftener and longer at Philip's face, for he could see it without noticing the hump, and it was really not a disagreeable face—very old-looking, Tom thought. He wondered how much older Philip was than himself. An anatomist—even a mere physiognomist—would have seen that the deformity of Philip's spine was not a congenital hump, but the result of an accident in infancy; but you do not expect from Tom any acquaintance with such distinctions: to him, Philip was simply a humpback. He had a vague notion that the deformity of Wakem's son had some relation to the lawyer's rascality, of which he had so often heard his father talk with hot emphasis; and he felt, too, a half-admitted fear of him as probably a spiteful fellow, who, not being able to fight you, had cunning ways of doing you a mischief by the sly. There was a hump-backed tailor in the neighbourhood of Mr Jacobs' academy, who was considered a very unamiable character, and was much hooted after by public-spirited boys solely on the ground of his unsatisfactory moral qualities; so that Tom was not without a basis of fact to go upon. Still, no face could be more unlike that ugly tailor's than this melancholy boy's face; the brown hair round it waved and curled at the ends like a girl's: Tom thought that truly pitiable. This Wakem was a pale, puny fellow, and it was quite clear he would not be able to play at anything worth speaking of: but he handled his pencil in an enviable manner, and was apparently making one thing after another without any trouble. What was he drawing? Tom was quite warm now, and wanted something new to be going forward. It was certainly more agreeable to have an ill-natured humpback as a companion than to stand looking out of the study window at the rain, and kicking his foot against the washboard in solitude; something would happen every day—"a quarrel or something;" and Tom thought he should rather like to show Philip that he had better not try his spiteful tricks on *him*. He suddenly walked across the hearth, and looked over Philip's paper.

"Why, that's a donkey with panniers—and a spaniel, and partridges in the corn!" he exclaimed, his tongue being completely loosed by surprise and admiration. "O my buttons! I wish I could draw like that. I'm to learn drawing this half—I wonder if I shall learn to make dogs and donkeys!"

"O, you can do them without learning," said Philip; "I never learned drawing."

"Never learned?" said Tom, in amazement. "Why, when I make dogs and horses, and those things, the heads and the legs won't come right; though I can see how they ought to be very well. I can make houses, and all sorts of chimneys—chimneys going all down the wall, and windows in the roof, and all that. But I daresay I could do dogs and horses if I was to try more," he added, reflecting that Philip might falsely suppose that he was going to "knock under," if he were too frank about the imperfection of his accomplishments.

"O yes," said Philip, "it's very easy. You've only to look well at things, and draw them over and over again. What you do wrong once, you can alter the next time."

"But haven't you been taught *any*thing?" said Tom, beginning to have a puzzled suspicion that Philip's crooked back might be the source of remarkable faculties. "I thought you'd been to school a long while."

"Yes," said Philip, smiling, "I've been taught Latin, and Greek, and mathematics,—and writing, and such things."

"O, but, I say, you don't like Latin, though, do you?" said Tom, lowering his voice confidentially.

"Pretty well; I don't care much about it," said Philip.

"Ah, but perhaps you haven't got into the *Propria quæ maribus*,"[1] said Tom, nodding his head sideways, as much as to say, "that was the test: it was easy talking till you came to *that*."

Philip felt some bitter complacency in the promising stupidity of this well-made active-looking boy; but made polite by his own extreme sensitiveness, as well as by his desire to conciliate, he checked his inclination to laugh, and said, quietly,

"I've done with the grammar; I don't learn that any more."

"Then you won't have the same lessons as I shall?" said Tom, with a sense of disappointment.

"No; but I daresay I can help you. I shall be very glad to help you if I can."

Tom did not say "Thank you," for he was quite absorbed in the thought that Wakem's son did not seem so spiteful a fellow as might have been expected.

"I say," he said presently, "do you love your father?"

"Yes," said Philip, colouring deeply; "don't you love yours?"

"O yes. . . . I only wanted to know," said Tom, rather ashamed of himself, now he saw Philip colouring and looking uncomfortable. He found much difficulty in adjusting his attitude of mind towards the son of Lawyer Wakem, and it had occurred to him that if Philip disliked his father, that fact might go some way towards clearing up his perplexity.

"Shall you learn drawing now?" he said, by way of changing the subject.

"No," said Philip. "My father wishes me to give all my time to other things now."

"What! Latin, and Euclid, and those things?" said Tom.

"Yes," said Philip, who had left off using his pencil, and was resting his head on one hand, while Tom was leaning forward on both elbows, and looking with increasing admiration at the dog and the donkey.

"And you don't mind that?" said Tom, with strong curiosity.

"No: I like to know what everybody else knows. I can study what I like by-and-by."

"I can't think why anybody should learn Latin," said Tom. "It's no good."

"It's part of the education of a gentleman," said Philip. "All gentlemen learn the same things."

"What! do you think Sir John Crake, the master of the harriers, knows Latin?" said Tom, who had often thought he should like to resemble Sir John Crake.

"He learnt it when he was a boy, of course," said Philip. "But I daresay he's forgotten it."

1. Masculine proper nouns.

"O, well, I can do that, then," said Tom, not with any epigrammatic intention, but with serious satisfaction at the idea that, as far as Latin was concerned, there was no hindrance to his resembling Sir John Crake. "Only you're obliged to remember it while you're at school, else you've got to learn ever so many lines of 'Speaker.'[2] Mr Stelling's very particular—did you know? He'll have you up ten times if you say 'nam' for 'jam' . . . he won't let you go a letter wrong, *I* can tell you."

"O, I don't mind," said Philip, unable to choke a laugh; "I can remember things easily. And there are some lessons I'm very fond of. I'm very fond of Greek history and everything about the Greeks. I should like to have been a Greek and fought the Persians, and then have come home and have written tragedies, or else have been listened to by everybody for my wisdom, like Socrates, and have died a grand death." (Philip, you perceive, was not without a wish to impress the well-made barbarian with a sense of his mental superiority.)

"Why, were the Greeks great fighters?" said Tom, who saw a vista in this direction. "Is there anything like David, and Goliath, and Samson, in the Greek history? Those are the only bits I like in the history of the Jews."

"O, there are very fine stories of that sort about the Greeks—about the heroes of early times who killed the wild beasts, as Samson did. And in the *Odyssey*—that's a beautiful poem—there's a more wonderful giant than Goliath—Polypheme, who had only one eye in the middle of his forehead; and Ulysses, a little fellow, but very wise and cunning, got a red-hot pine-tree and stuck it into this one eye, and made him roar like a thousand bulls."

"O, what fun!" said Tom, jumping away from the table, and stamping first with one leg and then the other. "I say, can you tell me all about those stories? Because I shan't learn Greek you know. . . . Shall I?" he added, pausing in his stamping with a sudden alarm, lest the contrary might be possible. "Does every gentleman learn Greek? . . . Will Mr Stelling make me begin with it, do you think?"

"No, I should think not—very likely not," said Philip. "But you may read those stories without knowing Greek. I've got them in English."

"O, but I don't like reading; I'd sooner have you tell them me. But only the fighting ones, you know. My sister Maggie is always wanting to tell me stories—but they're stupid things. Girls' stories always are. Can you tell a good many fighting stories?"

"O yes," said Philip; "lots of them, besides the Greek stories. I can tell you about Richard Cœur-de-Lion and Saladin, and about William Wallace, and Robert Bruce, and James Douglas[3]—I know no end."

2. Schoolbook by William Enfield (1774).
3. Scott's *The Talisman* (1825) tells of Richard the Lionheart's crusade against Saladin; *Tales of a Grandfather* (1827–29), a history of Scotland, features William Wallace, Robert Bruce, and James Douglas.

"You're older than I am, aren't you?" said Tom.

"Why, how old are *you*? I'm fifteen."

"I'm only going on fourteen," said Tom. "But I thrashed all the fellows at Jacobs'—that's where I was before I came here. And I beat 'em all at bandy and climbing. And I wish Mr Stelling would let us go fishing. *I* could show you how to fish. You *could* fish, couldn't you? It's only standing, and sitting still, you know."

Tom, in his turn, wished to make the balance dip in his favour. This hunchback must not suppose that his acquaintance with fighting stories put him on a par with an actual fighting hero, like Tom Tulliver. Philip winced under this allusion to his unfitness for active sports, and he answered almost peevishly—

"I can't bear fishing. I think people look like fools sitting watching a line hour after hour—or else throwing and throwing, and catching nothing."

"Ah, but you wouldn't say they looked like fools when they landed a big pike, I can tell you," said Tom, who had never caught anything that was "big" in his life, but whose imagination was on the stretch with indignant zeal for the honour of sport. Wakem's son, it was plain, had his disagreeable points, and must be kept in due check. Happily for the harmony of this first interview, they were now called to dinner, and Philip was not allowed to develop farther his unsound views on the subject of fishing. But Tom said to himself, that was just what he should have expected from a hunchback.

Chapter IV

"The Young Idea"[1]

The alternations of feeling in that first dialogue between Tom and Philip continued to mark their intercourse even after many weeks of schoolboy intimacy. Tom never quite lost the feeling that Philip, being the son of a "rascal," was his natural enemy, never thoroughly overcame his repulsion to Philip's deformity: he was a boy who adhered tenaciously to impressions once received: as with all minds in which mere perception predominates over thought and emotion, the external remained to him rigidly what it was in the first instance. But then, it was impossible not to like Philip's company when he was in a good humour; he could help one so well in one's Latin exercises, which Tom regarded as a kind of puzzle that could only be found out by a lucky chance; and he could tell such wonderful fighting stories about Hal of the Wynd,[2] for example, and other heroes who were especial favourites with Tom, because they

1. Line 1152 from James Thomson's *The Seasons*, "Spring" (1726–30).
2. Hero of Scott's *The Fair Maid of Perth* (1828).

laid about them with heavy strokes. He had small opinion of Saladin, whose scimitar could cut a cushion in two in an instant: who wanted to cut cushions? That was a stupid story, and he didn't care to hear it again. But when Robert Bruce, on the black pony, rose in his stirrups, and, lifting his good battle-axe, cracked at once the helmet and the skull of the too-hasty knight at Bannockburn, then Tom felt all the exaltation of sympathy, and if he had had a cocoa-nut at hand, he would have cracked it at once with the poker. Philip in his happier moods indulged Tom to the top of his bent, heightening the crash and bang and fury of every fight with all the artillery of epithets and similes at his command. But he was not always in a good humour or happy mood. The slight spurt of peevish susceptibility which had escaped him in their first interview, was a symptom of a perpetually-recurring mental ailment—half of it nervous irritability, half of it the heart-bitterness produced by the sense of his deformity. In these fits of susceptibility every glance seemed to him to be charged either with offensive pity or with ill-repressed disgust—at the very least it was an indifferent glance, and Philip felt indifference as a child of the south feels the chill air of a northern spring. Poor Tom's blundering patronage when they were out of doors together would sometimes make him turn upon the well-meaning lad quite savagely; and his eyes, usually sad and quiet, would flash with anything but playful lightning. No wonder Tom retained his suspicions of the humpback.

But Philip's self-taught skill in drawing was another link between them; for Tom found, to his disgust, that his new drawing-master gave him no dogs and donkeys to draw, but brooks and rustic bridges and ruins, all with a general softness of black-lead surface, indicating that nature, if anything, was rather satiny; and as Tom's feeling for the picturesque in landscape was at present quite latent, it is not surprising that Mr Goodrich's productions seemed to him an uninteresting form of art. Mr Tulliver, having a vague intention that Tom should be put to some business which included the drawing out of plans and maps, had complained to Mr Riley, when he saw him at Mudport, that Tom seemed to be learning nothing of that sort; whereupon that obliging adviser had suggested that Tom should have drawing-lessons. Mr Tulliver must not mind paying extra for drawing: let Tom be made a good draughtsman, and he would be able to turn his pencil to any purpose. So it was ordered that Tom should have drawing-lessons; and whom should Mr Stelling have selected as a master if not Mr Goodrich, who was considered quite at the head of his profession within a circuit of twelve miles round King's Lorton? By which means Tom learned to make an extremely fine point to his pencil, and to represent landscape with a "broad generality," which, doubtless from a narrow tendency in his mind to details, he thought extremely dull.

All this, you remember, happened in those dark ages when there were no schools of design—before schoolmasters were invariably men of scrupulous integrity, and before the clergy were all men of enlarged minds and varied culture. In those less-favoured days, it is no fable that there were other clergymen besides Mr Stelling who had narrow intellects and large wants, and whose income, by a logical confusion to which Fortune, being a female as well as blindfold, is peculiarly liable, was proportioned not to their wants but to their intellect—with which income has clearly no inherent relation. The problem these gentlemen had to solve was to readjust the proportion between their wants and their income; and since wants are not easily starved to death, the simpler method appeared to be—to raise their income. There was but one way of doing this; any of those low callings in which men are obliged to do good work at a low price were forbidden to clergymen: was it their fault if their only resource was to turn out very poor work at a high price? Besides, how should Mr Stelling be expected to know that education was a delicate and difficult business? any more than an animal endowed with a power of boring a hole through a rock should be expected to have wide views of excavation. Mr Stelling's faculties had been early trained to boring in a straight line, and he had no faculty to spare. But among Tom's contemporaries, whose fathers cast their sons on clerical instruction to find them ignorant after many days, there were many far less lucky than Tom Tulliver. Education was almost entirely a matter of luck—usually of ill-luck—in those distant days. The state of mind in which you take a billiard-cue or a dice-box in your hand is one of sober certainty compared with that of old-fashioned fathers, like Mr Tulliver, when they selected a school or a tutor for their sons. Excellent men, who had been forced all their lives to spell on an impromptu-phonetic system, and having carried on a successful business in spite of this disadvantage, had acquired money enough to give their sons a better start in life than they had had themselves, must necessarily take their chance as to the conscience and the competence of the schoolmaster whose circular fell in their way, and appeared to promise so much more than they would ever have thought of asking for, including the return of linen, fork, and spoon. It was happy for them if some ambitious draper of their acquaintance had not brought up his son to the Church, and if that young gentleman, at the age of four-and-twenty, had not closed his college dissipations by an imprudent marriage: otherwise, these innocent fathers, desirous of doing the best for their offspring, could only escape the draper's son by happening to be on the foundation of a grammar-school as yet unvisited by commissioners,[3] where two or three boys could have, all to themselves, the advantages of a large and lofty building, together with a head master, toothless, dim-eyed, and deaf, whose erudite indistinctness and inattention were

3. Grammar schools for local boys were supported by ancient foundations or endowments. In the nineteenth century, a series of government commissions investigated and redistributed these funds.

engrossed by them at the rate of three hundred pounds a-head—a ripe scholar, doubtless, when first appointed; but all ripeness beneath the sun has a further stage less esteemed in the market.

Tom Tulliver, then, compared with many other British youths of his time who have since had to scramble through life with some fragments of more or less relevant knowledge, and a great deal of strictly relevant ignorance, was not so very unlucky. Mr Stelling was a broad-chested healthy man, with the bearing of a gentleman, a conviction that a growing boy required a sufficiency of beef and a certain hearty kindness in him that made him like to see Tom looking well and enjoying his dinner; not a man of refined conscience, or with any deep sense of the infinite issues belonging to everyday duties; not quite competent to his high offices; but incompetent gentlemen must live, and without private fortune it is difficult to see how they could all live genteelly if they had nothing to do with education or government. Besides, it was the fault of Tom's mental constitution that his faculties could not be nourished on the sort of knowledge Mr Stelling had to communicate. A boy born with a deficient power of apprehending signs and abstractions must suffer the penalty of his congenital deficiency, just as if he had been born with one leg shorter than the other. A method of education sanctioned by the long practice of our venerable ancestors was not to give way before the exceptional dulness of a boy who was merely living at the time then present. And Mr Stelling was convinced that a boy so stupid at signs and abstractions must be stupid at everything else, even if that reverend gentleman could have taught him everything else. It was the practice of our venerable ancestors to apply that ingenious instrument the thumb-screw, and to tighten and tighten it in order to elicit non-existent facts; they had a fixed opinion to begin with, that the facts were existent, and what had they to do but to tighten the thumb-screw? In like manner, Mr Stelling had a fixed opinion that all boys with any capacity could learn what it was the only regular thing to teach: if they were slow, the thumb-screw must be tightened—the exercises must be insisted on with increased severity, and a page of Virgil be awarded as a penalty, to encourage and stimulate a too languid inclination to Latin verse.

The thumb-screw was a little relaxed, however, during this second half-year. Philip was so advanced in his studies, and so apt, that Mr Stelling could obtain credit by his facility, which required little help, much more easily than by the troublesome process of overcoming Tom's dulness. Gentlemen with broad chests and ambitious intentions do sometimes disappoint their friends by failing to carry the world before them. Perhaps it is, that high achievements demand some other unusual qualification besides an unusual desire for high prizes; perhaps it is that these stalwart gentlemen are rather indolent, their *divinæ particulum auræ*[4]

4. Fragment of the divine spirit (Horace, *Satires* 2.2.79).

being obstructed from soaring by a too hearty appetite. Some reason or other there was why Mr Stelling deferred the execution of many spirited projects—why he did not begin the editing of his Greek play, or any other work of scholarship, in his leisure hours, but, after turning the key of his private study with much resolution, sat down to one of Theodore Hook's[5] novels. Tom was gradually allowed to shuffle through his lessons with less rigour, and having Philip to help him, he was able to make some show of having applied his mind in a confused and blundering way, without being cross-examined into a betrayal that his mind had been entirely neutral in the matter. He thought school much more bearable under this modification of circumstances; and he went on contentedly enough, picking up a promiscuous education chiefly from things that were not intended as education at all. What was understood to be his education, was simply the practice of reading, writing, and spelling, carried on by an elaborate appliance of unintelligible ideas, and by much failure in the effort to learn by rote.

Nevertheless, there was a visible improvement in Tom under this training; perhaps because he was not a boy in the abstract, existing solely to illustrate the evils of a mistaken education, but a boy made of flesh and blood, with dispositions not entirely at the mercy of circumstances.

There was a great improvement in his bearing, for example, and some credit on this score was due to Mr Poulter, the village schoolmaster, who, being an old Peninsular soldier,[6] was employed to drill Tom—a source of high mutual pleasure. Mr Poulter, who was understood by the company at the Black Swan to have once struck terror into the hearts of the French, was no longer personally formidable. He had rather a shrunken appearance, and was tremulous in the mornings, not from age, but from the extreme perversity of the King's Lorton boys which nothing but gin could enable him to sustain with any firmness. Still, he carried himself with martial erectness, had his clothes scrupulously brushed, and his trousers tightly strapped; and on the Wednesday and Saturday afternoons, when he came to Tom, he was always inspired with gin and old memories, which gave him an exceptionally spirited air, as of a superannuated charger who hears the drum. The drilling-lessons were always protracted by episodes of warlike narrative, much more interesting to Tom than Philip's stories out of the *Iliad*; for there were no cannon in the *Iliad*, and, besides, Tom had felt some disgust on learning that Hector and Achilles might possibly never have existed. But the Duke of Wellington was really alive, and Bony[7] had not been long dead—therefore Mr Poulter's reminiscences of the Peninsular War were removed from all suspicion of being mythical. Mr Poulter, it

5. Prolific author of popular novels of the 1820s and 1830s about fashionable life.
6. Soldier fighting Napoleon's army in Portugal and Spain, 1809–14.
7. Napoleon Bonaparte (1769–1821).

appeared, had been a conspicuous figure at Talavera,[8] and had contributed not a little to the peculiar terror with which his regiment of infantry was regarded by the enemy. On afternoons, when his memory was more stimulated than usual, he remembered that the Duke of Wellington had (in strict privacy, lest jealousies should be awakened) expressed his esteem for that fine fellow Poulter. The very surgeon who attended him in the hospital after he had received his gunshot wound, had been profoundly impressed with the superiority of Mr Poulter's flesh: no other flesh would have healed in anything like the same time. On less personal matters connected with the important warfare in which he had been engaged, Mr Poulter was more reticent, only taking care not to give the weight of his authority to any loose notions concerning military history. Any one who pretended to a knowledge of what occurred at the siege of Badajos,[9] was especially an object of silent pity to Mr Poulter; he wished that prating person had been run down, and had the breath trampled out of him at the first go-off, as he himself had—he might talk about the siege of Badajos then! Tom did not escape irritating his drilling-master occasionally, by his curiosity concerning other military matters than Mr Poulter's personal experience.

"And General Wolfe,[1] Mr Poulter? wasn't he a wonderful fighter?" said Tom, who held the notion that all the martial heroes commemorated on the public-house signs were engaged in the war with Bony.

"Not at all!" said Mr Poulter, contemptuously. "Nothing o' the sort! . . . Heads up!" he added, in a tone of stern command, which delighted Tom, and made him feel as if he were a regiment in his own person.

"No, no!" Mr Poulter would continue, on coming to a pause in his discipline. "They'd better not talk to me about General Wolfe. He did nothing but die of his wound; that's a poor haction, I consider. Any other man 'ud have died o' the wounds I've had. . . . One of my sword-cuts 'ud ha' killed a fellow like General Wolfe."

"Mr Poulter," Tom would say, at any allusion to the sword, "I wish you'd bring your sword and do the sword-exercise!"

For a long while Mr Poulter only shook his head in a significant manner at this request, and smiled patronisingly, as Jupiter may have done when Semele urged her too ambitious request.[2] But one afternoon, when a sudden shower of heavy rain had detained Mr Poulter twenty minutes longer than usual at the Black Swan, the sword was brought—just for Tom to look at.

"And this is the real sword you fought with in all the battles, Mr Poulter?" said Tom, handling the hilt. "Has it ever cut a Frenchman's head off?"

8. Major victory for Wellington (1809).
9. Battle in southwest Spain.
1. General who captured Quebec for the British in 1759.
2. Semele persuaded her lover, Jupiter, to appear before her in his true form; his arrival as a thunderbolt killed her.

"Head off? Ah! and would, if he'd had three heads."

"But you had a gun and bayonet besides?" said Tom. "*I* should like the gun and bayonet best, because you could shoot 'em first and spear 'em after. Bang! Ps-s-s-s!" Tom gave the requisite pantomime to indicate the double enjoyment of pulling the trigger and thrusting the spear.

"Ah, but the sword's the thing when you come to close fighting," said Mr Poulter, involuntarily falling in with Tom's enthusiasm, and drawing the sword so suddenly that Tom leaped back with much agility.

"O but, Mr Poulter, if you're going to do the exercise," said Tom, a little conscious that he had not stood his ground as became an Englishman, "let me go and call Philip. He'll like to see you, you know."

"What! the humpbacked lad?" said Mr Poulter, contemptuously. "What's the use of *his* looking on?"

"O but he knows a great deal about fighting," said Tom, "and how they used to fight with bows and arrows, and battle-axes."

"Let him come then. I'll show him something different from his bows and arrows," said Mr Poulter, coughing, and drawing himself up, while he gave a little preliminary play to his wrist.

Tom ran in to Philip, who was enjoying his afternoon's holiday at the piano, in the drawing-room, picking out tunes for himself and singing them. He was supremely happy, perched like an amorphous bundle on the high stool, with his head thrown back, his eyes fixed on the opposite cornice, and his lips wide open, sending forth, with all his might, impromptu syllables to a tune of Arne's,[3] which had hit his fancy.

"Come, Philip," said Tom, bursting in; "don't stay roaring 'la la' there—come and see old Poulter do his sword-exercise in the carriage-house!"

The jar of this interruption—the discord of Tom's tones coming across the notes to which Philip was vibrating in soul and body, would have been enough to unhinge his temper, even if there had been no question of Poulter the drilling-master; and Tom, in the hurry of seizing something to say to prevent Mr Poulter from thinking he was afraid of the sword when he sprang away from it, had alighted on this proposition to fetch Philip—though he knew well enough that Philip hated to hear him mention his drilling-lessons. Tom would never have done so inconsiderate a thing except under the severe stress of his personal pride.

Philip shuddered visibly as he paused from his music. Then turning red, he said, with violent passion—

"Get away, you lumbering idiot! Don't come bellowing at me—you're not fit to speak to anything but a cart-horse!"

It was not the first time Philip had been made angry by him, but

3. Thomas Augustine Arne, composer of "Rule Brittania."

Tom had never before been assailed with verbal missiles that he understood so well.

"I'm fit to speak to something better than you—you poor-spirited imp!" said Tom, lighting up immediately at Philip's fire. "You know I won't hit you, because you're no better than a girl. But I'm an honest man's son, and *your* father's a rogue—everybody says so!"

Tom flung out of the room, and slammed the door after him, made strangely heedless by his anger; for to slam doors within the hearing of Mrs Stelling, who was probably not far off, was an offence only to be wiped out by twenty lines of Virgil. In fact, that lady did presently descend from her room, in double wonder at the noise and the subsequent cessation of Philip's music. She found him sitting in a heap on the hassock, and crying bitterly.

"What's the matter, Wakem? What was that noise about? Who slammed the door?"

Philip looked up, and hastily dried his eyes. "It was Tulliver who came in . . . to ask me to go out with him."

"And what are you in trouble about?" said Mrs Stelling.

Philip was not her favourite of the two pupils; he was less obliging than Tom, who was made useful in many ways. Still his father paid more than Mr Tulliver did, and she meant him to feel that she behaved exceedingly well to him. Philip, however, met her advances towards a good understanding very much as a caressed mollusc meets an invitation to show himself out of his shell. Mrs Stelling was not a loving, tender-hearted woman: she was a woman whose skirt sat well, who adjusted her waist and patted her curls with a preoccupied air when she inquired after your welfare. These things, doubtless, represent a great social power, but it is not the power of love—and no other power could win Philip from his personal reserve.

He said, in answer to her question, "My toothache came on, and made me hysterical again."

This had been the fact once, and Philip was glad of the recollection—it was like an inspiration to enable him to excuse his crying. He had to accept eau-de-cologne, and to refuse creosote[4] in consequence; but that was easy.

Meanwhile Tom, who had for the first time sent a poisoned arrow into Philip's heart, had returned to the carriage-house, where he found Mr Poulter, with a fixed and earnest eye, wasting the perfections of his sword-exercise on probably observant but inappreciative rats. But Mr Poulter was a host in himself; that is to say, he admired himself more than a whole army of spectators could have admired him. He took no notice of Tom's return, being too entirely absorbed in the cut and thrust—the solemn one, two, three, four; and Tom, not without a slight

4. Antiseptic liquid distilled from wood tar.

feeling of alarm at Mr Poulter's fixed eye and hungry-looking sword, which seemed impatient for something else to cut besides the air, admired the performance from as great a distance as possible. It was not until Mr Poulter paused and wiped the perspiration from his forehead, that Tom felt the full charm of the sword-exercise, and wished it to be repeated.

"Mr Poulter," said Tom, when the sword was being finally sheathed, "I wish you'd lend me your sword a little while to keep."

"No, no, young gentleman," said Mr Poulter, shaking his head decidedly, "you might do yourself some mischief with it."

"No, I'm sure I wouldn't—I'm sure I'd take care and not hurt myself. I shouldn't take it out of the sheath much, but I could ground arms with it, and all that."

"No, no, it won't do, I tell you; it won't do," said Mr Poulter, preparing to depart. "What 'ud Mr Stelling say to me?"

"O, I say, do, Mr Poulter! I'd give you my five-shilling piece if you'd let me keep the sword a week. Look here!" said Tom, reaching out the attractively large round of silver. The young dog calculated the effect as well as if he had been a philosopher.

"Well," said Mr Poulter, with still deeper gravity, "you must keep it out of sight, you know."

"O yes, I'll keep it under the bed," said Tom, eagerly, "or else at the bottom of my large box."

"And let me see, now, whether you can draw it out of the sheath without hurting yourself."

That process having been gone through more than once, Mr Poulter felt that he had acted with scrupulous conscientiousness, and said, "Well, now, Master Tulliver, if I take the crown-piece, it is to make sure as you'll do no mischief with the sword."

"O no, indeed, Mr Poulter," said Tom, delightedly handing him the crown-piece, and grasping the sword, which, he thought, might have been lighter with advantage.

"But if Mr Stelling catches you carrying it in?" said Mr Poulter, pocketing the crown-piece provisionally while he raised this new doubt.

"O, he always keeps in his up-stairs study on Saturday afternoons," said Tom, who disliked anything sneaking, but was not disinclined to a little stratagem in a worthy cause. So he carried off the sword in triumph, mixed with dread—dread that he might encounter Mr or Mrs Stelling—to his bedroom, where, after some consideration, he hid it in the closet behind some hanging clothes. That night he fell asleep in the thought that he would astonish Maggie with it when she came—tie it round his waist with his red comforter, and make her believe that the sword was his own, and that he was going to be a soldier. There was nobody but Maggie who would be silly enough to believe him, or whom he dared allow to know that he had a sword; and Maggie was really coming next week to see Tom, before she went to a boarding-school with Lucy.

If you think a lad of thirteen would not have been so childish, you must be an exceptionally wise man, who, although you are devoted to a civil calling, requiring you to look bland rather than formidable, yet never, since you had a beard, threw yourself into a martial attitude, and frowned before the looking-glass. It is doubtful whether our soldiers would be maintained if there were not pacific people at home who like to fancy themselves soldiers. War, like other dramatic spectacles, might possibly cease for want of a "public."

Chapter V

Maggie's Second Visit

This last breach between the two lads was not readily mended, and for some time they spoke to each other no more than was necessary. Their natural antipathy of temperament made resentment an easy passage to hatred, and in Philip the transition seemed to have begun: there was no malignity in his disposition, but there was a susceptibility that made him peculiarly liable to a strong sense of repulsion. The ox—we may venture to assert it on the authority of a great classic[1]—is not given to use his teeth as an instrument of attack; and Tom was an excellent bovine lad, who ran at questionable objects in a truly ingenious bovine manner; but he had blundered on Philip's tenderest point, and had caused him as much acute pain as if he had studied the means with the nicest precision and the most envenomed spite. Tom saw no reason why they should not make up this quarrel as they had done many others, by behaving as if nothing had happened; for though he had never before said to Philip that his father was a rogue, this idea had so habitually made part of his feeling as to the relation between himself and his dubious schoolfellow, whom he could neither like nor dislike, that the mere utterance did not make such an epoch to him as it did to Philip. And he had a right to say so, when Philip hectored over *him*, and called him names. But perceiving that his first advances towards amity were not met, he relapsed into his least favourable disposition towards Philip, and resolved never to appeal to him either about drawing or exercises again. They were only so far civil to each other as was necessary to prevent their state of feud from being observed by Mr Stelling, who would have "put down" such nonsense with great vigour.

When Maggie came, however, she could not help looking with growing interest at the new schoolfellow, although he was the son of that wicked Lawyer Wakem, who made her father so angry. She had arrived

1. I.e., Horace's *Satires*, 2.1.55.

in the middle of school-hours, and had sat by while Philip went through his lessons with Mr Stelling. Tom, some weeks ago, had sent her word that Philip knew no end of stories—not stupid stories like hers; and she was convinced now from her own observation that he must be very clever: she hoped he would think *her* rather clever too, when she came to talk to him. Maggie, moreover, had rather a tenderness for deformed things; she preferred the wry-necked lambs, because it seemed to her that the lambs which were quite strong and well made wouldn't mind so much about being petted; and she was especially fond of petting objects that would think it very delightful to be petted by her. She loved Tom very dearly, but she often wished that he *cared* more about her loving him.

"I think Philip Wakem seems a nice boy, Tom," she said, when they went out of the study together into the garden, to pass the interval before dinner. "He couldn't choose his father, you know; and I've read of very bad men who had good sons, as well as good parents who had bad children. And if Philip is good, I think we ought to be the more sorry for him because his father is not a good man. *You* like him, don't you?"

"O, he's a queer fellow," said Tom, curtly, "and he's as sulky as can be with me, because I told him his father was a rogue. And I'd a right to tell him so, for it was true—and *he* began it, with calling me names. But you stop here by yourself a bit, Magsie, will you? I've got something I want to do up-stairs."

"Can't I go too?" said Maggie, who, in this first day of meeting again, loved Tom's shadow.

"No, it's something I'll tell you about by-and-by, not yet," said Tom, skipping away.

In the afternoon the boys were at their books in the study, preparing the morrow's lessons, that they might have a holiday in the evening in honour of Maggie's arrival. Tom was hanging over his Latin grammar, moving his lips inaudibly like a strict but impatient Catholic repeating his tale of paternosters;[2] and Philip, at the other end of the room, was busy with two volumes, with a look of contented diligence that excited Maggie's curiosity; he did not look at all as if he were learning a lesson. She sat on a low stool at nearly a right angle with the two boys, watching first one and then the other; and Philip, looking off his book once towards the fireplace, caught the pair of questioning dark eyes fixed upon him. He thought this sister of Tulliver's seemed a nice little thing, quite unlike her brother; he wished *he* had a little sister. What was it, he wondered, that made Maggie's dark eyes remind him of the stories about princesses being turned into animals? . . . I think it was that her eyes were full of unsatisfied intelligence, and unsatisfied, beseeching affection.

"I say, Magsie," said Tom at last, shutting his books and putting them

2. Recitations of the Lord's Prayer.

away with the energy and decision of a perfect master in the art of leaving off, "I've done my lessons now. Come up-stairs with me."

"What is it?" said Maggie, when they were outside the door, a slight suspicion crossing her mind as she remembered Tom's preliminary visit up-stairs. "It isn't a trick you're going to play me, now?"

"No, no, Maggie," said Tom, in his most coaxing tone; "it's something you'll like *ever so.*"

He put his arm round her neck, and she put hers round his waist, and, twined together in this way, they went up-stairs.

"I say, Magsie, you must not tell anybody, you know," said Tom, "else I shall get fifty lines."

"Is it alive?" said Maggie, whose imagination had settled for the moment on the idea that Tom kept a ferret clandestinely.

"O, I shan't tell you," said he. "Now you go into that corner and hide your face, while I reach it out," he added, as he locked the bedroom door behind them. "I'll tell you when to turn round. You musn't squeal out, you know."

"O, but if you frighten me, I shall," said Maggie, beginning to look rather serious.

"You won't be frightened, you silly thing," said Tom. "Go and hide your face, and mind you don't peep."

"Of course I shan't peep," said Maggie, disdainfully; and she buried her face in the pillow like a person of strict honour.

But Tom looked round warily as he walked to the closet; then he stepped into the narrow space, and almost closed the door. Maggie kept her face buried without the aid of principle, for in that dream-suggestive attitude she had soon forgotten where she was, and her thoughts were busy with the poor deformed boy, who was so clever, when Tom called out, "Now then, Magsie!"

Nothing but long meditation and preconcerted arrangement of effects could have enabled Tom to present so striking a figure as he did to Maggie when she looked up. Dissatisfied with the pacific aspect of a face which had no more than the faintest hint of flaxen eyebrow, together with a pair of amiable blue-grey eyes and round pink cheeks that refused to look formidable, let him frown as he would before the looking-glass—(Philip had once told him of a man who had a horse-shoe frown,[3] and Tom had tried with all his frowning-might to make a horse-shoe on his forehead)—he had had recourse to that unfailing source of the terrible, burnt cork, and had made himself a pair of black eyebrows that met in a satisfactory manner over his nose, and were matched by a less carefully adjusted blackness about the chin. He had wound a red handkerchief round his cloth cap to give it the air of a turban, and his red comforter across his breast as a scarf—an amount of red which, with

3. From Scott's *Redgauntlet* (1824).

the tremendous frown on his brow, and the decision with which he grasped the sword, as he held it with its point resting on the ground, would suffice to convey an approximative idea of his fierce and blood-thirsty disposition.

Maggie looked bewildered for a moment, and Tom enjoyed that moment keenly; but in the next, she laughed, clapped her hands together, and said, "O Tom, you've made yourself like Bluebeard[4] at the show."

It was clear she had not been struck with the presence of the sword —it was not unsheathed. Her frivolous mind required a more direct appeal to its sense of the terrible, and Tom prepared for his master-stroke. Frowning with a double amount of intention, if not of corrugation, he (carefully) drew the sword from its sheath and pointed it at Maggie.

"O Tom, please don't," exclaimed Maggie, in a tone of suppressed dread, shrinking away from him into the opposite corner. "I *shall* scream—I'm sure I shall! O don't. I wish I'd never come up-stairs!"

The corners of Tom's mouth showed an inclination to a smile of complacency that was immediately checked as inconsistent with the severity of a great warrior. Slowly he let down the scabbard on the floor, lest it should make too much noise, and then said, sternly,—

"I'm the Duke of Wellington! March!" stamping forward with the right leg a little bent, and the sword still pointing towards Maggie, who, trembling, and with tear-filled eyes, got upon the bed, as the only means of widening the space between them.

Tom, happy in this spectator of his military performances, even though the spectator was only Maggie, proceeded, with the utmost exertion of his force, to such an exhibition of the cut and thrust as would necessarily be expected of the Duke of Wellington.

"Tom, I *will not* bear it—I *will* scream," said Maggie, at the first movement of the sword. "You'll hurt yourself; you'll cut your head off!"

"One—two," said Tom, resolutely, though at "two" his wrist trembled a little. "Three," came more slowly, and with it the sword swung downwards, and Maggie gave a loud shriek. The sword had fallen, with its edge on Tom's foot, and in a moment after, he had fallen too. Maggie leaped from the bed, still shrieking, and immediately there was a rush of footsteps towards the room. Mr Stelling, from his up-stairs study, was the first to enter. He found both the children on the floor. Tom had fainted, and Maggie was shaking him by the collar of his jacket, screaming, with wild eyes. She thought he was dead, poor child! and yet she shook him, as if that would bring him back to life. In another minute she was sobbing with joy because Tom had opened his eyes: she couldn't

4. A rich man in a French tale who marries women and then kills them.

sorrow yet that he had hurt his foot—it seemed as if all happiness lay in his being alive.

Chapter VI

A *Love-Scene*

Poor Tom bore his severe pain heroically, and was resolute in not "telling" of Mr Poulter more than was unavoidable: the five-shilling piece remained a secret even to Maggie. But there was a terrible dread weighing on his mind—so terrible that he dared not even ask the question which might bring the fatal "yes"—he dared not ask the surgeon or Mr Stelling, "Shall I be lame, sir?" He mastered himself so as not to cry out at the pain, but when his foot had been dressed, and he was left alone with Maggie seated by his bedside, the children sobbed together with their heads laid on the same pillow. Tom was thinking of himself walking about on crutches, like the wheelwright's son; and Maggie, who did not guess what was in his mind, sobbed for company. It had not occurred to the surgeon or to Mr Stelling to anticipate this dread in Tom's mind, and to reassure him by hopeful words. But Philip watched the surgeon out of the house, and waylaid Mr Stelling to ask the very question that Tom had not dared to ask for himself.

"I beg your pardon, sir—but does Mr Askern say Tulliver will be lame?"

"O no, O no," said Mr Stelling, "not permanently, only for a little while."

"Did he tell Tulliver so, sir, do you think?"

"No: nothing was said to him on the subject."

"Then may I go and tell him, sir?"

"Yes, to be sure: now you mention it, I daresay he may be troubling about that. Go to his bedroom, but be very quiet at present."

It had been Philip's first thought when he heard of the accident—"Will Tulliver be lame? It will be very hard for him if he is"—and Tom's hitherto unforgiven offences were washed out by that pity. Philip felt that they were no longer in a state of repulsion, but were being drawn into a common current of suffering and sad privation. His imagination did not dwell on the outward calamity and its future effect on Tom's life, but it made vividly present to him the probable state of Tom's feeling. Philip had only lived fourteen years, but those years had, most of them, been steeped in the sense of a lot irremediably hard.

"Mr Askern says you'll soon be all right again, Tulliver, did you know?" he said, rather timidly, as he stepped gently up to Tom's bed.

"I've just been to ask Mr Stelling, and he says you'll walk as well as ever again, by-and-by."

Tom looked up with that momentary stopping of the breath which comes with a sudden joy; then he gave a long sigh, and turned his blue-grey eyes straight on Philip's face, as he had not done for a fortnight or more. As for Maggie, this intimation of a possibility she had not thought of before, affected her as a new trouble; the bare idea of Tom's being always lame over-powered the assurance that such a misfortune was not likely to befall him, and she clung to him and cried afresh.

"Don't be a little silly, Magsie," said Tom, tenderly, feeling very brave now. "I shall soon get well."

"Good-bye, Tulliver," said Philip, putting out his small delicate hand, which Tom clasped immediately with his more substantial fingers.

"I say," said Tom, "ask Mr Stelling to let you come and sit with me sometimes, till I get up again, Wakem—and tell me about Robert Bruce, you know."

After that, Philip spent all his time out of school-hours with Tom and Maggie. Tom liked to hear fighting stories as much as ever, but he insisted strongly on the fact that those great fighters, who did so many wonderful things and came off unhurt, wore excellent armour from head to foot, which made fighting easy work, he considered. He should not have hurt his foot if he had had an iron shoe on. He listened with great interest to a new story of Philip's about a man who had a very bad wound in his foot, and cried out so dreadfully with the pain that his friends could bear with him no longer, but put him ashore on a desert island, with nothing but some wonderful poisoned arrows to kill animals with for food.[1]

"I didn't roar out a bit, you know," Tom said, "and I dare-say my foot was as bad as his. It's cowardly to roar."

But Maggie would have it that when anything hurt you very much, it was quite permissible to cry out, and it was cruel of people not to bear it. She wanted to know if Philoctetes had a sister, and why *she* didn't go with him on the desert island and take care of him.

One day, soon after Philip had told this story, he and Maggie were in the study alone together while Tom's foot was being dressed. Philip was at his books, and Maggie, after sauntering idly round the room, not caring to do anything in particular, because she would soon go to Tom again, went and leaned on the table near Philip to see what he was doing, for they were quite old friends now, and perfectly at home with each other.

"What are you reading about in Greek?" she said. "It's poetry—I can see that, because the lines are so short."

"It's about Philoctetes—the lame man I was telling you of yesterday,"

1. Philoctetes, whose story is most famously told by Sophocles in a play of the same name.

he answered, resting his head on his hand, and looking at her, as if he were not at all sorry to be interrupted. Maggie, in her absent way, continued to lean forward, resting on her arms and moving her feet about, while her dark eyes got more and more fixed and vacant, as if she had quite forgotten Philip and his book.

"Maggie," said Philip, after a minute or two, still leaning on his elbow and looking at her, "if you had had a brother like me, do you think you should have loved him as well as Tom?"

Maggie started a little on being roused from her reverie, and said, "What?" Philip repeated his question.

"O yes, better," she answered, immediately. "No, not better; because I don't think I *could* love you better than Tom. But I should be so sorry—*so sorry* for you."

Philip coloured: he had meant to imply, would she love him as well in spite of his deformity, and yet when she alluded to it so plainly, he winced under her pity. Maggie, young as she was, felt her mistake. Hitherto she had instinctively behaved as if she were quite unconscious of Philip's deformity: her own keen sensitiveness and experience under family criticism sufficed to teach her this as well as if she had been directed by the most finished breeding.

"But you are so very clever, Philip, and you can play and sing," she added, quickly. "I wish you *were* my brother. I'm very fond of you. And you would stay at home with me when Tom went out, and you would teach me everything—wouldn't you? Greek and everything?"

"But you'll go away soon, and go to school, Maggie," said Philip, "and then you'll forget all about me, and not care for me any more. And then I shall see you when you're grown up, and you'll hardly take any notice of me."

"O no, I shan't forget you, I'm sure," said Maggie, shaking her head very seriously. "I never forget anything, and I think about everybody when I'm away from them. I think about poor Yap—he's got a lump in his throat, and Luke says he'll die. Only don't you tell Tom, because it will vex him so. You never saw Yap: he's a queer little dog—nobody cares about him but Tom and me."

"Do you care as much about me as you do about Yap, Maggie?" said Philip, smiling rather sadly.

"O yes, I should think so," said Maggie, laughing.

"I'm very fond of *you*, Maggie; I shall never forget *you*," said Philip, "and when I'm very unhappy, I shall always think of you, and wish I had a sister with dark eyes, just like yours."

"Why do you like my eyes?" said Maggie, well pleased. She had never heard any one but her father speak of her eyes as if they had merit.

"I don't know," said Philip. "They're not like any other eyes. They seem trying to speak—trying to speak kindly. I don't like other people to look at me much, but I like you to look at me, Maggie."

"Why, I think you're fonder of me than Tom is," said Maggie, rather sorrowfully. Then, wondering how she could convince Philip that she could like him just as well, although he was crooked, she said,

"Should you like me to kiss you, as I do Tom? I will, if you like."

"Yes, very much: nobody kisses me."

Maggie put her arm round his neck and kissed him quite earnestly.

"There now," she said, "I shall always remember you, and kiss you when I see you again, if it's ever so long. But I'll go now, because I think Mr Askern's done with Tom's foot."

When their father came the second time, Maggie said to him, "O father, Philip Wakem is so very good to Tom—he is such a clever boy, and I *do* love him. And you love him too, Tom, don't you! *Say* you love him," she added, entreatingly.

Tom coloured a little as he looked at his father, and said, "I shan't be friends with him when I leave school, father; but we've made it up now, since my foot has been bad, and he's taught me to play at draughts, and I can beat him."

"Well, well," said Mr Tulliver, "if he's good to you, try and make him amends, and be good to *him*. He's a poor crooked creature, and takes after his dead mother. But don't you be getting too thick with him—he's got his father's blood in him too. Ay, ay, the grey colt may chance to kick like his black sire."

The jarring natures of the two boys effected what Mr Tulliver's admonition alone might have failed to effect: in spite of Philip's new kindness, and Tom's answering regard in this time of his trouble, they never became close friends. When Maggie was gone, and when Tom by-and-by began to walk about as usual, the friendly warmth that had been kindled by pity and gratitude died out by degrees, and left them in their old relation to each other. Philip was often peevish and contemptuous; and Tom's more specific and kindly impressions gradually melted into the old background of suspicion and dislike towards him as a queer fellow, a humpback, and the son of a rogue. If boys and men are to be welded together in the glow of transient feeling, they must be made of metal that will mix, else they inevitably fall asunder when the heat dies out.

Chapter VII

The Golden Gates Are Passed

So Tom went on even to the fifth half-year—till he was turned sixteen—at King's Lorton, while Maggie was growing with a rapidity which her aunts considered highly reprehensible, at Miss Firniss's boarding-school in the ancient town of Laceham on the Floss, with cousin Lucy for her companion. In her early letters to Tom she had always sent her love to Philip, and asked many questions about him, which were answered by brief sentences about Tom's toothache, and a turf-house which he was helping to build in the garden, with other items of that kind. She was pained to hear Tom say in the holidays that Philip was as queer as ever again, and often cross: they were no longer very good friends, she perceived; and when she reminded Tom that he ought always to love Philip for being so good to him when his foot was bad, he answered, "Well, it isn't my fault: *I* don't do anything to him." She hardly ever saw Philip during the remainder of their school-life; in the Midsummer holidays he was always away at the seaside, and at Christmas she could only meet him at long intervals in the streets of St Ogg's. When they did meet, she remembered her promise to kiss him, but, as a young lady who had been at a boarding-school, she knew now that such a greeting was out of the question, and Philip would not expect it. The promise was void, like so many other sweet, illusory promises of our childhood; void as promises made in Eden before the seasons were divided, and when the starry blossoms grew side by side with the ripening peach—impossible to be fulfilled when the golden gates had been passed.

But when their father was actually engaged in the long-threatened lawsuit, and Wakem, as the agent at once of Pivart and Old Harry, was acting against him, even Maggie felt, with some sadness, that they were not likely ever to have any intimacy with Philip again: the very name of Wakem made her father angry, and she had once heard him say, that if that crook-backed son lived to inherit his father's ill-gotten gains, there would be a curse upon him. "Have as little to do with him at school as you can, my lad," he said to Tom; and the command was obeyed the more easily because Mr Stelling by this time had two additional pupils; for though this gentleman's rise in the world was not of that meteor-like rapidity which the admirers of his extemporaneous eloquence had expected for a preacher whose voice demanded so wide a sphere, he had yet enough of growing prosperity to enable him to increase his expenditure in continued disproportion to his income.

As for Tom's school course, it went on with mill-like monotony, his mind continuing to move with a slow, half-stifled pulse in a medium of uninteresting or unintelligible ideas. But each vacation he brought home larger and larger drawings with the satiny rendering of landscape, and water-colours in vivid greens, together with manuscript books full of exercises and problems, in which the handwriting was all the finer because he gave his whole mind to it. Each vacation he brought home a new book or two, indicating his progress through different stages of history, Christian doctrine, and Latin literature; and that passage was not entirely without result, besides the possession of the books. Tom's ear and tongue had become accustomed to a great many words and phrases which are understood to be signs of an educated condition; and though he had never really applied his mind to any one of his lessons, the lessons had left a deposit of vague, fragmentary, ineffectual notions. Mr Tulliver, seeing signs of acquirement beyond the reach of his own criticism, thought it was probably all right with Tom's education: he observed, indeed, that there were no maps, and not enough "summing;" but he made no formal complaint to Mr Stelling. It was a puzzling business, this schooling; and if he took Tom away, where could he send him with better effect?

By the time Tom had reached his last quarter at King's Lorton, the years had made striking changes in him since the day we saw him returning from Mr Jacobs' academy. He was a tall youth now, carrying himself without the least awkwardness, and speaking without more shyness than was a becoming symptom of blended diffidence and pride: he wore his tail-coat and his stand-up collars, and watched the down on his lip with eager impatience, looking every day at his virgin razor, with which he had provided himself in the last holidays. Philip had already left—at the autumn quarter—that he might go to the south for the winter, for the sake of his health; and this change helped to give Tom the unsettled, exultant feeling that usually belongs to the last months before leaving school. This quarter, too, there was some hope of his father's lawsuit being decided: *that* made the prospect of home more entirely pleasurable. For Tom, who had gathered his view of the case from his father's conversation, had no doubt that Pivart would be beaten.

Tom had not heard anything from home for some weeks—a fact which did not surprise him, for his father and mother were not apt to manifest their affection in unnecessary letters—when, to his great surprise, on the morning of a dark cold day near the end of November, he was told, soon after entering the study at nine o'clock, that his sister was in the drawing-room. It was Mrs Stelling who had come into the study to tell him, and she left him to enter the drawing-room alone.

Maggie, too, was tall now, with braided and coiled hair: she was almost as tall as Tom, though she was only thirteen; and she really looked older than he did at that moment. She had thrown off her bonnet, her heavy braids were pushed back from her forehead, as if it would not bear that extra load, and her young face had a strangely worn look, as her eyes turned anxiously towards the door. When Tom entered she did not speak, but only went up to him, put her arms round his neck, and kissed him earnestly. He was used to various moods of hers, and felt no alarm at the unusual seriousness of her greeting.

"Why, how is it you're come so early this cold morning, Maggie? Did you come in the gig?" said Tom, as she backed towards the sofa, and drew him to her side.

"No, I came by the coach. I've walked from the turnpike."

"But how is it you're not at school? The holidays have not begun yet?"

"Father wanted me at home," said Maggie, with a slight trembling of the lip. "I came home three or four days ago."

"Isn't my father well?" said Tom, rather anxiously.

"Not quite," said Maggie. "He's very unhappy, Tom. The lawsuit is ended, and I came to tell you, because I thought it would be better for you to know it before you came home, and I didn't like only to send you a letter."

"My father hasn't lost?" said Tom, hastily, springing from the sofa, and standing before Maggie with his hands suddenly thrust in his pockets.

"Yes, dear Tom," said Maggie, looking up at him with trembling.

Tom was silent a minute or two, with his eyes fixed on the floor. Then he said—

"My father will have to pay a good deal of money, then?"

"Yes," said Maggie, rather faintly.

"Well, it can't be helped," said Tom, bravely, not translating the loss of a large sum of money into any tangible results. "But my father's very much vexed, I dare-say?" he added looking at Maggie, and thinking that her agitated face was only part of her girlish way of taking things.

"Yes," said Maggie, again faintly. Then, urged to fuller speech by Tom's freedom from apprehension, she said loudly and rapidly, as if the words *would* burst from her, "O Tom, he will lose the mill and the land, and everything; he will have nothing left."

Tom's eyes flashed out one look of surprise at her, before he turned pale, and trembled visibly. He said nothing, but sat down on the sofa again, looking vaguely out of the opposite window.

Anxiety about the future had never entered Tom's mind. His father had always ridden a good horse, kept a good house, and had the cheerful, confident air of a man who has plenty of property to fall back upon. Tom had never dreamed that his father would "fail;" *that* was a form of misfortune which he had always heard spoken of as a deep disgrace, and disgrace was an idea that he could not associate with any of his relations, least of all with his father. A proud sense of family respectability was part of the very air Tom had been born and brought up in. He knew there were people in St Ogg's who made a show without money to support it, and he had always heard such people spoken of by his own friends with contempt and reprobation. He had a strong belief, which was a life-long habit, and required no definite evidence to rest on, that his father could spend a great deal of money if he chose; and since his education at Mr Stelling's had given him a more expensive view of life, he had often thought that when he got older he would make a figure in the world, with his horse and dogs and saddle, and other accoutrements of a fine young man, and show himself equal to any of his contemporaries at St Ogg's, who might consider themselves a grade above him in society, because their fathers were professional men, or had large oil-mills. As to the prognostics and headshaking of his aunts and uncles, they had never produced the least effect on him, except to make him think that aunts and uncles were disagreeable society: he had heard them find fault in much the same way as long as he could remember. His father knew better than they did.

The down had come on Tom's lip, yet his thoughts and expectations had been hitherto only the reproduction, in changed forms, of the boyish dreams in which he had lived three years ago. He was awakened now with a violent shock.

Maggie was frightened at Tom's pale, trembling silence. There was something else to tell him—something worse. She threw her arms round him at last, and said, with a half sob—

"O Tom—dear, dear Tom, don't fret too much—try and bear it well."

Tom turned his cheek passively to meet her entreating kisses, and there gathered a moisture in his eyes, which he just rubbed away with his hand. The action seemed to rouse him, for he shook himself and said, "I shall go home with you, Maggie. Didn't my father say I was to go?"

"No, Tom, father didn't wish it," said Maggie, her anxiety about *his* feeling helping her to master her agitation. What *would* he do when she told him all? "But mother wants you to come—poor mother!—she cries so. O Tom, it's very dreadful at home."

Maggie's lips grew whiter, and she began to tremble almost as Tom had done. The two poor things clung closer to each other—both trembling—the one at an unshapen fear, the other at the image of a terrible certainty. When Maggie spoke, it was hardly above a whisper.

"And . . . and . . . poor father. . . ."

Maggie could not utter it. But the suspense was intolerable to Tom. A vague idea of going to prison, as a consequence of debt, was the shape his fears had begun to take.

"Where's my father?" he said, impatiently. "*Tell* me, Maggie."

"He's at home," said Maggie, finding it easier to reply to that question. "But," she added, after a pause, "not himself, . . . He fell off his horse. . . . He has known nobody but me ever since. . . . He seems to have lost his senses. . . . O, father, father. . . ."

With these last words, Maggie's sobs burst forth with the more violence for the previous struggle against them. Tom felt that pressure of the heart which forbids tears: he had no distinct vision of their troubles as Maggie had, who had been at home; he only felt the crushing weight of what seemed unmitigated misfortune. He tightened his arm almost convulsively round Maggie as she sobbed, but his face looked rigid and tearless—his eyes blank—as if a black curtain of cloud had suddenly fallen on his path.

But Maggie soon checked herself abruptly: a single thought had acted on her like a startling sound.

"We must set out, Tom—we must not stay—father will miss me—we must be at the turnpike at ten to meet the coach." She said this with hasty decision, rubbing her eyes, and rising to seize her bonnet.

Tom at once felt the same impulse, and rose too. "Wait a minute, Maggie," he said. "I must speak to Mr Stelling, and then we'll go."

He thought he must go to the study where the pupils were, but on his way he met Mr Stelling, who had heard from his wife that Maggie appeared to be in trouble when she asked for her brother; and, now that he thought the brother and sister had been alone long enough, was coming to inquire and offer his sympathy.

"Please, sir, I must go home," Tom said, abruptly, as he met Mr Stelling in the passage. "I must go back with my sister directly. My father's lost his lawsuit—he's lost all his property—and he's very ill."

Mr Stelling felt like a kind-hearted man; he foresaw a probable money loss for himself, but this had no appreciable share in his feeling, while he looked with grave pity at the brother and sister for whom youth and sorrow had begun together. When he knew how Maggie had come, and how eager she was to get home again, he hurried their departure, only whispering something to Mrs Stelling, who had followed him, and who immediately left the room.

Tom and Maggie were standing on the door-step, ready to set out, when Mrs Stelling came with a little basket, which she hung on Maggie's arms, saying, "Do remember to eat something on the way, dear." Maggie's heart went out towards this woman whom she had never liked, and she kissed her silently. It was the first sign within the poor child of that new sense which is the gift of sorrow—that susceptibility to the bare offices of humanity which raises them into a bond of loving fellowship, as to haggard men among the icebergs the mere presence of an ordinary comrade stirs the deep fountains of affection.

Mr Stelling put his hand on Tom's shoulder and said, "God bless you, my boy: let me know how you get on." Then he pressed Maggie's hand; but there were no audible good-byes. Tom had so often thought how joyful he should be the day he left school "for good!" And now his school years seemed like a holiday that had come to an end.

The two slight youthful figures soon grew indistinct on the distant road—were soon lost behind the projecting hedgerow.

They had gone forth together into their new life of sorrow, and they would never more see the sunshine undimmed by remembered cares. They had entered the thorny wilderness, and the golden gates of their childhood had for ever closed behind them.

Book Third

THE DOWNFALL

Chapter I

What Had Happened at Home

When Mr Tulliver first knew the fact that the lawsuit was decided against him, and that Pivart and Wakem were triumphant, every one who happened to observe him at the time thought that, for so confident and hot-tempered a man, he bore the blow remarkably well. He thought so himself: he thought he was going to show that if Wakem or anybody else considered him crushed, they would find themselves mistaken. He could not refuse to see that the costs of this protracted suit would take more than he possessed to pay them; but he appeared to himself to be full of expedients by which he could ward off any results but such as were tolerable, and could avoid the appearance of breaking down in the world. All the obstinacy and defiance of his nature, driven out of their old channel, found a vent for themselves in the immediate formation of plans by which he would meet his difficulties, and remain Mr Tulliver of Dorlcote Mill in spite of them. There was such a rush of projects in his brain, that it was no wonder his face was flushed when he came away from his talk with his attorney, Mr Gore, and mounted his horse to ride home from Lindum. There was Furley, who held the mortgage on the land—a reasonable fellow, who would see his own interest, Mr Tulliver was convinced, and who would be glad not only to purchase the whole estate including the mill and homestead, but would accept Mr Tulliver as tenant, and be willing to advance money to be repaid with high interest out of the profits of the business, which would be made over to him, Mr Tulliver only taking enough barely to maintain himself and his family. Who would neglect such a profitable investment? Certainly not Furley, for Mr Tulliver had determined that Furley should meet his plans with the utmost alacrity; and there are men whose brains have not yet been dangerously heated by the loss of a lawsuit, who are apt to see in their own interest or desires a motive for other men's actions. There was no doubt (in the miller's mind) that Furley would do just what was desirable; and if he did—why, things would not be so very much worse. Mr Tulliver and his family must live more meagerly and humbly, but it would only be till the profits of the business had paid off Furley's advances, and that might be while Mr Tulliver had still a good many years of life before him. It was clear that the costs of the suit could be paid without his being obliged to turn out of his old place, and look like a ruined man. It was certainly an awkward moment in his affairs. There was that suretyship[1] for poor Riley, who had died suddenly last April, and left his friend saddled with a debt of two hundred and fifty pounds—a fact which had helped to make Mr Tulliver's banking book less pleasant reading than a man might desire towards Christmas. Well! he had never been one of those poor-spirited sneaks who would refuse to give a helping hand to a fellow-traveller in this puzzling world. The really vexatious business was the fact that some months ago the creditor who had lent him the five hundred pounds to repay Mrs Glegg, had become uneasy about his money (set on by Wakem, of course), and Mr Tulliver, still confident that he should gain his suit, and finding it eminently inconvenient to raise the said sum until that desirable issue had taken place, had rashly acceded to the demand that he should give a bill of sale on his household furniture, and some other effects, as security in lieu of the bond. It was all one, he had said to himself: he should soon pay off the money, and there was no harm in giving that security any more than another. But now the consequences of this bill of sale occurred to him in a new light, and he remembered that the time was close at hand, when it would be enforced unless the money were repaid. Two months ago he would have declared stoutly that he would never be beholden to his wife's friends; but now he told himself as stoutly that it was nothing but right and natural that Bessy should go to the Pullets and explain the thing to them: they would hardly let Bessy's furniture be sold, and it might be security to Pullet if he advanced the money—there would, after all, be no gift or favour in the matter. Mr Tulliver would never have asked for anything from so poor-spirited a fellow for himself, but Bessy might do so if she liked.

It is precisely the proudest and most obstinate men who are the most liable to shift their position and contradict themselves in this sudden manner: everything is easier to them than to face the simple fact that they have been thoroughly defeated, and must begin life anew. And Mr Tulliver, you perceive, though nothing more than a superior miller and maltster, was as proud and obstinate as if he had been a very lofty personage, in whom such dispositions might be a source of that conspicuous, far-echoing tragedy, which sweeps the stage in regal robes and makes the dullest chronicler sublime. The pride and obstinacy of millers, and other insignificant people, whom you pass unnoticingly on the road

1. Guarantee to pay the debt of another person.

every day, have their tragedy too; but it is of that unwept, hidden sort, that goes on from generation to generation, and leaves no record—such tragedy, perhaps, as lies in the conflicts of young souls, hungry for joy, under a lot made suddenly hard to them, under the dreariness of a home where the morning brings no promise with it, and where the unexpectant discontent of worn and disappointed parents weighs on the children like a damp, thick air, in which all the functions of life are depressed; or such tragedy as lies in the slow or sudden death that follows on a bruised passion, though it may be a death that finds only a parish funeral. There are certain animals to which tenacity of position is a law of life—they can never flourish again, after a single wrench: and there are certain human beings to whom predominance is a law of life—they can only sustain humiliation so long as they can refuse to believe in it, and, in their own conception, predominate still.

Mr Tulliver was still predominating in his own imagination as he approached St Ogg's, through which he had to pass on his way homeward. But what was it that suggested to him, as he saw the Laceham coach entering the town, to follow it to the coach-office, and get the clerk there to write a letter, requiring Maggie to come home the very next day? Mr Tulliver's own hand shook too much under his excitement for him to write himself, and he wanted the letter to be given to the coachman to deliver at Miss Firniss's school in the morning. There was a craving which he would not account for to himself, to have Maggie near him—without delay—she must come back by the coach to-morrow.

To Mrs Tulliver, when he got home, he would admit no difficulties, and scolded down her burst of grief on hearing that the lawsuit was lost, by angry assertions that there was nothing to grieve about. He said nothing to her that night about the bill of sale, and the application to Mrs Pullet, for he had kept her in ignorance of the nature of that transaction, and had explained the necessity for taking an inventory of the goods as a matter connected with his will. The possession of a wife conspicuously one's inferior in intellect, is, like other high privileges, attended with a few inconveniences, and, among the rest, with the occasional necessity for using a little deception.

The next day Mr Tulliver was again on horseback in the afternoon, on his way to Mr Gore's office at St Ogg's. Gore was to have seen Furley in the morning, and to have sounded him in relation to Mr Tulliver's affairs. But he had not gone half-way when he met a clerk from Mr Gore's office, who was bringing a letter to Mr Tulliver. Mr Gore had been prevented by a sudden call of business from waiting at his office to see Mr Tulliver, according to appointment, but would be at his office at eleven to-morrow morning, and meanwhile had sent some important information by letter.

"O!" said Mr Tulliver, taking the letter, but not opening it. "Then tell Gore I'll see him to-morrow at eleven;" and he turned his horse.

The clerk, struck with Mr Tulliver's glistening excited glance, looked after him for a few moments, and then rode away. The reading of a letter was not the affair of an instant to Mr Tulliver; he took in the sense of a statement very slowly through the medium of written or even printed characters; so he had put the letter in his pocket, thinking he would open it in his arm-chair at home. But by-and-by it occurred to him that there might be something in the letter Mrs Tulliver must not know about, and if so, it would be better to keep it out of her sight altogether. He stopped his horse, took out the letter, and read it. It was only a short letter; the substance was, that Mr Gore had ascertained, on secret but sure authority, that Furley had been lately much straitened for money, and had parted with his securities—among the rest, the mortgage on Mr Tulliver's property, which he had transferred to——Wakem.

In half an hour after this, Mr Tulliver's own waggoner found him lying by the roadside insensible, with an open letter near him, and his grey horse snuffing uneasily about him.

When Maggie reached home that evening, in obedience to her father's call, he was no longer insensible. About an hour before, he had become conscious, and after vague, vacant looks around him, had muttered something about "a letter," which he presently repeated impatiently. At the instance of Mr Turnbull, the medical man, Gore's letter was brought and laid on the bed, and the previous impatience seemed to be allayed. The stricken man lay for some time with his eyes fixed on the letter, as if he were trying to knit up his thoughts by its help. But presently a new wave of memory seemed to have come and swept the other away; he turned his eyes from the letter to the door, and after looking uneasily, as if striving to see something his eyes were too dim for, he said, "The little wench."

He repeated the words impatiently from time to time, appearing entirely unconscious of everything except this one importunate want, and giving no sign of knowing his wife or any one else; and poor Mrs Tulliver, her feeble faculties almost paralysed by this sudden accumulation of troubles, went backwards and forwards to the gate to see if the Laceham coach were coming, though it was not yet time.

But it came at last, and set down the poor anxious girl, no longer the "little wench," except to her father's fond memory.

"O mother, what is the matter?" Maggie said, with pale lips, as her mother came towards her crying. She didn't think her father was ill, because the letter had come at his dictation from the office at St Ogg's.

But Mr Turnbull came now to meet her: a medical man is the good angel of the troubled house, and Maggie ran towards the kind old friend, whom she remembered as long as she could remember anything, with a trembling, questioning look.

"Don't alarm yourself too much, my dear," he said, taking her hand. "Your father has had a sudden attack, and has not quite recovered his memory. But he has been asking for you, and it will do him good to see you. Keep as quiet as you can; take off your things, and come upstairs with me."

Maggie obeyed, with that terrible beating of the heart which makes existence seem simply a painful pulsation. The very quietness with which Mr Turnbull spoke had frightened her susceptible imagination. Her father's eyes were still turned uneasily towards the door when she entered and met the strange, yearning, helpless look that had been seeking her in vain. With a sudden flash and movement, he raised himself in the bed—she rushed towards him, and clasped him with agonised kisses.

Poor child! it was very early for her to know one of those supreme moments in life when all we have hoped or delighted in, all we can dread or endure, falls away from our regard as insignificant—is lost, like a trivial memory, in that simple, primitive love which knits us to the beings who have been nearest to us, in their times of helplessness or of anguish.

But that flash of recognition had been too great a strain on the father's bruised, enfeebled powers. He sank back again in renewed insensibility and rigidity, which lasted for many hours, and was only broken by a flickering return of consciousness, in which he took passively everything that was given to him, and seemed to have a sort of infantine satisfaction in Maggie's near presence—such satisfaction as a baby has when it is returned to the nurse's lap.

Mrs Tulliver sent for her sisters, and there was much wailing and lifting up of hands below stairs: both uncles and aunts saw that the ruin of Bessy and her family was as complete as they had ever foreboded it, and there was a general family sense that a judgment had fallen on Mr Tulliver, which it would be an impiety to counteract by too much kindness. But Maggie heard little of this, scarcely ever leaving her father's bedside, where she sat opposite him with her hand on his. Mrs Tulliver wanted to have Tom fetched home, and seemed to be thinking more of her boy even than of her husband; but the aunts and uncles opposed this. Tom was better at school, since Mr Turnbull said there was no immediate danger, he believed. But at the end of the second day, when Maggie had become more accustomed to her father's fits of insensibility, and to the expectation that he would revive from them, the thought of Tom had become urgent with *her* too; and when her mother sate crying at night and saying, "My poor lad . . . it's nothing but right he should come home;" Maggie said, "Let me go for him, and tell him, mother: I'll go to-morrow morning if father doesn't know me and want me. It would be so hard for Tom to come home and not know anything about it beforehand."

And the next morning Maggie went, as we have seen. Sitting on the coach on their way home, the brother and sister talked to each other in sad, interrupted whispers.

"They say Mr Wakem has got a mortgage or something on the land, Tom," said Maggie. "It was the letter with that news in it that made father ill, they think."

"I believe that scoundrel's been planning all along to ruin my father," said Tom, leaping from the vaguest impressions to a definite conclusion. "I'll make him feel for it when I'm a man. Mind you never speak to Philip again."

"O, Tom!" said Maggie, in a tone of sad remonstrance; but she had no spirit to dispute anything then, still less to vex Tom by opposing him.

Chapter II

Mrs Tulliver's Teraphim,[1] *or Household Gods*

When the coach set down Tom and Maggie, it was five hours since she had started from home, and she was thinking with some trembling that her father had perhaps missed her, and asked for "the little wench" in vain. She thought of no other change that might have happened.

She hurried along the gravel-walk and entered the house before Tom; but in the entrance she was startled by a strong smell of tobacco. The parlour door was ajar—that was where the smell came from. It was very strange: could any visitor be smoking at a time like this? Was her mother there? If so, she must be told that Tom was come. Maggie, after this pause of surprise, was only in the act of opening the door when Tom came up, and they both looked into the parlour together. There was a coarse, dingy man, of whose face Tom had some vague recollection, sitting in his father's chair, smoking, with a jug and glass beside him.

The truth flashed on Tom's mind in an instant. To "have the bailiff in the house," and "to be sold up," were phrases which he had been used to, even as a little boy: they were part of the disgrace and misery of "failing," of losing all one's money, and being ruined—sinking into the condition of poor working people. It seemed only natural this should happen, since his father had lost all his property, and he thought of no more special cause for this particular form of misfortune than the loss of the lawsuit. But the immediate presence of this disgrace was so much keener an experience to Tom than the worst form of apprehension, that he felt at this moment as if his real trouble had only just begun: it was a touch on the irritated nerve compared with its spontaneous dull aching.

"How do you do, sir?" said the man, taking the pipe out of his mouth,

1. Images of household gods.

with rough, embarrassed civility. The two young startled faces made him a little uncomfortable.

But Tom turned away hastily without speaking: the sight was too hateful. Maggie had not understood the appearance of this stranger, as Tom had. She followed him, whispering, "Who can it be, Tom?—what is the matter?" Then, with a sudden undefined dread lest this stranger might have something to do with a change in her father, she rushed up-stairs, checking herself at the bedroom door to throw off her bonnet, and enter on tiptoe. All was silent there: her father was lying, heedless of everything around him, with his eyes closed as when she had left him. A servant was there, but not her mother.

"Where's my mother?" she whispered. The servant did not know.

Maggie hastened out, and said to Tom, "Father is lying quiet: let us go and look for my mother. I wonder where she is."

Mrs Tulliver was not down-stairs—not in any of the bed-rooms. There was but one room below the attic which Maggie had left unsearched: it was the store-room, where her mother kept all her linen and all the precious "best things" that were only unwrapped and brought out on special occasions. Tom, preceding Maggie as they returned along the passage, opened the door of this room, and immediately said, "Mother!"

Mrs Tulliver was seated there with all her laid-up treasures. One of the linen-chests was open: the silver teapot was unwrapped from its many folds of paper, and the best china was laid out on the top of the closed linen-chest; spoons and skewers and ladles were spread in rows on the shelves; and the poor woman was shaking her head and weeping, with a bitter tension of the mouth, over the mark, "Elizabeth Dodson," on the corner of some table-cloths she held in her lap.

She dropped them, and started up as Tom spoke.

"O my boy, my boy!" she said, clasping him round the neck. "To think as I should live to see this day! We're ruined . . . everything's going to be sold up . . . to think as your father should ha' married me to bring me to this! We've got nothing . . . we shall be beggars . . . we must go to the workhouse. . . ."

She kissed him, then seated herself again, and took another table-cloth on her lap, unfolding it a little way to look at the pattern, while the children stood by in mute wretchedness—their minds quite filled for the moment with the words "beggars" and "workhouse."

"To think o' these clothes as I spun myself," she went on, lifting things out and turning them over with an excitement all the more strange and piteous because the stout blond woman was usually so passive: if she had been ruffled before, it was at the surface merely: "and Job Haxey wove 'em, and brought the piece home on his back, as I remember standing at the door and seeing him come, before I ever thought o' marrying your father! And the pattern as I chose myself—and bleached so beautiful, and I marked 'em so as nobody ever saw such marking—they must cut the cloth to get it out, for it's a particular stitch. And they're all to be sold—and go into strange people's houses, and perhaps be cut with the knives, and wore out before I'm dead. You'll never have one of 'em, my boy," she said, looking up at Tom with her eyes full of tears, "and I meant 'em for you. I wanted you to have all o' this pattern. Maggie could have had the large check—it never shows so well when the dishes are on it."

Tom was touched to the quick, but there was an angry reaction immediately. His face flushed as he said—

"But will my aunts let them be sold, mother? Do they know about it? They'll never let your linen go, will they? Haven't you sent to them?"

"Yes, I sent Luke directly they'd put the bailies in, and your aunt Pullet's been—and, O dear, O dear, she cries so, and says your father's disgraced my family and made it the talk o' the country; and she'll buy the spotted cloths for herself, because she's never had so many as she wanted o' that pattern, and they shan't go to strangers, but she's got more checks a'ready nor she can do with." (Here Mrs Tulliver began to lay back the tablecloths in the chest, folding and stroking them automatically.) "And your uncle Glegg's been too, and he says things must be bought in for us to lie down on, but he must talk to your aunt; and they're all coming to consult. . . . But I know they'll none of 'em take my chany," she added, turning towards the cups and saucers—"for they all found fault with 'em when I bought 'em, 'cause o' the small gold sprig all over 'em, between the flowers. But there's none of 'em got better chany, not even your aunt Pullet herself,—and I bought it wi' my own money as I'd saved ever since I was turned fifteen; and the silver teapot, too—your father never paid for 'em. And to think as he should ha' married me, and brought me to this."

Mrs Tulliver burst out crying afresh, and she sobbed with her handkerchief at her eyes a few moments, but then removing it, she said in a deprecating way, still half-sobbing, as if she were called upon to speak before she could command her voice—

"And I *did* say to him times and times, 'Whativer you do, don't go to law'—and what more could I do? I've had to sit by while my own fortin's been spent, and what should ha' been my children's, too. You'll have niver a penny, my boy . . . but it isn't your poor mother's fault."

She put out one arm towards Tom, looking up at him piteously with her helpless, childish blue eyes. The poor lad went to her and kissed her, and she clung to him. For the first time Tom thought of his father with some reproach. His natural inclination to blame, hitherto kept entirely in abeyance towards his father by the predisposition to think him always right, simply on the ground that he was Tom Tulliver's father—was turned into this new channel by his mother's plaints, and with his indignation against Wakem there began to mingle some indignation of another sort. Perhaps his father might have helped bringing them all down in the world, and making people talk of them with contempt; but no one should talk long of Tom Tulliver with contempt. The natural strength and firmness of his nature was beginning to assert itself, urged by the double stimulus of resentment against his aunts, and the sense that he must behave like a man and take care of his mother.

"Don't fret, mother," he said, tenderly. "I shall soon be able to get money: I'll get a situation of some sort."

"Bless you, my boy!" said Mrs Tulliver, a little soothed. Then, looking round sadly, "But I shouldn't ha' minded so much if we could ha' kept the things wi' my name on 'em."

Maggie had witnessed this scene with gathering anger. The implied reproaches against her father—her father, who was lying there in a sort of living death—neutralised all her pity for griefs about table-cloths and china; and her anger on her father's account was heightened by some egotistic resentment at Tom's silent concurrence with her mother in shutting her out from the common calamity. She had become almost indifferent to her mother's habitual depreciation of her, but she was keenly alive to any sanction of it, however passive, that she might suspect in Tom. Poor Maggie was by no means made up of unalloyed devotedness, but put forth large claims for herself where she loved strongly. She burst out at last in an agitated, almost violent tone, "Mother, how can you talk so? as if you cared only for things with *your* name on, and not for what has my father's name too—and to care about anything but dear father himself!—when he's lying there, and may never speak to us again. Tom, you ought to say so too—you ought not to let any one find fault with my father."

Maggie, almost choked with mingled grief and anger, left the room, and took her old place on her father's bed. Her heart went out to him with a stronger movement than ever, at the thought that people would blame him. Maggie hated blame: she had been blamed all her life, and nothing had come of it but evil tempers. Her father had always defended and excused her, and her loving remembrance of his tenderness was a force within her that would enable her to do or bear anything for his sake.

Tom was a little shocked at Maggie's outburst—telling *him* as well as his mother what it was right to do! She ought to have learned better than have those hectoring, assuming manners, by this time. But he presently went into his father's room, and the sight there touched him in a way that effaced the slighter impressions of the previous hour. When Maggie saw how he was moved, she went to him and put her arm round his neck as he sat by the bed, and the two children forgot everything else in the sense that they had one father and one sorrow.

Chapter III

The Family Council

It was at eleven o'clock the next morning that the aunts and uncles came to hold their consultation. The fire was lighted in the large parlour, and poor Mrs Tulliver, with a confused impression that it was a great occasion, like a funeral, unbagged the bell-rope tassels, and unpinned the curtains, adjusting them in proper folds—looking round and shaking her head sadly at the polished tops and legs of the tables, which sister Pullet herself could not accuse of insufficient brightness.

Mr Deane was not coming—he was away on business; but Mrs Deane appeared punctually in that handsome new gig with the head to it, and the livery-servant driving it, which had thrown so clear a light on several traits in her character to some of her female friends in St Ogg's. Mr Deane had been advancing in the world as rapidly as Mr Tulliver had been going down in it; and in Mrs Deane's house the Dodson linen and plate were beginning to hold quite a subordinate position, as a mere supplement to the handsomer articles of the same kind, purchased in recent years: a change which had caused an occasional coolness in the sisterly intercourse between her and Mrs Glegg, who felt that Susan was getting "like the rest," and there would soon be little of the true Dodson spirit surviving except in herself, and, it might be hoped, in those nephews who supported the Dodson name on the family land, far away in the Wolds. People who live at a distance are naturally less faulty than those immediately under our own eyes; and it seems superfluous, when we consider the remote geographical position of the Ethiopians, and how very little the Greeks had to do with them, to inquire further why Homer calls them "blameless."[1]

Mrs Deane was the first to arrive; and when she had taken her seat in the large parlour, Mrs Tulliver came down to her with her comely face a little distorted, nearly as it would have been if she had been crying: she was not a woman who could shed abundant tears, except in moments when the prospect of losing her furniture became unusually vivid, but she felt how unfitting it was to be quite calm under present circumstances.

"O sister, what a world this is!" she exclaimed as she entered; "what trouble, O dear!"

Mrs Deane was a thin-lipped woman, who made small well-considered speeches on peculiar occasions, repeating them afterwards to her husband, and asking him if she had not spoken very properly.

"Yes, sister," she said, deliberately, "this is a changing world, and we don't know to-day what may happen to-morrow. But it's right to be

1. In book 1, line 423, of Homer's *Iliad*.

prepared for all things, and if trouble's sent, to remember as it isn't sent without a cause. I'm very sorry for you as a sister, and if the doctor orders jelly for Mr Tulliver, I hope you'll let me know: I'll send it willingly. For it is but right he should have proper attendance while he's ill."

"Thank you, Susan," said Mrs Tulliver, rather faintly, withdrawing her fat hand from her sister's thin one. "But there's been no talk o' jelly yet." Then after a moment's pause she added, "There's a dozen o' cut jelly-glasses up-stairs. . . . I shall niver put jelly into 'em no more."

Her voice was rather agitated as she uttered the last words, but the sound of wheels diverted her thoughts. Mr and Mrs Glegg were come, and were almost immediately followed by Mr and Mrs Pullet.

Mrs Pullet entered crying, as a compendious mode, at all times, of expressing what were her views of life in general, and what, in brief, were the opinions she held concerning the particular case before her.

Mrs Glegg had on her fuzziest front, and garments which appeared to have had a recent resurrection from rather a creasy form of burial; a costume selected with the high moral purpose of instilling perfect humility into Bessy and her children.

"Mrs G., won't you come nearer the fire?" said her husband, unwilling to take the more comfortable seat without offering it to her.

"You see I've seated myself here, Mr Glegg," returned this superior woman; "*you* can roast yourself, if you like."

"Well," said Mr Glegg, seating himself good-humouredly, "and how's the poor man up-stairs?"

"Dr Turnbull thought him a deal better this morning," said Mrs Tulliver; "he took more notice, and spoke to me; but he's never known Tom yet—looks at the poor lad as if he was a stranger, though he said something once about Tom and the pony. The doctor says his memory's gone a long way back, and he doesn't know Tom because he's thinking of him when he was little. Eh dear, eh dear!"

"I doubt it's the water got on his brain," said aunt Pullet, turning round from adjusting her cap in a melancholy way at the pier-glass. "It's much if he ever gets up again; and if he does, he'll most like be childish, as Mr Carr was, poor man! They fed him with a spoon as if he'd been a baby for three year. He'd quite lost the use of his limbs; but then he'd got a Bath chair,[2] and somebody to draw him; and that's what you won't have, I doubt, Bessy."

"Sister Pullet," said Mrs Glegg, severely, "if I understand right, we've come together this morning to advise and consult about what's to be done in this disgrace as has fallen upon the family, and not to talk o' people as don't belong to us. Mr Carr was none of our blood, nor noways connected with us, as I've ever heared."

2. Wheelchair.

"Sister Glegg," said Mrs Pullet, in a pleading tone, drawing on her gloves again, and stroking the fingers in an agitated manner, "if you've got anything disrespectful to say o' Mr Carr, I do beg of you as you won't say it to me. *I* know what he was," she added, with a sigh; "his breath was short to that degree as you could hear him two rooms off."

"Sophy!" said Mrs Glegg, with indignant disgust, "you *do* talk o' people's complaints till it's quite undecent. But I say again, as I said before, I didn't come away from home to talk about acquaintance, whether they'd short breath or long. If we aren't come together for one to hear what the other 'ull do to save a sister and her children from the parish, *I* shall go back. *One* can't act without the other, I suppose; it isn't to be expected as *I* should do everything."

"Well, Jane," said Mrs Pullet, "I don't see as you've been so very forrard at doing. So far as I know, this is the first time as here you've been, since it's been known as the bailiff's in the house; and I was here yesterday, and looked at all Bessy's linen and things, and I told her I'd buy in the spotted table-cloths. I couldn't speak fairer; for as for the teapot as she doesn't want to go out o' the family, it stands to sense I can't do with two silver teapots, not if it *hadn't* a straight spout—but the spotted damask I was allays fond on."

"I wish it could be managed so as my teapot and chany and the best castors needn't be put up for sale," said poor Mrs Tulliver, beseechingly, "and the sugar-tongs, the first things ever I bought."

"But that can't be helped, you know," said Mr Glegg. "If one o' the family chooses to buy 'em in, they can, but one thing must be bid for as well as another."

"And it isn't to be looked for," said uncle Pullet, with unwonted independence of idea, "as your own family should pay more for things nor they'll fetch. They may go for an old song by auction."

"O dear, O dear," said Mrs Tulliver, "to think o' my chany being sold i' that way—and I bought it when I was married, just as you did yours, Jane and Sophy: and I know you didn't like mine, because o' the sprig, but I was fond of it; and there's never been a bit broke, for I've washed it myself—and there's the tulips on the cups, and the roses, as anybody might go and look at 'em for pleasure. You wouldn't like *your* chany to go for an old song and be broke to pieces, though yours has got no colour in it, Jane—it's all white and flutted, and didn't cost so much as mine. And there's the castors—sister Deane, I can't think but you'd like to have the castors, for I've heard you say they're pretty."

"Well, I've no objection to buy some of the best things," said Mrs Deane, rather loftily; "we can do with extra things in our house."

"Best things!" exclaimed Mrs Glegg with severity, which had gathered intensity from her long silence. "It drives me past patience to hear you all talking o' best things, and buying in this, that, and the other, such as silver and chany. You must bring your mind to your circumstances,

Bessy, and not be thinking o' silver and chany; but whether you shall get so much as a flock bed to lie on, and a blanket to cover you, and a stool to sit on. You must remember, if you get 'em, it'll be because your friends have bought 'em for you, for you're dependent upon *them* for everything; for your husband lies there helpless, and hasn't got a penny i' the world to call his own. And it's for your own good I say this, for it's right you should feel what your state is, and what disgrace your husband's brought on your own family, as you've got to look to for everything—and be humble in your mind."

Mrs Glegg paused, for speaking with much energy for the good of others is naturally exhausting. Mrs Tulliver, always borne down by the family predominance of sister Jane, who had made her wear the yoke of a younger sister in very tender years, said pleadingly—

"I'm sure, sister, I've never asked anybody to do anything, only buy things as it 'ud be a pleasure to 'em to have, so as they mightn't go and be spoiled i' strange houses. I never asked anybody to buy the things in for me and my children; though there's the linen I spun, and I thought when Tom was born—I thought one o' the first things when he was lying i' the cradle, as all the things I'd bought wi' my own money, and been so careful of, 'ud go to him. But I've said nothing as I wanted my sisters to pay their money for me. What my husband has done for *his* sister's unknown, and we should ha' been better off this day if it hadn't been as he's lent money and never asked for it again."

"Come, come," said Mr Glegg, kindly, "don't let us make things too dark. What's done can't be undone. We shall make a shift among us to buy what's sufficient for you; though, as Mrs G. says, they must be useful, plain things. We mustn't be thinking o' what's unnecessary. A table, and a chair or two, and kitchen things, and a good bed, and suchlike. Why, I've seen the day when I shouldn't ha' known myself if I'd lain on sacking i'stead o' the floor. We get a deal o' useless things about us, only because we've got the money to spend."

"Mr Glegg," said Mrs G., "if you'll be kind enough to let me speak, i'stead o' taking the words out o' my mouth—I was going to say, Bessy, as it's fine talking for you to say as you've never asked us to buy anything for you; let me tell you, you *ought* to have asked us. Pray, how are you to be purvided for, if your own family don't help you? You must go to the parish, if they didn't. And you ought to know that, and keep it in mind, and ask us humble to do what we can for you, i'stead o' saying, and making a boast, as you've never asked us for anything."

"You talked o' the Mosses, and what Mr Tulliver's done for 'em," said uncle Pullet, who became unusually suggestive where advances of money were concerned. "Haven't *they* been anear you? They ought to do something, as well as other folks; and if he's lent 'em money, they ought to be made to pay it back."

"Yes, to be sure," said Mrs Deane; "I've been thinking so. How is it

Mr and Mrs Moss aren't here to meet us? It is but right they should do their share."

"O dear!" said Mrs Tulliver, "I never sent 'em word about Mr Tulliver, and they live so back'ard among the lanes at Basset, they niver hear anything only when Mr Moss comes to market. But I niver gave 'em a thought. I wonder Maggie didn't, though, for she was allays so fond of her aunt Moss."

"Why don't your children come in, Bessy?" said Mrs Pullet, at the mention of Maggie. "They should hear what their aunts and uncles have got to say: and Maggie—when it's me as have paid for half her schooling, she ought to think more of her aunt Pullet than of aunt Mosses. I may go off sudden when I get home to-day—there's no telling."

"If I'd had *my* way," said Mrs Glegg, "the children 'ud ha' been in the room from the first. It's time they knew who they've to look to, and it's right as *somebody* should talk to 'em, and let 'em know their condition i' life, and what they're come down to, and make 'em feel as they've got to suffer for their father's faults."

"Well, I'll go and fetch 'em, sister," said Mrs Tulliver, resignedly. She was quite crushed now, and thought of the treasures in the store-room with no other feeling than blank despair.

She went up-stairs to fetch Tom and Maggie, who were both in their father's room, and was on her way down again, when the sight of the store-room door suggested a new thought to her. She went towards it, and left the children to go down by themselves.

The aunts and uncles appeared to have been in warm discussion when the brother and sister entered—both with shrinking reluctance; for though Tom, with a practical sagacity which had been roused into activity by the strong stimulus of the new emotions he had undergone since yesterday, had been turning over in his mind a plan which he meant to propose to one of his aunts or uncles, he felt by no means amicably towards them, and dreaded meeting them all at once as he would have dreaded a large dose of concentrated physic, which was but just endurable in small draughts. As for Maggie, she was peculiarly depressed this morning: she had been called up, after brief rest, at three o'clock, and had that strange dreamy weariness which comes from watching in a sick-room through the chill hours of early twilight and breaking day—in which the outside daylight life seems to have no importance, and to be a mere margin to the hours in the darkened chamber. Their entrance interrupted the conversation. The shaking of hands was a melancholy and silent ceremony, till uncle Pullet observed, as Tom approached him—

"Well, young sir, we've been talking as we should want your pen and ink; you can write rarely now, after all your schooling, I should think."

"Ay, ay," said uncle Glegg, with admonition which he meant to be kind, "we must look to see the good of all this schooling, as your father's sunk so much money in, now—

"When land is gone and money's spent,
Then learning is most excellent.'

Now's the time, Tom, to let us see the good o' your learning. Let us see whether you can do better than I can, as have made my fortin without it. But I began wi' doing with little, you see: I could live on a basin o' porridge and a crust o' bread-and-cheese. But I doubt high living and high learning 'ull make it harder for you, young man, nor it was for me."

"But he must do it," interposed aunt Glegg, energetically, "whether it's hard or no. He hasn't got to consider what's hard; he must consider as he isn't to trusten to his friends to keep him in idleness and luxury: he's got to bear the fruits of his father's misconduct, and bring his mind to fare hard and to work hard. And he must be humble and grateful to his aunts and uncles for what they're doing for his mother and father, as must be turned out into the streets and go to the workhouse if they didn't help 'em. And his sister, too," continued Mrs Glegg, looking severely at Maggie, who had sat down on the sofa by her aunt Deane, drawn to her by the sense that she was Lucy's mother, "she must make up her mind to be humble and work; for there'll be no servants to wait on her any more—she must remember that. She must do the work o' the house, and she must respect and love her aunts as have done so much for her, and saved their money to leave to their nepheys and nieces."

Tom was still standing before the table in the centre of the group. There was a heightened colour in his face, and he was very far from looking humbled, but he was preparing to say, in a respectful tone, something he had previously meditated, when the door opened and his mother re-entered.

Poor Mrs Tulliver had in her hands a small tray, on which she had placed her silver teapot, a specimen teacup and saucer, the castors, and sugar-tongs.

"See here, sister," she said, looking at Mrs Deane, as she set the tray on the table, "I thought, perhaps, if you looked at the teapot again— it's a good while since you saw it—you might like the pattern better: it makes beautiful tea, and there's a stand and everything: you might use it for every day, or else lay it by for Lucy when she goes to housekeeping. I should be so loth for 'em to buy it at the Golden Lion," said the poor woman, her heart swelling, and the tears coming, "my teapot as I bought when I was married, and to think of its being scratched, and set before the travellers and folks, and my letters on it—see here, E. D.—and everybody to see 'em."

"Ah, dear, dear!" said aunt Pullet, shaking her head with deep sadness, "it's very bad—to think o' the family initials going about everywhere—it niver was so before: you're a very unlucky sister, Bessy. But what's the use o' buying the teapot, when there's the linen and spoons and everything to go, and some of 'em with your full name—and when it's got that straight spout, too."

"As to disgrace o' the family," said Mrs Glegg, "that can't be helped wi' buying teapots. The disgrace is, for one o' the family to ha' married a man as has brought her to beggary. The disgrace is, as they're to be sold up. We can't hinder the country from knowing that."

Maggie had started up from the sofa at the allusion to her father, but Tom saw her action and flushed face in time to prevent her from speaking. "Be quiet, Maggie," he said, authoritatively, pushing her aside. It was a remarkable manifestation of self-command and practical judgment in a lad of fifteen, that when his aunt Glegg ceased, he began to speak in a quiet and respectful manner, though with a good deal of trembling in his voice; for his mother's words had cut him to the quick.

"Then, aunt," he said, looking straight at Mrs Glegg, "if you think it's a disgrace to the family that we should be sold up, wouldn't it be better to prevent it altogether? And if you and my aunt Pullet," he continued, looking at the latter, "think of leaving any money to me and Maggie, wouldn't it be better to give it now, and pay the debt we're going to be sold up for, and save my mother from parting with her furniture?"

There was silence for a few moments, for every one, including Maggie, was astonished at Tom's sudden manliness of tone. Uncle Glegg was the first to speak.

"Ay, ay, young man—come now! You show some notion o' things. But there's the interest, you must remember; your aunts get five per cent on their money, and they'd lose that if they advanced it—you haven't thought o' that."

"I could work and pay that every year," said Tom, promptly. "I'd do anything to save my mother from parting with her things."

"Well done!" said uncle Glegg, admiringly. He had been drawing Tom out, rather than reflecting on the practicability of his proposal. But he had produced the unfortunate result of irritating his wife.

"Yes, Mr Glegg!" said that lady, with angry sarcasm. "It's pleasant work for you to be giving my money away, as you've pretended to leave at my own disposial. And my money, as was my own father's gift, and not yours, Mr Glegg; and I've saved it, and added to it myself, and had more to put out almost every year, and it's to go and be sunk in other folks' furniture, and encourage 'em in luxury and extravagance as they've no means of supporting; and I'm to alter my will, or have a codicil made, and leave two or three hundred less behind me when I die—me as have allays done right and been careful, and the eldest o' the family; and my money's to go and be squandered on them as have had the same chance as me, only they've been wicked and wasteful. Sister Pullet, *you* may do as you like, and you may let your husband rob you back again o' the money he's given you, but that isn't *my* sperrit."

"La, Jane, how fiery you are!" said Mrs Pullet. "I'm sure you'll have the blood in your head, and have to be cupped.[3] I'm sorry for Bessy and her children—I'm sure I think of 'em o' nights dreadful, for I sleep very bad wi' this new medicine: but it's no use for me to think o' doing anything, if you won't meet me half-way."

"Why, there's this to be considered," said Mr Glegg. "It's no use to pay off this debt and save the furniture, when there's all the law debts behind, as 'ud take every shilling, and more than could be made out o' land and stock, for I've made that out from Lawyer Gore. We'd need save our money to keep the poor man with, instead o' spending it on furniture as he can neither eat nor drink. You *will* be so hasty, Jane, as if I didn't know what was reasonable."

"Then speak accordingly, Mr Glegg!" said his wife, with slow, loud emphasis, bending her head towards him significantly.

Tom's countenance had fallen during this conversation, and his lip quivered; but he was determined not to give way. He would behave like a man. Maggie, on the contrary, after her momentary delight in Tom's speech, had relapsed into her state of trembling indignation. Her mother had been standing close by Tom's side, and had been clinging to his arm ever since he had last spoken: Maggie suddenly started up and stood in front of them, her eyes flashing like the eyes of a young lioness.

"Why do you come, then," she burst out, "talking and interfering with us and scolding us, if you don't mean to do anything to help my poor mother—your own sister—if you've no feeling for her when she's in trouble, and won't part with anything, though you would never miss it, to save her from pain? Keep away from us then, and don't come to find fault with my father—he was better than any of you—he was kind—he would have helped *you*, if you had been in trouble. Tom and I don't ever want to have any of your money, if you won't help my mother. We'd rather not have it! we'll do without you."

Maggie, having hurled her defiance at aunts and uncles in this way, stood still, with her large dark eyes glaring at them, as if she were ready to await all consequences.

Mrs Tulliver was frightened; there was something portentous in this mad outbreak; she did not see how life could go on after it. Tom was vexed; it was no *use* to talk so. The aunts were silent with surprise for some moments. At length, in a case of aberration such as this, comment presented itself as more expedient than any answer.

"You haven't seen the end o' your trouble wi' that child, Bessy," said Mrs Pullet; "she's beyond everything for boldness and unthankfulness.

3. Have blood drawn.

It's dreadful. I might ha' let alone paying for her schooling, for she's worse nor ever."

"It's no more than what I've allays said," followed Mrs Glegg. "Other folks may be surprised, but I'm not. I've said over and over again—years ago I've said—'Mark my words; that child 'ull come to no good: there isn't a bit of our family in her.' And as for her having so much schooling, I never thought well o' that. I'd my reasons when I said *I* wouldn't pay anything towards it."

"Come, come," said Mr Glegg, "let's waste no more time in talking—let's go to business. Tom now, get the pen and ink——"

While Mr Glegg was speaking, a tall dark figure was seen hurrying past the window.

"Why, there's Mrs Moss," said Mrs Tulliver. "The bad news must ha' reached her, then;" and she went out to open the door, Maggie eagerly following her.

"That's fortunate," said Mrs Glegg. "She can agree to the list o' things to be bought in. It's but right she should do her share when it's her own brother."

Mrs Moss was in too much agitation to resist Mrs Tulliver's movement, as she drew her into the parlour, automatically, without reflecting that it was hardly kind to take her among so many persons in the first painful moment of arrival. The tall, worn, dark-haired woman was a strong contrast to the Dodson sisters as she entered in her shabby dress, with her shawl and bonnet looking as if they had been hastily huddled on, and with that entire absence of self-consciousness which belongs to keenly-felt trouble. Maggie was clinging to her arm; and Mrs Moss seemed to notice no one else except Tom, whom she went straight up to and took by the hand.

"O my dear children," she burst out, "you've no call to think well o' me; I'm a poor aunt to you, for I'm one o' them as take all and give nothing. How's my poor brother?"

"Mr Turnbull thinks he'll get better," said Maggie. "Sit down, aunt Gritty. Don't fret."

"O my sweet child, I feel torn i' two," said Mrs Moss, allowing Maggie to lead her to the sofa, but still not seeming to notice the presence of the rest. "We've three hundred pounds o' my brother's money, and now he wants it, and you all want it, poor things!—and yet we must be sold up to pay it, and there's my poor children—eight of 'em, and the little un of all can't speak plain. And I feel as if I was a robber. But I'm sure I'd no thought as my brother. . . ."

The poor woman was interrupted by a rising sob.

"Three hundred pounds! O dear, dear," said Mrs Tulliver, who, when she had said that her husband had done "unknown" things for his sister, had not had any particular sum in her mind, and felt a wife's irritation at having been kept in the dark.

"What madness, to be sure!" said Mrs Glegg. "A man with a family! He'd no right to lend his money i' that way; and without security, I'll be bound, if the truth was known."

Mrs Glegg's voice had arrested Mrs Moss's attention, and, looking up, she said—

"Yes, there *was* security: my husband gave a note for it. We're not that sort o' people, neither of us, as 'ud rob my brother's children; and we looked to paying back the money, when the times got a bit better."

"Well, but now," said Mr Glegg, gently, "hasn't your husband no way o' raising this money? Because it 'ud be a little fortin, like, for these folks, if we can do without Tulliver's being made a bankrupt. Your husband's got stock: it is but right he should raise the money, as it seems to me—not but what I'm sorry for you, Mrs Moss."

"O sir, you don't know what bad luck my husband's had with his stock. The farm's suffering so as never was for want o' stock; and we've sold all the wheat, and we're behind with our rent . . . not but what we'd like to do what's right, and I'd sit up and work half the night, if it 'ud be any good . . . but there's them poor children . . . four of 'em such little uns. . . ."

"Don't cry so, aunt—don't fret," whispered Maggie, who had kept hold of Mrs Moss's hand.

"Did Mr Tulliver let you have the money all at once?" said Mrs Tulliver, still lost in the conception of things which had been "going on" without her knowledge.

"No; at twice," said Mrs Moss, rubbing her eyes and making an effort to restrain her tears. "The last was after my bad illness, four years ago, as everything went wrong, and there was a new note made then. What with illness and bad luck, I've been nothing but cumber[4] all my life."

"Yes, Mrs Moss," said Mrs Glegg, with decision. "Yours is a very unlucky family; the more's the pity for *my* sister."

"I set off in the cart as soon as ever I heard o' what had happened," said Mrs Moss, looking at Mrs Tulliver. "I should never ha' stayed away all this while, if you'd thought well to let me know. And it isn't as I'm thinking all about ourselves, and nothing about my brother—only the money was so on my mind, I couldn't help speaking about it. And my husband and me desire to do the right thing, sir," she added, looking at Mr Glegg, "and we'll make shift and pay the money, come what will, if that's all my brother's got to trust to. We've been used to trouble, and don't look for much else. It's only the thought o' my poor children pulls me i' two."

"Why, there's this to be thought on, Mrs Moss," said Mr Glegg, "and it's right to warn you;—if Tulliver's made a bankrupt, and he's got a

4. A burden, an encumbrance.

note-of-hand of your husband's for three hundred pounds, you'll be obliged to pay it: th' assignees 'ull come on you for it."

"O dear, O dear!" said Mrs Tulliver, thinking of the bankruptcy, and not of Mrs Moss's concern in it. Poor Mrs Moss herself listened in trembling submission, while Maggie looked with bewildered distress at Tom to see if *he* showed any signs of understanding this trouble, and caring about poor aunt Moss. Tom was only looking thoughtful, with his eyes on the table-cloth.

"And if he isn't made bankrupt," continued Mr Glegg, "as I said before, three hundred pounds 'ud be a little fortin for him, poor man. We don't know but what he may be partly helpless, if he ever gets up again. I'm very sorry if it goes hard with you, Mrs Moss—but my opinion is, looking at it one way, it'll be right for you to raise the money; and looking at it th' other way, you'll be obliged to pay it. You won't think ill o' me for speaking the truth."

"Uncle," said Tom, looking up suddenly from his meditative view of the table-cloth, "I don't think it would be right for my aunt Moss to pay the money, if it would be against my father's will for her to pay it; would it?"

Mr Glegg looked surprised for a moment or two before he said, "Why, no, perhaps not, Tom; but then he'd ha' destroyed the note, you know. We must look for the note. What makes you think it 'ud be against his will?"

"Why," said Tom, colouring, but trying to speak firmly, in spite of a boyish tremor, "I remember quite well, before I went to school to Mr Stelling, my father said to me one night, when we were sitting by the fire together, and no one else was in the room . . ."

Tom hesitated a little, and then went on.

"He said something to me about Maggie, and then he said, 'I've always been good to my sister, though she married against my will—and I've lent Moss money; but I shall never think of distressing him to pay it: I'd rather lose it. My children must not mind being the poorer for that.' And now my father's ill, and not able to speak for himself, I shouldn't like anything to be done contrary to what he said to me."

"Well, but then, my boy," said uncle Glegg, whose good feeling led him to enter into Tom's wish, but who could not at once shake off his habitual abhorrence of such recklessness as destroying securities, or alienating anything important enough to make an appreciable difference in a man's property, "we should have to make away wi' the note, you know, if we're to guard against what may happen, supposing your father's made bankrupt. . . ."

"Mr Glegg," interrupted his wife, severely, "mind what you're saying. You're putting yourself very forrard in other folks's business. If you speak rash, don't say it was my fault."

"That's such a thing as I never heared of before," said uncle Pullet, who had been making haste with his lozenge in order to express his amazement; "making away with a note! I should think anybody could set the constable on you for it."

"Well, but," said Mrs Tulliver, "if the note's worth all that money, why can't we pay it away, and save my things from going away? We've no call to meddle with your uncle and aunt Moss, Tom, if you think your father 'ud be angry when he gets well."

Mrs Tulliver had not studied the question of exchange, and was straining her mind after original ideas on the subject.

"Pooh, pooh, pooh! you women don't understand these things," said uncle Glegg. "There's no way o' making it safe for Mr and Mrs Moss but destroying the note."

"Then I hope you'll help me to do it, uncle," said Tom, earnestly. "If my father shouldn't get well, I should be very unhappy to think anything had been done against his will, that I could hinder. And I'm sure he meant me to remember what he said that evening. I ought to obey my father's wish about his property."

Even Mrs Glegg could not withhold her approval from Tom's words: she felt that the Dodson blood was certainly speaking in him, though, if his father had been a Dodson, there would never have been this wicked alienation of money. Maggie would hardly have restrained herself from leaping on Tom's neck, if her aunt Moss had not prevented her by herself rising and taking Tom's hand, while she said, with rather a choked voice—

"You'll never be the poorer for this, my dear boy, if there's a God above; and if the money's wanted for your father, Moss and me 'ull pay it, the same as if there was ever such security. We'll do as we'd be done by; for if my children have got no other luck, they've got an honest father and mother."

"Well," said Mr Glegg, who had been meditating after Tom's words, "we shouldn't be doing any wrong by the creditors, supposing your father *was* bankrupt. I've been thinking o' that, for I've been a creditor myself, and seen no end o' cheating. If he meant to give your aunt the money before ever he got into this sad work o' lawing, it's the same as if he'd made away with the note himself; for he'd made up his mind to be that much poorer. But there's a deal o' things to be considered, young man," Mr Glegg added, looking admonishingly at Tom, "when you come to money business, and you may be taking one man's dinner away to make another man's breakfast. You don't understand that, I doubt?"

"Yes, I do," said Tom, decidedly. "I know if I owe money to one man, I've no right to give it to another. But if my father had made up his mind to give my aunt the money before he was in debt, he had a right to do it."

"Well done, young man! I didn't think you'd been so sharp," said uncle Glegg, with much candour. "But perhaps your father *did* make away with the note. Let us go and see if we can find it in the chest."

"It's in my father's room. Let us go too, aunt Gritty," whispered Maggie.

Chapter IV

A Vanishing Gleam

Mr Tulliver, even between the fits of spasmodic rigidity which had recurred at intervals ever since he had been found fallen from his horse, was usually in so apathetic a condition that the exits and entrances into his room were not felt to be of great importance. He had lain so still, with his eyes closed, all this morning, that Maggie told her aunt Moss she must not expect her father to take any notice of them.

They entered very quietly, and Mrs Moss took her seat near the head of the bed, while Maggie sat in her old place on the bed, and put her hand on her father's, without causing any change in his face.

Mr Glegg and Tom had also entered, treading softly, and were busy selecting the key of the old oak chest from the bunch which Tom had brought from his father's bureau. They succeeded in opening the chest—which stood opposite the foot of Mr Tulliver's bed—and propping the lid with the iron holder, without much noise.

"There's a tin box," whispered Mr Glegg; "he'd most like put a small thing like a note in there. Lift it out, Tom; but I'll just lift up these deeds—they're the deeds o' the house and mill, I suppose—and see what there is under 'em."

Mr Glegg had lifted out the parchments, and had fortunately drawn back a little when the iron holder gave way, and the heavy lid fell with a loud bang, that resounded over the house.

Perhaps there was something in that sound more than the mere fact of the strong vibration that produced the instantaneous effects on the frame of the prostrate man, and for the time completely shook off the obstruction of paralysis. The chest had belonged to his father and his father's father, and it had always been rather a solemn business to visit it. All long-known objects, even a mere window fastening or a particular door-latch, have sounds which are a sort of recognised voice to us—a voice that will thrill and awaken, when it has been used to touch deep-lying fibres. In the same moment when all the eyes in the room were turned upon him, he started up and looked at the chest, the parchments in Mr Glegg's hand, and Tom holding the tin box, with a glance of perfect consciousness and recognition.

"What are you going to do with those deeds?" he said, in his ordinary tone of sharp questioning whenever he was irritated. "Come here, Tom. What do you do, going to my chest?"

Tom obeyed, with some trembling: it was the first time his father had recognised him. But instead of saying anything more to him, his father continued to look with a growing distinctness of suspicion at Mr Glegg and the deeds.

"What's been happening, then?" he said, sharply. "What are you meddling with my deeds for? Is Wakem laying hold of everything? . . . Why don't you tell me what you've been a-doing?" he added, impatiently, as Mr Glegg advanced to the foot of the bed before speaking.

"No, no, friend Tulliver," said Mr Glegg, in a soothing tone. "Nobody's getting hold of anything as yet. We only came to look and see what was in the chest. You've been ill, you know, and we've had to look after things a bit. But let's hope you'll soon be well enough to attend to everything yourself."

Mr Tulliver looked round him meditatively—at Tom, at Mr Glegg, and at Maggie; then suddenly appearing aware that some one was seated by his side at the head of the bed, he turned sharply round and saw his sister.

"Eh, Gritty!" he said, in the half-sad, affectionate tone in which he had been wont to speak to her. "What! you're there, are you? How could you manage to leave the children?"

"O, brother!" said good Mrs Moss, too impulsive to be prudent, "I'm thankful I'm come now to see you yourself again—I thought you'd never know us any more."

"What! have I had a stroke?" said Mr Tulliver, anxiously, looking at Mr Glegg.

"A fall from your horse—shook you a bit—that's all, I think," said Mr Glegg. "But you'll soon get over it, let's hope."

Mr Tulliver fixed his eyes on the bed-clothes, and remained silent for two or three minutes. A new shadow came over his face. He looked up at Maggie first, and said in a lower tone, "You got the letter, then, my wench?"

"Yes, father," she said, kissing him with a full heart. She felt as if her father were come back to her from the dead, and her yearning to show him how she had always loved him could be fulfilled.

"Where's your mother?" he said, so preoccupied that he received the kiss as passively as some quiet animal might have received it.

"She's down-stairs with my aunts, father: shall I fetch her?"

"Ay, ay: poor Bessy!" and his eyes turned towards Tom as Maggie left the room.

"You'll have to take care of 'em both if I die, you know, Tom. You'll be badly off, I doubt. But you must see and pay everybody. And mind—there's fifty pound o' Luke's as I put into the business—he gave it me a bit at a time, and he's got nothing to show for it. You must pay him first thing."

Uncle Glegg involuntarily shook his head, and looked more concerned than ever, but Tom said firmly—

"Yes, father. And haven't you a note from my uncle Moss for three hundred pounds? We came to look for that. What do you wish to be done about it, father?"

"Ah! I'm glad you thought o' that my lad," said Mr Tulliver. "I allays meant to be easy about that money, because o' your aunt. You mustn't mind losing the money, if they can't pay it—and it's like enough they can't. The note's in that box, mind! I allays meant to be good to you, Gritty," said Mr Tulliver, turning to his sister; "but, you know, you aggravated me when you would have Moss."

At this moment Maggie re-entered with her mother, who came in much agitated by the news that her husband was quite himself again.

"Well, Bessy," he said, as she kissed him, "you must forgive me if you're worse off than you ever expected to be. But it's the fault o' the law—it's none o' mine," he added, angrily. "It's the fault o' raskills! Tom—you mind this: if ever you've got the chance, you make Wakem smart. If you don't, you're a good-for-nothing son. You might horsewhip him—but he'd set the law on you—the law's made to take care o' raskills."

Mr Tulliver was getting excited, and an alarming flush was on his face. Mr Glegg wanted to say something soothing, but he was prevented by Mr Tulliver's speaking again to his wife. "They'll make a shift to pay everything, Bessy," he said, "and yet leave you your furniture; and your sisters 'll do something for you . . . and Tom 'll grow up . . . though what he's to be I don't know . . . I've done what I could . . . I've given him a eddication . . . and there's the little wench, she'll get married . . . but it's a poor tale. . . ."

The sanative effect of the strong vibration was exhausted, and with the last words the poor man fell again, rigid and insensible. Though this was only a recurrence of what had happened before, it struck all present as if it had been death, not only from its contrast with the completeness of the revival, but because his words had all had reference to the possibility that his death was near. But with poor Tulliver death was not to be a leap: it was to be a long descent under thickening shadows.

Mr Turnbull was sent for; but when he heard what had passed, he said this complete restoration, though only temporary, was a hopeful sign, proving that there was no permanent lesion to prevent ultimate recovery.

Among the threads of the past which the stricken man had gathered up, he had omitted the bill of sale; the flash of memory had only lit up prominent ideas, and he sank into forgetfulness again with half his humiliation unlearned.

But Tom was clear upon two points—that his uncle Moss's note must be destroyed, and that Luke's money must be paid, if in no other way, out of his own and Maggie's money now in the savings bank. There were subjects, you perceive, on which Tom was much quicker than on the niceties of classical construction, or the relations of a mathematical demonstration.

Chapter V

Tom Applies His Knife to the Oyster

The next day, at ten o'clock, Tom was on his way to St Ogg's, to see his uncle Deane, who was to come home last night, his aunt had said; and Tom had made up his mind that his uncle Deane was the right person to ask for advice about getting some employment. He was in a great way of business; he had not the narrow notions of uncle Glegg; and he had risen in the world on a scale of advancement which accorded with Tom's ambition.

It was a dark, chill, misty morning, likely to end in rain—one of those mornings when even happy people take refuge in their hopes. And Tom was very unhappy: he felt the humiliation as well as the prospective hardships of his lot with all the keenness of a proud nature; and with all his resolute dutifulness towards his father there mingled an irrepressible indignation against him which gave misfortune the less endurable aspect of a wrong. Since these were the consequences of going to law, his father was really blamable, as his aunts and uncles had always said he was; and it was a significant indication of Tom's character, that though he thought his aunts ought to do something more for his mother, he felt nothing like Maggie's violent resentment against them for showing no eager tenderness and generosity. There were no impulses in Tom that led him to expect what did not present itself to him as a right to be demanded. Why should people give away their money plentifully to those who had not taken care of their own money? Tom saw some justice in severity; and all the more, because he had confidence in himself that he should never deserve that just severity. It was very hard upon him that he should be put at this disadvantage in life by his father's want of prudence; but he was not going to complain and to find fault with people because they did not make everything easy for him. He would ask no one to help him, more than to give him work and pay him for it. Poor Tom was not without his hopes to take refuge in under the chill damp imprisonment of the December fog which seemed only like a part of his home troubles. At sixteen, the mind that has the strongest affinity for fact cannot escape illusion and self-flattery; and Tom, in sketching his future, had no other guide in arranging his facts than the suggestions of his own brave self-reliance. Both Mr Glegg and Mr Deane, he knew, had been very poor once: he did not want to save money slowly and retire on a moderate fortune like his uncle Glegg, but he would be like his uncle Deane—get a situation in some great house of business and rise fast. He had scarcely seen anything of his uncle Deane for the last three years—the two families had been getting wider apart; but for this very reason Tom was the more hopeful about applying to him. His uncle Glegg, he felt sure, would never encourage any spirited project, but he had a vague imposing idea of the resources at his uncle Deane's command. He had heard his father say, long ago, how Deane had made himself so valuable to Guest & Co. that they were glad enough to offer him a share in the business: that was what Tom resolved *he* would do. It was intolerable to think of being poor and looked down upon all one's life. He would provide for his mother and sister, and make every one say that he was a man of high character. He leaped over the years in this way, and in the haste of strong purpose and strong desire, did not see how they would be made up of slow days, hours, and minutes.

By the time he had crossed the stone bridge over the Floss and was entering St Ogg's, he was thinking that he would buy his father's mill and land again when he was rich enough, and improve the house and live there: he should prefer it to any smarter, newer place, and he could keep as many horses and dogs as he liked.

Walking along the street with a firm, rapid step, at this point in his reverie he was startled by some one who had crossed without his notice, and who said to him in a rough, familiar voice—

"Why, Master Tom, how's your father this morning?" It was a publican of St Ogg's—one of his father's customers.

Tom disliked being spoken to just then; but he said civilly, "He's still very ill, thank you."

"Ay, it's been a sore chance for you, young man, hasn't it?—this lawsuit turning out against him," said the publican, with a confused beery idea of being good-natured.

Tom reddened and passed on: he would have felt it like the handling of a bruise, even if there had been the most polite and delicate reference to his position.

"That's Tulliver's son," said the publican to a grocer standing on the adjacent door-step.

"Ah!" said the grocer, "I thought I knew his features. He takes after his mother's family: she was a Dodson. He's a fine, straight youth: what's he been brought up to?"

"Oh! to turn up his nose at his father's customers, and be a fine gentleman—not much else, I think."

Tom, roused from his dream of the future to a thorough consciousness of the present, made all the greater haste to reach the warehouse offices of Guest & Co., where he expected to find his uncle Deane. But this was Mr Deane's morning at the bank, a clerk told him, with some contempt for his ignorance: Mr Deane was not to be found in River Street on a Thursday morning.

At the bank Tom was admitted into the private room where his uncle was, immediately after sending in his name. Mr Deane was auditing accounts; but he looked up as Tom entered, and, putting out his hand, said, "Well, Tom, nothing fresh the matter at home, I hope? How's your father?"

"Much the same, thank you, uncle," said Tom, feeling nervous. "But I want to speak to you, please, when you're at liberty."

"Sit down, sit down," said Mr Deane, relapsing into his accounts, in which he and the managing-clerk remained so absorbed for the next half-hour that Tom began to wonder whether he should have to sit in this way till the bank closed—there seemed so little tendency towards a conclusion in the quiet monotonous procedure of these sleek, prosperous men of business. Would his uncle give him a place in the bank? it would be very dull, prosy work, he thought, writing there for ever to the loud ticking of a time-piece. He preferred some other way of getting rich. But at last there was a change: his uncle took a pen and wrote something with a flourish at the end.

"You'll just step up to Torry's now, Mr Spence, will you?" said Mr Deane, and the clock suddenly became less loud and deliberate in Tom's ears.

"Well, Tom," said Mr Deane, when they were alone, turning his substantial person a little in his chair, and taking out his snuff-box, "what's the business, my boy—what's the business?" Mr Deane, who had heard from his wife what had passed the day before, thought Tom was come to appeal to him for some means of averting the sale.

"I hope you'll excuse me for troubling you, uncle," said Tom, colouring, but speaking in a tone which, though tremulous, had a certain proud independence in it; "but I thought you were the best person to advise me what to do."

"Ah!" said Mr Deane, reserving his pinch of snuff, and looking at Tom with new attention, "let us hear."

"I want to get a situation, uncle, so that I may earn some money," said Tom, who never fell into circumlocution.

"A situation?" said Mr Deane, and then took his pinch of snuff with elaborate justice to each nostril. Tom thought snuff-taking a most provoking habit.

"Why, let me see, how old are you?" said Mr Deane, as he threw himself backward again.

"Sixteen—I mean, I am going in seventeen," said Tom, hoping his uncle noticed how much beard he had.

"Let me see—your father had some notion of making you an engineer, I think?"

"But I don't think I could get any money at that for a long while, could I?"

"That's true; but people don't get much money at anything, my boy, when they're only sixteen. You've had a good deal of schooling, however: I suppose you're pretty well up in accounts eh? You understand book-keeping?"

"No," said Tom, rather falteringly. "I was in Practice. But Mr Stelling says I write a good hand, uncle. That's my writing," added Tom, laying on the table a copy of the list he had made yesterday.

"Ah! that's good, that's good. But, you see, the best hand in the world 'll not get you a better place than a copying-clerk's, if you know nothing of book-keeping—nothing of accounts. And a copying-clerk's a cheap article. But what have you been learning at school, then?"

Mr Deane had not occupied himself with methods of education, and had no precise conception of what went forward in expensive schools.

"We learned Latin," said Tom, pausing a little between each item, as if he were turning over the books in his school-desk to assist his memory—"a good deal of Latin; and the last year I did Themes, one week in Latin and one in English; and Greek and Roman History; and Euclid; and I began Algebra, but I left it off again; and we had one day every week for Arithmetic. Then I used to have drawing-lessons; and there were several other books we either read or learned out of, English Poetry, and Horæ Paulinæ, and Blair's Rhetoric,[1] the last half."

Mr Deane tapped his snuff-box again, and screwed up his mouth: he felt in the position of many estimable persons when they had read the New Tariff, and found how many commodities were imported of which they knew nothing: like a cautious man of business, he was not going to speak rashly of a raw material in which he had had no experience. But the presumption was, that if it had been good for anything, so successful a man as himself would hardly have been ignorant of it. About Latin he had an opinion, and thought that in case of another war, since people would no longer wear hair-powder, it would be well to put a tax upon Latin, as a luxury much run upon by the higher classes, and not telling at all on the ship-owning department. But, for what he knew, the Horæ Paulinæ might be something less neutral. On the whole, this list of acquirements gave him a sort of repulsion towards poor Tom.

"Well," he said, at last, in rather a cold, sardonic tone, "you've had three years at these things—you must be pretty strong in 'em. Hadn't you better take up some line where they'll come in handy?"

Tom coloured, and burst out, with new energy—

"I'd rather not have any employment of that sort, uncle. I don't like Latin and those things. I don't know what I could do with them unless

1. William Paley's *Horæ Paulinæ; or the Truth of the Scripture History of St. Paul* . . . (1790); Hugh Blair's *Lectures on Rhetoric and Belles Lettres* (1783).

I went as usher[2] in a school; and I don't know them well enough for that: besides, I would as soon carry a pair of panniers. I don't want to be that sort of person. I should like to enter into some business where I can get on—a manly business, where I should have to look after things, and get credit for what I did. And I shall want to keep my mother and sister."

"Ah, young gentleman," said Mr Deane, with that tendency to repress youthful hopes which stout and successful men of fifty find one of their easiest duties, "that's sooner said than done—sooner said than done."

"But didn't *you* get on in that way, uncle?" said Tom, a little irritated that Mr Deane did not enter more rapidly into his views. "I mean, didn't you rise from one place to another through your abilities and good conduct?"

"Ay, ay, sir," said Mr Deane, spreading himself in his chair a little, and entering with great readiness into a retrospect of his own career. "But I'll tell you how I got on. It wasn't by getting astride a stick, and thinking it would turn into a horse if I sat on it long enough. I kept my eyes and ears open, sir, and I wasn't too fond of my own back, and I made my master's interest my own. Why, with only looking into what went on in the mill, I found out how there was a waste of five hundred a-year that might be hindered. Why, sir, I hadn't more schooling to begin with than a charity boy; but I saw pretty soon that I couldn't get on far without mastering accounts, and I learned 'em between working hours, after I'd been unlading. Look here." Mr Deane opened a book, and pointed to the page. "I write a good hand enough, and I'll match anybody at all sorts of reckoning by the head, and I got it all by hard work, and paid for it out of my own earnings—often out of my own dinner and supper. And I looked into the nature of all the things we had to do with in the business, and picked up knowledge as I went about my work, and turned it over in my head. Why, I'm no mechanic—I never pretended to be—but I've thought of a thing or two that the mechanics never thought of, and it's made a fine difference in our returns. And there isn't an article shipped or unshipped at our wharf but I know the quality of it. If I got places, sir, it was because I made myself fit for 'em. If you want to slip into a round hole, you must make a ball of yourself—that's where it is."

Mr Deane tapped his box again. He had been led on by pure enthusiasm in his subject, and had really forgotten what bearing this retrospective survey had on his listener. He had found occasion for saying the same thing more than once before, and was not distinctly aware that he had not his port-wine before him.

"Well, uncle," said Tom, with a slight complaint in his tone, "that's what I should like to do. Can't *I* get on in the same way?"

2. Assistant teacher.

"In the same way?" said Mr Deane, eyeing Tom with quiet deliberation. "There go two or three questions to that, Master Tom. That depends on what sort of material you are, to begin with, and whether you've been put into the right mill. But I'll tell you what it is. Your poor father went the wrong way to work in giving you an education. It wasn't my business, and I didn't interfere: but it is as I thought it would be. You've had a sort of learning that's all very well for a young fellow like our Mr Stephen Guest, who'll have nothing to do but sign cheques all his life, and may as well have Latin inside his head as any other sort of stuffing."

"But, uncle," said Tom, earnestly, "I don't see why the Latin need hinder me from getting on in business. I shall soon forget it all: it makes no difference to me. I had to do my lessons at school; but I always thought they'd never be of any use to me afterwards—I didn't care about them."

"Ay, ay, that's all very well," said Mr Deane; "but it doesn't alter what I was going to say. Your Latin and rigmarole may soon dry off you, but you'll be but a bare stick after that. Besides, it's whitened your hands and taken the rough work out of you. And what do you know? Why, you know nothing about book-keeping, to begin with, and not so much of reckoning as a common shopman. You'll have to begin at a low round of the ladder, let me tell you, if you mean to get on in life. It's no use forgetting the education your father's been paying for, if you don't give yourself a new un."

Tom bit his lips hard; he felt as if the tears were rising, and he would rather die than let them.

"You want me to help you to a situation," Mr Deane went on; "well, I've no fault to find with that. I'm willing to do something for you. But you youngsters nowadays think you're to begin with living well and working easy: you've no notion of running afoot before you get on horseback. Now, you must remember what you are—you're a lad of sixteen, trained to nothing particular. There's heaps of your sort, like so many pebbles, made to fit in nowhere. Well, you might be apprenticed to some business—a chemist's[3] and druggist's perhaps: your Latin might come in a bit there. . . ."

Tom was going to speak, but Mr Deane put up his hand and said—

"Stop! hear what I've got to say. You don't want to be a 'prentice—I know, I know—you want to make more haste—and you don't want to stand behind a counter. But if you're a copying-clerk, you'll have to stand behind a desk, and stare at your ink and paper all day: there isn't much out-look there, and you won't be much wiser at the end of the year than at the beginning. The world isn't made of pen, ink, and paper,

3. Pharmacist's.

and if you're to get on in the world, young man, you must know what the world's made of. Now the best chance for you 'ud be to have a place on a wharf, or in a warehouse, where you'd learn the smell of things —but you wouldn't like that, I'll be bound; you'd have to stand cold and wet, and be shouldered about by rough fellows. You're too fine a gentleman for that."

Mr Deane paused and looked hard at Tom, who certainly felt some inward struggle before he could reply.

"I would rather do what will be best for me in the end, sir: I would put up with what was disagreeable."

"That's well, if you can carry it out. But you must remember it isn't only laying hold of a rope—you must go on pulling. It's the mistake you lads make that have got nothing either in your brains or your pocket, to think you've got a better start in the world if you stick yourselves in a place where you can keep your coats clean, and have the shop-wenches take you for fine gentlemen. That wasn't the way *I* started, young man: when I was sixteen, my jacket smelt of tar, and I wasn't afraid of handling cheeses. That's the reason I can wear good broadcloth now, and have my legs under the same table with the heads of the best firms in St Ogg's."

Uncle Deane tapped his box, and seemed to expand a little under his waistcoat and gold chain, as he squared his shoulders in the chair.

"Is there any place at liberty that you know of now, uncle, that I should do for? I should like to set to work at once," said Tom, with a slight tremor in his voice.

"Stop a bit, stop a bit; we mustn't be in too great a hurry. You must bear in mind, if I put you in a place you're a bit young for, because you happen to be my nephew, I shall be responsible for you. And there's no better reason, you know, than your being my nephew; because it remains to be seen whether you're good for anything."

"I hope I should never do you any discredit, uncle," said Tom, hurt, as all boys are at the statement of the unpleasant truth that people feel no ground for trusting them. "I care about my own credit too much for that."

"Well done, Tom, well done! That's the right spirit, and I never refuse to help anybody if they've a mind to do themselves justice. There's a young man of two-and-twenty I've got my eye on now. I shall do what I can for that young man—he's got some pith in him. But then, you see, he's made good use of his time—a first-rate calculator—can tell you the cubic contents of anything in no time, and put me up the other day to a new market for Swedish bark;[4] he's uncommonly knowing in manufactures, that young fellow."

4. Bark used in tanning.

"I'd better set about learning book-keeping, hadn't I, uncle?" said Tom, anxious to prove his readiness to exert himself.

"Yes, yes, you can't do amiss there. But . . . ah, Spence, you're back again. Well, Tom, there's nothing more to be said just now, I think, and I must go to business again. Good-bye. Remember me to your mother."

Mr Deane put out his hand, with an air of friendly dismissal, and Tom had not courage to ask another question, especially in the presence of Mr Spence. So he went out again into the cold damp air. He had to call at his uncle Glegg's about the money in the Savings Bank, and by the time he set out again, the mist had thickened, and he could not see very far before him; but going along River Street again, he was startled, when he was within two yards of the projecting side of a shop-window, by the words "Dorlcote Mill" in large letters on a hand-bill, placed as if on purpose to stare at him. It was the catalogue of the sale to take place the next week—it was a reason for hurrying faster out of the town.

Poor Tom formed no visions of the distant future as he made his way homeward; he only felt that the present was very hard. It seemed a wrong towards him that his uncle Deane had no confidence in him—did not see at once that he should acquit himself well, which Tom himself was as certain of as of the day-light. Apparently he, Tom Tulliver, was likely to be held of small account in the world, and for the first time he felt a sinking of heart under the sense that he really was very ignorant, and could do very little. Who was that enviable young man, that could tell the cubic contents of things in no time, and make suggestions about Swedish bark? Swedish bark! Tom had been used to be so entirely satisfied with himself in spite of his breaking down in a demonstration, and construing *nunc illas promite vires*,[5] as "now promise those men;" but now he suddenly felt at a disadvantage, because he knew less than some one else knew. There must be a world of things connected with that Swedish bark, which, if he only knew them, might have helped him to get on. It would have been much easier to make a figure with a spirited horse and a new saddle.

Two hours ago, as Tom was walking to St Ogg's, he saw the distant future before him, as he might have seen a tempting stretch of smooth sandy beach beyond a belt of flinty shingles; he was on the grassy bank then, and thought the shingles might soon be passed. But now his feet were on the sharp stones; the belt of shingles had widened, and the stretch of sand had dwindled into narrowness.

"What did my uncle Deane say, Tom?" said Maggie, putting her arm through Tom's as he was warming himself rather drearily by the kitchen fire. "Did he say he would give you a situation?"

"No he didn't say that. He didn't quite promise me anything; he

5. I.e., now put forth those powers (Virgil, *Æneid* 5.191).

seemed to think I couldn't have a very good situation. I'm too young."

"But didn't he speak kindly, Tom?"

"Kindly? Pooh! what's the use of talking about that? I wouldn't care about his speaking kindly, if I could get a situation. But it's such a nuisance and bother—I've been at school all this while learning Latin and things—not a bit of good to me—and now my uncle says, I must set about learning book-keeping and calculation, and those things. He seems to make out I'm good for nothing."

Tom's mouth twitched with a bitter expression as he looked at the fire.

"O what a pity we haven't got Dominie Sampson," said Maggie, who couldn't help mingling some gaiety with their sadness. "If he had taught me book-keeping by double entry and after the Italian method, as he did Lucy Bertram,[6] I could teach you, Tom."

"*You* teach! Yes, I daresay. That's always the tone you take," said Tom.

"Dear Tom! I was only joking," said Maggie, putting her cheek against his coat-sleeve.

"But it's always the same, Maggie," said Tom, with the little frown he put on when he was about to be justifiably severe. "You're always setting yourself up above me and every one else, and I've wanted to tell you about it several times. You ought not to have spoken as you did to my uncles and aunts—you should leave it to me to take care of my mother and you, and not put yourself forward. You think you know better than any one, but you're almost always wrong. I can judge much better than you can."

Poor Tom! he had just come from being lectured and made to feel his inferiority: the reaction of his strong, self-asserting nature must take place somehow; and here was a case in which he could justly show himself dominant. Maggie's cheek flushed and her lip quivered with conflicting resentment and affection, and a certain awe as well as admiration of Tom's firmer and more effective character. She did not answer immediately; very angry words rose to her lips, but they were driven back again, and she said at last—

"You often think I'm conceited, Tom, when I don't mean what I say at all in that way. I don't mean to put myself above you—I know you behaved better than I did yesterday. But you are always so harsh to me, Tom."

With the last words the resentment was rising again.

"No, I'm not harsh," said Tom, with severe decision. "I'm always kind to you; and so I shall be: I shall always take care of you. But you must mind what I say."

Their mother came in now, and Maggie rushed away, that her burst

6. Characters from Scott's *Guy Mannering* (1815).

of tears, which she felt must come, might not happen till she was safe up-stairs. They were very bitter tears: everybody in the world seemed so hard and unkind to Maggie: there was no indulgence, no fondness, such as she imagined when she fashioned the world afresh in her own thoughts. In books there were people who were always agreeable or tender, and delighted to do things that made one happy, and who did not show their kindness by finding fault. The world outside the books was not a happy one, Maggie felt: it seemed to be a world where people behaved the best to those they did not pretend to love, and that did not belong to them. And if life had no love in it, what else was there for Maggie? Nothing but poverty and the companionship of her mother's narrow griefs—perhaps of her father's heart-cutting childish dependence. There is no hopelessness so sad as that of early youth, when the soul is made up of wants, and has no long memories, no superadded life in the life of others; though we who look on think lightly of such premature despair, as if our vision of the future lightened the blind sufferer's present.

Maggie in her brown frock, with her eyes reddened and her heavy hair pushed back, looking from the bed where her father lay, to the dull walls of this sad chamber which was the centre of her world, was a creature full of eager, passionate longings for all that was beautiful and glad; thirsty for all knowledge; with an ear straining after dreamy music that died away and would not come near to her; with a blind, unconscious yearning for something that would link together the wonderful impressions of this mysterious life, and give her soul a sense of home in it.

No wonder, when there is this contrast between the outward and the inward, that painful collisions come of it.[7]

Chapter VI

Tending to Refute the Popular Prejudice against the Present of a Pocket-Knife

In that dark time of December, the sale of the household furniture lasted beyond the middle of the second day. Mr Tulliver, who had begun, in his intervals of consciousness, to manifest an irritability which often appeared to have as a direct effect the recurrence of spasmodic rigidity and insensibility, had lain in this living death throughout the critical hours when the noise of the sale came nearest to his chamber. Mr Turnbull had decided that it would be a less risk to let him remain

7. The manuscript includes the following sentence, which was omitted from printed editions: "A girl of no startling appearance, and who will never be a Sappho or a Madame Roland or anything else that the world takes wide note of, may still hold forces within her as the living plant-seed does, which will make a way for themselves, often in a shattering, violent manner." (See the Riverside edition of the novel published by Houghton Mifflin and edited by Gordon S. Haight [1961].)

where he was, than to move him to Luke's cottage—a plan which the good Luke had proposed to Mrs Tulliver, thinking it would be very bad if the master were "to waken up" at the noise of the sale; and the wife and children had sat imprisoned in the silent chamber, watching the large prostrate figure on the bed, and trembling lest the blank face should suddenly show some response to the sounds which fell on their own ears with such obstinate, painful repetition.

But it was over at last—that time of importunate certainty and eye-straining suspense. The sharp sound of a voice, almost as metallic as the rap that followed it, had ceased; the tramping of footsteps on the gravel had died out. Mrs Tulliver's blond face seemed aged ten years by the last thirty hours: the poor woman's mind had been busy divining when her favourite things were being knocked down by the terrible hammer; her heart had been fluttering at the thought that first one thing and then another had gone to be identified as hers in the hateful publicity of the Golden Lion; and all the while she had to sit and make no sign of this inward agitation. Such things bring lines in well-rounded faces, and broaden the streaks of white among the hairs that once looked as if they had been dipped in pure sunshine. Already, at three o'clock, Kezia, the good-hearted, bad-tempered housemaid, who regarded all people that came to the sale as her personal enemies, the dirt on whose feet was of a peculiarly vile quality, had begun to scrub and swill with an energy much assisted by a continual low muttering against "folks as came to buy up other folks's things," and made light of "scrazing" the tops of mahogany tables over which better folks than themselves had had to—suffer a waste of tissue through evaporation. She was not scrubbing indiscriminately, for there would be further dirt of the same atrocious kind made by people who had still to fetch away their purchases: but she was bent on bringing the parlour, where that "pipe-smoking pig" the bailiff had sat, to such an appearance of scant comfort as could be given to it by cleanliness, and the few articles of furniture bought in for the family. Her mistress and the young folks should have their tea in it that night, Kezia was determined.

It was between five and six o'clock, near the usual tea-time, when she came up-stairs and said that Master Tom was wanted. The person who wanted him was in the kitchen, and in the first moments, by the imperfect fire and candle-light, Tom had not even an indefinite sense of any acquaintance with the rather broad-set but active figure, perhaps two years older than himself, that looked at him with a pair of blue eyes set in a disc of freckles, and pulled some curly red locks with a strong intention of respect. A low-crowned oilskin-covered hat, and a certain shiny deposit of dirt on the rest of the costume, as of tablets prepared for writing upon, suggested a calling that had to do with boats; but this did not help Tom's memory.

"Sarvant, Mister Tom," said he of the red locks, with a smile which seemed to break through a self-imposed air of melancholy. "You don't know me again, I doubt," he went on, as Tom continued to look at him inquiringly; "but I'd like to talk to you by yourself a bit, please."

"There's a fire i' the parlour, Master Tom," said Kezia, who objected to leaving the kitchen in the crisis of toasting.

"Come this way, then," said Tom, wondering if this young fellow belonged to Guest & Co.'s Wharf; for his imagination ran continually towards that particular spot, and uncle Deane might any time be sending for him to say that there was a situation at liberty.

The bright fire in the parlour was the only light that showed the few chairs, the bureau, the carpetless floor, and the one table—no, not the *one* table: there was a second table, in a corner, with a large Bible and a few other books upon it. It was this new strange bareness that Tom felt first, before he thought of looking again at the face which was also lit up by the fire, and which stole a half-shy, questioning glance at him as the entirely strange voice said—

"Why! you don't remember Bob, then, as you gen the pocket-knife to, Mr Tom?"

The rough-handled pocket-knife was taken out in the same moment, and the largest blade opened by way of irresistible demonstration.

"What! Bob Jakin?" said Tom—not with any cordial delight, for he felt a little ashamed of that early intimacy symbolised by the pocket-knife, and was not at all sure that Bob's motives for recalling it were entirely admirable.

"Ay, ay, Bob Jakin—if Jakin it must be, 'cause there's so many Bobs as you went arter the squerrils with, that day as I plumped right down from the bough, and bruised my shins a good un—but I got the squerril tight for all that, an' a scratter it was. An' this littlish blade's broke, you see, but I wouldn't hev a new 'un put in, 'cause they might be cheatin' me an' givin' me another knife istid, for there isn't such a blade i' the country—it's got used to my hand, like. An' there was niver nobody else gen me nothin' but what I got by my own sharpness, only you, Mr Tom; if it wasn't Bill Fawks as gen me the terrier pup istid o' drowndin' it, an' I had to jaw him a good un afore he'd give it me."

Bob spoke with a sharp and rather treble volubility, and got through his long speech with surprising despatch, giving the blade of his knife an affectionate rub on his sleeve when he had finished.

"Well, Bob," said Tom, with a slight air of patronage, the foregoing reminiscences having disposed him to be as friendly as was becoming, though there was no part of his acquaintance with Bob that he remembered better than the cause of their parting quarrel; "is there anything I can do for you?"

"Why, no, Mr Tom," answered Bob, shutting up his knife with a click and returning it to his pocket, where he seemed to be feeling for something else. "I shouldn't ha' come back upon you now ye're i' trouble, an' folks say as the master, as I used to frighten the birds for, an' he flogged me a bit for fun when he catched me eatin' the turnip, as they say he'll niver lift up his yead no more—I shouldn't ha' come now to ax you to gi' me another knife, 'cause you gen me one afore. If a chap gives me one black eye, that's enough for me: I shan't ax him for another afore I sarve him out; an' a good turn's worth as much as a bad un, anyhow. I shall niver grow down'ards again, Mr Tom, an' you war the little chap as I liked the best when *I* war a little chap, for all you leathered me, and wouldn't look at me again. There's Dick Brumby, there, I could leather him as much as I'd a mind; but lors! you get tired o' leatherin' a chap when you can niver make him see what you want him to shy at. I'n seen chaps as 'ud stand starin' at a bough till their eyes shot out, afore they'd see as a bird's tail warn't a leaf. It's poor work goin' wi' such raff—but you war allays a rare un at shying, Mr Tom, an' I could trusten to you for droppin' down wi' your stick in the nick o' time at a runnin' rat, or a stoat, or that, when I war a-beatin' the bushes."

Bob had drawn out a dirty canvass bag, and would perhaps not have paused just then if Maggie had not entered the room and darted a look of surprise and curiosity at him, whereupon he pulled his red locks again with due respect. But the next moment the sense of the altered room came upon Maggie with a force that overpowered the thought of Bob's presence. Her eyes had immediately glanced from him to the place where the bookcase had hung; there was nothing now but the oblong unfaded space on the wall, and below it the small table with the Bible and the few other books.

"O Tom," she burst out, clasping her hands, "where are the books? I thought my uncle Glegg said he would buy them—didn't he?—are those all they've left us?"

"I suppose so," said Tom, with a sort of desperate indifference. "Why should they buy many books when they bought so little furniture?"

"O but, Tom," said Maggie, her eyes filling with tears, as she rushed up to the table to see what books had been rescued. "Our dear old Pilgrim's Progress that you coloured with your little paints; and that picture of Pilgrim with a mantle on, looking just like a turtle—O dear!" Maggie went on, half sobbing as she turned over the few books. "I thought we should never part with that while we lived—everything is going away from us—the end of our lives will have nothing in it like the beginning!"

Maggie turned away from the table and threw herself into a chair, with the big tears ready to roll down her cheeks—quite blinded to the presence of Bob, who was looking at her with the pursuant gaze of an intelligent dumb animal, with perceptions more perfect than his comprehension.

"Well, Bob," said Tom, feeling that the subject of the books was unseasonable, "I suppose you just came to see me because we're in trouble? That was very good-natured of you."

"I'll tell you how it is, Master Tom," said Bob, beginning to untwist his canvass bag. "You see, I'n been with a barge this two 'ear—that's how I'n been gettin' my livin'—if it wasn't when I was tentin' the furnace, between whiles, at Torry's mill. But a fortni't ago I'd a rare bit o' luck —I allays thought I was a lucky chap, for I never set a trap but what I catched something; but this wasn't a trap, it was a fire i' Torry's mill, an' I doused it, else it 'ud ha' set th' oil alight, an' the genelman gen me ten suvreigns—he gen me 'em himself last week. An' he said first, I was a sperrited chap—but I knowed that afore—but then he outs wi' the ten suvreigns, an' that war summat new. Here they are—all but one!" Here Bob emptied the canvass bag on the table. "An' when I'd got 'em, my head was all of a boil like a kettle o' broth, thinkin' what sort o' life I should take to—for there war a many trades I'd thought on; for as for the barge, I'm clean tired out wi't, for it pulls the days out till they're as long as pigs' chitterlings. An' I thought first I'd ha' ferrets an' dogs, an' be a rat-catcher; an' then I thought as I should like a bigger way o' life, as I didn't know so well; for I'n seen to the bottom o' rat-catching; an' I thought, an' thought, till at last I settled I'd be a packman,[1] for they're knowin' fellers, the packmen are—an' I'd carry the lightest things I could i' my pack—an' there'd be a use for a feller's tongue, as is no use neither wi' rats nor barges. An' I should go about the country far an' wide, an' come round the women wi' my tongue, an' get my dinner hot at the public—lors! It 'ud be a lovely life!"

Bob paused, and then said, with defiant decision, as if resolutely turning his back on that paradisaic picture—

"But I don't mind about it—not a chip! An' I'n changed one o' the suvreigns to buy my mother a goose for dinner, an' I'n bought a blue plush wescoat, an' a sealskin cap—for if I meant to be a packman, I'd do it respectable. But I don't mind about it—not a chip! My yead isn't a turnip, an' I shall p'r'aps have a chance o' dousing another fire afore long. I'm a lucky chap. So I'll thank you to take the nine suvreigns, Mr Tom, and set yoursen up with 'em somehow—if it's true as the master's broke. They mayn't go fur enough—but they'll help."

Tom was touched keenly enough to forget his pride and suspicion.

"You're a very kind fellow, Bob," he said, colouring, with that little diffident tremor in his voice, which gave a certain charm even to Tom's pride and severity, "and I shan't forget you again, though I didn't know you this evening. But I can't take the nine sovereigns: I should be taking your little fortune from you, and they wouldn't do me much good either."

1. Peddler.

"Wouldn't they, Mr Tom?" said Bob, regretfully. "Now don't say so 'cause you think I want 'em. I aren't a poor chap. My mother gets a good penn'orth wi' picking feathers an' things; an' if she eats nothin' but bread-an'-water, it runs to fat. An' I'm such a lucky chap: an' I doubt you aren't quite so lucky, Mr Tom—th' old master isn't, anyhow—an' so you might take a slice o' my luck, an' no harm done. Lors! I found a leg o' pork i' the river one day: it had tumbled out o' one o' them round-sterned Dutchmen, I'll be bound. Come, think better on it, Mr Tom, for old 'quinetance sake—else I shall think you bear me a grudge."

Bob pushed the sovereigns forward, but before Tom could speak, Maggie, clasping her hands, and looking penitently at Bob, said—

"O, I'm so sorry, Bob—I never thought you were so good. Why, I think you're the kindest person in the world!"

Bob had not been aware of the injurious opinion for which Maggie was performing an inward act of penitence, but he smiled with pleasure at this handsome eulogy—especially from a young lass who, as he informed his mother that evening, had "such uncommon eyes, they looked somehow as they made him feel nohow."

"No, indeed, Bob, I can't take them," said Tom; "but don't think I feel your kindness less because I say no. I don't want to take anything from anybody, but to work my own way. And those sovereigns wouldn't help me much—they wouldn't, really—if I were to take them. Let me shake hands with you instead."

Tom put out his pink palm, and Bob was not slow to place his hard, grimy hand within it.

"Let me put the sovereigns in the bag again," said Maggie; "and you'll come and see us when you've bought your pack, Bob."

"It's like as if I'd come out o' make-believe, o' purpose to show 'em you," said Bob, with an air of discontent, as Maggie gave him the bag again, "a-taking 'em back i' this way. I *am* a bit of a Do, you know; but it isn't that sort o' Do:[2] it's on'y when a feller's a big rogue, or a big flat,[3] I like to let him in a bit, that's all."

"Now, don't you be up to any tricks, Bob," said Tom, "else you'll get transported[4] some day."

"No, no; not me, Mr Tom," said Bob, with an air of cheerful confidence. "There's no law again' fleabites. If I wasn't to take a fool in now and then, he'd niver get any wiser. But, lors! hev a suvreign to buy you and Miss summat, on'y for a token—just to match my pocket-knife."

While Bob was speaking he laid down the sovereign, and resolutely twisted up his bag again. Tom pushed back the gold, and said, "No, indeed, Bob; thank you heartily; but I can't take it." And Maggie, tak-

2. Con artist.
3. Dupe.
4. Sent overseas to a penal colony.

ing it between her fingers, held it up to Bob, and said, more persuasively—

"Not now—but perhaps another time. If ever Tom or my father wants help that you can give, we'll let you know—won't we, Tom? That's what you would like—to have us always depend on you as a friend that we can go to—isn't it, Bob?"

"Yes, Miss, and thank you," said Bob, reluctantly taking the money; "that's what I'd like—anything as you like. An' I wish you good-bye, Miss, and good-luck, Mr Tom, and thank you for shaking hands wi' me, *though* you wouldn't take the money."

Kezia's entrance, with very black looks, to inquire if she shouldn't bring in the tea now, or whether the toast was to get hardened to a brick, was a seasonable check on Bob's flux of words, and hastened his parting bow.

Chapter VII

How a Hen Takes to Stratagem

The days passed, and Mr Tulliver showed, at least to the eyes of the medical man, stronger and stronger symptoms of a gradual return to his normal condition: the paralytic obstruction was, little by little, losing its tenacity, and the mind was rising from under it with fitful struggles, like a living creature making its way from under a great snowdrift, that slides and slides again, and shuts up the newly-made opening.

Time would have seemed to creep to the watchers by the bed, if it had only been measured by the doubtful distant hope which kept count of the moments within the chamber; but it was measured for them by a fast-approaching dread which made the nights come too quickly. While Mr Tulliver was slowly becoming himself again, his lot was hastening towards its moment of most palpable change. The taxing-masters had done their work like any respectable gunsmith conscientiously preparing the musket, that; duly pointed by a brave arm, will spoil a life or two. Allocaturs, filing of bills in Chancery,[1] decrees of sale, are legal chain-shot or bomb-shells that can never hit a solitary mark, but must fall with widespread shattering. So deeply inherent is it in this life of ours that men have to suffer for each other's sins, so inevitably diffusive is human suffering, that even justice makes its victims, and we can conceive no retribution that does not spread beyond its mark in pulsations of unmerited pain.

By the beginning of the second week in January the bills were out advertising the sale, under a decree of Chancery, of Mr Tulliver's farming

1. Chancery: high court of equity; allocaturs: certificates allowing costs, issued at the termination of a legal action.

and other stock, to be followed by a sale of the mill and land, held in the proper after-dinner hour at the Golden Lion. The miller himself, unaware of the lapse of time, fancied himself still in that first stage of his misfortunes when expedients might be thought of; and often in his conscious hours talked in a feeble, disjointed manner, of plans he would carry out when he "got well." The wife and children were not without hope of an issue that would at least save Mr Tulliver from leaving the old spot, and seeking an entirely strange life. For uncle Deane had been induced to interest himself in this stage of the business. It would not, he acknowledged, be a bad speculation for Guest & Co. to buy Dorlcote Mill, and carry on the business, which was a good one, and might be increased by the addition of steam-power; in which case Tulliver might be retained as manager. Still Mr Deane would say nothing decided about the matter: the fact that Wakem held the mortgage on the land might put it into his head to bid for the whole estate, and further, to outbid the cautious firm of Guest & Co., who did not carry on business on sentimental grounds. Mr Deane was obliged to tell Mrs Tulliver something to that effect, when he rode over to the mill to inspect the books in company with Mrs Glegg: for she had observed that "if Guest & Co. would only think about it, Mr Tulliver's father and grandfather had been carrying on Dorlcote Mill long before the oil-mill of that firm had been so much as thought of." Mr Deane, in reply, doubted whether that was precisely the relation between the two mills which would determine their value as investments. As for uncle Glegg, the thing lay quite beyond his imagination; the good-natured man felt sincere pity for the Tulliver family, but his money was all locked up in excellent mortgages, and he could run no risk; that would be unfair to his own relatives; but he had made up his mind that Tulliver should have some new flannel waistcoats which he had himself renounced in favour of a more elastic commodity, and that he would buy Mrs Tulliver a pound of tea now and then; it would be a journey which his benevolence delighted in beforehand, to carry the tea, and see her pleasure on being assured it was the best black.

Still, it was clear that Mr Deane was kindly disposed towards the Tullivers. One day he had brought Lucy, who was come home for the Christmas holidays, and the little blond angel-head had pressed itself against Maggie's darker cheek with many kisses and some tears. These fair slim daughters keep up a tender spot in the heart of many a respectable partner in a respectable firm, and perhaps Lucy's anxious pitying questions about her poor cousins helped to make uncle Deane more prompt in finding Tom a temporary place in the warehouse, and in putting him in the way of getting evening lessons in book-keeping and calculation.

That might have cheered the lad and fed his hopes a little, if there had not come at the same time the much-dreaded blow of finding that his father must be a bankrupt, after all; at least, the creditors must be asked to take less than their due, which to Tom's untechnical mind was the same thing as bankruptcy. His father must not only be said to have "lost his property," but to have "failed"—the word that carried the worst obloquy to Tom's mind. For when the defendant's claim for costs had been satisfied, there would remain the friendly bill of Mr Gore, and the deficiency at the bank, as well as the other debts, which would make the assets shrink into unequivocal disproportion: "not more than ten or twelve shillings in the pound," predicted Mr Deane, in a decided tone, tightening his lips; and the words fell on Tom like a scalding liquid, leaving a continual smart.

He was sadly in want of something to keep up his spirits a little in the unpleasant newness of his position—suddenly transported from the easy carpeted ennui of study-hours at Mr Stelling's, and the busy idleness of castle-building in a "last half" at school, to the companionship of sacks and hides, and bawling men thundering down heavy weights at his elbow. The first step towards getting on in the world was a chill, dusty, noisy affair, and implied going without one's tea in order to stay in St Ogg's and have an evening lesson from a one-armed elderly clerk, in a room smelling strongly of bad tobacco. Tom's young pink-and-white face had its colours very much deadened by the time he took off his hat at home, and sat down with keen hunger to his supper. No wonder he was a little cross if his mother or Maggie spoke to him.

But all this while Mrs Tulliver was brooding over a scheme by which she, and no one else, would avert the result most to be dreaded, and prevent Wakem from entertaining the purpose of bidding for the mill. Imagine a truly respectable and amiable hen, by some portentous anomaly, taking to reflection and inventing combinations by which she might prevail on Hodge[2] not to wring her neck, or send her and her chicks to market: the result could hardly be other than much cackling and fluttering. Mrs Tulliver, seeing that everything had gone wrong, had begun to think that she had been too passive in life; and that, if she had applied her mind to business, and taken a strong resolution now and then, it would have been all the better for her and her family. Nobody, it appeared, had thought of going to speak to Wakem on this business of the mill; and yet, Mrs Tulliver reflected, it would have been quite the shortest method of securing the right end. It would have been of no use, to be sure, for Mr Tulliver to go—even if he had been able and willing—for he had been "going to law against Wakem" and abusing him for the last ten years; Wakem was always likely to have a spite against him. And now that Mrs Tulliver had come to the conclusion that her husband was very much in the wrong to bring her into this trouble, she

2. Generic name of an English rustic.

was inclined to think that his opinion of Wakem was wrong too. To be sure, Wakem had "put the bailies in the house, and sold them up;" but she supposed he did that to please the man that lent Mr Tulliver the money, for a lawyer had more folks to please than one, and he wasn't likely to put Mr Tulliver, who had gone to law with him, above everybody else in the world. The attorney might be a very reasonable man—why not? He had married a Miss Clint, and at the time Mrs Tulliver had heard of that marriage, the summer when she wore her blue satin spencer,[3] and had not yet any thoughts of Mr Tulliver, she knew no harm of Wakem. And certainly towards herself—whom he knew to have been a Miss Dodson—it was out of all possibility that he could entertain anything but goodwill, when it was once brought home to his observation that she, for her part, had never wanted to go to law, and indeed was at present disposed to take Mr Wakem's view of all subjects rather than her husband's. In fact, if that attorney saw a respectable matron like herself disposed "to give him good words," why shouldn't he listen to her representations? For she would put the matter clearly before him, which had never been done yet. And he would never go and bid for the mill on purpose to spite her, an innocent woman, who thought it likely enough that she had danced with him in their youth at Squire Darleigh's, for at those big dances she had often and often danced with young men whose names she had forgotten.

Mrs Tulliver hid these reasonings in her own bosom; for when she had thrown out a hint to Mr Deane and Mr Glegg, that she wouldn't mind going to speak to Wakem herself, they had said, "No, no, no," and "Pooh, pooh," and "Let Wakem alone," in the tone of men who were not likely to give a candid attention to a more definite exposition of her project; still less dared she mention the plan to Tom and Maggie, for "the children were always so against everything their mother said;" and Tom, she observed, was almost as much set against Wakem as his father was. But this unusual concentration of thought naturally gave Mrs Tulliver an unusual power of device and determination; and a day or two before the sale, to be held at the Golden Lion, when there was no longer any time to be lost, she carried out her plan by a stratagem. There were pickles in question—a large stock of pickles and ketchup which Mrs Tulliver possessed, and which Mr Hyndmarsh the grocer would certainly purchase if she could transact the business in a personal interview, so she would walk with Tom to St Ogg's that morning: and when Tom urged that she might let the pickles be, at present—he didn't like her to go about just yet—she appeared so hurt at this conduct in her son, contradicting her about pickles which she had made after the family receipts inherited from his own grandmother, who had died when

3. Short, close-fitting jacket.

his mother was a little girl, that he gave way, and they walked together until she turned towards Danish Street, where Mr Hyndmarsh retailed his grocery, not far from the offices of Mr Wakem.

That gentleman was not yet come to his office: would Mrs Tulliver sit down by the fire in his private room and wait for him? She had not long to wait before the punctual attorney entered, knitting his brow with an examining glance at the stout blond woman who rose, curtsying deferentially:—a tallish man, with an aquiline nose and abundant iron-grey hair. You have never seen Mr Wakem before, and are possibly wondering whether he was really as eminent a rascal, and as crafty, bitter an enemy of honest humanity in general, and of Mr Tulliver in particular, as he is represented to be in that eidolon[4] or portrait of him which we have seen to exist in the miller's mind.

It is clear that the irascible miller was a man to interpret any chance-shot that grazed him as an attempt on his own life, and was liable to entanglements in this puzzling world, which, due consideration had to his own infallibility, required the hypothesis of a very active diabolical agency to explain them. It is still possible to believe that the attorney was not more guilty towards him, than an ingenious machine, which performs its work with much regularity, is guilty towards the rash man who, venturing too near it, is caught up by some fly-wheel or other, and suddenly converted into unexpected mince-meat.

But it is really impossible to decide this question by a glance at his person: the lines and lights of the human countenance are like other symbols—not always easy to read without a key. On an *a priori* view of Wakem's aquiline nose, which offended Mr Tulliver, there was not more rascality than in the shape of his stiff shirt-collar, though this too, along with his nose, might have become fraught with damnatory meaning when once the rascality was ascertained.

"Mrs Tulliver, I think?" said Mr Wakem.

"Yes, sir. Miss Elizabeth Dodson as was."

"Pray be seated. You have some business with me?"

"Well sir, yes," said Mrs Tulliver, beginning to feel alarmed at her own courage, now she was really in presence of the formidable man, and reflecting that she had not settled with herself how she should begin. Mr Wakem felt in his waistcoat pockets, and looked at her in silence.

"I hope, sir," she began at last—"I hope, sir, you're not a-thinking as *I* bear you any ill-will because o' my husband's losing his lawsuit, and the bailies being put in, and the linen being sold—O dear! . . . for I wasn't brought up in that way. I'm sure you remember my father sir, for he was close friends with Squire Darleigh, and we allays went to the dances there—the Miss Dodsons—nobody could be more looked on—and justly, for

4. A phantasm.

there was four of us, and you're quite aware as Mrs Glegg and Mrs Deane are my sisters. And as for going to law, and losing money, and having sales before you're dead, I never saw anything o' that before I was married, nor for a long while after. And I'm not to be answerable for my bad luck i' marrying out o' my own family into one where the goings-on was different. And as for being drawn in t' abuse you as other folks abuse you, sir, *that* I niver was, and nobody can say it of me."

Mrs Tulliver shook her head a little, and looked at the hem of her pocket-handkerchief.

"I've no doubt of what you say, Mrs Tulliver," said Mr Wakem, with cold politeness. "But you have some question to ask me?"

"Well, sir, yes. But that's what I've said to myself—I've said you'd have some nat'ral feeling; and as for my husband, as hasn't been himself for this two months, I'm not a-defending him, in no way, for being so hot about th' erigation—not but what there's worse men, for he never wronged nobody of a shilling nor a penny, not willingly—and as for his fieriness and lawing, what could I do? And him struck as if it was with death when he got the letter as said you'd the hold upo' the land. But I can't believe but what you'll behave as a gentleman."

"What does all this mean, Mrs Tulliver?" said Mr Wakem, rather sharply. "What do you want to ask me?"

"Why, sir, if you'll be so good," said Mrs Tulliver, starting a little, and speaking more hurriedly, "if you'll be so good not to buy the mill an' the land—the land wouldn't so much matter, only my husband 'ull be like mad at your having it."

Something like a new thought flashed across Mr Wakem's face as he said, "Who told you I meant to buy it?"

"Why, sir, it's none o' my inventing; and I should never ha' thought of it, for my husband, as ought to know about the law, he allays used to say as lawyers had never no call to buy anything—either lands or houses—for they allays got 'em into their hands other ways. An' I should think that 'ud be the way with you, sir; and I niver said as you'd be the man to do contrairy to that."

"Ah, well, who was it that *did* say so?" said Wakem, opening his desk, and moving things about, with the accompaniment of an almost inaudible whistle.

"Why, sir, it was Mr Glegg and Mr Deane, as have all the management: and Mr Deane thinks as Guest & Co. 'ud buy the mill and let Mr Tulliver work it for 'em, if you didn't bid for it and raise the price. And it 'ud be such a thing for my husband to stay where he is, if he could get his living: for it was his father's before him, the mill was, and his grandfather built it, though I wasn't fond o' the noise of it, when first I was married, for there was no mills in our family—not the Dodsons'—and if I'd known as the mills had so much to do with the law, it wouldn't have been me as 'ud have been the first Dodson to marry one; but I went into it blindfold, that I did, erigation and everything."

"What! Guest & Co. will keep the mill in their own hands, I suppose, and pay your husband wages?"

"O dear, sir, it's hard to think of," said poor Mrs Tulliver, a little tear making its way, "as my husband should take wage. But it 'ud look more like what used to be, to stay at the mill than to go anywhere else: and if you'll only think—if you was to bid for the mill and buy it, my husband might be struck worse than he was before, and niver get better again as he's getting now."

"Well, but if I bought the mill, and allowed your husband to act as my manager in the same way, how then?" said Mr Wakem.

"O sir, I doubt he could niver be got to do it, not if the very mill stood still to beg and pray of him. For your name's like poison to him, it's so as never was; and he looks upon it as you've been the ruin of him all along, ever since you set the law on him about the road through the meadow—that's eight year ago, and he's been going on ever since—as I've allays told him he was wrong. . . ."

"He's a pig-headed, foul-mouthed fool!" burst out Mr Wakem, forgetting himself.

"O dear, sir!" said Mrs Tulliver, frightened at a result so different from the one she had fixed her mind on; "I wouldn't wish to contradict you, but it's like enough he's changed his mind with this illness—he's forgot a many things he used to talk about. And you wouldn't like to have a corpse on your mind, if he was to die; and they *do* say as it's allays unlucky when Dorlcote Mill changes hands, and the water might all run away, and *then* . . . not as I'm wishing you any ill-luck, sir, for I forgot to tell you as I remember your wedding as if it was yesterday—Mrs Wakem was a Miss Clint, I know *that*—and my boy, as there isn't a nicer, handsomer, straighter boy nowhere, to school with your son. . . ."

Mr Wakem rose, opened the door, and called to one of his clerks.

"You must excuse me for interrupting you, Mrs Tulliver; I have business that must be attended to; and I think there is nothing more necessary to be said."

"But if you *would* bear it in mind, sir," said Mrs Tulliver, rising, "and not run against me and my children; and I'm not denying Mr Tulliver's been in the wrong, but he's been punished enough, and there's worse men, for it's been giving to other folks has been his fault. He's done nobody any harm but himself and his family—the more's the pity—and I go and look at the bare shelves every day, and think where all my things used to stand."

"Yes, yes, I'll bear it in mind," said Mr Wakem, hastily, looking towards the open door.

"And if you'd please not to say as I've been to speak to you, for my son 'ud be very angry with me for demeaning myself, I know he would, and I've trouble enough without being scolded by my children."

Poor Mrs Tulliver's voice trembled a little, and she could make no answer to the attorney's "good morning," but curtsied and walked out in silence.

"Which day is it that Dorlcote Mill is to be sold? Where's the bill?" said Mr Wakem to his clerk when they were alone.

"Next Friday is the day: Friday, at six o'clock."

"Oh! just run to Winship's the auctioneer, and see if he's at home. I have some business for him: ask him to come up."

Although, when Mr Wakem entered his office that morning, he had had no intention of purchasing Dorlcote Mill, his mind was already made up: Mrs Tulliver had suggested to him several determining motives, and his mental glance was very rapid: he was one of those men who can be prompt without being rash, because their motives run in fixed tracks, and they have no need to reconcile conflicting aims.

To suppose that Wakem had the same sort of inveterate hatred towards Tulliver, that Tulliver had towards him, would be like supposing that a pike and a roach can look at each other from a similar point of view. The roach necessarily abhors the mode in which the pike gets his living, and the pike is likely to think nothing further even of the most indignant roach than that he is excellent good eating; it could only be when the roach choked him that the pike could entertain a strong personal animosity. If Mr Tulliver had ever seriously injured or thwarted the attorney, Wakem would not have refused him the distinction of being a special object of his vindictiveness. But when Mr Tulliver called Wakem a rascal at the market dinner-table, the attorney's clients were not a whit inclined to withdraw their business from him; and if, when Wakem himself happened to be present, some jocose cattle-feeder, stimulated by opportunity and brandy, made a thrust at him by alluding to old ladies' wills, he maintained perfect *sang froid*, and knew quite well that the majority of substantial men then present were perfectly contented with the fact that "Wakem was Wakem;" that is to say, a man who always knew the stepping-stones that would carry him through very muddy bits of practice. A man who had made a large fortune, had a handsome house among the trees at Tofton, and decidedly the finest stock of port-wine in the neighbourhood of St Ogg's, was likely to feel himself on a level with public opinion. And I am not sure that even honest Mr Tulliver himself, with his general view of law as a cockpit, might not, under opposite circumstances, have seen a fine appropriateness in the truth that "Wakem was Wakem;" since I have understood from persons versed in history, that mankind is not disposed to look narrowly into the conduct of great victors when their victory is on the right side. Tulliver, then, could be no obstruction to Wakem; on the contrary, he was a poor devil whom the lawyer had defeated several times—a hot-tempered fellow, who would always give you a handle against him. Wakem's conscience was not uneasy because he had used a few tricks against the miller: why should he hate that unsuccessful plaintiff—that pitiable, furious bull entangled in the meshes of a net?

Still, among the various excesses to which human nature is subject, moralists have never numbered that of being too fond of the people who openly revile us. The successful Yellow[5] candidate for the borough of Old Topping, perhaps, feels no pursuant meditative hatred toward the Blue editor who consoles his subscribers with vituperative rhetoric against Yellow men who sell their country, and are the demons of private life; but he might not be sorry, if law and opportunity favoured, to kick that Blue editor to a deeper shade of his favourite colour. Prosperous men take a little vengeance now and then, as they take a diversion, when it comes easily in their way, and is no hindrance to business; and such small unimpassioned revenges have an enormous effect in life, running through all degrees of pleasant infliction, blocking the fit men out of places, and blackening characters in unpremeditated talk. Still more, to see people who have been only insignificantly offensive to us, reduced in life and humiliated without any special efforts of ours, is apt to have a soothing, flattering influence: Providence, or some other prince of this world, it appears, has undertaken the task of retribution for us; and really, by an agreeable constitution of things, our enemies somehow *don't* prosper.

Wakem was not without this parenthetic vindictiveness towards the uncomplimentary miller; and now Mrs Tulliver had put the notion into his head, it presented itself to him as a pleasure to do the very thing that would cause Mr Tulliver the most deadly mortification,—and a pleasure of a complex kind, not made up of crude malice, but mingling with it the relish of self-approbation. To see an enemy humiliated gives a certain contentment, but this is jejune compared with the highly blent satisfaction of seeing him humiliated by your benevolent action or concession on his behalf. That is a sort of revenge which falls into the scale of virtue, and Wakem was not without an intention of keeping that scale respectably filled. He had once had the pleasure of putting an old enemy of his into one of the St Ogg's alms-houses, to the re-building of which he had given a large subscription; and here was an opportunity of providing for another by making him his own servant. Such things give a completeness to prosperity, and contribute elements of agreeable consciousness that are not dreamed of by that short-sighted, over-heated vindictiveness, which goes out of its way to wreak itself in direct injury. And Tulliver, with his rough tongue filed by a sense of obligation, would make a better servant than any chance-fellow who

5. Color of the Whig party; the Tory color was blue.

was cap-in-hand for a situation. Tulliver was known to be a man of proud honesty, and Wakem was too acute not to believe in the existence of honesty. He was given to observing individuals, not to judging of them according to maxims, and no one knew better than he that all men were not like himself. Besides, he intended to overlook the whole business of land and mill pretty closely: he was fond of these practical rural matters. But there were good reasons for purchasing Dorlcote Mill, quite apart from any benevolent vengeance on the miller. It was really a capital investment; besides, Guest & Co. were going to bid for it. Mr Guest and Mr Wakem were on friendly dining terms, and the attorney liked to predominate over a ship-owner and mill-owner who was a little too loud in the town affairs as well as in his table-talk. For Wakem was not a mere man of business: he was considered a pleasant fellow in the upper circles of St Ogg's—chatted amusingly over his port-wine, did a little amateur farming, and had certainly been an excellent husband and father: at church, when he went there, he sat under the handsomest of mural monuments erected to the memory of his wife. Most men would have married again under his circumstances, but he was said to be more tender to his deformed son than most men were to their best-shapen offspring. Not that Mr Wakem had not other sons besides Philip; but towards them he held only a chiaroscuro parentage,[6] and provided for them in a grade of life duly beneath his own. In this fact, indeed, there lay the clenching motive to the purchase of Dorlcote Mill. While Mrs Tulliver was talking, it had occurred to the rapid-minded lawyer, among all the other circumstances of the case, that this purchase would, in a few years to come, furnish a highly suitable position for a certain favourite lad whom he meant to bring on in the world.

These were the mental conditions on which Mrs Tulliver had undertaken to act persuasively, and had failed: a fact which may receive some illustration from the remark of a great philosopher, that fly-fishers fail in preparing their bait so as to make it alluring in the right quarter, for want of a due acquaintance with the subjectivity of fishes.

Chapter VIII

Daylight on the Wreck

It was a clear frosty January day on which Mr Tulliver first came downstairs: the bright sun on the chestnut boughs and the roofs opposite his window had made him impatiently declare that he would be caged up no longer: he thought everywhere would be more cheery under this sunshine than his bedroom; for he knew nothing of the bareness below, which made the flood of sunshine importunate, as if it had an unfeeling

6. I.e., illegitimate.

pleasure in showing the empty places, and the marks where well-known objects once had been. The impression on his mind that it was but yesterday when he received the letter from Mr Gore was so continually implied in his talk, and the attempts to convey to him the idea that many weeks had passed and much had happened since then, had been so soon swept away by recurrent forgetfulness, that even Mr Turnbull had begun to despair of preparing him to meet the facts by previous knowledge. The full sense of the present could only be imparted gradually by new experience—not by mere words, which must remain weaker than the impressions left by the *old* experience. This resolution to come down-stairs was heard with trembling by the wife and children. Mrs Tulliver said Tom must not go to St Ogg's at the usual hour—he must wait and see his father down-stairs: and Tom complied, though with an intense inward shrinking from the painful scene. The hearts of all three had been more deeply dejected than ever during the last few days. For Guest & Co. had not bought the mill: both mill and land had been knocked down to Wakem, who had been over the premises, and had laid before Mr Deane and Mr Glegg, in Mrs Tulliver's presence, his willingness to employ Mr Tulliver, in case of his recovery, as a manager of the business. This proposition had occasioned much family debating. Uncles and aunts were almost unanimously of opinion that such an offer ought not to be rejected when there was nothing in the way but a feeling in Mr Tulliver's mind, which, as neither aunts nor uncles shared it, was regarded as entirely unreasonable and childish—indeed, as a transferring towards Wakem of that indignation and hatred which Mr Tulliver ought properly to have directed against himself for his general quarrelsomeness, and his special exhibition of it in going to law. Here was an opportunity for Mr Tulliver to provide for his wife and daughter without any assistance from his wife's relations, and without that too evident descent into pauperism which makes it annoying to respectable people to meet the degraded member of the family by the wayside. Mr Tulliver, Mrs Glegg considered, must be made to feel, when he came to his right mind, that he could never humble himself enough; for *that* had come which she had always foreseen would come of his insolence in time past "to them as were the best friends he'd got to look to." Mr Glegg and Mr Deane were less stern in their views, but they both of them thought Tulliver had done enough harm by his hot-tempered crotchets, and ought to put them out of the question when a livelihood was offered him: Wakem showed a right feeling about the matter—*he* had no grudge against Tulliver. Tom had protested against entertaining the proposition: he shouldn't like his father to be under Wakem; he thought it would look mean-spirited; but his mother's main distress was the utter impossibility of ever "turning Mr Tulliver round about Wakem," or getting him to hear reason—no, they would all have to go and live in a pigsty on purpose to spite Wakem, who spoke "so as nobody could be fairer." Indeed, Mrs Tulliver's mind was reduced to such confusion by living in this strange medium of unaccountable sorrow, against which she continually appealed by asking, "O dear, what *have* I done to deserve worse than other women?" that Maggie began to suspect her poor mother's wits were quite going.

"Tom," she said, when they were out of their father's room together, "we *must* try to make father understand a little of what has happened before he goes down-stairs. But we must get my mother away. She will say something that will do harm. Ask Kezia to fetch her down, and keep her engaged with something in the kitchen."

Kezia was equal to the task. Having declared her intention of staying till the master could get about again, "wage or no wage," she had found a certain recompense in keeping a strong hand over her mistress, scolding her for "moithering" herself, and going about all day without changing her cap, and looking as if she was "mushed." Altogether, this time of trouble was rather a Saturnalian time to Kezia: she could scold her betters with unreproved freedom. On this particular occasion there were drying clothes to be fetched in: she wished to know if one pair of hands could do everything in-doors and out, and observed that *she* should have thought it would be good for Mrs Tulliver to put on her bonnet, and get a breath of fresh air by doing that needful piece of work. Poor Mrs Tulliver went submissively down-stairs: to be ordered about by a servant was the last remnant of her household dignities—she would soon have no servant to scold her.

Mr Tulliver was resting in his chair a little after the fatigue of dressing, and Maggie and Tom were seated near him, when Luke entered to ask if he should help master down-stairs.

"Ay, ay, Luke, stop a bit, sit down," said Mr Tulliver, pointing his stick towards a chair, and looking at him with that pursuant gaze which convalescent persons often have for those who have tended them, reminding one of an infant gazing about after its nurse. For Luke had been a constant night-watcher by his master's bed.

"How's the water now, eh, Luke?" said Mr Tulliver. "Dix hasn't been choking you up again, eh?"

"No, sir, it's all right."

"Ay, I thought not: he won't be in a hurry at that again, now Riley's been to settle him. That was what I said to Riley yesterday. . . . I said . . ."

Mr Tulliver leaned forward, resting his elbows on the arm-chair, and looking on the ground as if in search of something—striving after vanishing images like a man struggling against a doze. Maggie looked at Tom in mute distress—their father's mind was so far off the present, which would by-and-by thrust itself on his wandering consciousness!

Tom was almost ready to rush away, with that impatience of painful emotion which makes one of the differences between youth and maiden, man and woman.

"Father," said Maggie, laying her hand on his, "don't you remember that Mr Riley is dead?"

"Dead?" said Mr Tulliver, sharply, looking in her face with a strange, examining glance.

"Yes, he died of apoplexy nearly a year ago; I remember hearing you say you had to pay money for him; and he left his daughters badly off—one of them is under-teacher at Miss Firniss's, where I've been to school, you know. . . ."

"Ah?" said her father, doubtfully, still looking in her face. But as soon as Tom began to speak he turned to look at *him* with the same inquiring glances, as if he were rather surprised at the presence of these two young people. Whenever his mind was wandering in the far past, he fell into this oblivion of their actual faces: they were not those of the lad and the little wench who belonged to that past.

"It's a long while since you had the dispute with Dix, father," said Tom. "I remember your talking about it three years ago, before I went to school at Mr Stelling's. I've been at school there three years; don't you remember?"

Mr Tulliver threw himself backward again, losing the childlike outward glance under a rush of new ideas, which diverted him from external impressions.

"Ay, ay," he said, after a minute or two, "I've paid a deal o' money. . . . I was determined my son should have a good eddication: I'd none myself, and I've felt the miss of it. And he'll want no other fortin: that's what I say . . . if Wakem was to get the better of me again. . . ."

The thought of Wakem roused new vibrations, and after a moment's pause he began to look at the coat he had on, and to feel in his side-pocket. Then he turned to Tom, and said, in his old sharp way, "Where have they put Gore's letter?"

It was close at hand in a drawer, for he had often asked for it before.

"You know what there is in the letter, father?" said Tom, as he gave it to him.

"To be sure I do," said Mr Tulliver, rather angrily. "What o' that? If Furley can't take to the property, somebody else can: there's plenty o' people in the world besides Furley. But it's hindering—my not being well—go and tell 'em to get the horse in the gig, Luke: I can get down to St Ogg's well enough—Gore's expecting me."

"No, dear father!" Maggie burst out entreatingly, "it's a very long while since all that: you've been ill a great many weeks—more than two months—everything is changed."

Mr Tulliver looked at them all three alternately with a startled gaze: the idea that much had happened of which he knew nothing had often transiently arrested him before, but it came upon him now with entire novelty.

"Yes, father," said Tom, in answer to the gaze. "You needn't trouble your mind about business until you are quite well: everything is settled about that for the present—about the mill and the land and the debts."

"What's settled, then?" said his father, angrily.

"Don't you take on too much about it, sir," said Luke. "You'd ha' paid iverybody if you could—that's what I said to Master Tom—I said you'd ha' paid iverybody if you could."

Good Luke felt, after the manner of contented hard-working men whose lives have been spent in servitude, that sense of natural fitness in rank which made his master's downfall a tragedy to him. He was urged, in his slow way, to say something that would express his share in the family sorrow, and these words, which he had used over and over again to Tom when he wanted to decline the full payment of his fifty pounds out of the children's money, were the most ready to his tongue. They were just the words to lay the most painful hold on his master's bewildered mind.

"Paid everybody?" he said, with vehement agitation, his face flushing, and his eye lighting up. "Why . . . what . . . have they made me a *bankrupt*?"

"O father, dear father!" said Maggie, who thought that terrible word really represented the fact; "bear it well—because we love you—your children will always love you. Tom will pay them all; he says he will, when he's a man."

She felt her father beginning to tremble—his voice trembled too, as he said, after a few moments—

"Ay, my little wench, but I shall never live twice o'er."

"But perhaps you will live to see me pay everybody, father," said Tom, speaking with a great effort.

"Ah, my lad," said Mr Tulliver, shaking his head slowly, "but what's broke can never be whole again: it 'ud be your doing, not mine." Then, looking up at him, "You're only sixteen—it's an up-hill fight for you—but you mustn't throw it at your father; the raskills have been too many for him. I've given you a good eddication—that'll start you."

Something in his throat half-choked the last words; the flush which had alarmed his children because it had so often preceded a recurrence of paralysis, had subsided, and his face looked pale and tremulous. Tom said nothing: he was still struggling against his inclination to rush away. His father remained quiet a minute or two, but his mind did not seem to be wandering again.

"Have they sold me up, then?" he said, more calmly, as if he were possessed simply by the desire to know what had happened.

"Everything is sold, father; but we don't know all about the mill and the land yet," said Tom, anxious to ward off any question leading to the fact that Wakem was the purchaser.

"You must not be surprised to see the room look very bare downstairs, father," said Maggie; "but there's your chair and the bureau—*they're* not gone."

"Let us go—help me down, Luke—I'll go and see everything," said Mr Tulliver, leaning on his stick, and stretching out his other hand towards Luke.

"Ay, sir," said Luke, as he gave his arm to his master, "you'll make up your mind to't a bit better when you've seen iverything: you'll get used to't. That's what my mother says about her shortness o' breath—she says she's made friends wi't now, though she fought again' it sore when it fust come on."

Maggie ran on before to see that all was right in the dreary parlour, where the fire, dulled by the frosty sunshine, seemed part of the general shabbiness. She turned her father's chair, and pushed aside the table to make an easy way for him, and then stood with a beating heart to see him enter and look round for the first time. Tom advanced before him, carrying the leg-rest, and stood beside Maggie on the hearth. Of those two young hearts Tom's suffered the most unmixed pain, for Maggie, with all her keen susceptibility, yet felt as if the sorrow made larger room for her love to flow in, and gave breathing-space to her passionate nature. No true boy feels that: he would rather go and slay the Nemean lion,[1] or perform any round of heroic labours, than endure perpetual appeals to his pity, for evils over which he can make no conquest.

Mr Tulliver paused just inside the door, resting on Luke, and looking round him at all the bare places, which for him were filled with the shadows of departed objects—the daily companions of his life. His faculties seemed to be renewing their strength from getting a footing on this demonstration of the senses.

"Ah!" he said, slowly, moving towards his chair, "they've sold me up . . . they've sold me up."

Then seating himself, and laying down his stick, while Luke left the room, he looked round again.

"They've left the big Bible," he said. "It's got everything in—when I was born and married—bring it me, Tom."

The quarto[2] Bible was laid open before him at the fly-leaf, and while he was reading with slowly-travelling eyes, Mrs Tulliver entered the room, but stood in mute surprise to find her husband down already, and with the great Bible before him.

"Ah," he said, looking at a spot where his finger rested, "my mother was Margaret Beaton—she died when she was forty-seven: hers wasn't

1. Slaying the Nemean lion was the first of Hercules' twelve labors.
2. Size of a book, created by folding a printed sheet in four leaves, each measuring about 9½ by 12½ inches.

a long-lived family—we're our mother's children—Gritty and me are—we shall go to our last bed before long."

He seemed to be pausing over the record of his sister's birth and marriage, as if it were suggesting new thoughts to him: then he suddenly looked up at Tom, and said, in a sharp tone of alarm—

"They haven't come upo' Moss for the money as I lent him, have they?"

"No, father," said Tom; "the note was burnt."

Mr Tulliver turned his eyes on the page again, and presently said—

"Ah . . . Elizabeth Dodson . . . it's eighteen year since I married her. . . ."

"Come next Ladyday," said Mrs Tulliver, going up to his side and looking at the page.

Her husband fixed his eyes earnestly on her face.

"Poor Bessy," he said, "you was a pretty lass then—everybody said so—and I used to think you kept your good looks rarely. But you're sorely aged . . . don't you bear me ill-will. . . . I meant to do well by you . . . we promised one another for better or for worse. . . ."

"But I never thought it 'ud be so for worse as this," said poor Mrs Tulliver, with the strange scared look that had come over her of late; "and my poor father gave me away . . . and to come on so all at once. . . ."

"O mother," said Maggie, "don't talk in that way."

"No, I know you won't let your poor mother speak . . . that's been the way all my life . . . your father never minded what I said . . . it 'ud have been o' no use for me to beg and pray . . . and it 'ud be no use now, not if I was to go down o' my hands and knees. . . ."

"Don't say so, Bessy," said Mr Tulliver, whose pride, in these first moments of humiliation, was in abeyance to the sense of some justice in his wife's reproach. "If there's anything left as I could do to make you amends, I wouldn't say you nay."

"Then we might stay here and get a living, and I might keep among my own sisters . . . and me been such a good wife to you, and never crossed you from week's end to week's end . . . and they all say so . . . they say it 'ud be nothing but right . . . only you're so turned against Wakem."

"Mother," said Tom, severely, "this is not the time to talk about that."

"Let her be," said Mr Tulliver. "Say what you mean, Bessy."

"Why, now the mill and the land's all Wakem's, and he's got everything in his hands, what's the use o' setting your face against him?—when he says you may stay here, and speaks as fair as can be, and says you may manage the business, and have thirty shilling a-week, and a horse to ride about to market? And where have we got to put our heads? We must go into one o' the cottages in the village . . . and me and my children brought down to that . . . and all because you must set your mind against folks till there's no turning you."

Mr Tulliver had sunk back in his chair trembling.

"You may do as you like wi' me, Bessy," he said, in a low voice; "I've been the bringing of you to poverty . . . this world's too many for me. . . . I'm nought but a bankrupt—it's no use standing up for anything now."

"Father," said Tom, "I don't agree with my mother or my uncles, and I don't think you ought to submit to be under Wakem. I get a pound a-week now, and you can find something else to do when you get well."

"Say no more, Tom, say no more: I've had enough for this day. Give me a kiss, Bessy, and let us bear one another no ill-will: we shall never be young again. . . . This world's been too many for me."

Chapter IX

An Item Added to the Family Register

That first moment of renunciation and submission was followed by days of violent struggle in the miller's mind, as the gradual access of bodily strength brought with it increasing ability to embrace in one view all the conflicting conditions under which he found himself. Feeble limbs easily resign themselves to be tethered, and when we are subdued by sickness it seems possible to us to fulfil pledges which the old vigour comes back and breaks. There were times when poor Tulliver thought the fulfilment of his promise to Bessy was something quite too hard for human nature: he had promised her without knowing what she was going to say—she might as well have asked him to carry a ton weight on his back. But again, there were many feelings arguing on her side, besides the sense that life had been made hard to her by having married him. He saw a possibility, by much pinching, of saving money out of his salary towards paying a second dividend to his creditors, and it would not be easy elsewhere to get a situation such as he could fill. He had led an easy life, ordering much and working little, and had no aptitude for any new business. He must perhaps take to day-labour, and his wife must have help from her sisters—a prospect doubly bitter to him, now they had let all Bessy's precious things be sold, probably because they liked to set her against him, by making her feel that he had brought her to that pass. He listened to their admonitory talk, when they came to urge on him what he was bound to do for poor Bessy's sake, with averted eyes, that every now and then flashed on them furtively when their backs were turned. Nothing but the dread of needing their help could have made it an easier alternative to take their advice.

But the strongest influence of all was the love of the old premises where he had run about when he was a boy, just as Tom had done after him. The Tullivers had lived on this spot for generations, and he had sat listening on a low stool on winter evenings while his father talked of the old half-timbered mill that had been there before the last great floods which damaged it so that his grandfather pulled it down and built the new one. It was when he got able to walk about and look at all the old objects, that he felt the strain of this clinging affection for the old home as part of his life, part of himself. He couldn't bear to think of himself living on any other spot than this, where he knew the sound of every gate and door, and felt that the shape and colour of every roof and weather-stain and broken hillock was good, because his growing senses had been fed on them. Our instructed vagrancy, which has hardly time to linger by the hedgerows, but runs away early to the tropics, and is at home with palms and banyans,—which is nourished on books of travel, and stretches the theatre of its imagination to the Zambesi,[1]—can hardly get a dim notion of what an old-fashioned man like Tulliver felt for this spot, where all his memories centred, and where life seemed like a familiar smooth-handled tool that the fingers clutch with loving ease. And just now he was living in that freshened memory of the far-off time which comes to us in the passive hours of recovery from sickness.

"Ay, Luke," he said, one afternoon, as he stood looking over the orchard gate, "I remember the day they planted those apple-trees. My father was a huge man for planting—it was like a merrymaking to him to get a cart full o' young trees—and I used to stand i' the cold with him, and follow him about like a dog."

Then he turned round, and, leaning against the gate-post, looked at the opposite buildings.

"The old mill 'ud miss me, I think, Luke. There's a story as when the mill changes hands, the river's angry—I've heard my father say it many a time. There's no telling whether there mayn't be summat *in* the story, for this is a puzzling world, and Old Harry's got a finger in it—it's been too many for me, I know."

"Ay, sir," said Luke, with soothing sympathy, "what wi' the rust[2] on the wheat, an' the firin' o' the ricks an' that, as I've seen i' my time—things often looks comical: there's the bacon fat wi' our last pig runs away like butter—it leaves nought but a scratchin'."

"It's just as if it was yesterday, now," Mr Tulliver went on, "when my father began the malting.[3] I remember, the day they finished the malt-house, I thought summat great was to come of it; for we'd a plum-pudding that day and a bit of a feast, and I said to my mother—she was a fine dark-eyed woman, my mother was—the little wench 'ull be as like her as two peas."—Here Mr Tulliver put his stick between his legs,

1. River in southeastern Africa.
2. Destructive plant fungus.
3. Steeping grain in water for brewing or distilling.

and took out his snuff-box, for the greater enjoyment of this anecdote, which dropped from him in fragments, as if he every other moment lost narration in vision. "I was a little chap no higher much than my mother's knee—she was sore fond of us children, Gritty and me—and so I said to her, 'Mother,' I said, 'shall we have plum-pudding *every* day because o' the malt-house?' She used to tell me o' that till her dying day. She was but a young woman when she died, my mother was. But it's forty good year since they finished the malt-house, and it isn't many days out of 'em all, as I haven't looked out into the yard there, the first thing in the morning—all weathers, from year's end to year's end. I should go off my head in a new place. I should be like as if I'd lost my way. It's all hard, whichever way I look at it—the harness 'ull gall me—but it 'ud be summat to draw along the old road, instead of a new un."

"Ay, sir," said Luke, "you'd be a deal better here nor in some new place. I can't abide new places mysen: things is allays awk'ard—narrow-wheeled waggins, belike, and the stiles all another sort, an' oat-cake i' some places, tow'rt th' head o' the Floss, there. It's poor work, changing your country-side."

"But I doubt, Luke, they'll be for getting rid o' Ben, and making you do with a lad—and I must help a bit wi' the mill. You'll have a worse place."

"Ne'er mind, sir," said Luke, "I shan't plague mysen. I'n been wi' you twenty year, an' you can't get twenty year wi' whistlin' for 'em, no more nor you can make the trees grow: you mun wait till God A'mighty sends 'em. I can't abide new victual nor new faces, *I* can't—you niver know but what they'll gripe you."

The walk was finished in silence after this, for Luke had disburthened himself of thoughts to an extent that left his conversational resources quite barren, and Mr Tulliver had relapsed from his recollections into a painful meditation on the choice of hardships before him. Maggie noticed that he was unusually absent that evening at tea; and afterwards he sat leaning forward in his chair, looking at the ground, moving his lips, and shaking his head from time to time. Then he looked hard at Mrs Tulliver, who was knitting opposite him, then at Maggie, who, as she bent over her sewing, was intensely conscious of some drama going forward in her father's mind. Suddenly he took up the poker and broke the large coal fiercely.

"Dear heart, Mr Tulliver, what can you be thinking of?" said his wife, looking up in alarm: "it's very wasteful, breaking the coal, and we've got hardly any large coal left, and I don't know where the rest is to come from."

"I don't think you're quite so well to-night, are you, father?" said Maggie; "you seem uneasy."

"Why, how is it Tom doesn't come?" said Mr Tulliver, impatiently.

"Dear heart! is it time? I must go and get his supper," said Mrs Tulliver, laying down her knitting, and leaving the room.

"It's nigh upon half-past eight," said Mr Tulliver. "He'll be here soon. Go, go and get the big Bible, and open it at the beginning, where everything's set down. And get the pen and ink."

Maggie obeyed, wondering: but her father gave no further orders, and only sat listening for Tom's footfall on the gravel, apparently irritated by the wind, which had risen, and was roaring so as to drown all other sounds. There was a strange light in his eyes that rather frightened Maggie: *she* began to wish that Tom would come, too.

"There he is, then," said Mr Tulliver, in an excited way, when the knock came at last. Maggie went to open the door, but her mother came out of the kitchen, hurriedly, saying, "Stop a bit, Maggie; I'll open it."

Mrs Tulliver had begun to be a little frightened at her boy, but she was jealous of every office others did for him.

"Your supper's ready by the kitchen-fire, my boy," she said, as he took off his hat and coat. "You shall have it by yourself, just as you like, and I won't speak to you."

"I think my father wants Tom, mother," said Maggie; "he must come into the parlour first."

Tom entered with his usual saddened evening face, but his eyes fell immediately on the open Bible and the inkstand, and he glanced with a look of anxious surprise at his father, who was saying—

"Come, come, you're late—I want you."

"Is there anything the matter, father?" said Tom.

"You sit down—all of you," said Mr Tulliver, peremptorily. "And, Tom, sit down here; I've got something for you to write i' the Bible."

They all three sat down, looking at him. He began to speak, slowly, looking first at his wife.

"I've made up my mind, Bessy, and I'll be as good as my word to you. There'll be the same grave made for us to lie down in, and we mustn't be bearing one another ill-will. I'll stop in the old place, and I'll serve under Wakem—and I'll serve him like an honest man: there's no Tulliver but what's honest, mind that, Tom"—here his voice rose: "they'll have it to throw up against me as I paid a dividend—but it wasn't my fault—it was because there's raskills in the world. They've been too many for me, and I must give in. I'll put my neck in harness—for you've a right to say as I've brought you into trouble, Bessy—and I'll serve him as honest as if he was no raskill: I'm an honest man, though I shall never hold my head up no more—I'm a tree as is broke—a tree as is broke."

He paused, and looked on the ground. Then suddenly raising his head, he said, in a louder yet deeper tone—

"But I won't forgive him! I know what they say—he never meant me any harm—that's the way Old Harry props up the raskills—he's been at the bottom of everything—but he's a fine gentleman—I know, I know. I shouldn't ha' gone to law, they say. But who made it so as there was no arbitratin', and no justice to be got? It signifies nothing to him—I know that; he's one o' them fine gentlemen as get money by doing business for poorer folks, and when he's made beggars of 'em he'll give 'em charity. I won't forgive him! I wish he might be punished with shame till his own son 'ud like to forget him. I wish he may do summat as they'd make him work at the treadmill! But he won't—he's too big a raskill to let the law lay hold on him. And you mind this, Tom—you never forgive him, neither, if you mean to be my son. There'll maybe come a time when you may make him feel—it'll never come to me—I'n got my head under the yoke. Now write—write it i' the Bible."

"O father, what?" said Maggie, sinking down by his knee, pale and trembling. "It's wicked to curse and bear malice."

"It isn't wicked, I tell you," said her father, fiercely. "It's wicked as the raskills should prosper—it's the devil's doing. Do as I tell you, Tom. Write."

"What am I to write, father?" said Tom, with gloomy submission.

"Write as your father, Edward Tulliver, took service under John Wakem, the man as had helped to ruin him, because I'd promised my wife to make her what amends I could for her trouble, and because I wanted to die in th' old place, where I was born and my father was born. Put that i' the right words—you know how—and then write, as I don't forgive Wakem, for all that; and for all I'll serve him honest, I wish evil may befall him. Write that."

There was a dead silence as Tom's pen moved along the paper: Mrs Tulliver looked scared, and Maggie trembled like a leaf.

"Now let me hear what you've wrote," said Mr Tulliver. Tom read aloud, slowly.

"Now write—write as you'll remember what Wakem's done to your father, and you'll make him and his feel it, if ever the day comes. And sign your name Thomas Tulliver."

"O no, father, dear father!" said Maggie, almost choked with fear. "You shouldn't make Tom write that."

"Be quiet, Maggie!" said Tom. "I *shall* write it."

Book Fourth

THE VALLEY OF HUMILIATION

Chapter I

A Variation of Protestantism Unknown to Bossuet[1]

Journeying down the Rhone[2] on a summer's day, you have perhaps felt the sunshine made dreary by those ruined villages which stud the banks in certain parts of its course, telling how the swift river once rose, like an angry, destroying god, sweeping down the feeble generations whose breath is in their nostrils, and making their dwellings a desolation.[3] Strange contrast, you may have thought, between the effect produced on us by these dismal remnants of commonplace houses, which in their best days were but the sign of a sordid life, belonging in all its details to our own vulgar era; and the effect produced by those ruins on the castled Rhine,[4] which have crumbled and mellowed into such harmony with the green and rocky steeps, that they seem to have a natural fitness, like the mountain-pine: nay, even in the day when they were built they must have had this fitness, as if they had been raised by an earth-born race, who had inherited from their mighty parent a sublime instinct of form. And that was a day of romance! If those robber-barons were somewhat grim and drunken ogres, they had a certain grandeur of the wild beast in them—they were forest boars with tusks, tearing and rending, not the ordinary domestic grunter; they represented the demon forces for ever in collision with beauty, virtue, and the gentle uses of life; they made a fine contrast in the picture with the wandering minstrel, the soft-lipped princess, the pious recluse, and the timid Israelite. That was a time of colour, when the sunlight fell on glancing steel and floating banners; a time of adventure and fierce struggle—nay, of living, religious art and religious enthusiasm; for were not cathedrals built in those days,

1. Seventeenth-century French Protestant bishop, author of *Histoire des variations des églises protestantes* (History of variations of Protestant churches) (1688).
2. Major river of France, originating in the Swiss Alps.
3. "Their dwellings a desolation": from Jeremiah 51:42–43; "whose breath is in their nostrils": from Genesis 7:22.
4. Major river of northern Europe, originating in Switzerland.

and did not great emperors leave their Western palaces to die before the infidel strongholds in the sacred East? Therefore it is that these Rhine castles thrill me with a sense of poetry: they belong to the grand historic life of humanity, and raise up for me the vision of an epoch. But these dead-tinted, hollow-eyed, angular skeletons of villages on the Rhone oppress me with the feeling that human life—very much of it—is a narrow, ugly, grovelling existence, which even calamity does not elevate, but rather tends to exhibit in all its bare vulgarity of conception; and I have a cruel conviction that the lives these ruins are the traces of, were part of a gross sum of obscure vitality, that will be swept into the same oblivion with the generations of ants and beavers.

Perhaps something akin to this oppressive feeling may have weighed upon you in watching this old-fashioned family life on the banks of the Floss, which even sorrow hardly suffices to lift above the level of the tragi-comic. It is a sordid life, you say, this of the Tullivers and Dodsons—irradiated by no sublime principles, no romantic visions, no active, self-renouncing faith—moved by none of those wild, uncontrollable passions which create the dark shadows of misery and crime—without that primitive rough simplicity of wants, that hard submissive ill-paid toil, that childlike spelling-out of what nature has written, which gives its poetry to peasant life. Here, one has conventional worldly notions and habits without instruction and without polish—surely the most prosaic form of human life: proud respectability in a gig of unfashionable build: worldliness without side-dishes. Observing these people narrowly, even when the iron hand of misfortune has shaken them from their unquestioning hold on the world, one sees little trace of religion, still less of a distinctively Christian creed. Their belief in the Unseen, so far as it manifests itself at all, seems to be rather of a pagan kind; their moral notions, though held with strong tenacity, seem to have no standard beyond hereditary custom. You could not live among such people; you are stifled for want of an outlet towards something beautiful, great, or noble; you are irritated with these dull men and women, as a kind of population out of keeping with the earth on which they live—with this rich plain where the great river flows for ever onward, and links the small pulse of the old English town with the beatings of the world's mighty heart. A vigorous superstition, that lashes its gods or lashes its own back, seems to be more congruous with the mystery of the human lot, than the mental condition of these emmet-like Dodsons and Tullivers.

I share with you this sense of oppressive narrowness; but it is necessary that we should feel it, if we care to understand how it acted on the lives of Tom and Maggie—how it has acted on young natures in many generations, that in the onward tendency of human things have risen above the mental level of the generation before them, to which they have been nevertheless tied by the strongest fibres of their hearts. The suffering, whether of martyr or victim, which belongs to every historical advance of mankind, is represented in this way in every town, and by hundreds of obscure hearths; and we need not shrink from this comparison of small things with great; for does not science tell us that its highest striving is after the ascertainment of a unity which shall bind the smallest things with the greatest? In natural science, I have understood, there is nothing petty to the mind that has a large vision of relations, and to which every single object suggests a vast sum of conditions. It is surely the same with the observation of human life.

Certainly the religious and moral ideas of the Dodsons and Tullivers were of too specific a kind to be arrived at deductively, from the statement that they were part of the Protestant population of Great Britain. Their theory of life had its core of soundness, as all theories must have on which decent and prosperous families have been reared and have flourished; but it had the very slightest tincture of theology. If, in the maiden days of the Dodson sisters, their Bibles opened more easily at some parts than others, it was because of dried tulip-petals, which had been distributed quite impartially, without preference for the historical, devotional, or doctrinal. Their religion was of a simple, semi-pagan kind, but there was no heresy in it—if heresy properly means choice—for they didn't know there was any other religion, except that of chapel-goers,[5] which appeared to run in families, like asthma. How *should* they know? The vicar of their pleasant rural parish was not a controversialist, but a good hand at whist, and one who had a joke always ready for a blooming female parishioner. The religion of the Dodsons consisted in revering whatever was customary and respectable: it was necessary to be baptised, else one could not be buried in the churchyard, and to take the sacrament before death as a security against more dimly understood perils; but it was of equal necessity to have the proper pall-bearers and well-cured hams at one's funeral, and to leave an unimpeachable will. A Dodson would not be taxed with the omission of anything that was becoming, or that belonged to that eternal fitness of things which was plainly indicated in the practice of the most substantial parishioners, and in the family traditions—such as, obedience to parents, faithfulness to kindred, industry, rigid honesty, thrift, the thorough scouring of wooden and copper utensils, the hoarding of coins likely to disappear from the currency, the production of first-rate commodities for the market, and the general preference for whatever was home-made. The Dodsons were a very proud race, and their pride lay in the utter frustration of all desire to tax them with a breach of traditional duty or propriety. A wholesome pride in many respects, since it identified honour with perfect integrity, thoroughness of work, and faithfulness to admitted rules: and society owes some worthy qualities in many of her members

5. Dissenters from the established Church of England.

to mothers of the Dodson class, who made their butter and their fromenty[6] well, and would have felt disgraced to make it otherwise. To be honest and poor was never a Dodson motto, still less to seem rich though being poor; rather, the family badge was to be honest and rich; and not only rich, but richer than was supposed. To live respected, and have the proper bearers at your funeral, was an achievement of the ends of existence that would be entirely nullified if, on the reading of your will, you sank in the opinion of your fellow-men, either by turning out to be poorer than they expected, or by leaving your money in a capricious manner, without strict regard to degrees of kin. The right thing was to correct them severely, if they were other than a credit to the family, but still not to alienate from them the smallest rightful share in the family shoe-buckles and other property. A conspicuous quality in the Dodson character was its genuineness; its vices and virtues alike were phases of a proud, honest egoism, which had a hearty dislike to whatever made against its own credit and interest, and would be frankly hard of speech to inconvenient "kin," but would never forsake or ignore them—would not let them want bread, but only require them to eat it with bitter herbs.[7]

The same sort of traditional belief ran in the Tulliver veins, but it was carried in richer blood, having elements of generous imprudence, warm affection, and hot-tempered rashness. Mr Tulliver's grandfather had been heard to say that he was descended from one Ralph Tulliver, a wonderfully clever fellow, who had ruined himself. It is likely enough that the clever Ralph was a high liver, rode spirited horses, and was very decidedly of his own opinion. On the other hand, nobody had ever heard of a Dodson who had ruined himself: it was not the way of that family.

If such were the views of life on which the Dodsons and Tullivers had been reared in the praiseworthy past of Pitt and high prices,[8] you will infer from what you already know concerning the state of society in St Ogg's, that there had been no highly modifying influence to act on them in their maturer life. It was still possible, even in that later time of anti-Catholic preaching, for people to hold many pagan ideas, and believe themselves good church-people notwithstanding; so we need hardly feel any surprise at the fact that Mr Tulliver, though a regular church-goer, recorded his vindictiveness on the fly-leaf of his Bible. It was not that any harm could be said concerning the vicar of that charming rural parish to which Dorlcote Mill belonged: he was a man of excellent family, an irreproachable bachelor, of elegant pursuits,—had taken honours, and held a fellowship. Mr Tulliver regarded him with dutiful respect, as he did everything else belonging to the church-service;

6. Also called "frumenty," a dish of sweetened, boiled wheat and milk.
7. From Exodus 12:8.
8. Willliam Pitt, prime minister, 1783–1801. Prices were high during part of his term.

but he considered that church was one thing and common-sense another, and he wanted nobody to tell *him* what common-sense was. Certain seeds which are required to find a nidus[9] for themselves under unfavourable circumstances, have been supplied by nature with an apparatus of hooks, so that they will get a hold on very unreceptive surfaces. The spiritual seed which had been scattered over Mr Tulliver had apparently been destitute of any corresponding provision, and had slipped off to the winds again, from a total absence of hooks.

Chapter II

The Torn Nest is Pierced by the Thorns

There is something sustaining in the very agitation that accompanies the first shocks of trouble, just as an acute pain is often a stimulus, and produces an excitement which is transient strength. It is in the slow, changed life that follows—in the time when sorrow has become stale, and has no longer an emotive intensity that counteracts its pain—in the time when day follows day in dull unexpectant sameness, and trial is a dreary routine;—it is then that despair threatens; it is then that the peremptory hunger of the soul is felt, and eye and ear are strained after some unlearned secret of our existence, which shall give to endurance the nature of satisfaction.

This time of utmost need was come to Maggie, with her short span of thirteen years. To the usual precocity of the girl, she added that early experience of struggle, of conflict between the inward impulse and outward fact, which is the lot of every imaginative and passionate nature; and the years since she hammered the nails into her wooden Fetish among the worm-eaten shelves of the attic, had been filled with so eager a life in the triple world of Reality, Books, and Waking Dreams, that Maggie was strangely old for her years in everything except in her entire want of that prudence and self-command which were the qualities that made Tom manly in the midst of his intellectual boyishness. And now her lot was beginning to have a still, sad monotony, which threw her more than ever on her inward self. Her father was able to attend to business again, his affairs were settled, and he was acting as Wakem's manager on the old spot. Tom went to and fro every morning and evening, and became more and more silent in the short intervals at home: what was there to say? One day was like another, and Tom's interest in life, driven back and crushed on every other side, was concentrating itself into the one channel of ambitious resistance to misfortune. The peculiarities of his father and mother were very irksome to

9. A place where spores or seeds develop.

him, now they were laid bare of all the softening accompaniments of an easy prosperous home; for Tom had very clear prosaic eyes, not apt to be dimmed by mists of feeling or imagination. Poor Mrs Tulliver, it seemed, would never recover her old self—her placid household activity: how could she? The objects among which her mind had moved complacently were all gone—all the little hopes, and schemes, and speculations, all the pleasant little cares about her treasures which had made the world quite comprehensible to her for a quarter of a century, since she had made her first purchase of the sugar-tongs, had been suddenly snatched away from her, and she remained bewildered in this empty life. Why that should have happened to her which had not happened to other women, remained an insoluble question by which she expressed her perpetual ruminating comparison of the past with the present. It was piteous to see the comely woman getting thinner and more worn under a bodily as well as mental restlessness, which made her often wander about the empty house after her work was done, until Maggie, becoming alarmed about her, would seek her, and bring her down by telling her how it vexed Tom that she was injuring her health by never sitting down and resting herself. Yet amidst this helpless imbecility there was a touching trait of humble self-devoting maternity, which made Maggie feel tenderly towards her poor mother amidst all the little wearing griefs caused by her mental feebleness. She would let Maggie do none of the work that was heaviest and most soiling to the hands, and was quite peevish when Maggie attempted to relieve her from her grate-brushing and scouring: "Let it alone, my dear; your hands 'ull get as hard as hard," she would say: "it's your mother's place to do that. I can't do the sewing—my eyes fail me." And she would still brush and carefully tend Maggie's hair, which she had become reconciled to, in spite of its refusal to curl, now it was so long and massy. Maggie was not her pet child, and, in general, would have been much better if she had been quite different; yet the womanly heart, so bruised in its small personal desires, found a future to rest on in the life of this young thing, and the mother pleased herself with wearing out her own hands to save the hands that had so much more life in them.

But the constant presence of her mother's regretful bewilderment was less painful to Maggie than that of her father's sullen incommunicative depression. As long as the paralysis was upon him, and it seemed as if he might always be in a childlike condition of dependence—as long as he was still only half-awakened to his trouble, Maggie had felt the strong tide of pitying love almost as an inspiration, a new power, that would make the most difficult life easy for his sake; but now, instead of childlike dependence there had come a taciturn hard concentration of purpose, in strange contrast with his old vehement communicativeness and high spirit; and this lasted from day to day, and from week to week, the dull eye never brightening with any eagerness or any joy. It is something cruelly incomprehensible to youthful natures, this sombre sameness in middle-aged and elderly people, whose life has resulted in disappointment and discontent, to whose faces a smile becomes so strange that the sad lines all about the lips and brow seem to take no notice of it, and it hurries away again for want of a welcome. "Why will they not kindle up and be glad sometimes?" thinks young elasticity. "It would be so easy if the only liked to do it." And these leaden clouds that never part are apt to create impatience even in the filial affection that streams forth in nothing but tenderness and pity in the time of more obvious affliction.

Mr Tulliver lingered nowhere away from home: he hurried away from market, he refused all invitations to stay and chat, as in old times, in the houses where he called on business. He could not be reconciled with his lot: there was no attitude in which his pride did not feel its bruises; and in all behaviour towards him, whether kind or cold, he detected an allusion to the change in his circumstances. Even the days on which Wakem came to ride round the land and inquire into the business, were not so black to him as those market-days on which he had met several creditors who had accepted a composition from him. To save something towards the repayment of those creditors, was the object towards which he was now bending all his thoughts and efforts; and under the influence of this all-compelling demand of his nature, the somewhat profuse man, who hated to be stinted or to stint any one else in his own house, was gradually metamorphosed into the keen-eyed grudger of morsels. Mrs Tulliver could not economise enough to satisfy him, in their food and firing; and he would eat nothing himself but what was of the coarsest quality. Tom, though depressed and strongly repelled by his father's sullenness, and the dreariness of home, entered thoroughly into his father's feelings about paying the creditors; and the poor lad brought his first quarter's money, with a delicious sense of achievement, and gave it to his father to put into the tin box which held the savings. The little store of sovereigns in the tin box seemed to be the only sight that brought a faint beam of pleasure into the miller's eyes—faint and transient, for it was soon dispelled by the thought that the time would be long—perhaps longer than his life—before the narrow savings could remove the hateful incubus of debt. A deficit of more than five hundred pounds, with the accumulating interest, seemed a deep pit to fill with the savings from thirty shillings a-week, even when Tom's probable savings were to be added. On this one point there was entire community of feeling in the four widely differing beings who sat round the dying fire of sticks, which made a cheap warmth for them on the verge of bed-time. Mrs Tulliver carried the proud integrity of the Dodsons in her blood, and had been brought up to think that to wrong people of their money, which was another phrase for debt, was a sort of moral pillory: it would have been wickedness, to her mind, to have run counter to her husband's desire to "do the right thing," and retrieve his name. She had a confused dreamy notion that, if the creditors were all paid, her plate and linen ought to come back to her; but she had an inbred perception that while people owed money they were unable to pay, they couldn't rightly call anything their own. She murmured a little that Mr Tulliver so peremptorily refused to receive anything in repayment from Mr and Mrs Moss; but to all his requirements of household economy she was submissive to the point of denying herself the cheapest indulgences of mere flavour: her only rebellion was to smuggle into the kitchen something that would make rather a better supper than usual for Tom.

These narrow notions about debt, held by the old-fashioned Tullivers, may perhaps excite a smile on the faces of many readers in these days of wide commercial views and wide philosophy, according to which everything rights itself without any trouble of ours: the fact that my tradesman is out of pocket by me, is to be looked at through the serene certainty that somebody else's tradesman is in pocket by somebody else; and since there must be bad debts in the world, why, it is mere egoism not to like that we in particular should make them instead of our fellow-citizens. I am telling the history of very simple people, who had never had any illuminating doubts as to personal integrity and honour.

Under all this grim melancholy and narrowing concentration of desire, Mr Tulliver retained the feeling towards his "little wench" which made her presence a need to him, though it would not suffice to cheer him. She was still the desire of his eyes; but the sweet spring of fatherly love was now mingled with bitterness, like everything else. When Maggie laid down her work at night, it was her habit to get a low stool and sit by her father's knee, leaning her cheek against it. How she wished he would stroke her head, or give some sign that he was soothed by the sense that he had a daughter who loved him! But now she got no answer to her little caresses, either from her father or from Tom—the two idols of her life. Tom was weary and abstracted in the short intervals when he was at home, and her father was bitterly preoccupied with the thought that the girl was growing up—was shooting up into a woman; and how was she to do well in life? She had a poor chance for marrying, down in the world as they were. And he hated the thought of her marrying poorly, as her aunt Gritty had done: *that* would be a thing to make him turn in his grave—the little wench so pulled down by children and toil, as her aunt Moss was. When uncultured minds, confined to a narrow range of personal experience, are under the pressure of continued misfortune, their inward life is apt to become a perpetually repeated round of sad and bitter thoughts: the same words, the same scenes are revolved over and over again, the same mood accompanies them—the end of the year finds them as much what they were at the beginning as if they were machines set to a recurrent series of movements.

The sameness of the days was broken by few visitors. Uncles and aunts paid only short visits now: of course, they could not stay to meals, and the constraint caused by Mr Tulliver's savage silence, which seemed to add to the hollow resonance of the bare uncarpeted room when the aunts were talking, heightened the unpleasantness of these family visits on all sides, and tended to make them rare. As for other acquaintances—there is a chill air surrounding those who are down in the world, and people are glad to get away from them, as from a cold room: human beings, mere men and women, without furniture, without anything to offer you, who have ceased to count as anybody, present an embarrassing negation of reasons for wishing to see them, or of subjects on which to converse with them. At that distant day, there was a dreary isolation in the civilised Christian society of these realms for families that had dropped below their original level, unless they belonged to a sectarian church, which gets some warmth of brotherhood by walling in the sacred fire.

Chapter III

A Voice from the Past

One afternoon, when the chestnuts were coming into flower, Maggie had brought her chair outside the front door, and was seated there with a book on her knees. Her dark eyes had wandered from the book, but they did not seem to be enjoying the sunshine which pierced the screen of jasmine on the projecting porch at her right, and threw leafy shadows on her pale round cheek; they seemed rather to be searching for something that was not disclosed by the sunshine. It had been a more miserable day than usual: her father, after a visit of Wakem's, had had a paroxysm of rage, in which for some trifling fault he had beaten the boy who served in the mill. Once before, since his illness, he had had a similar paroxysm, in which he had beaten his horse, and the scene had left a lasting terror in Maggie's mind. The thought had risen, that some time or other he might beat her mother if she happened to speak in her feeble way at the wrong moment. The keenest of all dread with her was, lest her father should add to his present misfortune the wretchedness of doing something irretrievably disgraceful. The battered school-book of Tom's which she held on her knees could give her no fortitude under the pressure of that dread, and again and again her eyes had filled with tears, as they wandered vaguely, seeing neither the chestnut-trees nor the distant horizon, but only future scenes of home-sorrow.

Suddenly she was roused by the sound of the opening gate and of footsteps on the gravel. It was not Tom who was entering, but a man in a seal-skin cap and a blue plush waistcoat, carrying a pack on his back, and followed closely by a bull-terrier of brindled coat and defiant aspect.

"O Bob, it's you!" said Maggie, starting up with a smile of pleased recognition, for there had been no abundance of kind acts to efface the recollection of Bob's generosity; "I'm so glad to see you."

"Thank you, Miss," said Bob, lifting his cap and showing a delighted face, but immediately relieving himself of some accompanying embarrassment by looking down at his dog, and saying in a tone of disgust, "Get out wi' you, you thunderin' sawney!"[1]

"My brother is not at home yet, Bob," said Maggie; "he is always at St Ogg's in the daytime."

"Well, Miss," said Bob, "I should be glad to see Mr Tom—but that isn't just what I'm come for—look here!"

Bob was in the act of depositing his pack on the door-step, and with it a row of small books fastened together with string. Apparently, however, they were not the object to which he wished to call Maggie's attention, but rather something which he had carried under his arm, wrapped in a red handkerchief.

"See here!" he said again, laying the red parcel on the others and unfolding it; "you won't think I'm a-makin' too free, Miss, I hope, but I lighted on these books, and I thought they might make up to you a bit for them as you've lost; for I heared you speak o' picturs—an' as for picturs, *look* here!"

The opening of the red handkerchief had disclosed a superannuated "Keepsake" and six or seven numbers of a "Portrait Gallery,"[2] in royal octavo; and the emphatic request to look referred to a portrait of George the Fourth in all the majesty of his depressed cranium and voluminous neckcloth.

"There's all sorts o' genelmen here," Bob went on, turning over the leaves with some excitement, "wi' all sorts o' noses—an' some bald an' some wi' wigs—Parlament genelmen, I reckon. An' here," he added, opening the "Keepsake," "*here's* ladies for you, some wi' curly hair and some wi' smooth, an' some a-smiling wi' their heads o' one side, an' some as if they was goin' to cry—look here—a-sittin' on the ground out o' door, dressed like the ladies I'n seen get out o' the carriages at the balls in th' Old Hall there. My eyes, I wonder what the chaps wear as go a-courtin' em! I sot up till the clock was gone twelve last night a-lookin' at 'em—I did—till they stared at me out o' the picturs as if they'd know when I spoke to 'em. But, lors! I shouldn't know what to say to 'em. They'll be more fittin' company for you, Miss; and the man

1. Fool.
2. "Portrait Gallery": books of portrait engravings; "Keepsake": literary annual of fashionable life containing verse and illustrations.

at the book-stall, he said they banged iverything for picturs—he said they was a fust-rate article."

"And you've bought them for me, Bob?" said Maggie, deeply touched by this simple kindness. "How very, very good of you! But I'm afraid you gave a great deal of money for them."

"Not me!" said Bob. "I'd ha' gev three times the money if they'll make up to you a bit for them as was sold away from you, Miss. For I'n niver forgot how you looked when you fretted about the books bein' gone—it's stuck by me as if it was a pictur hingin' before me. An' when I see'd the book open upo' the stall, wi' the lady lookin' out of it wi' eyes a bit like your'n when you was frettin'—you'll excuse my takin' the liberty, Miss—I thought I'd make free to buy it for you, an' then I bought the books full o' genelmen to match—an' then"—here Bob took up the small stringed packet of books—"I thought you might like a bit more print as well as the picturs, an' I got these for a say-so—they're cram-full o' print, an' I thought they'd do no harm comin' along wi' these bettermost books. An' I hope you won't say me nay, an' tell me as you won't have 'em, like Mr Tom did wi' the suvreigns."

"No, indeed, Bob," said Maggie, "I'm very thankful to you for thinking of me, and being so good to me and Tom. I don't think any one ever did such a kind thing for me before. I haven't many friends who care for me."

"Hev a dog, Miss!—they're better friends nor any Christian," said Bob, laying down his pack again, which he had taken up with the intention of hurrying away; for he felt considerable shyness in talking to a young lass like Maggie, though, as he usually said of himself, "his tongue overrun him" when he began to speak. "I can't give you Mumps, 'cause he'd break his heart to go away from me—eh, Mumps, what do you say, you riff-raff?"—(Mumps declined to express himself more diffusely than by a single affirmative movement of his tail.) "But I'd get you a pup, Miss, an' welcome."

"No, thank you, Bob. We have a yard dog, and I mayn't keep a dog of my own."

"Eh, that's a pity: else there's a pup—if you didn't mind about it not being thoroughbred: its mother acts in the Punch show—an uncommon sensable bitch—she means more sense wi' her bark nor half the chaps can put into their talk from breakfast to sundown. There's one chap carries pots,—a poor low trade as any on the road,—he says, 'Why, Toby's nought but a mongrel—there's nought to look at in her.' But I says to him, 'Why, what are you yoursen but a mongrel? There wasn't much pickin' o' *your* feyther an' mother, to look at you.' Not but what I like a bit o' breed myself, but I can't abide to see one cur grinnin' at another. I wish you good-evenin', Miss," added Bob, abruptly taking up his pack again, under the consciousness that his tongue was acting in an undisciplined manner.

"Won't you come in the evening some time, and see my brother, Bob?" said Maggie.

"Yes, Miss, thank you—another time. You'll give my duty to him, if you please. Eh, he's a fine growed chap, Mr Tom is; he took to growin' i' the legs, an' *I* didn't."

The pack was down again, now—the hook of the stick having somehow gone wrong.

"You don't call Mumps a cur, I suppose?" said Maggie, divining that any interest she showed in Mumps would be gratifying to his master.

"No, Miss, a fine way off that," said Bob, with a pitying smile; "Mumps is as fine a cross as you'll see anywhere along the Floss, an' I'n been up it wi' the barge times enow. Why, the gentry stops to look at him; but you won't catch Mumps a-looking at the gentry much—he minds his own business, he does."

The expression of Mumps's face, which seemed to be tolerating the superfluous existence of objects in general, was strongly confirmatory of this high praise.

"He looks dreadfully surly," said Maggie. "Would he let me pat him?"

"Ay, that would he, and thank you. He knows his company, Mumps does. He isn't a dog as 'ull be caught wi' gingerbread: he'd smell a thief a good deal stronger nor the gingerbread—he would. Lors, I talk to him by th' hour together, when I'm walking i' lone places, and if I'n done a bit o' mischief, I allays tell him. I'n got no secrets but what Mumps knows 'em. He knows about my big thumb, he does."

"Your big thumb—what's that, Bob?" said Maggie.

"That's what it is, Miss," said Bob, quickly, exhibiting a singularly broad specimen of that difference between the man and the monkey. "It tells i' measuring out the flannel, you see. I carry flannel, 'cause it's light for my pack, an it's dear stuff, you see, so a big thumb tells. I clap my thumb at the end o' the yard and cut o' the hither side of it, and the old women aren't up to't."

"But, Bob," said Maggie, looking serious, "that's cheating: I don't like to hear you say that."

"Don't you, Miss?" said Bob, regretfully. "Then I'm sorry I said it. But I'm so used to talking to Mumps, an' he doesn't mind a bit o' cheating, when it's them skinflint women, as haggle an' haggle, an' 'ud like to get their flannel for nothing, an' 'ud niver ask theirselves how I got my dinner out on't. I niver cheat anybody as doesn't want to cheat me, Miss—lors, I'm a honest chap, I am; only I must hev a bit o' sport, an' now I don't go wi' the ferrets, I'n got no varmint to come over but them haggling women. I wish you good-evening, Miss."

"Good-bye, Bob. Thank you very much for bringing me the books. And come again to see Tom."

"Yes, Miss," said Bob, moving on a few steps; then turning half round, he said, "I'll leave off that trick wi' my big thumb, if you don't think well on me for it, Miss—but it 'ud be a pity, it would. I couldn't find another trick so good—an' what 'ud be the use o' havin' a big thumb? It might as well ha' been narrow."

Maggie, thus exalted into Bob's directing Madonna, laughed in spite of herself; at which her worshipper's blue eyes twinkled too, and under these favouring auspices he touched his cap and walked away.

The days of chivalry are not gone, notwithstanding Burke's grand dirge over them:[3] they live still in that far-off worship paid by many a youth and man to the woman of whom he never dreams that he shall touch so much as her little finger or the hem of her robe. Bob, with the pack on his back, had as respectful an adoration for this dark-eyed maiden as if he had been a knight in armour calling aloud on her name as he pricked on to the fight.

That gleam of merriment soon died away from Maggie's face, and perhaps only made the returning gloom deeper by contrast. She was too dispirited even to like answering questions about Bob's present of books, and she carried them away to her bedroom, laying them down there and seating herself on her one stool, without caring to look at them just yet. She leaned her cheek against the window-frame, and thought that the light-hearted Bob had a lot much happier than hers.

Maggie's sense of loneliness, and utter privation of joy, had deepened with the brightness of advancing spring. All the favourite out-door nooks about home, which seemed to have done their part with her parents in nurturing and cherishing her, were now mixed up with the home-sadness, and gathered no smile from the sunshine. Every affection, every delight the poor child had had, was like an aching nerve to her. There was no music for her any more—no piano, no harmonised voices, no delicious stringed instruments, with their passionate cries of imprisoned spirits sending a strange vibration through her frame. And of all her school-life there was nothing left her now but her little collection of school-books, which she turned over with a sickening sense that she knew them all, and they were all barren of comfort. Even at school she had often wished for books with *more* in them: everything she had learned there seemed like the ends of long threads that snapped immediately. And now—without the indirect charm of school-emulation—Télémaque[4] was mere bran; so were the hard dry questions on Christian Doctrine: there was no flavour in them—no strength. Sometimes Maggie thought she could have been contented with absorbing fancies; if she could have had all Scott's novels and all Byron's poems!—then, perhaps, she might have found happiness enough to dull her sensibility to her actual daily life. And yet . . . they were hardly what she wanted. She could make dream-worlds of her own—but no dream-world would satisfy

3. In Edmund Burke's *Reflections on the Revolution in France* (1790).
4. The hero of a didactic romance by François Fénelon, *Les Aventures de Télémaque* (The adventures of Télémaque) (1699).

her now. She wanted some explanation of this hard, real life: the unhappy-looking father, seated at the dull breakfast-table; the childish, bewildered mother; the little sordid tasks that filled the hours, or the more oppressive emptiness of weary, joyless leisure; the need of some tender, demonstrative love; the cruel sense that Tom didn't mind what she thought or felt, and that they were no longer playfellows together; the privation of all pleasant things that had come to *her* more than to others: she wanted some key that would enable her to understand, and, in understanding, endure, the heavy weight that had fallen on her young heart. If she had been taught "real learning and wisdom, such as great men knew," she thought she should have held the secrets of life; if she had only books, that she might learn for herself what wise men knew! Saints and martyrs had never interested Maggie so much as sages and poets. She knew little of saints and martyrs, and had gathered, as a general result of her teaching, that they were a temporary provision against the spread of Catholicism, and had all died at Smithfield.[5]

In one of these meditations it occurred to her that she had forgotten Tom's school-books, which had been sent home in his trunk. But she found the stock unaccountably shrunk down to the few old ones which had been well thumbed—the Latin Dictionary and Grammar, a Delectus, a torn Eutropius, the well-worn Virgil, Aldrich's Logic,[6] and the exasperating Euclid. Still, Latin, Euclid, and Logic would surely be a considerable step in masculine wisdom—in that knowledge which made men contented, and even glad to live. Not that the yearning for effectual wisdom was quite unmixed: a certain mirage would now and then rise on the desert of the future, in which she seemed to see herself honoured for her surprising attainments. And so the poor child, with her soul's hunger and her illusions of self-flattery, began to nibble at this thick-rinded fruit of the tree of knowledge, filling her vacant hours with Latin, geometry, and the forms of the syllogism, and feeling a gleam of triumph now and then that her understanding was quite equal to these peculiarly masculine studies. For a week or two she went on resolutely enough, though with an occasional sinking of heart, as if she had set out toward the Promised Land alone, and found it a thirsty, trackless, uncertain journey. In the severity of her early resolution, she would take Aldrich out into the fields, and then look off her book towards the sky, where the lark was twinkling, or to the reeds and bushes by the river, from which the waterfowl rustled forth on its anxious, awkward flight—with a startled sense that the relation between Aldrich and this living world was extremely remote for her. The discouragement deepened as the days went on, and the eager heart gained faster and faster on the patient mind. Somehow, when she sat at the window with her book, her eyes *would* fix themselves blankly on the out-door sunshine; then they would

5. Site of Protestant martyrdom under the Catholic Queen Mary (1553–58).
6. Henry Aldrich, *Artis Logicae Compendium* (1691); Eutropius: history of ancient Rome.

fill with tears, and sometimes, if her mother was not in the room, the studies would all end in sobbing. She rebelled against her lot, she fainted under its loneliness, and fits even of anger and hatred towards her father and mother, who were so unlike what she would have them to be—towards Tom, who checked her, and met her thought or feeling always by some thwarting difference—would flow out over her affections and conscience like a lava stream, and frighten her with a sense that it was not difficult for her to become a demon. Then her brain would be busy with wild romances of a flight from home in search of something less sordid and dreary: she would go to some great man—Walter Scott, perhaps—and tell him how wretched and how clever she was, and he would surely do something for her. But, in the middle of her vision, her father would perhaps enter the room for the evening, and, surprised that she sat still without noticing him, would say, complainingly, "Come, am I to fetch my slippers myself?" The voice pierced through Maggie like a sword: there was another sadness besides her own, and she had been thinking of turning her back on it and forsaking it.

This afternoon, the sight of Bob's cheerful freckled face had given her discontent a new direction. She thought it was part of the hardship of her life that there was laid upon her the burthen of larger wants than others seemed to feel—that she had to endure this wide hopeless yearning for that something, whatever it was, that was greatest and best on this earth. She wished she could have been like Bob, with his easily satisfied ignorance, or like Tom, who had something to do on which he could fix his mind with a steady purpose, and disregard everything else. Poor child! as she leaned her head against the window-frame, with her hands clasped tighter and tighter, and her foot beating the ground, she was as lonely in her trouble as if she had been the only girl in the civilised world of that day who had come out of her school-life with a soul untrained for inevitable struggles—with no other part of her inherited share in the hard-won treasures of thought, which generations of painful toil have laid up for the race of men, than shreds and patches of feeble literature and false history—with much futile information about Saxon and other kings of doubtful example—but unhappily quite without that knowledge of the irreversible laws within and without her, which, governing the habits, becomes morality, and, developing the feelings of submission and dependence, becomes religion:—as lonely in her trouble as if every other girl besides herself had been cherished and watched over by elder minds, not forgetful of their own early time, when need was keen and impulse strong.

At last Maggie's eyes glanced down on the books that lay on the window-shelf, and she half forsook her reverie to turn over listlessly the leaves of the "Portrait Gallery," but she soon pushed this aside to examine the little row of books tied together with string. "Beauties of the Spectator," "Rasselas," "Economy of Human Life," "Gregory's Letters"—

she knew the sort of matter that was inside all these: the "Christian Year"—that seemed to be a hymn-book, and she laid it down again; but *Thomas à Kempis*?[7]—the name had come across her in her reading, and she felt the satisfaction, which every one knows, of getting some ideas to attach to a name that strays solitary in the memory. She took up the little, old, clumsy book with some curiosity: it had the corners turned down in many places, and some hand, now for ever quiet, had made at certain passages strong pen-and-ink marks, long since browned by time. Maggie turned from leaf to leaf, and read where the quiet hand pointed . . . "Know that the love of thyself doth hurt thee more than anything in the world. . . . If thou seekest this or that, and wouldst be here or there to enjoy thy own will and pleasure, thou shalt never be quiet nor free from care: for in everything somewhat will be wanting, and in every place there will be some that will cross thee. . . . Both above and below, which way soever thou dost turn thee, everywhere thou shalt find the Cross: and everywhere of necessity thou must have patience, if thou wilt have inward peace, and enjoy an everlasting crown. . . . If thou desire to mount unto this height, thou must set out courageously, and lay the axe to the root, that thou mayst pluck up and destroy that hidden inordinate inclination to thyself, and unto all private and earthly good. On this sin, that a man inordinately loveth himself, almost all dependeth, whatsoever is thoroughly to be overcome; which evil being once overcome and subdued, there will presently ensue great peace and tranquillity. . . . It is but little thou sufferest in comparison of them that have suffered so much, were so strongly tempted, so grievously afflicted, so many ways tried and exercised. Thou oughtest therefore to call to mind the more heavy sufferings of others, that thou mayest the easier bear thy little adversities. And if they seem not little unto thee, beware lest thy impatience be the cause thereof. . . . Blessed are those ears that receive the whispers of the divine voice, and listen not to the whisperings of the world. Blessed are those ears which hearken not unto the voice which soundeth outwardly, but unto the Truth, which teacheth inwardly. . . ."

A strange thrill of awe passed through Maggie while she read, as if she had been wakened in the night by a strain of solemn music, telling of beings whose souls had been astir while hers was in stupor. She went on from one brown mark to another, where the quiet hand seemed to point, hardly conscious that she was reading—seeming rather to listen while a low voice said—

7. *Spectator*: a periodical edited by Joseph Addison and Richard Steele, 1711–12; "Rasselas": *Rasselas. The Prince of Abissinia. A Tale* (1759) by Samuel Johnson; "Economy of Human Life": *The Economy of Human Life* (1802) by Robert Dodsley; "Gregory's Letters": either *Letters on the Evidences, Doctrines, and Duties of the Christian Religion* (1811) by Olinthus Gilbert Gregory or the letters of Pope Gregory I; "Christian Year": *The Christian Year* (1827) by John Keble; *Thomas à Kempis: Imitation of Christ* (1470), popular mystical work by the Augustinian monk.

"Why dost thou here gaze about, since this is not the place of thy rest? In heaven ought to be thy dwelling, and all earthly things are to be looked on as they forward they journey thither. All things pass away, and thou together with them. Beware thou cleave not unto them, lest thou be entangled and perish. . . . If a man should give all his substance, yet it is as nothing. And if he should do great penances, yet are they but little. And if he should attain to all knowledge, he is yet far off. And if he should be of great virtue, and very fervent devotion, yet is there much wanting; to wit, one thing, which is most necessary for him. What is that? That having left all, he leave himself, and go wholly out of himself, and retain nothing of self-love. . . . I have often said unto thee, and now again I say the same, Forsake thyself, resign thyself, and thou shalt enjoy much inward peace. . . . Then shall all vain imaginations, evil perturbations, and superfluous cares fly away; then shall immoderate fear leave thee, and inordinate love shall die."

Maggie drew a long breath and pushed her heavy hair back, as if to see a sudden vision more clearly. Here, then, was a secret of life that would enable her to renounce all other secrets—here was a sublime height to be reached without the help of outward things—here was insight, and strength, and conquest, to be won by means entirely within her own soul, where a supreme Teacher was waiting to be heard. It flashed through her like the suddenly apprehended solution of a problem, that all the miseries of her young life had come from fixing her heart on her own pleasure, as if that were the central necessity of the universe; and for the first time she saw the possibility of shifting the position from which she looked at the gratification of her own desires—of taking her stand out of herself, and looking at her own life as an insignificant part of a divinely-guided whole. She read on and on in the old book, devouring eagerly the dialogues with the invisible Teacher, the pattern of sorrow, the source of all strength; returning to it after she had been called away, and reading till the sun went down behind the willows. With all the hurry of an imagination that could never rest in the present, she sat in the deepening twilight forming plans of self-humiliation and entire devotedness; and, in the ardour of first discovery, renunciation seemed to her the entrance into that satisfaction which she had so long been craving in vain. She had not perceived—how could she until she had lived longer?—the inmost truth of the old monk's outpourings, that renunciation remains sorrow, though a sorrow borne willingly. Maggie was still panting for happiness, and was in ecstasy because she had found the key to it. She knew nothing of doctrines and systems—of mysticism or quietism; but this voice out of the far-off middle ages was the direct communication of a human soul's belief and experience, and came to Maggie as an unquestioned message.

I supposed that is the reason why the small old-fashioned book, for which you need only pay sixpence at a book-stall, works miracles to this day, turning bitter waters into sweetness: while expensive sermons and treatises, newly issues, leave all things as they were before. It was written down by a hand that waited for the heart's prompting; it is the chronicle of a solitary, hidden anguish, struggle, trust and triumph—not written on velvet cushions to teach endurance to those who are treading with bleeding feet on the stones. And so it remains to all time a lasting record of human needs and human consolations: the voice of a brother who, ages ago, felt and suffered and renounced—in the cloister, perhaps, with serge gown and tonsured head, with much chanting and long fasts, and with a fashion of speech different from ours—but under the same silent far-off heavens, and with the same passionate desires, the same strivings, the same failures, the same weariness.

In writing the history of unfashionable families, one is apt to fall into a tone of emphasis which is very far from being the tone of good society, where principles and beliefs are not only of an extremely moderate kind, but are always presupposed, no subjects being eligible but such as can be touched with a light and graceful irony. But then, good society has its claret and its velvet-carpets, its dinner-engagements six weeks deep, its opera and its faëry ball-rooms; rides off its ennui on thoroughbred horses, lounges at the club, has to keep clear of crinoline vortices, gets it science done by Faraday,[8] and its religion by the superior clergy who are to be met in the best houses: how should it have time or need for belief and emphasis? But good society, floated on gossamer wings of light irony, is of very expensive production; requiring nothing less than a wide and arduous national life condensed in unfragrant deafening factories, cramping itself in mines, sweating at furnaces, grinding, hammering, weaving under more or less oppression of carbonic acid—or else, spread over sheepwalks, and scattered in lonely houses and huts on the clayey or chalky corn-lands, where the rainy days look dreary. This wide national life is based entirely on emphasis—the emphasis of want, which urges it into all the activities necessary for the maintenance of good society and light irony: it spends it heavy years often in a chill, uncarpeted fashion, amidst family discord unsoftened by long corridors. Under such circumstances, there are many among its myriads of souls who have absolutely needed an emphatic belief: life in this unpleasurable shape demanding some solution even to unspeculative minds; just as you inquire into the stuffing of your couch when anything galls you there, whereas eider-down and perfect French springs excite no question. Some have an emphatic belief in alcohol, and seek their *ekstasis*[9] or outside standing-ground in gin; but the rest require something that good society calls "enthusiasm," something that will present motives in an entire absence of high prizes, something that will give patience and feed human love when the limbs ache with weariness, and human looks are

8. Michael Faraday, eminent nineteenth-century scientist and lecturer.
9. Religious ecstasy (Greek).

hard upon us—something, clearly, that lies outside personal desires, that includes resignation for ourselves and active love for what is not ourselves. Now and then, that sort of enthusiasm finds a far-echoing voice that comes from an experience springing out of the deepest need. And it was by being brought within the long lingering vibrations of such a voice that Maggie, with her girl's face and unnoted sorrows, found an effort and a hope that helped her through years of loneliness, making out a faith for herself without the aid of established authorities and appointed guides—for they were not at hand, and her need was pressing. From what you know of her, you will not be surprised that she threw some exaggeration and wilfulness, some pride and impetuosity, even into her self-renunciation: her own life was still a drama for her, in which she demanded of herself that her part should be played with intensity. And so it came to pass that she often lost the spirit of humility by being excessive in the outward act; she often strove after too high a flight, and came down with her poor little half-fledged wings dabbled in the mud. For example, she not only determined to work at plain sewing, that she might contribute something towards the fund in the tin box, but she went, in the first instance, in her zeal of self-mortification, to ask for it at a linen-shop in St Ogg's, instead of getting it in a more quiet and indirect way; and could see nothing but what was entirely wrong and unkind, nay, persecuting, in Tom's reproof of her for this unnecessary act. "I don't like *my* sister to do such things," said Tom; "*I'll* take care that the debts are paid, without your lowering yourself in that way." Surely there was some tenderness and bravery mingled with the worldliness and self-assertion of that little speech; but Maggie held it as dross, overlooking the grains of gold, and took Tom's rebuke as one of her outward crosses. Tom was very hard to her, she used to think, in her long night-watchings—to her who had always loved him so; and then she strove to be contented with that hardness, and to require nothing. That is the path we all like when we set out on our abandonment of egoism—the path of martyrdom and endurance, where the palm-branches grow, rather than the steep highway of tolerance, just allowance, and self-blame, where there are no leafy honours to be gathered and worn.

The old books, Virgil, Euclid, and Aldrich—that wrinkled fruit of the tree of knowledge—had been all laid by; for Maggie had turned her back on the vain ambition to share the thoughts of the wise. In her first ardour she flung away the books with a sort of triumph that she had risen above the need of them; and if they had been her own, she would have burned them, believing that she would never repent. She read so eagerly and constantly in her three books, the Bible, Thomas-à-Kempis, and the "Christian Year" (no longer rejected as a "hymn-book"), that they filled her mind with a continual stream of rhythmic memories; and she was too ardently learning to see all nature and life in the light of her new faith, to need any other material for her mind to work on, as she sat with her well-plied needle, making shirts and other complicated stitchings, falsely called "plain"—by no means plain to Maggie, since wristband and sleeve and the like had a capability of being sewed in wrong side outwards in moments of mental wandering.

Hanging diligently over her sewing, Maggie was a sight any one might have been pleased to look at. That new inward life of hers, notwithstanding some volcanic upheavings of imprisoned passions, yet shone out in her face with a tender soft light that mingled itself as added loveliness with the gradually enriched colour and outline of her blossoming youth. Her mother felt the change in her with a sort of puzzled wonder that Maggie should be "growing up so good;" it was amazing that this once "contrairy" child was become so submissive, so backward to assert her own will. Maggie used to look up from her work and find her mother's eyes fixed upon her; they were watching and waiting for the large young glance, as if her elder frame got some needful warmth from it. The mother was getting fond of her tall, brown girl, the only bit of furniture now on which she could bestow her anxiety and pride; and Maggie, in spite of her own ascetic wish to have no personal adornment, was obliged to give way to her mother about her hair, and submit to have the abundant black locks plaited into a coronet on the summit of her head, after the pitiable fashion of those antiquated times.

"Let your mother have that bit o' pleasure, my dear," said Mrs Tulliver; "I'd trouble enough with your hair once."

So Maggie, glad of anything that would soothe her mother, and cheer their long day together, consented to the vain decoration, and showed a queenly head above her old frocks—steadily refusing, however, to look at herself in the glass. Mrs Tulliver liked to call the father's attention to Maggie's hair and other unexpected virtues, but he had a brusque reply to give.

"I knew well enough what she'd be, before now—it's nothing new to me. But it's a pity she isn't made o' commoner stuff—she'll be thrown away, I doubt: there'll be nobody to marry her as is fit for her."

And Maggie's graces of mind and body fed his gloom. He sat patiently enough while she read him a chapter, or said something timidly when they were alone together about trouble being turned into a blessing. He took it all as part of his daughter's goodness, which made his misfortunes the sadder to him because they damaged her chance in life. In a mind charged with an eager purpose and an unsatisfied vindictiveness, there is no room for new feelings: Mr Tulliver did not want spiritual consolation—he wanted to shake off the degradation of debt, and to have his revenge.

Book Fifth

WHEAT AND TARES[1]

Chapter I

In the Red Deeps

The family sitting-room was a long room with a window at each end; one looking towards the croft and along the Ripple to the banks of the Floss, the other into the mill-yard. Maggie was sitting with her work against the latter window when she saw Mr Wakem entering the yard, as usual, on his fine black horse; but not alone, as usual. Some one was with him—a figure in a cloak, on a handsome pony. Maggie had hardly time to feel that it was Philip come back, before they were in front of the window, and he was raising his hat to her; while his father, catching the movement by a side-glance, looked sharply round at them both.

Maggie hurried away from the window and carried her work up-stairs; for Mr Wakem sometimes came in and inspected the books, and Maggie felt that the meeting with Philip would be robbed of all pleasure in the presence of the two fathers. Some day, perhaps, she should see him when they could just shake hands, and she could tell him that she remembered his goodness to Tom, and the things he had said to her in the old days, though they could never be friends any more. It was not at all agitating to Maggie to see Philip again: she retained her childish gratitude and pity towards him, and remembered his cleverness; and in the early weeks of her loneliness she had continually recalled the image of him among the people who had been kind to her in life; often wishing she had him for a brother and a teacher, as they had fancied it might have been, in their talk together. But that sort of wishing had been banished along with other dreams that savoured of seeking her own will; and she thought, besides, that Philip might be altered by his life abroad—he might have become worldly, and really not care about her saying anything to him now. And yet, his face was wonderfully little altered—it was only a larger, more manly copy of the pale small-featured

1. From Matthew 13:24–30.

boy's face, with the grey eyes and the boyish waving brown hair: there was the old deformity to awaken the old pity; and after all her meditations, Maggie felt that she really *should* like to say a few words to him. He might still be melancholy, as he always used to be, and like her to look at him kindly. She wondered if he remembered how he used to like her eyes; with that thought Maggie glanced towards the square looking-glass which was condemned to hang with its face towards the wall, and she half-started from her seat to reach it down; but she checked herself and snatched up her work, trying to repress the rising wishes by forcing her memory to recall snatches of hymns, until she saw Philip and his father returning along the road, and she could go down again.

It was far on in June now, and Maggie was inclined to lengthen the daily walk which was her one indulgence; but this day and the following she was so busy with work which must be finished that she never went beyond the gate, and satisfied her need of the open air by sitting out of doors. One of her frequent walks, when she was not obliged to go to St Ogg's, was to a spot that lay beyond what was called the "Hill"—an insignificant rise of ground crowned by trees, lying along the side of the road which ran by the gates of Dorlcote Mill. Insignificant I call it, because in height it was hardly more than a bank: but there may come moments when Nature makes a mere bank a means towards a fateful result, and that is why I ask you to imagine this high bank crowned with trees, making an uneven wall for some quarter of a mile along the left side of Dorlcote Mill and the pleasant fields behind it, bounded by the murmuring Ripple. Just where this line of bank sloped down again to the level, a by-road turned off and led to the other side of the rise, where it was broken into very capricious hollows and mounds by the working of an exhausted stone-quarry—so long exhausted that both mounds and hollows were now clothed with brambles and trees, and here and there by a stretch of grass which a few sheep kept closenibbled. In her childish days Maggie held this place, called the Red Deeps, in very great awe, and needed all her confidence in Tom's bravery to reconcile her to an excursion thither—visions of robbers and fierce animals haunting every hollow. But now it had the charm for her which any broken ground, any mimic rock and ravine, have for the eyes that rest habitually on the level; especially in summer, when she could sit on a grassy hollow under the shadow of a branching ash, stooping aslant from the steep above her, and listen to the hum of insects, like tiniest bells on the garment of Silence, or see the sunlight piercing the distant boughs, as if to chase and drive home the truant heavenly blue of the wild hyacinths. In this June time too, the dog-roses were in their glory, and that was an additional reason why Maggie should direct her walk to the Red Deeps, rather than to any other spot, on the first day she was free to wander at her will—a pleasure she loved so well, that sometimes, in her ardours of renunciation, she thought she ought to deny herself the frequent indulgence in it.

You may see her now, as she walks down the favourite turning, and enters the Deeps by a narrow path through a group of Scotch firs—her tall figure and old lavender gown visible through an hereditary black silk shawl of some wide-meshed net-like material; and now she is sure of being unseen, she takes off her bonnet and ties it over her arm. One would certainly suppose her to be farther on in life than her seventeenth year—perhaps because of the slow resigned sadness of the glance, from which all search and unrest seem to have departed, perhaps because her broad-chested figure has the mould of early womanhood. Youth and health have withstood well the involuntary and voluntary hardships of her lot, and the nights in which she has lain on the hard floor for a penance have left no obvious trace; the eyes are liquid, the brown cheek is firm and rounded, the full lips are red. With her dark colouring and jet crown surmounting her tall figure, she seems to have a sort of kinship with the grand Scotch firs, at which she is looking up as if she loved them well. Yet one has a sense of uneasiness in looking at her—a sense of opposing elements, of which a fierce collision is imminent: surely there is a hushed expression, such as one often sees in older faces under borderless caps, out of keeping with the resistant youth, which one expects to flash out in a sudden, passionate glance, that will dissipate all the quietude, like a damp fire leaping out again when all seemed safe.

But Maggie herself was not uneasy at this moment. She was calmly enjoying the free air, while she looked up at the old fir-trees, and thought that those broken ends of branches were the records of past storms, which had only made the red stems soar higher. But while her eyes were still turned upward, she became conscious of a moving shadow cast by the evening sun on the grassy path before her, and looked down with a startled gesture to see Philip Wakem, who first raised his hat, and then, blushing deeply, came forward to her and put out his hand. Maggie, too, coloured with surprise, which soon gave way to pleasure. She put out her hand and looked down at the deformed figure before her with frank eyes, filled for the moment with nothing but the memory of her child's feelings—a memory that was always strong in her. She was the first to speak.

"You startled me," she said, smiling faintly; "I never meet any one here. How came you to be walking here? Did you come to meet *me*?"

It was impossible not to perceive that Maggie felt herself a child again.

"Yes, I did," said Philip, still embarrassed: "I wished to see you very much. I watched a long while yesterday on the bank near your house to see if you would come out, but you never came. Then I watched again to-day, and when I saw the way you took, I kept you in sight and came down the bank, behind there. I hope you will not be displeased with me."

"No," said Maggie, with simple seriousness, walking on, as if she meant Philip to accompany her, "I'm very glad you came, for I wished very much to have an opportunity of speaking to you. I've never forgotten how good you were long ago to Tom, and me too; but I was not sure that you would remember us so well. Tom and I have had a great deal of trouble since then, and I think *that* makes one think more of what happened before the trouble came."

"I can't believe that you have thought of me so much as I have thought of you," said Philip, timidly. "Do you know, when I was away, I made a picture of you as you looked that morning in the study when you said you would not forget me."

Philip drew a large miniature-case from his pocket, and opened it. Maggie saw her old self leaning on a table, with her black locks hanging down behind her ears, looking into space with strange, dreamy eyes. It was a water-colour sketch, of real merit as a portrait.

"O dear," said Maggie, smiling, and flushed with pleasure, "what a queer little girl I was! I remember myself with my hair in that way, in that pink frock. I really *was* like a gypsy. I daresay I am now," she added, after a little pause; "am I like what you expected me to be?"

The words might have been those of a coquette, but the full bright glance Maggie turned on Philip was not that of a coquette. She really did hope he liked her face as it was now, but it was simply the rising again of her innate delight in admiration and love. Philip met her eyes and looked at her in silence for a long moment, before he said, quietly, "No, Maggie."

The light died out a little from Maggie's face, and there was a slight trembling of the lip. Her eyelids fell lower, but she did not turn away her head, and Philip continued to look at her. Then he said, slowly—

"You are very much more beautiful than I thought you would be."

"Am I?" said Maggie, the pleasure returning in a deeper flush. She turned her face away from him and took some steps, looking straight before her in silence, as if she were adjusting her consciousness to this new idea. Girls are so accustomed to think of dress as the main ground of vanity, that, in abstaining from the looking-glass, Maggie had thought more of abandoning all care for adornment than of renouncing the contemplation of her face. Comparing herself with elegant, wealthy young ladies, it had not occurred to her that she could produce any effect with her person. Philip seemed to like the silence well. He walked by her side, watching her face, as if that sight left no room for any other wish. They had passed from among the fir-trees, and had now come to a green hollow almost surrounded by an amphitheatre of the pale pink dog-roses. But as the light about them had brightened, Maggie's face had lost its glow. She stood still when they were in the hollows, and, looking at Philip again, she said, in a serious, sad voice—

"I wish we could have been friends—I mean, if it would have been good and right for us. But that is the trial I have to bear in everything: I may not keep anything I used to love when I was little. The old books went; and Tom is different—and my father. It is like death. I must part with everything I cared for when I was a child. And I must part with you: we must never take any notice of each other again. That was what I wanted to speak to you for. I wanted to let you know that Tom and I can't do as we like about such things, and that if I behave as if I had forgotten all about you, it is not out of envy or pride—or—or any bad feeling."

Maggie spoke with more and more sorrowful gentleness as she went on, and her eyes began to fill with tears. The deepening expression of pain on Philip's face gave him a stronger resemblance to his boyish self, and made the deformity appeal more strongly to her pity.

"I know—I see all that you mean," he said, in a voice that had become feebler from discouragement: "I know what there is to keep us apart on both sides. But it is not right, Maggie—don't you be angry with me, I am so used to call you Maggie in my thoughts—it is not right to sacrifice everything to other people's unreasonable feelings. I would give up a great deal for *my* father; but I would not give up a friendship or—or an attachment of any sort, in obedience to any wish of his that I didn't recognise as right."

"I don't know," said Maggie, musingly. "Often, when I have been angry and discontented, it has seemed to me that I was not bound to give up anything; and I have gone on thinking till it has seemed to me that I could think away all my duty. But no good has ever come of that—it was an evil state of mind. I'm quite sure that whatever I might do, I should wish in the end that I had gone without anything for myself, rather than have made my father's life harder to him."

"But would it make his life harder if we were to see each other sometimes?" said Philip. He was going to say something else, but checked himself.

"O, I'm sure he wouldn't like it. Don't ask me why, or anything about it," said Maggie, in a distressed tone. "My father feels so strongly about some things. He is not at all happy."

"No more am I," said Philip, impetuously: "*I* am not happy."

"Why?" said Maggie, gently. "At least—I ought not to ask—but I'm very, very sorry."

Philip turned to walk on, as if he had not patience to stand still any longer, and they went out of the hollow, winding amongst the trees and bushes in silence. After that last word of Philip's, Maggie could not bear to insist immediately on their parting.

"I've been a great deal happier," she said at last, timidly, "since I have given up thinking about what is easy and pleasant, and being discontented because I couldn't have my own will. Our life is determined for us—and it makes the mind very free when we give up wishing, and only think of bearing what is laid upon us, and doing what is given us to do."

"But I can't give up wishing," said Philip, impatiently. "It seems to me we can never give up longing and wishing while we are thoroughly alive. There are certain things we feel to be beautiful and good, and we *must* hunger after them. How can we ever be satisfied without them until our feelings are deadened? I delight in fine pictures—I long to be able to paint such. I strive and strive, and can't produce what I want. That is pain to me, and always *will* be pain, until my faculties lose their keenness, like aged eyes. Then there are many other things I long for"—here Philip hesitated a little, and then said—"things that other men have, and that will always be denied me. My life will have nothing great or beautiful in it; I would rather not have lived."

"O, Philip," said Maggie, "I wish you didn't feel so." But her heart began to beat with something of Philip's discontent.

"Well then," said he, turning quickly round and fixing his grey eyes entreatingly in her face, "I should be contented to live, if you would let me see you sometimes." Then, checked by a fear which her face suggested, he looked away again, and said, more calmly, "I have no friend to whom I can tell everything—no one who cares enough about me; and if I could only see you now and then, and you would let me talk to you a little, and show me that you cared for me—and that we may always be friends in heart, and help each other—then I might come to be glad of life."

"But how can I see you, Philip?" said Maggie, falteringly. (Could she really do him good? It would be very hard to say "good-bye" this day, and not speak to him again. Here was a new interest to vary the days —it was so much easier to renounce the interest before it came.)

"If you would let me see you here sometimes—walk with you here —I would be contented if it were only once or twice in a month. *That* could injure no one's happiness, and it would sweeten my life. Besides," Philip went on, with all the inventive astuteness of love at one-and-twenty, "if there is any enmity between those who belong to us, we ought all the more to try and quench it by our friendship—I mean, that by our influence on both sides we might bring about a healing of the wounds that have been made in the past, if I could know everything about them. And I don't believe there is any enmity in my own father's mind: I think he has proved the contrary."

Maggie shook her head slowly, and was silent, under conflicting thoughts. It seemed to her inclination, that to see Philip now and then, and keep up the bond of friendship with him, was something not only innocent, but good: perhaps she might really help him to find contentment as she had found it. The voice that said this made sweet music to Maggie; but athwart it there came an urgent monotonous warning from another voice which she had been learning to obey: the warning that such interviews implied secrecy—implied doing something she would dread to be discovered in—something that, if discovered, must cause anger and pain; and that the admission of anything so near doubleness would act as a spiritual blight. Yet the music would swell out again, like chimes borne onward by a recurrent breeze, persuading her that the wrong lay all in the faults and weaknesses of others, and that there was such a thing as futile sacrifice for one to the injury of another. It was very cruel for Philip that he should be shrunk from, because of an unjustifiable vindictiveness towards his father—poor Philip, whom some people would shrink from only because he was deformed. The idea that he might become her lover, or that her meeting him could cause disapproval in that light, had not occurred to her; and Philip saw the absence of this idea clearly enough—saw it with a certain pang, although it made her consent to his request the less unlikely. There was bitterness to him in the perception that Maggie was almost as frank and unconstrained towards him as when she was a child.

"I can't say either yes or no," she said at last, turning round and walking towards the way she had come; "I must wait, lest I should decide wrongly. I must seek for guidance."

"May I come again, then—to-morrow—or the next day—or next week?"

"I think I had better write," said Maggie, faltering again. "I have to go to St Ogg's sometimes, and I can put the letter in the post."

"O no," said Philip, eagerly; "that would not be so well. My father might see the letter—and—he has not any enmity, I believe, but he views things differently from me: he thinks a great deal about wealth and position. Pray let me come here once more. *Tell* me when it shall be; or if you can't tell me, I will come as often as I can till I do see you."

"I think it must be so, then," said Maggie, "for I can't be quite certain of coming here any particular evening."

Maggie felt a great relief in adjourning the decision. She was free now to enjoy the minutes of companionship; she almost thought she might linger a little; the next time they met she should have to pain Philip by telling him her determination.

"I can't help thinking," she said, looking smilingly at him, after a few moments of silence, "how strange it is that we should have met and talked to each other, just as if it had been only yesterday when we parted at Lorton. And yet we must both be very much altered in those five years—I think it is five years. How was it you seemed to have a sort of feeling that I was the same Maggie?—I was not quite so sure that you would be the same: I know you are so clever, and you must have seen and learnt so much to fill your mind: I was not quite sure you would care about me now."

"I have never had any doubt that you would be the same, whenever I might see you," said Philip. "I mean, the same in everything that made me like you better than any one else. I don't want to explain that: I don't think any of the strongest effects our natures are susceptible of can ever be explained. We can neither detect the process by which they are arrived at, nor the mode in which they act on us. The greatest of painters only once painted a mysteriously divine child;[2] he couldn't have told how he did it, and we can't tell why we feel it to be divine. I think there are stores laid up in our human nature that our understandings can make no complete inventory of. Certain strains of music affect me so strangely—I can never hear them without their changing my whole attitude of mind for a time, and if the effect would last, I might be capable of heroisms."

"Ah! I know what you mean about music—*I* feel so," said Maggie, clasping her hands with her old impetuosity. "At least," she added, in a saddened tone, "I used to feel so when I had any music; I never have any now except the organ at church."

"And you long for it, Maggie?" said Philip, looking at her with affectionate pity. "Ah, you can have very little that is beautiful in your life. Have you many books? You were so fond of them when you were a little girl."

They were come back to the hollow, round which the dog-roses grew, and they both paused under the charm of the faëry evening light, reflected from the pale pink clusters.

"No, I have given up books," said Maggie, quietly, "except a very, very few."

Philip had already taken from his pocket a small volume, and was looking at the back, as he said—

"Ah, this is the second volume, I see, else you might have liked to take it home with you. I put it in my pocket because I am studying a scene for a picture."

Maggie had looked at the back too, and saw the title: it revived an old impression with overmastering force.

" 'The Pirate,' "[3] she said, taking the book from Philip's hands. "O, I began that once; I read to where Minna is walking with Cleveland, and I could never get to read the rest. I went on with it in my own head, and I made several endings; but they were all unhappy. I could never make a happy ending out of that beginning. Poor Minna! I wonder what is the real end. For a long while I couldn't get my mind away

2. The *Sistine Madonna* of Raphael, Italian Renaissance painter.
3. Scott novel (1821).

from the Shetland Isles—I used to feel the wind blowing on me from the rough sea."

Maggie spoke rapidly, with glistening eyes.

"Take that volume home with you, Maggie," said Philip, watching her with delight. "I don't want it now. I shall make a picture of you instead—you, among the Scotch firs and the slanting shadows."

Maggie had not heard a word he had said: she was absorbed in a page at which she had opened. But suddenly she closed the book, and gave it back to Philip, shaking her head with a backward movement, as if to say "avaunt" to floating visions.

"Do keep it, Maggie," said Philip, entreatingly; "it will give you pleasure."

"No, thank you," said Maggie, putting it aside with her hand and walking on. "It would make me in love with this world again, as I used to be—it would make me long to see and know many things—it would make me long for a full life."

"But you will not always be shut up in your present lot: why should you starve your mind in that way? It is narrow asceticism—I don't like to see you persisting in it, Maggie. Poetry and art and knowledge are sacred and pure."

"But not for me—not for me," said Maggie, walking more hurriedly. "Because I should want too much. I must wait—this life will not last long."

"Don't hurry away from me without saying 'good-bye,' Maggie," said Philip, as they reached the group of Scotch firs, and she continued still to walk along without speaking. "I must not go any farther, I think, must I?"

"O no, I forgot; good-bye," said Maggie, pausing, and putting out her hand to him. The action brought her feeling back in a strong current to Philip; and after they had stood looking at each other in silence for a few moments, with their hands clasped, she said, withdrawing her hand,

"I'm very grateful to you for thinking of me all those years. It is very sweet to have people love us. What a wonderful, beautiful thing it seems that God should have made your heart so that you could care about a queer little girl whom you only knew for a few weeks! I remember saying to you, that I thought you cared for me more than Tom did."

"Ah, Maggie," said Philip, almost fretfully, "you would never love me so well as you love your brother."

"Perhaps not," said Maggie, simply; "but then, you know, the first thing I ever remember in my life is standing with Tom by the side of the Floss, while he held my hand: everything before that is dark to me. But I shall never forget you—though we must keep apart."

"Don't say so, Maggie," said Philip. "If I kept that little girl in my mind for five years, didn't I earn some part in her? She ought not to take herself quite away from me."

"Not if I were free," said Maggie; "but I am not—I must submit." She hesitated a moment, and then added, "And I wanted to say to you, that you had better not take more notice of my brother than just bowing to him. He once told me not to speak to you again, and he doesn't change his mind. . . . O dear, the sun is set. I am too long away. Good-bye." She gave him her hand once more.

"I shall come here as often as I can, till I see you again, Maggie. Have some feeling for *me* as well as for others."

"Yes, yes, I have," said Maggie, hurrying away, and quickly disappearing behind the last fir-tree; though Philip's gaze after her remained immovable for minutes as if he saw her still.

Maggie went home, with an inward conflict already begun; Philip went home to do nothing but remember and hope. You can hardly help blaming him severely. He was four or five years older than Maggie, and had a full consciousness of his feeling towards her to aid him in foreseeing the character his contemplated interviews with her would bear in the opinion of a third person. But you must not suppose that he was capable of a gross selfishness, or that he could have been satisfied without persuading himself that he was seeking to infuse some happiness into Maggie's life—seeking this even more than any direct ends for himself. He could give her sympathy—he could give her help. There was not the slightest promise of love towards him in her manner; it was nothing more than the sweet girlish tenderness she had shown him when she was twelve: perhaps she would never love him—perhaps no woman ever *could* love him: well, then, he would endure that; he should at least have the happiness of seeing her—of feeling some nearness to her. And he clutched passionately the possibility that she *might* love him: perhaps the feeling would grow, if she could come to associate him with that watchful tenderness which her nature would be so keenly alive to. If any woman could love him, surely Maggie was that woman: there was such wealth of love in her, and there was no one to claim it all. Then—the pity of it, that a mind like hers should be withering in its very youth, like a young forest-tree, for want of the light and space it was formed to flourish in! Could he not hinder that, by persuading her out of her system of privation? He would be her guardian angel; he would do anything, bear anything, for her sake—except not seeing her.

Chapter II

Aunt Glegg Learns the Breadth of Bob's Thumb

While Maggie's life-struggles had lain almost entirely within her own soul, one shadowy army fighting another, and the slain shadows for ever rising again, Tom was engaged in a dustier, noisier warfare, grappling with more substantial obstacles, and gaining more definite conquests. So it has been since the days of Hecuba, and of Hector, Tamer of horses:[1] inside the gates, the women with streaming hair and uplifted hands offering prayers, watching the world's combat from afar, filling their long, empty days with memories and fears: outside, the men, in fierce struggle with things divine and human, quenching memory in the stronger light of purpose, losing the sense of dread and even of wounds in the hurrying ardour of action.

From what you have seen of Tom, I think he is not a youth of whom you would prophesy failure in anything he had thoroughly wished: the wagers are likely to be on his side, notwithstanding his small success in the classics. For Tom had never desired success in this field of enterprise; and for getting a fine flourishing growth of stupidity there is nothing like pouring out on a mind a good amount of subjects in which it feels no interest. But now Tom's strong will bound together his integrity, his pride, his family regrets, and his personal ambition, and made them one force, concentrating his efforts and surmounting discouragements. His uncle Deane, who watched him closely, soon began to conceive hopes of him, and to be rather proud that he had brought into the employment of the firm a nephew who appeared to be made of such good commercial stuff. The real kindness of placing him in the warehouse first was soon evident to Tom, in the hints his uncle began to throw out, that after a time he might perhaps be trusted to travel at certain seasons, and buy in for the firm various vulgar commodities with which I need not shock refined ears in this place; and it was doubtless with a view to this result that Mr Deane, when he expected to take his wine alone, would tell Tom to step in and sit with him an hour, and would pass that hour in much lecturing and catechising concerning articles of export and import, with an occasional excursus of more indirect utility on the relative advantages to the merchants of St Ogg's of having goods brought in their own and in foreign bottoms—a subject on which Mr Deane, as a shipowner, naturally threw off a few sparks when he got warmed with talk and wine. Already, in the second year, Tom's salary was raised; but all, except the price of his dinner and clothes, went home into the tin box; and he shunned comradeship, lest it should

1. In Homer's *Iliad* (book 24) Hecuba laments the death of her son Hector, the Trojan hero. "Tamer of horses" is Homer's epithet for Hector and other warriors.

lead him into expenses in spite of himself. Not that Tom was moulded on the spooney type of the Industrious Apprentice;[2] he had a very strong appetite for pleasure—would have liked to be a Tamer of horses, and to make a distinguished figure in all neighbouring eyes, dispensing treats and benefits to others with well-judged liberality, and being pronounced one of the finest young fellows of those parts; nay, he determined to achieve these things sooner or later; but his practical shrewdness told him that the means to such achievements could only lie for him in present abstinence and self-denial: there were certain milestones to be passed, and one of the first was the payment of his father's debts. Having made up his mind on that point, he strode along without swerving, contracting some rather saturnine sternness, as a young man is likely to do who has a premature call upon him for self-reliance. Tom felt intensely that common cause with his father which springs from family pride, and was bent on being irreproachable as a son; but his growing experience caused him to pass much silent criticism on the rashness and imprudence of his father's past conduct: their dispositions were not in sympathy, and Tom's face showed little radiance during his few home hours. Maggie had an awe of him, against which she struggled as something unfair to her consciousness of wider thoughts and deeper motives; but it was of no use to struggle. A character at unity with itself—that performs what it intends, subdues every counteracting impulse, and has no visions beyond the distinctly possible—is strong by its very negations.

You may imagine that Tom's more and more obvious unlikeness to his father was well fitted to conciliate the maternal aunts and uncles; and Mr Deane's favourable reports and predictions to Mr Glegg concerning Tom's qualifications for business, began to be discussed amongst them with various acceptance. He was likely, it appeared, to do the family credit, without causing it any expense and trouble. Mrs Pullet had always thought it strange if Tom's excellent complexion, so entirely that of the Dodsons, did not argue a certainty that he would turn out well, his juvenile errors of running down the peacock, and general disrespect to his aunts, only indicating a tinge of Tulliver blood which he had doubtless outgrown. Mr Glegg, who had contracted a cautious liking for Tom ever since his spirited and sensible behaviour when the execution was in the house, was now warming into a resolution to further his prospects actively—some time, when an opportunity offered of doing so in a prudent manner, without ultimate loss; but Mrs Glegg observed that she was not given to speak without book, as some people were; that those who said least were most likely to find their words made good; and that when the right moment came, it would be seen who could do something better than talk. Uncle Pullet, after silent meditation for a period of several lozenges, came distinctly to the conclusion, that when

2. Industrious Apprentice: from William Hogarth's series *Industry and Idleness* (1747); spooney: foolish.

a young man was likely to do well, it was better not to meddle with him.

Tom, meanwhile, had shown no disposition to rely on any one but himself, though, with a natural sensitiveness towards all indications of favourable opinion, he was glad to see his uncle Glegg look in on him sometimes in a friendly way during business hours, and glad to be invited to dine at his house, though he usually preferred declining on the ground that he was not sure of being punctual. But about a year ago, something had occurred which induced Tom to test his uncle Glegg's friendly disposition.

Bob Jakin, who rarely returned from one of his rounds without seeing Tom and Maggie, awaited him on the bridge as he was coming home from St Ogg's one evening, that they might have a little private talk. He took the liberty of asking if Mr Tom had ever thought of making money by trading a bit on his own account. Trading, how? Tom wished to know. Why, by sending out a bit of a cargo to foreign ports; because Bob had a particular friend who had offered to do a little business for him in that way in Laceham goods, and would be glad to serve Mr Tom on the same footing. Tom was interested at once, and begged for full explanation; wondering he had not thought of this plan before. He was so well pleased with the prospect of a speculation that might change the slow process of addition into multiplication, that he at once determined to mention the matter to his father, and get his consent to appropriate some of the savings in the tin box to the purchase of a small cargo. He would rather not have consulted his father, but he had just paid his last quarter's money into the tin box, and there was no other resource. All the savings were there; for Mr Tulliver would not consent to put the money out at interest lest he should lose it. Since he had speculated in the purchase of some corn, and had lost by it, he could not be easy without keeping the money under his eye.

Tom approached the subject carefully, as he was seated on the hearth with his father that evening, and Mr Tulliver listened, leaning forward in his arm-chair and looking up in Tom's face with a sceptical glance. His first impulse was to give a positive refusal, but he was in some awe of Tom's wishes, and since he had had the sense of being an "unlucky" father, he had lost some of his old peremptoriness and determination to be master. He took the key of the bureau from his pocket, got out the key of the large chest, and fetched down the tin box—slowly, as if he were trying to defer the moment of a painful parting. Then he seated himself against the table, and opened the box with that little padlock-key which he fingered in his waistcoat pocket in all vacant moments. There they were, the dingy bank-notes and the bright sovereigns, and he counted them out on the table—only a hundred and sixteen pounds in two years, after all the pinching.

"How much do you want, then?" he said, speaking as if the words burnt his lips.

"Suppose I begin with the thirty-six pounds, father?" said Tom.

Mr Tulliver separated this sum from the rest, and, keeping his hand over it, said,—

"It's as much as I can save out o' my pay in a year."

"Yes, father: it is such slow work—saving out of the little money we get. And in this way we might double our savings."

"Ay, my lad," said the father, keeping his hand on the money, "but you might lose it—you might lose a year o' my life—and I haven't got many."

Tom was silent.

"And you know I wouldn't pay a dividend with the first hundred, because I wanted to see it all in a lump—and when I see it, I'm sure on't. If you trust to luck, it's sure to be against me. It's Old Harry's got the luck in his hands; and if I lose one year, I shall never pick it up again—death 'ull o'ertake me."

Mr Tulliver's voice trembled, and Tom was silent for a few minutes before he said,—

"I'll give it up, father, since you object to it so strongly."

But, unwilling to abandon the scheme altogether, he determined to ask his uncle Glegg to venture twenty pounds, on condition of receiving five per cent of the profits. That was really a very small thing to ask. So when Bob called the next day at the wharf to know the decision, Tom proposed that they should go together to his uncle Glegg's to open the business; for his diffident pride clung to him, and made him feel that Bob's tongue would relieve him from some embarrassment.

Mr Glegg, at the pleasant hour of four in the afternoon of a hot August day, was naturally counting his wall-fruit[3] to assure himself that the sum total had not varied since yesterday. To him entered Tom, in what appeared to Mr Glegg very questionable companionship: that of a man with a pack on his back—for Bob was equipped for a new journey—and of a huge brindled bull-terrier, who walked with a slow swaying movement from side to side, and glanced from under his eyelids with a surly indifference which might after all be a cover to the most offensive designs. Mr Glegg's spectacles, which had been assisting him in counting the fruit, made these suspicious details alarmingly evident to him.

"Heigh! heigh! keep that dog back, will you?" he shouted, snatching up a stake and holding it before him as a shield when the visitors were within three yards of him.

"Get out wi' you, Mumps," said Bob, with a kick. "He's as quiet as a lamb, sir,"—an observation which Mumps corroborated by a low growl as he retreated behind his master's legs.

3. The fruit of trees grown against a wall.

"Why, what ever does this mean, Tom?" said Mr Glegg. "Have you brought information about the scoundrels as cut my trees?" If Bob came in the character of "information," Mr Glegg saw reasons for tolerating some irregularity.

"No, sir," said Tom: "I came to speak to you about a little matter of business of my own."

"Ay—well; but what has this dog got to do with it?" said the old gentleman, getting mild again.

"It's my dog, sir," said the ready Bob. "An' it's me as put Mr Tom up to the bit o' business; for Mr Tom's been a friend o' mine iver since I was a little chap: fust thing iver I did was frightenin' the birds for th' old master. An' if a bit o' luck turns up, I'm allays thinkin' if I can let Mr Tom have a pull at it. An' it's a downright roarin' shame, as when he's got the chance o' making a bit o' money wi' sending goods out—ten or twelve per zent clear, when freight an' commission's paid—as he shouldn't lay hold o' the chance for want o' money. An' when there's the Laceham goods—lors! they're made o' purpose for folks as want to send out a little carguy; light, an' take up no room—you may pack twenty pound so as you can't see the passill: an' they're manifacturs as please fools, so I reckon they aren't like to want a market. An I'd go to Laceham an' buy in the goods for Mr Tom along wi' my own. An' there's the shupercargo o' the bit of a vessel as is goin' to take 'em out. I know him partic'lar; he's a solid man, an' got a family i' the town here. Salt, his name is—an' a briny chap he is too—an' if you don't believe me, I can take you to him."

Uncle Glegg stood open-mouthed with astonishment at this unembarrassed loquacity, with which his understanding could hardly keep pace. He looked at Bob, first over his spectacles, then through them, then over them again; while Tom, doubtful of his uncle's impression, began to wish he had not brought this singular Aaron or mouthpiece:[4] Bob's talk appeared less seemly, now some one besides himself was listening to it.

"You seem to be a knowing fellow," said Mr Glegg, at last.

"Ay, sir, you say true," returned Bob, nodding his head aside; "I think my head's all alive inside like an old cheese, for I'm so full o' plans, one knocks another over. If I hadn't Mumps to talk to, I should get top-heavy an' tumble in a fit. I suppose it's because I niver went to school much. That's what I jaw my old mother for. I says, 'You should ha' sent me to school a bit more,' I says—'an' then I could ha' read i' the books like fun, an' kep' my head cool an' empty.' Lors, she's fine an' comfor'ble now, my old mother is: she ates her baked meat an' taters as often as she likes. For I'm gettin' so full o' money, I must hev a wife

4. From Exodus 4:10–16, where God instructs Moses, who fears he doesn't speak fluently, to use his brother Aaron as his mouthpiece.

to spend it for me. But it's botherin', a wife is—and Mumps mightn't like her."

Uncle Glegg, who regarded himself as a jocose man since he had retired from business, was beginning to find Bob amusing, but he had still a disapproving observation to make, which kept his face serious.

"Ah," he said, "I should think you're at a loss for ways o' spending your money, else you wouldn't keep that big dog, to eat as much as two Christians. It's shameful—shameful!" But he spoke more in sorrow than in anger, and quickly added—

"But, come now, let's hear more about this business, Tom. I suppose you want a little sum to make a venture with. But where's all your own money? You don't spend it all—eh?"

"No, sir," said Tom, colouring; "but my father is unwilling to risk it, and I don't like to press him. If I could get twenty or thirty pounds to begin with, I could pay five per cent for it, and then I could gradually make a little capital of my own, and do without a loan."

"Ay . . . ay," said Mr Glegg, in an approving tone; "that's not a bad notion, and I won't say as I wouldn't be your man. But it 'ull be as well for me to see this Salt, as you talk on. And then . . . here's this friend o' yours offers to buy the goods for you. Perhaps you've got somebody to stand surety for you if the money's put into your hands?" added the cautious old gentleman, looking over his spectacles at Bob.

"I don't think that's necessary, uncle," said Tom. "At least, I mean it would not be necessary for me, because I know Bob well; but perhaps it would be right for you to have some security."

"You get your percentage out o' the purchase, I suppose?" said Mr Glegg, looking at Bob.

"No, sir," said Bob, rather indignantly; "I didn't offer to get a apple for Mr Tom, o' purpose to hev a bite out of it myself. When I play folks tricks there'll be more fun in 'em nor that."

"Well, but it's nothing but right you should have a small percentage," said Mr Glegg. "I've no opinion o' transactions where folks do things for nothing. It allays looks bad."

"Well, then," said Bob, whose keenness saw at once what was implied, "I'll tell you what I get by't, an' it's money in my pocket in the end:—I make myself look big, wi' makin' a bigger purchase. That's what I'm thinking on. Lors! I'm a 'cute chap—I am."

"Mr Glegg, Mr Glegg," said a severe voice from the open parlour window, "pray are you coming in to tea?—or are you going to stand talking with packmen till you get murdered in the open daylight?"

"Murdered?" said Mr Glegg; "what's the woman talking of? Here's your nephey Tom come about a bit o' business."

"Murdered—yes—it isn't many 'sizes[5] ago since a packman murdered

5. Session of the assizes, the periodic English county court.

a young woman in a lone place, and stole her thimble, and threw her body into a ditch."

"Nay, nay," said Mr Glegg, soothingly, "you're thinking o' the man wi' no legs, as drove a dog-cart."

"Well, it's the same thing, Mr Glegg—only you're fond o' contradicting what I say; and if my nephey's come about business, it 'ud be more fitting if you'd bring him into the house, and let his aunt know about it, instead o' whispering in corners, in that plotting, underminding way."

"Well, well," said Mr Glegg, "we'll come in now."

"You needn't stay here," said the lady to Bob, in a loud voice, adapted to the moral not the physical distance between them. "We don't want anything. I don't deal wi' packmen. Mind you shut the gate after you."

"Stop a bit; not so fast," said Mr Glegg: "I haven't done with this young man yet. Come in, Tom; come in," he added, stepping in at the French window.

"Mr Glegg," said Mrs G., in a fatal tone, "if you're going to let that man and his dog in on my carpet, before my very face, be so good as to let me know. A wife's got a right to ask that, I hope."

"Don't you be uneasy, mum," said Bob, touching his cap. He saw at once that Mrs Glegg was a bit of game worth running down, and longed to be at the sport; "we'll stay out upo' the gravel here—Mumps and me will. Mumps knows his company—he does. I might hish at him by th' hour together, before he'd fly at a real gentlewoman like you. It's wonderful how he knows which is the good-looking ladies—and's partic'lar fond of 'em when they've good shapes. Lors!" added Bob, laying down his pack on the gravel, "it's a thousand pities such a lady as you shouldn't deal with a packman, i'stead o' goin' into these new-fangled shops, where there's half-a-dozen fine gents wi' their chins propped up wi' a stiff stock, a-looking like bottles wi' ornamental stoppers, an' all got to get their dinner out of a bit o' calico: it stan's to reason you must pay three times the price you pay a packman, as is the nat'ral way o' gettin' goods—an' pays no rent, an' isn't forced to throttle himself till the lies are squeezed out on him, whether he will or no. But lors! mum, you know what it is better nor I do—*you* can see through them shopmen, I'll be bound."

"Yes, I reckon I can, and through the packmen too," observed Mrs Glegg, intending to imply that Bob's flattery had produced no effect on *her*; while her husband, standing behind her with his hands in his pockets and legs apart, winked and smiled with conjugal delight at the probability of his wife's being circumvented.

"Ay, to be sure, mum," said Bob. "Why, you must ha' dealt wi' no end o' packmen when you war a young lass—before the master here had the luck to set eyes on you. I know where you lived, I do—seen th' house many a time—close upon Squire Darleigh's—a stone house wi' steps. . . ."

"Ah, that it had," said Mrs Glegg, pouring out the tea. "You know something o' my family then . . . are you akin to that packman with a squint in his eye, as used to bring th' Irish linen?"

"Look you there now!" said Bob, evasively. "Didn't I know as you'd remember the best bargains you've made in your life was made wi' packmen? Why, you see, even a squintin' packman's better nor a shopman as can see straight. Lors! if I'd had the luck to call at the stone house wi' my pack, as lies here,"—stooping and thumping the bundle emphatically with his fist,—"an th' handsome young lasses all stannin' out on the stone steps, it 'ud ha' been summat like openin' a pack—that would. It's on'y the poor houses now as a packman calls on, if it isn't for the sake o' the sarvant-maids. They're paltry times—these are. Why, mum, look at the printed cottons now, an' what they was when you wore 'em—why, you wouldn't put such a thing on now, I can see. It must be first-rate quality—the manifactur as you'd buy—summat as 'ud wear as well as your own faitures."

"Yes, better quality nor any you're like to carry: you've got nothing first-rate but brazenness, I'll be bound," said Mrs Glegg, with a triumphant sense of her insurmountable sagacity. "Mr Glegg, are you going ever to sit down to your tea? Tom, there's a cup for you."

"You speak true there, mum," said Bob. "My pack isn't for ladies like you. The time's gone by for that. Bargains picked up dirt cheap! A big o' damage here an' there, as can be cut out, or else niver seen i' the wearin'; but not fit to offer to rich folks as can pay for the look o' things as nobody sees. I'm not the man as 'ud offer t' open my pack to *you*, mum: no, no; I'm a imperent chap, as you say—these times makes folks imperent—but I'm not up to the mark o' that."

"Why, what goods do you carry in your pack?" said Mrs Glegg. "Fine-coloured things, I suppose—shawls an' that?"

"All sorts, mum, all sorts," said Bob, thumping his bundle; "but let us say no more about that, if *you* please. I'm here upo' Mr Tom's business, an' I'm not the man to take up the time wi' my own."

"And pray, what *is* this business as is to be kept from me?" said Mrs Glegg, who, solicited by a double curiosity, was obliged to let the one-half wait.

"A little plan o' nephey Tom's here," said good-natured Mr Glegg; "and not altogether a bad un, I think. A little plan for making money: that's the right sort o' plan for young folks as have got their fortin to make, eh, Jane?"

"But I hope it isn't a plan where he expects iverything to be done for him by his friends: that's what the young folks think of mostly nowadays. And pray, what has this packman got to do wi' what goes on in our family? Can't you speak for yourself, Tom, and let your aunt know things, as a nephey should?"

"This is Bob Jakin, aunt," said Tom, bridling the irritation that aunt Glegg's voice always produced. "I've known him ever since we were little boys. He's a very good fellow, and always ready to do me a kindness. And he has had some experience in sending goods out—a small part of a cargo as a private speculation; and he thinks, if I could begin to do a little in the same way, I might make some money. A large interest is got in that way."

"Large int'rest?" said aunt Glegg, with eagerness; "and what do you call large int'rest?"

"Ten or twelve per cent, Bob says, after expenses are paid."

"Then why wasn't I let to know o' such things before, Mr Glegg?" said Mrs Glegg, turning to her husband, with a deep grating tone of reproach. "Haven't you allays told me as there was no getting more nor five per cent?"

"Pooh, pooh, nonsense, my good woman," said Mr Glegg. "You couldn't go into trade, could you? You can't get more than five per cent with security."

"But I can turn a bit o' money for you, an' welcome, mum," said Bob, "if you'd like to risk it—not as there's any risk to speak on. But if you'd a mind to lend a bit o' money to Mr Tom, he'd pay you six or seven per zent, an' get a trifle for himself as well; an' a good-natur'd lady like you 'ud like the feel o' the money better if your nephey took part on it."

"What do you say, Mrs G.?" said Mr Glegg. "I've a notion, when I've made a bit more inquiry, as I shall perhaps start Tom here with a bit of a nest-egg—he'll pay me int'rest, you know—an' if you've got some little sums lyin' idle twisted up in a stockin' toe, or that . . ."

"Mr Glegg, it's beyond iverything! You'll go and give information to the tramps next, as they may come and rob me."

"Well, well, as I was sayin', if you like to join me wi' twenty pounds, you can—I'll make it fifty. That'll be a pretty good nest-egg—eh, Tom?"

"You're not counting on me, Mr Glegg, I hope," said his wife. "You could do fine things wi' my money, I don't doubt."

"Very well," said Mr Glegg, rather snappishly, "then we'll do without you. I shall go with you to see this Salt," he added, turning to Bob.

"And now, I suppose, you'll go all the other way, Mr Glegg," said Mrs G., "and want to shut me out o' my own nephey's business. I never said I wouldn't put money into it—I don't say as it shall be twenty pounds, though you're so ready to say it for me—but he'll see some day as his aunt's in the right not to risk the money she's saved for him till it's proved as it won't be lost."

"Ay, that's a pleasant sort o' risk, that is," said Mr Glegg, indiscreetly winking at Tom, who couldn't avoid smiling. But Bob stemmed the injured lady's outburst.

"Ay, mum," he said, admiringly, "you know what's what—you do. An it's nothing but fair. *You* see how the first bit of a job answers, an' then you'll come down handsome. Lors, it's a fine thing to hev good kin. I got my bit of a nest-egg, as the master calls it, all by my own sharpness—ten suvreigns it was—wi' dousing the fire at Torry's mill, an' it's growed an' growed by a bit an' a bit, till I'n got a matter o' thirty pound to lay out, besides makin' my mother comfor'ble. I should get more, on'y I'm such a soft wi' the women—I can't help lettin' 'em hev such good bargains. There's this bundle, now" (thumping it lustily), "any other chap 'ud make a pretty penny out on it. But me! . . . lors, I shall sell 'em for pretty near what I paid for 'em."

"Have you got a bit of good net, now?" said Mrs Glegg, in a patronising tone, moving from the tea-table, and folding her napkin.

"Eh, mum, not what you'd think it worth your while to look at. I'd scorn to show it you. It 'ud be an insult to you."

"But let me see," said Mrs Glegg, still patronising. "If they're damaged goods, they're like enough to be a bit the better quality."

"No, mum. I know my place," said Bob, lifting up his pack and shouldering it. "I'm not going t' expose the lowness o' my trade to a lady like you. Packs is come down i' the world: it 'ud cut you to th' heart to see the difference. I'm at your sarvice, sir, when you've a mind to go and see Salt."

"All in good time," said Mr Glegg, really unwilling to cut short the dialogue. "Are you wanted at the wharf, Tom?"

"No, sir; I left Stowe in my place."

"Come, put down your pack, and let me see," said Mrs Glegg, drawing a chair to the window, and seating herself with much dignity.

"Don't you ask it, mum," said Bob, entreatingly.

"Make no more words," said Mrs Glegg, severely, "but do as I tell you."

"Eh, mum, I'm loth—that I am," said Bob, slowly depositing his pack on the step, and beginning to untie it with unwilling fingers. "But what you order shall be done" (much fumbling in pauses between the sentences). "It's not as you'll buy a single thing on me. . . . I'd be sorry for you to do it . . . for think o' them poor women up i' the villages there, as niver stir a hundred yards from home . . . it 'ud be a pity for anybody to buy up their bargains. Lors, it's as good as a junketing to 'em when they see me wi' my pack . . . an' I shall niver pick up such bargains for 'em again. Least ways, I've no time now, for I'm off to Laceham. See here, now," Bob went on, becoming rapid again, and holding up a scarlet woollen kerchief with an embroidered wreath in the corner; "here's a thing to make a lass's mouth water, an' on'y two shillin'—an' why? Why, 'cause there's a bit of a moth-hole i' this plain end. Lors, I think the moths an' the mildew was sent by Providence o' purpose to cheapen the goods a bit for the good-lookin' women as han't got much money. If it hadn't been for the moths, now, every hankicher on 'em 'ud ha' gone to the rich handsome ladies, like you, mum, at five shillin' apiece—not a farthin' less; but what does the moth do? Why, it nibbles off three shillin' o' the price i' no time, an' then a packman like me can carry't to the poor lasses as live under the dark thack,[6] to make a bit of a blaze for 'em. Lors, it's as good as a fire, to look at such a hankicher!"

Bob held it at a distance for admiration, but Mrs Glegg said sharply—

"Yes, but nobody wants a fire this time o' year. Put these coloured things by—let me look at your nets, if you've got em."

"Eh, mum, I told you how it 'ud be," said Bob, flinging aside the coloured things with an air of desperation. "I knowed it 'ud turn again' you to look at such paltry articles as I carry. Here's a piece o' figured muslin now—what's the use o' you lookin' at it? You might as well look at poor folks's victual, mum—it 'ud on'y take away your appetite. There's a yard i' the middle on't as the pattern's all missed—lors, why it's a muslin as the Princess Victoree might ha' wore—but," added Bob, flinging it behind him on to the turf, as if to save Mrs Glegg's eyes, "it'll be bought up by the huckster's wife at Fibb's End—that's where *it*'ll go—ten shillin' for the whole lot—ten yards, countin' the damage un—five-an'-twenty shillin' 'ud ha' been the price—not a penny less. But I'll say no more, mum; it's nothing to you—a piece o' muslin like that; you can afford to pay three times the money for a thing as isn't half so good. It's nets *you* talked on; well, I've got a piece as 'ull serve you to make fun on. . . ."

"Bring me that muslin," said Mrs Glegg: "it's a buff—I'm partial to buff."

"Eh, but a *damaged* thing," said Bob, in a tone of deprecating disgust. "You'd do nothing with it, mum—you'd give it to the cook, I know you would—an' it 'ud be a pity—she'd look too much like a lady in it—it's unbecoming for servants."

"Fetch it, and let me see you measure it," said Mrs Glegg, authoritatively.

Bob obeyed with ostentatious reluctance.

"See what there is over measure!" he said, holding forth the extra half-yard, while Mrs Glegg was busy examining the damaged yard, and throwing her head back to see how far the fault would be lost on a distant view.

"I'll give you six shilling for it," she said, throwing it down with the air of a person who mentions an ultimatum.

6. Thatched roof.

"Didn't I tell you now, mum, as it 'ud hurt your feelings to look at my pack? That damaged bit's turned your stomach now—I see it has," said Bob, wrapping the muslin up with the utmost quickness, and apparently about to fasten up his pack. "You're used to seein' a different sort o' article carried by packmen, when you lived at the stone house. Packs is come down i' the world; I told you that: *my* goods are for common folks. Mrs Pepper 'ull give me ten shillin' for that muslin, an' be sorry as I didn't ask her more. Such articles answer i' the wearin'—they keep their colour till the threads melt away i' the wash-tub, an' that won't be while *I*'m a young un."

"Well, seven shilling," said Mrs Glegg.

"Put it out o' your mind, mum, now do," said Bob. "Here's a bit o' net, then, for you to look at before I tie up my pack: just for you to see what my trade's come to: spotted and sprigged, you see, beautiful, but yallow—'s been lyin' by an' got the wrong colour. I could niver ha' bought such net, if it hadn't been yallow. Lors, it's took me a deal o' study to know the vally o' such articles; when I begun to carry a pack, I was as ignirant as a pig—net or calico was all the same to me. I thought them things the most vally as was the thickest. I was took in dreadful—for I'm a straightforrard chap—up to no tricks, mum. I can on'y say my nose is my own, for if I went beyond, I should lose myself pretty quick. An' I gev five-an'-eightpence for that piece o' net—if I was to tell y' anything else I should be tellin' you fibs: an five-an'-eightpence I shall ask for it—not a penny more—for it's a woman's article, an' I like to 'commodate the women. Five-an'-eightpence for six yards—as cheap as if it was only the dirt on it as was paid for."

"I don't mind having three yards of it," said Mrs Glegg.

"Why, there's but six altogether," said Bob. "No, mum, it isn't worth your while; you can go to the shop to-morrow an' get the same pattern ready whitened. It's on'y three times the money—what's that to a lady like you?" He gave an emphatic tie to his bundle.

"Come, lay me out that muslin," said Mrs Glegg. "Here's eight shilling for it."

"You *will* be jokin', mum," said Bob, looking up with a laughing face; "I see'd you was a pleasant lady when I fust come to the winder."

"Well, put it me out," said Mrs Glegg, peremptorily.

"But if I let you have it for ten shillin', mum, you'll be so good as not tell nobody. I should be a laughin'-stock—the trade 'ud hoot me, if they knowed it. I'm obliged to make believe as I ask more nor I do for my goods, else they'd find out I was a flat. I'm glad you don't insist upo' buyin' the net, for then I should ha' lost my two best bargains for Mrs Pepper o' Fibb's End—an' she's a rare customer."

"Let me look at the net again," said Mrs Glegg, yearning after the cheap spots and sprigs, now they were vanishing.

"Well, I can't deny *you*, mum," said Bob, handing it out. "Eh! see what a pattern now! Real Laceham goods. Now, this is the sort o' article I'm recommendin' Mr Tom to send out. Lors, it's a fine thing for anybody as has got a bit o' money—these Laceham goods 'ud make it breed like maggits. If I was a lady wi' a bit o' money!—why, I know one as put thirty pound into them goods—a lady wi' a cork leg; but as sharp—you wouldn't catch *her* runnin' her head into a sack: *she*'d see her way clear out o' anything afore she'd be in a hurry to start. Well, she let out thirty pound to a young man in the drapering line, and he laid it out i' Laceham goods, an' a shupercargo o' my acquinetance (not Salt) took 'em out, an' she got her eight per zent fust go off—an' now you can't hold her but she must be sendin' out carguies wi' every ship, till she's gettin' as rich as a Jew. Bucks her name is—she doesn't live i' this town. Now then, mum, if you'll please to give me the net. . . ."

"Here's fifteen shilling, then, for the two," said Mrs Glegg. "But it's a shameful price."

"Nay, mum, you'll niver say that when you're upo' your knees i' church i' five years' time. I'm makin' you a present o' th' articles—I am, indeed. That eightpence shaves off my profit as clean as a razor. Now then, sir," continued Bob, shouldering his pack, "if you please, I'll be glad to go and see about makin' Mr Tom's fortin. Eh, I wish I'd got another twenty pound to lay out for *my*sen: I shouldn't stay to say my Catechism afore I knowed what to do wi't."

"Stop a bit, Mr Glegg," said the lady, as her husband took his hat, "you never *will* give me the chance o' speaking. You'll go away now, and finish everything about this business, and come back and tell me it's too late for me to speak. As if I wasn't my nephey's own aunt, and th' head o' the family on his mother's side! and laid by guineas, all full weight, for him—as he'll know who to respect when I'm laid in my coffin."

"Well, Mrs G., say what you mean," said Mr G., hastily.

"Well, then, I desire as nothing may be done without my knowing. I don't say as I shan't venture twenty pounds, if you make out as everything's right and safe. And if I do, Tom," concluded Mrs Glegg, turning impressively to her nephew, "I hope you'll allays bear it in mind and be grateful for such an aunt. I mean you to pay me interest, you know—I don't approve o' giving; we niver looked for that in *my* family."

"Thank you, aunt," said Tom, rather proudly. "I prefer having the money only lent to me."

"Very well: that's the Dodson sperrit," said Mrs Glegg, rising to get her knitting with the sense that any further remark after this would be bathos.

Salt—that eminently "briny chap"—having been discovered in a cloud of tobacco-smoke at the Anchor Tavern, Mr Glegg commenced inquiries which turned out satisfactorily enough to warrant the advance of the "nest-egg," to which aunt Glegg contributed twenty pounds; and in this modest beginning you see the ground of a fact which might otherwise surprise you—namely, Tom's accumulation of a fund, unknown to his father, that promised in no very long time to meet the more tardy process of saving, and quite cover the deficit. When once his attention had been turned to this source of gain, Tom determined to make the most of it, and lost no opportunity of obtaining information and extending his small enterprises. In not telling his father, he was influenced by that strange mixture of opposite feelings which often gives equal truth to those who blame an action and those who admire it: partly, it was that disinclination to confidence which is seen between near kindred—that family repulsion which spoils the most sacred relations of our lives; partly, it was the desire to surprise his father with a great joy. He did not see that it would have been better to soothe the interval with a new hope, and prevent the delirium of a too sudden elation.

At the time of Maggie's first meeting with Philip, Tom had already nearly a hundred and fifty pounds of his own capital; and while they were walking by the evening light in the Red Deeps, he, by the same evening light, was riding into Laceham, proud of being on his first journey on behalf of Guest & Co., and revolving in his mind all the chances that by the end of another year he should have doubled his gains, lifted off the obloquy of debt from his father's name, and perhaps—for he should be twenty-one—have got a new start for himself, on a higher platform of employment. Did he not deserve it? He was quite sure that he did.

Chapter III

The Wavering Balance

I said that Maggie went home that evening from the Red Deeps with a mental conflict already begun. You have seen clearly enough, in her interview with Philip, what that conflict was. Here suddenly was an opening in the rocky wall which shut in the narrow valley of humiliation, where all her prospect was the remote unfathomed sky; and some of the memory-haunting earthly delights were no longer out of her reach. She might have books, converse, affection—she might hear tidings of the world from which her mind had not yet lost its sense of exile; and it would be a kindness to Philip too, who was pitiable—clearly not happy; and perhaps here was an opportunity indicated for making her mind more worthy of its highest service—perhaps the noblest, completest devoutness could hardly exist without some width of knowledge: *must* she always live in this resigned imprisonment? It was so blameless, so good a thing that there should be friendship between her and Philip;

the motives that forbade it were so unreasonable—so unchristian! But the severe monotonous warning came again and again—that she was losing the simplicity and clearness of her life by admitting a ground of concealment, and that, by forsaking the simple rule of renunciation, she was throwing herself under the seductive guidance of illimitable wants. She thought she had won strength to obey the warning before she allowed herself the next week to turn her steps in the evening to the Red Deeps. But while she was resolved to say an affectionate farewell to Philip, how she looked forward to that evening walk in the still, fleckered shade of the hollows, away from all that was harsh and unlovely; to the affectionate admiring looks that would meet her; to the sense of comradeship that childish memories would give to wiser, older talk; to the certainty that Philip would care to hear everything she said, which no one else cared for! It was a half-hour that it would be very hard to turn her back upon, with the sense that there would be no other like it. Yet she said what she meant to say; she looked firm as well as sad.

"Philip, I have made up my mind—it is right that we should give each other up, in everything but memory. I could not see you without concealment—stay, I know what you are going to say—it is other people's wrong feelings that make concealment necessary; but concealment is bad, however it may be caused. I feel that it would be bad for me, for us both. And then, if our secret were discovered, there would be nothing but misery—dreadful anger; and then we must part after all, and it would be harder, when we were used to seeing each other."

Philip's face had flushed, and there was a momentary eagerness of expression, as if he had been about to resist this decision with all his might. But he controlled himself, and said, with assumed calmness, "Well, Maggie, if we must part, let us try and forget it for one half-hour: let us talk together a little while—for the last time."

He took her hand, and Maggie felt no reason to withdraw it: his quietness made her all the more sure she had given him great pain, and she wanted to show him how unwillingly she had given it. They walked together hand in hand in silence.

"Let us sit down in the hollow," said Philip, "where we stood the last time. See how the dog-roses have strewed the ground, and spread their opal petals over it!"

They sat down at the roots of the slanting ash.

"I've begun my picture of you among the Scotch firs, Maggie," said Philip, "so you must let me study your face a little, while you stay—since I am not to see it again. Please, turn your head this way."

This was said in an entreating voice, and it would have been very hard of Maggie to refuse. The full lustrous face, with the bright black coronet, looked down like that of a divinity well pleased to be worshipped, on the pale-hued, small-featured face that was turned up to it.

"I shall be sitting for my second portrait then," she said, smiling. "Will it be larger than the other?"

"O yes, much larger. It is an oil-painting. You will look like a tall Hamadryad,[1] dark and strong and noble, just issued from one of the fir-trees, when the stems are casting their afternoon shadows on the grass."

"You seem to think more of painting than of anything now, Philip?"

"Perhaps I do," said Philip, rather sadly; "but I think of too many things—sow all sorts of seeds, and get no great harvest from any one of them. I'm cursed with susceptibility in every direction, and effective faculty in none. I care for painting and music; I care for classic literature, and mediæval literature, and modern literature: I flutter all ways, and fly in none."

"But surely that is a happiness to have so many tastes—to enjoy so many beautiful things—when they are within your reach," said Maggie, musingly. "It always seemed to me a sort of clever stupidity only to have one sort of talent—almost like a carrier-pigeon."

"It might be a happiness to have many tastes if I were like other men," said Philip, bitterly. "I might get some power and distinction by mere mediocrity, as they do; at least I should get those middling satisfactions which make men contented to do without great ones. I might think society at St Ogg's agreeable then. But nothing could make life worth the purchase-money of pain to me, but some faculty that would lift me above the dead level of provincial existence. Yes—there is one thing: a passion answers as well as a faculty."

Maggie did not hear the last words: she was struggling against the consciousness that Philip's words had set her own discontent vibrating again as it used to do.

"I understand what you mean," she said, "though I know so much less than you do. I used to think I could never bear life if it kept on being the same every day, and I must always be doing things of no consequence, and never know anything greater. But, dear Philip, I think we are only like children, that some one who is wiser is taking care of. Is it not right to resign ourselves entirely, whatever may be denied us? I have found great peace in that for the last two or three years—even joy in subduing my own will."

"Yes, Maggie," said Philip, vehemently; "and you are shutting yourself up in a narrow self-delusive fanaticism; which is only a way of escaping pain by starving into dulness all the highest powers of your nature. Joy and peace are not resignation: resignation is the willing endurance of a pain that is not allayed—that you don't expect to be allayed. Stupefaction is not resignation: and it is stupefaction to remain in ignorance—to shut up all the avenues by which the life of your fellow-men might become known to you. I am not resigned: I am not sure that life is long enough

1. Tree nymph.

to learn that lesson. *You* are not resigned: you are only trying to stupefy yourself."

Maggie's lips trembled; she felt there was some truth in what Philip said, and yet there was a deeper consciousness that, for any immediate application it had to her conduct, it was no better than falsity. Her double impression corresponded to the double impulse of the speaker. Philip seriously believed what he said, but he said it with vehemence because it made an argument against the resolution that opposed his wishes. But Maggie's face, made more childlike by the gathering tears, touched him with a tenderer, less egoistic feeling. He took her hand and said gently—

"Don't let us think of such things in this short half-hour, Maggie. Let us only care about being together. . . . We shall be friends in spite of separation. . . . We shall always think of each other. I shall be glad to live as long as you are alive, because I shall think there may always come a time when I can—when you will let me help you in some way."

"What a dear, good brother you would have been, Philip," said Maggie, smiling through the haze of tears. "I think you would have made as much fuss about me, and been as pleased for me to love you, as would have satisfied even me. You would have loved me well enough to bear with me, and forgive me everything. That was what I always longed that Tom should do. I was never satisfied with a *little* of anything. That is why it is better for me to do without earthly happiness altogether. . . . I never felt that I had enough music—I wanted more instruments playing together—I wanted voices to be fuller and deeper. Do you ever sing now, Philip?" she added abruptly, as if she had forgotten what went before.

"Yes," he said, "every day, almost. But my voice is only middling—like everything else in me."

"O sing me something—just one song. I *may* listen to that before I go—something you used to sing at Lorton on a Saturday afternoon, when we had the drawing-room all to ourselves, and I put my apron over my head to listen."

"*I* know," said Philip, and Maggie buried her face in her hands, while he sang *sotto voce*, "Love in her eyes sits playing;"[2] and then said, "That's it, isn't it?"

"O no, I won't stay," said Maggie, starting up. "It will only haunt me. Let us walk, Philip. I must go home."

She moved away, so that he was obliged to rise and follow her.

"Maggie," he said, in a tone of remonstrance, "don't persist in this wilful, senseless privation. It makes me wretched to see you benumbing and cramping your nature in this way. You were so full of life when you were a child: I thought you would be a brilliant woman—all wit

2. Aria from Handel's *Acis and Galatea* (1732).

and bright imagination. And it flashes out in your face still, until you draw that veil of dull quiescence over it."

"Why do you speak so bitterly to me, Philip?" said Maggie.

"Because I foresee it will not end well: you can never carry on this self-torture."

"I shall have strength given me," said Maggie, tremulously.

"No, you will not, Maggie: no one has strength given to do what is unnatural. It is mere cowardice to seek safety in negations. No character becomes strong in that way. You will be thrown into the world some day, and then every rational satisfaction of your nature that you deny now, will assault you like a savage appetite."

Maggie started and paused, looking at Philip with alarm in her face. "Philip, how dare you shake me in this way? You are a tempter."

"No, I am not; but love gives insight, Maggie, and insight often gives foreboding. *Listen* to me—*let* me supply you with books; do let me see you sometimes—be your brother and teacher, as you said at Lorton. It is less wrong that you should see me than that you should be committing this long suicide."

Maggie felt unable to speak. She shook her head and walked on in silence, till they came to the end of the Scotch firs, and she put out her hand in sign of parting.

"Do you banish me from this place for ever, then, Maggie? Surely I may come and walk in it sometimes? If I meet you by chance, there is no concealment in that?"

It is the moment when our resolution seems about to become irrevocable—when the fatal iron gates are about to close upon us—that tests our strength. Then, after hours of clear reasoning and firm conviction, we snatch at any sophistry that will nullify our long struggles, and bring us the defeat that we love better than victory.

Maggie felt her heart leap at this subterfuge of Philip's, and there passed over her face that almost imperceptible shock which accompanies any relief. He saw it, and they parted in silence.

Philip's sense of the situation was too complete for him not to be visited with glancing fears lest he had been intervening too presumptuously in the action of Maggie's conscience—perhaps for a selfish end. But no!—he persuaded himself his end was not selfish. He had little hope that Maggie would ever return the strong feeling he had for her; and it must be better for Maggie's future life, when these petty family obstacles to her freedom had disappeared, that the present should not be entirely sacrificed, and that she should have some opportunity of culture—some interchange with a mind above the vulgar level of those she was now condemned to live with. If we only look far enough off for the consequence of our actions, we can always find some point in the combination of results by which those actions can be justified: by adopting the point of view of a Providence who arranges results, or of a philosopher who traces them, we shall find it possible to obtain perfect complacency in choosing to do what is most agreeable to us in the present moment. And it was in this way that Philip justified his subtle efforts to overcome Maggie's true prompting against a concealment that would introduce doubleness into her own mind, and might cause new misery to those who had the primary natural claim on her. But there was a surplus of passion in him that made him half independent of justifying motives. His longing to see Maggie, and make an element in her life, had in it some of that savage impulse to snatch an offered joy, which springs from a life in which the mental and bodily constitution have made pain predominate. He had not his full share in the common good of men: he could not even pass muster with the insignificant, but must be singled out for pity, and excepted from what was a matter of course with others. Even to Maggie he was an exception: it was clear that the thought of his being her lover had never entered her mind.

Do not think too hardly of Philip. Ugly and deformed people have great need of unusual virtues, because they are likely to be extremely uncomfortable without them: but the theory that unusual virtues spring by a direct consequence out of personal disadvantages, as animals get thicker wool in severe climates, is perhaps a little overstrained. The temptations of beauty are much dwelt upon, but I fancy they only bear the same relation to those of ugliness, as the temptation to excess at a feast, where the delights are varied for eye and ear as well as palate, bears to the temptations that assail the desperation of hunger. Does not the Hunger Tower[3] stand as the type of the utmost trial to what is human in us?

Philip had never been soothed by that mother's love which flows out to us in the greater abundance because our need is greater, which clings to us the more tenderly because we are the less likely to be winners in the game of life; and the sense of his father's affection and indulgence towards him was marred by the keener perception of his father's faults. Kept aloof from all practical life as Philip had been, and by nature half feminine in sensitiveness, he had some of the woman's intolerant repulsion towards worldliness and the deliberate pursuit of sensual enjoyment; and this one strong natural tie in his life—his relation as a son—was like an aching limb to him. Perhaps there is inevitably something morbid in a human being who is in any way unfavourably excepted from ordinary conditions, until the good force has had time to triumph; and it has rarely had time for that at two-and-twenty. That force was present in Philip in much strength, but the sun himself looks feeble through the morning mists.

3. The tower in which Dante's Ugolino is confined with his children without food and driven by hunger to eat their corpses (*Inferno*, canto 33).

Chapter IV

Another Love-Scene

Early in the following April, nearly a year after that dubious parting you have just witnessed, you may, if you like, again see Maggie entering the Red Deeps through the group of Scotch firs. But it is early afternoon and not evening, and the edge of sharpness in the spring air makes her draw her large shawl close about her and trip along rather quickly; though she looks round, as usual, that she may take in the sight of her beloved trees. There is a more eager, inquiring look in her eyes than there was last June, and a smile is hovering about her lips, as if some playful speech were awaiting the right hearer. The hearer was not long in appearing.

"Take back your *Corinne*,"[1] said Maggie, drawing a book from under her shawl. "You were right in telling me she would do me no good; but you were wrong in thinking I should wish to be like her."

"Wouldn't you really like to be a tenth Muse,[2] then, Maggie?" said Philip, looking up in her face as we look at a first parting in the clouds that promises us a bright heaven once more.

"Not at all," said Maggie, laughing. "The Muses were uncomfortable goddesses, I think—obliged always to carry rolls and musical instruments about with them. If I carried a harp in this climate, you know, I must have a green baise cover for it—and I should be sure to leave it behind me by mistake."

"You agree with me in not liking Corinne, then?"

"I didn't finish the book," said Maggie. "As soon as I came to the blond-haired young lady reading in the park, I shut it up, and determined to read no further. I foresaw that that light-complexioned girl would win away all the love from Corinne and make her miserable. I'm determined to read no more books where the blond-haired women carry away all the happiness. I should begin to have a prejudice against them. If you could give me some story, now, where the dark woman triumphs, it would restore the balance. I want to avenge Rebecca and Flora MacIvor, and Minna[3] and all the rest of the dark unhappy ones. Since you are my tutor, you ought to preserve my mind from prejudices—you are always arguing against prejudices."

"Well, perhaps you will avenge the dark women in your own person, and carry away all the love from your cousin Lucy. She is sure to have some handsome young man of St Ogg's at her feet now: and you have

1. Novel by Madame de Staël (1807), in which the dark-haired, literary heroine loses her lover to her half-sister, the fair-haired, conventional Lucille.
2. In Greek mythology, there were nine Muses who presided over the arts and sciences.
3. The dark-haired women in Scott's *Ivanhoe* (1820), *Waverley* (1814), and *The Pirate* (1822), respectively.

only to shine upon him—your fair little cousin will be quite quenched in your beams."

"Philip, that is not pretty of you, to apply my nonsense to anything real," said Maggie, looking hurt. "As if I, with my old gowns and want of all accomplishments, could be a rival of dear little Lucy, who knows and does all sorts of charming things, and is ten times prettier than I am—even if I were odious and base enough to wish to be her rival. Besides, I never go to aunt Deane's when any one is there: it is only because dear Lucy is good, and loves me, that she comes to see me, and will have me go to see her sometimes."

"Maggie," said Philip, with surprise, "it is not like you to take playfulness literally. You must have been in St Ogg's this morning, and brought away a slight infection of dulness."

"Well," said Maggie, smiling, "if you meant that for a joke, it was a poor one; but I thought it was a very good reproof. I thought you wanted to remind me that I am vain, and wish every one to admire me most. But it isn't for that, that I'm jealous for the dark women—not because I'm dark myself. It's because I always care the most about the unhappy people: if the blond girl were forsaken, I should like *her* best. I always take the side of the rejected lover in the stories."

"Then you would never have the heart to reject one yourself—should you, Maggie?" said Philip, flushing a little.

"I don't know," said Maggie, hesitatingly. Then with a bright smile —"I think perhaps I could if he were very conceited; and yet, if he got extremely humiliated afterwards, I should relent."

"I've often wondered, Maggie," Philip said, with some effort, "whether you wouldn't really be more likely to love a man that other women were not likely to love."

"That would depend on what they didn't like him for," said Maggie, laughing. "He might be very disagreeable. He might look at me through an eye-glass stuck in his eye, making a hideous face, as young Torry does. I should think other women are not fond of that; but I never felt any pity for young Torry. I've never any pity for conceited people, because I think they carry their comfort about with them."

"But suppose, Maggie—suppose it was a man who was not conceited—who felt he had nothing to be conceited about—who had been marked from childhood for a peculiar kind of suffering—and to whom you were the day-star of his life—who loved you, worshipped you, so entirely that he felt it happiness enough for him if you would let him see you at rare moments. . . ."

Philip paused with a pang of dread lest his confession should cut short this very happiness—a pang of the same dread that had kept his love mute through long months. A rush of self-consciousness told him that he was besotted to have said all this. Maggie's manner this morning had been as unconstrained and indifferent as ever.

But she was not looking indifferent now. Struck with the unusual emotion in Philip's tone, she had turned quickly to look at him, and as he went on speaking, a great change came over her face—a flush and slight spasm of the features such as we see in people who hear some news that will require them to readjust their conceptions of the past. She was quite silent, and, walking on towards the trunk of a fallen tree, she sat down, as if she had no strength to spare for her muscles. She was trembling.

"Maggie," said Philip, getting more and more alarmed in every fresh moment of silence, "I was a fool to say it—forget that I've said it. I shall be contented if things can be as they were."

The distress with which he spoke urged Maggie to say something. "I am so surprised, Philip—I had not thought of it." And the effort to say this brought the tears down too.

"Has it made you hate me, Maggie?" said Philip, impetuously. "Do you think I'm a presumptuous fool?"

"O Philip!" said Maggie, "how can you think I have such feelings?—as if I were not grateful for *any* love. But . . . but I had never thought of your being my lover. It seemed so far off—like a dream—only like one of the stories one imagines—that I should ever have a lover."

"Then can you bear to think of me as your lover, Maggie?" said Philip, seating himself by her, and taking her hand, in the elation of a sudden hope. "*Do* you love me?"

Maggie turned rather pale: this direct question seemed not easy to answer. But her eyes met Philip's, which were in this moment liquid and beautiful with beseeching love. She spoke with hesitation, yet with sweet, simple, girlish tenderness.

"I think I could hardly love any one better: there is nothing but what I love you for." She paused a little while, and then added, "But it will be better for us not to say any more about it—won't it, dear Philip? You know we couldn't even be friends, if our friendship were discovered. I have never felt that I was right in giving way about seeing you—though it has been so precious to me in some ways; and now the fear comes upon me strongly again, that it will lead to evil."

"But no evil has come, Maggie; and if you had been guided by that fear before, you would only have lived through another dreary benumbing year, instead of reviving into your real self."

Maggie shook her head. "It has been very sweet, I know—all the talking together, and the books, and the feeling that I had the walk to look forward to, when I could tell you the thoughts that had come into my head while I was away from you. But it has made me restless: it has made me think a great deal about the world; and I have impatient thoughts again—I get weary of my home—and then it cuts me to the heart afterwards, that I should ever have felt weary of my father and mother. I think what you call being benumbed was better—better for me—for then my selfish desires were benumbed."

Philip had risen again, and was walking backwards and forwards impatiently.

"No, Maggie, you have wrong ideas of self-conquest, as I've often told you. What you call self-conquest—blinding and deafening yourself to all but one train of impressions—is only the culture of monomania in a nature like yours."

He had spoken with some irritation, but now he sat down by her again, and took her hand.

"Don't think of the past now, Maggie; think only of our love. If you can really cling to me with all your heart, every obstacle will be overcome in time: we need only wait. I can live on hope. Look at me, Maggie; tell me again, it is possible for you to love me. Don't look away from me to that cloven tree; it is a bad omen."

She turned her large dark glance upon him with a sad smile.

"Come, Maggie, say one kind word, or else you were better to me at Lorton. You asked me if I should like you to kiss me—don't you remember?—and you promised to kiss me when you met me again. You never kept the promise."

The recollection of that childish time came as a sweet relief to Maggie. It made the present moment less strange to her. She kissed him almost as simply and quietly as she had done when she was twelve years old. Philip's eyes flashed with delight, but his next words were words of discontent.

"You don't seem happy enough, Maggie: you are forcing yourself to say you love me, out of pity."

"No, Philip," said Maggie, shaking her head, in her old childish way; "I'm telling you the truth. It is all new and strange to me; but I don't think I could love any one better than I love you. I should like always to live with you—to make you happy. I have always been happy when I have been with you. There is only one thing I will not do for your sake: I will never do anything to wound my father. You must never ask that from me."

"No, Maggie: I will ask nothing—I will bear everything—I'll wait another year only for a kiss, if you will only give me the first place in your heart."

"No," said Maggie, smiling, "I won't make you wait so long as that." But then, looking serious again, she added, as she rose from her seat—

"But what would your own father say, Philip? O, it is quite impossible we can ever be more than friends—brother and sister in secret, as we have been. Let us give up thinking of everything else."

"No, Maggie, I can't give you up—unless you are deceiving me—unless you really only care for me as if I were your brother. Tell me the truth."

"Indeed, I do, Philip. What happiness have I ever had so great as being with you?—since I was a little girl—the days Tom was good to me. And your mind is a sort of world to me: you can tell me all I want to know. I think I should never be tired of being with you."

They were walking hand in hand, looking at each other; Maggie, indeed, was hurrying along, for she felt it time to be gone. But the sense that their parting was near, made her more anxious lest she should have unintentionally left some painful impression on Philip's mind. It was one of those dangerous moments when speech is at once sincere and deceptive—when feeling, rising high above its average depth, leaves flood-marks which are never reached again.

They stopped to part among the Scotch firs.

"Then my life will be filled with hope, Maggie—and I shall be happier than other men, in spite of all? We *do* belong to each other—for always—whether we are apart or together?"

"Yes, Philip: I should like never to part: I should like to make your life very happy."

"I am waiting for something else—I wonder whether it will come."

Maggie smiled, with glistening tears, and then stooped her tall head to kiss the pale face that was full of pleading, timid love—like a woman's.

She had a moment of real happiness then—a moment of belief that, if there were sacrifice in this love, it was all the richer and more satisfying.

She turned away and hurried home, feeling that in the hour since she had trodden this road before, a new era had begun for her. The tissue of vague dreams must now get narrower and narrower, and all the threads of thought and emotion be gradually absorbed in the woof of her actual daily life.

Chapter V

The Cloven Tree

Secrets are rarely betrayed or discovered according to any programme our fear has sketched out. Fear is almost always haunted by terrible dramatic scenes, which recur in spite of the best-argued probabilities against them; and during a year that Maggie had had the burthen of concealment on her mind, the possibility of discovery had continually presented itself under the form of a sudden meeting with her father or Tom when she was walking with Philip in the Red Deeps. She was aware that this was not one of the most likely events; but it was the scene that most completely symbolised her inward dread. Those slight indirect suggestions which are dependent on apparently trivial coincidences and incalculable states of mind, are the favourite machinery of Fact, but are not the stuff in which imagination is apt to work.

Certainly one of the persons about whom Maggie's fears were farthest from troubling themselves was her aunt Pullet, on whom, seeing that she did not live in St Ogg's, and was neither sharp-eyed nor sharp-tempered, it would surely have been quite whimsical of them to fix rather than on aunt Glegg. And yet the channel of fatality—the pathway of the lightning—was no other than aunt Pullet. She did not live at St Ogg's, but the road from Garum Firs lay by the Red Deeps, at the end opposite that by which Maggie entered.

The day after Maggie's last meeting with Philip, being a Sunday on which Mr Pullet was bound to appear in funeral hat-band and scarf at St Ogg's church, Mrs Pullet made this the occasion of dining with sister Glegg, and taking tea with poor sister Tulliver. Sunday was the one day in the week on which Tom was at home in the afternoon; and to-day the brighter spirits he had been in of late had flowed over in unusually cheerful open chat with his father, and in the invitation, "Come, Magsie, you come too!" when he strolled out with his mother in the garden to see the advancing cherry-blossoms. He had been better pleased with Maggie since she had been less odd and ascetic; he was even getting rather proud of her: several persons had remarked in his hearing that his sister was a very fine girl. To-day there was a peculiar brightness in her face, due in reality to an under-current of excitement, which had as much doubt and pain as pleasure in it; but it might pass for a sign of happiness.

"You look very well, my dear," said aunt Pullet, shaking her head sadly, as they sat round the tea-table. "I niver thought your girl 'ud be so good-looking, Bessy. But you must wear pink my dear: that blue thing as your aunt Glegg gave you turns you into a crowflower. Jane never *was* tasty. Why don't you wear that gown o' mine?"

"It is so pretty and so smart, aunt. I think it's too showy for me—at least for my other clothes, that I must wear with it."

"To be sure, it 'ud be unbecoming if it wasn't well known you've got them belonging to you as can afford to give you such things when they've done with 'em themselves. It stands to reason I must give my own niece clothes now and then—such things as *I* buy every year, and never wear anything out. And as for Lucy, there's no giving to her, for she's got everything o' the choicest: sister Deane may well hold her head up, though she looks dreadful yallow, poor thing—I doubt this liver complaint 'ull carry her off. That's what this new vicar, this Dr Kenn, said in the funeral sermon to-day."

"Ah, he's a wonderful preacher, by all account—isn't he, Sophy?" said Mrs Tulliver.

"Why, Lucy had got a collar on this blessed day," continued Mrs Pullet, with her eyes fixed in a ruminating manner, "as I don't say I haven't got as good, but I must look out my best to match it."

"Miss Lucy's called the bell o' St Ogg's, they say: that's a cur'ous word," observed Mr Pullet, on whom the mysteries of etymology sometimes fell with an oppressive weight.

"Pooh!" said Mr Tulliver, jealous for Maggie, "she's a small thing, not much of a figure. But fine feathers make fine birds. I see nothing to admire so much in those diminutive women; they look silly by the side o' the men—out o' proportion. When I chose my wife, I chose her the right size—neither too little nor too big."

The poor wife, with her withered beauty, smiled complacently.

"But the men aren't *all* big," said uncle Pullet, not without some self-reference; "a young fellow may be good-looking and yet not be a six-foot, like Master Tom here."

"Ah, it's poor talking about littleness and bigness,—anybody may think it's a mercy they're straight," said aunt Pullet. "There's that mis-made son o' Lawyer Wakem's—I saw him at church to-day. Dear, dear! to think o' the property he's like to have; and they say he's very queer and lonely—doesn't like much company. I shouldn't wonder if he goes out of his mind; for we never come along the road but he's a-scrambling out o' the trees and brambles at the Red Deeps."

This wide statement, by which Mrs Pullet represented the fact that she had twice seen Philip at the spot indicated, produced an effect on Maggie which was all the stronger because Tom sate opposite her, and she was intensely anxious to look indifferent. At Philip's name she had blushed, and the blush deepened every instant from consciousness, until the mention of the Red Deeps made her feel as if the whole secret were betrayed, and she dared not even hold her tea-spoon lest she should show how she trembled. She sat with her hands clasped under the table, not daring to look round. Happily, her father was seated on the same side with herself, beyond her uncle Pullet, and could not see her face without stooping forward. Her mother's voice brought the first relief—turning the conversation; for Mrs Tulliver was always alarmed when the name of Wakem was mentioned in her husband's presence. Gradually Maggie recovered composure enough to look up; her eyes met Tom's, but he turned away his head immediately; and she went to bed that night wondering if he had gathered any suspicion from her confusion. Perhaps not: perhaps he would think it was only her alarm at her aunt's mention of Wakem before her father: that was the interpretation her mother had put on it. To her father, Wakem was like a disfiguring disease, of which he was obliged to endure the consciousness, but was exasperated to have the existence recognised by others; and no amount of sensitiveness in her about her father could be surprising, Maggie thought.

But Tom was too keen-sighted to rest satisfied with such an interpretation: he had seen clearly enough that there was something distinct from anxiety about her father in Maggie's excessive confusion. In trying to recall all the details that could give shape to his suspicions, he remembered only lately hearing his mother scold Maggie for walking in the Red Deeps when the ground was wet, and bringing home shoes clogged with red soil: still Tom, retaining all his old repulsion for Philip's deformity, shrank from attributing to his sister the probability of feeling more than a friendly interest in such an unfortunate exception to the common run of men. Tom's was a nature which had a sort of superstitious repugnance to everything exceptional. A love for a deformed man would be odious in any woman—in a sister intolerable. But if she had been carrying on any kind of intercourse whatever with Philip, a stop must be put to it at once: she was disobeying her father's strongest feelings and her brother's express commands, besides compromising herself by secret meetings. He left home the next morning in that watchful state of mind which turns the most ordinary course of things into pregnant coincidences.

That afternoon, about half-past three o'clock, Tom was standing on the wharf, talking with Bob Jakin about the probability of the good ship Adelaide coming in, in a day or two, with results highly important to both of them.

"Eh," said Bob, parenthetically, as he looked over the fields on the other side of the river, "there goes that crooked young Wakem. I know him or his shadder as far off as I can see 'em: I'm allays lighting on him o' that side the river."

A sudden thought seemed to have darted through Tom's mind. "I must go, Bob," he said, "I've something to attend to," hurrying off to the warehouse, where he left notice for some one to take his place—he was called away home on peremptory business.

The swiftest pace and the shortest road took him to the gate, and he was pausing to open it deliberately, that he might walk into the house with an appearance of perfect composure, when Maggie came out at the front door in bonnet and shawl. His conjecture was fulfilled, and he waited for her at the gate. She started violently when she saw him.

"Tom, how is it you are come home? Is there anything the matter?" Maggie spoke in a low tremulous voice.

"I'm come to walk with you to the Red Deeps and meet Philip Wakem," said Tom, the central fold in his brow, which had become habitual with him, deepening as he spoke.

Maggie stood helpless—pale and cold. By some means, then, Tom knew everything. At last she said, "I'm not going," and turned round.

"Yes, you are; but I want to speak to you first. Where is my father?"

"Out on horseback."

"And my mother?"

"In the yard, I think, with the poultry."

"I can go in, then, without her seeing me?"

They walked in together, and Tom, entering the parlour, said to Maggie, "Come in here."

She obeyed, and he closed the door behind her.

"Now, Maggie, tell me this instant everything that has passed between you and Philip Wakem."

"Does my father know anything?" said Maggie, still trembling.

"No," said Tom, indignantly. "But he *shall* know, if you attempt to use deceit towards me any further."

"I don't wish to use deceit," said Maggie, flushing into resentment at hearing this word applied to her conduct.

"Tell me the whole truth then."

"Perhaps you know it."

"Never mind whether I know it or not. Tell me exactly what has happened, or my father shall know everything."

"I tell it for my father's sake, then."

"Yes, it becomes you to profess affection for your father, when you have despised his strongest feelings."

"You never do wrong, Tom," said Maggie, tauntingly.

"Not if I know it," answered Tom, with proud sincerity. "But I have nothing to say to you, beyond this: tell me what has passed between you and Philip Wakem. When did you first meet him in the Red Deeps?"

"A year ago," said Maggie, quietly. Tom's severity gave her a certain fund of defiance, and kept her sense of error in abeyance. "You need ask me no more questions. We have been friendly a year. We have met and walked together often. He has lent me books."

"Is that all?" said Tom, looking straight at her with his frown.

Maggie paused a moment; then, determined to make an end of Tom's right to accuse her of deceit, she said, haughtily—

"No, not quite all. On Saturday he told me that he loved me. I didn't think of it before then—I had only thought of him as an old friend."

"And you *encouraged* him?" said Tom, with an expression of disgust.

"I told him that I loved him too."

Tom was silent a few moments, looking on the ground and frowning, with his hands in his pockets. At last, he looked up, and said, coldly—

"Now, then, Maggie, there are but two courses for you to take; either you vow solemnly to me, with your hand on my father's Bible, that you will never have another meeting or speak another word in private with Philip Wakem, or you refuse, and I tell my father everything; and this month, when by my exertions he might be made happy once more, you will cause him the blow of knowing that you are a disobedient, deceitful daughter, who throws away her own respectability by clandestine meetings with the son of a man that has helped to ruin her father. Choose!" Tom ended with cold decision, going up to the large Bible, drawing it forward, and opening it at the fly-leaf, where the writing was.

It was a crushing alternative to Maggie.

"Tom," she said, urged out of pride into pleading, "don't ask me that. I will promise you to give up all intercourse with Philip, if you will let me see him once, or even only write to him and explain everything—to give it up as long as it would ever cause any pain to my father. . . . I feel something for Philip too. *He* is not happy."

"I don't wish to hear anything of your feelings; I have said exactly what I mean: choose—and quickly, lest my mother should come in."

"If I give you my word, that will be as strong a bond to me as if I laid my hand on the Bible. I don't require that to bind me."

"Do what *I* require," said Tom. "I can't trust you, Maggie. There is no consistency in you. Put your hand on this Bible, and say, 'I renounce all private speech and intercourse with Philip Wakem from this time forth.' Else you will bring shame on us all, and grief on my father; and what is the use of my exerting myself and giving up everything else for the sake of paying my father's debts, if you are to bring madness and vexation on him, just when he might be easy and hold up his head once more?"

"O Tom—*will* the debts be paid soon?" said Maggie, clasping her hands, with a sudden flash of joy across her wretchedness.

"If things turn out as I expect," said Tom. "But," he added, his voice trembling with indignation, "while I have been contriving and working that my father may have some peace of mind before he dies—working for the respectability of our family—you have done all you can to destroy both."

Maggie felt a deep movement of compunction: for the moment, her mind ceased to contend against what she felt to be cruel and unreasonable, and in her self-blame she justified her brother.

"Tom," she said, in a low voice, "it was wrong of me—but I was so lonely—and I was sorry for Philip. And I think enmity and hatred are wicked."

"Nonsense!" said Tom. "Your duty was clear enough. Say no more; but promise, in the words I told you."

"I *must* speak to Philip once more."

"You will go with me now and speak to him."

"I give you my word not to meet him or write to him again without your knowledge. That is the only thing I will say. I will put my hand on the Bible if you like."

"Say it, then."

Maggie laid her hand on the page of manuscript and repeated the promise. Tom closed the book, and said, "Now, let us go."

Not a word was spoken as they walked along. Maggie was suffering in anticipation of what Philip was about to suffer, and dreading the galling words that would fall on him from Tom's lips; but she felt it was in vain to attempt anything but submission. Tom had his terrible clutch on her conscience and her deepest dread: she writhed under the demonstrable truth of the character he had given to her conduct, and yet her whole soul rebelled against it as unfair from its incompleteness. He, meanwhile, felt the impetus of his indignation diverted towards Philip. He did not know how much of an old boyish repulsion and of mere personal pride and animosity was concerned in the bitter severity of the words by which he meant to do the duty of a son and a brother. Tom was not given to inquire subtly into his own motives, any more than into other matters of an intangible kind; he was quite sure that his own motives as well as actions were good, else he would have had nothing to do with them.

Maggie's only hope was that something might, for the first time, have prevented Philip from coming. Then there would be delay—then she might get Tom's permission to write to him. Her heart beat with double violence when they got under the Scotch firs. It was the last moment of suspense, she thought; Philip always met her soon after she got beyond them. But they passed across the more open green space, and entered the narrow bushy path by the mound. Another turning, and they came so close upon him that both Tom and Philip stopped suddenly within a yard of each other. There was a moment's silence, in which Philip darted a look of inquiry at Maggie's face. He saw an answer there, in the pale parted lips, and the terrified tension of the large eyes. Her imagination, always rushing extravagantly beyond an immediate impression, saw her tall strong brother grasping the feeble Philip bodily, crushing him and trampling on him.

"Do you call this acting the part of a man and a gentleman, sir?" Tom said, in a voice of harsh scorn, as soon as Philip's eyes were turned on him again.

"What do you mean?" answered Philip, haughtily.

"Mean? Stand farther from me, lest I should lay hands on you, and I'll tell you what I mean. I mean, taking advantage of a young girl's foolishness and ignorance to get her to have secret meetings with you. I mean, daring to trifle with the respectability of a family that has a good and honest name to support."

"I deny that," interrupted Philip, impetuously. "I could never trifle with anything that affected your sister's happiness. She is dearer to me than she is to you; I honour her more than you can ever honour her; I would give up my life to her."

"Don't talk high-flown nonsense to me, sir! Do you mean to pretend that you didn't know it would be injurious to her to meet you here week after week? Do you pretend you had any right to make professions of love to her, even if you had been a fit husband for her, when neither her father nor your father would ever consent to a marriage between you? And *you—you* to try and worm yourself into the affections of a handsome girl who is not eighteen, and has been shut out from the world by her father's misfortunes! That's your crooked notion of honour, is it? I call it base treachery—I call it taking advantage of circumstances to win what's too good for you—what you'd never get by fair means."

"It is manly of you to talk in this way to *me*," said Philip, bitterly, his whole frame shaken by violent emotions. "Giants have an immemorial right to stupidity and insolent abuse. You are incapable even of understanding what I feel for your sister. I feel so much for her that I could even desire to be at friendship with *you*."

"I should be very sorry to understand your feelings," said Tom, with scorching contempt. "What I wish is that you should understand *me*—that I shall take care of *my* sister, and that if you dare to make the least attempt to come near her, or to write to her, or to keep the slightest hold on her mind, your puny, miserable body, that ought to have put some modesty into your mind, shall not protect you. I'll thrash you—I'll hold you up to public scorn. Who wouldn't laugh at the idea of *your* turning lover to a fine girl?"

"Tom, I will not bear it—I will listen no longer," Maggie burst out, in a convulsed voice.

"Stay, Maggie!" said Philip, making a strong effort to speak. Then, looking at Tom, "You have dragged your sister here, I suppose, that she may stand by while you threaten and insult me. These naturally seemed to you the right means to influence me. But you are mistaken. Let your sister speak. If she says she is bound to give me up, I shall abide by her wishes to the slightest word."

"It was for my father's sake, Philip," said Maggie, imploringly. "Tom threatens to tell my father—and he couldn't bear it: I have promised, I have vowed solemnly, that we will not have any intercourse without my brother's knowledge."

"It is enough, Maggie. *I* shall not change; but I wish you to hold yourself entirely free. But trust me—remember that I can never seek for anything but good to what belongs to you."

"Yes," said Tom, exasperated by this attitude of Philip's, "you can talk of seeking good for her and what belongs to her now: did you seek her good before?"

"I did—at some risk, perhaps. But I wished her to have a friend for life—who would cherish her, who would do her more justice than a coarse and narrow-minded brother, that she has always lavished her affections on."

"Yes, my way of befriending her is different from yours; and I'll tell you what is my way. I'll save her from disobeying and disgracing her father: I'll save her from throwing herself away on you—from making herself a laughing-stock—from being flouted by a man like *your* father, because she's not good enough for his son. You know well enough what sort of justice and cherishing you were preparing for her. I'm not to be imposed upon by fine words: I can see what actions mean. Come away, Maggie."

He seized Maggie's right wrist as he spoke, and she put out her left hand. Philip clasped it an instant, with one eager look, and then hurried away.

Tom and Maggie walked on in silence for some yards. He was still holding her wrist tightly, as if he were compelling a culprit from the scene of action. At last Maggie, with a violent snatch, drew her hand away, and her pent-up, long-gathered irritation burst into utterance.

"Don't suppose that I think you are right, Tom, or that I bow to your will. I despise the feelings you have shown in speaking to Philip: I detest your insulting unmanly allusions to his deformity. You have been reproaching other people all your life—you have been always sure you yourself are right: it is because you have not a mind large enough to see that there is anything better than your own conduct and your own petty aims."

"Certainly," said Tom, coolly. "I don't see that your conduct is better, or your aims either. If your conduct, and Philip Wakem's conduct, has been right, why are you ashamed of its being known? Answer me that. I know what I have aimed at in my conduct, and I've succeeded: pray, what good has your conduct brought to you or any one else?"

"I don't want to defend myself," said Maggie, still with vehemence: "I know I've been wrong—often, continually. But yet, sometimes when I have done wrongs, it has been because I have feelings that you would be the better for, if you had them. If *you* were in fault ever—if you had done anything very wrong, I should be sorry for the pain it brought you; I should not want punishment to be heaped on you. But you have always enjoyed punishing me—you have always been hard and cruel to me: even when I was a little girl, and always loved you better than any one else in the world, you would let me go crying to bed without forgiving me. You have no pity: you have no sense of your own imperfection and your own sins. It is a sin to be hard; it is not fitting for a mortal—for a Christian. You are nothing but a Pharisee.[1] You thank God for nothing but your own virtues—you think they are great enough to win you everything else. You have not even a vision of feelings by the side of which your shining virtues are mere darkness!"

"Well," said Tom, with cold scorn, "if your feelings are so much better than mine, let me see you show them in some other way than by conduct that's likely to disgrace us all—than by ridiculous flights first into one extreme and then into another. Pray, how have you shown your love, that you talk of, either to me or my father? By disobeying and deceiving us. I have a different way of showing my affection."

"Because you are a man, Tom, and have power, and can do something in the world."

"Then, if you can do nothing, submit to those that can."

1. In the Bible, a sect noted for strict adherence to the letter of the law.

"So I *will* submit to what I acknowledge and feel to be right. I will submit even to what is unreasonable from my father, but I will not submit to it from you. You boast of your virtues as if they purchased you a right to be cruel and unmanly as you've been to-day. Don't suppose I would give up Philip Wakem in obedience to you. The deformity you insult would make me cling to him and care for him the more."

"Very well—that is your view of things," said Tom, more coldly than ever; "you need say no more to show me what a wide distance there is between us. Let us remember that in future, and be silent."

Tom went back to St Ogg's, to fulfil an appointment with his uncle Deane, and receive directions about a journey on which he was to set out the next morning.

Maggie went up to her own room to pour out all that indignant remonstrance, against which Tom's mind was close barred, in bitter tears. Then, when the first burst of unsatisfied anger was gone by, came the recollection of that quiet time before the pleasure which had ended in to-day's misery had perturbed the clearness and simplicity of her life. She used to think in that time that she had made great conquests, and won a lasting stand on serene heights above worldly temptations and conflict. And here she was down again in the thick of a hot strife with her own and others' passions. Life was not so short, then, and perfect rest was not so near as she had dreamed when she was two years younger. There was more struggle for her—perhaps more falling. If she had felt that she was entirely wrong, and that Tom had been entirely right, she could sooner have recovered more inward harmony; but now her penitence and submission were constantly obstructed by resentment that would present itself to her no otherwise than as a just indignation. Her heart bled for Philip: she went on recalling the insults that had been flung at him with so vivid a conception of what he had felt under them, that it was almost like a sharp bodily pain to her, making her beat the floor with her foot, and tighten her fingers on her palm.

And yet, how was it that she was now and then conscious of a certain dim background of relief in the forced separation from Philip? Surely it was only because the sense of a deliverance from concealment was welcome at any cost.

Chapter VI

The Hard-Won Triumph

Three weeks later, when Dorlcote Mill was at its prettiest moment in all the year—the great chestnuts in blossom, and the grass all deep and daisied—Tom Tulliver came home to it earlier than usual in the evening, and as he passed over the bridge, he looked with the old deep-rooted affection at the respectable red brick house, which always seemed cheerful and inviting outside, let the rooms be as bare and the hearts as sad as they might, inside. There is a very pleasant light in Tom's blue-grey eyes as he glances at the house-windows: that fold in his brow never disappears, but it is not unbecoming; it seems to imply a strength of will that may possibly be without harshness, when the eyes and mouth have their gentlest expression. His firm step becomes quicker, and the corners of his mouth rebel against the compression which is meant to forbid a smile.

The eyes in the parlour were not turned towards the bridge just then, and the group there was sitting in unexpectant silence—Mr Tulliver in his arm-chair, tired with a long ride, and ruminating with a worn look, fixed chiefly on Maggie, who was bending over her sewing while her mother was making the tea.

They all looked up with surprise when they heard the well-known foot.

"Why, what's up now, Tom?" said his father. "You're a bit earlier than usual."

"O, there was nothing more for me to do, so I came away. Well, mother!"

Tom went up to his mother and kissed her, a sign of unusual good-humour with him. Hardly a word or look had passed between him and Maggie in all the three weeks; but his usual incommunicativeness at home prevented this from being noticeable to their parents.

"Father," said Tom, when they had finished tea, "do you know exactly how much money there is in the tin box?"

"Only a hundred and ninety-three pound," said Mr Tulliver. "You've brought less o' late—but young fellows like to have their own way with their money. Though I didn't do as I liked before *I* was of age." He spoke with rather timid discontent.

"Are you quite sure that's the sum, father?" said Tom: "I wish you would take the trouble to fetch the tin box down. I think you have perhaps made a mistake."

"How should I make a mistake?" said his father, sharply. "I've counted it often enough; but I can fetch it, if you won't believe me."

It was always an incident Mr Tulliver liked, in his gloomy life, to fetch the tin box and count the money.

"Don't go out of the room, mother," said Tom, as he saw her moving when his father was gone up-stairs.

"And isn't Maggie to go?" said Mrs Tulliver; "because somebody must take away the things."

"Just as she likes," said Tom, indifferently.

That was a cutting word to Maggie. Her heart had leaped with the sudden conviction that Tom was going to tell their father the debts could be paid—and Tom would have let her be absent when that news was told! But she carried away the tray, and came back immediately. The feeling of injury on her own behalf could not predominate at that moment.

Tom drew to the corner of the table near his father when the tin box was set down and opened, and the red evening light falling on them made conspicuous the worn, sour gloom of the dark-eyed father and the suppressed joy in the face of the fair-complexioned son. The mother and Maggie sat at the other end of the table, the one in blank patience, the other in palpitating expectation.

Mr Tulliver counted out the money, setting it in order on the table, and then said, glancing sharply at Tom—

"There now! you see I was right enough."

He paused, looking at the money with bitter despondency.

"There's more nor three hundred wanting—it'll be a fine while before *I* can save that. Losing that forty-two pound wi' the corn was a sore job. This world's been too many for me. It's took four year to lay *this* by—it's much if I'm above ground for another four year. . . . I must trusten to you to pay 'em," he went on, with a trembling voice, "if you keep i' the same mind now you're coming o' age. . . . But you're like enough to bury me first."

He looked up in Tom's face with a querulous desire for some assurance.

"No, father," said Tom, speaking with energetic decision, though there was tremor discernible in his voice too, "you will live to see the debts all paid. You shall pay them with your own hand."

His tone implied something more than mere hopefulness or resolution. A slight electric shock seemed to pass through Mr Tulliver, and he kept his eyes fixed on Tom with a look of eager inquiry, while Maggie, unable to restrain herself, rushed to her father's side and knelt down by him. Tom was silent a little while before he went on.

"A good while ago, my uncle Glegg lent me a little money to trade with, and that has answered. I have three hundred and twenty pounds in the bank."

His mother's arms were round his neck as soon as the last words were uttered, and she said, half-crying—

"O, my boy, I knew you'd make iverything right again, when you got a man."

But his father was silent: the flood of emotion hemmed in all power of speech. Both Tom and Maggie were struck with fear lest the shock of joy might even be fatal. But the blessed relief of tears came. The broad chest heaved, the muscles of the face gave way, and the grey-haired man burst into loud sobs. The fit of weeping gradually subsided, and he sat quiet, recovering the regularity of his breathing. At last he looked up at his wife and said, in a gentle tone—

"Bessy, you must come and kiss me now—the lad has made you amends. You'll see a bit o' comfort again, belike."

When she had kissed him, and he had held her hand a minute, his thoughts went back to the money.

"I wish you'd brought me the money to look at, Tom," he said, fingering the sovereigns on the table; "I should ha' felt surer."

"You shall see it to-morrow, father," said Tom. "My uncle Deane has appointed the creditors to meet to-morrow at the Golden Lion, and he has ordered a dinner for them at two o'clock. My uncle Glegg and he will both be there. It was advertised in the *Messenger* on Saturday."

"Then Wakem knows on't!" said Mr Tulliver, his eye kindling with triumphant fire. "Ah!" he went on, with a long-drawn guttural enunciation, taking out his snuff-box, the only luxury he had left himself, and tapping it with something of his old air of defiance—"I'll get from under *his* thumb now—though I *must* leave th' old mill. I thought I could ha' held out to die here—but I can't. . . . We've got a glass o' nothing in the house, have we, Bessy?"

"Yes," said Mrs Tulliver, drawing out her much-reduced bunch of keys, "there's some brandy sister Deane brought me when I was ill."

"Get it me, then, get it me. I feel a bit weak."

"Tom, my lad," he said, in a stronger voice, when he had taken some brandy-and-water, "you shall make a speech to 'em. I'll tell 'em it's you as got the best part o' the money. They'll see I'm honest at last, and ha' got an honest son. Ah! Wakem 'ud be fine and glad to have a son like mine—a fine straight fellow—i'stead o' that poor crooked creatur! You'll prosper i' the world, my lad; you'll maybe see the day when Wakem and his son 'ull be a round or two below you. You'll like enough be ta'en into partnership, as your uncle Deane was before you—you're in the right way for't; and then there's nothing to hinder your getting rich. . . . And if ever you're rich enough—mind this—try and get th' old mill again."

Mr Tulliver threw himself back in his chair: his mind, which had so long been the home of nothing but bitter discontent and foreboding, suddenly filled, by the magic of joy, with visions of good fortune. But some subtle influence prevented him from foreseeing the good fortune as happening to himself.

"Shake hands wi' me, my lad," he said, suddenly putting out his hand. "It's a great thing when a man can be proud as he's got a good son. I've had *that* luck."

Tom never lived to taste another moment so delicious as that; and Maggie couldn't help forgetting her own grievances. Tom *was* good; and in the sweet humility that springs in us all in moments of true admiration and gratitude, she felt that the faults he had to pardon in her had never been redeemed, as his faults were. She felt no jealousy this evening that, for the first time, she seemed to be thrown into the background in her father's mind.

There was much more talk before bed-time. Mr Tulliver naturally wanted to hear all the particulars of Tom's trading adventures, and he listened with growing excitement and delight. He was curious to know what had been said on every occasion—if possible, what had been thought; and Bob Jakin's part in the business threw him into peculiar outbursts of sympathy with the triumphant knowingness of that remarkable packman. Bob's juvenile history, so far as it had come under Mr Tulliver's knowledge, was recalled with that sense of astonishing promise it displayed, which is observable in all reminiscences of the childhood of great men.

It was well that there was this interest of narrative to keep under the vague but fierce sense of triumph over Wakem, which would otherwise have been the channel his joy would have rushed into with dangerous force. Even as it was, that feeling from time to time gave threats of its ultimate mastery, in sudden bursts of irrelevant exclamation.

It was long before Mr Tulliver got to sleep that night, and the sleep, when it came, was filled with vivid dreams. At half-past five o'clock in the morning, when Mrs Tulliver was already rising, he alarmed her by starting up with a sort of smothered shout, and looking round in a bewildered way at the walls of the bedroom.

"What's the matter, Mr Tulliver?" said his wife. He looked at her, still with a puzzled expression, and said at last—

"Ah!—I was dreaming . . . did I make a noise? . . . I thought I'd got hold of him."

Chapter VII

A Day of Reckoning

Mr Tulliver was an essentially sober man—able to take his glass and not averse to it, but never exceeding the bounds of moderation. He had naturally an active Hotspur temperament, which did not crave liquid fire to set it a-glow; his impetuosity was usually equal to an exciting occasion without any such reinforcements; and his desire for the brandy-and-water implied that the too sudden joy had fallen with a dangerous shock on a frame depressed by four years of gloom and unaccustomed hard fare. But that first doubtful tottering moment passed, he seemed to gather strength with his gathering excitement; and the next day, when he was seated at table with his creditors, his eye kindling and his cheek flushed with the consciousness that he was about to make an honourable figure once more, he looked more like the proud, confident, warm-hearted and warm-tempered Tulliver of old times, than might have seemed possible to any one who had met him a week before, riding along as had been his wont for the last four years since the sense of failure and debt had been upon him—with his head hanging down, casting brief, unwilling looks on those who forced themselves on his notice. He made his speech, asserting his honest principles with his old confident eagerness, alluding to the rascals and the luck that had been against him, but that he had triumphed over, to some extent, by hard efforts and the aid of a good son; and winding up with the story of how Tom had got the best part of the needful money. But the streak of irritation and hostile triumph seemed to melt for a little while into purer fatherly pride and pleasure, when, Tom's health having been proposed, and uncle Deane having taken occasion to say a few words of eulogy on his general character and conduct, Tom himself got up and made the single speech of his life. It could hardly have been briefer: he thanked the gentlemen for the honour they had done him. He was glad that he had been able to help his father in proving his integrity and regaining his honest name; and, for his own part, he hoped he should never undo that work and disgrace that name. But the applause that followed was so great, and Tom looked so gentlemanly as well as tall and straight, that Mr Tulliver remarked, in an explanatory manner, to his friends on his right and left, that he had spent a deal of money on his son's education.

The party broke up in very sober fashion at five o'clock. Tom remained in St Ogg's to attend to some business, and Mr Tulliver mounted his horse to go home, and describe the memorable things that had been said and done, to "poor Bessy and the little wench." The air of excitement that hung about him was but faintly due to good cheer or any stimulus but the potent wine of triumphant joy. He did not choose any back street to-day, but rode slowly, with uplifted head and free glances, along the principal street all the way to the bridge. Why did he not happen to meet Wakem? The want of that coincidence vexed him, and set his mind at work in an irritating way. Perhaps Wakem was gone out of town to-day on purpose to avoid seeing or hearing anything of an honourable action, which might well cause him some unpleasant twinges. If Wakem were to meet him then, Mr Tulliver would look straight at him, and the rascal would perhaps be forsaken a little by his cool domineering impudence. He would know by-and-by that an honest man was not going to serve *him* any longer, and lend his honesty to fill a pocket already over-full of dishonest gains. Perhaps the luck was beginning to turn; perhaps the devil didn't always hold the best cards in this world.

Simmering in this way, Mr Tulliver approached the yard-gates of Dorlcote Mill, near enough to see a well-known figure coming out of them on a fine black horse. They met about fifty yards from the gates, between the great chestnuts and elms and the high bank.

"Tulliver," said Wakem, abruptly, in a haughtier tone than usual, "what a fool's trick you did—spreading those hard lumps on that Far Close. I told you how it would be; but you men never learn to farm with any method."

"Oh!" said Tulliver, suddenly boiling up. "Get somebody else to farm for you, then, as 'll ask *you* to teach him."

"You have been drinking, I suppose," said Wakem, really believing that this was the meaning of Tulliver's flushed face and sparkling eyes.

"No, I've not been drinking," said Tulliver; "I want no drinking to help me make up my mind as I'll serve no longer under a scoundrel."

"Very well! you may leave my premises to-morrow, then: hold your insolent tongue and let me pass." (Tulliver was backing his horse across the road to hem Wakem in.)

"No, I *shan't* let you pass," said Tulliver, getting fiercer. "I shall tell you what I think of you first. You're too big a raskill to get hanged—you're . . ."

"Let me pass, you ignorant brute, or I'll ride over you."

Mr Tulliver, spurring his horse and raising his whip, made a rush forward, and Wakem's horse, rearing and staggering backward, threw his rider from the saddle and sent him sideways on the ground. Wakem had had the presence of mind to loose the bridle at once, and as the horse only staggered a few paces and then stood still, he might have risen and remounted without more inconvenience than a bruise and a shake. But before he could rise, Tulliver was off his horse too. The sight of the long-hated predominant man down and in his power, threw him into a frenzy of triumphant vengeance, which seemed to give him preternatural agility and strength. He rushed on Wakem, who was in the act of trying to recover his feet, grasped him by the left arm so as to press Wakem's whole weight on the right arm, which rested on the ground, and flogged him fiercely across the back with his riding-whip. Wakem shouted for help, but no help came, until a woman's scream was heard, and the cry of "Father, father!"

Suddenly, Wakem felt, something had arrested Mr Tulliver's arm; for the flogging ceased, and the grasp on his own arm was relaxed.

"Get away with you—go!" said Tulliver, angrily. But it was not to Wakem that he spoke. Slowly the lawyer rose, and, as he turned his head, saw that Tulliver's arms were being held by a girl—rather by the fear of hurting the girl that clung to him with all her young might.

"O Luke—mother—come and help Mr Wakem!" Maggie cried, as she heard the longed-for footsteps.

"Help me on to that low horse," said Wakem to Luke, "then I shall perhaps manage: though—confound it—I think this arm is sprained."

With some difficulty, Wakem was heaved on to Tulliver's horse. Then he turned toward the miller and said, with white rage, "You'll suffer for this, sir. Your daughter is a witness that you've assaulted me."

"I don't care," said Mr Tulliver, in a thick, fierce voice; "go and show your back, and tell 'em I thrashed you. Tell 'em I've made things a bit more even i' the world."

"Ride my horse home with me," said Wakem to Luke. "By the Tofton Ferry—not through the town."

"Father, come in!" said Maggie, imploringly. Then, seeing that Wakem had ridden off, and that no further violence was possible, she slackened her hold and burst into hysteric sobs, while poor Mrs Tulliver stood by in silence, quivering with fear. But Maggie became conscious that as she was slackening her hold, her father was beginning to grasp her and lean on her. The surprise checked her sobs.

"I feel ill—faintish," he said. "Help me in, Bessy—I'm giddy—I've a pain i' the head."

He walked in slowly, propped by his wife and daughter, and tottered into his arm-chair. The almost purple flush had given way to paleness, and his hand was cold.

"Hadn't we better send for the doctor?" said Mrs Tulliver.

He seemed to be too faint and suffering to hear her; but presently, when she said to Maggie, "Go and see for somebody to fetch the doctor," he looked up at her with full comprehension, and said, "Doctor? no—no doctor. It's my head—that's all. Help me to bed."

Sad ending to the day that had risen on them all like a beginning of better times! But mingled seed must bear a mingled crop.

In half an hour after his father had lain down Tom came home. Bob Jakin was with him—come to congratulate "the old master," not without some excusable pride that he had had his share in bringing about Mr Tom's good-luck; and Tom had thought his father would like nothing better, as a finish to the day, than a talk with Bob. But now Tom could only spend the evening in gloomy expectation of the unpleasant consequences that must follow on this mad outbreak of his father's long-smothered hate. After the painful news had been told, he sat in silence: he had not spirit or inclination to tell his mother and sister anything about the dinner—they hardly cared to ask it. Apparently the mingled thread in the web of their life was so curiously twisted together, that there could be no joy without a sorrow coming close upon it. Tom was dejected by the thought that his exemplary effort must always be baffled by the wrong-doing of others: Maggie was living through, over and over again, the agony of the moment in which she had rushed to throw herself on her father's arm—with a vague, shuddering foreboding of wretched scenes to come. Not one of the three felt any particular alarm about Mr Tulliver's health: the symptoms did not recall his former dangerous attack, and it seemed only a necessary consequence that his violent passion and effort of strength, after many hours of unusual excitement, should have made him feel ill. Rest would probably cure him.

Tom, tired out by his active day, fell asleep soon, and slept soundly: it seemed to him as if he had only just come to bed, when he waked to see his mother standing by him in the grey light of early morning.

"My boy, you must get up this minute: I've sent for the doctor, and your father wants you and Maggie to come to him."

"Is he worse, mother?"

"He's been very ill all night with his head, but he doesn't say it's worse—he only said sudden, 'Bessy, fetch the boy and girl. Tell 'em to make haste.' "

Maggie and Tom threw on their clothes hastily in the chill grey light, and reached their father's room almost at the same moment. He was watching for them with an expression of pain on his brow, but with sharpened anxious consciousness in his eyes. Mrs Tulliver stood at the foot of the bed, frightened and trembling, looking worn and aged from disturbed rest. Maggie was at the bedside first, but her father's glance was towards Tom, who came and stood next to her.

"Tom, my lad, it's come upon me as I shan't get up again. . . . This world's been too many for me, my lad, but you've done what you could to make things a bit even. Shake hands wi' me again, my lad, before I go away from you."

The father and son clasped hands and looked at each other an instant. Then Tom said, trying to speak firmly—

"Have you any wish, father—that I can fulfil, when . . ."

"Ay, my lad . . . you'll try and get the old mill back."

"Yes, father."

"And there's your mother—you'll try and make her amends, all you can, for my bad luck . . . and there's the little wench. . . ."

The father turned his eyes on Maggie with a still more eager look, while she, with a bursting heart, sank on her knees, to be closer to the dear, time-worn face which had been present with her through long years, as the sign of her deepest love and hardest trial.

"You must take care of her, Tom . . . don't you fret, my wench . . . there'll come somebody as'll love you and take your part . . . and you must be good to her, my lad. I was good to *my* sister. Kiss me, Maggie. . . . Come, Bessy. . . . You'll manage to pay for a brick grave, Tom, so as your mother and me can lie together."

He looked away from them all when he had said this, and lay silent for some minutes, while they stood watching him, not daring to move. The morning light was growing clearer for them, and they could see the heaviness gathering in his face, and the dulness in his eyes. But at last he looked towards Tom and said—

"I had my turn—I beat him. That was nothing but fair. I never wanted anything but what was fair."

"But, father, dear father," said Maggie, an unspeakable anxiety predominating over her grief, "you forgive him—you forgive every one now?"

He did not move his eyes to look at her, but he said—

"No, my wench. I don't forgive him. . . . What's forgiving to do? I can't love a raskill. . . ."

His voice had become thicker; but he wanted to say more, and moved his lips again and again, struggling in vain to speak. At length the words forced their way.

"Does God forgive raskills? . . . but if He does, He won't be hard wi' me."

Book Sixth

THE GREAT TEMPTATION

Chapter I

A Duet in Paradise

The well-furnished drawing-room, with the open grand piano, and the pleasant outlook down a sloping garden to a boat-house by the side of the Floss, is Mr Deane's. The neat little lady in mourning, whose light-brown ringlets are falling over the coloured embroidery with which her fingers are busy, is of course Lucy Deane; and the fine young man who is leaning down from his chair to snap the scissors in the extremely abbreviated face of the "King Charles"[1] lying on the young lady's feet, is no other than Mr Stephen Guest, whose diamond ring, attar of roses, and air of nonchalant leisure, at twelve o'clock in the day, are the graceful and odoriferous result of the largest oil-mill and the most extensive wharf in St Ogg's. There is an apparent triviality in the action with the scissors, but your discernment perceives at once that there is a design in it which makes it eminently worthy of a large-headed, long-limbed young man; for you see that Lucy wants the scissors, and is compelled, reluctant as she may be, to shake her ringlets back, raise her soft hazel eyes, smile playfully down on the face that is so very nearly on a level with her knee, and, holding out her little shell-pink palm, to say—

"My scissors, please, if you can renounce the great pleasure of persecuting my poor Minny."

The foolish scissors have slipped too far over the knuckles, it seems, and Hercules holds out his entrapped fingers hopelessly.

"Confound the scissors! The oval lies the wrong way. Please, draw them off for me."

"Draw them off with your other hand," says Miss Lucy, roguishly.

"O, but that's my left hand: I'm not left-handed." Lucy laughs, and the scissors are drawn off with gentle touches from tiny tips, which naturally dispose Mr Stephen for a repetition *da capo*.[2] Accordingly, he

1. English toy spaniel.
2. From the beginning (a musical term).

watches for the release of the scissors, that he may get them into his possession again.

"No, no," said Lucy, sticking them in her band, "you shall not have my scissors again—you have strained them already. Now don't set Minny growling again. Sit up and behave properly, and then I will tell you some news."

"What is that?" said Stephen, throwing himself back and hanging his right arm over the corner of his chair. He might have been sitting for his portrait, which would have represented a rather striking young man of five-and-twenty, with a square forehead, short dark-brown hair standing erect, with a slight wave at the end, like a thick crop of corn, and a half-ardent, half-sarcastic glance from under his well-marked horizontal eye-brows. "Is it very important news?"

"Yes—very. Guess."

"You are going to change Minny's diet, and give him three ratafias[3] soaked in a dessert-spoonful of cream daily?"

"Quite wrong."

"Well, then, Dr Kenn has been preaching against buckram, and you ladies have all been sending him a round-robin, saying—'This is a hard doctrine; who can bear it?' "

"For shame!" said Lucy, adjusting her little mouth gravely. "It is rather dull of you not to guess my news, because it is about something I mentioned to you not very long ago."

"But you have mentioned many things to me not long ago. Does your feminine tyranny require that when you say the thing you mean is one of several things, I should know it immediately by that mark?"

"Yes, I know you think I am silly."

"I think you are perfectly charming."

"And my silliness is part of my charm?"

"I didn't say *that*."

"But I know you like women to be rather insipid. Philip Wakem betrayed you: he said so one day when you were not here."

"O, I know Phil is fierce on that point; he makes it quite a personal matter. I think he must be love-sick for some unknown lady—some exalted Beatrice[4] whom he met abroad."

"By the by!" said Lucy, pausing in her work, "it has just occurred to me that I have never found out whether my cousin Maggie will object to see Philip, as her brother does. Tom will not enter a room where Philip is, if he knows it: perhaps Maggie may be the same, and then we shan't be able to sing our glees[5]—shall we?"

"What! is your cousin coming to stay with you?" said Stephen, with a look of slight annoyance.

3. Sweet biscuits made of almond paste.
4. Dante's beloved, whom he idealized in his poems.
5. Unaccompanied songs for three or more voices.

"Yes; that was my news, which you have forgotten. She's going to leave her situation, where she has been nearly two years, poor thing—ever since her father's death; and she will stay with me a month or two—many months, I hope."

"And am I bound to be pleased at that news?"

"O no, not at all," said Lucy, with a little air of pique. "*I* am pleased, but that, of course, is no reason why *you* should be pleased. There is no girl in the world I love so well as my cousin Maggie."

"And you will be inseparable, I suppose, when she comes. There will be no possibility of a *tête-à-tête* with you any more, unless you can find an admirer for her, who will pair off with her occasionally. What is the ground of dislike to Philip? He might have been a resource."

"It is a family quarrel with Philip's father. There were very painful circumstances, I believe. I never quite understood them, or knew them all. My uncle Tulliver was unfortunate and lost all his property, and I think he considered Mr Wakem was somehow the cause of it. Mr Wakem bought Dorlcote Mill, my uncle's old place, where he always lived. You must remember my uncle Tulliver, don't you?"

"No," said Stephen, with rather supercilious indifference. "I've always known the name, and I daresay I knew the man by sight, apart from his name. I know half the names and faces in the neighbourhood in that detached, disjointed way."

"He was a very hot-tempered man. I remember, when I was a little girl, and used to go to see my cousins, he often frightened me by talking as if he were angry. Papa told me there was a dreadful quarrel, the very day before my uncle's death, between him and Mr Wakem, but it was hushed up. That was when you were in London. Papa says my uncle was quite mistaken in many ways: his mind had become embittered. But Tom and Maggie must naturally feel it very painful to be reminded of these things. They have had so much—so very much trouble. Maggie was at school with me six years ago, when she was fetched away because of her father's misfortunes, and she has hardly had any pleasure since, I think. She has been in a dreary situation in a school since uncle's death, because she is determined to be independent, and not live with aunt Pullet; and I could hardly wish her to come to me then, because dear mamma was ill, and everything was so sad. That is why I want her to come to me now, and have a long, long holiday."

"Very sweet and angelic of you," said Stephen, looking at her with an admiring smile; "and all the more so if she has the conversational qualities of her mother."

"Poor aunty! You are cruel to ridicule her. She is very valuable to *me*, I know. She manages the house beautifully—much better than any stranger would—and she was a great comfort to me in mamma's illness."

"Yes, but in point of companionship, one would prefer that she should be represented by her brandy-cherries and cream-cakes. I think with a shudder that her daughter will always be present in person, and have no agreeable proxies of that kind—a fat, blonde girl, with round blue eyes, who will stare at us silently."

"O yes!" exclaimed Lucy, laughing wickedly and clapping her hands, "that is just my cousin Maggie. You must have seen her!"

"No, indeed: I'm only guessing what Mrs Tulliver's daughter must be; and then if she is to banish Philip, our only apology for a tenor, that will be an additional bore."

"But I hope that may not be. I think I will ask you to call on Philip and tell him Maggie is coming to-morrow. He is quite aware of Tom's feeling, and always keeps out of his way; so he will understand, if you tell him, that I asked you to warn him not to come until I write to ask him."

"I think you had better write a pretty note for me to take: Phil is so sensitive, you know, the least thing might frighten him off coming at all, and we had hard work to get him. I can never induce him to come to the Park: he doesn't like my sisters, I think. It is only your faëry touch that can lay his ruffled feathers."

Stephen mastered the little hand that was straying towards the table, and touched it lightly with his lips. Little Lucy felt very proud and happy. She and Stephen were in that stage of courtship which makes the most exquisite moment of youth, the freshest blossom-time of passion—when each is sure of the other's love, but no formal declaration has been made, and all its mutual divination, exalting the most trivial word, the lightest gesture, into thrills delicate and delicious as wafted jasmine scent. The explicitness of an engagement wears off this finest edge of susceptibility; it is jasmine gathered and presented in a large bouquet.

"But it is really odd that you should have hit so exactly on Maggie's appearance and manners," said the cunning Lucy, moving to reach her desk, "because she might have been like her brother, you know; and Tom has not round eyes; and he is as far as possible from staring at people."

"O, I suppose he is like the father: he seems to be as proud as Lucifer. Not a brilliant companion, though, I should think."

"I like Tom. He gave me my Minny when I lost Lolo; and papa is very fond of him: he says Tom has excellent principles. It was through him that his father was able to pay all his debts before he died."

"Oh, ah; I've heard about that. I heard your father and mine talking about it a little while ago, after dinner, in one of their interminable discussions about business. They think of doing something for young Tulliver: he saved them from a considerable loss by riding home in some marvellous way, like Turpin,[6] to bring them news about the stoppage

6. With great speed and recklessness. Dick Turpin, eighteenth-century highwayman, was hanged for stealing horses.

of a bank, or something of that sort. But I was rather drowsy at the time."

Stephen rose from his seat, and sauntered to the piano, humming in falsetto, "Graceful Consort," as he turned over the volume of "The Creation,"[7] which stood open on the desk.

"Come and sing this," he said, when he saw Lucy rising.

"What! 'Graceful Consort?' I don't think it suits your voice."

"Never mind; it exactly suits my feeling, which, Philip will have it, is the grand element of good singing. I notice men with indifferent voices are usually of that opinion."

"Philip burst into one of his invectives against 'The Creation' the other day," said Lucy, seating herself at the piano. "He says it has a sort of sugared complacency and flattering make-believe in it, as if it were written for the birthday fête of a German Grand-Duke."

"O pooh! He is the fallen Adam with a soured temper. We are Adam and Eve unfallen, in paradise. Now, then—the recitative, for the sake of the moral. You will sing the whole duty of woman—'And from obedience grows my pride and happiness.' "

"O no, I shall not respect an Adam who drags the *tempo*, as you will," said Lucy, beginning to play the duet.

Surely the only courtship unshaken by doubts and fears, must be that in which the lovers can sing together. The sense of mutual fitness that springs from the two deep notes fulfilling expectation just at the right moment between the notes of the silvery soprano, from the perfect accord of descending thirds and fifths, from the preconcerted loving chase of a fugue, is likely enough to supersede any immediate demand for less impassioned forms of agreement. The contralto will not care to catechise the bass; the tenor will foresee no embarrassing dearth of remark in evenings spent with the lovely soprano. In the provinces, too, where music was so scarce in that remote time, how could the musical people avoid falling in love with each other? Even political principle must have been in danger of relaxation under such circumstances; and the violin, faithful to rotten boroughs,[8] must have been tempted to fraternise in a demoralising way with a reforming violoncello. In this case, the linnet-throated soprano, and the full-toned bass, singing,

> "With thee delight is ever new,
> With thee is life incessant bliss,"

believed what they sang all the more *because* they sang it.

"Now for Raphael's great song," said Lucy, when they had finished the duet. "You do the 'heavy beasts' to perfection."

7. Haydn oratorio (1798), of which "Graceful Consort" is an air.
8. Districts that retained electoral power disproportionate to their population. Reformers urged their abolition, which was accomplished by the Reform Bill of 1832.

"That sounds complimentary," said Stephen, looking at his watch. "By Jove, it's nearly half-past one. Well, I can just sing this."

Stephen delivered with admirable ease the deep notes representing the tread of the heavy beasts: but when a singer has an audience of two, there is room for divided sentiments. Minny's mistress was charmed; but Minny, who had intrenched himself, trembling, in his basket as soon as the music began, found this thunder so little to his taste that he leaped out and scampered under the remotest *chiffonière*,[9] as the most eligible place in which a small dog could await the crack of doom.

"Adieu, 'graceful consort,' " said Stephen, buttoning his coat across when he had done singing, and smiling down from his tall height, with the air of rather a patronising lover, at the little lady on the music-stool. "My bliss is not incessant, for I must gallop home. I promised to be there at lunch."

"You will not be able to call on Philip, then? It is of no consequence: I have said everything in my note."

"You will be engaged with your cousin to-morrow, I suppose?"

"Yes, we are going to have a little family-party. My cousin Tom will dine with us; and poor aunty will have her two children together for the first time. It will be very pretty; I think a great deal about it."

"But I may come the next day?"

"O yes! Come and be introduced to my cousin Maggie—though you can hardly be said not to have seen her, you have described her so well."

"Good-bye, then." And there was that slight pressure of the hands, and momentary meeting of the eyes, which will often leave a little lady with a slight flush and smile on her face that do not subside immediately when the door is closed, and with an inclination to walk up and down the room rather than to seat herself quietly at her embroidery, or other rational and improving occupation. At least this was the effect on Lucy; and you will not, I hope, consider it an indication of vanity predominating over more tender impulses, that she just glanced in the chimney-glass as her walk brought her near it. The desire to know that one has not looked an absolute fright during a few hours of conversation, may be construed as lying within the bonds of a laudable benevolent consideration for others. And Lucy had so much of this benevolence in her nature that I am inclined to think her small egoisms were impregnated with it, just as there are people not altogether unknown to you, whose small benevolences have a predominant and somewhat rank odour of egoism. Even now, that she is walking up and down with a little triumphant flutter of her girlish heart at the sense that she is loved by the person of chief consequence in her small world, you may see in her hazel eyes an ever-present sunny benignity, in which the momentary harmless flashes of personal vanity are quite lost; and if she is happy in

9. High, narrow chest of drawers.

thinking of her lover, it is because the thought of him mingles readily with all the gentle affections and good-natured offices with which she fills her peaceful days. Even now, her mind, with that instantaneous alternation which makes two currents of feeling or imagination seem simultaneous, is glancing continually from Stephen to the preparations she has only half finished in Maggie's room. Cousin Maggie should be treated as well as the grandest lady-visitor—nay, better, for she should have Lucy's best prints and drawings in her bedroom, and the very finest bouquet of spring flowers on her table. Maggie would enjoy all that—she was so fond of pretty things! And there was poor aunt Tulliver, that no one made any account of—she was to be surprised with the present of a cap of superlative quality, and to have her health drunk in a gratifying manner, for which Lucy was going to lay a plot with her father this evening. Clearly, she had not time to indulge in long reveries about her own happy love-affairs. With this thought she walked towards the door, but paused there.

"What's the matter, then, Minny?" she said, stooping in answer to some whimpering of that small quadruped, and lifting his glossy head against her pink cheek. "Did you think I was going without you? Come, then, let us go and see Sinbad."

Sinbad was Lucy's chestnut horse, that she always fed with her own hand when he was turned out in the paddock. She was fond of feeding dependent creatures, and knew the private tastes of all the animals about the house, delighting in the little rippling sounds of her canaries when their beaks were busy with fresh seed, and in the small nibbling pleasures of certain animals which, lest she should appear too trivial, I will here call "the more familiar rodents."

Was not Stephen Guest right in his decided opinion that this slim maiden of eighteen was quite the sort of wife a man would not be likely to repent of marrying?—a woman who was loving and thoughtful for other women, not giving them Judas-kisses with eyes askance on their welcome defects, but with real care and vision for their half-hidden pains and mortifications, with long ruminating enjoyment of little pleasures prepared for them? Perhaps the emphasis of his admiration did not fall precisely on this rarest quality in her—perhaps he approved his own choice of her chiefly because she did not strike him as a remarkable rarity. A man likes his wife to be pretty: well, Lucy was pretty, but not to a maddening extent. A man likes his wife to be accomplished, gentle, affectionate, and not stupid; and Lucy had all these qualifications. Stephen was not surprised to find himself in love with her, and was conscious of excellent judgment in preferring her to Miss Leyburn, the daughter of the county member,[1] although Lucy was only the daughter of his father's subordinate partner; besides, he had had to defy and overcome

1. I.e., member of Parliament.

a slight unwillingness and disappointment in his father and sisters—a circumstance which gives a young man an agreeable consciousness of his own dignity. Stephen was aware that he had sense and independence enough to choose the wife who was likely to make him happy, unbiassed by any indirect considerations. He meant to choose Lucy: she was a little darling, and exactly the sort of woman he had always most admired.

Chapter II

First Impressions

"He is very clever, Maggie," said Lucy. She was kneeling on a footstool at Maggie's feet, after placing that dark lady in the large crimson-velvet chair. "I feel sure you will like him. I hope you will."

"I shall be very difficult to please," said Maggie, smiling, and holding up one of Lucy's long curls, that the sunlight might shine through it. "A gentleman who thinks he is good enough for Lucy must expect to be sharply criticised."

"Indeed, he's a great deal too good for me. And sometimes, when he is away, I almost think it can't really be that he loves me. But I can never doubt it when he is with me—though I couldn't bear any one but you to know that I feel in that way, Maggie."

"Oh, then, if I disapprove of him you can give him up, since you are not engaged," said Maggie, with playful gravity.

"I would rather not be engaged. When people are engaged, they begin to think of being married soon," said Lucy, too thoroughly preoccupied to notice Maggie's joke; "and I should like everything to go on for a long while just as it is. Sometimes I am quite frightened lest Stephen should say that he has spoken to papa; and from something that fell from papa the other day, I feel sure he and Mr Guest are expecting that. And Stephen's sisters are very civil to me now. At first, I think they didn't like his paying me attention; and that was natural. It *does* seem out of keeping that I should ever live in a great place like the Park House—such a little insignificant thing as I am."

"But people are not expected to be large in proportion to the houses they live in, like snails," said Maggie, laughing. "Pray, are Mr Guest's sisters giantesses?"

"O no; and not handsome—that is, not very," said Lucy, half-penitent at this uncharitable remark. "But *he* is—at least he is generally considered very handsome."

"Though you are unable to share that opinion?"

"O, I don't know," said Lucy, blushing pink over brow and neck. "It is a bad plan to raise expectation; you will perhaps be disappointed. But

I have prepared a charming surprise for *him*; I shall have a glorious laugh against him. I shall not tell you what it is, though."

Lucy rose from her knees and went to a little distance, holding her pretty head on one side, as if she had been arranging Maggie for a portrait, and wished to judge of the general effect.

"Stand up a moment, Maggie."

"What is your pleasure now?" said Maggie, smiling languidly as she rose from her chair and looked down on her slight, aërial cousin, whose figure was quite subordinate to her faultless drapery of silk and crape.

Lucy kept her contemplative attitude a moment or two in silence, and then said—

"I can't think what witchery it is in you, Maggie, that makes you look best in shabby clothes; though you really must have a new dress now. But do you know, last night I was trying to fancy you in a handsome fashionable dress, and do what I would, that old limp merino would come back as the only right thing for you. I wonder if Marie Antoinette looked all the grander when her gown was darned at the elbows. Now, if *I* were to put anything shabby on, I should be quite unnoticeable—I should be a mere rag."

"O, quite," said Maggie, with mock gravity. "You would be liable to be swept out of the room with the cobwebs and carpet-dust, and to find yourself under the grate, like Cinderella. Mayn't I sit down now?"

"Yes, now you may," said Lucy, laughing. Then, with an air of serious reflection, unfastening her large jet brooch, "But you must change brooches, Maggie; that little butterfly looks silly on you."

"But won't that mar the charming effect of my consistent shabbiness?" said Maggie, seating herself submissively, while Lucy knelt again and unfastened the contemptible butterfly. "I wish my mother were of your opinion, for she was fretting last night because this is my best frock. I've been saving my money to pay for some lessons: I shall never get a better situation without more accomplishments."

Maggie gave a little sigh.

"Now, don't put on that sad look again," said Lucy, pinning the large brooch below Maggie's fine throat. "You're forgetting that you've left that dreary schoolroom behind you, and have no little girls' clothes to mend."

"Yes," said Maggie. "It is with me as I used to think it would be with the poor uneasy white bear I saw at the show. I thought he must have got so stupid with the habit of turning backwards and forwards in that narrow space, that he would keep doing it if they set him free. One gets a bad habit of being unhappy."

"But I shall put you under a discipline of pleasure that will make you lose that bad habit," said Lucy, sticking the black butterfly absently in her own collar, while her eyes met Maggie's affectionately.

"You dear, tiny thing," said Maggie, in one of her bursts of loving admiration, "you enjoy other people's happiness so much, I believe you would do without any of your own. I wish I were like you."

"I've never been tried in that way," said Lucy. "I've always been so happy. I don't know whether I could bear much trouble; I never had any but poor mamma's death. You *have* been tried, Maggie; and I'm sure you feel for other people quite as much as I do."

"No, Lucy," said Maggie, shaking her head slowly, "I don't enjoy their happiness as you do—else I should be more contented. I do feel for them when they are in trouble; I don't think I could ever bear to make any one *un*happy; and yet I often hate myself, because I get angry sometimes at the sight of happy people. I think I get worse as I get older—more selfish. That seems very dreadful."

"Now, Maggie!" said Lucy, in a tone of remonstrance, "I don't believe a word of that. It is all a gloomy fancy—just because you are depressed by a dull, wearisome life."

"Well, perhaps it is," said Maggie, resolutely clearing away the clouds from her face with a bright smile, and throwing herself backward in her chair. "Perhaps it comes from the school diet—watery rice-pudding spiced with Pinnock. Let us hope it will give way before my mother's custards and this charming Geoffrey Crayon."[1]

Maggie took up the "Sketch Book," which lay by her on the table.

"Do I look fit to be seen with this little brooch?" said Lucy, going to survey the effect in the chimney-glass.

"O no, Mr Guest will be obliged to go out of the room again if he sees you in it. Pray make haste and put another on."

Lucy hurried out of the room, but Maggie did not take the opportunity of opening her book: she let it fall on her knees, while her eyes wandered to the window, where she could see the sunshine falling on the rich clumps of spring flowers and on the long hedge of laurels—and beyond, the silvery breadth of the dear old Floss, that at this distance seemed to be sleeping in a morning holiday. The sweet fresh garden-scent came through the open window, and the birds were busy flitting and alighting, gurgling and singing. Yet Maggie's eyes began to fill with tears. The sight of the old scenes had made the rush of memories so painful, that even yesterday she had only been able to rejoice in her mother's restored comfort and Tom's brotherly friendliness as we rejoice in good news of friends at a distance, rather than in the presence of a happiness which we share. Memory and imagination urged upon her a sense of privation too keen to let her taste what was offered in the transient present: her future, she thought, was likely to be worse than her past, for after her years of contented renunciation, she had slipped back into desire and

1. Pseudonym of early nineteenth-century American writer Washington Irving, author of *The Sketch Book of Geoffrey Crayon, Gent.* (1820).

longing: she found joyless days of distasteful occupation harder and harder—she found the image of the intense and varied life she yearned for, and despaired of, becoming more and more importunate. The sound of the opening door roused her, and, hastily wiping away her tears, she began to turn over the leaves of her book.

"There is one pleasure, I know, Maggie, that your deepest dismalness will never resist," said Lucy, beginning to speak as soon as she entered the room. "That is music, and I mean you to have quite a riotous feast of it. I mean you to get up your playing again, which used to be so much better than mine, when we were at Laceham."

"You would have laughed to see me playing the little girls' tunes over and over to them, when I took them to practice," said Maggie, "just for the sake of fingering the dear keys again. But I don't know whether I could play anything more difficult now than 'Begone, dull care!' "[2]

"I know what a wild state of joy you used to be in when the glee-men came round," said Lucy, taking up her embroidery, "and we might have all those old glees that you used to love so, if I were certain that you don't feel exactly as Tom does about some things."

"I should have thought there was nothing you might be more certain of," said Maggie, smiling.

"I ought rather to have said, one particular thing. Because if you feel just as he does about that, we shall want our third voice. St Ogg's is so miserably provided with musical gentlemen. There are really only Stephen and Philip Wakem who have any knowledge of music, so as to be able to sing a part."

Lucy had looked up from her work as she uttered the last sentence, and saw that there was a change in Maggie's face.

"Does it hurt you to hear the name mentioned, Maggie? If it does, I will not speak of him again. I know Tom will not see him if he can avoid it."

"I don't feel at all as Tom does on that subject," said Maggie, rising and going to the window as if she wanted to see more of the landscape. "I've always liked Philip Wakem ever since I was a little girl, and saw him at Lorton. He was so good when Tom hurt his foot."

"O, I'm so glad!" said Lucy. "Then you won't mind his coming sometimes, and we can have much more music than we could without him. I'm very fond of poor Philip, only I wish he were not so morbid about his deformity. I suppose it *is* his deformity that makes him so sad—and sometimes bitter. It is certainly very piteous to see his poor little crooked body and pale face among great strong people."

"But, Lucy," said Maggie, trying to arrest the prattling stream. . . .

"Ah, there is the door-bell. That must be Stephen," Lucy went on,

2. Seventeenth-century air.

not noticing Maggie's faint effort to speak. "One of the things I most admire in Stephen is, that he makes a greater friend of Philip than any one."

It was too late for Maggie to speak now: the drawing-room door was opening, and Minny was already growling in a small way at the entrance of a tall gentleman, who went up to Lucy and took her hand with a half-polite, half-tender glance and tone of inquiry, which seemed to indicate that he was unconscious of any other presence.

"Let me introduce you to my cousin, Miss Tulliver," said Lucy, turning with wicked enjoyment towards Maggie, who now approached from the farther window. "This is Mr Stephen Guest."

For one instant Stephen could not conceal his astonishment at the sight of this tall dark-eyed nymph with her jet-black coronet of hair; the next, Maggie felt herself, for the first time in her life, receiving the tribute of a very deep blush and a very deep bow from a person towards whom she herself was conscious of timidity. This new experience was very agreeable to her—so agreeable, that it almost effaced her previous emotion about Philip. There was a new brightness in her eyes, and a very becoming flush on her cheek, as she seated herself.

"I hope you perceive what a striking likeness you drew the day before yesterday," said Lucy, with a pretty laugh of triumph. She enjoyed her lover's confusion—the advantage was usually on his side.

"This designing cousin of yours quite deceived me, Miss Tulliver," said Stephen, seating himself by Lucy, and stooping to play with Minny—only looking at Maggie furtively. "She said you had light hair and blue eyes."

"Nay, it was you who said so," remonstrated Lucy. "I only refrained from destroying your confidence in your own second-sight."

"I wish I could always err in the same way," said Stephen, "and find reality so much more beautiful than my preconceptions."

"Now you have proved yourself equal to the occasion," said Maggie, "and said what it was incumbent on you to say under the circumstances."

She flashed a slightly defiant look at him: it was clear to her that he had been drawing a satirical portrait of her beforehand. Lucy had said he was inclined to be satirical, and Maggie had mentally supplied the addition—"and rather conceited."

"An alarming amount of devil there," was Stephen's first thought. The second, when she had bent over her work, was, "I wish she would look at me again." The next was to answer:

"I suppose all phrases of mere compliment have their turn to be true. A man is occasionally grateful when he says 'thank you.' It's rather hard upon him that he must use the same words with which all the world declines a disagreeable invitation—don't you think so, Miss Tulliver?"

"No," said Maggie, looking at him with her direct glance; "if we use common words on a great occasion, they are the more striking, because they are felt at once to have a particular meaning, like old banners, or everyday clothes, hung up in a sacred place."

"Then my compliment ought to be eloquent," said Stephen, really not quite knowing what he said while Maggie looked at him, "seeing that the words were so far beneath the occasion."

"No compliment can be eloquent, except as an expression of indifference," said Maggie, flushing a little.

Lucy was rather alarmed: she thought Stephen and Maggie were not going to like each other. She had always feared lest Maggie should appear too odd and clever to please that critical gentleman. "Why, dear Maggie," she interposed, "you have always pretended that you are too fond of being admired; and now, I think, you are angry because some one ventures to admire you."

"Not at all," said Maggie; "I like too well to feel that I am admired, but compliments never make me feel that."

"I will never pay you a compliment again, Miss Tulliver," said Stephen.

"Thank you; that will be a proof of respect."

Poor Maggie! She was so unused to society that she could take nothing as a matter of course, and had never in her life spoken from the lips merely, so that she must necessarily appear absurd to more experienced ladies, from the excessive feeling she was apt to throw into very trivial incidents. But she was even conscious herself of a little absurdity in this instance. It was true she had a theoretic objection to compliments, and had once said impatiently to Philip, that she didn't see why women were to be told with a simper that they were beautiful, any more than old men were to be told that they were venerable: still, to be so irritated by a common practice in the case of a stranger like Mr Stephen Guest, and to care about his having spoken slightingly of her before he had seen her, was certainly unreasonable, and as soon as she was silent she began to be ashamed of herself. It did not occur to her that her irritation was due to the pleasanter emotion which preceded it, just as when we are satisfied with a sense of glowing warmth, an innocent drop of cold water may fall upon us as a sudden smart.

Stephen was too well-bred not to seem unaware that the previous conversation could have been felt embarrassing, and at once began to talk of impersonal matters, asking Lucy if she knew when the bazaar was at length to take place, so that there might be some hope of seeing her rain the influence of her eyes on objects more grateful than those worsted flowers that were growing under her fingers.

"Some day next month, I believe," said Lucy. "But your sisters are doing more for it than I am: they are to have the largest stall."

"Ah, yes; but they carry on their manufactures in their own sitting-room, where I don't intrude on them. I see you are not addicted to the fashionable vice of fancy-work, Miss Tulliver," said Stephen, looking at Maggie's plain hemming.

"No," said Maggie, "I can do nothing more difficult or more elegant than shirt-making."

"And your plain sewing is so beautiful, Maggie," said Lucy, "that I think I shall beg a few specimens of you to show as fancy-work. Your exquisite sewing is quite a mystery to me—you used to dislike that sort of work so much in old days."

"It is a mystery easily explained, dear," said Maggie, looking up quietly. "Plain sewing was the only thing I could get money by; so I was obliged to try and do it well."

Lucy, good and simple as she was, could not help blushing a little: she did not quite like that Stephen should know that—Maggie need not have mentioned it. Perhaps there was some pride in the confession: the pride of poverty that will not be ashamed of itself. But if Maggie had been the queen of coquettes she could hardly have invented a means of giving greater piquancy to her beauty in Stephen's eyes: I am not sure that the quiet admission of plain sewing and poverty would have done alone, but assisted by the beauty, they made Maggie more unlike other women even than she had seemed at first.

"But I can knit, Lucy," Maggie went on, "if that will be of any use for your bazaar."

"O yes, of infinite use. I shall set you to work with scarlet wool tomorrow. But your sister is the most enviable person," continued Lucy, turning to Stephen, "to have the talent of modelling. She is doing a wonderful bust of Dr Kenn entirely from memory."

"Why, if she can remember to put the eyes very near together, and the corners of the mouth very far apart, the likeness can hardly fail to be striking in St Ogg's."

"Now that is very wicked of you," said Lucy, looking rather hurt. "I didn't think you would speak disrespectfully of Dr Kenn."

"I say anything disrespectful of Dr Kenn? Heaven forbid! But I am not bound to respect a libellous bust of him. I think Kenn one of the finest fellows in the world. I don't care much about the tall candlesticks he has put on the communion-table, and I shouldn't like to spoil my temper by getting up to early prayers every morning. But he's the only man I ever knew personally who seems to me to have anything of the real apostle in him—a man who has eight hundred a-year, and is contented with deal furniture and boiled beef because he gives away two-thirds of his income. That was a very fine thing of him—taking into his house that poor lad Grattan who shot his mother by accident. He sacrifices more time than a less busy man could spare, to save the poor fellow from getting into a morbid state of mind about it. He takes the lad out with him constantly, I see."

"That is beautiful," said Maggie, who had let her work fall, and was listening with keen interest. "I never knew any one who did such things."

"And one admires that sort of action in Kenn all the more," said Stephen, "because his manners in general are rather cold and severe. There's nothing sugary and maudlin about him."

"O, I think he's a perfect character!" said Lucy, with pretty enthusiasm.

"No; there I can't agree with you," said Stephen, shaking his head with sarcastic gravity.

"Now, what fault can you point out in him?"

"He's an Anglican."

"Well, those are the right views, I think," said Lucy, gravely.

"That settles the question in the abstract," said Stephen, "but not from a parliamentary point of view. He has set the Dissenters and the Church people by the ears; and a rising senator like myself, of whose services the country is very much in need, will find it inconvenient when he puts up for the honour of representing St Ogg's in Parliament."

"Do you really think of that?" said Lucy, her eyes brightening with a proud pleasure that made her neglect the argumentative interests of Anglicanism.

"Decidedly—whenever old Mr Leyburn's public spirit and gout induce him to give way. My father's heart is set on it; and gifts like mine, you know"—here Stephen drew himself up, and rubbed his large white hands over his hair with playful self-admiration—"gifts like mine involve great responsibilities. Don't you think so, Miss Tulliver?"

"Yes," said Maggie, smiling, but not looking up; "so much fluency and self-possession should not be wasted entirely on private occasions."

"Ah, I see how much penetration you have," said Stephen. "You have discovered already that I am talkative and impudent. Now superficial people never discern that—owing to my manner, I suppose."

"She doesn't look at me when I talk of myself," he thought, while his listeners were laughing. "I must try other subjects."

Did Lucy intend to be present at the meeting of the Book Club next week? was the next question. Then followed the recommendation to choose Southey's "Life of Cowper," unless she were inclined to be philosophical, and startle the ladies of St Ogg's by voting for one of the Bridgewater Treatises. Of course Lucy wished to know what these alarmingly learned books were; and as it is always pleasant to improve the minds of ladies by talking to them at ease on subjects of which they know nothing, Stephen became quite brilliant in an account of Buckland's Treatise, which he had just been reading.[3] He was rewarded by seeing Maggie let her work fall, and gradually get so absorbed in his

3. The eight *Bridgewater Treatises on the Power, Wisdom, and Goodness of God as Manifested in the Creation* (1833–36), commissioned by the eighth earl of Bridgewater; William Buckland's *Geology and Mineralogy Considered with Reference to Natural Theology* appeared in 1836.

wonderful geological story that she sat looking at him, leaning forward with crossed arms, and with an entire absence of self-consciousness, as if he had been the snuffiest of old professors, and she a downy-lipped alumnus.[4] He was so fascinated by this clear, large gaze, that at last he forgot to look away from it occasionally towards Lucy; but she, sweet child, was only rejoicing that Stephen was proving to Maggie how clever he was, and that they would certainly be good friends after all.

"I will bring you the book, shall I, Miss Tulliver?" said Stephen, when he found the stream of his recollections running rather shallow. "There are many illustrations in it that you will like to see."

"O, thank you," said Maggie, blushing with returning self-consciousness at this direct address, and taking up her work again.

"No, no," Lucy interposed. "I must forbid your plunging Maggie in books. I shall never get her away from them; and I want her to have delicious do-nothing days, filled with boating, and chatting, and riding, and driving: that is the holiday she needs."

"Apropos!" said Stephen, looking at his watch. "Shall we go out for a row on the river now? The tide will suit for us to go the Tofton way, and we can walk back."

That was a delightful proposition to Maggie, for it was years since she had been on the river. When she was gone to put on her bonnet, Lucy lingered to give an order to the servant, and took the opportunity of telling Stephen that Maggie had no objection to seeing Philip, so that it was a pity she had sent that note the day before yesterday. But she would write another to-morrow and invite him.

"I'll call and beat him up to-morrow," said Stephen, "and bring him with me in the evening, shall I? My sisters will want to call on you when I tell them your cousin is with you. I must leave the field clear for them in the morning."

"O yes, pray bring him," said Lucy. "And you *will* like Maggie, shan't you?" she added, in a beseeching tone. "Isn't she a dear, noble-looking creature?"

"Too tall," said Stephen, smiling down upon her, "and a little too fiery. She is not my type of woman, you know."

Gentlemen, you are aware, are apt to impart these imprudent confidences to ladies concerning their unfavourable opinion of sister fair ones. That is why so many women have the advantage of knowing that they are secretly repulsive to men who have self-denyingly made ardent love to them. And hardly anything could be more distinctively characteristic of Lucy, than that she both implicitly believed what Stephen said, and was determined that Maggie should not know it. But you, who have a higher logic than the verbal to guide you, have already

4. Student.

foreseen, as the direct sequence to that unfavourable opinion of Stephen's, that he walked down to the boat-house calculating, by the aid of a vivid imagination, that Maggie must give him her hand at least twice in consequence of this pleasant boating plan, and that a gentleman who wishes ladies to look at him is advantageously situated when he is rowing them in a boat. What then? Had he fallen in love with this surprising daughter of Mrs Tulliver at first sight? Certainly not. Such passions are never heard of in real life. Besides, he was in love already, and half-engaged to the dearest little creature in the world; and he was not a man to make a fool of himself in any way. But when one is five-and-twenty, one has not chalk-stones[5] at one's finger-ends that the touch of a handsome girl should be entirely indifferent. It was perfectly natural and safe to admire beauty and enjoy looking at it—at least under such circumstances as the present. And there was really something very interesting about this girl, with her poverty and troubles: it was gratifying to see the friendship between the two cousins. Generally, Stephen admitted, he was not fond of women who had any peculiarity of character—but here the peculiarity seemed really of a superior kind; and provided one is not obliged to marry such women, why, they certainly make a variety in social intercourse.

Maggie did not fulfil Stephen's hope by looking at him during the first quarter of an hour: her eyes were too full of the old banks that she knew so well. She felt lonely, cut off from Philip—the only person who had ever seemed to love her devotedly, as she had always longed to be loved. But presently the rhythmic movement of the oars attracted her, and she thought she should like to learn how to row. This roused her from her reverie, and she asked if she might take an oar. It appeared that she required much teaching, and she became ambitious. The exercise brought the warm blood into her cheeks, and made her inclined to take her lesson merrily.

"I shall not be satisfied until I can manage both oars, and row you and Lucy," she said, looking very bright as she stepped out of the boat. Maggie, we know, was apt to forget the thing she was doing, and she had chosen an inopportune moment for her remark: her foot slipped, but happily Mr Stephen Guest held her hand, and kept her up with a firm grasp.

"You have not hurt yourself at all, I hope?" he said, bending to look in her face with anxiety. It was very charming to be taken care of in that kind graceful manner by some one taller and stronger than one's self. Maggie had never felt just in the same way before.

When they reached home again, they found uncle and aunt Pullet seated with Mrs Tulliver in the drawing-room, and Stephen hurried away, asking leave to come again in the evening.

5. Chalk-like deposits in the tissues and joints of the hands and feet associated with gout.

"And pray bring with you the volume of Purcell[6] that you took away," said Lucy. "I want Maggie to hear your best songs."

Aunt Pullet, under the certainty that Maggie would be invited to go out with Lucy, probably to Park House, was much shocked at the shabbiness of her clothes, which, when witnessed by the higher society of St Ogg's, would be a discredit to the family, that demanded a strong and prompt remedy; and the consultation as to what would be most suitable to this end from among the superfluities of Mrs Pullet's wardrobe, was one that Lucy as well as Mrs Tulliver entered into with some zeal. Maggie must really have an evening-dress as soon as possible, and she was about the same height as aunt Pullet.

"But she's so much broader across the shoulders than I am—it's very ill-convenient," said Mrs Pullet, "else she might wear that beautiful black brocade o' mine without any alteration; and her arms are beyond everything," added Mrs Pullet, sorrowfully, as she lifted Maggie's large round arm. "She'd never get my sleeves on."

"O never mind that, aunt: pray send us the dress," said Lucy. "I don't mean Maggie to have long sleeves, and I have abundance of black lace for trimming. Her arms will look beautiful."

"Maggie's arms *are* a pretty shape," said Mrs Tulliver. "They're like mine used to be—only mine was never brown: I wish she'd had *our* family skin."

"Nonsense, aunty!" said Lucy, patting her aunt Tulliver's shoulder, "you don't understand those things. A painter would think Maggie's complexion beautiful."

"May be, my dear," said Mrs Tulliver, submissively. "You know better than I do. Only when I was young a brown skin wasn't thought well on among respectable folks."

"No," said uncle Pullet, who took intense interest in the ladies' conversation as he sucked his lozenges. "Though there was a song about the 'Nut-brown Maid,' too; I think she was crazy—crazy Kate,[7]—but I can't justly remember."

"O dear, dear!" said Maggie, laughing, but impatient; "I think that will be the end of *my* brown skin, if it is always to be talked about so much."

6. Henry Purcell, seventeenth-century composer of vocal music.
7. "Crazy Kate": unlucky lover in Cowper's *The Task* (1785); "Nut-brown Maid": ballad included in *Percy's Reliques of Ancient English Poetry* (1765).

Chapter III

Confidential Moments

When Maggie went up to her bedroom that night, it appeared that she was not at all inclined to undress. She set down her candle on the first table that presented itself, and began to walk up and down her room, which was a large one, with a firm, regular, and rather rapid step, which showed that the exercise was the instinctive vent of strong excitement. Her eyes and cheeks had an almost feverish brilliancy; her head was thrown backward, and her hands were clasped with the palms outward, and with that tension of the arms which is apt to accompany mental absorption.

Had anything remarkable happened?

Nothing that you are not likely to consider in the highest degree unimportant. She had been hearing some fine music sung by a fine bass voice—but then it was sung in a provincial, amateur fashion, such as would have left a critical ear much to desire. And she was conscious of having been looked at a great deal, in rather a furtive manner, from beneath a pair of well-marked horizontal eyebrows, with a glance that seemed somehow to have caught the vibratory influence of the voice. Such things could have had no perceptible effect on a thoroughly well-educated young lady, with a perfectly balanced mind, who had had all the advantages of fortune, training, and refined society. But if Maggie had been that young lady, you would probably have known nothing about her: her life would have had so few vicissitudes that it could hardly have been written; for the happiest women, like the happiest nations, have no history.[1]

In poor Maggie's highly-strung, hungry nature—just come away from a third-rate schoolroom, with all its jarring sounds and petty round of tasks—these apparently trivial causes had the effect of rousing and exalting her imagination in a way that was mysterious to herself. It was not that she thought distinctly of Mr Stephen Guest, or dwelt on the indications that he looked at her with admiration; it was rather that she felt the half-remote presence of a world of love and beauty and delight, made up of vague, mingled images from all the poetry and romance she had ever read, or had ever woven in her dreamy reveries. Her mind glanced back once or twice to the time when she had courted privation, when she had thought all longing, all impatience was subdued; but that condition seemed irrecoverably gone, and she recoiled from the remembrance of it. No prayer, no striving now, would bring back that negative peace: the battle of her life, it seemed, was not to be decided

1. Eliot is referring to an aphorism by Montesquieu, the French social and political philosopher (1689–1755): "Happy the People whose Annals are blank in History-Books!"

in that short and easy way—by perfect renunciation at the very threshold of her youth. The music was vibrating in her still—Purcell's music, with its wild passion and fancy—and she could not stay in the recollection of that bare, lonely past. She was in her brighter aërial world again, when a little tap came at the door: of course it was her cousin, who entered in ample white dressing-gown.

"Why, Maggie, you naughty child, haven't you begun to undress?" said Lucy, in astonishment. "I promised not to come and talk to you, because I thought you must be tired. But here you are, looking as if you were ready to dress for a ball. Come, come, get on your dressing-gown, and unplait your hair."

"Well, *you* are not very forward," retorted Maggie, hastily reaching her own pink cotton gown, and looking at Lucy's light-brown hair brushed back in curly disorder.

"O, I have not much to do. I shall sit down and talk to you till I see you are really on the way to bed."

While Maggie stood and unplaited her long black hair over her pink drapery, Lucy sat down near the toilette-table, watching her with affectionate eyes, and head a little aside, like a pretty spaniel. If it appears to you at all incredible that young ladies should be led on to talk confidentially in a situation of this kind, I will beg you to remember that human life furnishes many exceptional cases.

"You really *have* enjoyed the music to-night, haven't you, Maggie?"

"O yes, that is what prevents me from feeling sleepy. I think I should have no other mortal wants, if I could always have plenty of music. It seems to infuse strength into my limbs, and ideas into my brain. Life seems to go on without effort, when I am filled with music. At other times one is conscious of carrying a weight."

"And Stephen has a splendid voice, hasn't he?"

"Well, perhaps we are neither of us judges of that," said Maggie, laughing, as she seated herself and tossed her long hair back. "You are not impartial, and *I* think any barrel-organ splendid."

"But tell me what you think of him, now. Tell me exactly—good and bad too."

"O, I think you should humiliate him a little. A lover should not be so much at ease, and so self-confident. He ought to tremble more."

"Nonsense, Maggie! As if any one could tremble at me! You think he is conceited—I see that. But you don't dislike him, do you?"

"Dislike him! No. Am I in the habit of seeing such charming people, that I should be very difficult to please? Besides, how could I dislike any one that promised to make you happy, you dear thing!" Maggie pinched Lucy's dimpled chin.

"We shall have more music to-morrow evening," said Lucy, looking happy already, "for Stephen will bring Philip Wakem with him."

"O Lucy, I can't see him," said Maggie, turning pale. "At least, I could not see him without Tom's leave."

"Is Tom such a tyrant as that?" said Lucy, surprised. "I'll take the responsibility, then—tell him it was my fault."

"But, dear," said Maggie, falteringly, "I promised Tom very solemnly—before my father's death—I promised him I would not speak to Philip without his knowledge and consent. And I have a great dread of opening the subject with Tom—of getting into a quarrel with him again."

"But I never heard of anything so strange and unreasonable. What harm can poor Philip have done? May I speak to Tom about it?"

"O no, pray don't, dear," said Maggie. "I'll go to him myself tomorrow, and tell him that you wish Philip to come. I've thought before of asking him to absolve me from my promise, but I've not had the courage to determine on it."

They were both silent for some moments, and then Lucy said—

"Maggie, you have secrets from me, and I have none from you."

Maggie looked meditatively away from Lucy. Then she turned to her and said, "I *should* like to tell you about Philip. But, Lucy, you must not betray that you know it to any one—least of all to Philip himself, or to Mr Stephen Guest."

The narrative lasted long, for Maggie had never before known the relief of such an outpouring: she had never before told Lucy anything of her inmost life; and the sweet face bent towards her with sympathetic interest, and the little hand pressing hers, encouraged her to speak on. On two points only she was not expansive. She did not betray fully what still rankled in her mind as Tom's great offence—the insults he had heaped on Philip. Angry as the remembrance still made her, she could not bear that any one else should know it all—both for Tom's sake and Philip's. And she could not bear to tell Lucy of the last scene between her father and Wakem, though it was this scene which she had ever since felt to be a new barrier between herself and Philip. She merely said, she saw now that Tom was, on the whole, right in regarding any prospect of love and marriage between her and Philip as put out of the question by the relation of the two families. Of course Philip's father would never consent.

"There, Lucy, you have had my story," said Maggie, smiling, with the tears in her eyes. "You see I am like Sir Andrew Aguecheek[2]—*I was adored once.*"

"Ah, now I see how it is you know Shakespeare and everything, and have learned so much since you left school; which always seemed to me witchcraft before—part of your general uncanniness," said Lucy.

2. Maggie is quoting a line spoken by Sir Andrew Aguecheek, a foolish knight in Shakespeare's *Twelfth Night* (2.3.181).

She mused a little with her eyes downward, and then added, looking at Maggie, "It is very beautiful that you should love Philip: I never thought such a happiness would befall him. And in my opinion, you ought not to give him up. There are obstacles now; but they may be done away with in time."

Maggie shook her head.

"Yes, yes," persisted Lucy; "I can't help being hopeful about it. There is something romantic in it—out of the common way—just what everything that happens to you ought to be. And Philip will adore you like a husband in a fairy tale. O, I shall puzzle my small brain to contrive some plot that will bring everybody into the right mind, so that you may marry Philip, when I marry—somebody else. Wouldn't that be a pretty ending to all my poor, poor Maggie's troubles?"

Maggie tried to smile, but shivered, as if she felt a sudden chill.

"Ah, dear, you are cold," said Lucy. "You must go to bed; and so must I. I dare not think what time it is."

They kissed each other, and Lucy went away—possessed of a confidence which had a strong influence over her subsequent impressions. Maggie had been thoroughly sincere: her nature had never found it easy to be otherwise. But confidences are sometimes blinding, even when they are sincere.

Chapter IV

Brother and Sister

Maggie was obliged to go to Tom's lodgings in the middle of the day, when he would be coming in to dinner, else she would not have found him at home. He was not lodging with entire strangers. Our friend Bob Jakin had, with Mumps's tacit consent, taken not only a wife about eight months ago, but also one of those queer old houses pierced with surprising passages, by the water-side, where, as he observed, his wife and mother could keep themselves out of mischief by letting out two "pleasure-boats," in which he had invested some of his savings, and by taking in a lodger for the parlour and spare bedroom. Under these circumstances, what could be better for the interests of all parties, sanitary considerations apart, than that the lodger should be Mr Tom?

It was Bob's wife who opened the door to Maggie. She was a tiny woman, with the general physiognomy of a Dutch doll, looking, in comparison with Bob's mother, who filled up the passage in the rear, very much like one of those human figures which the artist finds conveniently standing near a colossal statue to show the proportions. The tiny woman curtsied and looked up at Maggie with some awe as soon as she had opened the door; but the words, "Is my brother at home?"

which Maggie uttered smilingly, made her turn round with sudden excitement, and say—

"Eh, mother, mother—tell Bob!—it's Miss Maggie! Come in, Miss, for goodness do," she went on, opening a side door, and endeavouring to flatten her person against the wall to make the utmost space for the visitor.

Sad recollections crowded on Maggie as she entered the small parlour, which was now all that poor Tom had to call by the name of "home" —that name which had once, so many years ago, meant for both of them the same sum of dear familiar objects. But everything was not strange to her in this new room: the first thing her eyes dwelt on was the large old Bible, and the sight was not likely to disperse the old memories. She stood without speaking.

"If you please to take the privilege o' sitting down, Miss," said Mrs Jakin, rubbing her apron over a perfectly clean chair, and then lifting up the corner of that garment and holding it to her face with an air of embarrassment, as she looked wonderingly at Maggie.

"Bob is at home, then?" said Maggie, recovering herself, and smiling at the bashful Dutch doll.

"Yes, Miss; but I think he must be washing and dressing himself—I'll go and see," said Mrs Jakin, disappearing.

But she presently came back walking with new courage a little way behind her husband, who showed the brilliancy of his blue eyes and regular white teeth in the doorway, bowing respectfully.

"How do you do, Bob?" said Maggie, coming forward and putting out her hand to him; "I always meant to pay your wife a visit, and I shall come another day on purpose for that, if she will let me. But I was obliged to come to-day, to speak to my brother."

"He'll be in before long, Miss. He's doin' finely, Mr Tom is: he'll be one o' the first men hereabouts—you'll see that."

"Well, Bob, I'm sure he'll be indebted to you, whatever he becomes: he said so himself only the other night, when he was talking of you."

"Eh, Miss, that's his way o' takin' it. But I think the more on't when he says a thing, because his tongue doesn't overshoot him as mine does. Lors! I'm no better nor a tilted bottle, I arn't—I can't stop mysen when once I begin. But you look rarely, Miss—it does me good to see you. What do you say now, Prissy?"—here Bob turned to his wife. "Isn't it all come true as I said? Though there isn't many sorts o' goods as I can't over-praise when I set my tongue to't."

Mrs Bob's small nose seemed to be following the example of her eyes in turning up reverentially towards Maggie, but she was able now to smile and curtsy, and say, "I'd looked forrard like aenything to seein' you, Miss, for my husband's tongue's been runnin' on you, like as if he was light-headed, iver since first he come a-courtin' on me."

"Well, well," said Bob, looking rather silly. "Go an' see after the taters, else Mr Tom 'ull have to wait for 'em."

"I hope Mumps is friendly with Mrs Jakin, Bob," said Maggie, smiling. "I remember you used to say, he wouldn't like your marrying."

"Eh, Miss," said Bob, grinning, "he made up his mind to't when he see'd what a little un she was. He pretends not to see her mostly, or else to think as she isn't full-growed. But about Mr Tom, Miss," said Bob, speaking lower and looking serious, "he's as close as a iron biler,[1] he is; but I'm a 'cutish chap, an' when I've left off carrying my pack, an' am at a loose end, I've got more brains nor I know what to do wi', an' I'm forced to busy myself wi' other folks's insides. An' it worrets me as Mr Tom 'ull sit by himself so glumpish, a-knittin' his brow, an' a-lookin' at the fire of a night. He should be a bit livelier now—a fine young fellow like him. My wife says, when she goes in sometimes, an' he takes no notice of her, he sits lookin' into the fire, and frownin' as if he was watchin' folks at work in it."

"He thinks so much about business," said Maggie.

"Ay," said Bob, speaking lower; "but do you think it's nothin' else, Miss? He's close, Mr Tom is; but I'm a 'cute chap, I am, an' I thought tow'rt last Christmas as I'd found out a soft place in him. It was about a little black spaniel—a rare bit o' breed—as he made a fuss to get. But since then summat's come over him, as he's set his teeth again' things more nor iver, for all he's had such good-luck. An' I wanted to tell *you*, Miss, 'cause I thought you might work it out of him a bit, now you're come. He's a deal too lonely, and doesn't go into company enough."

"I'm afraid I have very little power over him, Bob," said Maggie, a good deal moved by Bob's suggestion. It was a totally new idea to her mind, that Tom could have his love troubles. Poor fellow!—and in love with Lucy too! But it was perhaps a mere fancy of Bob's too officious brain. The present of the dog meant nothing more than cousinship and gratitude. But Bob had already said, "Here's Mr Tom," and the outer door was opening.

"There's no time to spare, Tom," said Maggie, as soon as Bob had left the room. "I must tell you at once what I came about, else I shall be hindering you from taking your dinner."

Tom stood with his back against the chimney-piece, and Maggie was seated opposite the light. He noticed that she was tremulous, and he had a presentiment of the subject she was going to speak about. The presentiment made his voice colder and harder as he said, "What is it?"

This tone roused a spirit of resistance in Maggie, and she put her request in quite a different form from the one she had predetermined on. She rose from her seat, and, looking straight at Tom, said—

"I want you to absolve me from my promise about Philip Wakem.

1. Boiler.

Or rather, I promised you not to see him without telling you. I am come to tell you that I wish to see him."

"Very well," said Tom, still more coldly.

But Maggie had hardly finished speaking in that chill, defiant manner, before she repented, and felt the dread of alienation from her brother.

"Not for myself, dear Tom. Don't be angry. I shouldn't have asked it, only that Philip, you know, is a friend of Lucy's, and she wishes him to come—has invited him to come this evening; and I told her I couldn't see him without telling you. I shall only see him in the presence of other people. There will never be anything secret between us again."

Tom looked away from Maggie, knitting his brow more strongly for a little while. Then he turned to her and said, slowly and emphatically—

"You know what is my feeling on that subject, Maggie. There is no need for my repeating anything I said a year ago. While my father was living, I felt bound to use the utmost power over you, to prevent you from disgracing him as well as yourself, and all of us. But now I must leave you to your own choice. You wish to be independent—you told me so after my father's death. My opinion is not changed. If you think of Philip Wakem as a lover again, you must give up me."

"I don't wish it, dear Tom—at least as things are: I see that it would lead to misery. But I shall soon go away to another situation, and I should like to be friends with him again while I am here. Lucy wishes it."

The severity of Tom's face relaxed a little.

"I shouldn't mind your seeing him occasionally at my uncle's—I don't want you to make a fuss on the subject. But I have no confidence in you, Maggie. You would be led away to do anything."

That was a cruel word. Maggie's lip began to tremble.

"Why will you say that, Tom? It is very hard of you. Have I not done and borne everything as well as I could? And I have kept my word to you—when—when. . . . My life has not been a happy one, any more than yours."

She was obliged to be childish—the tears would come. When Maggie was not angry, she was as dependent on kind or cold words as a daisy on the sunshine or the cloud: the need of being loved would always subdue her, as, in old days, it subdued her in the worm-eaten attic. The brother's goodness came uppermost at this appeal, but it could only show itself in Tom's fashion. He put his hand gently on her arm, and said, in the tone of a kind pedagogue—

"Now listen to me, Maggie. I'll tell you what I mean. You're always in extremes—you have no judgment and self-command; and yet you think you know best, and will not submit to be guided. You know I didn't wish you to take a situation. My aunt Pullet was willing to give you a good home, and you might have lived respectably amongst your relations, until I could have provided a home for you with my mother. And that is what I should like to do. I wished my sister to be a lady, and I would always have taken care of you, as my father desired, until you were well married. But your ideas and mine never accord, and you will not give way. Yet you might have sense enough to see that a brother, who goes out into the world and mixes with men, necessarily knows better what is right and respectable for his sister than she can know herself. You think I am not kind; but my kindness can only be directed by what I believe to be good for you."

"Yes—I know—dear Tom," said Maggie, still half-sobbing, but trying to control her tears. "I know you would do a great deal for me: I know how you work, and don't spare yourself. I am grateful to you. But, indeed, you can't quite judge for me—our natures are very different. You don't know how differently things affect me from what they do you."

"Yes, I *do* know: I know it too well. I know how differently you must feel about all that affects our family, and your own dignity as a young woman, before you could think of receiving secret addresses from Philip Wakem. If it was not disgusting to me in every other way, I should object to my sister's name being associated for a moment with that of a young man whose father must hate the very thought of us all, and would spurn you. With any one but you, I should think it quite certain that what you witnessed just before my father's death would secure you from ever thinking again of Philip Wakem as a lover. But I don't feel certain of it with you—I never feel certain about anything with *you*. At one time you take pleasure in a sort of perverse self-denial, and at another you have not resolution to resist a thing that you know to be wrong."

There was a terrible cutting truth in Tom's words—that hard rind of truth which is discerned by unimaginative, unsympathetic minds. Maggie always writhed under this judgment of Tom's: she rebelled and was humiliated in the same moment: it seemed as if he held a glass before her to show her her own folly and weakness—as if he were a prophetic voice predicting her future fallings—and yet, all the while, she judged him in return: she said inwardly that he was narrow and unjust, that he was below feeling those mental needs which were often the source of the wrong-doing or absurdity that made her life a planless riddle to him.

She did not answer directly: her heart was too full, and she sat down, leaning her arm on the table. It was no use trying to make Tom feel that she was near to him. He always repelled her. Her feeling under his words was complicated by the allusion to the last scene between her father and Wakem; and at length that painful, solemn memory surmounted the immediate grievance. No! She did not think of such things with frivolous indifference, and Tom must not accuse her of that. She looked up at him with a grave, earnest gaze, and said—

"I can't make you think better of me, Tom, by anything I can say.

But I am not so shut out from all your feelings as you believe me to be. I see as well as you do, that from our position with regard to Philip's father—not on other grounds—it would be unreasonable—it would be wrong for us to entertain the idea of marriage; and I have given up thinking of him as a lover. . . . I am telling you the truth, and you have no right to disbelieve me: I have kept my word to you, and you have never detected me in a falsehood. I should not only not encourage, I should carefully avoid, any intercourse with Philip on any other footing than that of quiet friendship. You may think that I am unable to keep my resolutions; but at least you ought not to treat me with hard contempt on the ground of faults that I have not committed yet."

"Well, Maggie," said Tom, softening under this appeal, "I don't want to overstrain matters. I think, all things considered, it will be best for you to see Philip Wakem, if Lucy wishes him to come to the house. I believe what you say—at least you believe it yourself, I know: I can only warn you. I wish to be as good a brother to you as you will let me."

There was a little tremor in Tom's voice as he uttered the last words, and Maggie's ready affection came back with as sudden a glow as when they were children, and bit their cake together as a sacrament of conciliation. She rose and laid her hand on Tom's shoulder.

"Dear Tom, I know you mean to be good. I know you have had a great deal to bear, and have done a great deal. I should like to be a comfort to you—not to vex you. You don't think I'm altogether naughty, now, do you?"

Tom smiled at the eager face: his smiles were very pleasant to see when they did come, for the grey eyes could be tender underneath the frown.

"No, Maggie."

"I may turn out better than you expect."

"I hope you will."

"And may I come some day and make tea for you, and see this extremely small wife of Bob's again?"

"Yes; but trot away now, for I've no more time to spare," said Tom, looking at his watch.

"Not to give me a kiss?"

Tom bent to kiss her cheek, and then said—

"There! Be a good girl. I've got a great deal to think of to-day. I'm going to have a long consultation with my uncle Deane this afternoon."

"You'll come to aunt Glegg's to-morrow? We're going all to dine early, that we may go there to tea. You *must* come: Lucy told me to say so."

"O pooh! I've plenty else to do," said Tom, pulling his bell violently, and bringing down the small bell-rope.

"I'm frightened—I shall run away," said Maggie, making a laughing retreat; while Tom, with masculine philosophy, flung the bell-rope to the farther end of the room—not very far either: a touch of human experience which I flatter myself will come home to the bosoms of not a few substantial or distinguished men who were once at an early stage of their rise in the world, and were cherishing very large hopes in very small lodgings.

Chapter V

Showing That Tom Had Opened the Oyster

"And now we've settled this Newcastle business, Tom," said Mr Deane, that same afternoon, as they were seated in the private room at the Bank together, "there's another matter I want to talk to you about. Since you're likely to have rather a smoky, unpleasant time of it at Newcastle for the next few weeks, you'll want a good prospect of some sort to keep up your spirits."

Tom waited less nervously than he had done on a former occasion in this apartment, while his uncle took out his snuff-box and gratified each nostril with deliberate impartiality.

"You see, Tom," said Mr Deane, at last, throwing himself backward, "the world goes on at a smarter pace now than it did when I was a young fellow. Why, sir, forty years ago, when I was much such a strapping youngster as you, a man expected to pull between the shafts the best part of his life, before he got the whip in his hand. The looms went slowish, and fashions didn't alter quite so fast: I'd a best suit that lasted me six years. Everything was on a lower scale, sir—in point of expenditure, I mean. It's this steam, you see, that has made the difference: it drives on every wheel double pace, and the wheel of fortune along with 'em, as our Mr Stephen Guest said at the anniversary dinner (he hits these things off wonderfully, considering he's seen nothing of business). I don't find fault with the change, as some people do. Trade, sir, opens a man's eyes; and if the population is to get thicker upon the ground, as it's doing, the world must use its wits at inventions of one sort or other. I know I've done my share as an ordinary man of business. Somebody has said it's a fine thing to make two ears of corn grew where only one grew before; but, sir, it's a fine thing, too, to further the exchange of commodities, and bring the grains of corn to the mouths that are hungry. And that's our line of business; and I consider it as honourable a position as a man can hold, to be connected with it."

Tom knew that the affair his uncle had to speak of was not urgent; Mr Deane was too shrewd and practical a man to allow either his reminiscences or his snuff to impede the progress of trade. Indeed, for the last month or two, there had been hints thrown out to Tom which enabled him to guess that he was going to hear some proposition for his own benefit. With the beginning of the last speech he had stretched out his legs, thrust his hands in his pockets, and prepared himself for some introductory diffuseness, tending to show that Mr Deane had succeeded by his own merit, and that what he had to say to young men in general was, that if they didn't succeed too, it was because of their own demerit. He was rather surprised, then, when his uncle put a direct question to him.

"Let me see—it's going on for seven years now since you applied to me for a situation—eh, Tom?"

"Yes, sir; I'm three-and-twenty now," said Tom.

"Ah—it's as well not to say that, though: for you'd pass for a good deal older, and age tells well in business. I remember your coming very well: I remember I saw there was some pluck in you, and that was what made me give you encouragement. And I'm happy to say, I was right—I'm not often deceived. I was naturally a little shy at pushing my nephew, but I'm happy to say you've done me credit, sir; and if I'd had a son o' my own, I shouldn't have been sorry to see him like you."

Mr Deane tapped his box and opened it again, repeating in a tone of some feeling—"No, I shouldn't have been sorry to see him like you."

"I'm very glad I've given you satisfaction, sir; I've done my best," said Tom, in his proud, independent way.

"Yes, Tom, you've given me satisfaction. I don't speak of your conduct as a son; though that weighs with me in my opinion of you. But what I have to do with, as a partner in our firm, is the qualities you've shown as a man o' business. Ours is a fine business—a splendid concern, sir—and there's no reason why it shouldn't go on growing: there's a growing capital, and growing outlets for it; but there's another thing that's wanted for the prosperity of every concern, large or small, and that's men to conduct it—men of the right habits; none o' your flashy fellows, but such as are to be depended on. Now this is what Mr Guest and I see clear enough. Three years ago, we took Gell into the concern: we gave him a share in the oil-mill. And why? Why, because Gell was a fellow whose services were worth a premium. So it will always be, sir. So it was with me. And though Gell is pretty near ten years older than you, there are other points in your favour."

Tom was getting a little nervous as Mr Deane went on speaking; he was conscious of something he had in his mind to say, which might not be agreeable to his uncle, simply because it was a new suggestion rather than an acceptance of the proposition he foresaw.

"It stands to reason," Mr Deane went on, when he had finished his new pinch, "that your being my nephew weighs in your favour; but I don't deny that if you'd been no relation of mine at all, your conduct in that affair of Pelley's bank would have led Mr Guest and myself to make some acknowledgment of the service you've been to us; and, backed by your general conduct and business ability, it has made us determine on giving you a share in the business—a share which we shall be glad to increase as the years go on. We think that'll be better, on all grounds, than raising your salary. It'll give you more importance, and prepare you better for taking some of the anxiety off my shoulders by-and-by. I'm equal to a good deal o' work at present, thank God; but I'm getting older—there's no denying that. I told Mr Guest I would open the subject to you; and when you come back from this northern business, we can go into particulars. This is a great stride for a young fellow of three-and-twenty, but I'm bound to say you've deserved it."

"I'm very grateful to Mr Guest and you, sir; of course I feel the most indebted to *you*, who first took me into the business, and have taken a good deal of pains with me since."

Tom spoke with a slight tremor, and paused after he had said this.

"Yes, yes," said Mr Deane. "I don't spare pains when I see they'll be of any use. I gave myself some trouble with Gell—else he wouldn't have been what he is."

"But there's one thing I should like to mention to you, uncle. I've never spoken to you of it before. If you remember, at the time my father's property was sold, there was some thought of your firm buying the Mill: I know you thought it would be a very good investment, especially if steam were applied."

"To be sure, to be sure. But Wakem outbid us—he'd made up his mind to that. He's rather fond of carrying everything over other people's heads."

"Perhaps it's of no use my mentioning it at present," Tom went on, "but I wish you to know what I have in my mind about the Mill. I've a strong feeling about it. It was my father's dying wish that I should try and get it back again whenever I could: it was in his family for five generations. I promised my father; and besides that, I'm attached to the place. I shall never like any other so well. And if it should ever suit your views to buy it for the firm, I should have a better chance of fulfilling my father's wish. I shouldn't have liked to mention the thing to you, only you've been kind enough to say my services have been of some value. And I'd give up a much greater chance in life for the sake of having the Mill again—I mean, having it in my own hands, and gradually working off the price."

Mr Deane had listened attentively, and now looked thoughtful.

"I see, I see," he said, after a while; "the thing would be possible, if there were any chance of Wakem's parting with the property. But that I *don't* see. He's put that young Jetsome in the place; and he had his reasons when he bought it, I'll be bound."

"He's a loose fish, that young Jetsome," said Tom. "He's taking to drinking, and they say he's letting the business go down. Luke told me about it—our old miller. He says, he shan't stay unless there's an alteration. I was thinking, if things went on in that way, Wakem might be more willing to part with the Mill. Luke says he's getting very sour about the way things are going on."

"Well, I'll turn it over, Tom. I must inquire into the matter, and go into it with Mr Guest. But, you see, it's rather striking out a new branch, and putting you to that, instead of keeping you where you are, which was what we'd wanted."

"I should be able to manage more than the mill when things were once set properly going, sir. I want to have plenty of work. There's nothing else I care about much."

There was something rather sad in that speech from a young man of three-and-twenty, even in uncle Deane's business-loving ears.

"Pooh, pooh! you'll be having a wife to care about one of these days, if you get on at this pace in the world. But as to this Mill, we mustn't reckon on our chickens too early. However, I promise you to bear it in mind, and when you come back we'll talk of it again. I am going to dinner now. Come and breakfast with us to-morrow morning, and say good-bye to your mother and sister before you start."

Chapter VI

Illustrating the Laws of Attraction

It is evident to you now, that Maggie had arrived at a moment in her life which must be considered by all prudent persons as a great opportunity for a young woman. Launched into the higher society of St Ogg's, with a striking person, which had the advantage of being quite unfamiliar to the majority of beholders, and with such moderate assistance of costume as you have seen foreshadowed in Lucy's anxious colloquy with aunt Pullet, Maggie was certainly at a new starting-point in life. At Lucy's first evening-party, young Torry fatigued his facial muscles more than usual in order that "the dark-eyed girl there, in the corner," might see him in all the additional style conferred by his eye-glass; and several young ladies went home intending to have short sleeves with black lace, and to plait their hair in a broad coronet at the back of their head—"That cousin of Miss Deane's looked so very well." In fact, poor Maggie, with all her inward consciousness of a painful past and her presentiment of a troublous future, was on the way to become an object of some envy—a topic of discussion in the newly-established billiard-room, and between fair friends who had no secrets from each other on the subject of trimmings. The Miss Guests, who associated chiefly on terms of condescension with the families of St Ogg's, and were the glass of fashion there, took some exception to Maggie's manners. She had a way of not assenting at once to the observations current in good society, and of saying that she didn't know whether those observations were true or not, which gave her an air of *gaucherie*,[1] and impeded the even flow of conversation; but it is a fact capable of an amiable interpretation, that ladies are not the worst disposed towards a new acquaintance of their own sex because she has points of inferiority. And Maggie was so entirely without those pretty airs of coquetry which had the traditional reputation of driving gentlemen to despair, that she won some feminine pity for being so ineffective in spite of her beauty. She had not had many advantages, poor thing! and it must be admitted there was no pretension about her: her abruptness and unevenness of manner were plainly the result of her secluded and lowly circumstances. It was only a wonder that there was no tinge of vulgarity about her, considering what the rest of poor Lucy's relations were: an allusion which always made the Miss Guests shudder a little. It was not agreeable to think of any connection by marriage with such people as the Gleggs and the Pullets; but it was of no use to contradict Stephen, when once he had set his mind on anything, and certainly there was no possible objection to Lucy in herself—no one could help liking her. She would naturally desire that the Miss Guests should behave kindly to this cousin of whom she was so fond, and Stephen would make a great fuss if they were deficient in civility. Under these circumstances the invitations to Park House were not wanting; and elsewhere, also, Miss Deane was too popular and too distinguished a member of society in St Ogg's for any attention towards her to be neglected.

Thus Maggie was introduced for the first time to the young lady's life, and knew what it was to get up in the morning without any imperative reason for doing one thing more than another. This new sense of leisure and unchecked enjoyment amidst the soft-breathing airs and garden-scents of advancing spring—amidst the new abundance of music, and lingering strolls in the sunshine, and the delicious dreaminess of gliding on the river—could hardly be without some intoxicating effect on her, after her years of privation; and even in the first week Maggie began to be less haunted by her sad memories and anticipations. Life was certainly very pleasant just now: it was becoming very pleasant to dress in the evening, and to feel that she was one of the beautiful things of this spring-time. And there were admiring eyes always awaiting her now; she was no longer an unheeded person, liable to be chid, from whom attention was continually claimed, and on whom no one felt bound to confer any. It was pleasant, too, when Stephen and Lucy were gone out riding, to sit down at the piano alone, and find that the old fitness between her fingers and the keys remained, and revived, like a sympathetic kinship not to be worn out by separation—to get the tunes she had heard the evening before, and repeat them again and again until she had found out a way of producing them so as to make them a more

1. Awkwardness.

pregnant, passionate language to her. The mere concord of octaves was a delight to Maggie, and she would often take up a book of studies rather than any melody, that she might taste more keenly by abstraction the more primitive sensation of intervals. Not that her enjoyment of music was of the kind that indicates a great specific talent; it was rather that her sensibility to the supreme excitement of music was only one form of that passionate sensibility which belonged to her whole nature, and made her faults and virtues all merge in each other—made her affections sometimes an impatient demand, but also prevented her vanity from taking the form of mere feminine coquetry and device, and gave it the poetry of ambition. But you have known Maggie a long while, and need to be told, not her characteristics, but her history, which is a thing hardly to be predicted even from the completest knowledge of characteristics. For the tragedy of our lives is not created entirely from within. "Character," says Novalis, in one of his questionable aphorisms—"character is destiny."[2] But not the whole of our destiny. Hamlet, Prince of Denmark, was speculative and irresolute, and we have a great tragedy in consequence. But if his father had lived to a good old age, and his uncle had died an early death, we can conceive Hamlet's having married Ophelia, and got through life with a reputation of sanity, notwithstanding many soliloquies, and some moody sarcasms towards the fair daughter of Polonius, to say nothing of the frankest incivility to his father-in-law.

Maggie's destiny, then, is at present hidden, and we must wait for it to reveal itself like the course of an unmapped river: we only know that the river is full and rapid, and that for all rivers there is the same final home. Under the charm of her new pleasures, Maggie herself was ceasing to think, with her eager prefiguring imagination, of her future lot; and her anxiety about her first interview with Philip was losing its predominance: perhaps, unconsciously to herself, she was not sorry that the interview had been deferred.

For Philip had not come the evening he was expected, and Mr Stephen Guest brought word that he was gone to the coast—probably, he thought, on a sketching expedition; but it was not certain when he would return. It was just like Philip—to go off in that way without telling any one. It was not until the twelfth day that he returned, to find both Lucy's notes awaiting him: he had left before he knew of Maggie's arrival.

Perhaps one had need be nineteen again to be quite convinced of the feelings that were crowded for Maggie into those twelve days—of the length to which they were stretched for her by the novelty of her experience in them, and the varying attitudes of her mind. The early days of an acquaintance almost always have this importance for us, and fill up a larger space in our memory than longer subsequent periods, which

2. Novalis is the pseudonym of Friedrich von Hardenberg, eighteenth-century poet and novelist. The aphorism appears in the posthumous *Heinrich von Ofterdingen* (1802).

have been less filled with discovery and new impressions. There were not many hours in those ten days in which Mr Stephen Guest was not seated by Lucy's side, or standing near her at the piano, or accompanying her on some out-door excursion: his attentions were clearly becoming more assiduous; and that was what every one had expected. Lucy was very happy: all the happier because Stephen's society seemed to have become much more interesting and amusing since Maggie had been there. Playful discussions—sometimes serious ones—were going forward, in which both Stephen and Maggie revealed themselves, to the admiration of the gentle unobtrusive Lucy; and it more than once crossed her mind what a charming quartet they should have through life when Maggie married Philip. Is it an inexplicable thing that a girl should enjoy her lover's society the more for the presence of a third person, and be without the slightest spasm of jealousy that the third person had the conversation habitually directed to her? Not when that girl is as tranquil-hearted as Lucy, thoroughly possessed with a belief that she knows the state of her companions' affections, and not prone to the feelings which shake such a belief in the absence of positive evidence against it. Besides, it was Lucy by whom Stephen sat, to whom he gave his arm, to whom he appealed as the person sure to agree with him; and every day there was the same tender politeness towards her, the same consciousness of her wants and care to supply them. Was there really the same?—it seemed to Lucy that there was more; and it was no wonder that the real significance of the change escaped her. It was a subtle act of conscience in Stephen that even he himself was not aware of. His personal attentions to Maggie were comparatively slight, and there had even sprung up an apparent distance between them, that prevented the renewal of that faint resemblance to gallantry into which he had fallen the first day in the boat. If Stephen came in when Lucy was out of the room—if Lucy left them together, they never spoke to each other: Stephen, perhaps, seemed to be examining books on music, and Maggie bent her head assiduously over her work. Each was oppressively conscious of the other's presence, even to the finger-ends. Yet each looked and longed for the same thing to happen the next day. Neither of them had begun to reflect on the matter, or silently to ask, "To what does all this tend?" Maggie only felt that life was revealing something quite new to her; and she was absorbed in the direct, immediate experience, without any energy left for taking account of it and reasoning about it. Stephen wilfully abstained from self-questioning, and would not admit to himself that he felt an influence which was to have any determining effect on his conduct. And when Lucy came into the room again, they were once more unconstrained: Maggie could contradict Stephen and laugh at him, and he could recommend to her consideration the example of that most charming heroine, Miss Sophia

Western, who had a great "respect for the understandings of men."[3] Maggie could look at Stephen—which, for some reason or other, she always avoided when they were alone; and he could even ask her to play his accompaniment for him, since Lucy's fingers were so busy with that bazaar-work; and lecture her on hurrying the *tempo*, which was certainly Maggie's weak point.

One day—it was the day of Philip's return—Lucy had formed a sudden engagement to spend the evening with Mrs Kenn, whose delicate state of health, threatening to become confirmed illness through an attack of bronchitis, obliged her to resign her functions at the coming bazaar into the hands of other ladies, of whom she wished Lucy to be one. The engagement had been formed in Stephen's presence, and he had heard Lucy promise to dine early and call at six o'clock for Miss Torry, who brought Mrs Kenn's request.

"Here is another of the moral results of this idiotic bazaar," Stephen burst forth, as soon as Miss Torry had left the room—"taking young ladies from the duties of the domestic hearth into scenes of dissipation among urn-rugs and embroidered reticules![4] I should like to know what is the proper function of women, if it is not to make reasons for husbands to stay at home, and still stronger reasons for bachelors to go out. If this goes on much longer, the bonds of society will be dissolved."

"Well, it will not go on much longer," said Lucy, laughing, "for the bazaar is to take place on Monday week."

"Thank heaven!" said Stephen. "Kenn himself said the other day, that he didn't like this plan of making vanity do the work of charity; but just as the British public is not reasonable enough to bear direct taxation, so St Ogg's has not got force of motive enough to build and endow schools without calling in the force of folly."

"Did he say so?" said little Lucy, her hazel eyes opening wide with anxiety. "I never heard him say anything of that kind: I thought he approved of what we were doing."

"I'm sure he approves *you*," said Stephen, smiling at her affectionately; "your conduct in going out to-night looks vicious, I own, but I know there is benevolence at the bottom of it."

"O, you think too well of me," said Lucy, shaking her head, with a pretty blush, and there the subject ended. But it was tacitly understood that Stephen would not come in the evening, and on the strength of that tacit understanding he made his morning visit the longer, not saying good-bye until after four.

Maggie was seated in the drawing-room alone, shortly after dinner, with Minny on her lap, having left her uncle to his wine and his nap, and her mother to the compromise between knitting and nodding,

3. Heroine of Henry Fielding's *Tom Jones* (1749). The reference is to book 17, chapter 3.
4. Reticules: small workbags; urn-rug: pad for under tea urn.

which, when there was no company, she always carried on in the dining-room till tea-time. Maggie was stooping to caress the tiny silken pet, and comforting him for his mistress's absence, when the sound of a footstep on the gravel made her look up, and she saw Mr Stephen Guest walking up the garden, as if he had come straight from the river. It was very unusual to see him so soon after dinner! He often complained that their dinner-hour was late at Park House. Nevertheless, there he was, in his black dress: he had evidently been home, and must have come again by the river. Maggie felt her cheeks glowing and her heart beating: it was natural she should be nervous, for she was not accustomed to receive visitors alone. He had seen her look up through the open window, and raised his hat as he walked towards it, to enter that way instead of by the door. He blushed too, and certainly looked as foolish as a young man of some wit and self-possession can be expected to look, as he walked in with a roll of music in his hand, and said, with an air of hesitating improvisation—

"You are surprised to see me again, Miss Tulliver—I ought to apologise for coming upon you by surprise, but I wanted to come into the town, and I got our man to row me; so I thought I would bring these things from the 'Maid of Artois'[5] for your cousin: I forgot them this morning. Will you give them to her?"

"Yes," said Maggie, who had risen confusedly with Minny in her arms, and now, not quite knowing what else to do, sat down again.

Stephen laid down his hat, with the music, which rolled on the floor, and sat down in the chair close by her. He had never done so before, and both he and Maggie were quite aware that it was an entirely new position.

"Well, you pampered minion!"[6] said Stephen, leaning to pull the long curly ears that drooped over Maggie's arm. It was not a suggestive remark, and as the speaker did not follow it up by further development, it naturally left the conversation at a stand-still. It seemed to Stephen like some action in a dream, that he was obliged to do, and wonder at himself all the while—to go on stroking Minny's head. Yet it was very pleasant: he only wished he dared look at Maggie, and that she would look at him—let him have one long look into those deep strange eyes of hers, and then he would be satisfied, and quite reasonable after that. He thought it was becoming a sort of monomania with him, to want that long look from Maggie; and he was racking his invention continually to find out some means by which he could have it without its appearing singular and entailing subsequent embarrassment. As for Maggie, she had no distinct thought—only the sense of a presence like that of a closely-hovering broad-winged bird in the darkness, for she was unable to look up, and saw nothing but Minny's black wavy coat.

5. Michael William Balfe's opera (1836).
6. Favorite.

But this must end some time—perhaps it ended very soon, and only *seemed* long, as a minute's dream does. Stephen at last sat upright sideways in his chair, leaning one hand and arm over the back and looking at Maggie. What should he say?

"We shall have a splendid sunset, I think; shan't you go out and see it?"

"I don't know," said Maggie. Then, courageously raising her eyes and looking out of the window, "If I'm not playing cribbage with my uncle."

A pause: during which Minny is stroked again, but has sufficient insight not to be grateful for it—to growl rather.

"Do you like sitting alone?"

A rather arch look came over Maggie's face, and, just glancing at Stephen, she said, "Would it be quite civil to say 'yes'?"

"It *was* rather a dangerous question for an intruder to ask," said Stephen, delighted with that glance, and getting determined to stay for another. "But you will have more than half an hour to yourself after I am gone," he added, taking out his watch. "I know Mr Deane never comes in till half-past seven."

Another pause, during which Maggie looked steadily out of the window, till by a great effort she moved her head to look down at Minny's back again, and said—

"I wish Lucy had not been obliged to go out. We lose our music."

"We shall have a new voice to-morrow night," said Stephen. "Will you tell your cousin that our friend Philip Wakem is come back? I saw him as I went home."

Maggie gave a little start—it seemed hardly more than a vibration that passed from head to foot in an instant. But the new images summoned by Philip's name, dispersed half the oppressive spell she had been under. She rose from her chair with a sudden resolution, and, laying Minny on his cushion, went to reach Lucy's large work-basket from its corner. Stephen was vexed and disappointed: he thought, perhaps Maggie didn't like the name of Wakem to be mentioned to her in that abrupt way—for he now recalled what Lucy had told him of the family quarrel. It was of no use to stay any longer. Maggie was seating herself at the table with her work, and looking chill and proud: and he—he looked like a simpleton for having come. A gratuitous, entirely superfluous visit of that sort was sure to make a man disagreeable and ridiculous. Of course it was palpable to Maggie's thinking, that he had dined hastily in his own room for the sake of setting off again and finding her alone.

A boyish state of mind for an accomplished young gentleman of five-and-twenty, not without legal knowledge! But a reference to history, perhaps, may make it not incredible.

At this moment Maggie's ball of knitting-wool rolled along the ground, and she started up to reach it. Stephen rose too, and, picking up the ball, met her with a vexed complaining look that gave his eyes quite a new expression to Maggie, whose own eyes met them as he presented the ball to her.

"Good-bye," said Stephen, in a tone that had the same beseeching discontent as his eyes. He dared not put out his hand—he thrust both hands into his tail-pockets as he spoke. Maggie thought she had perhaps been rude.

"Won't you stay?" she said timidly, not looking away, for that would have seemed rude again.

"No, thank you," said Stephen, looking still into the half-unwilling, half-fascinated eyes, as a thirsty man looks towards the track of the distant brook. "The boat is waiting for me. . . . You'll tell your cousin?"

"Yes."

"That I brought the music, I mean?"

"Yes."

"And that Philip is come back."

"Yes." (Maggie did not notice Philip's name this time.)

"Won't you come out a little way into the garden?" said Stephen, in a still gentler tone, but the next moment he was vexed that she did not say "No," for she moved away now towards the open window, and he was obliged to take his hat and walk by her side. But he thought of something to make him amends.

"Do take my arm," he said, in a low tone, as if it were a secret.

There is something strangely winning to most women in that offer of the firm arm: the help is not wanted physically at that moment, but the sense of help—the presence of strength that is outside them and yet theirs—meets a continual want of the imagination. Either on that ground or some other, Maggie took the arm. And they walked together round the grass plot and under the drooping green of the laburnums, in the same dim dreamy state as they had been in a quarter of an hour before; only that Stephen had had the look he longed for, without yet perceiving in himself the symptoms of returning reasonableness, and Maggie had darting thoughts across the dimness:—how came she to be there?—why had she come out? Not a word was spoken. If it had been, each would have been less intensely conscious of the other.

"Take care of this step," said Stephen, at last.

"O, I will go in now," said Maggie, feeling that the step had come like a rescue. "Good evening."

In an instant she had withdrawn her arm, and was running back to the house. She did not reflect that this sudden action would only add to the embarrassing recollections of the last half-hour. She had no thought left for that. She only threw herself into the low arm-chair, and burst into tears.

"O Philip, Philip, I wish we were together again—so quietly—in the Red Deeps."

Stephen looked after her a moment, then went on to the boat, and was soon landed at the wharf. He spent the evening in the billiard-room, smoking one cigar after another, and losing "lives"[7] at pool. But he would not leave off. He was determined not to think—not to admit any more distinct remembrance than was urged upon him by the perpetual presence of Maggie. He was looking at her, and she was on his arm.

But there came the necessity of walking home in the cool starlight, and with it the necessity of cursing his own folly, and bitterly determining that he would never trust himself alone with Maggie again. It was all madness: he was in love, thoroughly attached to Lucy, and engaged—engaged as strongly as an honourable man need be. He wished he had never seen this Maggie Tulliver, to be thrown into a fever by her in this way: she would make a sweet, strange, troublesome, adorable wife to some man or other, but he would never have chosen her himself. Did she feel as he did? He hoped she did—not. He ought not to have gone. He would master himself in future. He would make himself disagreeable to her—quarrel with her perhaps. Quarrel with her? Was it possible to quarrel with a creature who had such eyes—defying and deprecating, contradicting and clinging, imperious and beseeching—full of delicious opposites. To see such a creature subdued by love for one would be a lot worth having—to another man.

There was a muttered exclamation which ended this inward soliloquy, as Stephen threw away the end of his last cigar, and, thrusting his hands into his pockets, stalked along at a quieter pace through the shrubbery. It was not of a benedictory kind.

Chapter VII

Philip Re-Enters

The next morning was very wet: the sort of morning on which male neighbours who have no imperative occupation at home are likely to pay their fair friends an illimitable visit. The rain, which has been endurable enough for the walk or ride one way, is sure to become so heavy, and at the same time so certain to clear up by-and-by, that nothing but an open quarrel can abbreviate the visit: latent detestation will not do at all. And if people happen to be lovers, what can be so delightful, in England, as a rainy morning? English sunshine is dubious; bonnets are never quite secure; and if you sit down on the grass, it may lead to catarrhs. But the rain is to be depended on. You gallop through it in a mackintosh, and presently find yourself in the seat you like best—a little above or a little below the one on which your goddess sits (it is the same thing to the metaphysical mind, and that is the reason why women are

7. Chances; each player had three per game.

at once worshipped and looked down upon), with a satisfactory confidence that there will be no lady-callers.

"Stephen will come earlier this morning, I know," said Lucy: "he always does when it's rainy."

Maggie made no answer. She was angry with Stephen: she began to think she should dislike him; and if it had not been for the rain, she would have gone to her aunt Glegg's this morning, and so have avoided him altogether. As it was, she must find some reason for remaining out of the room with her mother.

But Stephen did not come earlier, and there was another visitor—a nearer neighbour—who preceded him. When Philip entered the room, he was going merely to bow to Maggie, feeling that their acquaintance was a secret which he was bound not to betray; but when she advanced towards him and put out her hand, he guessed at once that Lucy had been taken into her confidence. It was a moment of some agitation to both, though Philip had spent many hours in preparing for it; but like all persons who have passed through life with little expectation of sympathy, he seldom lost his self-control, and shrank with the most sensitive pride from any noticeable betrayal of emotion. A little extra paleness, a little tension of the nostril when he spoke, and the voice pitched in rather a higher key, that to strangers would seem expressive of cold indifference, were all the signs Philip usually gave of an inward drama that was not without its fierceness. But Maggie, who had little more power of concealing the impressions made upon her than if she had been constructed of musical strings, felt her eyes getting larger with tears as they took each other's hands in silence. They were not painful tears: they had rather something of the same origin as the tears women and children shed when they have found some protection to cling to, and look back on the threatened danger. For Philip, who a little while ago was associated continually in Maggie's mind with the sense that Tom might reproach her with some justice, had now, in this short space, become a sort of outward conscience to her, that she might fly to for rescue and strength. Her tranquil, tender affection for Philip, with its root deep down in her childhood, and its memories of long quiet talk confirming by distinct successive impressions the first instinctive bias—the fact that in him the appeal was more strongly to her pity and womanly devotedness than to her vanity or other egoistic excitability of her nature, seemed now to make a sort of sacred place, a sanctuary where she could find refuge from an alluring influence which the best part of herself must resist, which must bring horrible tumult within, wretchedness without. This new sense of her relation to Philip nullified the anxious scruples she would otherwise have felt, lest she should overstep the limit of intercourse with him that Tom would sanction; and she put out her hand to him, and felt the tears in her eyes without any consciousness of an inward check. The scene was just what Lucy expected, and her kind heart delighted in bringing Philip and Maggie together again; though, even with all *her* regard for Philip, she could not resist the impression that her cousin Tom had some excuse for feeling shocked at the physical incongruity between the two—a prosaic person like cousin Tom, who didn't like poetry and fairy tales. But she began to speak as soon as possible, to set them at ease.

"This was very good and virtuous of you," she said, in her pretty treble, like the low conversational notes of little birds, "to come so soon after your arrival. And as it is, I think I will pardon you for running away in an inopportune manner, and giving your friends no notice. Come and sit down here," she went on, placing the chair that would suit him best, "and you shall find yourself treated mercifully."

"You will never govern well, Miss Deane," said Philip as he seated himself, "because no one will ever believe in your severity. People will always encourage themselves in misdemeanours by the certainty that you will be indulgent."

Lucy gave some playful contradiction, but Philip did not hear what it was, for he had naturally turned towards Maggie, and she was looking at him with that open, affectionate scrutiny, which we give to a friend from whom we have been long separated. What a moment their parting had been! And Philip felt as if he were only in the morrow of it. He felt this so keenly—with such intense, detailed remembrance—with such passionate revival of all that had been said and looked in their last conversation—that with that jealousy and distrust which in diffident natures is almost inevitably linked with a strong feeling, he thought he read in Maggie's glance and manner the evidence of a change. The very fact that he feared and half expected it, would be sure to make this thought rush in, in the absence of positive proof to the contrary.

"I am having a great holiday, am I not?" said Maggie. "Lucy is like a fairy godmother: she has turned me from a drudge into a princess in no time. I do nothing but indulge myself all day long, and she always finds out what I want before I know it myself."

"I'm sure she is the happier for having you, then," said Philip. "You must be better than a whole menagerie of pets to her. And you look well—you are benefiting by the change."

Artificial conversation of this sort went on a little while, till Lucy, determined to put an end to it, exclaimed, with a good imitation of annoyance, that she had forgotten something, and was quickly out of the room.

In a moment Maggie and Philip leaned forward, and the hands were clasped again, with a look of sad contentment like that of friends who meet in the memory of recent sorrow.

"I told my brother I wished to see you, Philip—I asked him to release me from my promise, and he consented."

Maggie, in her impulsiveness, wanted Philip to know at once the position they must hold towards each other; but she checked herself. The things that had happened since he had spoken of his love for her were so painful that she shrank from being the first to allude to them. It seemed almost like an injury towards Philip even to mention her brother—her brother who had insulted him. But he was thinking too entirely of her to be sensitive on any other point at that moment.

"Then we can at least be friends, Maggie? There is nothing to hinder that now?"

"Will not your father object?" said Maggie, withdrawing her hand.

"I should not give you up on any ground but your own wish, Maggie," said Philip, colouring. "There are points on which I should always resist my father, as I used to tell you. *That* is one."

"Then there is nothing to hinder our being friends, Philip—seeing each other and talking to each other while I am here: I shall soon go away again. I mean to go very soon—to a new situation."

"Is that inevitable, Maggie?"

"Yes: I must not stay here long. It would unfit me for the life I must begin again at last. I can't live in dependence—I can't live with my brother—though he is very good to me. He would like to provide for me; but that would be intolerable to me."

Philip was silent a few moments, and then said, in that high, feeble voice which with him indicated the resolute suppression of emotion:—

"Is there no other alternative, Maggie? Is that life, away from those who love you, the only one you will allow yourself to look forward to?"

"Yes, Philip," she said, looking at him pleadingly, as if she entreated him to believe that she was compelled to this course. "At least, as things are; I don't know what may be in years to come. But I begin to think there can never come much happiness to me from loving: I have always had so much pain mingled with it. I wish I could make myself a world outside it, as men do."

"Now, you are returning to your old thought in a new form, Maggie—the thought I used to combat," said Philip, with a slight tinge of bitterness. "You want to find out a mode of renunciation that will be an escape from pain. I tell you again, there is no such escape possible except by perverting or mutilating one's nature. What would become of me, if I tried to escape from pain? Scorn and cynicism would be my only opium; unless I could fall into some kind of conceited madness, and fancy myself a favourite of Heaven because I am not a favourite with men."

The bitterness had taken on some impetuosity as Philip went on speaking: the words were evidently an outlet for some immediate feeling of his own, as well as an answer to Maggie. There was a pain pressing on him at that moment. He shrank with proud delicacy from the faintest allusion to the words of love—of plighted love that had passed between them. It would have seemed to him like reminding Maggie of a promise;

it would have had for him something of the baseness of compulsion. He could not dwell on the fact that he himself had not changed; for that too would have had the air of an appeal. His love for Maggie was stamped, even more than the rest of his experience, with the exaggerated sense that he was an exception—that she, that every one, saw him in the light of an exception.

But Maggie was conscience-stricken.

"Yes, Philip," she said, with her childish contrition when he used to chide her, "you are right, I know. I do always think too much of my own feelings, and not enough of others'—not enough of yours. I had need have you always to find fault with me and teach me: so many things have come true that you used to tell me."

Maggie was resting her elbow on the table, leaning her head on her hand and looking at Philip with half-penitent dependent affection, as she said this; while he was returning her gaze with an expression that, to her consciousness, gradually became less vague—became charged with a specific recollection. Had his mind flown back to something that *she* now remembered?—something about a lover of Lucy's? It was a thought that made her shudder: it gave new definiteness to her present position, and to the tendency of what had happened the evening before. She moved her arm from the table, urged to change her position by that positive physical oppression at the heart that sometimes accompanies a sudden mental pang.

"What is the matter, Maggie? Has something happened?" Philip said, inexpressible anxiety—his imagination being only too ready to weave everything that was fatal to them both.

"No—nothing," said Maggie, rousing her latent will. Philip must not have that odious thought in his mind: she would banish it from her own. "Nothing," she repeated, "except in my own mind. You used to say I should feel the effect of my starved life, as you called it, and I do. I am too eager in my enjoyment of music and all luxuries, now they are come to me."

She took up her work and occupied herself resolutely, while Philip watched her, really in doubt whether she had anything more than this general allusion in her mind. It was quite in Maggie's character to be agitated by vague self-reproach. But soon there came a violent well-known ring at the door-bell resounding through the house.

"O what a startling announcement!" said Maggie, quite mistress of herself, though not without some inward flutter. "I wonder where Lucy is."

Lucy had not been deaf to the signal, and after an interval long enough for a few solicitous but not hurried inquiries, she herself ushered Stephen in.

"Well, old fellow," he said, going straight up to Philip and shaking him heartily by the hand, bowing to Maggie in passing, "it's glorious to have you back again; only I wish you'd conduct yourself a little less like a sparrow with a residence on the house-top, and not go in and out constantly without letting the servants know. This is about the twentieth time I've had to scamper up those countless stairs to that painting-room of yours, all to no purpose, because your people thought you were at home. Such incidents embitter friendship."

"I've so few visitors—it seems hardly worth while to leave notice of my exit and entrances," said Philip, feeling rather oppressed just then by Stephen's bright strong presence and strong voice.

"Are you quite well this morning, Miss Tulliver?" said Stephen, turning to Maggie with stiff politeness, and putting out his hand with the air of fulfilling a social duty.

Maggie gave the tips of her fingers, and said, "Quite well, thank you," in a tone of proud indifference. Philip's eyes were watching them keenly; but Lucy was used to seeing variations in their manner to each other, and only thought with regret that there was some natural antipathy which every now and then surmounted their mutual goodwill. "Maggie is not the sort of woman Stephen admires, and she is irritated by something in him which she interprets as conceit," was the silent observation that accounted for everything to guileless Lucy. Stephen and Maggie had no sooner completed this studied greeting than each felt hurt by the other's coldness. And Stephen, while rattling on in questions to Philip about his recent sketching expedition, was thinking all the more about Maggie because he was not drawing her into the conversation as he had invariable done before. "Maggie and Philip are not looking happy," thought Lucy: "this first interview has been saddening to them."

"I think we people who have not been galloping," she said to Stephen, "are all a little damped by the rain. Let us have some music. We ought to take advantage of having Philip and you together. Give us the duet in 'Masaniello:'[1] Maggie has not heard that, and I know it will suit her."

"Come, then," said Stephen, going towards the piano, and giving a foretaste of the tune in his deep "brum-brum," very pleasant to hear.

"You, please, Philip—you play the accompaniment," said Lucy, "and then I can go on with my work. You *will* like to play, shan't you?" she added, with a pretty inquiring look, anxious, as usual, lest she should have proposed what was not pleasant to another; but with yearnings towards her unfinished embroidery.

Philip had brightened at the proposition, for there is no feeling, perhaps, except the extremes of fear and grief, that does not find relief in music—that does not make a man sing or play the better; and Philip had an abundance of pent-up feeling at this moment, as complex as any trio or quartet that was ever meant to express love and jealousy, and resignation and fierce suspicion, all at the same time.

1. English title of Daniel F. E. Auber's opera *La Muette de Portici* (The mute girl of Portici) (1828).

"O yes," he said, seating himself at the piano, "it is a way of eking out one's imperfect life and being three people at once—to sing and make the piano sing, and hear them both all the while—or else to sing and paint."

"Ah, there you are an enviable fellow. I can do nothing with my hands," said Stephen. "That has generally been observed in men of great administrative capacity, I believe. A tendency to predominance of the reflective powers in me!—haven't you observed that, Miss Tulliver?"

Stephen had fallen by mistake into his habit of playful appeal to Maggie, and she could not repress the answering flush and epigram.

"I *have* observed a tendency to predominance," she said, smiling; and Philip at that moment devoutly hoped that she found the tendency disagreeable.

"Come, come," said Lucy; "music, music! We will discuss each other's qualities another time."

Maggie always tried in vain to go on with her work when music began. She tried harder than ever to-day; for the thought that Stephen knew how much she cared for his singing was one that no longer roused a merely playful resistance; and she knew, too, that it was his habit always to stand so that he could look at her. But it was of no use: she soon threw her work down, and all her intentions were lost in the vague state of emotion produced by the inspiring duet—emotion that seemed to make her at once strong and weak: strong for all enjoyment, weak for all resistance. When the strain passed into the minor, she half-started from her seat with the sudden thrill of that change. Poor Maggie! She looked very beautiful when her soul was being played on in this way by the inexorable power of sound. You might have seen the slightest perceptible quivering through her whole frame as she leaned a little forward, clasping her hands as if to steady herself; while her eyes dilated and brightened into that wide-open, childish expression of wondering delight, which always came back in her happiest moments. Lucy, who at other times had always been at the piano when Maggie was looking in this way, could not resist the impulse to steal up to her and kiss her. Philip, too, caught a glimpse of her now and then round the open book on the desk, and felt that he had never before seen her under so strong an influence.

"More, more!" said Lucy, when the duet had been encored. "Something spirited again. Maggie always says she likes a great rush of sound."

"It must be 'Let us take the road,'[2] then," said Stephen—"so suitable for a wet morning. But are you prepared to abandon the most sacred duties of life, and come and sing with us?"

"O yes," said Lucy, laughing. "If you will look out the 'Beggar's Opera' from the large canterbury.[3] It has a dingy cover."

2. Chorus from John Gay's *The Beggar's Opera* (1728).
3. Cabinet with partitions for storing music.

"That is a great clue, considering there are about a score covers here of rival dinginess," said Stephen, drawing out the canterbury.

"O, play something the while, Philip," said Lucy, noticing that his fingers were wandering over the keys. "What is that you are falling into?—something delicious that I don't know."

"Don't you know that?" said Philip, bringing out the tune more definitely. "It's from the *Somnambula*—'Ah! perchè non posso odiarti.'[4] I don't know the opera, but it appears the tenor is telling the heroine that he shall always love her though she may forsake him. You've heard me sing it to the English words, 'I love thee still.' "

It was not quite unintentionally that Philip had wandered into this song, which might be an indirect expression to Maggie of what he could not prevail on himself to say to her directly. Her ears had been open to what he was saying, and when he began to sing, she understood the plaintive passion of the music. That pleading tenor had no very fine qualities as a voice, but it was not quite new to her: it had sung to her by snatches, in a subdued way, among the grassy walks and hollows, and underneath the leaning ash-tree in the Red Deeps. There seemed to be some reproach in the words—did Philip mean that? She wished she had assured him more distinctly in their conversation that she desired not to renew the hope of love between them, *only* because it clashed with her inevitable circumstances. She was touched, not thrilled by the song: it suggested distinct memories and thoughts, and brought quiet regret in the place of excitement.

"That's the way with you tenors," said Stephen, who was waiting with music in his hand while Philip finished the song. "You demoralise the fair sex by warbling your sentimental love and constancy under all sorts of vile treatment. Nothing short of having your heads served up in a dish like that mediæval tenor or troubadour,[5] would prevent you from expressing your entire resignation. I must administer an antidote, while Miss Deane prepares to tear herself away from her bobbins."

Stephen rolled out, with saucy energy—

"Shall I, wasting in despair,
Die because a woman's fair?"[6]

and seemed to make all the air in the room alive with a new influence. Lucy, always proud of what Stephen did, went towards the piano with laughing, admiring looks at him; and Maggie, in spite of her resistance to the spirit of the song and to the singer, was taken hold of and shaken by the invisible influence—was borne along by a wave too strong for her.

4. I.e., *Sonnambula*, opera by Vincenzo Bellini (1831); 'Ah! perché non posso odearti': Ah why can I not hate you.
5. Guillem de Cabestanh, Provençal troubadour who was killed by the husband of his beloved; his heart was served up to her and she subsequently killed herself.
6. From a song by George Wither (1622).

But, angrily resolved not to betray herself, she seized her work, and went on making false stitches and pricking her fingers with much perseverance, not looking up or taking notice of what was going forward, until all the three voices united in "Let us take the road."

I am afraid there would have been a subtle, stealing gratification in her mind if she had known how entirely this saucy, defiant Stephen was occupied with her: how he was passing rapidly from a determination to treat her with ostentatious indifference to an irritating desire for some sign of inclination from her—some interchange of subdued word or look with her. It was not long before he found an opportunity, when they had passed to the music of "The Tempest."[7] Maggie, feeling the need of a footstool, was walking across the room to get one, when Stephen, who was not singing just then, and was conscious of all her movements, guessed her want, and flew to anticipate her, lifting the footstool with an entreating look at her, which made it impossible not to return a glance of gratitude. And then, to have the footstool placed carefully by a too self-confident personage—not *any* self-confident personage, but one in particular, who suddenly looks humble and anxious, and lingers, bending still, to ask if there is not some draught in that position between the window and the fireplace, and if he may not be allowed to move the work-table for her—these things will summon a little of the too-ready, traitorous tenderness into a woman's eyes, compelled as she is in her girlish time to learn her life-lessons in very trivial language. And to Maggie such things had not been everyday incidents, but were a new element in her life, and found her keen appetite for homage quite fresh. That tone of gentle solicitude obliged her to look at the face that was bent towards her, and to say, "No, thank you;" and nothing could prevent that mutual glance from being delicious to both, as it had been the evening before.

It was but an ordinary act of politeness in Stephen; it had hardly taken two minutes; and Lucy, who was singing, scarcely noticed it. But to Philip's mind, filled already with a vague anxiety that was likely to find a definite ground for itself in any trivial incident, this sudden eagerness in Stephen, and the change in Maggie's face, which was plainly reflecting a beam from his, seemed so strong a contrast with the previous overwrought signs of indifference, as to be charged with painful meaning. Stephen's voice, pouring in again, jarred upon his nervous susceptibility as if it had been the clang of sheet-iron, and he felt inclined to make the piano shriek in utter discord. He had really seen no communicable ground for suspecting any unusual feeling between Stephen and Maggie: his own reason told him so, and he wanted to go home at once that he might reflect coolly on these false images, till he had convinced himself of their nullity. But then, again, he wanted to stay as long as Stephen

7. Either Thomas Arne's music (1746) for the songs from Shakespeare's play, or Purcell's setting for Dryden's adaptation (1695).

stayed—always to be present when Stephen was present with Maggie. It seemed to poor Philip so natural, nay, inevitable, that any man who was near Maggie should fall in love with her! There was no promise of happiness for her if she were beguiled into loving Stephen Guest; and this thought emboldened Philip to view his own love for her in the light of a less unequal offering. He was beginning to play very falsely under this deafening inward tumult, and Lucy was looking at him in astonishment, when Mrs Tulliver's entrance to summon them to lunch came as an excuse for abruptly breaking off the music.

"Ah, Mr Philip," said Mr Deane, when they entered the dining-room, "I've not seen you for a long while. Your father's not at home, I think, is he? I went after him to the office the other day, and they said he was out of town."

"He's been to Mudport on business for several days," said Philip; "but he's come back now."

"As fond of his farming hobby as ever, eh?"

"I believe so," said Philip, rather wondering at this sudden interest in his father's pursuits.

"Ah!" said Mr Deane, "he's got some land in his own hands on this side the river as well as the other, I think?"

"Yes, he has."

"Ah!" continued Mr Deane, as he dispensed the pigeon-pie; "he must find farming a heavy item—an expensive hobby. I never had a hobby myself—never would give in to that. And the worst of all hobbies are those that people think they can get money at. They shoot their money down like corn out of a sack then."

Lucy felt a little nervous under her father's apparently gratuitous criticism of Mr Wakem's expenditure. But it ceased there, and Mr Deane became unusually silent and meditative during his luncheon. Lucy, accustomed to watch all indications in her father, and having reasons, which had recently become strong, for an extra interest in what referred to the Wakems, felt an unusual curiosity to know what had prompted her father's questions. His subsequent silence made her suspect there had been some special reason for them in his mind.

With this idea in her head, she resorted to her usual plan when she wanted to tell or ask her father anything particular: she found a reason for her aunt Tulliver to leave the dining-room after dinner, and seated herself on a small stool at her father's knee. Mr Deane, under those circumstances, considered that he tasted some of the most agreeable moments his merits had purchased him in life, notwithstanding that Lucy, disliking to have her hair powdered with snuff, usually began by mastering his snuff-box on such occasions.

"You don't want to go to sleep yet, papa, *do* you?" she said, as she brought up her stool and opened the large fingers that clutched the snuff-box.

"Not yet," said Mr Deane, glancing at the reward of merit in the decanter. "But what do *you* want?" he added, pinching the dimpled chin fondly. "To coax some more sovereigns out of my pocket for your bazaar? Eh?"

"No, I have no base motives at all to-day. I only want to talk, not to beg. I want to know what made you ask Philip Wakem about his father's farming to-day, papa? It seemed rather odd, because you never hardly say anything to him about his father; and why should you care about Mr Wakem's losing money by his hobby?"

"Something to do with business," said Mr Deane, waving his hands, as if to repel intrusion into that mystery.

"But, papa, you always say Mr Wakem has brought Philip up like a girl: how came you to think you should get any business knowledge out of him? Those abrupt questions sounded rather oddly. Philip thought them queer."

"Nonsense, child!" said Mr Deane, willing to justify his social demeanour, with which he had taken some pains in his upward progress. "There's a report that Wakem's mill and farm on the other side of the river—Dorlcote Mill, your uncle Tulliver's, you know—isn't answering so well as it did. I wanted to see if your friend Philip would let anything out about his father's being tired of farming."

"Why? Would you buy the mill, papa, if he would part with it?" said Lucy, eagerly. "O, tell me everything—here, you shall have your snuff-box if you'll tell me. Because Maggie says all their hearts are set on Tom's getting back the mill some time. It was one of the last things her father said to Tom, that he must get back the mill."

"Hush, you little puss," said Mr Deane, availing himself of the restored snuff-box. "You must not say a word about this thing—do you hear? There's very little chance of their getting the mill, or of anybody's getting it out of Wakem's hands. And if he knew that we wanted it with a view to the Tullivers getting it again, he'd be the less likely to part with it. It's natural, after what happened. He behaved well enough to Tulliver before; but a horsewhipping is not likely to be paid for with sugar-plums."

"Now, papa," said Lucy, with a little air of solemnity, "will you trust me? You must not ask me all my reasons for what I'm going to say—but I have very strong reasons. And I'm very cautious—I am, indeed."

"Well, let us hear."

"Why, I believe, if you will let me take Philip Wakem into our confidence—let me tell him all about your wish to buy, and what it's for—that my cousins wish to have it, and why they wish to have it—I believe Philip would help to bring it about. I know he would desire to do it."

"I don't see how that can be, child," said Mr Deane, looking puzzled.

"Why should *he* care?"—then, with a sudden penetrating look at his daughter, "You don't think the poor lad's fond of you, and so you can make him do what you like?" (Mr Deane felt quite safe about his daughter's affections.)

"No, papa; he cares very little about me—not so much as I care about him. But I have a reason for being quite sure of what I say. Don't you ask me. And if you ever guess, don't tell me. Only give me leave to do as I think fit about it."

Lucy rose from her stool to seat herself on her father's knee, and kissed him with that last request.

"Are you sure you won't do mischief, now?" he said, looking at her with delight.

"Yes, papa, quite sure. I'm very wise; I've got all your business talents. Didn't you admire my accompt-book, now, when I showed it you?"

"Well, well, if this youngster will keep his counsel, there won't be much harm done. And to tell the truth, I think there's not much chance for us any other way. Now, let me go off to sleep."

Chapter VIII

Wakem in a New Light

Before three days had passed after the conversation you have just overheard between Lucy and her father, she had contrived to have a private interview with Philip during a visit of Maggie's to her aunt Glegg. For a day and a night Philip turned over in his mind with restless agitation all that Lucy had told him in that interview, till he had thoroughly resolved on a course of action. He thought he saw before him now a possibility of altering his position with respect to Maggie, and removing at least one obstacle between them. He laid his plan and calculated all his moves with the fervid deliberation of a chess-player in the days of his first ardour, and was amazed himself at his sudden genius as a tactician. His plan was as bold as it was thoroughly calculated. Having watched for a moment when his father had nothing more urgent on his hands than the newspaper, he went behind him, laid a hand on his shoulder, and said—

"Father, will you come into my sanctum, and look at my new sketches? I've arranged them now."

"I'm getting terribly stiff in the joints, Phil, for climbing those stairs of yours," said Wakem, looking kindly at his son as he laid down his paper. "But come along, then."

"This is a nice place for you, isn't it, Phil?—a capital light that from the roof, eh?" was, as usual, the first thing he said on entering the painting-room. He liked to remind himself and his son too that his fatherly indulgence had provided the accommodation. He had been a good father. Emily would have nothing to reproach him with there, if she came back again from her grave.

"Come, come," he said, putting his double eye-glass over his nose, and seating himself to take a general view while he rested, "you've got a famous show here. Upon my word, I don't see that your things aren't as good as that London artist's—what's his name—that Leyburn gave so much money for."

Philip shook his head and smiled. He had seated himself on his painting-stool, and had taken a lead pencil in his hand, with which he was making strong marks to counteract the sense of tremulousness. He watched his father get up, and walk slowly round, good-naturedly dwelling on the pictures much larger than his amount of genuine taste for landscape would have prompted, till he stopped before a stand on which two pictures were placed—one much larger than the other—the smaller one in a leather case.

"Bless me! what have you here?" said Wakem, startled by a sudden transition from landscape to portrait. "I thought you'd left off figures. Who are these?"

"They are the same person," said Philip, with calm promptness, "at different ages."

"And what person?" said Wakem, sharply fixing his eyes with a growing look of suspicion on the larger picture.

"Miss Tulliver. The small one is something like what she was when I was at school with her brother at King's Lorton: the larger one is not quite so good a likeness of what she was when I came from abroad."

Wakem turned round fiercely, with a flushed face, letting his eye-glass fall, and looking at his son with a savage expression for a moment, as if he was ready to strike that daring feebleness from the stool. But he threw himself into the arm-chair again, and thrust his hands into his trouser-pockets, still looking angrily at his son, however. Philip did not return the look, but sat quietly watching the point of his pencil.

"And do you mean to say, then, that you have had any acquaintance with her since you came from abroad?" said Wakem, at last, with that vain effort which rage always makes to throw as much punishment as it desires to inflict into words and tones, since blows are forbidden.

"Yes: I saw a great deal of her for a whole year before her father's death. We met often in that thicket—the Red Deeps—near Dorlcote Mill. I love her dearly: I shall never love any other woman. I have thought of her ever since she was a little girl."

"Go on, sir!—and you have corresponded with her all this while?"

"No. I never told her I loved her till just before we parted, and she promised her brother not to see me again or to correspond with me. I am not sure that she loves me, or would consent to marry me. But if she would consent—if she *did* love me well enough—I should marry her."

"And this is the return you make me for all the indulgences I've heaped on you?" said Wakem, getting white, and beginning to tremble under an enraged sense of impotence before Philip's calm defiance and concentration of purpose.

"No, father," said Philip, looking up at him for the first time. "I don't regard it as a return. You have been an indulgent father to me; but I have always felt that it was because you had an affectionate wish to give me as much happiness as my unfortunate lot would admit of—not that it was a debt you expected me to pay by sacrificing all my chances of happiness to satisfy feelings of yours, which I can never share."

"I think most sons would share their father's feelings in this case," said Wakem, bitterly. "The girl's father was an ignorant mad brute, who was within an inch of murdering me. The whole town knows it. And the brother is just as insolent, only in a cooler way. He forbade her seeing you, you say; he'll break every bone in your body, for your greater happiness, if you don't take care. But you seem to have made up your mind: you have counted the consequences, I suppose. Of course you are independent of me: you can marry this girl to-morrow, if you like: you are a man of five-and-twenty—you can go your way, and I can go mine. We need have no more to do with each other."

Wakem rose and walked towards the door, but something held him back, and instead of leaving the room, he walked up and down it. Philip was slow to reply, and when he spoke, his tone had a more incisive quietness and clearness than ever.

"No: I can't marry Miss Tulliver, even if she would have me—if I have only my own resources to maintain her with. I have been brought up to no profession. I can't offer her poverty as well as deformity."

"Ah, *there* is a reason for your clinging to me, doubtless," said Wakem, still bitterly, though Philip's last words had given him a pang: they had stirred a feeling which had been a habit for a quarter of a century. He threw himself into the chair again.

"I expected all this," said Philip. "I know these scenes are often happening between father and son. If I were like other men of my age, I might answer your angry words by still angrier—we might part—I should marry the woman I love, and have a chance of being as happy as the rest. But if it will be a satisfaction to you to annihilate the very object of everything you've done for me, you have an advantage over most fathers: you can completely deprive me of the only thing that would make my life worth having."

Philip paused, but his father was silent.

"You know best what satisfaction you would have, beyond that of gratifying a ridiculous rancour worthy only of wandering savages."

"Ridiculous rancour!" Wakem burst out. "What do you mean? Damn it! is a man to be horsewhipped by a boor and love him for it? Besides, there's that cold, proud devil of a son, who said a word to me I shall not forget when we had the settling. He would be as pleasant a mark for a bullet as I know—if he were worth the expense."

"I don't mean your resentment towards them," said Philip, who had his reasons for some sympathy with this view of Tom, "though a feeling of revenge is not worth much, that you should care to keep it. I mean your extending the enmity to a helpless girl, who has too much sense and goodness to share their narrow prejudices. *She* has never entered into the family quarrels."

"What does that signify? We don't ask what a woman does—we ask whom she belongs to. It's altogether a degrading thing to you—to think of marrying old Tulliver's daughter."

For the first time in the dialogue, Philip lost some of his self-control, and coloured with anger.

"Miss Tulliver," he said, with bitter incisiveness, "has the only grounds of rank that anything but vulgar folly can suppose to belong to the middle class: she is thoroughly refined, and her friends, whatever else they may be, are respected for irreproachable honour and integrity. All St Ogg's, I fancy, would pronounce her to be more than my equal."

Wakem darted a glance of fierce question at his son; but Philip was not looking at him, and with a certain penitent consciousness went on, in a few moments, as if in amplification of his last words—

"Find a single person in St Ogg's who will not tell you that a beautiful creature like her would be throwing herself away on a pitiable object like me."

"Not she!" said Wakem, rising again, and forgetting everything else in a burst of resentful pride, half fatherly, half personal. "It would be a deuced fine match for her. It's all stuff about an accidental deformity, when a girl's really attached to a man."

"But girls are not apt to get attached under those circumstances," said Philip.

"Well, then," said Wakem, rather brutally, trying to recover his previous position, "if she doesn't care for you, you might have spared yourself the trouble of talking to me about her—and you might have spared me the trouble of refusing my consent to what was never likely to happen."

Wakem strode to the door, and, without looking round again, banged it after him.

Philip was not without confidence that his father would be ultimately wrought upon as he had expected, by what had passed; but the scene had jarred upon his nerves, which were as sensitive as a woman's. He determined not to go down to dinner: he couldn't meet his father again that day. It was Wakem's habit, when he had no company at home, to go out in the evening—often as early as half-past seven; and as it was far on in the afternoon now, Philip locked up his room and went out for a long ramble, thinking he would not return until his father was out of the house again. He got into a boat, and went down the river to a favourite village, where he dined, and lingered till it was late enough for him to return. He had never had any sort of quarrel with his father before, and had a sickening fear that this contest, just begun, might go on for weeks—and what might not happen in that time? He would not allow himself to define what that involuntary question meant. But if he could once be in the position of Maggie's accepted, acknowledged lover, there would be less room for vague dread. He went up to his painting-room again, and threw himself, with a sense of fatigue, into the arm-chair, looking round absently at the views of water and rock that were ranged around, till he fell into a doze, in which he fancied Maggie was slipping down a glistening, green, slimy channel of a waterfall, and he was looking on helpless, till he was awakened by what seemed a sudden, awful crash.

It was the opening of the door, and he could hardly have dozed more than a few moments, for there was no perceptible change in the evening light. It was his father who entered; and when Philip moved to vacate the chair for him, he said—

"Sit still. I'd rather walk about."

He stalked up and down the room once or twice, and then, standing opposite Philip with his hand thrust in his side-pockets, he said, as if continuing a conversation that had not been broken off—

"But this girl seems to have been fond of you, Phil, else she wouldn't have met you in that way."

Philip's heart was beating rapidly, and a transient flush passed over his face like a gleam. It was not quite easy to speak at once.

"She liked me at King's Lorton, when she was a little girl, because I used to sit with her brother a great deal when he had hurt his foot. She had kept that in her memory, and thought of me as a friend of a long while ago. She didn't think of me as a lover, when she met me."

"Well, but you made love to her at last. What did she say then?" said Wakem, walking about again.

"She said she *did* love me then."

"Confound it, then, what else do you want? Is she a jilt?"

"She was very young then," said Philip, hesitatingly. "I'm afraid she hardly knew what she felt. I'm afraid our long separation, and the idea that events must always divide us, may have made a difference."

"But she's in the town. I've seen her at church. Haven't you spoken to her since you came back?"

"Yes, at Mr Deane's. But I couldn't renew my proposals to her on several grounds. One obstacle would be removed if you would give your consent—if you would be willing to think of her as a daughter-in-law."

Wakem was silent a little while, pausing before Maggie's picture.

"She's not the sort of woman your mother was, though, Phil," he said, at last. "I saw her at church—she's handsomer than this—deuced fine eyes and fine figure, I saw; but rather dangerous and unmanageable, eh?"

"She's very tender and affectionate; and so simple—without the airs and petty contrivances other women have."

"Ah?" said Wakem. Then looking round at his son, "But your mother looked gentler: she had that brown wavy hair and grey eyes, like yours. You can't remember her very well. It was a thousand pities I'd no likeness of her."

"Then, shouldn't you be glad for me to have the same sort of happiness, father—to sweeten my life for me? There can never be another tie so strong to you as that which began eight-and-twenty years ago, when you married my mother, and you have been tightening it ever since."

"Ah, Phil—you're the only fellow that knows the best of me," said Wakem, giving his hand to his son. "We must keep together if we can. And now, what am I to do? You must come down-stairs and tell me. Am I to go and call on this dark-eyed damsel?"

The barrier once thrown down in this way, Philip could talk freely to his father of their entire relation with the Tullivers—of the desire to get the mill and land back into the family—and of its transfer to Guest & Co. as an intermediate step. He could venture now to be persuasive and urgent, and his father yielded with more readiness than he had calculated on.

"I don't care about the mill," he said at last, with a sort of angry compliance. "I've had an infernal deal of bother lately about the mill. Let them pay me for my improvements, that's all. But there's one thing you needn't ask me. I shall have no direct transactions with young Tulliver. If you like to swallow him, for his sister's sake, you may; but I've no sauce that will make him go down."

I leave you to imagine the agreeable feelings with which Philip went to Mr Deane the next day, to say that Mr Wakem was ready to open the negotiations, and Lucy's pretty triumph as she appealed to her father whether she had not proved her great business abilities. Mr Deane was rather puzzled, and suspected that there had been something "going on" among the young people to which he wanted a clue. But to men of Mr Deane's stamp, what goes on among the young people is as extraneous to the real business of life as what goes on among the birds and butterflies—until it can be shown to have a malign bearing on monetary affairs. And in this case the bearing appeared to be entirely propitious.

Chapter IX

Charity in Full-Dress

The culmination of Maggie's career as an admired member of society in St Ogg's was certainly the day of the bazaar, when her simple, noble beauty, clad in a white muslin of some soft-floating kind, which I suspect must have come from the stores of aunt Pullet's wardrobe, appeared with marked distinction among the more adorned and conventional women around her. We perhaps never detect how much of our social demeanour is made up of artificial airs, until we see a person who is at once beautiful and simple: without the beauty, we are apt to call simplicity awkwardness. The Miss Guests were much too well-bred to have any of the grimaces and affected tones that belong to pretentious vulgarity; but their stall being next to the one where Maggie sat, it seemed newly obvious to-day that Miss Guest held her chin too high, and that Miss Laura spoke and moved continually with a view to effect.

All well-drest St Ogg's and its neighbourhood were there; and it would have been worth while to come, even from a distance, to see the fine old hall, with its open roof and carved oaken rafters, and great oaken folding-doors, and light shed down from a height on the many-coloured show beneath: a very quaint place, with broad faded stripes painted on the walls, and here and there a show of heraldic animals of a bristly, long-snouted character, the cherished emblems of a noble family once the seigniors of this now civic hall. A grand arch, cut in the upper wall at one end, surmounted an oaken orchestra, with an open room behind it, where hothouse plants and stalls for refreshments were disposed: an agreeable resort for gentlemen, disposed to loiter, and yet to exchange the occasional crush down below for a more commodious point of view. In fact, the perfect fitness of this ancient building for an admirable modern purpose, that made charity truly elegant, and led through vanity up to the supply of a deficit, was so striking that hardly a person entered the room without exchanging the remark more than once. Near the great arch over the orchestra was the stone oriel with painted glass, which was one of the venerable inconsistencies of the old hall; and it was close by this that Lucy had her stall, for the convenience of certain large plain articles which she had taken charge of for Mrs Kenn. Maggie had begged to sit at the open end of the stall, and to have the sale of these articles rather than of bead-mats and other elaborate products, of which she had but a dim understanding. But it soon appeared that the gentlemen's dressing-gowns, which were among her commodities, were objects of such general attention and inquiry, and excited so troublesome a curiosity as to their lining and comparative merits, together with a determination to test them by trying on, as to make her post a very conspicuous one. The ladies who had commodities of their own to sell, and did not want dressing-gowns, saw at once the frivolity and bad taste of this masculine preference for goods which any tailor could furnish; and it is possible that the emphatic notice of various kinds which was drawn towards Miss Tulliver on this public occasion, threw a very strong and unmistakeable light on her subsequent conduct in many minds then present. Not that anger, on account of spurned beauty, can dwell in the celestial breasts of charitable ladies, but rather, that the errors of persons who have once been much admired necessarily take a deeper tinge from the mere force of contrast; and also, that to-day Maggie's conspicuous position, for the first time, made evident certain characteristics which were subsequently felt to have an explanatory bearing. There was something rather bold in Miss Tulliver's direct gaze, and something undefinably coarse in the style of her beauty, which placed her, in the opinion of all feminine judges, far below her cousin Miss Deane; for the ladies of St Ogg's had now completely ceded to Lucy their hypothetic claims on the admiration of Mr Stephen Guest.

As for dear little Lucy herself, her late benevolent triumph about the Mill, and all the affectionate projects she was cherishing for Maggie and Philip, helped to give her the highest spirits to-day, and she felt nothing but pleasure in the evidence of Maggie's attractiveness. It is true, she was looking very charming herself, and Stephen was paying her the utmost attention on this public occasion; jealously buying up the articles he had seen under her fingers in the process of making, and gaily helping her to cajole the male customers into the purchase of the most effeminate futilities. He chose to lay aside his hat and wear a scarlet fez of her embroidering; but by superficial observers this was necessarily liable to be interpreted less as a compliment to Lucy than as a mark of coxcombry. "Guest is a great coxcomb," young Torry observed; "but then he is a privileged person in St Ogg's—he carries all before him: if another fellow did such things, everybody would say he made a fool of himself."

And Stephen purchased absolutely nothing from Maggie, until Lucy said, in rather a vexed under-tone—

"See, now; all the things of Maggie's knitting will be gone, and you will not have bought one. There are those deliciously soft warm things for the wrists—do buy them."

"Oh, no," said Stephen, "they must be intended for imaginative persons, who can chill themselves on this warm day by thinking of the frosty Caucasus.[1] Stern reason is my forte, you know. You must get Philip to buy those. By the way, why doesn't he come?"

"He never likes going where there are many people, though I enjoined him to come. He said he would buy up any of my goods that the rest of the world rejected. But now, do go and buy something of Maggie."

1. Reference to Shakespeare's *Richard II*, 1.3.294–95; the Caucasus are a mountain chain between the Caspian Sea and the Black Sea.

"No, no—see—she has got a customer: there is old Wakem himself just coming up."

Lucy's eyes turned with anxious interest towards Maggie, to see how she went through this first interview, since a sadly memorable time, with a man towards whom she must have so strange a mixture of feelings; but she was pleased to notice that Wakem had tact enough to enter at once into talk about the bazaar wares, and appear interested in purchasing, smiling now and then kindly at Maggie, and not calling on her to speak much, as if he observed that she was rather pale and tremulous.

"Why, Wakem is making himself particularly amiable to your cousin," said Stephen, in an under-tone to Lucy; "is it pure magnanimity? you talked of a family quarrel."

"O, that will soon be quite healed, I hope," said Lucy, becoming a little indiscreet in her satisfaction, and speaking with an air of significance. But Stephen did not appear to notice this, and as some lady-purchasers came up, he lounged on towards Maggie's end, handling trifles and standing aloof until Wakem, who had taken out his purse, had finished his transactions.

"My son came with me," he overheard Wakem saying, "but he has vanished into some other part of the building, and has left all these charitable gallantries to me. I hope you'll reproach him for his shabby conduct."

She returned his smile and bow without speaking, and he turned away, only then observing Stephen, and nodding to him. Maggie, conscious that Stephen was still there, busied herself with counting money, and avoided looking up. She had been well pleased that he had devoted himself to Lucy to-day, and had not come near her. They had begun the morning with an indifferent salutation, and both had rejoiced in being aloof from each other, like a patient who has actually done without his opium, in spite of former failures in resolution. And during the last few days they had even been making up their minds to failures, looking to the outward events that must soon come to separate them, as a reason for dispensing with self-conquest in detail.

Stephen moved step by step as if he were being unwillingly dragged, until he had got round the open end of the stall, and was half hidden by a screen of draperies. Maggie went on counting her money till she suddenly heard a deep gentle voice saying, "Aren't you very tired? Do let me bring you something—some fruit or jelly—mayn't I?"

The unexpected tones shook her like a sudden accidental vibration of a harp close by her.

"O no, thank you," she said, faintly, and only half-looking up for an instant.

"You look so pale," Stephen insisted, in a more entreating tone. "I'm sure you're exhausted. I must disobey you, and bring something."

"No, indeed, I couldn't take it."

"Are you angry with me? What have I done? *Do* look at me."

"Pray, go away," said Maggie, looking at him helplessly, her eyes glancing immediately from him to the opposite corner of the orchestra, which was half hidden by the folds of the old faded green curtain. Maggie had no sooner uttered this entreaty than she was wretched at the admission it implied; but Stephen turned away at once, and, following her upward glance, he saw Philip Wakem seated in the half-hidden corner, so that he could command little more than that angle of the hall in which Maggie sat. An entirely new thought occurred to Stephen, and, linking itself with what he had observed of Wakem's manner, and with Lucy's reply to his observation, it convinced him that there had been some former relation between Philip and Maggie beyond that childish one of which he had heard. More than one impulse made him immediately leave the hall and go up-stairs to the refreshment-room, where, walking up to Philip, he sat down behind him, and put his hand on his shoulder.

"Are you studying for a portrait, Phil," he said, "or for a sketch of that oriel window? By George! it makes a capital bit from this dark corner, with the curtain just marking it off."

"I have been studying expression," said Philip, curtly.

"What! Miss Tulliver's? It's rather of the savage-moody order to-day, I think—something of the fallen princess serving behind a counter. Her cousin sent me to her with a civil offer to get her some refreshment, but I have been snubbed, as usual. There's a natural antipathy between us, I suppose: I have seldom the honour to please her."

"What a hypocrite you are!" said Philip, flushing angrily.

"What! because experience must have told me that I'm universally pleasing? I admit the law, but there's some disturbing force here."

"I am going," said Philip, rising abruptly.

"So am I—to get a breath of fresh air; this place gets oppressive. I think I have done suit and service long enough."

The two friends walked down-stairs together without speaking. Philip turned through the outer door into the courtyard, but Stephen, saying, "O, by the by, I must call in here," went on along the passage to one of the rooms at the other end of the building, which were appropriated to the town library. He had the room all to himself, and a man requires nothing less than this, when he wants to dash his cap on the table, throw himself astride a chair, and stare at a high brick wall with a frown which would not have been beneath the occasion if he had been slaying "the giant Python."[2] The conduct that issues from a moral conflict has often so close a resemblance to vice, that the distinction escapes all outward judgments, founded on a mere comparison of actions. It is clear to you,

2. Dragon slain by Apollo.

I hope, that Stephen was not a hypocrite—capable of deliberate doubleness for a selfish end; and yet his fluctuations between the indulgence of a feeling and the systematic concealment of it, might have made a good case in support of Philip's accusation.

Meanwhile, Maggie sat at her stall cold and trembling, with that painful sensation in the eyes which comes from resolutely repressed tears. Was her life to be always like this?—always bringing some new source of inward strife? She heard confusedly the busy indifferent voices around her, and wished her mind could flow into that easy, babbling current. It was at this moment that Dr Kenn, who had quite lately come into the hall, and was now walking down the middle with his hands behind him, taking a general view, fixed his eyes on Maggie for the first time, and was struck with the expression of pain on her beautiful face. She was sitting quite still, for the stream of customers had lessened at this late hour in the afternoon: the gentlemen had chiefly chosen the middle of the day, and Maggie's stall was looking rather bare. This, with her absent, pained expression, finished the contrast between her and her companions, who were all bright, eager, and busy. He was strongly arrested. Her face had naturally drawn his attention as a new and striking one at church, and he had been introduced to her during a short call on business at Mr Deane's, but he had never spoken more than three words to her. He walked towards her now, and Maggie, perceiving some one approaching, roused herself to look up and be prepared to speak. She felt a childlike, instinctive relief from the sense of uneasiness in this exertion, when she saw it was Dr Kenn's face that was looking at her: that plain, middle-aged face, with a grave, penetrating kindness in it, seeming to tell of a human being who had reached a firm, safe strand, but was looking with helpful pity towards the strugglers still tossed by the waves, had an effect on Maggie at this moment which was afterwards remembered by her as if it had been a promise. The middle-aged, who have lived through their strongest emotions, but are yet in the time when memory is still half passionate and not merely contemplative, should surely be a sort of natural priesthood, whom life has disciplined and consecrated to be the refuge and rescue of early stumblers and victims of self-despair. Most of us, at some moment in our young lives, would have welcomed a priest of that natural order in any sort of canonicals or uncanonicals, but had to scramble upwards into all the difficulties of nineteen entirely without such aid, as Maggie did.

"You find your office rather a fatiguing one, I fear, Miss Tulliver?" said Dr Kenn.

"It is, rather," said Maggie, simply, not being accustomed to simper amiable denials of obvious facts.

"But I can tell Mrs Kenn that you have disposed of her goods very quickly," he added; "she will be very much obliged to you."

"O, I have done nothing: the gentlemen came very fast to buy the dressing-gowns and embroidered waistcoats, but I think any of the other ladies would have sold more: I didn't know what to say about them."

Dr Kenn smiled. "I hope I'm going to have you as a permanent parishioner now, Miss Tulliver—am I? You have been at a distance from us hitherto."

"I have been a teacher in a school, and I'm going into another situation of the same kind very soon."

"Ah? I was hoping you would remain among your friends, who are all in this neighbourhood, I believe."

"O, *I must go*," said Maggie, earnestly, looking at Dr Kenn with an expression of reliance, as if she had told him her history in those three words. It was one of those moments of implicit revelation which will sometimes happen even between people who meet quite transiently—on a mile's journey, perhaps, or when resting by the wayside. There is always this possibility of a word or look from a stranger to keep alive the sense of human brotherhood.

Dr Kenn's ear and eye took in all the signs that this brief confidence of Maggie's was charged with meaning.

"I understand," he said; "you feel it right to go. But that will not prevent our meeting again, I hope: it will not prevent my knowing you better, if I can be of any service to you."

He put out his hand and pressed hers kindly before he turned away.

"She has some trouble or other at heart," he thought. "Poor child! she looks as if she might turn out to be one of

'The souls by nature pitched too high,
By suffering plunged too low.'[3]

There's something wonderfully honest in those beautiful eyes."

It may be surprising that Maggie, among whose many imperfections an excessive delight in admiration and acknowledged supremacy were not absent now, any more than when she was instructing the gypsies with a view towards achieving a royal position among them, was not more elated on a day when she had had the tribute of so many looks and smiles, together with that satisfactory consciousness which had necessarily come from being taken before Lucy's cheval-glass,[4] and made to look at the full length of her tall beauty, crowned by the night of her massy hair. Maggie had smiled at herself then, and for the moment had forgotten everything in the sense of her own beauty. If that state of mind could have lasted, her choice would have been to have Stephen Guest at her feet, offering her a life filled with all luxuries, with daily incense of adoration near and distant, and with all possibilities of culture at her command. But there were things in her stronger than vanity—passion, and affection, and long deep memories of early discipline and effort, of

3. From Keble's *Christian Year* (1827), LXXIV.
4. Full-length mirror that can be tilted.

early claims on her love and pity; and the stream of vanity was soon swept along and mingled inperceptibly with that wider current which was at its highest force to-day, under the double urgency of the events and inward impulses brought by the last week.

Philip had not spoken to her himself about the removal of obstacles between them on his father's side—he shrank from that; but he had told everything to Lucy, with the hope that Maggie, being informed through her, might give him some encouraging sign that their being brought thus much nearer to each other was a happiness to her. The rush of conflicting feelings was too great for Maggie to say much when Lucy, with a face breathing playful joy, like one of Correggio's cherubs,[5] poured forth her triumphant revelation; and Lucy could hardly be surprised that she could do little more than cry with gladness at the thought of her father's wish being fulfilled, and of Tom's getting the Mill again in reward for all his hard striving. The details of preparation for the bazaar had then come to usurp Lucy's attention for the next few days, and nothing had been said by the cousins on subjects that were likely to rouse deeper feelings. Philip had been to the house more than once, but Maggie had had no private conversation with him, and thus she had been left to fight her inward battle without interference.

But when the bazaar was fairly ended, and the cousins were alone again, resting together at home, Lucy said—

"You must give up going to stay with your aunt Moss the day after to-morrow, Maggie: write a note to her, and tell her you have put it off at my request, and I'll send the man with it. She won't be displeased; you'll have plenty of time to go by-and-by; and I don't want you to go out of the way just now."

"Yes, indeed I must go, dear; I can't put it off. I wouldn't leave aunt Gritty out for the world. And I shall have very little time, for I'm going away to a new situation on the 25th of June."

"Maggie!" said Lucy, almost white with astonishment.

"I didn't tell you, dear," said Maggie, making a great effort to command herself, "because you've been so busy. But some time ago I wrote to our old governess, Miss Firniss, to ask her to let me know if she met with any situation that I could fill, and the other day I had a letter from her telling me that I could take three orphan pupils of hers to the coast during the holidays, and then make trial of a situation with her as teacher. I wrote yesterday to accept the offer."

Lucy felt so hurt that for some moments she was unable to speak.

"Maggie," she said at last, "how could you be so unkind to me—not to tell me—to take *such* a step—and now!" She hesitated a little, and then added—"And Philip? I thought everything was going to be so

5. Figures portrayed by the Italian painter (1494–1534).

happy. O Maggie—what is the reason? Give it up; let me write. There is nothing now to keep you and Philip apart."

"Yes," said Maggie, faintly. "There is Tom's feeling. He said I must give him up if I married Philip. And I know he would not change—at least not for a long while—unless something happened to soften him."

"But I will talk to him: he's coming back this week. And this good news about the Mill will soften him. And I'll talk to him about Philip. Tom's always very compliant to me: I don't think he's so obstinate."

"But I must go," said Maggie, in a distressed voice. "I must leave some time to pass. Don't press me to stay, dear Lucy."

Lucy was silent for two or three minutes, looking away and ruminating. At length she knelt down by her cousin, and, looking up in her face with anxious seriousness, said—

"Maggie, is it that you don't love Philip well enough to marry him?—tell me—trust me."

Maggie held Lucy's hands tightly in silence a little while. Her own hands were quite cold. But when she spoke, her voice was quite clear and distinct.

"Yes, Lucy, I would choose to marry him. I think it would be the best and highest lot for me—to make his life happy. He loved me first. No one else could be quite what he is to me. But I can't divide myself from my brother for life. I must go away, and wait. Pray, don't speak to me again about it."

Lucy obeyed in pain and wonder. The next word she said was—

"Well, dear Maggie, at least you will go to the dance at Park House to-morrow, and have some music and brightness, before you go to pay these dull, dutiful visits. Ah! here come aunty and the tea."

Chapter X

The Spell Seems Broken

The suite of rooms opening into each other at Park House looked duly brilliant with lights and flowers and the personal splendours of sixteen couples, with attendant parents and guardians. The focus of brilliancy was the long drawing-room, where the dancing went forward, under the inspiration of the grand piano; the library, into which it opened at one end, had the more sober illumination of maturity, with caps and cards; and at the other end, the pretty sitting-room with a conservatory attached, was left as an occasional cool retreat. Lucy, who had laid aside her black for the first time, and had her pretty slimness set off by an abundant dress of white crape, was the acknowledged queen of the occasion; for this was one of the Miss Guests' thoroughly condescending parties, including no member of any aristocracy higher than that of St Ogg's, and stretching to the extreme limits of commercial and professional gentility.

Maggie at first refused to dance, saying that she had forgotten all the figures—it was so many years since she had danced at school; and she was glad to have that excuse, for it is ill dancing with a heavy heart. But at length the music wrought in her young limbs, and the longing came; even though it was the horrible young Torry, who walked up a second time to try and persuade her. She warned him that she could not dance anything but a country-dance; but he, of course, was willing to wait for that high felicity, meaning only to be complimentary when he assured her at several intervals that it was a "great bore" that she couldn't waltz—he would have liked so much to waltz with her. But at last it was the turn of the good old-fashioned dance which has the least of vanity and the most of merriment in it, and Maggie quite forgot her troublous life in a childlike enjoyment of that half-rustic rhythm which seems to banish pretentious etiquette. She felt quite charitably towards young Torry, as his hand bore her along and held her up in the dance; her eyes and cheeks had that fire of young joy in them which will flame out if it can find the least breath to fan it; and her simple black dress, with its bit of black lace, seemed like the dim setting of a jewel.

Stephen had not yet asked her to dance—had not yet paid her more than a passing civility. Since yesterday, that inward vision of her which perpetually made part of his consciousness, had been half-screened by the image of Philip Wakem, which came across it like a blot: there was some attachment between her and Philip; at least there was an attachment on his side, which made her feel in some bondage. Here then, Stephen told himself, was another claim of honour which called on him to resist the attraction that was continually threatening to over-power him. He told himself so; and yet he had once or twice felt a certain savage resistance, and at another moment a shuddering repugnance, to this intrusion of Philip's image, which almost made it a new incitement to rush towards Maggie and claim her for himself. Nevertheless he had done what he meant to do this evening: he had kept aloof from her; he had hardly looked at her; and he had been gaily assiduous to Lucy. But now his eyes were devouring Maggie: he felt inclined to kick young Torry out of the dance, and take his place. Then he wanted the dance to end that he might get rid of his partner. The possibility that he too should dance with Maggie, and have her hand in his so long, was beginning to possess him like a thirst. But even now their hands were meeting in the dance—were meeting still to the very end of it, though they were far off each other.

Stephen hardly knew what happened, or in what automatic way he got through the duties of politeness in the interval, until he was free and saw Maggie seated alone again, at the farther end of the room. He made his way towards her round the couples that were forming for the waltz, and when Maggie became conscious that she was the person he sought, she felt, in spite of all the thoughts that had gone before, a glowing gladness at heart. Her eyes and cheeks were still brightened with her childlike enthusiasm in the dance; her whole frame was set to joy and tenderness; even the coming pain could not seem bitter—she was ready to welcome it as a part of life, for life at this moment seemed a keen vibrating consciousness poised above pleasure or pain. This one, this last night, she might expand unrestrainedly in the warmth of the present, without those chill eating thoughts of the past and the future.

"They're going to waltz again," said Stephen, bending to speak to her, with that glance and tone of subdued tenderness which young dreams create to themselves in the summer woods when low cooing voices fill the air. Such glances and tones bring the breath of poetry with them into a room that is half-stifling with glaring gas and hard flirtation.

"They are going to waltz again: it is rather dizzy work to look on, and the room is very warm. Shall we walk about a little?"

He took her hand and placed it within his arm, and they walked on into the sitting-room, where the tables were strewn with engravings for the accommodation of visitors who would not want to look at them. But no visitors were here at this moment. They passed on into the conservatory.

"How strange and unreal the trees and flowers look with the lights among them," said Maggie, in a low voice. "They look as if they belonged to an enchanted land, and would never fade away:—I could fancy they were all made of jewels."

She was looking at the tier of geraniums as she spoke, and Stephen made no answer: but he was looking at her—and does not a supreme poet[1] blend light and sound into one, calling darkness mute, and light eloquent? Something strangely powerful there was in the light of Stephen's long gaze, for it made Maggie's face turn towards it and look upward at it—slowly, like a flower at the ascending brightness. And they walked unsteadily on, without feeling that they were walking—without feeling anything but that long grave mutual gaze which has the solemnity belonging to all deep human passion. The hovering thought that they must and would renounce each other made this moment of mute confession more intense in its rapture.

But they had reached the end of the conservatory, and were obliged to pause and turn. The change of movement brought a new consciousness to Maggie: she blushed deeply, turned away her head, and drew her arm from Stephen's, going up to some flowers to smell them. Stephen stood motionless, and still pale.

1. Dante.

"O, may I get this rose?" said Maggie, making a great effort to say something, and dissipate the burning sense of irretrievable confession. "I think I am quite wicked with roses—I like to gather them and smell them till they have no scent left."

Stephen was mute; he was incapable of putting a sentence together, and Maggie bent her arm a little upward towards the large half-opened rose that had attracted her. Who has not felt the beauty of a woman's arm?—the unspeakable suggestions of tenderness that lie in the dimpled elbow, and all the varied gently-lessening curves down to the delicate wrist, with its tiniest, almost imperceptible nicks in the firm softness. A woman's arm touched the soul of a great sculptor two thousand years ago, so that he wrought an image of it for the Parthenon[2] which moves us still as it clasps lovingly the time-worn marble of a headless trunk. Maggie's was such an arm as that—and it had the warm tints of life.

A mad impulse seized on Stephen; he darted towards the arm, and showered kisses on it, clasping the wrist.

But the next moment Maggie snatched it from him, and glared at him like a wounded war-goddess, quivering with rage and humiliation.

"How dare you?"—she spoke in a deeply-shaken, half-smothered voice. "What right have I given you to insult me?"

She darted from him into the adjoining room, and threw herself on the sofa, panting and trembling.

A horrible punishment was come upon her for the sin of allowing a moment's happiness that was treachery to Lucy, to Philip—to her own better soul. That momentary happiness had been smitten with a blight—a leprosy: Stephen thought more lightly of *her* than he did of Lucy.

As for Stephen, he leaned back against the framework of the conservatory, dizzy with the conflict of passions—love, rage, and confused despair: despair at his want of self-mastery, and despair that he had offended Maggie.

The last feeling surmounted every other: to be by her side again and entreat forgiveness was the only thing that had the force of a motive for him, and she had not been seated more than a few minutes when he came and stood humbly before her. But Maggie's bitter rage was unspent.

"Leave me to myself, if you please," she said, with impetuous haughtiness, "and for the future avoid me."

Stephen turned away, and walked backwards and forwards at the other end of the room. There was the dire necessity of going back into the dancing-room again, and he was beginning to be conscious of that. They had been absent so short a time, that when he went in again the waltz was not ended.

2. The figure of Demeter or Persephone among the Elgin marbles, from the Parthenon; sold to the British Museum in 1816.

Maggie, too, was not long before she re-entered. All the pride of her nature was stung into activity: the hateful weakness which had dragged her within reach of this wound to her self-respect, had at least wrought its own cure. The thoughts and temptations of the last month should all be flung away into an unvisited chamber of memory: there was nothing to allure her now; duty would be easy, and all the old calm purposes would reign peacefully once more. She re-entered the drawing-room still with some excited brightness in her face, but with a sense of proud self-command that defied anything to agitate her. She refused to dance again, but she talked quite readily and calmly with every one who addressed her. And when they got home that night, she kissed Lucy with a free heart, almost exulting in this scorching moment, which had delivered her from the possibility of another word or look that would have the stamp of treachery towards that gentle, unsuspicious sister.

The next morning Maggie did not set off to Basset quite so soon as she had expected. Her mother was to accompany her in the carriage, and household business could not be despatched hastily by Mrs Tulliver. So Maggie, who had been in a hurry to prepare herself, had to sit waiting, equipped for the drive, in the garden. Lucy was busy in the house wrapping up some bazaar presents for the younger ones at Basset, and when there was a loud ring at the door-bell, Maggie felt some alarm lest Lucy should bring out Stephen to her: it was sure to be Stephen.

But presently the visitor came out into the garden alone, and seated himself by her on the garden-chair. It was not Stephen.

"We can just catch the tips of the Scotch firs, Maggie, from this seat," said Philip.

They had taken each other's hands in silence, but Maggie had looked at him with a more complete revival of the old childlike affectionate smile than he had seen before, and he felt encouraged.

"Yes," she said, "I often look at them, and wish I could see the low sunlight on the stems again. But I have never been that way but once—to the churchyard, with my mother."

"I have been there—I go there—continually," said Philip. "I have nothing but the past to live upon."

A keen remembrance and keen pity impelled Maggie to put her hand in Philip's. They had so often walked hand-in-hand!

"I remember all the spots," she said—"just where you told me of particular things—beautiful stories that I had never heard of before."

"You will go there again soon—won't you, Maggie?" said Philip, getting timid. "The Mill will soon be your brother's home again."

"Yes; but I shall not be there," said Maggie. "I shall only hear of that happiness. I am going away again—Lucy has not told you, perhaps?"

"Then the future will never join on to the past again, Maggie? That book is quite closed?"

The grey eyes that had so often looked up at her with entreating worship, looked up at her now, with a last struggling ray of hope in them, and Maggie met them with her large sincere gaze.

"That book never will be closed, Philip," she said, with grave sadness; "I desire no future that will break the ties of the past. But the tie to my brother is one of the strongest. I can do nothing willingly that will divide me always from him."

"Is that the only reason that would keep us apart for ever, Maggie?" said Philip, with a desperate determination to have a definite answer.

"The only reason," said Maggie, with calm decision. And she believed it. At that moment she felt as if the enchanted cup had been dashed to the ground.[3] The reactionary excitement that gave her a proud self-mastery had not subsided, and she looked at the future with a sense of calm choice.

They sat hand-in-hand without looking at each other or speaking for a few minutes: in Maggie's mind the first scenes of love and parting were more present than the actual moment, and she was looking at Philip in the Red Deeps.

Philip felt that he ought to have been thoroughly happy in that answer of hers: she was as open and transparent as a rock-pool. Why was he not thoroughly happy? Jealousy is never satisfied with anything short of an omniscience that would detect the subtlest fold of the heart.

Chapter XI

In the Lane

Maggie had been four days at her aunt Moss's, giving the early June sunshine quite a new brightness in the care-dimmed eyes of that affectionate woman, and making an epoch for her cousins great and small, who were learning her words and actions by heart, as if she had been a transient avatar of perfect wisdom and beauty.

She was standing on the causeway with her aunt and a group of cousins feeding the chickens, at that quiet moment in the life of the farmyard before the afternoon milking-time. The great buildings round the hollow yard were as dreary and tumble-down as ever, but over the old garden-wall the straggling rose-bushes were beginning to toss their summer weight, and the grey wood and old bricks of the house, on its higher level, had a look of sleepy age in the broad afternoon sunlight, that suited the quiescent time. Maggie, with her bonnet over her arm, was smiling down at the hatch of small fluffy chickens, when her aunt exclaimed—

3. A reference to a famous episode in Edmund Spenser's *The Faerie Queene* (1590–96), 2.12.57, in which the knight of Temperance flings a cup to the ground with which he is tempted in the Bower of Bliss. In *Comus* (1634) John Milton alludes to this episode when the Lady's brothers smash the enchanter's cup with which he tries to seduce her.

"Goodness me! who is that gentleman coming in at the gate?"

It was a gentleman on a tall bay horse; and the flanks and neck of the horse were streaked black with fast riding. Maggie felt a beating at head and heart—horrible as the sudden leaping to life of a savage enemy who had feigned death.

"Who is it, my dear?" said Mrs Moss, seeing in Maggie's face the evidence that she knew.

"It is Mr Stephen Guest," said Maggie, rather faintly. "My cousin Lucy's——a gentleman who is very intimate at my cousin's."

Stephen was already close to them, had jumped off his horse, and now raised his hat as he advanced.

"Hold the horse, Willy," said Mrs Moss to the twelve-year-old boy.

"No, thank you," said Stephen, pulling at the horse's impatiently tossing head. "I must be going again immediately. I have a message to deliver to you, Miss Tulliver—on private business. May I take the liberty of asking you to walk a few yards with me?"

He had a half-jaded, half-irritated look, such as a man gets when he has been dogged by some care or annoyance that makes his bed and his dinner of little use to him. He spoke almost abruptly, as if his errand were too pressing for him to trouble himself about what would be thought by Mrs Moss of his visit and request. Good Mrs Moss, rather nervous in the presence of this apparently haughty gentleman, was inwardly wondering whether she would be doing right or wrong to invite him again to leave his horse and walk in, when Maggie, feeling all the embarrassment of the situation, and unable to say anything, put on her bonnet, and turned to walk towards the gate.

Stephen turned too, and walked by her side, leading his horse.

Not a word was spoken till they were out in the lane, and had walked four or five yards, when Maggie, who had been looking straight before her all the while, turned again to walk back, saying, with haughty resentment—

"There is no need for me to go any farther. I don't know whether you consider it gentlemanly and delicate conduct to place me in a position that forced me to come out with you—or whether you wished to insult me still further by thrusting an interview upon me in this way."

"Of course you are angry with me for coming," said Stephen, bitterly. "Of course it is of no consequence what a man has to suffer—it is only your woman's dignity that you care about."

Maggie gave a slight start, such as might have come from the slightest possible electric shock.

"As if it were not enough that I'm entangled in this way—that I'm mad with love for you—that I resist the strongest passion a man can feel, because I try to be true to other claims—but you must treat me as if I were a coarse brute, who would willingly offend you. And when, if

I had my own choice, I should ask you to take my hand, and my fortune, and my whole life, and do what you liked with them! I know I forgot myself. I took an unwarrantable liberty. I hate myself for having done it. But I repented immediately—I've been repenting ever since. You ought not to think it unpardonable: a man who loves with his whole soul, as I do you, is liable to be mastered by his feelings for a moment; but you know—you must believe—that the worst pain I could have is to have pained you—that I would give the world to recall the error."

Maggie dared not speak—dared not turn her head. The strength that had come from resentment was all gone, and her lips were quivering visibly. She could not trust herself to utter the full forgiveness that rose in answer to that confession.

They were come nearly in front of the gate again, and she paused, trembling.

"You must not say these things—I must not hear them," she said, looking down in misery, as Stephen came in front of her, to prevent her from going farther towards the gate. "I'm very sorry for any pain you have to go through; but it is of no use to speak."

"Yes, it *is* of use," said Stephen, impetuously. "It would be of use if you would treat me with some sort of pity and consideration, instead of doing me vile injustice in your mind. I could bear everything more quietly if I knew you didn't hate me for an insolent coxcomb. Look at me—see what a hunted devil I am: I've been riding thirty miles every day to get away from the thought of you."

Maggie did not—dared not look. She had already seen the harassed face. But she said, gently—

"I don't think any evil of you."

"Then, dearest, look at me," said Stephen, in deepest, tenderest tones of entreaty. "Don't go away from me yet. Give me a moment's happiness—make me feel you've forgiven me."

"Yes, I do forgive you," said Maggie, shaken by those tones, and all the more frightened at herself. "But pray let me go in again. Pray go away."

A great tear fell from under her lowered eyelids.

"I can't go away from you—I can't leave you," said Stephen, with still more passionate pleading. "I shall come back again if you send me away with this coldness—I can't answer for myself. But if you will go with me only a little way, I can live on that. You see plainly enough that your anger has only made me ten times more unreasonable."

Maggie turned. But Tancred, the bay horse, began to make such spirited remonstrances against this frequent change of direction, that Stephen, catching sight of Willy Moss peeping through the gate, called out, "Here! just come and hold my horse for five minutes."

"O no," said Maggie, hurriedly, "my aunt will think it so strange."

"Never mind," Stephen answered, impatiently; "they don't know the people at St Ogg's. Lead him up and down just here, for five minutes," he added to Willy, who was now close to them; and then he turned to Maggie's side, and they walked on. It was clear that she *must* go on now.

"Take my arm," said Stephen, entreatingly; and she took it, feeling all the while as if she were sliding downwards in a nightmare.

"There is no end to this misery," she began, struggling to repel the influence by speech. "It is wicked—base—ever allowing a word or look that Lucy—that others might not have seen. Think of Lucy."

"I do think of her—bless her. If I didn't——" Stephen had laid his hand on Maggie's that rested on his arm, and they both felt it difficult to speak.

"And I have other ties," Maggie went on, at last, with a desperate effort,—"even if Lucy did not exist."

"You are engaged to Philip Wakem?" said Stephen, hastily. "Is it so?"

"I consider myself engaged to him—I don't mean to marry any one else."

Stephen was silent again until they had turned out of the sun into a side lane, all grassy and sheltered. Then he burst out impetuously—

"It is unnatural—it is horrible. Maggie, if you loved me as I love you, we should throw everything else to the winds for the sake of belonging to each other. We should break all these mistaken ties that were made in blindness, and determine to marry each other."

"I would rather die than fall into that temptation," said Maggie, with deep, slow distinctness—all the gathered spiritual force of painful years coming to her aid in this extremity. She drew her arm from his as she spoke.

"Tell me, then, that you don't care for me," he said, almost violently. "Tell me that you love some one else better."

It darted through Maggie's mind that here was a mode of releasing herself from outward struggle—to tell Stephen that her whole heart was Philip's. But her lips would not utter that, and she was silent.

"If you do love me, dearest," said Stephen, gently, taking up her hand again and laying it within his arm, "it is better—it is right that we should marry each other. We can't help the pain it will give. It is come upon us without our seeking: it is natural—it has taken hold of me in spite of every effort I have made to resist it. God knows, I've been trying to be faithful to tacit engagements, and I've only made things worse—I'd better have given way at first."

Maggie was silent. If it were *not* wrong—if she were once convinced of that, and need no longer beat and struggle against this current, soft and yet strong as the summer stream!

"Say 'yes,' dearest," said Stephen, leaning to look entreatingly in her face. "What could we care about in the whole world beside, if we belonged to each other?"

Her breath was on his face—his lips were very near hers—but there was a great dread dwelling in his love for her.

Her lips and eyelids quivered; she opened her eyes full on his for an instant, like a lovely wild animal timid and struggling under caresses, and then turned sharp round towards home again.

"And after all," he went on, in an impatient tone, trying to defeat his own scruples as well as hers, "I am breaking no positive engagement: if Lucy's affections had been withdrawn from me and given to some one else, I should have felt no right to assert a claim on her. If you are not absolutely pledged to Philip, we are neither of us bound."

"You don't believe that—it is not your real feeling," said Maggie, earnestly. "You feel, as I do, that the real tie lies in the feelings and expectations we have raised in other minds. Else all pledges might be broken, when there was no outward penalty. There would be no such thing as faithfulness."

Stephen was silent: he could not pursue that argument; the opposite conviction had wrought in him too strongly through his previous time of struggle. But it soon presented itself in a new form.

"The pledge *can't* be fulfilled," he said, with impetuous insistance. "It is unnatural: we can only pretend to give ourselves to any one else. There is wrong in that too—there may be misery in it for *them* as well as for us. Maggie, you must see that—you do see that."

He was looking eagerly at her face for the least sign of compliance; his large, firm, gentle grasp was on her hand. She was silent for a few moments, with her eyes fixed on the ground; then she drew a deep breath, and said, looking up at him with solemn sadness—

"O it is difficult—life is very difficult! It seems right to me sometimes that we should follow our strongest feeling;—but then, such feelings continually come across the ties that all our former life has made for us—the ties that have made others dependent on us—and would cut them in two. If life were quite easy and simple, as it might have been in paradise, and we could always see that one being first towards whom . . . I mean, if life did not make duties for us before love comes, love would be a sign that two people ought to belong to each other. But I see—I feel it is not so now: there are things we must renounce in life; some of us must resign love. Many things are difficult and dark to me; but I see one thing quite clearly—that I must not, cannot, seek my own happiness by sacrificing others. Love is natural; but surely pity and faithfulness and memory are natural too. And they would live in me still, and punish me if I did not obey them. I should be haunted by the suffering I had caused. Our love would be poisoned. Don't urge me; help me—help me, *because* I love you."

Maggie had become more and more earnest as she went on; her face had become flushed, and her eyes fuller and fuller of appealing love. Stephen had the fibre of nobleness in him that vibrated to her appeal: but in the same moment—how could it be otherwise?—that pleading beauty gained new power over him.

"Dearest," he said, in scarcely more than a whisper, while his arm stole round her, "I'll do, I'll bear anything you wish. But—one kiss—one—the last—before we part."

One kiss—and then a long look—until Maggie said tremulously, "Let me go—let us make haste back."

She hurried along, and not another word was spoken. Stephen stood still and beckoned when they came within sight of Willy and the horse, and Maggie went on through the gate. Mrs Moss was standing alone at the door of the old porch: she had sent all the cousins in, with kind thoughtfulness. It might be a joyful thing that Maggie had a rich and handsome lover, but she would naturally feel embarrassed at coming in again:—and it might *not* be joyful. In either case, Mrs Moss waited anxiously to receive Maggie by herself. The speaking face told plainly enough that, if there was joy, it was of a very agitating, dubious sort.

"Sit down here a bit, my dear." She drew Maggie into the porch, and sat down on the bench by her:—there was no privacy in the house.

"O aunt Gritty, I'm very wretched. I wish I could have died when I was fifteen. It seemed so easy to give things up then—it is so hard now."

The poor child threw her arms round her aunt's neck, and fell into long, deep sobs.

Chapter XII

A Family Party

Maggie left her good aunt Gritty at the end of the week, and went to Garum Firs to pay her visit to aunt Pullet according to agreement. In the mean time very unexpected things had happened, and there was to be a family party at Garum to discuss and celebrate a change in the fortunes of the Tullivers, which was likely finally to carry away the shadow of their demerits like the last limb of an eclipse, and cause their hitherto obscured virtues to shine forth in full-rounded splendour. It is pleasant to know that a new ministry just come into office are not the only fellow-men who enjoy a period of high appreciation and full-blown eulogy: in many respectable families throughout this realm, relatives becoming creditable meet with a similar cordiality of recognition, which, in its fine freedom from the coercion of any antecedents, suggests the hopeful possibility that we may some day without any notice find ourselves in full millennium, with cockatrices who have ceased to bite, and wolves that no longer show their teeth with any but the blandest intentions.

Lucy came so early as to have the start even of aunt Glegg; for she longed to have some undisturbed talk with Maggie about the wonderful news. It seemed—did it not? said Lucy, with her prettiest air of wisdom—as if everything, even other people's misfortunes (poor creatures!) were conspiring now to make poor dear aunt Tulliver, and cousin Tom, and naughty Maggie too, if she were not obstinately bent on the contrary, as happy as they deserved to be after all their troubles. To think that the very day—the *very day*—after Tom had come back from Newcastle, that unfortunate young Jetsome, whom Mr Wakem had placed at the Mill, had been pitched off his horse in a drunken fit, and was lying at St Ogg's in a dangerous state, so that Wakem had signified his wish that the new purchasers should enter on the premises at once! It was very dreadful for that unhappy young man, but it did seem as if the misfortune had happened then, rather than at any other time, in order that cousin Tom might all the sooner have the fit reward of his exemplary conduct—papa thought so very highly of him. Aunt Tulliver must certainly go to the Mill now, and keep house for Tom: that was rather a loss to Lucy in the matter of household comfort; but then, to think of poor aunty being in her old place again, and gradually getting comforts about her there!

On this last point Lucy had her cunning projects, and when she and Maggie had made their dangerous way down the bright stairs into the handsome parlour, where the very sunbeams seemed cleaner than elsewhere, she directed her manœuvres, as any other great tactician would have done, against the weaker side of the enemy.

"Aunt Pullet," she said, seating herself on the sofa, and caressingly adjusting that lady's floating cap-string, "I want you to make up your mind what linen and things you will give Tom towards housekeeping; because you're always so generous—you give such nice things, you know; and if you set the example, aunt Glegg will follow."

"That she never can, my dear," said Mrs Pullet, with unusual vigour, "for she hasn't got the linen to follow suit wi' mine, I can tell you. She'd niver the taste, not if she'd spend the money. Big checks and live things, like stags and foxes, all her table-linen is—not a spot nor a diamont among 'em. But it's poor work, dividing one's linen before one dies—I niver thought to ha' done that, Bessy," Mrs Pullet continued, shaking her head and looking at her sister Tulliver, "when you and me chose the double diamont, the first flax iver we'd spun—and the Lord knows where yours is gone."

"I'd no choice, I'm sure, sister," said poor Mrs Tulliver, accustomed to consider herself in the light of an accused person. "I'm sure it was no wish o' mine, iver, as I should lie awake o' nights thinking o' my best bleached linen all over the country."

"Take a peppermint, Mrs Tulliver," said uncle Pullet, feeling that he was offering a cheap and wholesome form of comfort, which he was recommending by example.

"O but, aunt Pullet," said Lucy, "you've so much beautiful linen. And suppose you had had daughters! Then you must have divided it, when they were married."

"Well, I don't say as I won't do it," said Mrs Pullet, "for now Tom's so lucky, it's nothing but right his friends should look on him and help him. There's the table-cloths I bought at your sale, Bessy; it was nothing but good natur' o' me to buy 'em, for they've been lying in the chest ever since. But I'm not going to give Maggie any more o' my Indy muslin and things, if she's to go into service again, when she might stay and keep me company, and do my sewing for me, if she wasn't wanted at her brother's."

"Going into service," was the expression by which the Dodson mind represented to itself the position of teacher or governess, and Maggie's return to that menial condition, now circumstances offered her more eligible prospects, was likely to be a sore point with all her relatives, besides Lucy. Maggie in her crude form, with her hair down her back, and altogether in a state of dubious promise, was a most undesirable niece; but now she was capable of being at once ornamental and useful. The subject was revived in aunt and uncle Glegg's presence, over the tea and muffins.

"Hegh, hegh!" said Mr Glegg, good-naturedly patting Maggie on the back, "nonsense, nonsense! Don't let us hear of you taking a place again, Maggie. Why, you must ha' picked up half-a-dozen sweethearts at the bazaar: isn't there one of 'em the right sort of article? Come, now?"

"Mr Glegg," said his wife, with that shade of increased politeness in her severity which she always put on with her crisper fronts, "you'll excuse me, but you're far too light for a man of your years. It's respect and duty to her aunts, and the rest of her kin as are so good to her, should have kept my niece from fixing about going away again without consulting us—not sweethearts, if I'm to use such a word, though it was never heared in *my* family."

"Why, what did they call us, when we went to see 'em, then, eh, neighbour Pullet? They thought us sweet enough then," said Mr Glegg, winking pleasantly, while Mr Pullet, at the suggestion of sweetness, took a little more sugar.

"Mr Glegg," said Mrs G., "if you're going to be undelicate, let me know."

"La, Jane, your husband's only joking," said Mrs Pullet; "let him joke while he's got health and strength. There's poor Mr Tilt got his mouth drawn all o' one side, and couldn't laugh if he was to try."

"I'll trouble you for the muffineer,[1] then, Mr Glegg," said Mrs G., "if I may be so bold to interrupt your joking. Though it's other people must see the joke in a niece's putting a slight on her mother's eldest sister, as is the head o' the family; and only coming in and out on short visits, all the time she's been in the town, and then settling to go away without my knowledge—as I'd laid caps out on purpose for her to make 'em up for me,—and me as have divided my money so equal——"

"Sister," Mrs Tulliver broke in, anxiously, "I'm sure Maggie never thought o' going away without staying at your house as well as the others. Not as it's my wish she should go away at all—but quite contrairy. I'm sure I'm innocent. I've said over and over again, 'My dear, you've no call to go away.' But there's ten days or a fortnight Maggie 'll have before she's fixed to go: she can stay at your house just as well, and I'll step in when I can, and so will Lucy."

"Bessy," said Mrs Glegg, "if you'd exercise a little more thought, you might know I should hardly think it was worth while to unpin a bed, and go to all that trouble now, just at the end o' the time, when our house isn't above a quarter of an hour's walk from Mr Deane's. She can come the first thing in the morning, and go back the last at night, and be thankful she's got a good aunt so close to her to come and sit with. I know *I* should, when I was her age."

"La, Jane," said Mrs Pullet, "it 'ud do your beds good to have somebody to sleep in 'em. There's that striped room smells dreadful mouldy, and the glass mildewed like anything. I'm sure I thought I should be struck with death when you took me in."

"O, there is Tom!" exclaimed Lucy, clapping her hands. "He's come on Sindbad, as I told him. I was afraid he was not going to keep his promise."

Maggie jumped up to kiss Tom as he entered, with strong feeling, at this first meeting since the prospect of returning to the Mill had been opened to him; and she kept his hand, leading him to the chair by her side. To have no cloud between herself and Tom was still a perpetual yearning in her, that had its root deeper than all change. He smiled at her very kindly this evening, and said, "Well, Magsie, how's aunt Moss?"

"Come, come, sir," said Mr Glegg, putting out his hand. "Why, you're such a big man, you carry all before you, it seems. You're come into your luck a good deal earlier than us old folks did—but I wish you joy, I wish you joy. You'll get the Mill all for your own again, some day, I'll be bound. You won't stop half-way up the hill."

"But I hope he'll bear in mind as it's his mother's family as he owes it to," said Mrs Glegg. "If he hadn't had them to take after, he'd ha' been poorly off. There was never any failures, nor lawing, nor wastefulness in our family—nor dying without wills——"

1. Shaker for sprinkling sugar on muffins, or a covered dish for keeping toasted muffins hot.

"No, nor sudden deaths," said aunt Pullet; "allays the doctor called in. But Tom had the Dodson skin: I said that from the first. And I don't know what *you* mean to do, sister Glegg, but I mean to give him a table-cloth of all my three biggest sizes but one, besides sheets. I don't say what more I shall do; but *that* I shall do, and if I should die to-morrow, Mr Pullet, you'll bear it in mind—though you'll be blundering with the keys, and never remember as that on the third shelf o' the left-hand wardrobe, behind the night-caps with the broad ties—not the narrow-frilled uns—is the key o' the drawer in the Blue Room, where the key o' the Blue Closet is. You'll make a mistake, and I shall niver be worthy to know it. You've a memory for my pills and draughts, wonderful—I'll allays say that of you—but you're lost among the keys." This gloomy prospect of the confusion that would ensue on her decease, was very affecting to Mrs Pullet.

"You carry it too far, Sophy—that locking in and out," said Mrs Glegg, in a tone of some disgust at this folly. "You *go* beyond your own family. There's nobody can say I don't lock up; but I do what's reasonable, and no more. And as for the linen, I shall look out what's serviceable, to make a present of to my nephey: I've got cloth as has never been whittened, better worth having than other people's fine holland; and I hope he'll lie down in it and think of his aunt."

Tom thanked Mrs Glegg, but evaded any promise to meditate nightly on her virtues; and Mr Glegg effected a diversion for him by asking about Mr Deane's intentions concerning steam.

Lucy had had her far-sighted views in begging Tom to come on Sindbad. It appeared, when it was time to go home, that the man-servant was to ride the horse, and cousin Tom was to drive home his mother and Lucy. "You must sit by yourself, aunty," said that contriving young lady, "because I must sit by Tom; I've a great deal to say to him."

In the eagerness of her affectionate anxiety for Maggie, Lucy could not persuade herself to defer a conversation about her with Tom, who, she thought, with such a cup of joy before him as this rapid fulfilment of his wish about the Mill, must become pliant and flexible. Her nature supplied her with no key to Tom's; and she was puzzled as well as pained to notice the unpleasant change on his countenance when she gave him the history of the way in which Philip had used his influence with his father. She had counted on this revelation as a great stroke of policy, which was to turn Tom's heart towards Philip at once, and, besides that, prove that the elder Wakem was ready to receive Maggie with all the honours of a daughter-in-law. Nothing was wanted, then, but for dear Tom, who always had that pleasant smile when he looked at cousin Lucy, to turn completely round, say the opposite of what he had always said before, and declare that he, for his part, was delighted that all the old grievances should be healed, and that Maggie should have Philip with all suitable despatch: in cousin Lucy's opinion nothing could be easier.

But to minds strongly marked by the positive and negative qualities that create severity—strength of will, conscious rectitude of purpose, narrowness of imagination and intellect, great power of self-control, and a disposition to exert control over others—prejudices come as the natural food of tendencies which can get no sustenance out of that complex, fragmentary, doubt-provoking knowledge which we call truth. Let a prejudice be bequeathed, carried in the air, adopted by hearsay, caught in through the eye—however it may come, these minds will give it a habitation: it is something to assert strongly and bravely, something to fill up the void of spontaneous ideas, something to impose on others with the authority of conscious right: it is at once a staff and a baton. Every prejudice that will answer these purposes is self-evident. Our good upright Tom Tulliver's mind was of this class: his inward criticism of his father's faults did not prevent him from adopting his father's prejudice; it was a prejudice against a man of lax principle and lax life, and it was a meeting-point for all the disappointed feelings of family and personal pride. Other feelings added their force to produce Tom's bitter repugnance to Philip, and to Maggie's union with him; and notwithstanding Lucy's power over her strong-willed cousin, she got nothing but a cold refusal ever to sanction such a marriage: "but of course Maggie could do as she liked—she had declared her determination to be independent. For Tom's part, he held himself bound by his duty to his father's memory, and by every manly feeling, never to consent to any relation with the Wakems."

Thus, all that Lucy had effected by her zealous mediation was to fill Tom's mind with the expectation that Maggie's perverse resolve to go into a situation again would presently metamorphose itself, as her resolves were apt to do, into something equally perverse, but entirely different—a marriage with Philip Wakem.

Chapter XIII

Borne Along by the Tide

In less than a week Maggie was at St Ogg's again,—outwardly in much the same position as when her visit there had just begun. It was easy for her to fill her mornings apart from Lucy without any obvious effort; for she had her promised visits to pay to her aunt Glegg, and it was natural that she should give her mother more than usual of her companionship in these last weeks, especially as there were preparations to be thought of for Tom's housekeeping. But Lucy would hear of no pretext for her remaining away in the evenings: she must always come from aunt Glegg's before dinner—"else what shall I have of you?" said Lucy, with a tearful pout that could not be resisted. And Mr Stephen Guest had unaccountably taken to dining at Mr Deane's as often as possible, instead of avoiding that, as he used to do. At first he began his mornings with a resolution that he would not dine there—not even go in the evening, till Maggie was away. He had even devised a plan of starting off on a journey in this agreeable June weather: the headaches which he had constantly been alleging as a ground for stupidity and silence were a sufficient ostensible motive. But the journey was not taken, and by the fourth morning no distinct resolution was formed about the evenings: they were only foreseen as times when Maggie would still be present for a little while—when one more touch, one more glance, might be snatched. For, why not? There was nothing to conceal between them: they knew—they had confessed their love, and they had renounced each other: they were going to part. Honour and conscience were going to divide them: Maggie, with that appeal from her inmost soul, had decided it; but surely they might cast a lingering look at each other across the gulf, before they turned away never to look again till that strange light had for ever faded out of their eyes.

Maggie, all this time, moved about with a quiescence and even torpor of manner, so contrasted with her usual fitful brightness and ardour, that Lucy would have had to seek some other cause for such a change, if she had not been convinced that the position in which Maggie stood between Philip and her brother, and the prospect of her self-imposed wearisome banishment, were quite enough to account for a large amount of depression. But under this torpor there was a fierce battle of emotions, such as Maggie in all her life of struggle had never known or foreboded: it seemed to her as if all the worst evil in her had lain in ambush till now, and had suddenly started up full-armed, with hideous, overpowering strength! There were moments in which a cruel selfishness seemed to be getting possession of her: why should not Lucy—why should not Philip suffer? *She* had had to suffer through many years of her life; and who had renounced anything for her? And when something like that fulness of existence—love, wealth, ease, refinement, all that her nature craved—was brought within her reach, why was she to forego it, that another might have it—another, who perhaps needed it less? But amidst all this new passionate tumult there were the old voices making themselves heard with rising power, till, from time to time, the tumult seemed quelled. *Was* that existence which tempted her the full existence she dreamed? Where, then, would be all the memories of early striving—all the deep pity for another's pain, which had been nurtured in her through years of affection and hardship—all the divine presentiment of something higher than mere personal enjoyment, which had made the sacredness of life? She might as well hope to enjoy walking by maiming her feet, as hope to enjoy an existence in which she set out by maiming the faith and sympathy that were the best organs of her soul. And then, if pain were so hard to *her*, what was it to others?—"Ah, God! preserve me from inflicting—give me strength to bear it."—How had she sunk into this struggle with a temptation that she would once have thought herself as secure from, as from deliberate crime? When was that first hateful moment in which she had been conscious of a feeling that clashed with her truth, affection, and gratitude, and had not shaken it from her with horror, as if it had been a loathsome thing?—And yet, since this strange, sweet, subduing influence did not, should not, conquer her—since it was to remain simply her own suffering . . . her mind was meeting Stephen's in that thought of his, that they might still snatch moments of mute confession before the parting came. For was not he suffering too? She saw it daily—saw it in the sickened look of fatigue with which, as soon as he was not compelled to exert himself, he relapsed into indifference towards everything but the possibility of watching her. Could she refuse sometimes to answer that beseeching look which she felt to be following her like a low murmur of love and pain? She refused it less and less, till at last the evening for them both was sometimes made of a moment's mutual gaze: they thought of it till it came, and when it had come, they thought of nothing else. One other thing Stephen seemed now and then to care for, and that was, to sing: it was a way of speaking to Maggie. Perhaps he was not distinctly conscious that he was impelled to it by a secret longing—running counter to all his self-confessed resolves—to deepen the hold he had on her. Watch your own speech, and notice how it is guided by your less conscious purposes, and you will understand that contradiction in Stephen.

Philip Wakem was a less frequent visitor, but he came occasionally in the evening, and it happened that he was there when Lucy said, as they sat out on the lawn, near sunset—

"Now Maggie's tale of visits to aunt Glegg is completed, I mean that we shall go out boating every day until she goes. She has not had half enough boating because of these tiresome visits, and she likes it better than anything. Don't you, Maggie?"

"Better than any sort of locomotion, I hope you mean," said Philip, smiling at Maggie, who was lolling backward in a low garden-chair, "else she will be selling her soul to that ghostly boatman who haunts the Floss—only for the sake of being drifted in a boat for ever."

"Should you like to be her boatman?" said Lucy. "Because, if you would, you can come with us and take an oar. If the Floss were but a quiet lake instead of a river, we should be independent of any gentleman, for Maggie can row splendidly. As it is, we are reduced to ask services of knights and squires, who do not seem to offer them with great alacrity."

She looked playful reproach at Stephen, who was sauntering up and down, and was just singing in pianissimo falsetto—

"The thirst that from the soul doth rise,
Doth ask a drink divine."[1]

He took no notice, but still kept aloof: he had done so frequently during Philip's recent visits.

"You don't seem inclined for boating," said Lucy, when he came to sit down by her on the bench. "Doesn't rowing suit you now?"

"O, I hate a large party in a boat," he said, almost irritably. "I'll come when you have no one else."

Lucy coloured, fearing that Philip would be hurt: it was quite a new thing for Stephen to speak in that way; but he had certainly not been well of late. Philip coloured too, but less from a feeling of personal offence than from a vague suspicion that Stephen's moodiness had some relation to Maggie, who had started up from her chair as he spoke, and had walked towards the hedge of laurels to look at the descending sunlight on the river.

"As Miss Deane didn't know she was excluding others by inviting me," said Philip, "I am bound to resign."

"No, indeed, you shall not," said Lucy, much vexed. "I particularly wish for your company to-morrow. The tide will suit at half-past ten: it will be a delicious time for a couple of hours to row to Luckreth and walk back, before the sun gets too hot. And how can you object to four people in a boat?" she added, looking at Stephen.

"I don't object to the people, but the number," said Stephen, who had recovered himself, and was rather ashamed of his rudeness. "If I voted for a fourth at all, of course it would be you, Phil. But we won't divide the pleasure of escorting the ladies; we'll take it alternately. I'll go the next day."

This incident had the effect of drawing Philip's attention with freshened solicitude towards Stephen and Maggie; but when they re-entered the house, music was proposed, and Mrs Tulliver and Mr Deane being occupied with cribbage, Maggie sat apart near the table where the books and work were placed—doing nothing, however, but listening abstractedly to the music. Stephen presently turned to a duet which he insisted that Lucy and Philip should sing: he had often done the same thing before; but this evening Philip thought he divined some double intention in every word and look of Stephen's, and watched him keenly—angry with himself all the while for this clinging suspicion. For had not Maggie virtually denied any ground for his doubts on her side? and she was truth itself: it was impossible not to believe her word and glance when they had last spoken together in the garden. Stephen might be strongly fascinated by her (what was more natural?), but Philip felt himself rather base for intruding on what must be his friend's painful secret. Still, he

1. From Ben Jonson's, "Drink to Me Only with Thine Eyes" (1616).

watched. Stephen, moving away from the piano, sauntered slowly towards the table near which Maggie sat, and turned over the newspapers, apparently in mere idleness. Then he seated himself with his back to the piano, dragging a newspaper under his elbow, and thrusting his hand through his hair, as if he had been attracted by some bit of local news in the *Laceham Courier*. He was in reality looking at Maggie, who had not taken the slightest notice of his approach. She had always additional strength of resistance when Philip was present, just as we can restrain our speech better in a spot that we feel to be hallowed. But at last she heard the word "dearest" uttered in the softest tone of pained entreaty, like that of a patient who asks for something that ought to have been given without asking. She had never heard that word since the moments in the lane at Basset, when it had come from Stephen again and again, almost as involuntarily as if it had been an inarticulate cry. Philip could hear no word, but he had moved to the opposite side of the piano, and could see Maggie start and blush, raise her eyes an instant towards Stephen's face, but immediately look apprehensively towards himself. It was not evident to her that Philip had observed her; but a pang of shame, under the sense of this concealment, made her move from her chair and walk to her mother's side to watch the game at cribbage.

Philip went home soon after in a state of hideous doubt mingled with wretched certainty. It was impossible for him now to resist the conviction that there was some mutual consciousness between Stephen and Maggie; and for half the night his irritable, susceptible nerves were pressed upon almost to frenzy by that one wretched fact: he could attempt no explanation that would reconcile it with her words and actions. When, at last, the need for belief in Maggie rose to its habitual predominance, he was not long in imagining the truth:—she was struggling, she was banishing herself—this was the clue to all he had seen since his return. But athwart that belief there came other possibilities that would not be driven out of sight. His imagination wrought out the whole story: Stephen was madly in love with her; he must have told her so; she had rejected him, and was hurrying away. But would he give her up, knowing—Philip felt the fact with heart-crushing despair—that she was made half helpless by her feeling towards him?

When the morning came, Philip was too ill to think of keeping his engagement to go in the boat. In his present agitation he could decide on nothing: he could only alternate between contradictory intentions. First, he thought he must have an interview with Maggie, and entreat her to confide in him; then again, he distrusted his own interference. Had he not been thrusting himself on Maggie all along? She had uttered words long ago in her young ignorance; it was enough to make her hate him that these should be continually present with her as a bond. And had he any right to ask her for a revelation of feelings which she had evidently intended to withhold from him? He would not trust himself to see her, till he had assured himself that he could act from pure anxiety for her, and not from egoistic irritation. He wrote a brief note to Stephen, and sent it early by the servant, saying that he was not well enough to fulfil his engagement to Miss Deane. Would Stephen take his excuse, and fill his place?

Lucy had arranged a charming plan, which had made her quite content with Stephen's refusal to go in the boat. She discovered that her father was to drive to Lindum this morning at ten: Lindum was the very place she wanted to go to, to make purchases—important purchases, which must by no means be put off to another opportunity; and aunt Tulliver must go too, because she was concerned in some of the purchases.

"You will have your row in the boat just the same, you know," she said to Maggie when they went out of the breakfast-room and up-stairs together; "Philip will be here at half-past ten, and it is a delicious morning. Now, don't say a word against it, you dear dolorous thing. What is the use of my being a fairy godmother, if you set your face against all the wonders I work for you? Don't think of awful cousin Tom: you may disobey him a little."

Maggie did not persist in objecting. She was almost glad of the plan; for perhaps it would bring her some strength and calmness to be alone with Philip again: it was like revisiting the scene of a quieter life, in which the very struggles were repose, compared with the daily tumult of the present. She prepared herself for the boat, and at half-past ten sat waiting in the drawing-room.

The ring of the door-bell was punctual, and she was thinking with half-sad, affectionate pleasure of the surprise Philip would have in finding that he was to be with her alone, when she distinguished a firm rapid step across the hall, that was certainly not Philip's: the door opened, and Stephen Guest entered.

In the first moment they were both too much agitated to speak; for Stephen had learned from the servant that the others were gone out. Maggie had started up and sat down again, with her heart beating violently; and Stephen, throwing down his cap and gloves, came and sat by her in silence. She thought Philip would be coming soon; and with great effort—for she trembled visibly—she rose to go to a distant chair.

"He is not coming," said Stephen, in a low tone. "*I* am going in the boat."

"O, we can't go," said Maggie, sinking into her chair again. "Lucy did not expect—she would be hurt. Why is not Philip come?"

"He is not well; he asked me to come instead."

"Lucy is gone to Lindum," said Maggie, taking off her bonnet, with hurried, trembling fingers. "We must not go."

"Very well," said Stephen, dreamily, looking at her, as he rested his arm on the back of his chair. "Then we'll stay here."

He was looking into her deep, deep eyes—far-off and mysterious as the starlit blackness, and yet very near, and timidly loving. Maggie sat perfectly still—perhaps for moments, perhaps for minutes—until the helpless trembling had ceased, and there was a warm glow on her cheek.

"The man is waiting—he has taken the cushions," she said. "Will you go and tell him?"

"What shall I tell him?" said Stephen, almost in a whisper. He was looking at the lips now.

Maggie made no answer.

"Let us go," Stephen murmured, entreatingly, rising, and taking her hand to raise her too. "We shall not be long together."

And they went. Maggie felt that she was being led down the garden among the roses, being helped with firm tender care into the boat, having the cushion and cloak arranged for her feet, and her parasol opened for her (which she had forgotten)—all by this stronger presence that seemed to bear her along without any act of her own will, like the added self which comes with the sudden exalting influence of a strong tonic—and she felt nothing else. Memory was excluded.

They glided rapidly along, Stephen rowing, helped by the backward-flowing tide, past the Tofton trees and houses—on between the silent sunny fields and pastures, which seemed filled with a natural joy that had no reproach for theirs. The breath of the young, unwearied day, the delicious rhythmic dip of the oars, the fragmentary song of a passing bird heard now and then, as if it were only the overflowing of brim-full gladness, the sweet solitude of a twofold consciousness that was mingled into one by that grave untiring gaze which need not be averted—what else could there be in their minds for the first hour? Some low, subdued, languid exclamation of love came from Stephen from time to time, as he went on rowing idly, half automatically: otherwise, they spoke no word; for what could words have been but an inlet to thought? and thought did not belong to that enchanted haze in which they were enveloped—it belonged to the past and the future that lay outside the haze. Maggie was only dimly conscious of the banks, as they passed them, and dwelt with no recognition on the villages: she knew there were several to be passed before they reached Luckreth, where they always stopped and left the boat. At all times she was so liable to fits of absence, that she was likely enough to let her way-marks pass unnoticed.

But at last Stephen, who had been rowing more and more idly, ceased to row, laid down the oars, folded his arms, and looked down on the water as if watching the pace at which the boat glided without his help. This sudden change roused Maggie. She looked at the far-stretching fields—at the banks close by—and felt that they were entirely strange to her. A terrible alarm took possession of her.

"O, have we passed Luckreth—where we were to stop?" she exclaimed, looking back to see if the place were out of sight. No village was to be seen. She turned round again, with a look of distressed questioning at Stephen.

He went on watching the water, and said, in a strange, dreamy, absent tone, "Yes—a long way."

"O what shall I do?" cried Maggie, in an agony. "We shall not get home for hours—and Lucy—O God, help me!"

She clasped her hands and broke into a sob, like a frightened child: she thought of nothing but of meeting Lucy, and seeing her look of pained surprise and doubt—perhaps of just upbraiding.

Stephen moved and sat near her, and gently drew down the clasped hands.

"Maggie," he said, in a deep tone of slow decision, "let us never go home again—till no one can part us—till we are married."

The unusual tone, the startling words, arrested Maggie's sob, and she sat quite still—wondering: as if Stephen might have seen some possibilities that would alter everything, and annul the wretched facts.

"See, Maggie, how everything has come without our seeking—in spite of all our efforts. We never thought of being alone together again: it has all been done by others. See how the tide is carrying us out—away from all those unnatural bonds that we have been trying to make faster round us—and trying in vain. It will carry us on to Torby, and we can land there, and get some carriage, and hurry on to York and then to Scotland—and never pause a moment till we are bound to each other, so that only death can part us. It is the only right thing, dearest: it is the only way of escaping from this wretched entanglement. Everything has concurred to point it out to us. We have contrived nothing, we have thought of nothing ourselves."

Stephen spoke with deep, earnest pleading. Maggie listened—passing from her startled wonderment to the yearning after that belief, that the tide was doing it all—that she might glide along with the swift, silent stream, and not struggle any more. But across that stealing influence came the terrible shadow of past thoughts; and the sudden horror lest now, at last, the moment of fatal intoxication was close upon her, called up feelings of angry resistance towards Stephen.

"Let me go!" she said, in an agitated tone, flashing an indignant look at him, and trying to get her hands free. "You have wanted to deprive me of any choice. You knew we were come too far—you have dared to take advantage of my thoughtlessness. It is unmanly to bring me into such a position."

Stung by this reproach, he released her hands, moved back to his former place, and folded his arms, in a sort of desperation at the difficulty Maggie's words had made present to him. If she would not consent to go on, he must curse himself for the embarrassment he had led her into. But the reproach was the unendurable thing: the one thing worse than parting with her was, that she should feel he had acted unworthily towards her. At last he said, in a tone of suppressed rage—

"I didn't notice that we had passed Luckreth till we had got to the next village; and then it came into my mind that we would go on. I can't justify it: I ought to have told you. It is enough to make you hate me—since you don't love me well enough to make everything else indifferent to you, as I do you. Shall I stop the boat, and try to get you out here? I'll tell Lucy that I was mad—and that you hate me—and you shall be clear of me for ever. No one can blame you, because I have behaved unpardonably to you."

Maggie was paralysed: it was easier to resist Stephen's pleading, than this picture he had called up of himself suffering while she was vindicated—easier even to turn away from his look of tenderness than from this look of angry misery, that seemed to place her in selfish isolation from him. He had called up a state of feeling in which the reasons which had acted on her conscience seemed to be transmuted into mere self-regard. The indignant fire in her eyes was quenched, and she began to look at him with timid distress. She had reproached him for being hurried into irrevocable trespass—she, who had been so weak herself.

"As if I shouldn't feel what happened to you—just the same," she said, with reproach of another kind—the reproach of love, asking for more trust. This yielding to the idea of Stephen's suffering was more fatal than the other yielding, because it was less distinguishable from that sense of others' claims which was the moral basis of her resistance.

He felt all the relenting in her look and tone—it was heaven opening again. He moved to her side, and took her hand, leaning his elbow on the back of the boat, and saying nothing. He dreaded to utter another word, he dreaded to make another movement, that might provoke another reproach or denial from her. Life hung on her consent: everything else was hopeless, confused, sickening misery. They glided along in this way, both resting in that silence as in a haven, both dreading lest their feelings should be divided again—till they became aware that the clouds had gathered, and that the slightest perceptible freshening of the breeze was growing and growing, so that the whole character of the day was altered.

"You will be chill, Maggie, in this thin dress. Let me raise the cloak over your shoulders. Get up an instant, dearest."

Maggie obeyed: there was an unspeakable charm in being told what to do, and having everything decided for her. She sat down again covered with the cloak, and Stephen took to his oars again, making haste; for they must try to get to Torby as fast as they could. Maggie was hardly conscious of having said or done anything decisive. All yielding is attended with a less vivid consciousness than resistance; it is the partial sleep of thought; it is the submergence of our own personality by another.

Every influence tended to lull her into acquiescence: that dreamy gliding in the boat, which had lasted for four hours, and had brought some weariness and exhaustion—the recoil of her fatigued sensations from the impracticable difficulty of getting out of the boat at this unknown distance from home, and walking for long miles—all helped to bring her into more complete subjection to that strong mysterious charm which made a last parting from Stephen seem the death of all joy, and made the thought of wounding him like the first touch of the torturing iron before which resolution shrank. And then there was the present happiness of being with him, which was enough to absorb all her languid energy.

Presently Stephen observed a vessel coming after them. Several vessels, among them the steamer to Mudport, had passed them with the early tide, but for the last hour they had seen none. He looked more and more eagerly at this vessel, as if a new thought had come into his mind along with it, and then he looked at Maggie hesitatingly.

"Maggie, dearest," he said, at last, "if this vessel should be going to Mudport, or to any convenient place on the coast northward, it would be our best plan to get them to take us on board. You are fatigued—and it may soon rain—it may be a wretched business, getting to Torby in this boat. It's only a trading-vessel, but I daresay you can be made tolerably comfortable. We'll take the cushions out of the boat. It is really our best plan. They'll be glad enough to take us: I've got plenty of money about me; I can pay them well."

Maggie's heart began to beat with reawakened alarm at this new proposition; but she was silent—one course seemed as difficult as another.

Stephen hailed the vessel. It was a Dutch vessel going to Mudport, the English mate informed him, and, if this wind held, would be there in less than two days.

"We had got out too far with our boat," said Stephen. "I was trying to make for Torby. But I'm afraid of the weather; and this lady—my wife—will be exhausted with fatigue and hunger. Take us on board—will you?—and haul up the boat. I'll pay you well."

Maggie, now really faint and trembling with fear, was taken on board, making an interesting object of contemplation to admiring Dutchmen. The mate feared the lady would have a poor time of it on board, for they had no accommodation for such entirely unlooked-for passengers—no private cabin larger than an old-fashioned church-pew. But at least they had Dutch cleanliness, which makes all other inconveniences tolerable; and the boat-cushions were spread into a couch for Maggie on the poop with all alacrity. But to pace up and down the deck leaning on Stephen—being upheld by his strength—was the first change that she needed: then came food, and then quiet reclining on the cushions, with the sense that no new resolution *could* be taken that day. Everything must wait till to-morrow. Stephen sat beside her with her hand in his; they could only speak to each other in low tones; only look at each other now and then, for it would take a long while to dull the curiosity of the five men on board, and reduce these handsome young strangers to that minor degree of interest, which belongs, in a sailor's regard, to all objects nearer than the horizon. But Stephen was triumphantly happy. Every other thought or care was thrown into unmarked perspective by the certainty that Maggie must be his. The leap had been taken now: he had been tortured by scruples, he had fought fiercely with overmastering inclination, he had hesitated; but repentance was impossible. He murmured forth in fragmentary sentences his happiness—his adoration—his tenderness—his belief that their life together must be heaven—that her presence with him would give rapture to every common day—that to satisfy her lightest wish was dearer to him than all other bliss—that everything was easy for her sake, except to part with her, and now they never *would* part; he would belong to her for ever, and all that was his was hers—had no value for him except as it was hers. Such things, uttered in low broken tones by the one voice that has first stirred the fibre of young passion, have only a feeble effect—on experienced minds at a distance from them. To poor Maggie they were very near: they were like nectar held close to thirsty lips: there was, there *must* be, then, a life for mortals here below which was not hard and chill—in which affection would no longer be self-sacrifice. Stephen's passionate words made the vision of such a life more fully present to her than it had ever been before; and the vision for the time excluded all realities—all except the returning sun-gleams which broke out on the waters as the evening approached, and mingled with the visionary sunlight of promised happiness—all except the hand that pressed hers, and the voice that spoke to her, and the eyes that looked at her with grave, unspeakable love.

There was to be no rain, after all; the clouds rolled off to the horizon again, making the great purple rampart and long purple isles of that wondrous land which reveals itself to us when the sun goes down—the land that the evening star watches over. Maggie was to sleep all night on the poop; it was better than going below; and she was covered with the warmest wrappings the ship could furnish. It was still early, when the fatigues of the day brought on a drowsy longing for perfect rest, and she laid down her head, looking at the faint dying flush in the west, where the one golden lamp was getting brighter and brighter. Then she looked up at Stephen, who was still seated by her, hanging over her as he leaned his arm against the vessel's side. Behind all the delicious visions of these last hours, which had flowed over her like a soft stream, and made her entirely passive, there was the dim consciousness that the condition was a transient one, and that the morrow must bring back the old life of struggle—that there were thoughts which would presently avenge themselves for this oblivion. But now nothing was distinct to her: she was being lulled to sleep with that soft stream still flowing over her, with those delicious visions melting and fading like the wondrous aërial land of the west.

Chapter XIV

Waking

When Maggie was gone to sleep, Stephen, weary too with his unaccustomed amount of rowing, and with the intense inward life of the last twelve hours, but too restless to sleep, walked and lounged about the deck with his cigar far on into midnight, not seeing the dark water—hardly conscious there were stars—living only in the near and distant future. At last fatigue conquered restlessness, and he rolled himself up in a piece of tarpauling on the deck near Maggie's feet.

She had fallen asleep before nine, and had been sleeping for six hours before the faintest hint of a midsummer daybreak was discernible. She awoke from that vivid dreaming which makes the margin of our deeper rest: She was in a boat on the wide water with Stephen, and in the gathering darkness something like a star appeared, that grew and grew till they saw it was the Virgin seated in St Ogg's boat, and it came nearer and nearer, till they saw the Virgin was Lucy and the boatman was Philip—no, not Philip, but her brother, who rowed past without looking at her; and she rose to stretch out her arms and call to him, and their own boat turned over with the movement, and they began to sink, till with one spasm of dread she seemed to awake, and find she was a child again in the parlour at evening twilight, and Tom was not really angry. From the soothed sense of that false waking she passed to the real waking—to the plash of water against the vessel, and the sound of a footstep on the deck, and the awful starlit sky. There was a moment of utter bewilderment before her mind could get disentangled from the confused web of dreams; but soon the whole terrible truth urged itself upon her. Stephen was not by her now: she was alone with her own memory and her own dread. The irrevocable wrong that must blot her life had been committed: she had brought sorrow into the lives of others—into the lives that were knit up with hers by trust and love. The feeling of a few short weeks had hurried her into the sins her nature had most recoiled from—breach of faith and cruel selfishness; she had rent the ties that had given meaning to duty, and had made herself an outlawed soul, with no guide but the wayward choice of her own passion. And where would that lead her?—where had it led her now? She had said she would rather die than fall into that temptation. She felt it now—now that the consequences of such a fall had come before the outward act was completed. There was at least this fruit from all her years of striving after the highest and best—that her soul, though betrayed, beguiled, ensnared, could never deliberately consent to a choice of the lower. And a choice of what? O God—not a choice of joy, but of conscious cruelty and hardness; for could she ever cease to see before her Lucy and Philip, with their murdered trust and hopes? Her life with Stephen could have no sacredness: she must for ever sink and wander vaguely, driven by uncertain impulse; for she had let go the clue of life—that clue which once in the far-off years her young need had clutched so strongly. She had renounced all delights then, before she knew them, before they had come within her reach. Philip had been right when he told her that she knew nothing of renunciation: she had thought it was quiet ecstasy; she saw it face to face now—that sad patient loving strength which holds the clue of life—and saw that the thorns were for ever pressing on its brow. The yesterday, which could never be revoked—if she could have changed it now for any length of inward silent endurance, she would have bowed beneath that cross with a sense of rest.

Daybreak came and the reddening eastern light, while her past life was grasping her in this way, with that tightening clutch which comes in the last moments of possible rescue. She could see Stephen now lying on the deck still fast asleep, and with the sight of him there came a wave of anguish that found its way in a long-suppressed sob. The worst bitterness of parting—the thought that urged the sharpest inward cry for help, was the pain it must give to *him*. But surmounting everything was the horror at her own possible failure, the dread lest her conscience should be benumbed again, and not rise to energy till it was too late. —Too late! it was too late already not to have caused misery: too late for everything, perhaps, but to rush away from the last act of baseness —the tasting of joys that were wrung from crushed hearts.

The sun was rising now, and Maggie started up with the sense that a day of resistance was beginning for her. Her eyelashes were still wet with tears, as with her shawl over her head, she sat looking at the slowly-rounding sun. Something roused Stephen too, and, getting up from his hard bed, he came to sit beside her. The sharp instinct of anxious love saw something to give him alarm in the very first glance. He had a hovering dread of some resistance in Maggie's nature that he would be unable to overcome. He had the uneasy consciousness that he had robbed her of perfect freedom yesterday: there was too much native honour in him, for him not to feel that, if her will should recoil, his conduct would have been odious, and she would have a right to reproach him.

But Maggie did not feel that right: she was too conscious of fatal weakness in herself—too full of the tenderness that comes with the foreseen need for inflicting a wound. She let him take her hand when he came to sit down beside her, and smiled at him—only with rather a sad glance; she could say nothing to pain him till the moment of possible parting was nearer. And so they drank their cup of coffee together, and walked about the deck, and heard the captain's assurance that they should be in at Mudport by five o'clock, each with an inward burthen; but in him it was an undefined fear, which he trusted to the coming hours to dissipate; in her it was a definite resolve on which she was trying silently to tighten her hold. Stephen was continually, through the morning, expressing his anxiety at the fatigue and discomfort she was suffering, and alluded to landing and to the change of motion and repose she would have in a carriage, wanting to assure himself more completely by presupposing that everything would be as he had arranged it. For a long while Maggie contented herself with assuring him that she had had a good night's rest, and that she didn't mind about being on the vessel—it was not like being on the open sea—it was only a little less pleasant than being in a boat on the Floss. But a suppressed resolve will betray itself in the eyes, and Stephen became more and more uneasy as the day advanced, under the sense that Maggie had entirely lost her passiveness. He longed, but did not dare, to speak of their marriage—of where they would go after it, and the steps he would take to inform his father, and the rest, of what had happened. He longed to assure himself of a tacit assent from her. But each time he looked at her, he gathered a stronger dread of the new, quiet sadness with which she met his eyes. And they were more and more silent.

"Here we are in sight of Mudport," he said, at last. "Now, dearest," he added, turning towards her with a look that was half-beseeching, "the worst part of your fatigue is over. On the land we can command swiftness. In another hour and a half we shall be in a chaise together—and that will seem rest to you after this."

Maggie felt it was time to speak: it would only be unkind now to assent by silence. She spoke in the lowest tone, as he had done, but with distinct decision.

"We shall not be together—we shall have parted."

The blood rushed to Stephen's face.

"We shall not," he said. "I'll die first."

It was as he had dreaded—there was a struggle coming. But neither of them dared to say another word, till the boat was let down, and they were taken to the landing-place. Here there was a cluster of gazers and passengers awaiting the departure of the steamboat to St Ogg's. Maggie had a dim sense, when she had landed, and Stephen was hurrying her along on his arm, that some one had advanced towards her from that cluster as if he were coming to speak to her. But she was hurried along, and was indifferent to everything but the coming trial.

A porter guided them to the nearest inn and posting-house, and Stephen gave the order for the chaise as they passed through the yard.

Maggie took no notice of this, and only said, "Ask them to show us into a room where we can sit down."

When they entered, Maggie did not sit down, and Stephen, whose face had a desperate determination in it, was about to ring the bell, when she said, in a firm voice:—

"I'm not going: we must part here."

"Maggie," he said, turning round towards her, and speaking in the tones of a man who feels a process of torture beginning, "do you mean to kill me? What is the use of it now? The whole thing is done."

"No, it is not done," said Maggie. "Too much is done—more than we can ever remove the trace of. But I will go no farther. Don't try to prevail with me again. I couldn't choose yesterday."

What was he to do? He dared not go near her—her anger might leap out, and make a new barrier. He walked backwards and forwards in maddening perplexity.

"Maggie," he said at last, pausing before her, and speaking in a tone of imploring wretchedness, "have some pity—hear me—forgive me for what I did yesterday. I will obey you now—I will do nothing without your full consent. But don't blight our lives for ever by a rash perversity that can answer no good purpose to any one—that can only create new evils. Sit down, dearest; wait—think what you are going to do. Don't treat me as if you couldn't trust me."

He had chosen the most effective appeal; but Maggie's will was fixed unswervingly on the coming wrench. She had made up her mind to suffer.

"We must not wait," she said, in a low but distinct voice; "we must part at once."

"We *can't* part, Maggie," said Stephen, more impetuously. "I can't bear it. What is the use of inflicting that misery on me? the blow—whatever it may have been—has been struck now. Will it help any one else that you should drive me mad?"

"I will not begin any future, even for you," said Maggie, tremulously, "with a deliberate consent to what ought not to have been. What I told you at Basset I feel now: I would rather have died than fall into this temptation. It would have been better if we had parted for ever then. But we must part now."

"We will *not* part," Stephen burst out, instinctively placing his back against the door—forgetting everything he had said a few moments before; "I will not endure it. You'll make me desperate—I shan't know what I do."

Maggie trembled. She felt that the parting could not be effected suddenly. She must rely on a slower appeal to Stephen's better self—she must be prepared for a harder task than that of rushing away while resolution was fresh. She sat down. Stephen, watching her with that look of desperation which had come over him like a lurid light, approached slowly from the door, seated himself close beside her, and grasped her hand. Her heart beat like the heart of a frightened bird; but this direct opposition helped her. She felt her determination growing stronger.

"Remember what you felt weeks ago," she began, with beseeching earnestness—"remember what we both felt—that we owed ourselves to others, and must conquer every inclination which could make us false to that debt. We have failed to keep our resolutions; but the wrong remains the same."

"No, it does *not* remain the same," said Stephen. "We have proved that it was impossible to keep our resolutions. We have proved that the feeling which draws us towards each other is too strong to be overcome: that natural law surmounts every other; we can't help what it clashes with."

"It is not so, Stephen—I'm quite sure that is wrong. I have tried to think it again and again; but I see, if we judged in that way, there would be a warrant for all treachery and cruelty—we should justify breaking the most sacred ties that can ever be formed on earth. If the past is not to bind us, where can duty lie? We should have no law but the inclination of the moment."

"But there are ties that can't be kept by mere resolution," said Stephen, starting up and walking about again. "What is outward faithfulness? Would they have thanked us for anything so hollow as constancy without love?"

Maggie did not answer immediately. She was undergoing an inward as well as an outward contest. At last she said, with a passionate assertion of her conviction, as much against herself as against him—

"That seems right—at first; but when I look further, I'm sure it is *not* right. Faithfulness and constancy mean something else besides doing what is easiest and pleasantest to ourselves. They mean renouncing whatever is opposed to the reliance others have in us—whatever would cause misery to those whom the course of our lives has made dependent on us. If we—if I had been better, nobler, those claims would have been so strongly present with me—I should have felt them pressing on my heart so continually, just as they do now in the moments when my conscience is awake—that the opposite feeling would never have grown in me, as it has done: it would have been quenched at once—I should have prayed for help so earnestly—I should have rushed away as we rush from hideous danger. I feel no excuse for myself—none. I should never have failed towards Lucy and Philip as I have done, if I had not been weak, selfish, and hard—able to think of their pain without a pain to myself that would have destroyed all temptation. O, what is Lucy feeling now? She believed in me—she loved me—she was so good to me. Think of her. . . ."

Maggie's voice was getting choked as she uttered these last words.

"I *can't* think of her," said Stephen, stamping as if with pain. "I can think of nothing but you, Maggie. You demand of a man what is impossible. I felt that once; but I can't go back to it now. And where is the use of *your* thinking of it, except to torture me? You can't save them from pain now; you can only tear yourself from me, and make my life worthless to me. And even if we could go back, and both fulfil our engagements—if that were possible now—it would be hateful—horrible, to think of your ever being Philip's wife—of your ever being the wife of a man you didn't love. We have both been rescued from a mistake."

A deep flush came over Maggie's face, and she couldn't speak. Stephen saw this. He sat down again, taking her hand in his, and looking at her with passionate entreaty.

"Maggie! Dearest! If you love me, you are mine. Who can have so great a claim on you as I have? My life is bound up in your love. There is nothing in the past that can annul our right to each other: it is the first time we have either of us loved with our whole heart and soul."

Maggie was still silent for a little while—looking down. Stephen was in a flutter of new hope: he was going to triumph. But she raised her eyes and met his with a glance that was filled with the anguish of regret—not with yielding.

"No—not with my whole heart and soul, Stephen," she said, with timid resolution. "I have never consented to it with my whole mind. There are memories, and affections, and longings after perfect goodness, that have such a strong hold on me; they would never quit me for long; they would come back and be pain to me—repentance. I couldn't live in peace if I put the shadow of a wilful sin between myself and God. I have caused sorrow already—I know—I feel it; but I have never deliberately consented to it: I have never said, 'They shall suffer, that I may have joy.' It has never been my will to marry you: if you were to win consent from the momentary triumph of my feeling for you, you would not have my whole soul. If I could wake back again into the time before yesterday, I would choose to be true to my calmer affections, and live without the joy of love."

Stephen loosed her hand, and, rising impatiently, walked up and down the room in suppressed rage.

"Good God!" he burst out, at last, "what a miserable thing a woman's love is to a man's! I could commit crimes for you—and you can balance and choose in that way. But you *don't* love me: if you had a tithe of the feeling for me that I have for you, it would be impossible to you to think for a moment of sacrificing me. But it weighs nothing with you that you are robbing me of *my* life's happiness."

Maggie pressed her fingers together almost convulsively as she held them clasped on her lap. A great terror was upon her, as if she were ever and anon seeing where she stood by great flashes of lightning, and then again stretched forth her hands in the darkness.

"No—I don't sacrifice you—I couldn't sacrifice you," she said, as soon as she could speak again; "but I can't believe in a good for you, that I feel—that we both feel is a wrong towards others. We can't choose happiness either for ourselves or for another: we can't tell where that will lie. We can only choose whether we will indulge ourselves in the present moment, or whether we will renounce that, for the sake of obeying the divine voice within us—for the sake of being true to all the motives that sanctify our lives. I know this belief is hard: it has slipped away from me again and again; but I have felt that if I let it go for ever, I should have no light through the darkness of this life."

"But, Maggie," said Stephen, seating himself by her again, "is it possible you don't see that what happened yesterday has altered the whole position of things? What infatuation is it—what obstinate prepossession that blinds you to that? It is too late to say what we might have done or what we ought to have done. Admitting the very worst view of what has been done, it is a fact we must act on now; our position is altered; the right course is no longer what it was before. We must accept our own actions and start afresh from them. Suppose we had been married yesterday? It is nearly the same thing. The effect on others would not have been different. It would only have made this difference to ourselves," Stephen added, bitterly, "that you might have acknowledged then that your tie to me was stronger than to others."

Again a deep flush came over Maggie's face, and she was silent. Stephen thought again that he was beginning to prevail—he had never yet believed that he should *not* prevail: there are possibilities which our minds shrink from too completely for us to fear them.

"Dearest," he said, in his deepest, tenderest tone, leaning towards her, and putting his arm round her, "you *are* mine now—the world believes it—duty must spring out of that now: in a few hours you will be legally mine, and those who had claims on us will submit—they will see that there was a force which declared against their claims."

Maggie's eyes opened wide in one terrified look at the face that was close to hers, and she started up—pale again.

"O, I can't do it," she said, in a voice almost of agony—"Stephen—don't ask me—don't urge me. I can't argue any longer—I don't know what is wise; but my heart will not let me do it. I see—I feel their trouble now: it is as if it were branded on my mind. *I* have suffered, and had no one to pity me; and now I have made others suffer. It would never leave me; it would embitter your love to me. I *do* care for Philip—in a different way: I remember all we said to each other; I know how he thought of me as the one promise of his life. He was given to me that I might make his lot less hard; and I have forsaken him. And Lucy—she has been deceived—she who trusted me more than any one.

I cannot marry you: I cannot take a good for myself that has been wrung out of their misery. It is not the force that ought to rule us—this that we feel for each other; it would rend me away from all that my past life has made dear and holy to me. I can't set out on a fresh life, and forget that: I must go back to it, and cling to it, else I shall feel as if there were nothing firm beneath my feet."

"Good God, Maggie!" said Stephen, rising too and grasping her arm, "you rave. How can you go back without marrying me? You don't know what will be said, dearest. You see nothing as it really is."

"Yes, I do. But they will believe me. I will confess everything. Lucy will believe me—she will forgive you, and—and—O, *some* good will come by clinging to the right. Dear, dear Stephen, let me go!—don't drag me into deeper remorse. My whole soul has never consented—it does not consent now."

Stephen let go her arm, and sank back on his chair, half stunned by despairing rage. He was silent a few moments, not looking at her; while her eyes were turned towards him yearningly, in alarm at this sudden change. At last he said, still without looking at her—

"Go, then—leave me—don't torture me any longer—I can't bear it."

Involuntarily she leaned towards him and put out her hand to touch his. But he shrank from it as if it had been burning iron, and said again—

"Leave me."

Maggie was not conscious of a decision as she turned away from that gloomy averted face, and walked out of the room: it was like an automatic action that fulfils a forgotten intention. What came after? A sense of stairs descended as if in a dream—of flagstones—of a chaise and horses standing—then a street, and a turning into another street where a stage-coach was standing, taking in passengers—and the darting thought that that coach would take her away, perhaps towards home. But she could ask nothing yet; she only got into the coach.

Home—where her mother and brother were—Philip—Lucy—the scene of her very cares and trials—was the haven towards which her mind tended—the sanctuary where sacred relics lay—where she would be rescued from more falling. The thought of Stephen was like a horrible throbbing pain, which yet, as such pains do, seemed to urge all other thoughts into activity. But among her thoughts, what others would say and think of her conduct was hardly present. Love and deep pity and remorseful anguish left no room for that.

The coach was taking her to York—farther away from home; but she did not learn that until she was set down in the old city at midnight. It was no matter: she could sleep there, and start home the next day. She had her purse in her pocket, with all her money in it—a bank-note and a sovereign: she had kept it in her pocket from forgetfulness, after going out to make purchases the day before yesterday.

Did she lie down in the gloomy bedroom of the old inn that night with her will bent unwaveringly on the path of penitent sacrifice? The great struggles of life are not so easy as that; the great problems of life are not so clear. In the darkness of that night she saw Stephen's face turned towards her in passionate, reproachful misery; she lived through again all the tremulous delights of his presence with her that made existence an easy floating in a stream of joy, instead of a quiet resolved endurance and effort. The love she had renounced came back upon her with a cruel charm, she felt herself opening her arms to receive it once more; and then it seemed to slip away and fade and vanish, leaving only the dying sound of a deep thrilling voice that said, "Gone—for ever gone."

Book Seventh

THE FINAL RESCUE

Chapter I

The Return to the Mill

Between four and five o'clock on the afternoon of the fifth day from that on which Stephen and Maggie had left St Ogg's, Tom Tulliver was standing on the gravel-walk outside the old house at Dorlcote Mill. He was master there now: he had half-fulfilled his father's dying wish, and by years of steady self-government and energetic work he had brought himself near to the attainment of more than the old respectability which had been the proud inheritance of the Dodsons and Tullivers.

But Tom's face, as he stood in the hot still sunshine of that summer afternoon, had no gladness, no triumph in it. His mouth wore its bitterest expression, his severe brow its hardest and deepest fold, as he drew down his hat farther over his eyes to shelter them from the sun, and, thrusting his hands deep into his pockets, began to walk up and down the gravel. No news of his sister had been heard since Bob Jakin had come back in the steamer from Mudport, and put an end to all improbable suppositions of an accident on the water by stating that he had seen her land from a vessel with Mr Stephen Guest. Would the next news be that she was married—or what? Probably that she was not married: Tom's mind was set to the expectation of the worst that could happen—not death, but disgrace.

As he was walking with his back towards the entrance gate, and his face towards the rushing mill-stream, a tall dark-eyed figure, that we know well, approached the gate, and paused to look at him, with a fast-beating heart. Her brother was the human being of whom she had been most afraid, from her childhood upwards: afraid with that fear which springs in us when we love one who is inexorable, unbending, unmodifiable—with a mind that we can never mould ourselves upon, and yet that we cannot endure to alienate from us. That deep-rooted fear was shaking Maggie now; but her mind was unswervingly bent on returning to her brother, as the natural refuge that had been given her.

In her deep humiliation under the retrospect of her own weakness—in her anguish at the injury she had inflicted—she almost desired to endure the severity of Tom's reproof, to submit in patient silence to that harsh disapproving judgment against which she had so often rebelled: it seemed no more than just to her now—who was weaker than she was? She craved that outward help to her better purpose which would come from complete, submissive confession—from being in the presence of those whose looks and words would be a reflection of her own conscience.

Maggie had been kept on her bed at York for a day with that prostrating headache which was likely to follow on the terrible strain of the previous day and night. There was an expression of physical pain still about her brow and eyes, and her whole appearance, with her dress so long unchanged, was worn and distressed. She lifted the latch of the gate and walked in—slowly. Tom did not hear the gate; he was just then close upon the roaring dam: but he presently turned, and, lifting up his eyes, saw the figure whose worn look and loneliness seemed to him a confirmation of his worst conjectures. He paused, trembling and white with disgust and indignation.

Maggie paused too—three yards before him. She felt the hatred in his face: felt it rushing through her fibres; but she must speak.

"Tom," she began, faintly, "I am come back to you—I am come back home—for refuge—to tell you everything."

"You will find no home with me," he answered, with tremulous rage. "You have disgraced us all. You have disgraced my father's name. You have been a curse to your best friends. You have been base—deceitful; no motives are strong enough to restrain you. I wash my hands of you for ever. You don't belong to me."

Their mother had come to the door now. She stood paralysed by the double shock of seeing Maggie and hearing Tom's words.

"Tom," said Maggie, with more courage, "I am perhaps not so guilty as you believe me to be. I never meant to give way to my feelings. I struggled against them. I was carried too far in the boat to come back on Tuesday. I came back as soon as I could."

"I can't believe in you any more," said Tom, gradually passing from the tremulous excitement of the first moment to cold inflexibility. "You have been carrying on a clandestine relation with Stephen Guest—as you did before with another. He went to see you at my aunt Moss's; you walked alone with him in the lanes; you must have behaved as no modest girl would have done to her cousin's lover, else that could never have happened. The people at Luckreth saw you pass—you passed all the other places; you knew what you were doing. You have been using Philip Wakem as a screen to deceive Lucy—the kindest friend you ever had. Go and see the return you have made her: she's ill—unable to speak—my mother can't go near her, lest she should remind her of *you*."

Maggie was half stunned—too heavily pressed upon by her anguish even to discern any difference between her actual guilt and her brother's accusations, still less to vindicate herself.

"Tom," she said, crushing her hands together under her cloak, in the effort to speak again. "Whatever I have done, I repent it bitterly. I want to make amends. I will endure anything. I want to be kept from doing wrong again."

"What *will* keep you?" said Tom, with cruel bitterness. "Not religion; not your natural feelings of gratitude and honour. And he—he would deserve to be shot, if it were not——But you are ten times worse than he is. I loathe your character and your conduct. You struggled with your feelings, you say. Yes! *I* have had feelings to struggle with; but I conquered them. I have had a harder life than you have had; but I have found *my* comfort in doing my duty. But I will sanction no such character as yours: the world shall know that *I* feel the difference between right and wrong. If you are in want, I will provide for you—let my mother know. But you shall not come under my roof. It is enough that I have to bear the thought of your disgrace: the sight of you is hateful to me."

Slowly Maggie was turning away with despair in her heart. But the poor frightened mother's love leaped out now, stronger than all dread.

"My child! I'll go with you. You've got a mother."

O the sweet rest of that embrace to the heart-stricken Maggie! More helpful than all wisdom is one draught of simple human pity that will not forsake us.

Tom turned and walked into the house.

"Come in, my child," Mrs Tulliver whispered. "He'll let you stay and sleep in my bed. He won't deny that, if I ask him."

"No, mother," said Maggie, in a low tone, like a moan. "I will never go in."

"Then wait for me outside. I'll get ready and come with you."

When his mother appeared with her bonnet on, Tom came out to her in the passage, and put money into her hands.

"My house is yours, mother, always," he said. "You will come and let me know everything you want—you will come back to me."

Poor Mrs Tulliver took the money, too frightened to say anything. The only thing clear to her was the mother's instinct, that she would go with her unhappy child.

Maggie was waiting outside the gate; she took her mother's hand, and they walked a little way in silence.

"Mother," said Maggie, at last, "we will go to Luke's cottage. Luke will take me in. He was very good to me when I was a little girl."

"He's got no room for us, my dear, now; his wife's got so many children. I don't know where to go, if it isn't to one o' your aunts; and I hardly durst," said poor Mrs Tulliver, quite destitute of mental resources in this extremity.

Maggie was silent a little while, and then said—

"Let us go to Bob Jakin's, mother: his wife will have room for us, if they have no other lodger."

So they went on their way to St Ogg's—to the old house by the riverside.

Bob himself was at home, with a heaviness at heart which resisted even the new joy and pride of possessing a two months' old baby, quite the liveliest of its age that had ever been born to prince or packman. He would perhaps not so thoroughly have understood all the dubiousness of Maggie's appearance with Mr Stephen Guest on the quay at Mudport, if he had not witnessed the effect it produced on Tom when he went to report it; and since then, the circumstances which in any case gave a disastrous character to her elopement, had passed beyond the more polite circles of St Ogg's, and had become matter of common talk, accessible to the grooms and errand-boys. So that when he opened the door and saw Maggie standing before him in her sorrow and weariness, he had no questions to ask, except one, which he dared only ask himself, Where was Mr Stephen Guest? Bob, for his part, hoped he might be in the warmest department of an asylum understood to exist in the other world for gentlemen who are likely to be in fallen circumstances there.

The lodgings were vacant, and both Mrs Jakin the larger and Mrs Jakin the less were commanded to make all things comfortable for "the old Missis and the young Miss"—alas! that she was still "Miss." The ingenious Bob was sorely perplexed as to how this result could have come about—how Mr Stephen Guest could have gone away from her, or could have let her go away from him, when he had the chance of keeping her with him. But he was silent, and would not allow his wife to ask him a question; would not present himself in the room, lest it should appear like intrusion and a wish to pry; having the same chivalry towards dark-eyed Maggie, as in the days when he had bought her the memorable present of books.

But after a day or two Mrs Tulliver was gone to the Mill again for a few hours to see to Tom's household matters. Maggie had wished this: after the first violent outburst of feeling, which came as soon as she had no longer any active purpose to fulfil, she was less in need of her mother's presence; she even desired to be alone with her grief. But she had been solitary only a little while in the old sitting-room that looked on the river, when there came a tap at the door, and turning round her sad face as she said, "Come in," she saw Bob enter with the baby in his arms and Mumps at his heels.

"We'll go back, if it disturbs you, Miss," said Bob.

"No," said Maggie, in a low voice, wishing she could smile.

Bob, closing the door behind him, came and stood before her.

"You see, we've got a little un, Miss, and I wanted you to look at it, and take it in your arms, if you'd be so good. For we made free to name it after you, and it 'ud be better for your takin' a bit o' notice on it."

Maggie could not speak, but she put out her arms to receive the tiny baby, while Mumps snuffed at it anxiously, to ascertain that this transference was all right. Maggie's heart had swelled at this action and speech of Bob's: she knew well enough that it was a way he had chosen to show his sympathy and respect.

"Sit down, Bob," she said presently, and he sat down in silence, finding his tongue unmanageable in quite a new fashion, refusing to say what he wanted it to say.

"Bob," she said, after a few moments, looking down at the baby, and holding it anxiously, as if she feared it might slip from her mind and her fingers, "I have a favour to ask of you."

"Don't you speak so, Miss," said Bob, grasping the skin of Mumps's neck; "if there's anything I can do for you, I should look upon it as a day's earnings."

"I want you to go to Dr Kenn's, and ask to speak to him, and tell him that I am here, and should be very grateful if he would come to me while my mother is away. She will not come back till evening."

"Eh, Miss—I'd do it in a minute—it is but a step; but Dr Kenn's wife lies dead—she's to be buried to-morrow—died the day I come from Mudport. It's all the more pity she should ha' died just now, if you want him. I hardly like to go a-nigh him yet."

"O, no, Bob," said Maggie, "we must let it be—till after a few days, perhaps—when you hear that he is going about again. But perhaps he may be going out of town—to a distance," she added, with a new sense of despondency at this idea.

"Not he, Miss," said Bob. "*He'll* none go away. He isn't one o' them gentlefolks as go to cry at waterin'-places when their wives die: he's got summat else to do. He looks fine an' sharp after the parish—he does. He christened the little un, an' he was *at* me to know what I did of a Sunday, as I didn't come to church. But I told him I was upo' the travel three parts o' the Sundays—an' then I'm so used to bein' on my legs, I can't sit so long on end—'an' lors, sir,' says I, 'a packman can do wi' a small 'lowance o' church: it tastes strong,' says I; 'there's no call to lay it on thick.' Eh, Miss, how good the little un is wi' you! It's like as if it knowed you: it partly does, I'll be bound—like the birds know the mornin'."

Bob's tongue was now evidently loosed from its unwonted bondage, and might even be in danger of doing more work than was required of it. But the subjects on which he longed to be informed were so steep and difficult of approach, that his tongue was likely to run on along the level rather than to carry him on that unbeaten road. He felt this, and was silent again for a little while, ruminating much on the possible forms in which he might put a question. At last he said, in a more timid voice than usual,—

"Will you give me leave to ask you only one thing, Miss?"

Maggie was rather startled, but she answered, "Yes, Bob, if it is about myself—not about any one else."

"Well, Miss, it's this: *Do* you owe anybody a grudge?"

"No, not any one," said Maggie, looking up at him inquiringly. "Why?"

"O, lors, Miss," said Bob, pinching Mumps's neck harder than ever, "I wish you did—an' 'ud tell me—I'd leather him till I couldn't see—I would—an' the Justice might do what he liked to me arter."

"O, Bob," said Maggie, smiling faintly, "you're a very good friend to me. But I shouldn't like to punish any one, even if they'd done me wrong; I've done wrong myself too often."

This view of things was puzzling to Bob, and threw more obscurity than ever over what could possibly have happened between Stephen and Maggie. But further questions would have been too intrusive, even if he could have framed them suitably, and he was obliged to carry baby away again to an expectant mother.

"Happen you'd like Mumps for company, Miss," he said when he had taken the baby again. "He's rare company—Mumps is—he knows iverything, an' makes no bother about it. If I tell him, he'll lie before you an' watch you—as still—just as he watches my pack. You'd better let me leave him a bit; he'll get fond on you. Lors, it's a fine thing to hev a dumb brute fond on you; it'll stick to you, an' make no jaw."

"Yes, do leave him, please," said Maggie. "I think I should like to have Mumps for a friend."

"Mumps, lie down there," said Bob, pointing to a place in front of Maggie, "an' niver do you stir till you're spoke to."

Mumps lay down at once, and made no sign of restlessness when his master left the room.

Chapter II

St Ogg's Passes Judgment

It was soon known throughout St Ogg's that Miss Tulliver was come back: she had not, then, eloped in order to be married to Mr Stephen Guest—at all events, Mr Stephen Guest had not married her—which came to the same thing, so far as her culpability was concerned. We judge others according to results; how else?—not knowing the process by which results are arrived at. If Miss Tulliver, after a few months of well-chosen travel, had returned as Mrs Stephen Guest—with a post-marital *trousseau*, and all the advantages possessed even by the most unwelcome wife of an only son, public opinion, which at St Ogg's, as elsewhere, always knew what to think, would have judged in strict consistency with those results. Public opinion, in these cases, is always of the feminine gender—not the world, but the world's wife: and she would have seen, that two handsome young people—the gentleman of quite the first family in St Ogg's—having found themselves in a false position, had been led into a course which, to say the least of it, was highly injudicious, and productive of sad pain and disappointment, especially to that sweet young thing, Miss Deane. Mr Stephen Guest had certainly not behaved well; but then, young men were liable to those sudden infatuated attachments; and bad as it might seem in Mrs Stephen Guest to admit the faintest advances from her cousin's lover (indeed it *had* been said that she was actually engaged to young Wakem—old Wakem himself had mentioned it), still she was very young—"and a deformed young man, you know!—and young Guest so very fascinating; and, they say, he positively worships her (to be sure, that can't last!) and he ran away with her in the boat quite against her will—and what could she do? She couldn't come back then: no one would have spoken to her; and how very well that maize-coloured satinette becomes her complexion! It seems as if the folds in front were quite come in; several of her dresses are made so;—they say he thinks nothing too handsome to buy for her. Poor Miss Deane! She is very pitiable; but then, there was no positive engagement; and the air at the coast will do her good. After all, if young Guest felt no more for her than *that*, it was better for her not to marry him. What a wonderful marriage for a girl like Miss Tulliver—quite romantic! Why, young Guest will put up for the borough at the next election. Nothing like commerce nowadays! That young Wakem nearly went out of his mind—he always *was* rather queer; but he's gone abroad again to be out of the way—quite the best thing for a deformed young man. Miss Unit declares she will never visit Mr and Mrs Stephen Guest—such nonsense! pretending to be better than other people. Society couldn't be carried on if we inquired into private conduct in that way—and Christianity tells us to think no evil—and my belief is, that Miss Unit had no cards sent her."

But the results, we know, were not of a kind to warrant this extenuation of the past. Maggie had returned without a *trousseau*, without a husband—in that degraded and outcast condition to which error is well known to lead; and the world's wife, with that fine instinct which is given her for the preservation of Society, saw at once that Miss Tulliver's conduct had been of the most aggravated kind. Could anything be more detestable? A girl so much indebted to her friends—whose mother as well as herself had received so much kindness from the Deanes—to lay the design of winning a young man's affections away from her own cousin, who had behaved like a sister to her! Winning his affections? That was not the phrase for such a girl as Miss Tulliver: it would have been more correct to say that she had been actuated by mere unwomanly boldness and unbridled passion. There was always something questionable about her. That connection with young Wakem, which, they said, had been carried on for years, looked very ill—disgusting, in fact! But with a girl of that disposition!—To the world's wife there had always been something in Miss Tulliver's very physique that a refined instinct felt to be prophetic of harm. As for poor Mr Stephen Guest, he was rather pitiable than otherwise: a young man of five-and-twenty is not to be too severely judged in these cases—he is really very much at the mercy of a designing bold girl. And it was clear that he had given way in spite of himself: he had shaken her off as soon as he could; indeed, their having parted so soon looked very black indeed—*for her*. To be sure, he had written a letter, laying all the blame on himself, and telling the story in a romantic fashion so as to try and make her appear quite innocent: of course he would do that! But the refined instinct of the world's wife was not to be deceived: providentially!—else what would become of Society? Why, her own brother had turned her from his door: he had seen enough, you might be sure, before he would do that. A truly respectable young man—Mr Tom Tulliver: quite likely to rise in the world! His sister's disgrace was naturally a heavy blow to him. It was to be hoped that she would go out of the neighbourhood—to America, or anywhere—so as to purify the air of St Ogg's from the taint of her presence, extremely dangerous to daughters there! No good could happen to her: it was only to be hoped she would repent, and that God would have mercy on her: He had not the care of Society on His hands—as the world's wife had.

It required nearly a fortnight for fine instinct to assure itself of these inspirations; indeed, it was a whole week before Stephen's letter came, telling his father the facts, and adding that he was gone across to Holland—had drawn upon the agent at Mudport for money—was incapable of any resolution at present.

Maggie, all this while, was too entirely filled with a more agonising anxiety to spend any thought on the view that was being taken of her conduct by the world of St Ogg's: anxiety about Stephen—Lucy—Philip—beat on her poor heart in a hard, driving, ceaseless storm of mingled love, remorse, and pity. If she had thought of rejection and injustice at all, it would have seemed to her that they had done their worst—that she could hardly feel any stroke from them intolerable since the words she had heard from her brother's lips. Across all her anxiety for the loved and the injured, those words shot again and again, like a horrible pang that would have brought misery and dread even into a heaven of delights. The idea of ever recovering happiness never glimmered in her mind for a moment; it seemed as if every sensitive fibre in her were too entirely preoccupied by pain ever to vibrate again to another influence. Life stretched before her as one act of penitence, and all she craved, as she dwelt on her future lot, was something to guarantee her from more falling: her own weakness haunted her like a vision of hideous possibilities, that made no peace conceivable except such as lay in the sense of a sure refuge.

But she was not without practical intentions: the love of independence was too strong an inheritance and a habit for her not to remember that she must get her bread; and when other projects looked vague, she fell back on that of returning to her plain sewing, and so getting enough to pay for her lodging at Bob's. She meant to persuade her mother to return to the Mill by-and-by, and live with Tom again; and somehow or other she would maintain herself at St Ogg's. Dr Kenn would perhaps help her and advise her. She remembered his parting words at the bazaar. She remembered the momentary feeling of reliance that had sprung in her when he was talking with her, and she waited with yearning expectation for the opportunity of confiding everything to him. Her mother called every day at Mr Deane's to learn how Lucy was: the report was always sad—nothing had yet roused her from the feeble passivity which had come on with the first shock. But of Philip, Mrs Tulliver had learned nothing: naturally, no one whom she met would speak to her about what related to her daughter. But at last she summoned courage to go and see sister Glegg, who of course would know everything, and had been even to see Tom at the Mill in Mrs Tulliver's absence, though he had said nothing of what had passed on the occasion.

As soon as her mother was gone, Maggie put on her bonnet. She had resolved on walking to the Rectory and asking to see Dr Kenn: he was in deep grief—but the grief of another does not jar upon us in such circumstances. It was the first time she had been beyond the door since her return; nevertheless her mind was so bent on the purpose of her walk, that the unpleasantness of meeting people on the way, and being stared at, did not occur to her. But she had no sooner passed beyond the narrower streets which she had to thread from Bob's dwelling, than she became aware of unusual glances cast at her; and this consciousness made her hurry along nervously, afraid to look to right or left. Presently, however, she came full on Mrs and Miss Turnbull, old acquaintances of her family; they both looked at her strangely, and turned a little aside without speaking. All hard looks were pain to Maggie, but her self-reproach was too strong for resentment: no wonder they will not speak to me, she thought—they are very fond of Lucy. But now she knew that she was about to pass a group of gentlemen, who were standing at the door of the billiard-rooms, and she could not help seeing young Torry step out a little with his glass at his eye, and bow to her with that air of nonchalance which he might have bestowed on a friendly barmaid. Maggie's pride was too intense for her not to feel that sting, even in the midst of her sorrow; and for the first time the thought took strong hold of her that she would have other obloquy cast on her besides that which was felt to be due to her breach of faith towards Lucy. But she was at the Rectory now; there, perhaps, she would find something else than retribution. Retribution may come from any voice: the hardest, cruelest, most imbruted urchin at the street-corner can inflict it: surely help and pity are rarer things—more needful for the righteous to bestow.

She was shown up at once, after being announced, into Dr Kenn's study, where he sat amongst piled-up books, for which he had little appetite, leaning his cheek against the head of his youngest child, a girl of three. The child was sent away with the servant, and when the door was closed, Dr Kenn said, placing a chair for Maggie,—

"I was coming to see you, Miss Tulliver; you have anticipated me; I am glad you did."

Maggie looked at him with her childlike directness as she had done at the bazaar, and said, "I want to tell you everything." But her eyes filled fast with tears as she said it, and all the pent-up excitement of her humiliating walk would have its vent before she could say more.

"Do tell me everything," Dr Kenn said, with quiet kindness in his grave firm voice. "Think of me as one to whom a long experience has been granted, which may enable him to help you."

In rather broken sentences, and with some effort at first, but soon with the greater ease that came from a sense of relief in the confidence, Maggie told the brief story of a struggle that must be the beginning of a long sorrow. Only the day before, Dr Kenn had been made acquainted with the contents of Stephen's letter, and he had believed them at once, without the confirmation of Maggie's statement. That involuntary plaint of hers, "O, *I must go*," had remained with him as the sign that she was undergoing some inward conflict.

Maggie dwelt the longest on the feeling which had made her come back to her mother and brother, which made her cling to all the memories of the past. When she had ended, Dr Kenn was silent for some minutes: there was a difficulty on his mind. He rose, and walked up and down the hearth with his hands behind him. At last he seated himself again, and said, looking at Maggie—

"Your prompting to go to your nearest friends—to remain where all the ties of your life have been formed—is a true prompting, to which the Church in its original constitution and discipline responds—opening its arms to the penitent—watching over its children to the last—never abandoning them until they are hopelessly reprobate. And the Church ought to represent the feeling of the community, so that every parish should be a family knit together by Christian brotherhood under a spiritual father. But the ideas of discipline and Christian fraternity are entirely relaxed—they can hardly be said to exist in the public mind: they hardly survive except in the partial, contradictory form they have taken in the narrow communities of schismatics; and if I were not supported by the firm faith that the Church must ultimately recover the full force of that constitution which is alone fitted to human needs, I should often lose heart at observing the want of fellowship and sense of mutual responsibility among my own flock. At present everything seems tending towards the relaxation of ties—towards the substitution of wayward choice for the adherence to obligation, which has its roots in the past. Your conscience and your heart have given you true light on this point, Miss Tulliver; and I have said all this that you may know what my wish about you—what my advice to you—would be, if they sprang from my own feeling and opinion unmodified by counteracting circumstances."

Dr Kenn paused a little while. There was an entire absence of effusive benevolence in his manner; there was something almost cold in the gravity of his look and voice. If Maggie had not known that his benevolence was persevering in proportion to its reserve, she might have been chilled and frightened. As it was, she listened expectantly, quite sure that there would be some effective help in his words. He went on.

"Your inexperience of the world, Miss Tulliver, prevents you from anticipating fully the very unjust conceptions that will probably be formed concerning your conduct—conceptions which will have a baneful effect, even in spite of known evidence to disprove them."

"O, I do—I begin to see," said Maggie, unable to repress this utterance of her recent pain. "I know I shall be insulted: I shall be thought worse than I am."

"You perhaps do not yet know," said Dr Kenn, with a touch of more personal pity, "that a letter is come which ought to satisfy every one who has known anything of you, that you chose the steep and difficult path of a return to the right, at the moment when that return was most of all difficult."

"Oh—where is he?" said poor Maggie, with a flush and tremor that no presence could have hindered.

"He is gone abroad: he has written of all that passed to his father. He has vindicated you to the utmost; and I hope the communication of that letter to your cousin will have a beneficial effect on her."

Dr Kenn waited for her to get calm again before he went on.

"That letter, as I said, ought to suffice to prevent false impressions concerning you. But I am bound to tell you, Miss Tulliver, that not only the experience of my whole life, but my observation within the last three days, makes me fear that there is hardly any evidence which will save you from the painful effect of false imputations. The persons who are the most incapable of a conscientious struggle such as yours, are precisely those who will be likely to shrink from you; because they will not believe in your struggle. I fear your life here will be attended not only with much pain, but with many obstructions. For this reason—and for this only—I ask you to consider whether it will not perhaps be better for you to take a situation at a distance, according to your former intention. I will exert myself at once to obtain one for you."

"O, if I could but stop here!" said Maggie. "I have no heart to begin a strange life again. I should have no stay. I should feel like a lonely wanderer—cut off from the past. I have written to the lady who offered me a situation to excuse myself. If I remained here, I could perhaps atone in some way to Lucy—to others: I could convince them that I'm sorry. And," she added, with some of the old proud fire flashing out, "I will not go away because people say false things of me. They shall learn to retract them. If I must go away at last, because—because others wish it, I will not go now."

"Well," said Dr Kenn, after some consideration, "if you determine on that, Miss Tulliver, you may rely on all the influence my position gives me. I am bound to aid and countenance you by the very duties of my office as a parish priest. I will add, that personally I have a deep interest in your peace of mind and welfare."

"The only thing I want is some occupation that will enable me to get my bread and be independent," said Maggie. "I shall not want much. I can go on lodging where I am."

"I must think over the subject maturely," said Dr Kenn, "and in a few days I shall be better able to ascertain the general feeling. I shall come to see you: I shall bear you constantly in mind."

When Maggie had left him, Dr Kenn stood ruminating with his hands behind him, and his eyes fixed on the carpet, under a painful sense of doubt and difficulty. The tone of Stephen's letter, which he had read, and the actual relations of all the persons concerned, forced upon him powerfully the idea of an ultimate marriage between Stephen and Maggie as the least evil; and the impossibility of their proximity in St Ogg's on any other supposition, until after years of separation, threw an insurmountable prospective difficulty over Maggie's stay there. On the other hand, he entered with all the comprehension of a man who had known spiritual conflict, and lived through years of devoted service to his fellow-men, into that state of Maggie's heart and conscience which made the consent to the marriage a desecration to her: her conscience must not be tampered with: the principle on which she had acted was a safer guide than any balancing of consequences. His experience told him that intervention was too dubious a responsibility to be lightly incurred: the possible issue either of an endeavour to restore the former relations with Lucy and Philip, or of counselling submission to this irruption of a new feeling, was hidden in a darkness all the more impenetrable because each immediate step was clogged with evil.

The great problem of the shifting relation between passion and duty is clear to no man who is capable of apprehending it: the question whether the moment has come in which a man has fallen below the possibility of a renunciation that will carry any efficacy, and must accept the sway of a passion against which he had struggled as a trespass, is one for which we have no master-key that will fit all cases. The casuists[1] have become a byword of reproach; but their perverted spirit of minute discrimination was the shadow of a truth to which eyes and hearts are too often fatally sealed—the truth, that moral judgments must remain false and hollow, unless they are checked and enlightened by a perpetual reference to the special circumstances that mark the individual lot.

All people of broad, strong sense have an instinctive repugnance to the men of maxims; because such people early discern that the mysterious complexity of our life is not to be embraced by maxims, and that to lace ourselves up in formulas of that sort is to repress all the divine promptings and inspirations that spring from growing insight and sympathy. And the man of maxims is the popular representative of the minds that are guided in their moral judgment solely by general rules, thinking that these will lead them to justice by a ready-made patent method, without the trouble of exerting patience, discrimination, impartiality—without any care to assure themselves whether they have the insight that comes from a hardly-earned estimate of temptation, or from a life vivid and intense enough to have created a wide fellow-feeling with all that is human.

Chapter III

Showing That Old Acquaintances Are Capable of Surprising Us

When Maggie was at home again, her mother brought her news of an unexpected line of conduct in aunt Glegg. As long as Maggie had not been heard of, Mrs Glegg had half-closed her shutters and drawn down her blinds: she felt assured that Maggie was drowned: that was far more probable than that her niece and legatee should have done anything to wound the family honour in the tenderest point. When, at last, she learned from Tom that Maggie had come home, and gathered from him what was her explanation of her absence, she burst forth in severe reproof of Tom for admitting the worst of his sister until he was compelled. If you were not to stand by your "kin" as long as there was a shred of honour attributable to them, pray what were you to stand by? Lightly to admit conduct in one of your own family that would force you to alter your will, had never been the way of the Dodsons; and though Mrs Glegg had always augured ill of Maggie's future at a time when other people were perhaps less clear-sighted, yet fair-play was a jewel, and it was not for her own friends to help to rob the girl of her fair fame, and to cast her out from family shelter to the scorn of the outer world, until she had become unequivocally a family disgrace. The cir-

1. Those skilled in the science or doctrine of dealing with cases of conscience and resolving questions of right and wrong; often used pejoratively.

cumstances were unprecedented in Mrs Glegg's experience—nothing of that kind had happened among the Dodsons before; but it was a case in which her hereditary rectitude and personal strength of character found a common channel along with her fundamental ideas of clanship, as they did in her life-long regard to equity in money matters. She quarrelled with Mr Glegg, whose kindness, flowing entirely into compassion for Lucy, made him as hard in his judgment of Maggie as Mr Deane himself was; and, fuming against her sister Tulliver because she did not at once come to her for advice and help, shut herself up in her own room with Baxter's "Saints' Rest" from morning till night, denying herself to all visitors, till Mr Glegg brought from Mr Deane the news of Stephen's letter. Then Mrs Glegg felt that she had adequate fighting-ground—then she laid aside Baxter, and was ready to meet all comers. While Mrs Pullet could do nothing but shake her head and cry, and wish that cousin Abbot had died, or any number of funerals had happened rather than this, which had never happened before, so that there was no knowing how to act, and Mrs Pullet could never enter St Ogg's again, because "acquaintances" knew of it all,—Mrs Glegg only hoped that Mrs Wooll, or any one else, would come to her with their false tales about her own niece, and she would know what to say to that ill-advised person!

Again she had a scene of remonstrance with Tom, all the more severe in proportion to the greater strength of her present position. But Tom, like other immovable things, seemed only the more rigidly fixed under that attempt to shake him. Poor Tom! he judged by what he had been able to see; and the judgment was painful enough to himself. He thought he had the demonstration of facts observed through years by his own eyes which gave no warning of their imperfection, that Maggie's nature was utterly untrustworthy, and too strongly marked with evil tendencies to be safely treated with leniency: he would act on that demonstration at any cost; but the thought of it made his days bitter to him. Tom, like every one of us, was imprisoned within the limits of his own nature, and his education had simply glided over him, leaving a slight deposit of polish: if you are inclined to be severe on his severity, remember that the responsibility of tolerance lies with those who have the wider vision. There had arisen in Tom a repulsion towards Maggie that derived its very intensity from their early childish love in the time when they had clasped tiny fingers together, and their later sense of nearness in a common duty and a common sorrow: the sight of her, as he had told her, was hateful to him. In this branch of the Dodson family aunt Glegg found a stronger nature than her own—a nature in which family feeling had lost the character of clanship by taking on a doubly deep dye of personal pride. Mrs Glegg allowed that Maggie ought to be punished—she was not a woman to deny that—she knew what conduct was; but punished in proportion to the misdeeds proved against her, not to those which were cast upon her by people outside her own family, who might wish to show that their own kin were better.

"Your aunt Glegg scolded me so as niver was, my dear," said poor Mrs Tulliver, when she came back to Maggie, "as I didn't go to her before—she said it wasn't for her to come to me first. But she spoke like a sister, too: *having* she allays was, and hard to please—O dear!—but she's said the kindest word as has ever been spoke by you yet, my child. For she says, for all she's been so set again' having one extry in the house, and making extry spoons and things, and putting her about in her ways, you shall have a shelter in her house, if you'll go to her dutiful, and she'll uphold you against folks as say harm of you when they've no call. And I told her I thought you couldn't bear to see anybody but me, you were so beat down with trouble; but she said, '*I* won't throw ill words at her—there's them out o' th' family 'ull be ready enough to do that. But I'll give her good advice; an' she must be humble.' It's wonderful o' Jane; for I'm sure she used to throw everything I did wrong at me—if it was the raisin wine as turned out bad, or the pies too hot—or whativer it was."

"O mother," said poor Maggie, shrinking from the thought of all the contact her bruised mind would have to bear, "tell her I'm very grateful—I'll go to see her as soon as I can; but I can't see any one just yet, except Dr Kenn. I've been to him—he will advise me, and help me to get some occupation. I can't live with any one, or be dependent on them, tell aunt Glegg; I must get my own bread. But did you hear nothing of Philip—Philip Wakem? Have you never seen any one that has mentioned him?"

"No, my dear: but I've been to Lucy's, and I saw your uncle, and he says they got her to listen to the letter, and she took notice o' Miss Guest, and asked questions, and the doctor thinks she's on the turn to be better. What a world this is—what trouble, O dear! The law was the first beginning, an' it's gone from bad to worse, all of a sudden, just when the luck seemed on the turn." This was the first lamentation that Mrs Tulliver had let slip to Maggie, but old habit had been revived by the interview with sister Glegg.

"My poor, poor mother!" Maggie burst out, cut to the heart with pity and compunction, and throwing her arms round her mother's neck, "I was always naughty and troublesome to you. And now you might have been happy if it hadn't been for me."

"Eh, my dear," said Mrs Tulliver, leaning towards the warm young cheek; "I must put up wi' my children—I shall never have no more; and if they bring me bad luck, I must be fond on it—there's nothing else much to be fond on, for my furnitur' went long ago. And you'd got to be very good once; I can't think how it's turned out the wrong way so!"

Still two or three more days passed, and Maggie heard nothing of Philip; anxiety about him was becoming her predominant trouble, and she summoned courage at last to inquire about him of Dr Kenn, on his next visit to her. He did not even know if Philip was at home. The elder Wakem was made moody by an accumulation of annoyance: the disappointment in this young Jetsome, to whom, apparently, he was a good deal attached, had been followed close by the catastrophe to his son's hopes after he had done violence to his own strong feeling by conceding to them, and had incautiously mentioned this concession in St Ogg's —and he was almost fierce in his brusqueness when any one asked him a question about his son. But Philip could hardly have been ill, or it would have been known through the calling in of the medical man; it was probable that he was gone out of the town for a little while. Maggie sickened under this suspense, and her imagination began to live more and more persistently in what Philip was enduring. What did he believe about her?

At last Bob brought her a letter, without a post-mark, directed in a hand which she knew familiarly in the letters of her own name—a hand in which her name had been written long ago, in a pocket Shakespeare which she possessed. Her mother was in the room, and Maggie, in violent agitation, hurried up-stairs that she might read the letter in solitude. She read it with a throbbing brow.

"Maggie,—I believe in you—I know you never meant to deceive me—I know you tried to keep faith to me, and to all. I believed this before I had any other evidence of it than your own nature. The night after I last parted from you I suffered torments. I had seen what convinced me that you were not free; that there was another whose presence had a power over you which mine never possessed; but through all the suggestions—almost murderous suggestions—of rage and jealousy, my mind made its way to belief in your truthfulness. I was sure that you meant to cleave to me, as you had said; that you had rejected him; that you struggled to renounce him, for Lucy's sake and for mine. But I could see no issue that was not fatal for *you*; and that dread shut out the very thought of resignation. I foresaw that he would not relinquish you, and I believed then, as I believe now, that the strong attraction which drew you together proceeded only from one side of your characters, and belonged to that partial, divided action of our nature which makes half the tragedy of the human lot. I have felt the vibration of chords in your nature that I have continually felt the want of in his. But perhaps I am wrong; perhaps I feel about you as the artist does about the scene over which his soul has brooded with love: he would tremble to see it confided to other hands; he would never believe that it could bear for another all the meaning and the beauty it bears for him.

"I dared not trust myself to see you that morning; I was filled with selfish passion; I was shattered by a night of conscious delirium. I told you long ago that I had never been resigned even to the mediocrity of my powers: how could I be resigned to the loss of the one thing which had ever come to me on earth, with the promise of such deep joy as would give a new and blessed meaning to the foregoing pain—the promise of another self that would lift my aching affection into the divine rapture of an ever-springing, ever-satisfied want?

"But the miseries of that night had prepared me for what came before the next. It was no surprise to me. I was certain that he had prevailed on you to sacrifice everything to him, and I waited with equal certainty to hear of your marriage. I measured your love and his by my own. But I was wrong, Maggie. There is something stronger in you than your love for him.

"I will not tell you what I went through in that interval. But even in its utmost agony—even in those terrible throes that love must suffer before it can be disembodied of selfish desire—my love for you sufficed to withhold me from suicide, without the aid of any other motive. In the midst of my egoism, I yet could not bear to come like a death-shadow across the feast of your joy. I could not bear to forsake the world in which you still lived and might need me; it was part of the faith I had vowed to you—to wait and endure. Maggie, that is a proof of what I write now to assure you of—that no anguish I have had to bear on your account has been too heavy a price to pay for the new life into which I have entered in loving you. I want you to put aside all grief because of the grief you have caused me. I was nurtured in the sense of privation; I never expected happiness; and in knowing you, in loving you, I have had, and still have, what reconciles me to life. You have been to my affections what light, what colour is to my eyes—what music is to the inward ear; you have raised a dim unrest into a vivid consciousness. The new life I have found in caring for your joy and sorrow more than for what is directly my own, has transformed the spirit of rebellious murmuring into that willing endurance which is the birth of strong sympathy. I think nothing but such complete and intense love could have initiated me into that enlarged life which grows and grows by appropriating the life of others; for before, I was always dragged back from it by ever-present painful self-consciousness. I even think sometimes that this gift of transferred life which has come to me in loving you, may be a new power to me.

"Then—dear one—in spite of all, you have been the blessing of my life. Let no self-reproach weigh on you because of me. It is I who should rather reproach myself for having urged my feelings upon you, and hurried you into words that you have felt as fetters. You meant to be true to those words; you *have* been true. I can measure your sacrifice by what I have known in only one half-hour of your presence with me, when I dreamed that you might love me best. But, Maggie, I have no just claim on you for more than affectionate remembrance.

"For some time I have shrunk from writing to you, because I have shrunk even from the appearance of wishing to thrust myself before you, and so repeating my original error. But you will not misconstrue me. I know that we must keep apart for a long while; cruel tongues would force us apart, if nothing else did. But I shall not go away. The place where you are is the one where my mind must live, wherever I might travel. And remember that I am unchangeably yours: yours—not with selfish wishes, but with a devotion that excludes such wishes.

"God comfort you,—my loving, large-souled Maggie. If every one else has misconceived you, remember that you have never been doubted by him whose heart recognised you ten years ago.

"Do not believe any one who says I am ill, because I am not seen out of doors. I have only had nervous headaches—no worse than I have sometimes had them before. But the over-powering heat inclines me to be perfectly quiescent in the day-time. I am strong enough to obey any word which shall tell me that I can serve you by word or deed.

"Yours, to the last,

"Philip Wakem."

As Maggie knelt by the bed sobbing, with that letter pressed under her, her feelings again and again gathered themselves in a whispered cry, always in the same words:

"O God, is there any happiness in love that could make me forget *their* pain?"

Chapter IV

Maggie and Lucy

By the end of the week Dr Kenn had made up his mind that there was only one way in which he could secure to Maggie a suitable living at St Ogg's. Even with his twenty years' experience as a parish priest, he was aghast at the obstinate continuance of imputations against her in the face of evidence. Hitherto he had been rather more adored and appealed to than was quite agreeable to him; but now, in attempting to open the ears of women to reason, and their consciences to justice, on behalf of Maggie Tulliver, he suddenly found himself as powerless as he was aware he would have been if he had attempted to influence the shape of bonnets. Dr Kenn could not be contradicted; he was listened to in silence; but when he left the room, a comparison of opinions among his hearers yielded much the same result as before. Miss Tulliver had undeniably acted in a blamable manner; even Dr Kenn did not deny that: how, then, could he think so lightly of her as to put that favourable interpretation on everything she had done? Even on the supposition that required the utmost stretch of belief—namely, that none of the things said about Miss Tulliver were true—still, since they *had* been said about her, they had cast an odour round her which must cause her to be shrunk from by every woman who had to take care of her own reputation—and of Society. To have taken Maggie by the hand and said, "I will not believe unproved evil of you: my lips shall not utter it; my ears shall be closed against it; I, too, am an erring mortal, liable to stumble, apt to come short of my most earnest efforts; your lot has been harder than mine, your temptation greater; let us help each other to stand and walk without more falling;"—to have done this would have demanded courage, deep pity, self-knowledge, generous trust—would have demanded a mind that tasted no piquancy in evil-speaking, that felt no self-exaltation in condemning, that cheated itself with no large words into the belief that life can have any moral end, any high religion, which excludes the striving after perfect truth, justice, and love towards the individual men and women who come across our own path. The ladies of St Ogg's were not beguiled by any wide speculative conceptions; but they had their favourite abstraction, called Society, which served to make their consciences perfectly easy in doing what satisfied their own egoism—thinking and speaking the worst of Maggie Tulliver, and turning their backs upon her. It was naturally disappointing to Dr Kenn, after two years of superfluous incense from his feminine parishioners, to find them suddenly maintaining their views in opposition to his; but then, they maintained them in opposition to a Higher Authority, which they had venerated longer. That Authority had furnished a very explicit answer to persons who might inquire where their social duties began, and might be inclined to take wide views as to the starting-point. The answer had not turned on the ultimate good of Society, but on "a certain man" who was found in trouble by the wayside.[1]

Not that St Ogg's was empty of women with some tenderness of heart and conscience: probably it had as fair a proportion of human goodness in it as any other small trading town of that day. But until every good man is brave, we must expect to find many good women timid: too timid even to believe in the correctness of their own best promptings, when these would place them in a minority. And the men at St Ogg's were not all brave by any means: some of them were even fond of scandal—and to an extent that might have given their conversation an effeminate character, if it had not been distinguished by masculine jokes, and by an occasional shrug of the shoulders at the mutual hatred of women. It was the general feeling of the masculine mind at St Ogg's

1. A reference to the parable of the good Samaritan (Luke 10:29–37).

that women were not to be interfered with in their treatment of each other.

And thus every direction in which Dr Kenn had turned in the hope of procuring some kind recognition and some employment for Maggie, proved a disappointment to him. Mrs James Torry could not think of taking Maggie as a nursery governess, even temporarily—a young woman about whom "such things had been said," and about whom "gentlemen joked;" and Miss Kirke, who had a spinal complaint, and wanted a reader and companion, felt quite sure that Maggie's mind must be of a quality with which she, for her part, could not risk *any* contact. Why did not Miss Tulliver accept the shelter offered her by her aunt Glegg?—it did not become a girl like her to refuse it. Or else, why did she not go out of the neighbourhood, and get a situation where she was not known? (It was not, apparently, of so much importance that she should carry her dangerous tendencies into strange families unknown at St Ogg's.) She must be very bold and hardened to wish to stay in a parish where she was so much stared at and whispered about.

Dr Kenn, having great natural firmness, began, in the presence of this opposition, as every firm man would have done, to contract a certain strength of determination over and above what would have been called forth by the end in view. He himself wanted a daily governess for his younger children; and though he had hesitated in the first instance to offer this position to Maggie, the resolution to protest with the utmost force of his personal and priestly character against her being crushed and driven away by slander, was now decisive. Maggie gratefully accepted an employment that gave her duties as well as a support: her days would be filled now, and solitary evenings would be a welcome rest. She no longer needed the sacrifice her mother made in staying with her, and Mrs Tulliver was persuaded to go back to the Mill.

But now it began to be discovered that Dr Kenn, exemplary as he had hitherto appeared, had his crotchets—possibly his weaknesses. The masculine mind of St Ogg's smiled pleasantly, and did not wonder that Kenn liked to see a fine pair of eyes daily, or that he was inclined to take so lenient a view of the past; the feminine mind, regarded at that period as less powerful, took a more melancholy view of the case. If Dr Kenn should be beguiled into marrying that Miss Tulliver! It was not safe to be too confident, even about the best of men: an apostle had fallen, and wept bitterly afterwards; and though Peter's denial[2] was not a close precedent, his repentance was likely to be.

Maggie had not taken her daily walks to the Rectory for many weeks, before the dreadful possibility of her some time or other becoming the Rector's wife had been talked of so often in confidence, that ladies were beginning to discuss how they should behave to her in that position.

2. Of Christ (Luke 22:62).

For Dr Kenn, it had been understood, had sat in the schoolroom half an hour one morning, when Miss Tulliver was giving her lessons; nay, he had sat there every morning: he had once walked home with her—he almost *always* walked home with her—and if not, he went to see her in the evening. What an artful creature she was! What a *mother* for those children! It was enough to make poor Mrs Kenn turn in her grave, that they should be put under the care of this girl only a few weeks after her death. Would he be so lost to propriety as to marry her before the year was out? The masculine mind was sarcastic, and thought *not*.

The Miss Guests saw an alleviation to the sorrow of witnessing a folly in their Rector: at least their brother would be safe; and their knowledge of Stephen's tenacity was a constant ground of alarm to them, lest he should come back and marry Maggie. They were not among those who disbelieved their brother's letter; but they had no confidence in Maggie's adherence to her renunciation of him; they suspected that she had shrunk rather from the elopement than from the marriage, and that she lingered in St Ogg's, relying on his return to her. They had always thought her disagreeable; they now thought her artful and proud; having quite as good grounds for that judgment as you and I probably have for many strong opinions of the same kind. Formerly they had not altogether delighted in the contemplated match with Lucy, but now their dread of a marriage between Stephen and Maggie added its momentum to their genuine pity and indignation on behalf of the gentle forsaken girl, in making them desire that he should return to her. As soon as Lucy was able to leave home, she was to seek relief from the oppressive heat of this August by going to the coast with the Miss Guests; and it was in their plans that Stephen should be induced to join them. On the very first hint of gossip concerning Maggie and Dr Kenn, the report was conveyed in Miss Guest's letter to her brother.

Maggie had frequent tidings through her mother, or aunt Glegg, or Dr Kenn, of Lucy's gradual progress towards recovery, and her thoughts tended continually towards her uncle Deane's house: she hungered for an interview with Lucy, if it were only for five minutes—to utter a word of penitence, to be assured by Lucy's own eyes and lips that she did not believe in the willing treachery of those whom she had loved and trusted. But she knew that even if her uncle's indignation had not closed his house against her, the agitation of such an interview would have been forbidden to Lucy. Only to have seen her without speaking, would have been some relief; for Maggie was haunted by a face cruel in its very gentleness: a face that had been turned on hers with glad sweet looks of trust and love from the twilight time of memory; changed now to a sad and weary face by a first heart-stroke. And as the days passed on, that pale image became more and more distinct; the picture grew and grew into more speaking definiteness under the avenging hand of remorse; the soft hazel eyes, in their look of pain, were bent for ever on Maggie, and pierced her the more because she could see no anger in them. But Lucy was not yet able to go to church, or any place where Maggie could see her; and even the hope of that departed, when the news was told her by aunt Glegg, that Lucy was really going away in a few days to Scarborough with the Miss Guests, who had been heard to say that they expected their brother to meet them there.

Only those who have known what hardest inward conflict is, can know what Maggie felt as she sat in her loneliness the evening after hearing that news from Mrs Glegg—only those who have known what it is to dread their own selfish desires as the watching mother would dread the sleeping-potion that was to still her own pain.

She sat without candle in the twilight, with the window wide open towards the river; the sense of oppressive heat adding itself undistinguishably to the burthen of her lot. Seated on a chair against the window, with her arm on the window-sill, she was looking blankly at the flowing river, swift with the backward-rushing tide—struggling to see still the sweet face in its unreproaching sadness, that seemed now from moment to moment to sink away and be hidden behind a form that thrust itself between, and made darkness. Hearing the door open, she thought Mrs Jakin was coming in with her supper, as usual; and with that repugnance to trivial speech which comes with languor and wretchedness, she shrank from turning round and saying she wanted nothing: good little Mrs Jakin would be sure to make some well-meant remarks. But the next moment, without her having discerned the sound of a footstep, she felt a light hand on her shoulder, and heard a voice close to her saying, "Maggie!"

The face was there—changed, but all the sweeter: the hazel eyes were there, with their heart-piercing tenderness.

"Maggie!" the soft voice said. "Lucy!" answered a voice with a sharp ring of anguish in it; and Lucy threw her arms round Maggie's neck, and leaned her pale cheek against the burning brow.

"I stole out," said Lucy, almost in a whisper, while she sat down close to Maggie and held her hand, "when papa and the rest were away. Alice is come with me. I asked her to help me. But I must only stay a little while, because it is so late."

It was easier to say that at first than to say anything else. They sat looking at each other. It seemed as if the interview must end without more speech, for speech was very difficult. Each felt that there would be something scorching in the words that would recall the irretrievable wrong. But soon, as Maggie looked, every distinct thought began to be overflowed by a wave of loving penitence, and words burst forth with a sob.

"God bless you for coming, Lucy."

The sobs came thick on each other after that.

"Maggie, dear, be comforted," said Lucy now, putting her cheek against Maggie's again. "Don't grieve." And she sat still, hoping to soothe Maggie with that gentle caress.

"I didn't mean to deceive you, Lucy," said Maggie, as soon as she could speak. "It always made me wretched that I felt what I didn't like you to know. . . . It was because I thought it would all be conquered, and you might never see anything to wound you."

"I know, dear," said Lucy. "I know you never meant to make me unhappy. . . . It is a trouble that has come on us all: —you have more to bear than I have—and you gave him up, when . . . you did what it must have been very hard to do."

They were silent again a little while, sitting with clasped hands, and cheeks leaned together.

"Lucy," Maggie began again, "*he* struggled too. He wanted to be true to you. He will come back to you. Forgive him—he will be happy then. . . ."

These words were wrung forth from Maggie's deepest soul, with an effort like the convulsed clutch of a drowning man. Lucy trembled and was silent.

A gentle knock came at the door. It was Alice, the maid, who entered and said—

"I daredn't stay any longer, Miss Deane. They'll find it out, and there 'll be such anger at your coming out so late."

Lucy rose and said, "Very well, Alice—in a minute."

"I'm to go away on Friday, Maggie," she added, when Alice had closed the door again. "When I come back, and am strong, they will let me do as I like. I shall come to you when I please then."

"Lucy," said Maggie, with another great effort, "I pray to God continually that I may never be the cause of sorrow to you any more."

She pressed the little hand that she held between hers, and looked up into the face that was bent over hers. Lucy never forgot that look.

"Maggie," she said, in a low voice, that had the solemnity of confession in it, "you are better than I am. I can't . . ."

She broke off there, and said no more. But they clasped each other again in a last embrace.

Chapter V

The Last Conflict

In the second week of September, Maggie was again sitting in her lonely room, battling with the old shadowy enemies that were for ever slain and rising again. It was past midnight, and the rain was beating heavily against the window, driven with fitful force by the rushing, loud-moaning wind. For, the day after Lucy's visit, there had been a sudden change in the weather: the heat and drought had given way to cold variable winds, and heavy falls of rain at intervals; and she had been forbidden to risk the contemplated journey until the weather should become more settled. In the counties higher up the Floss, the rains had been continuous, and the completion of the harvest had been arrested. And now, for the last two days, the rains on this lower course of the river had been incessant, so that the old men had shaken their heads and talked of sixty years ago, when the same sort of weather, happening about the equinox, brought on the great floods, which swept the bridge away, and reduced the town to great misery. But the younger generation, who had seen several small floods, thought lightly of these sombre recollections and forebodings; and Bob Jakin, naturally prone to take a hopeful view of his own luck, laughed at his mother when she regretted their having taken a house by the river-side; observing that but for that they would have had no boats, which were the most lucky of possessions in case of a flood that obliged them to go to a distance for food.

But the careless and the fearful were alike sleeping in their beds now. There was hope that the rain would abate by the morrow; threatenings of a worse kind, from sudden thaws after falls of snow, had often passed off in the experience of the younger ones; and at the very worst, the banks would be sure to break lower down the river when the tide came in with violence, and so the waters would be carried off, without causing more than temporary inconvenience, and losses that would be felt only by the poorer sort, whom charity would relieve.

All were in their beds now, for it was past midnight: all, except some solitary watchers such as Maggie. She was seated in her little parlour towards the river with one candle, that left everything dim in the room, except a letter which lay before her on the table. That letter which had come to her to-day, was one of the causes that had kept her up far on into the night—unconscious how the hours were going—careless of seeking rest—with no image of rest coming across her mind, except of that far, far off rest, from which there would be no more waking for her into this struggling earthly life.

Two days before Maggie received that letter, she had been to the Rectory for the last time. The heavy rain would have prevented her from going since; but there was another reason. Dr Kenn, at first enlightened only by a few hints as to the new turn which gossip and slander had taken in relation to Maggie, had recently been made more fully aware of it by an earnest remonstrance from one of his male parishioners against the indiscretion of persisting in the attempt to overcome the prevalent feeling in the parish by a course of resistance. Dr Kenn, having a conscience void of offence in the matter, was still inclined to persevere—was still averse to give way before a public sentiment that was odious and contemptible; but he was finally wrought upon by the consideration of the peculiar responsibility attached to his office, of avoiding the appearance of evil—an "appearance" that is always dependent on the average quality of surrounding minds. Where these minds are low and gross, the area of that "appearance" is proportionately widened. Perhaps he was in danger of acting from obstinacy; perhaps it was his duty to succumb: conscientious people are apt to see their duty in that which is the most painful course; and to recede was always painful to Dr Kenn. He made up his mind that he must advise Maggie to go away from St Ogg's for a time; and he performed that difficult task with as much delicacy as he could, only stating in vague terms that he found his attempt to countenance her stay was a source of discord between himself and his parishioners, that was likely to obstruct his usefulness as a clergyman. He begged her to allow him to write to a clerical friend of his, who might possibly take her into his own family as governess; and, if not, would probably know of some other available position for a young woman in whose welfare Dr Kenn felt a strong interest.

Poor Maggie listened with a trembling lip: she could say nothing but a faint "thank you—I shall be grateful;" and she walked back to her lodgings, through the driving rain, with a new sense of desolation. She must be a lonely wanderer; she must go out among fresh faces, that would look at her wonderingly, because the days did not seem joyful to her; she must begin a new life, in which she would have to rouse herself to receive new impressions—and she was so unspeakably, sickeningly weary! There was no home, no help for the erring: even those who pitied were constrained to hardness. But ought she to complain? Ought she to shrink in this way from the long penance of life, which was all the possibility she had of lightening the load to some other sufferers, and so changing that passionate error into a new force of unselfish human love? All the next day she sat in her lonely room, with a window darkened by the cloud and the driving rain, thinking of that future, and wrestling for patience:—for what repose could poor Maggie ever win except by wrestling?

And on the third day—this day of which she had just sat out the close—the letter had come which was lying on the table before her.

The letter was from Stephen. He was come back from Holland: he was at Mudport again, unknown to any of his friends; and had written to her from that place, enclosing the letter to a person whom he trusted in St Ogg's. From beginning to end it was a passionate cry of reproach: an appeal against her useless sacrifice of him—of herself: against that perverted notion of right which led her to crush all his hopes, for the sake of a mere idea, and not any substantial good—*his* hopes, whom she loved, and who loved her with that single overpowering passion, that worship, which a man never gives to a woman more than once in his life.

"They have written to me that you are to marry Kenn. As if I should believe that! Perhaps they have told you some such fables about me. Perhaps they tell you I have been 'travelling.' My body has been dragged about somewhere; but *I* have never travelled from the hideous place where you left me—where I started up from the stupor of helpless rage to find you gone.

"Maggie! whose pain can have been like mine? Whose injury is like mine? Who besides me has met that long look of love that has burnt itself into my soul, so that no other image can come there? Maggie, call me back to you!—call me back to life and goodness! I am banished from both now. I have no motives: I am indifferent to everything. Two months have only deepened the certainty that I can never care for life without you. Write me one word—say 'Come!' In two days I should be with you. Maggie—have you forgotten what it was to be together?—to be within reach of a look—to be within hearing of each other's voice?"

When Maggie first read this letter she felt as if her real temptation had only just begun. At the entrance of the chill dark cavern, we turn with unworn courage from the warm light; but how, when we have trodden far in the damp darkness, and have begun to be faint and weary—how, if there is a sudden opening above us, and we are invited back again to the life-nourishing day? The leap of natural longing from under the pressure of pain is so strong, that all less immediate motives are likely to be forgotten—till the pain has been escaped from.

For hours Maggie felt as if her struggle had been in vain. For hours every other thought that she strove to summon was thrust aside by the image of Stephen waiting for the single word that would bring him to her. She did not *read* the letter: she heard him uttering it, and the voice shook her with its old strange power. All the day before she had been filled with the vision of a lonely future through which she must carry the burthen of regret, upheld only by clinging faith. And here—close within her reach—urging itself upon her even as a claim—was another future, in which hard endurance and effort were to be exchanged for easy delicious leaning on another's loving strength! And yet that promise of joy in the place of sadness did not make the dire force of the temptation to Maggie. It was Stephen's tone of misery, it was the doubt in the justice of her own resolve, that made the balance tremble, and made her once start from her seat to reach the pen and paper, and write "Come!"

But close upon that decisive act, her mind recoiled; and the sense of contradiction with her past self in her moments of strength and clearness, came upon her like a pang of conscious degradation. No—she must wait; she must pray; the light that had forsaken her would come again: she should feel again what she had felt, when she had fled away, under an inspiration strong enough to conquer agony—to conquer love: she should feel again what she had felt when Lucy stood by her, when Philip's letter had stirred all the fibres that bound her to the calmer past.

She sat quite still, far on into the night: with no impulse to change her attitude, without active force enough even for the mental act of prayer: only waiting for the light that would surely come again. It came with the memories that no passion could long quench: the long past came back to her, and with it the fountains of self-renouncing pity and affection, of faithfulness and resolve. The words that were marked by the quiet hand in the little old book that she had long ago learned by heart, rushed even to her lips, and found a vent for themselves in a low murmur that was quite lost in the loud driving of the rain against the window and the loud moan and roar of the wind: "I have received the Cross, I have received it from Thy hand; I will bear it, and bear it till death, as Thou hast laid it upon me."

But soon other words rose that could find no utterance but in a sob: "Forgive me, Stephen! It will pass away. You will come back to her."

She took up the letter, held it to the candle, and let it burn slowly on the hearth. To-morrow she would write to him the last word of parting.

"I will bear it, and bear it till death. . . . But how long it will be before death comes! I am so young, so healthy. How shall I have patience and strength? Am I to struggle and fall and repent again?—has life other trials as hard for me still?"

With that cry of self-despair, Maggie fell on her knees against the table, and buried her sorrow-stricken face. Her soul went out to the Unseen Pity that would be with her to the end. Surely there was something being taught her by this experience of great need; and she must be learning a secret of human tenderness and long-suffering, that the less erring could hardly know? "O God, if my life is to be long, let me live to bless and comfort——"

At that moment Maggie felt a startling sensation of sudden cold about her knees and feet: it was water flowing under her. She started up: the stream was flowing under the door that led into the passage. She was not bewildered for an instant—she knew it was the flood!

The tumult of emotion she had been enduring for the last twelve hours seemed to have left a great calm in her: without screaming, she hurried with the candle up-stairs to Bob Jakin's bedroom. The door was ajar; she went in and shook him by the shoulder.

"Bob, the flood is come! it is in the house! let us see if we can make the boats safe."

She lighted his candle, while the poor wife, snatching up her baby, burst into screams; and then she hurried down again to see if the waters were rising fast. There was a step down into the room at the door leading from the staircase; she saw that the water was already on a level with the step. While she was looking, something came with a tremendous crash against the window, and sent the leaded panes and the old wooden frame-work inwards in shivers,—the water pouring in after it.

"It is the boat!" cried Maggie. "Bob, come down to get the boats!"

And without a moment's shudder of fear, she plunged through the water, which was rising fast to her knees, and by the glimmering light of the candle she had left on the stairs, she mounted on to the window-sill, and crept into the boat, which was left with the prow lodging and protruding through the window. Bob was not long after her, hurrying without shoes or stockings, but with the lanthorn in his hand.

"Why, they're both here—both the boats," said Bob, as he got into the one where Maggie was. "It's wonderful this fastening isn't broke too, as well as the mooring."

In the excitement of getting into the other boat, unfastening it, and mastering an oar, Bob was not struck with the danger Maggie incurred. We are not apt to fear for the fearless, when we are companions in their danger, and Bob's mind was absorbed in possible expedients for the safety of the helpless in-doors. The fact that Maggie had been up, had waked him, and had taken the lead in activity, gave Bob a vague impression of her as one who would help to protect, not need to be protected. She too had got possession of an oar, and had pushed off, so as to release the boat from the overhanging window-frame.

"The water's rising so fast," said Bob, "I doubt it 'll be in at the chambers before long—th' house is so low. I've more mind to get Prissy and the child and the mother into the boat, if I could, and trusten to the water—for th' old house is none so safe. And if I let go the boat . . . but *you*," he exclaimed, suddenly lifting the light of his lanthorn on Maggie, as she stood in the rain with the oar in her hand and her black hair streaming.

Maggie had no time to answer, for a new tidal current swept along the line of the houses, and drove both the boats out on to the wide water, with a force that carried them far past the meeting current of the river.

In the first moments Maggie felt nothing, thought of nothing, but that she had suddenly passed away from that life which she had been dreading: it was the transition of death, without its agony—and she was alone in the darkness with God.

The whole thing had been so rapid—so dream-like—that the threads of ordinary association were broken: she sank down on the seat clutching the oar mechanically, and for a long while had no distinct conception of her position. The first thing that waked her to fuller consciousness was the cessation of the rain, and a perception that the darkness was divided by the faintest light, which parted the overhanging gloom from the immeasurable watery level below. She was driven out upon the flood:—that awful visitation of God which her father used to talk of—which had made the nightmare of her childish dreams. And with that thought there rushed in the vision of the old home—and Tom—and her mother—they had all listened together.

"O God, where am I? Which is the way home?" she cried out, in the dim loneliness.

What was happening to them at the Mill? The flood had once nearly destroyed it. They might be in danger—in distress: her mother and her brother, alone there, beyond reach of help! Her whole soul was strained now on that thought; and she saw the long-loved faces looking for help into the darkness, and finding none.

She was floating in smooth water now—perhaps far on the over-flooded fields. There was no sense of present danger to check the outgoing of her mind to the old home; and she strained her eyes against the curtain of gloom that she might seize the first sight of her whereabout—that she might catch some faint suggestion of the spot towards which all her anxieties tended.

O how welcome, the widening of that dismal watery level—the gradual uplifting of the cloudy firmament—the slowly defining blackness of objects above the glassy dark! Yes—she must be out on the fields—those were the tops of hedgerow trees. Which way did the river lie? Looking behind her, she saw the lines of black trees: looking before her, there were none: then, the river lay before her. She seized an oar and began to paddle the boat forward with the energy of wakening hope: the dawning seemed to advance more swiftly, now she was in action; and she could soon see the poor dumb beasts crowding piteously on a mound where they had taken refuge. Onward she paddled and rowed by turns in the growing twilight: her wet clothes clung round her, and her streaming hair was dashed about by the wind, but she was hardly conscious of any bodily sensations—except a sensation of strength, inspired by mighty emotion. Along with the sense of danger and possible rescue for those long-remembered beings at the old home, there was an undefined sense of reconcilement with her brother: what quarrel, what harshness, what unbelief in each other can subsist in the presence of a great calamity, when all the artificial vesture of our life is gone, and we are all one with each other in primitive mortal needs? Vaguely, Maggie felt this;—in the strong resurgent love towards her brother that swept away all the later impressions of hard, cruel offence and misunderstanding, and left only the deep, underlying, unshakable memories of early union.

But now there was a large dark mass in the distance, and near to her Maggie could discern the current of the river. The dark mass must be—yes, it was—St Ogg's. Ah, now she knew which way to look for the first glimpse of the well-known trees—the grey willows, the now yellowing chestnuts—and above them the old roof! But there was no colour, no shape yet: all was faint and dim. More and more strongly the energies seemed to come and put themselves forth, as if her life were a stored-up force that was being spent in this hour, unneeded for any future.

She must get her boat into the current of the Floss, else she would never be able to pass the Ripple and approach the house: this was the thought that occurred to her, as she imagined with more and more vividness the state of things round the old home. But then she might be carried very far down, and be unable to guide her boat out of the current again. For the first time distinct ideas of danger began to press upon her; but there was no choice of courses, no room for hesitation, and she floated into the current. Swiftly she went now, without effort; more and more clearly in the lessening distance and the growing light she began to discern the objects that she knew must be the well-known trees and roofs; nay, she was not far off a rushing muddy current that must be the strangely altered Ripple.

Great God! there were floating masses in it, that might dash against her boat as she passed, and cause her to perish too soon. What were those masses?

For the first time Maggie's heart began to beat in an agony of dread. She sat helpless—dimly conscious that she was being floated along—more intensely conscious of the anticipated clash. But the horror was transient: it passed away before the on-coming warehouses of St Ogg's: she had passed the mouth of the Ripple, then: *now*, she must use all her skill and power to manage the boat and get it if possible out of the current. She could see now that the bridge was broken down: she could see the masts of a stranded vessel far out over the watery field. But no boats were to be seen moving on the river—such as had been laid hands on were employed in the flooded streets.

With new resolution, Maggie seized her oar, and stood up again to paddle; but the now ebbing tide added to the swiftness of the river, and she was carried along beyond the bridge. She could hear shouts from the windows overlooking the river, as if the people there were calling to her. It was not till she had passed on nearly to Tofton that she could get the boat clear of the current. Then with one yearning look towards her uncle Deane's house that lay farther down the river, she took to both her oars and rowed with all her might across the watery fields, back towards the Mill. Colour was beginning to awake now, and as she approached the Dorlcote fields, she could discern the tints of the trees—could see the old Scotch firs far to the right, and the home chestnuts—Oh! how deep they lay in the water: deeper than the trees on this side the hill. And the roof of the Mill—where was it? Those heavy fragments hurrying down the Ripple—what had they meant? But it was not the house—the house stood firm; drowned up to the first story, but still firm—or was it broken in at the end towards the Mill?

With panting joy that she was there at last—joy that overcame all distress—Maggie neared the front of the house. At first she heard no sound: she saw no object moving. Her boat was on a level with the upstairs windows. She called out in a loud piercing voice,

"Tom, where are you? Mother, where are you? Here is Maggie!"

Soon, from the window of the attic in the central gable, she heard Tom's voice:

"Who is it? Have you brought a boat?"

"It is I, Tom—Maggie. Where is mother?"

"She is not here: she went to Garum, the day before yesterday. I'll come down to the lower window."

"Alone, Maggie?" said Tom, in a voice of deep astonishment, as he opened the middle window on a level with the boat.

"Yes, Tom: God has taken care of me, to bring me to you. Get in quickly. Is there no one else?"

"No," said Tom, stepping into the boat, "I fear the man is drowned: he was carried down the Ripple, I think, when part of the Mill fell with the crash of trees and stones against it: I've shouted again and again, and there has been no answer. Give me the oars, Maggie."

It was not till Tom had pushed off and they were on the wide water—he face to face with Maggie—that the full meaning of what had happened rushed upon his mind. It came with so overpowering a force—it was such a new revelation to his spirit, of the depths in life, that had lain beyond his vision which he had fancied so keen and clear—that he was unable to ask a question. They sat mutely gazing at each other: Maggie with eyes of intense life looking out from a weary, beaten face—Tom pale with a certain awe and humiliation. Thought was busy though the lips were silent: and though he could ask no question, he guessed a story of almost miraculous divinely-protected effort. But at last a mist gathered over the blue-grey eyes, and the lips found a word they could utter: the old childish—"Magsie!"

Maggie could make no answer but a long deep sob of that mysterious wondrous happiness that is one with pain.

As soon as she could speak, she said, "We will go to Lucy, Tom: we'll go and see if she is safe, and then we can help the rest."

Tom rowed with untired vigour, and with a different speed from poor Maggie's. The boat was soon in the current of the river again, and soon they would be at Tofton.

"Park House stands high up out of the flood," said Maggie. "Perhaps they have got Lucy there."

Nothing else was said; a new danger was being carried towards them by the river. Some wooden machinery had just given way on one of the wharves, and huge fragments were being floated along. The sun was rising now, and the wide area of watery desolation was spread out in dreadful clearness around them—in dreadful clearness floated onwards the hurrying, threatening masses. A large company in a boat that was working its way along under the Tofton houses, observed their danger, and shouted, "Get out of the current!"

But that could not be done at once, and Tom, looking before him, saw death rushing on them. Huge fragments, clinging together in fatal fellowship, made one wide mass across the stream.

"It is coming, Maggie!" Tom said, in a deep hoarse voice, loosing the oars, and clasping her.

The next instant the boat was no longer seen upon the water—and the huge mass was hurrying on in hideous triumph.

But soon the keel of the boat reappeared, a black speck on the golden water.

The boat reappeared—but brother and sister had gone down in an embrace never to be parted: living through again in one supreme moment the days when they had clasped their little hands in love, and roamed the daisied fields together.

Conclusion

Nature repairs her ravages—repairs them with her sunshine, and with human labour. The desolation wrought by that flood, had left little visible trace on the face of the earth, five years after. The fifth autumn was rich in golden corn-stacks, rising in thick clusters among the distant hedgerows; the wharves and warehouses on the Floss were busy again, with echoes of eager voices, with hopeful lading and unlading.

And every man and woman mentioned in this history was still living—except those whose end we know.

Nature repairs her ravages—but not all. The uptorn trees are not rooted again; the parted hills are left scarred: if there is a new growth, the trees are not the same as the old, and the hills underneath their green vesture bear the marks of the past rending. To the eyes that have dwelt on the past, there is no thorough repair.

Dorlcote Mill was rebuilt. And Dorlcote churchyard,—where the brick grave that held a father whom we know, was found with the stone laid prostrate upon it after the flood,—had recovered all its grassy order and decent quiet.

Near that brick grave there was a tomb erected, very soon after the flood, for two bodies that were found in close embrace; and it was visited at different moments by two men who both felt that their keenest joy and keenest sorrow were for ever buried there.

One of them visited the tomb again with a sweet face beside him—but that was years after.

The other was always solitary. His great companionship was among the trees of the Red Deeps, where the buried joy seemed still to hover —like a revisiting spirit.

The tomb bore the names of Tom and Maggie Tulliver, and below the names it was written—

"In their death they were not divided."[1]

THE END

1. David's lament for Saul and his son Jonathan, David's beloved (2 Samuel 1:23).

BACKGROUNDS AND CONTEMPORARY REACTIONS

Backgrounds

EXCERPTS FROM LETTERS†

George Eliot to John Blackwood,[1] August 17, 1859

* * *

I'm glad my story cleaves to you. At present, I have no hope that it will affect people as strongly as Adam has done. The characters are on a lower level generally, and the environment less romantic. But my stories grow in me like plants, and this is only in the leaf-bud. I have faith that the flower will come. Not enough faith, though, to make me like the idea of beginning to print till the flower is fairly out—till I know the end as well as the beginning.

* * *

George Henry Lewes to John Blackwood,[2] September 6, 1859

My dear Blackwood

Your letter, with the checque, was sent on to me here where we are rusticating and zoologizing, and I hope getting up some health to stock us for the autumn and winter. We tried North Wales, and then ran across here; and although Weymouth does not turn out what we wanted, we made a discovery yesterday which will repay all. G.E. is in high spirits, having found a Mill and Millstream to his heart's content; and we are going to hire a laborer's cottage for a day or two, and live a poetical primitive life, the results of which will appear in Maggie—who by the way becomes more fascinating than ever, and Tom more intensely boyish.

* * *

† From *The George Eliot Letters*, ed. Gordon S. Haight, 9 vols. (New Haven: Yale UP, 1954–78) 3: 133, 145, 240, 243, 244, 245, 269, 285, 299, 317–18, 362, 374, 394, 397; 8: 465–66. Reprinted by permission of Yale University Press.

1. John Blackwood was George Eliot's publisher.
2. George Henry Lewes was George Eliot's common-law husband, with whom she lived from 1854 until he died in 1878. (They could not marry because he could not obtain a divorce from his first wife.)

George Eliot to John Blackwood, January 3, 1860

* * *

I suppose it will be well to announce the new book in February (in Maga), will it not? We are demurring about the title. Mr. Lewes is beginning to prefer *"The House of Tulliver, or, Life on the Floss,"* to our old notion of "Sister Maggi." *"The Tullivers, or, Life on the Floss,"* has the advantage of slipping easily off the lazy English tongue, but it is after too common a fashion (The Newcomes, The Bertrams, etc. etc. etc.). Then, there is *"The Tulliver Family, or Life on the Floss."* Pray meditate and give us your opinion.

* * *

George Henry Lewes to John Blackwood, January 4, 1860

* * *

Ponder on these titles.

1. Sister Maggie. (That sounds *rather* like a child's story)
2. The House of Tulliver or Life on the Floss.
3. The Tulliver Family or Life on the Floss.
4. Maggie Tulliver.
5. The Tullivers.

It will be well now to begin announcing it in lists—if not the title at any rate the fact of a new novel being in the press.

* * *

John Blackwood to George Eliot, January 6, 1860

My Dear Madam

It is a real pleasure to receive such a letter as yours, which I got yesterday. Since then we have all been considering the various Titles proposed, and this morning it suddenly came across me that

The Mill on the Floss

would be an appropriate Title and in some respects more appropriate and curiously exciting than any of those suggested. It has too a sort of poetical sound.

The Major and I rather inclined for Sister Maggie, but as the early part of the story is so much about children I think Lewes' objection is valid. Mr. Simpson to whom we showed the proposed titles was for the House of Tulliver or Life on the Floss, but now we all incline for The

Mill. The Title however is of no great moment and whatever you fix upon will be best.

* * *

George Eliot to John Blackwood, January 6, 1860

My dear Sir

"The Mill on the Floss" be it then! The only objections are, that the Mill is not *strictly* on the Floss, being on its small tributary, and that the title is of rather laborious utterance. But I think these objections do not deprive it of its advantage over "The Tullivers, or Life on the Floss,"—the only alternative, so far as we can see. Pray give the casting vote.

* * *

George Henry Lewes to John Blackwood, March 5, 1860

* * *

Mrs. Lewes is getting her eyes redder and *swollener* every morning as she lives through her tragic story. But there is such a strain of poetry to relieve the tragedy that the more she cries, and the readers cry, the better say I. She is anxious to hear your opinion of the part you have got; although she knows you don't like disagreeable and uncomfortable situations.

* * *

George Eliot to John Blackwood, April 3, 1860

* * *

I think Rome will at last chase away Maggie and the Mill from my thoughts: I hope it will, for she and her sorrows have clung to me painfully. As for the book, I can see nothing in it just now but the absence of things that might have been there. In fact, the third volume has the material of a novel compressed into it. I tremble rather, to hear of its reception, lest high hopes should be speedily checked. But then, I am always in a state of fear, more or less rational; and if any good news comes, it will be the more welcome. You will hardly have anything to tell by the time you receive this letter, and perhaps it will be worth while for you to wait till something more than the fact of the subscription has turned up. But I know you will write just as soon as the kindest consideration can prompt.

* * *

George Eliot to William Blackwood,[3] May 27, 1860

My dear Major Blackwood

I am much obliged to you for writing at once, and so scattering some clouds which had gathered over my mind in consequence of an indication or two in Mr. John Blackwood's previous letter. The "Times" article arrived on Sunday. It is written in a generous spirit, and with so high a degree of intelligence, that I am rather alarmed lest the misapprehensions it exhibits should be due to my defective presentation, rather than to any failure on the part of the critic. I have certainly fulfilled my intention very badly if I have made the Dodson honesty appear "mean and uninteresting," or made the payment of one's debts appear a contemptible virtue in comparison with any sort of "Bohemian" qualities. So far as my own feeling and intention are concerned, no one class of persons or form of character is held up to reprobation or to exclusive admiration. Tom is painted with as much love and pity as Maggie, and I am so far from hating the Dodsons myself, that I am rather aghast to find them ticketed with such very ugly adjectives.

* * *

George Eliot to John Blackwood, July 9, 1860

My dear Sir

I return Sir Edward's critical letter,[4] which I have read with much interest. On two points I recognize the justice of his criticism. First, that Maggie is made to appear too passive in the scene of quarrel in the Red Deeps. If my book were still in MS., I should—now that the defect is suggested to me—alter, or rather expand that scene. Secondly, that the tragedy is not adequately prepared. This is a defect which I felt even while writing the third volume, and have felt ever since the MS. left me. The "*epische Breite*"[5] into which I was beguiled by love of my subject in the two first volumes, caused a want of proportionate fulness in the treatment of the third, which I shall always regret.

The other chief point of criticism—Maggie's position towards Stephen—is too vital a part of my whole conception and purpose for

3. John Blackwood's brother. See page 451 for the review in *The Times* to which he refers.
4. A letter from Sir Edward Bulwer-Lytton, a prominent novelist and man of letters, reprinted on page 448.
5. Epic breadth (German).

me to be converted to the condemnation of it. If I am wrong there—if I did not really know what my heroine would feel and do under the circumstances in which I deliberately placed her, I ought not to have written this book at all, but quite a different book, if any. If the ethics of art do not admit the truthful presentation of a character essentially noble but liable to great error—error that is anguish to its own nobleness—*then*, it seems to me, the ethics of art are too narrow, and must be widened to correspond with a widening psychology.

But it is good for me to know how my tendencies as a writer clash with the conclusions of a highly accomplished mind, that I may be warned into examining well whether my discordancy with those conclusions may not arise rather from an idiosyncrasy of mine, than from a conviction which is argumentatively justifiable.

I hope you will thank Sir Edward on my behalf for the trouble he has taken to put his criticism into a form specific enough to be useful. I feel his taking such trouble to be at once a tribute and a kindness. If printed criticisms were usually written with only half the same warrant of knowledge, and with an equal sincerity of intention, I should read them without fear of fruitless annoyance. I remain, my dear Sir,

Always yours truly
Marian Evans Lewes.

George Eliot to François D'Albert-Durade,[6] December 6, 1860

* * *

I think it will be wise to adopt the title you suggest "le Moulin de Dorlcote" instead of "sur la Floss"; but on this point I leave you to decide according to your final impressions, when the decision becomes necessary. Here in England the public is about equally divided in opinion about my two last books—some preferring "Adam," some "The Mill"; but I agree with you that the French readers are likely to find the first volume of the latter too long. My delight in the pictures of childhood led me into what the Germans call an "epic breadth," which to many may perhaps be an epic tediousness. * * *

6. A close friend of Eliot's with whom she lived for five months during her stay in Geneva in 1849–50 and who later became her French translator.

George Eliot to François D'Albert-Durade, January 29, 1861

* * *

I see that you think there are many readers who will prefer 'The Mill' to 'Adam.' To my feeling, there is more thought and a profounder veracity in 'The Mill' than in 'Adam', but Adam is more complete, and better balanced. My love of the childhood scenes made me linger over them; so that I could not develop as fully as I wished the concluding "Book" in which the tragedy occurs, and which I had looked forward to with much attention and premeditation from the beginning. My books don't seem to belong to me after I have once written them; and I find myself delivering opinions about them as if I had nothing to do with them. I am not afraid that you will be unable to distinguish that frankness from self-conceit.

George Eliot to John Blackwood, March 30, 1861

* * * There is an article on the Mill in McMillan's Mag.[7] which is worth reading. I cannot of course agree with the writer in all his regrets: if I could have done so, I should not have written the book I did write, but quite another. Still it is a comfort to me to read any criticism which recognizes the high responsibilities of literature that undertakes to represent life. The ordinary tone about art is, that the artist may do what he will, provided he pleases the public.

* * *

George Eliot to John Blackwood, April 4, 1861

* * * And letters drop in from time to time giving me words of strong encouragement—especially about the Mill; so that I have reason to be cheerful, and to believe that where one has a large public, one's words must hit their mark. If it were not for that, special cases of misinterpretation might paralyze me. For example, when you read McMillan, pray notice how my critic attributes to me a disdain for Tom: as if it were not *my* respect for Tom which infused itself into my reader—as if he could have respected Tom, if I had not painted him with respect; the exhibition of the *right* on both sides being the very soul of my intention in the story. However, I ought to be satisfied if I have roused the feeling that does justice to both sides.

* * *

7. See page 458 for the review to which she refers.

Emily Davies to Jane Crow,[8] August 21, 1869

My dear Jane

I went to see Mrs. Lewes this afternoon, and though I did not stay very long, she said a great deal. We spoke of her health, which is such that she has scarcely ever had the feeling of being really well or can work without a sense of drag, but it does not come to an illness, and she is afraid she inherits from her father, longevity. The anxiety about Mr. Lewes's son upsets her a good deal, "but one hates oneself for being perturbed." Then she remarked how easily one fell both into any little vice that belongs to us, after being disturbed in it, and spoke of the state of perturbation as entirely caused by not being sufficiently occupied with large interests. I referred to something in Felix Holt about Mr. Lyon's preoccupation which set him above small cares, and said what an enviable state it must be. She said Yes, one only knew it by contrast, by the sense of the want of it.

Somehow we got to talk of the Mill on the Floss. She said her sole purpose in writing it was to show the conflict which is going on everywhere when the younger generation with its higher culture comes into collision with the older, and in which, she said, so many young hearts make shipwreck far worse than Maggie. I asked if she had known actual people like the Dodsons, and she said "Oh, so much worse." She thought those Dodsons very nice people and that we owe much to them for keeping up the sense of respectability, which was the only religion possible to the mass of the English people. Their want of education made a theoretic or dogmatic religion impossible, and sincce the Reformation, an imaginative religion had not been possible. It had all been drained away. She considers that in the Mill on the Floss, everything is softened, as compared with real life. Her own experience she said was worse. It was impossible for her to write an autobiography, but she wished that somebody else could do it, it might be useful—or, that she could do it herself. She could do it better than any one else, because she could do it impartially, judging herself, and showing how wrong *she* was. She spoke of having come into collision with her father and being on the brink of being turned out of his house. And she dwelt a little on how much fault there is on the side of the young in such cases, of their ignorance of life, and the narrowness of their intellectual superiority.

Then we got to talk of fiction, and she was eager to explain the difference between prosaic and poetical fiction—that what is prosaic in ordinary novels is not the presence of the realistic element, without

8. Emily Davies was the leader of the campaign to open higher education in England to women and an acquaintance of Eliot's. Jane Crow was secretary of the Society for Promoting the Employment of Women and a childhood friend of Davies.

which the tragedy cannot be given [shown]—she herself is obliged to see and feel every minutest detail—but in the absence of anything suggesting the ideal, the higher life. She seems quite oppressed with the quantity of second rate art everywhere about. It gives her such a sense of nausea that it makes it almost impossible to her to write—"such a quantity of dialogue about everything, every hole and corner being ransacked, every possible incident seized upon," not *well* done, but done in such abundance that good art is discouraged and the higher standard works are thrust aside. She was anxious to impress upon me what she felt about the difference between prosaic and poetical work, because she thought I might disseminate it. She said in an appealing tone "Then when you talk to young people and teachers, you *will* advise against indiscriminate reading?"

She thinks she has done very little, in quantity. She cannot write what she does not care about. She had not that kind of ability. Whatever she had done, she has studied for. Before she began to write the Mill on the Floss, she had it all in her mind, and read about the Trent to make sure that the physical conditions of some English river were such as to make the inundation possible, and assured herself that the population in its neighbourhood was such as to justify her picture. It is still amazing to me, though she seemed only to feel how *little* she had done, how she has managed to get through so much work, actual hard labour, in the time. A great deal of it must have been very rapidly done.

Mrs. Lewes said a good deal besides what I have put down. She thinks people who write regularly for the Press are almost sure to be spoiled by it. There is so much dishonesty, people's work being praised because they belong to the confederacy. She spoke very strongly about the wickedness of not paying one's debts. She thinks it worse than drunkenness, not in its consequences, but in the character itself. . . .

GEORGE ELIOT

Brother and Sister†[1]

I

I cannot choose but think upon the time
When our two lives grew like two buds that kiss

† From *Complete Poems. Scenes of Clerical Life* (New York: C. T. Brainard, 1892) 391–96.

1. This sonnet sequence, first published in 1869, derives from the same autobiographical materials as *The Mill on the Floss*.

At lightest thrill from the bee's swinging chime,
Because the one so near the other is.

He was the elder and a little man
Of forty inches, bound to show no dread,
And I the girl that puppy-like now ran,
Now lagged behind my brother's larger tread.

I held him wise, and when he talked to me
Of snakes and birds, and which God loved the best,
I thought his knowledge marked the boundary
Where men grew blind, though angels knew the rest.

If he said "Hush!" I tried to hold my breath;
Wherever he said "Come!" I stepped in faith.

II

Long years have left their writing on my brow,
But yet the freshness and the dew-fed beam
Of those young mornings are about me now,
When we two wandered toward the far-off stream

With rod and line. Our basket held a store
Baked for us only, and I thought with joy
That I should have my share, though he had more,
Because he was the elder and a boy.

The firmaments of daisies since to me
Have had those mornings in their opening eyes,
The bunchéd cowslip's pale transparency
Carries that sunshine of sweet memories,

And wild-rose branches take their finest scent
From those blest hours of infantine content.

III

Our mother bade us keep the trodden ways,
Stroked down my tippet, set my brother's frill,[2]
Then with the benediction of her gaze
Clung to us lessening, and pursued us still

Across the homestead to the rookery elms,
Whose tall old trunks had each a grassy mound,

2. Frill: an ornamental edging; tippet: a small cape.

So rich for us, we counted them as realms
With varied products: here were earth-nuts found,

And here the Lady-fingers in deep shade;
Here sloping toward the Moat the rushes grew,
The large to split for pith, the small to braid;
While over all the dark rooks cawing flew,

  And made a happy strange solemnity,
  A deep-toned chant from life unknown to me.

IV

Our meadow-path had memorable spots:
One where it bridged a tiny rivulet,
Deep hid by tangled blue Forget-me-knots;
And all along the waving grasses met

My little palm, or nodded to my cheek,
When flowers with upturned faces gazing drew
My wonder downward, seeming all to speak
With eyes of souls that dumbly heard and knew.

Then came the copse, where wild things rushed unseen,
And black-scathed grass betrayed the past abode
Of mystic gypsies, who still lurked between
Me and each hidden distance of the road.

  A gypsy once had startled me at play,
  Blotting with her dark smile my sunny day.

V

Thus rambling we were schooled in deepest lore,
And learned the meanings that give words a soul,
The fear, the love, the primal passionate store,
Whose shaping impulses make manhood whole.

Those hours were seed to all my after good;
My infant gladness, through eye, ear, and touch,
Took easily as warmth a various food
To nourish the sweet skill of loving much.

For who in age shall roam the earth and find
Reasons for loving that will strike out love
With sudden rod from the hard year-pressed mind?
Were reasons sown as thick as stars above,

'Tis love must see them, as the eyes see light:
Day is but Number to the darkened sight.

VI

Our brown canal was endless to my thought;
And on its banks I sat in dreamy peace,
Unknowing how the good I loved was wrought,
Untroubled by the fear that it would cease.

Slowly the barges floated into view,
Rounding a grassy hill to me sublime
With some Unknown beyond it, whither flew
The parting cuckoo toward a fresh spring-time.

The wide-arched bridge, the scented elder-flowers,
The wondrous watery rings that died too soon,
The echoes of the quarry, the still hours
With white robe sweeping on the shadeless noon,

Were but my growing self, are part of me,
My present Past, my root of piety.

VII

Those long days measured by my little feet
Had chronicles which yield me many a text;
Where irony still finds an image meet
Of full-grown judgments in this world perplext.

One day my brother left me in high charge,
To mind the rod, while he went seeking bait,
And bade me, when I saw a nearing barge,
Snatch out the line, lest he should come too late.

Proud of the task, I watched with all my might
For one whole minute, till my eyes grew wide,
Till sky and earth took on a strange new light
And seemed a dream-world floating on some tide—

A fair pavilioned boat for me alone
Bearing me onward through the vast unknown.

VIII

But sudden came the barge's pitch-black prow,
Nearer and angrier came my brother's cry,

And all my soul was quivering fear, when lo!
Upon the imperilled line, suspended high,

A silver perch! My guilt that won the prey,
Now turned to merit, had a guerdon rich
Of hugs and praises, and made merry play,
Until my triumph reached its highest pitch

When all at home were told the wondrous feat,
And how the little sister had fished well.
In secret, though my fortune tasted sweet,
I wondered why this happiness befell.

"The little lass had luck," the gardener said:
And so I learned, luck was with glory wed.

IX

We had the selfsame world enlarged for each
By loving difference of girl and boy:
The fruit that hung on high beyond my reach
He plucked for me, and oft he must employ

A measuring glance to guide my tiny shoe
Where lay firm stepping-stones, or call to mind
"This thing I like my sister may not do
For she is little, and I must be kind."

Thus boyish Will the nobler mastery learned
Where inward vision over impulse reigns,
Widening its life with separate life discerned,
A Like unlike, a Self that self restrains.

His years with others must the sweeter be
For those brief days he spent in loving me.

X

His sorrow was my sorrow, and his joy
Sent little leaps and laughs through all my frame;
My doll seemed lifeless and no girlish toy
Had any reason when my brother came.

I knelt with him at marbles, marked his fling
Cut the ringed stem and make the apple drop,
Or watched him winding close the spiral string
That looped the orbits of the humming top.

Grasped by such fellowship my vagrant thought
Ceased with dream-fruit dream-wishes to fulfil;
My aëry-picturing fantasy was taught
Subjection to the harder, truer skill

That seeks with deeds to grave a thought-tracked line,
And by "What is," "What will be" to define.

XI

School parted us; we never found again
That childish world where our two spirits mingled
Like scents from varying roses that remain
One sweetness, nor can evermore be singled

Yet the twin habit of that early time
Lingered for long about the heart and tongue:
We had been natives of one happy clime,
And its dear accent to our utterance clung,

Till the dire years whose awful name is Change
Had grasped our souls still yearning in divorce,
And pitiless shaped them in two forms that range
Two elements which sever their life's course.

But were another childhood-world my share,
I would be born a little sister there.

Contemporary Reactions

From *Spectator*, April 7, 1860

The Mill on the Floss

The new story by the author of *Adam Bede* is full of power—a vague word to use, but, as far as any one word can stamp a whole work of art, it is the only word with any approach to fitness in it. The story is in the main the record of the struggle of a young girl towards a noble life—a life she can intensely feel to be alone worthy of a woman, but which she has not the simple strength of will and act to realize at once in its directness. Few persons in the novel-dramas which make so much of our literature now-a-days are so distinctly embodied and vividly coloured as the Maggie Tulliver who has just been introduced as a new guest in so many thousand English homes. Her love for her brother—clinging, exacting in its excess of lovingness, but still thoughtlessly unselfish, is painted with wonderful minuteness. Very few writers can enter into the thoughts of children, can follow out their little trains of half-reasonings, and detect the ways and methods by which they arrive at conclusions: and of those few, George Eliot seems to us, in the present day, to possess in the highest degree the gift of knowing the child-soul in those things which are common to all children. * * *

In the new story, the author describes Maggie Tulliger from her childhood upwards, and traces the influence of all the home associations on the young girl's mind. Her active mind, her spirit sensitive to all things, her heart with a hunger and thirst to be loved, are analyzed with a wondrous instinctive knowledge of the inner workings of a child's mind. All the persons around her leave some kind of impression on her. Her father is a man of narrow culture, with that consciousness of its narrowness which indicates the power of a nature much broader, and which is shown most in his love for "his little wench"—the wayward child he clings to half-blindly, not understanding her mind but understanding that he loves her. His love for her keeps alive in her a most wholesome and healthy tenderness. But the very native limits of his mind still leave much of the depths of her feeling unsounded. Towards her brother, she is imperatively attracted. His boyhood is also drawn; the lines are few, the touches seem but mere accidental tints left by the pencil, but the character is painted to the very life. The plain practical turn of the boy's mind, his involuntary contempt for imperfections he does not share, his passive bewilderment as to things he cannot learn, and his quiet undemonstrative energy in going through with the work before him: are the main characteristics of the portrait. The manner in which he meets his sister's love—frank and sincere in his amount of love when he shows it, equally frank and sincere when, by withholding it, he awards her what he considers deserved punishment—but which to her mind, morbidly sensitive, is an abyss of pain he can never by any possibility realize to his narrow solid mind—is a curious instance of the power the author has of tracing, with rare insight, not alone the inner workings of two very different natures, but the effect the two natures have upon one another. There is not much depth or variety in the brother's character, but the truth with which it is done indicates the richness of the artist's power who, in her second-rate characters, follows the firm outline her cunning hand has traced as conscientously as in fulfilling the more gracious task of working out the leading figures of the great design.

The next influence on Maggie's character brings into light new revelations of the spirit within her. Philip Wakem, a deformed young man, son of her father's bitter enemy, a hard-griping solicitor, has been partially known to her from childhood. He, thoughtful and perceptive, has watched her and been won by the strange beauty of her character, not inaptly expressed by deep wild eyes, with wondrous power of expressing all her beauty and all her weakness—all her deep heart-wish to be noble, all her fitfulness in striving to fulfil the high ideal she can so quickly conceive. He can see in her a beauty of soul not visible to herself. He can interpret her thoughts, better than she can, and detect in her intermittent asceticism a mere stunting of emotions that ought to have full play. The awakening of the girl's higher faculties under the influence of a mind of wider range and finer tone than her own is indicated, and the effect of the circumstances of her childhood and youth on her manners, speech, and actions, is shown so naturally, that one for a time quite forgets the artist and her art. Maggie is no exceptional girl in any way. * * *

* * * the wayward little child, "naughty" to the last degree, quick in her "ways," is natural enough, and the growth of her characteristics bears all the impress of the facts around her. Her mental conflicts are not alone analyzed in her childhood and youth and in relation to all her home ties. As life advances, two kinds of love contend for mastery within her; she remembers her first awakening to higher things at the dawn of womanhood, and her first lover keeps a place in her thoughts which he never forfeits. It is almost impossible to those who have not read the book to describe how delicately and clearly the author brings before us the distinction between Maggie loving Philip Wakem and

Maggie loving Stephen Guest. The contending thoughts are so natural; they seem inevitable, and through every weak word, every unconscious betrayal, bringing complication and suffering into the story—keenly as one feels them, as if they were painful scenes we saw acted before our eyes—we still have an instinctive sense that they are unavoidable, that they could not be left unspoken, or undone. There are parts of the story where the style gives a kind of consciousness of reality, as if you heard the words spoken by a voice shaken with the emotions so well described; there are passages of dialogue where the love between men and women is expressed more naturally and powerfully, we think, than in any novel we ever read. Rising fresh from the perusal, we may overrate the power of these passages, and attribute to style or words what may be due to situations the interest of which is prepared by skilful construction; but we think there can be no mistaking the wondrous human passion that animates the scenes between the two lovers—bound to others in honour, yet clinging together with such appealing love.

Some parts of the story are likely to be misunderstood at first reading; some passages appeared to us out of harmony and some incidents forced, until the very last pages threw a light over the whole. It is the epic of a human soul, traced through childhood, development, and temptation. The sordid scenes at Dorlcote Mill—described with photographic truth and minute manner-painting worthy of Miss Austen—are still interesting only in their effect on Maggie; her impatience is more natural, and her impetuous aspiration after something higher than her home-surroundings stands out more distinctly. The character of Mrs. Tulliver and her three sisters,—with all their family fretfulness and peculiarities, their idolatry of the "properties,"—supply not only a background dull and mean enough for the bright, bold, dark-eyed girl, but furnish an excuse for much that is erring in her "ways." You feel that, in such a home, a child like Maggie would inevitably grow up into a woman such as Maggie Tulliver is. Her native glow of love and sense of beauty lead her perforce into the path traced out. In this novel, therefore, we have reproduced the old grand element of interest which the Greek drama possessed, the effect of circumstances upon man; but you have, in addition, that analysis of the inner mind, of which *Hamlet* stands in literature the greatest example. In the case of Maggie, we have a career regarded both from the inside and from the outside; we feel the throbbing of her heart at each new sensation, and we see, as it were, from our own stand-point, the outward facts that awaken her to new life. On sweeps the river of life and of destiny; the flood resistless, the waters strong: men and homes, and old associations of outer life, are swept away for miles, or engulphed; all around drifts from its moorings; and, as spectators, we watch the roll of the resistless tide. On comes one young girl, alone upon a raft, hardly saved from the flood; she strives against the current, but is still swept along, and now we are made conscious of her thoughts and feelings. We see not alone the river of life, with its hard facts floated away, and its merciless waters, but we are conscious of every thought of the victim. We follow back to the heart the retreating blood that has left the cheek pale; we know every gleam of hope and pang of despair that runs through mind and soul, as the familiar landmarks are passed, and she is drifted down with the flood. We do not remember any novel where the interest so clearly centres round the one character, where every fact—the smallest—is read with deep attention, because it may affect her—as in real life the very name of a town or street, or even shop, remembered in connexion with some one person much beloved, has at once a new vivid life. Not that Maggie is made actually powerful in her influence on the other persons, but that everything she does, or anything done to her, is of interest, and thus the whole story takes a noble unity.

* * *

From *Saturday Review*, April 14, 1860

The Mill on the Floss

A year ago, most readers who had just finished *Adam Bede* would have been greatly surprised to hear two things which we now know to be true. It would have been very strange news that *Adam Bede* waas written by a woman, and it would have been equally surprising to learn that within a twelvemonth the authoress would produce another tale quite worthy to rank beside its predecessor. Now that we are wise after the event, we can detect many subtle signs of female authorship in *Adam Bede*; but at the time it was generally accepted as the work of a man. To speak the simple truth, without affectation of politeness, it was thought to be too good for a woman's story. It turns out that a woman was not only able to write it, but that she did not write it by any lucky accident. The *Mill on the Floss* may not, perhaps, be so popular as *Adam Bede*, but it shows no falling off nor any exhaustion of power. We may think ourselves very fortunate to have a third female novelist not inferior to Miss Austen and Miss Bronté; and it so happens that there is much in the works of this new writer that reminds us of these two well-known novelists without anything like copying. George Eliot has a minuteness of painting and a certain archness of style that are quite after the manner of Miss Austen, while the wide scope of her remarks, and her delight in depicting strong and wayward feelings, show that she belongs to the generation of Currer Bell, and not to that of the quiet authoress of *Emma*. Where all excel, it is of no use to draw up a sort of literary class-list, and pronounce an opinion as to the comparative merits of these three writers; but no one can now doubt that the lady who, with the usual pretty affectation of her sex, likes to look on paper as much like a man as possible, and so calls herself George Eliot, has established her place in the first rank of our female novelists.

She has done us all one great kindness, for she has opened up a field that is perfectly new. She has, for the first time in fiction, invented or disclosed the family life of the English farmer, and the class to which he belongs. She paints farmers and their wives and children, and their equals in the little villages and towns around them, and brings before us their settled opinions, convictions, and humours. Both in her present novel and in *Adam Bede* she throws the date of her story back a few years, and paints the farmers of a past generation. * * *

* * * The most conspicuous of these characters are three sisters who belong to the family of Dodson, and are possessed with an immovable belief in the innate superiority of everything Dodson. These sisters have married three men dissimilar enough in taste and temper to have each an individual and distinct existence, and yet with a general resemblance in the cast and level of their minds which stamps them as belonging to the same class and generation. There is nothing in which George Eliot succeeds more conspicuously than in this very nice art of making her characters like real people, and yet shading them off into the large group which she is describing. Some notion of what it requires to make a good novelist may be obtained by reflecting on all that is implied in the delineation of three farmer's daughters and their husbands with separate and probable characters, and in allotting them suitable conversation, and following the turns and shifts of their minds within the narrow limits of the matters that may be supposed to interest them. It is this profusion of delineative power that marks the *Mill on the Floss*, and the delineations are given both by minute touches of description and by dialogues. To write dialogue is much harder than merely to describe, and George Eliot trusts greatly to the talk of her farmers' wives in order to make her conception of these sisters come vividly before us. Both in the description and in the dialogue there are exhibited a neatness of finish, a comprehensiveness of detail, and a relish for subdued comedy that constantly bring back to our recollection the best productions of Miss Austen's genius. Like Miss Austen, too, George Eliot possesses the art of taking the reader into her confidence. We seem to share with the authoress the fun of the play she is showing us. She joins us in laughing at her characters and yet this is done so lightly and with such tact that the continuity of the story is not broken. Every one must remember the consummate skill with which Miss Austen manages this, and if we do not quite like to acknowledge that our old favourite has been equalled, we must allow that George Eliot performs the same neat stroke of art with a success that is little inferior.

Portraiture, however, and the description of farmers and their wives, only occupies one portion of George Eliot's thoughts. There is a side of her mind which is entirely unlike that of Miss Austen, and which brings her much closer to Charlotte Brontë. She is full of meditation on some of the most difficult problems of life. She occupies herself with the destinies, the possibilities, and the religious position of all the people of whom she cares to think. Especially she seems haunted with the thought of the amazing discrepancy between what she calls "the emmet-life" of these British farmers, and the ideal of Christianity. She dwells on the pettiness, the narrowness, the paganism of their character. She even takes a pleasure in making the contrast as strong as she can. In her stern determination to paint what she conceives to be the truth, to soften nothing and not to exalt and elevate where she profoundly believes all to be poor and low, she shocks us with traits of character that are exceptional, however possible. In the *Mill on the Floss* an old miller is ruined, and the fault, as he thinks, lies at the door of a roguish lawyer. When he finds his ruin is accomplished, he solemnly takes the family Bible, and in the fly-leaf records a curse against his enemy. Usually, however, the proceedings of the Dodsons and their set are much milder. It is the gossip, the stinginess, the total absence of all spirituality in the farmer circles that weigh upon George Eliot. She has set herself to imagine how such influences would tell upon an exception to the set, in a lively, imaginative, impulsive girl, the daughter of the Dodson married to the miller. The history of this girl is taken up when she is seven years old, and is continued until she has been for some time a young woman. She goes through great outward trials, in addition to the perpetual suffering inflicted on her by relations who entirely misunderstand her. She has a period in which fiction is everything to her, and she consoles herself for all that reality imposes on her by the delightful dreams of the imagination. When her suffering becomes too intense, she takes refuge in mystical religion. Later on, she seems to accept the doctrine inculcated by one of her lovers, that resignation cannot be the highest end of human life, as it is merely negative. She then passes into a stage where she is absorbed in the fierce moral conflicts awakened by a passion to which she thinks it wrong to yield. All this is entirely in the vein of Charlotte Brontë, and the *Mill on the Floss* shows that George Eliot has thought as keenly and profoundly as the authoress of *Jane Eyre* on the peculiar difficulties and sorrows encountered by a girl of quick feeling and high aspirations under adverse outward circumstances. But the objection which we feel to difficult moral problems being handled in fiction is certainly not removed by the writings of either of these gifted women. What does it all come to except that human life is inexplicable, and that women who feel this find the feeling painful? It is true that a girl like the heroine of the *Mill on the Floss* is not an improbable character, Many a girl in the obscurity of an uncongenial home has first taken to ascetic and mystical religion, and then had doubts forced on her whether such a religion could give her peace. But because they really occur, it does not follow that spiritual doubts and conflicts are a proper subject for a novelist. Fiction has, in such matters, the great defect that it encourages both the writer and the reader to treat the most solemn problems of human life as things that are to be started, discussed, and laid aside at pleasure. The conduct of the story always affords an opening to escape from the responsibility of definite thought. It does even more than afford an opening—it forces the mind to escape from reflection into the study of outward life. The subjects started are, therefore, always too large for the manner in which they are handled. When women like George Eliot and Currer Bell are writing, we are perhaps too interested in their style, in the freshness of their thoughts, and in the story they are telling, to care much for the abandonment of the moral difficulties that have been raised. But no one who considers how much harm the light, trifling, and inadequate discussion of great subjects does in the present day, can have much pleasure in finding that a novelist powerful enough to become the example and excuse of lesser writers exhibits ascetic religion as a temporary phase in a young woman's career.

Passion, and especially the passion of love, is so avowedly the chief subject of the modern novel that we can scarcely quarrel with a novelist because the passion she chooses to describe is of a very intense kind. We all know that love is neither a smooth-going nor a strictly decorous and prudential affair, and there are many emotions in female breasts, even when the sufferer is judged by her acquaintance to be an ordinary sort of person, which would shock friends and critics if put down in black and white. But there is a kind of love-making which seems to possess a strange fascination for the modern female novelist. Currer Bell and George Eliot, and we may add George Sand, all like to dwell on love as a strange overmastering force which, through the senses, captivates and enthrals the soul. They linger on the description of the physical sensations that accompany the meeting of hearts in love. Curiously, too, they all like to describe these sensations as they conceive them to exist in men. We are bound to say that their conceptions are true and adequate. But we are not sure that it is quite consistent with feminine delicacy to lay so much stress on the bodily feelings of the other sex. No one could be less open to the charge of thinking lightly of purity than George Eliot. She proclaims in every page the infinite gain of virtue. In her new novel she has set herself to describe the triumph of principle over feeling, as in *Adam Bede* she described the dreadful results of giving feeling the victory. But she lets her fancy run on things which are not wrong, but are better omitted from the scope of female meditation. The heroine, for example, is in love with a man who passionately loves her, but as each is pre-engaged, they are separated by duty and honour. All goes on very well until one day the lover, when alone with the heroine, takes to watching her arm. Its beauties are minutely described, as well as the effect gradually produced on him. At last, in a transport of passion, he rushes forward, seizes on the lovely arm, and covers it with kisses. There is nothing wrong in writing about such an act, and it is the sort of thing that does sometimes happen in real life; but we cannot think that the conflict of sensation and principle raised in a man's mind by gazing at a woman's arm is a theme that a female novelist can touch on without leaving behind a feeling of hesitation, if not repulsion, in the reader. In points like these, it may be observed that men are more delicate than women. There are very few men who would not shrink from putting into words what they might imagine to be the physical effects of love in a woman. Perhaps we may go further, and say that the whole delineation of passionate love, as painted by modern female novelists, is open to very serious criticism. There are emotions over which we ought to throw a veil; and no one can say that, in order to portray an ardent and tender love, it is necessary to describe the conquest of a beautiful arm over honour and principle. As it seems to us, the defect of the *Mill on the Floss* is that there is too much that is painful in it. And the authoress is so far led away by her reflections on moral problems and her interest in the phases of triumphant passion, that she sacrifices her story. We have such entire changes of circumstances, and the characters are exhibited under such totally different conditions of age and mental development, that we get to care nothing for them. The third volume seems to belong to quite a new story. The Dodsons have faded away, and the young woman with the overmastering passion is very slightly connected with the little Maggie of the Mill who makes her appearance at the beginning of the novel. As in *Adam Bede*, the interest fades off towards the end; and we are not sorry when the tremendous machinery of a flood is called in to drown off two of the principal characters. We hope that some time George Eliot will give us a tale less painful and less discursive. There is something in the world and in the quiet walks of English lower life besides fierce mental struggles and wild love. We do not see why we should not be treated to a story that would do justice to George Eliot's powers, and yet form a pleasing and consistent whole.

Sir Edward Bulwer-Lytton to John Blackwood,[1] April 14, 1860[†]

My dear Sir

I have just finished the Mill on the Floss and can assure you of my very high opinion of its many beauties. That rare and minute knowledge

1. Bulwer-Lytton was a prominent novelist and man of letters; Blackwood was Eliot's publisher. Eliot responds to Bulwer-Lytton's views in her letter to Blackwood of July 9, 1860, reprinted on page 430.

† From *The George Eliot Letters*, ed. Gordon S. Haight, 9 vols. (New Haven: Yale UP, 1978) 8: 261–62. Reprinted by permission of Yale University Press.

of the female heart which struck me so forcibly in A. Bede is here brought out with more variety, and in more richness of humour. All the Dodson sisters are wonderful. I feel it a great relief to get rid of the Provincial Dialect, and the language of Dialogue in the rural characters is extremely natural without vulgarity and full of point and playfulness. The only criticism I should here make is that here and there is a little unconscious imitation of Dickens; not more so perhaps than so fascinating and popular a genius as his would inevitably cause in persons writing somewhat after him and resorting to somewhat the same classes of Society for characters. Putting that aside, the general style is admirable.

In the 1st Volume as to construction and position I did not see a fault. Tom and Maggie as children are most beautifully drawn. Towards the latter part of the 2nd Volume I began to fear that there might be the same fault (as *I* think it) which I found in Ad. Bede. viz.: the want of clear perception and close study of what I call 'position' in Narrative. There is position in Narrative as well as Drama, and it can never be neglected without more or less injury to the story. In fact it comprises much of what the antient Critics meant by "the Becoming." No character should be placed in a position that does not become the conceptions already formed of that character, and it is in vain to reply that there is no violation of the Natural in such a position. The Natural that belongs to the Individual Character *is* violated. There is nothing for instance of the "unbecoming" or "false position" in the beating of Thersites; it becomes him to be beat. But if Achilles had kicked Agammenon for taking away Briseis it might be quite natural in Achilles to do so, but it would have been "unbecoming" so far as Agammenon was concerned, and it would have been difficult afterwards to respect him as the King of Men.

Now when Tom and Maggie go to meet Phillip, Maggie is put into a false position as regards the previous description of her hasty generous impulsive character to stand by and listen with so little interruption to her brother's coarse abuse of Phillip, and her natural fear must have been felt that Phillip would think she had brought Tom there, and it was a sort of treachery, and her inevitable impulse would have been to burst out with profound sympathy for Phillip. She is brought here as it is, for no sufficient cause in the plot, merely to witness her lover's humiliation and the situation is untrue to the courage of her character. Hence she loses somewhat in interest after that scene. But this is unimportant compared to the error, as I think, of her whole position towards Stephen. It may be quite natural that she should take that liking to him, but it is a position at variance with all that had before been Heroic about her. The *indulgence* of such a sentiment for the affianced of a friend under whose roof she was, was a treachery and a meanness according to the Ethics of Art, and nothing can afterwards lift the character into e hold on us. The refusal to marry Stephen fails to do so. This me to another view of a fault in the same direction. In studying incident the very remarkable writer does not eno[ugh] weigh what eeable or Disagreeable. Now the Disagreeable should be carefully avoided. You may have the painful, the terrible, the horrible, even; but the *disagreeable* should be shunned. For instance, it is a disagreeable and unworthy position for Phillip to treat so lightly *the blows* his father had received from the *father* of the woman he wants to marry, and Phillip sinks in dignity on acc[oun]t of it. Lastly—the Tragic should be prepared for and seem to come step by step as if unavoidable. But that is not the case here.

One feels from the time that Maggie's father *dies* in consequence of his meeting with Phillip's father that the end cannot be happy, but the steps that lead towards an end so gloomy are not sufficiently marked and solemn and when the Drowning comes at last, it fails accordingly in the pathos and terror it would otherwise excite; there has not been even sufficient care taken to make that final reconciliation in death of brother and sister as touching as it should be. Tom indeed has been by that time set so far apart from his sister that he can't be jerked back into the old boyish love of a sudden, and we don't see *why* he should be drowned at all. These are to my mind defects that belong to the same class of defects as those in Ad. Bede but they are not so marked, and these defects did not prevent or even injure the great popularity of Adam Bede. Neither will they in this case. I even doubt whether they will be visible to most readers. Where such defects really tell (even supposing I am right, which I may not be) is 10 or 20 years hence in the *duration* of a work. They scarcely touch its first sale or the author's immediate reputation.

I have been more lengthy in dwelling on faults real or supposed, because I measure the author by a very high standard. I know no female author with such grasp of character, such deep cuts into secret recesses of the heart, such ease and power of language, such charming combination of unaffected pathos and delicate affluent humour. And on the whole I like the Book even better than Adam Bede—which is indeed saying a great deal.

Yours
E. B. L.

[E. S. Dallas][1]

From *The Times*, May 19, 1860

The Mill on the Floss

"George Eliot" is as great as ever. She has produced a second novel, equal to her first in power, although not in interest. As far as interest is concerned, indeed, it would have been exceedingly difficult to repeat the triumph of *Adam Bede*, in which the author contrived to paint the lily and to gild refined gold by adding the charm of a delightful philosophy to the pleasure of a good story. The reader will at once remember that he could not help liking all the characters in that history. The general influence of the book was to reconcile us to human nature, to make us think better of our fellow men, to make us feel that in the weakest there is something to be admired, in the worst something to be loved, to draw us nearer to each other by showing how completely we are one, and so to give us not only the temporary delight of listening to a pleasant tale, but also the permanent good of an increased sympathy with our kind. It was comparatively easy to excite our interest in the doings of persons towards whom we were led to entertain such friendly feelings. We treasured all their sayings, we watched eagerly all their movements, we were curious as to all their thoughts. The author, apparently afraid of repeating herself, and determined to avoid the imputation of representing the world as too good and sugary, now introduces us to a very different set of personages. A majority of the characters brought together in these three volumes are unpleasant companions, prosaic, selfish, nasty. We are launched into a world of pride, vainglory, and hypocrisy, envy, hatred and malice, and all uncharitableness. Everybody is quarrelling with everybody in a small mean way; and we have the petty gossip and malignant slander of village worthies painted to the life. These are not promising materials, but the authoress has impressed her genius for them, and, relying on her marvellous powers of delineation, has felt that by the mere force of truth she could command our attention and compel applause. We doubt, indeed, whether Miss Lydia Languish will care much for this novel, and we are almost afraid to dwell on the nature of the theme which "George Eliot" has chosen, lest the timid reader should be repulsed, and we should suggest an allusion to the supposed impossibility of making a silk purse out of a sow's ear. As to the fact that here we have the silk purse there can be no mistake, but it would require the genius of "George Eliot" to describe

1. Dallas was a reviewer and critic on the staff of *The Times*. For Eliot's response to this review, see her letter to William Blackwood, May 27, 1860, page 430.

by what magic it is produced out of materials that appear to be singularly barren of silk.

We can only indicate what lies on the surface, and we must attribute a great part of "George Eliot's" triumph to the charm of her style. She plays with her subject; there is no appearance of effort; even when she is most serious she is half sportive; even when she has reached her climaxes she is entirely at her ease. This pervading humour is very pleasant, and takes the reader unawares. It does not much matter what is the subject with which such a mind as "George Elliot" plays; the result is sure to be amusing. One of our poets has declared, that in the meanest flowers he found thoughts that were too deep for tears; he might have added, too deep for anybody to care about them. It is not every topic that spontaneously yields the elements of tears and tragedy. The elements of comedy are much more universal, and "George Eliot" manages to make us smile through her novel, and to be tickled by incongruities that in less skilful hands would be as thorns and briars to vex the reader. In the three volumes there is not a dull page. The style is singularly apt and rich, and its felicities are not the result of tricks. Onward it flows and bears us along with a resistless force, and before we can get tired of the sometimes prosy interlocuters of the drama, the author steps in and rouses our attention with a wise remark or a pleasant reflection that shows the wideness of her reading, the closeness of her observation, and the maturity of her thought. It seems, too, not less easy for her to make her characters speak than to speak herself. As if her descriptions were not vivid enough, she prefers to make her characters speak for themselves, and the dialogue is sustained with marvellous ability—the slightest shades of difference between the personages being rendered with great subtlety. This is remarkably displayed in the representation of the odious Dodson family, in which the family likeness is strictly preserved, while the individual traits are not lost. Relying on her imitative power in this respect, and on the fascination which a truthful picture exerts over every mind, "George Eliot" has invited our attention to the hard realities of a life in which none but a true genius could find the elements of a successful novel.

The two leading characteristics of almost all the personages to whom we are introduced are honesty and pugnacity, and these flow from one and the same source. A strong character, such as is here described, that feels its own strength, delights in it, and is proud of it—is honest, because dishonesty is a weakness, not because it is an injury to others. The Dodson family are stingy, selfish wretches, who give no sympathy and require none, who would let a neighbour starve, and let a brother be bankrupt when a very little assistance would save him from the disgrace; but they would not touch a penny that is not theirs, there is no legal obligation which they would not discharge, they would scorn the approach of a lie. They would be truthful and honest, not as a social duty, but as a personal pride—because nobody should have it in his or her power to say that they were weak enough to neglect a manifest obligation. From the same source of self-satisfied strength comes pugnacity in all its forms of rivalry and contradiction, jealousies and criticisms, lawsuits, and slanders, and blows. Everybody in this tale is repelling everybody, and life is in the strictest sense a battle. Even the good angel of the story, that little Maggie, who is full of affection, and whose affection is continually leading her into blunders and misfortunes, is first of all introduced to us while she is indulging an unnatural ferocity towards her doll, whose head she is punching—driving a nail into it as Jael drove one into the temples of Sisera. Her brother Tom, who is the next important personage in the little community, is chiefly remarkable for self-assertion and hardheaded resistance of fate—his strong wrestling with adversity, and his anxiety to punish the slightest offence. Her father, Mr. Tulliver, is the incarnation of pugnacity. Her uncles and aunts are nothing if not critical, and after bickering among themselves for days together, and crowing over each other in the pride of imaginary conquest, look out upon their little parish with somewhat of the dissatisfaction which made the most renowned of victors lament that there were no more worlds to conquer. Two of the most remarkable scenes in the book are quite characteristic. The one is when old Tulliver, having lost the mill, agrees to remain in it as the servant of his enemy, who had come into possession. Excellent result of adversity, we say—the man has learned to forgive in resigning himself to the service of one who had done him the greatest of injuries. The nature of his religion, however, soon appears in the vow which he requests his son to register in the family Bible. * * * In the end the Tullivers manage to pay all their debts and to square accounts with the world. The moment this object has been achieved poor old Tulliver determines to be revenged on his foe, and at once proceeds to knock him down, which he does so vigorously as to bring upon himself a fit of illness ending in death. * * * This life of proud self-assertion that on the bad side presents itself in an incessant bickering, and on the best side appears as a devotion to justice and truth for selfish ends, may become interesting by being made heroic. The Brontes—both Charlotte and Emily—were fond of depicting this character, and by their account, by the account of Mrs. Gaskell, and by that of "George Eliot," it is a character that abounds in the northern counties. But when Charlotte or Emily Bronte dealt with such a nature, they ennobled or, at least, magnified it. In their pages we looked on men essentially selfish and unsociable—men encased in armour of proof against all encroachment—men who wronged nobody, and who vowed that nobody should wrong them. But the selfish isolation of such characters was lit up with passion, was justified or expiated by long suffering from some overwhelming wrong, was idealized by being joined to the possession of great intellectual powers. "George Eliot" has attempted a more difficult task. She takes these characters as we find them in real life—in all their intrinsic littleness. She paints them as she finds them—snapping at each other over the tea-table; eyeing each other enviously at church; privately plotting how to astonish each other by some extraordinary display; putting the worst construction on every word and act; officiously proffering advice and predicting calamity; living with perfect content their sordid life of vulgar respectability. The first half of the novel is devoted to the exhibition of this degraded species of existence, which is dissected with a masterly hand. Although it is the least exalting part of the work, it is the part of which the reader will carry away the most vivid recollection. The Dodson family will live for ever, and they inspire the work. With a self-denial which we cannot but admire, the author has resolutely set herself the task of delineating, without exaggeration, without extenuation, with minute accuracy, the sort of life which thousands upon thousands of our countrymen lead—a life that outwardly is most respectable, but inherently is most degraded—so degraded, indeed, that the very virtues which adorn it are scarcely to be distinguished from vices. We may be told that honesty is always honesty, and that if people arrive at true results we should not investigate too curiously their devious roads and their stumbling gait in travelling to the desired end. That is the practical philosophy of society, but now and then it is well that motives should be tested, and that we should see how much nearer than the Pharisee the publican and the sinner are to the kingdom of Heaven—how easily treachery may lurk in a kiss, and how naturally honesty may be as mean and detestable as a lie.

When "George Eliot" got exactly half through her work she foresaw the criticisms which a novel based on such a foundation would certainly provoke and she commenced her fourth book * * * by uttering against her story all that the most savage critic can have it in his heart to say. She compares the ruined villages that stud the banks of the Rhone in certain parts of its course with the ruined castles that crumble on the Rhine, and she contrasts the interests awakened by the one and by the other. * * * "George Eliot" expects her readers to be oppressed by a feeling of the same sort as they survey the sort of life that is depicted in these volumes, in which men and women are represented like ants upon an anthill—full of activity, full of intelligence, full of contrivance, but without any felt relation to the unseen world, brutish in their understanding, and going down to the grave like the brutes that perish. This emmetlike life of the Tullivers and Dodsons is essentially, as "George Eliot" preaches, a sordid life—irradiated by no sublime principles, no romantic visions, no active, self-renouncing faith, moved by none of those wild, uncontrollable passions which create the dark shadows of crime and misery—without that primitive rough simplicity of wants, that hard, submissive, ill-paid toil, that childlike spelling out of what nature has written, which gives its poetry to peasant life—a life so sordid that even sorrow hardly suffices to lift it above the level of the tragi-comic. We commend these half-dozen pages, in which the author, midway in her work, has stopped to criticize it and to explain her intention to the notice of all who wish to understand, as well as to enjoy what a writer of undoubted genius has invited us to read. Without attending to the clue thus furnished by the author, her object will be overlooked and full justice will not be done to her work. We must point out, however, that the object which the author has set herself of painting in all its nakedness, hideousness, and littleness the life of respectable brutishness which so many persons lead, illumined by not one ray of spiritual influence, by no suspicion of a higher life, of another world, of a surrounding divinity,—lifts the present work out of the category of ordinary novels. The author is attempting not merely to amuse us as a novelist, but, as a preacher, to make us think and feel. The riddle of life as it is here expounded is more like a Greek tragedy than a modern novel. In form we have the modern novel, with its every-day incidents and its humorous descriptions, but in spirit we have the Greek play, with its mysterious allusions and its serious import. In the highest sense we might call this a religious novel, only that description is liable to be misunderstood, and especially as religion is chiefly "conspicuous by its absence." We read on, wondering what is the meaning of the story, wondering why these mean, prosaic people, the Dodsons ever live; wondering why a brilliant novelist asks us to make their acquaintance and to become interested in their paltry existence, when suddenly the author breaks in upon us with the criticism to which we have already referred, and which we have partly quoted. She says in effect:—"You, reader, are oppressed by all this meanness—disgusted at all this hardness—perplexed that I should think it worthy of your notice. I perfectly agree with you; but such is life, and it is in the midst of such a life, the most marked quality of which is the utter absence of poetry or religion, that many of us grow up—it was in the midst of such a desert that my little heroine, Maggie, bloomed into beauty. It is well that these things should be impressed upon us, and that we should lay them to heart."

In fulfilling this portion of her task, which occupies exactly the first half of the novel, the author has very clearly helped herself out of a difficulty. It is difficult to describe adults leading a purely bestial life of vulgar respectability without rendering the picture simply repulsive. But the life of children is essentially an animal life,—a life, therefore, that to a certain extent accords with the brutish habits of mature personages; with this great difference, however,—that what is repulsive in the mature is amusing in the young. We do not expect boys and girls to have a strong sense of invisible things,—to be very spiritual in their aims—to make any striking display of poetry, sentiment, or religion. We wink at their enormities in sweets, we laugh at their savage tyrannies, and we take them for what they are—dear little animals, and nothing more.

"George Eliot" relieves the repulsiveness of the insect life which she has exhibited in the Dodson family by making her bigger insects all revolve around these two little creatures, Maggie and Tom Tulliver. Her description of the childlife is unique. No one has yet ventured to paint the childlife in all its prosaic reality. * * * "George Eliot," in approaching the subject, determined, as best agreeing with the general scope of her novel, to paint reality; and she has pictured the boy and girl life with the most amusing fidelity. We see all the little squabbling and domineering that goes on among children; we see them disgracefully intent on raspberry tart; we see the boy, after he has eaten up his share, mysteriously surveying his sister's, and wondering whether she will spare him a bit; we see the pleasure which they take in first tickling a toad, and then smashing it with a stone; we see all the envies, and cruelties, and gluttonies that in men would be revolting, but are only grotesque in these funny little animals.

The light of the story is Maggie, who has a warm heart, abounding in sympathy and longing for a return of her affection. Unfortunately, none of the personages by whom she is surrounded is capable of returning it, and "the little wench" finds herself at sixes and sevens with her family circle and with all the world. Almost the only one that has a kind word for her is her father, who immensely admires her cleverness. Her mother does not care for her,—cares more for her silver teapot and her spotted linen. Her brother despises her for her dependence and tenderness. Her uncles and aunts have no mercy on her. In these circumstances a hunchback falls in love with her, and she returns his affection. But herein she committed a great wrong, inasmuch as her lover, Philip Wakem, is son of the man accursed by her father, and against whom the fearful vow of vengeance was registered in the family Bible. Here she had a great struggle between duty and inclination,—the duty which she owed to her sick father, who might be killed if he heard of his daughter's intimacy with the son of his enemy, and the inclination to make herself and her lover happy; but the former prevailed. She found some peace and content in a mystical piety, which inculcated self-denial to the verge of asceticism as the true gateway to happiness. She had afterwards a yet fierce struggle to encounter. While still cherishing the memory of her renounced hunchback she received the attentions of a more likely man—who, unhappily, was all but engaged to her cousin. Her heart has been half won, when back comes the hunchback. Vows are renewed, but suddenly there is a shuffling of lovers; the new lover runs away with Maggie, and we expect that the story is to end in a maarriage. Here, however, comes the tug of war. Maggie will not obey passion in preference to duty. She remembers her own promise to the hunchback; she knows that the lover who has lured her away is the accepted suitor of her cousin, whom she would not wrong for the world, and so she insists on returning to her friends at the mill. She returns; but virtue must be its own reward, for she returns with a reputation blighted. The good people of St. Ogg's treat her as an outcast. Had she married the man who stole her away, thus jilting the hunchback and stabbing her cousin with the most cruel ingratitude, society would have received her with tolerance and eventually smiled on a rich man's wife. But simply to resist the devil—to come back unmarried though innocent, was too much for the worthy Dodson family—too much even for her brother, who turned her out of his house. There was no room in the world for her—there was little more chance of happiness. As we wonder what her fate will be, and begin half to suppose that the author is laying a train for a second shuffling of lovers, and so allotting her pairs that each shall be happy in the end, a sudden flood comes to put a stop to our speculations, for Maggie is drowned in it along with her brother Tom, and the motto of the novel is justified, "In their death they were not divided."

In the latter half of the novel it is that Maggie and Tom cease to be children; and here, also, we cease to be oppressed as before with that intolerable Dodson family, who are likely to have a proud preeminence in fiction as the most thorny set of people ever introduced into a tale. Other personages are introduced, and especially the character of Bob Jakin, the pedlar, is developed into something very entertaining. The incidents are nothing. "George Eliot" is not very strong in her incidents, and there are several points in the plot about which questions might be raised. It is in the description of character that she chiefly excels, and in the art of making the characters exhibit themselves. Her analysis of what is passing in the mind is very fine, and "George Eliot" takes her place as not one whit behind the greatest of our lady novelists, if she is not, indeed, before them all. Aunt Glegg, and Sister Pullett, and Mr. Pullett, and Luke, and the Rev. Walter Stelling, and Dr. Kenn, and Mr. Stephen Guest, are all admirably drawn; and, if it were not rather a mean thing in a critic to pick out the plums from a first-rate novel, we could give many quotations of their good sayings. Let the reader have his pleasure undisturbed by previous nibbling. But again we say that for the full appreciation of the present novel the object of it must not be forgotten; and that object is, to establish the contrast between a life of utter respectability and a life of stumbling and dubious, but still honest and noble, aspiration. Err as she may, sin as she may, the very faults of Maggie are more to be respected and loved than the hard consistency of her brother Tom and the Pharisaical rigidity of the Dodson family. One must not press the maxim too far, and we protest by anticipation against the novels that are sure to be written on the model of the present one, showing that it is a grand thing to lead a Bohemian life, and that respectability and the payment of one's debts is necessarily mean and uninteresting. In its own place, however, it contains a truth which ought to be attended to, and which a writer so sober as "George Eliot" is not likely to overstrain.

[DINAH MULOCK][1]

From *Macmillan's Magazine*, April 1861

* * *

Of "The Mill on the Floss," in a literary point of view, there can be but one opinion—that, as a work of art, it is as perfect as the novel can well be made: superior even to "Adam Bede." For the impression it gives of *power*, evenly cultivated and clear sighted,—the power of creation, amalgamating real materials into a foreplanned ideal scheme; the power of selection able to distinguish at once the fit and the unfit, choosing the one and rejecting the other, so as to make every part not only complete as to itself, but as to its relation with a well-balanced whole—the "Mill on the Floss" is one of the finest imaginative works in our language. In its diction, too: how magnificently rolls on that noble Saxon English—terse and clear, yet infinitely harmonious, keeping in its most simple common-place flow a certain majesty and solemnity which reminds one involuntarily of the deep waters of the Floss. The fatal Floss, which runs through the whole story like a Greek fate or a Gothic destiny—ay, from the very second chapter, when

> "Maggie, Maggie," continued the mother, in a tone of half-coaxing fretfulness, as this small mistake of nature entered the room, "where's the use o' my telling you to keep away from the water? You'll tumble in and be drownded some day, an' then you'll be sorry you didn't do as mother told you."

This is a mere chance specimen of the care over small things—the exquisite polish of each part, that yet never interferes with the breadth of the whole—which marks this writer as one of the truest *artists*, in the highest sense, of our or any other age.

Another impression made strongly by the first work of "George Eliot," and repeated by "his" (we prefer to respect the pseudonym) second, is the earnestness, sincerity, and heart nobility of the author. Though few books are freer from that morbid intrusion of self in which many writers of fiction indulge, no one can lay down "The Mill on the Floss" without a feeling of having held commune with a mind of rare individuality, with a judgment active and clear, and with a moral nature, conscientious, generous, religious, and pure. It is to this moral nature, this noblest

1. Dinah Mulock, later Dinah Mulock Craik, was a popular and prolific writer of novels, poems, children's books, and essays. In a letter, George Eliot refused to consider herself "a rival of Miss Mulock—a writer who is read only by novel readers, pure and simple, never by people of high culture." For Eliot's response to this review, which she did not know was written by Mulock, see her letters to John Blackwood of March 30 and April 4, 1861, page 432.

half of all literary perfectness, in our author, as in all other authors, that we now make appeal.

"George Eliot," or any other conscientious novelist, needs not to be told that he who appropriates this strange phantasmagoria of human life, to re-paint and re-arrange by the light of his own imagination, takes materials not his own, nor yet his reader's. He deals with mysteries which, in their entirety, belong alone to the Maker of the universe. By the force of his intellect, the quick sympathies of his heart, he may pierce into them a little way—farther, perhaps, than most people—but at best only a little way. He will be continually stopped by things he cannot understand—matters too hard for him, which make him feel, the more deeply and humbly as he grows more wise, how we are, at best,

> "Like infants crying in the dark,
> "And with no language but a cry."

If by his dimly-beheld, one-sided, fragmentary representations, which mimic untruly the great picture of life, this cry, either in his own voice, or in the involuntary utterance of his readers, rises into an accusation against God, how awful is his responsibility, how tremendous the evil that he may originate!

We doubt not, the author of the "Mill on the Floss" would shudder at the suspicion of this sort of involuntary blasphemy, and yet such is the tendency of the book and its story.

A very simple story. A girl of remarkable gifts—mentally, physically, and morally; born, like thousands more, of parents far inferior to herself—struggles through a repressed chlidhood, a hopeless youth: brought suddenly out of this darkness into the glow of a first passion for a man who, ignoble as he may be, is passionately in earnest with regard to her: she is tempted to treachery, and sinks into a great error, her extrication out of which, without involving certain misery and certain wrong to most or all around her, is simply an impossibility. The author cuts the Gordian knot by creating a flood on the Floss, which wafts this poor child out of her troubles and difficulties into the other world.

Artistically speaking, this end is very fine. Towards it the tale has gradually climaxed. From such a childhood as that of *Tom* and *Maggie Tulliver*, nothing could have come but the youth *Tom* and the girl *Maggie*, as we find them throughout that marevellous third volume: changed, indeed, but still keeping the childish images of little *Tom* and little *Maggie*, of Dorlcote Mill. Ay, even to the hour, when with that sense of the terrible exalted into the sublime, which only genius can make us feel—we see them go down to the deeps of the Floss "in an embrace never to be parted: living through again, in one supreme moment, the days when they had clasped their little hands in love, and roamed through the daisied fields together."

So far as exquisite literary skill, informed and vivified by the highest order of imaginative power, can go, this story is perfect. But take it from another point of view. Ask, what good will it do?—whether it will lighten any burdened heart, help any perplexed spirit, comfort the sorrowful, succour the tempted, or bring back the erring into the way of peace; and what is the answer? Silence.

Let us reconsider the story, not artistically, but morally.

Here is a human being, placed during her whole brief life—her hapless nineteen years—under circumstances the hardest and most fatal that could befal one of her temperament. She has all the involuntary egotism and selfishness of a nature that, while eagerly craving for love, loves ardently and imaginatively rather than devotedly; and the only love that might have at once humbled and raised her, by showing her how far nobler it was than her own—Philip's—is taken from her in early girlhood. Her instincts of right, true as they are, have never risen into principles; her temptations to vanity, and many other faults, are wild and fierce; yet not human help ever comes near her to strengthen the one or subdue the other. This *may* be true to nature, and yet we think it is not. Few of us, calmly reviewing our past, can feel that we have ever been left so long and so utterly without either outward aid, or the inner voice—never silent in a heart like poor *Maggie's*. It is, in any case, a perilous doctrine to preach—the doctrine of overpowering circumstances.

Again, notwithstanding the author's evident yearning over *Maggie*, and disdain for *Tom*, we cannot but feel that if people are to be judged by the only fair human judgment, of how far they act up to what they believe in, *Tom*, so far as his light goes, is a finer character than his sister. He alone has the self-denial to do what he does not like, for the sake of doing right; he alone has the self-command to smother his hopeless love, and live on, a brave, hard-working life; he, except in his injustice to poor *Maggie*, has at least the merit of having made no one else miserable. Perfectly true is what he says, though he says it in a Pharisaical way, "Yes, *I* have had feelings to struggle with, but I conquered them. I have had a harder life than you have had, but I have found *my* comfort in doing my duty." Nay, though perhaps scarcely intended, Bob Jakin's picture of the solitary lad, "as close as an iron biler," who "sits by himself so glumpish, aknittin' his brow, an' a-lookin' at the fire of a night," is in its way as pathetic as *Maggie's* helpless cry to Dr. Kenn, at the bazaar, "O, I must go."

In the whole history of this fascinating *Maggie* there is a picturesque piteousness which somehow confuses one's sense of right and wrong. Yet what—we cannot help asking—what is to become of the hundreds of clever girls, born of uncongenial parents, hemmed in with unsympathising kindred of the Dodson sort, blest with no lover on whom to bestow their strong affections, no friend to whom to cling for guidance and support? They must fight their way, heaven help them! alone and unaided, through cloud and darkness, to the light. And, thank heaven, hundreds of them do, and live to hold out a helping hand afterwards to thousands more. "The "middle-aged" (says "George Eliot," in this very book), "who have lived through their strongest emotions, but are yet in the time when memory is still half-passionate and not merely contemplative, should surely be a sort of natural priesthood, whom life has disciplined and consecrated to be the refuge and rescue of early stumblers and victims of self-despair."

Will it help these—such a picture as *Maggie*, who, with all her high aspirations and generous qualities, is, throughout her poor young life, a stay and comfort to no human being, but, on the contrary, a source of grief and injury to every one connected with her? If we are to judge character by results—not by grand imperfect essays, but by humbler fulfilments—of how much more use in the world were even fond, shallow *Lucy*, and narrow-minded *Tom*, than this poor *Maggie*, who seems only just to have caught hold of the true meaning and beauty of existence in that last pathetic prayer, "If my life is to be long, let me live to bless and comfort," when she is swept away out of our sight and love for ever.

True this is, as we have said, a magnificent ending for the book; but is it for the life—the one human life which this author has created so vividly and powerfully, that we argue concerning it as if we had actually known it? Will it influence for good any other real lives—this passionately written presentment of temptation never conquered, or just so far that we see its worst struggle as but beginning; of sorrows which teach nothing, or teach only bitterness; of love in its most delicious, most deadly phase; love blind, selfish, paramount, seeing no future but possession, and, that hope gone, no alternative but death—death, welcomed as the solution of all difficulties, the escape from all pain?

Is this right? Is it a creed worthy of an author who has pre-eminently what all novelists should have, "the brain of a man and the heart of a woman," united with what we may call a sexless intelligence, clear and calm, able to observe, and reason, and guide mortal passions, as those may, who have come out of the turmoil of the flesh into the region of ministering spirits, "αγγελοι," messengers between God and man? What if the messenger testify falsely? What if the celestial trumpet give forth an uncertain sound?

Yet let us be just. There are those who argue that this—perhaps the finest ending, artistically, of any modern novel, is equally fine in a moral sense: that the death of *Maggie* and *Tom* is a glorious Euthanasia, showing that when even at the eleventh hour, temptation is conquered, error atoned, and love reconciled, the life is complete: its lesson has been learnt, its work done; there is nothing more needed but the *vade in pacem* to an immediate heaven. This, if the author so meant it, was an idea grand, noble, Christian: as Christian (be it said with reverence) as the doctrine preached by the Divine Pardoner of all sinners to the sinner beside whom He died—"To-day shalt thou be with me in paradise." But the conception ought to have been worked out so plainly that no reader could mistake it. We should not have been left to feel, as we do feel, undecided whether this death was a translation or an escape: whether if they had not died, *Maggie* would not have been again the same *Maggie*, always sinning and always repenting; and *Tom* the same *Tom*, hard and narrow-minded, though the least ray of love and happiness cast over his gloomy life, might have softened and made a thoroughly good man of him. The author ought to have satisfied us entirely as to the radical change in both; else we fall back upon the same dreary creed of overpowering circumstances: of human beings struggling for ever in a great quagmire of unconquerable temptations, inevitable and hopeless woe. A creed more fatal to every noble effort and brave self-restraint—above all to that humble faith in the superior Will which alone should govern ours—can hardly be conceived. It is true that there occur sometimes in life positions so complex and overwhelming, that plain right and wrong become confused; until the most righteous and religious man is hardly able to judge clearly or act fairly. But to meet such positions is one thing, to *invent* them is another. It becomes a serious question whether any author—who, great as his genius may be, sees not farther than mortal intelligence can—is justified in leading his readers into a labyrinth, the way out of which he does not, first, see clearly himself, and next, is able to make clear to them, so as to leave them mentally and morally at rest, free from all perplexity and uncertainty.

Now, uncertainty is the prevailing impression with which we close "the Mill on the Floss." We are never quite satisfied in our detestation of the *Dodson* family, the more odious because so dreadfully natural that we feel we all are haunted by some of the race, could name them among our own connections, perhaps have even received kindnesses from a *Mrs. Pullet*, a *Mrs. Glegg*, or a *Mrs. Tulliver*. We are vexed with ourselves for being so angry with stern, honest, upright, business-like *Tom*—so contemptuously indifferent to gentle unsuspicious *Lucy*, with her universal kindness, extending from "the more familiar rodents" to her silly *aunt Tulliver*. We question much whether such a generous girl as *Maggie* would have fallen in love with *Stephen* at all; whether she would not from the first have regarded him simply as her cousin's lover, and if his passion won anything from her, it would but have been the half-angry half-sorrowful disdain which a high-minded woman could not help feeling towards a man who forgot duty and honour in selfish love, even though the love were for herself. And, last and chief perplexity of all, we feel that, granting the case as our author puts it, the mischief done, the mutual passion mutually confessed, *Stephen's* piteous arguments have some justice on their side. The wrong done to him in *Maggie's* forsaking him was almost as great as the wrong previously done to *Philip* and *Lucy*:—whom no self-sacrifice on her part or *Stephen's* could ever have made happy again.

And, to test the matter, what reader will not confess, with a vague sensation of uneasy surprise, to have taken far less interest in all the good injured personages of the story, than in this mad *Stephen* and treacherous *Maggie*? Who that is capable of understanding—as a thing which has been or is, or may one day be—the master-passion that furnishes the key to so many lives, will not start to find how vividly this book revives it, or wakens it, or places it before him as a future possibility? Who does not think with a horribly delicious feeling, of such a crisis, when right and wrong, bliss and bale, justice and conscience, seem swept from their boundaries, and a whole existence of *Dodsons*, *Lucys*, and *Tom Tullivers*, appears worth nothing compared to the ecstacy of that "one kiss—the last" between *Stephen* and *Maggie* in the lane?

Is this right? The spell once broken—broken with the closing of the book—every high and pure and religious instinct within us answers unhesitatingly—"No."

It is *not* right to paint *Maggie* only as she is in her strong, unsatisfied, erring youth—and leave her there, her doubts unresolved, her passions unregulated, her faults unatoned and unforgiven: to cut her off ignobly and accidentally, leaving two acts, one her recoil of conscience with regard to *Stephen*, and the other her instinctive self-devotion in going to rescue *Tom*, as the sole noble landmarks of a life that had in it every capability for good with which a woman could be blessed. It is *not* right to carry us on through these three marvelous volumes, and leave us at the last standing by the grave of the brother and sister, ready to lift up an accusatory cry, less to a beneficent Deity than to the humanly-invented Arimanes of the universe.—"Why should such things be? Why hast Thou made us thus?"

But it may be urged, that fiction has its counterpart, and worse, in daily truth. How many perplexing histories do we not know of young lives blighted, apparently by no fault of their own; of blameless lives dragged into irresistible temptations; of high natures so meshed in by circumstances that they, as well as we, judging them from without, can hardly distinguish right from wrong, guilt from innocence; of living and loveable beings so broken down by unmerited afflictions, that when at last they come to an end, we look on the poor dead face with a sense of thankfulness that there at least,

> "There is no other thing expressed
> But long disquiet merged in rest."

All this is most true, *so far as we see*. But we never can see, not even the wisest and greatest of us, anything like *the whole* of even the meanest and briefest human life. We never can know through what fiery trial of temptation, nay, even sin,—for sin itself appears sometimes in the wonderful alchemy of the universe to be used as an agent for good,—a strong soul is being educated into a saintly minister to millions of weaker souls: coming to them with the authority of one whom suffering has taught how to heal suffering; nay, whom the very fact of having sinned once, has made more deeply to pity, so as more easily to rescue sinners. And, lastly, we never can comprehend, unless by experience, that exceeding peace—the "peace which passeth all understanding," which is oftentimes seen in those most heavily and hopelessly afflicted: those who have lost all, and gained their own souls: whereof they possess themselves in patience: waiting until the "supreme moment" of which our author speaks, but which is to them not an escape from the miseries of this world, but a joyful entrance into the world ever-lasting.

Ay, thank heaven, though the highest human intellect may fail to hear it, there are millions of human hearts yet living and throbbing, or mouldering quietly into dust, who have felt, all through the turmoil or silence of existence, though lasting for threescore years and ten, a continual still small voice, following them to the end: "Fear not: for I am thy *God*."

Would that in some future book, as poweful as "The Mill on the Floss," the author might become a true "Αγγελος," and teach us this!

HENRY JAMES[1]

The Novels of George Eliot[†]

* * *

Of the four English stories, "The Mill on the Floss" seems to me to have most dramatic continuity, in distinction from that descriptive, discursive method of narration which I have attempted to indicate. After Hetty Sorrel, I think Maggie Tulliver the most successful of the author's young women, and after Tito Melema, Tom Tulliver is the best of her young men. English novels abound in pictures of childhood; but I know of none more truthful and touching than the early pages of this work. Poor erratic Maggie is worth a hundred of her positive brother, and yet on the very threshold of life she is compelled to accept him as her master. He falls naturally into the man's privilege of always being in

1. Henry James (1843–1916) was a major expatriate American novelist. He became a British citizen in 1915.

† From *The Atlantic Monthly* October 1866: 489–90.

the right. * * * The following scene is more than a reminiscence; it is a real retrospect. Tom and Maggie are sitting upon the bough of an elder-tree, eating jam-puffs. At last only one remains, and Tom undertakes to divide it.

* * *

The portions of the story which bear upon the Dodson family are in their way not unworthy of Balzac; only that, while our author has treated its peculiarities humorously, Balzac would have treated them more seriously, almost solemnly. We are reminded of him by the attempt to classify the Dodsons socially in a scientific manner, and to accumulate small examples of their idiosyncrasies. I do not mean to say that the resemblance is very deep. The chief defect—indeed, the only serious one—in "The Mill on the Floss" is its conclusion. Such a conclusion is in itself assuredly not illegitimate, and there is nothing in the fact of the flood, to my knowledge, essentially unnatural: what I object to is its relation to the preceding part of the story. The story is told as if it were destined to have, if not a strictly happy termination, at least one within ordinary probabilities. As it stands, the *dénouement* shocks the reader most painfully. Nothing has prepared him for it; the story does not move towards it; it casts no shadow before it. Did such a *dénouement* lie within the author's intentions from the first, or was it a tardy expedient for the solution of Maggie's difficulties? This question the reader asks himself, but of course he asks it in vain. For my part, although, as long as humanity is subject to floods and earthquakes, I have no objection to see them made use of in novels, I would in this particular case have infinitely preferred that Maggie should have been left to her own devices. I understand the author's scruples, and to a certain degree I respect them. A lonely spinsterhood seemed but a dismal consummation of her generous life; and yet, as the author conceives, it was unlikely that she would return to Stephen Guest. I respect Maggie profoundly; but nevertheless I ask, Was this after all so unlikely? I will not try to answer the question. I have shown enough courage in asking it. But one thing is certain: a *dénouement* by which Maggie should have called Stephen back would have been extremely interesting, and would have had far more in its favor than can be put to confusion by a mere exclamation of horror.

ALGERNON CHARLES SWINBURNE[1]

[The Flaw in *The Mill on the Floss*][†]

* * *

And now we must regretfully and respectfully consider of what quality and what kind may be the faults which deform the best and ripest work of Charlotte Brontë's chosen rival. Few or none, I should suppose, of her most passionate and intelligent admirers would refuse to accept 'The Mill on the Floss' as on the whole at once the highest and the purest and the fullest example of her magnificent and matchless powers—for matchless altogether, as I have already insisted, they undoubtedly are in their own wide and fruitful field of work. The first two-thirds of the book suffice to compose perhaps the very noblest of tragic as well as of humorous prose idyls in the language; comprising, as they likewise do, one of the sweetest as well as saddest and tenderest as well as subtlest examples of dramatic analysis—a study in that kind as soft and true as Rousseau's, as keen and true as Browning's, as full as either's of the fine and bitter sweetness of a pungent and fiery fidelity. But who can forget the horror of inward collapse, the sickness of spiritual reaction, the reluctant incredulous rage of disenchantment and disgust, with which he first came upon the thrice unhappy third part? The two first volumes have all the intensity and all the perfection of George Sand's best work, tempered by all the simple purity and interfused with all the stainless pathos of Mrs. Gaskell's; they carry such affluent weight of thought and shine with such warm radiance of humour as invigorates and illuminates the work of no other famous woman; they have the fiery clarity of crystal or of lightning; * * * But what shall any one say of the upshot? If we are really to take it on trust, to confront it as a contingent or conceivable possibility, resting our reluctant faith on the authority of so great a female writer, that a woman of Maggie Tulliver's kind can be moved to any sense but that of bitter disgust and sickening disdain by a thing—I will not write, a man—of Stephen Guest's; if we are to accept as truth and fact, however astonishing and revolting, so shameful an avowal, so vile a revelation as this; in that ugly and lamentable case, our only remark, as our only comfort, must be that now at least the last word of realism has surely been spoken, the last abyss of cynicism has surely been sounded and laid bare. * * *

* * * My faith will not digest at once the first two volumes and the third volume of 'The Mill on the Floss'; my conscience or credulity has not gorge enough for such a gulp. Whatever capacity for belief is in me

1. Swinburne (1837–1909) was a prominent poet and critic.

† From A *Note on Charlotte Brontë* (London: Chatto and Windus, 1877) 28–38.

I find here impaled once more as on the horns of that old divine's dilemma between the irreconcilable attributes of goodness and omnipotence in the supposed Creator of suffering and of sin.

* * *

* * * The hideous transformation by which Maggie is debased—were it but for an hour—into the willing or yielding companion of Stephen's flight would probably and deservedly have been resented as a brutal and vulgar outrage on the part of a male novelist. But the man never lived, I do believe, who could have done such a thing as this: as the man, I should suppose, does not exist who could make for the first time the acquaintance of Mr. Stephen Guest with no incipient sense of a twitching in his fingers and a tingling in his toes at the notion of any contact between Maggie Tulliver and a cur so far beneath the chance of promotion to the notice of his horsewhip, or elevation to the level of his boot.

Here then is the patent flaw, here too plainly is the flagrant blemish, which defaces and degrades the very crown and flower of George Eliot's wonderful and most noble work; no rent or splash on the raiment, no speck or scar on the skin of it, but a cancer in the very bosom, a gangrene in the very flesh. It is a radical and mortal plague-spot, corrosive and incurable; in the apt and accurate phrase of Rabelais, 'an enormous solution of continuity.' No washing or trimming, no pruning or purging, could eradicate or efface it; it could only be removable by amputation and remediable by cautery.

JOHN RUSKIN[1]

[The Vulgarity of *The Mill on the Floss*][†]

* * *

All healthy and helpful literature sets simple bars between right and wrong; assumes the possibility, in men and women, of having healthy minds in healthy bodies, and loses no time in the diagnosis of fever or dyspepsia in either; least of all in the particular kind of fever which signifies the ungoverned excess of any appetite or passion. The "dulness" which many modern readers inevitably feel, and some modern blockheads think it creditable to allege, in Scott, consists not a little in his absolute purity from every loathsome element or excitement of the lower passions; so that people who live habitually in Satyric or hircine con-

1. Ruskin (1819–1900) was one of the great Victorian prose writers, whose works included art criticism, aesthetic theory, and social criticism.

† From *The Complete Works of John Ruskin*, ed. E. T. Cook and Alexandra Wedderburn, vol. 34 (London: George Allen, 1903–1912) 376–77.

ditions of thought find him as insipid as they would a picture of Angelico's. The accurate and trenchant separation between him and the common railrod-station novelist is that, in his total method of conception, only lofty character is worth describing at all; and it becomes interesting, not by its faults, but by the difficulties and accidents of the fortune through which it passes, while, in the railway novel, interest is obtained with the vulgar reader for the vilest character, because the author describes carefully to his recognition the blotches, burrs and pimples in which the paltry nature resembles his own. *The Mill on the Floss* is perhaps the most striking instance extant of this study of cutaneous disease. There is not a single person in the book of the smallest importance to anybody in the world but themselves, or whose qualities deserved so much as a line of printer's type in their description. There is no girl alive, fairly clever, half educated, and unluckily related, whose life has not at least as much in it as Maggie's, to be described and to be pitied. Tom is a clumsy and cruel lout, with the making of better things in him (and the same may be said of nearly every Englishman at present smoking and elbowing his way through the ugly world his blunders have contributed to the making of); while the rest of the characters are simply the sweepings out of a Pentonville omnibus.

CRITICISM

LESLIE STEPHEN[1]

[The Heroine of *The Mill on the Floss*][†]

Adam Bede had not been long in the hands of readers when a new novel was begun. At the end of April 1859 George Eliot had finished a short story called "The Lifted Veil"—taken up as "a resource when her head was too stupid for more important work"—and was about to "rewrite" the first two chapters of the novel which ultimately received the name of *The Mill on the Floss.* The first volume was finished before October, the second on 16th January, and the third on 21st March 1860. It appeared at the beginning of April, rivalled *Adam Bede* in its immediate popularity, and sustained or increased her reputation with the most thoughtful readers. In one respect, as already intimated, it is clearly the most interesting of all her books. In the *Scenes of Clerical Life* she had made use of the stories current in the early domestic circle; in *Adam Bede* she had drawn a portrait of that circle itself; and she now took herself for a heroine, and the first two volumes become virtually a spiritual autobiography. The title originally suggested, "Sister Maggie," is really the most appropriate. The external circumstances have, of course, been altered. The scenery is supposed to be in Lincolnshire, and the town of St. Ogg's is said to represent Gainsborough. But her native district still supplies the details. The "round pool," to which she had gone on fishing expeditions with her brother, and the "Red Deeps," which had been a favourite haunt, are transported from Griff to Dorlcote Mill. The attic to which Maggie retires in the mill is the attic to which George Eliot had retired in her father's house. Her brother, we are told, had already detected her in her first story. She was now revealed, not only to him, but to her old neighbours, by the closeness of her descriptions. The important point, however, is her identity with the heroine. The elder Tullivers do not represent her parents; and the brother Tom, it is to be hoped, was at most vaguely suggested by the real Isaac Evans. But Maggie Tulliver, spite of certain modifications—the remarkable personal beauty, for example, which has for good reasons to be bestowed upon her—evidently represents as clearly as possible what George Eliot would have been had she been transplanted in her infancy to some slightly different family in the same district. Although many of the best novels in the language are autobiographical, there is hardly one which gives so vivid and direct a representation of the writer's most intimate characteristics. It is proper, I believe, to speak of such writing as "subjective"—an epithet which sometimes suggests an erroneous infer-

1. Leslie Stephen (1832–1904) was a prominent man of letters and Virginia Woolf's father.
† From *George Eliot* (New York: The Macmillan Company, 1909) 86–104.

ence. Every genuine description is subjective in the sense that it must give the writer's own impressions, and is not a mere adoption of language which has recorded the impressions of others. But it need not be "subjective" in the sense of giving the individual peculiarities alone. Self-knowledge implies also knowledge of our common human nature. The novelist speaks for us because he speaks for himself. The actual "confession," of course, depends for its interest upon the interest of the character revealed; and if that character be one of great moral and intellectual power, and an impressive incarnation of an interesting type of the human species, the direct utterance of its emotions has a peculiar fascination. "To my feeling," said George Eliot, "there is more thought and a profounder veracity in *The Mill* than in *Adam*; but *Adam* is more complete and better balanced. My love of the childhood scenes made me linger over them, so that I could not develop as fully as I wished the concluding 'book,' in which the tragedy occurs, and which I had looked forward to with much attention and premeditation from the beginning." Bulwer had made this criticism, and had also found fault with the scene in which Maggie accepts Tom's dictation too passively. She admitted that he was right in both cases, and both remarks were, as we shall see, significant. *The Mill on the Floss*, indeed, considered simply as a story, obviously suffers from the disproportionate development of the earlier part; but I do not think that any reader could wish for a change which would sacrifice the revelation of character to the requirements of the plot. Taken by itself, the first part of *The Mill* represents to my mind the culmination of George Eliot's power. Maggie is one example of the feminine type which occurs with important modifications in most of the other stories. But George Eliot throws herself so frankly into Maggie's position, gives her "double" such reality by the wayward foibles associated with her nobler impulses, and dwells so lovingly upon all her joys and sorrows, that the character glows with a more tender and poetic charm than any of her other heroines. I suppose that Dinah Morris would be placed higher in the scale of morality; but if the test of a heroine's merits be the reader's disposition to fall in love with her (and that, I confess, is my own), I hold that Maggie is worth a wilderness of Dinahs.

One result of this sympathy with her heroine is conspicuous. No book, I imagine, ever set forth so clearly and touchingly the glamour with which the childish imagination invests the trivial and commonplace. There is enough poetry in all of us in our earlier years to enable us to appreciate the truth, though rare genius is required to recall so vividly the old associations and to bring out so tenderly their pathetic side. We all have enough poetry left beneath our layers of commonplace to share Maggie's emotions in the attic, with its high-pitched roof, its worm-eaten floors and shelves, and dark rafters festooned with cobwebs, where she keeps her "Fetish": the trunk of an old doll, into whose head she drives nails in emulation of Jael's feat as pictured in the Family

Bible. We can understand, too, the "dim delicious awe" produced by the "resolute din, the unresting motion of the great stones" in the mill, where the meal pours down till the very spider-nets look like a fairy bulwark. Maggie speculated especially upon the "fat floury spiders," and their probable relations to spiders of the outside world. Toads and earwigs become actors in other little romances. She confides to her little cousin that Mrs. Earwig is running so fast to fetch a doctor for a small earwig that has fallen into the hot copper. Brother Tom shows his matter-of-fact character by smashing the earwig "as a superfluous yet easy means of proving the entire unreality" of such a story. The imaginative faculty transfigures toads and earwigs and invests with mystery the round pool, framed with willows and tall reeds, where she delights in the "whispers and dreamy silences," and listens to the "light dipping sounds of the rising fish and the gentle rustling as if the willows and the reeds and the water lend their happy whispering also." Her life is to change, but the old joy can never be quite lost. "Our delight in the sunshine on the deep-bladed grass to-day would be no more than the faint perception of wearied souls if it were not for the sunshine and the grass in the far-off years which still live in us and transform our perception into love."

Meanwhile, however, imagination is a faculty which has its disadvantages when it is placed in uncongenial surroundings. Its possessor or victim has to suffer terrible raps over the knuckles from the Tom Tullivers. "Those bitter sorrows of childhood!" she exclaims, "when sorrow is all new and strange, when hope has not yet got wings to fly beyond the days and weeks, and the space from summer to summer seems measureless!" George Eliot insists upon this text, and the absurdity of telling a child that its real troubles are to come. "We have sobbed piteously, standing with tiny bare legs above our little socks, when we have lost sight of a mother or nurse," but we can no longer revive the poignancy of the moment. "Surely if we could recall that early bitterness and the dim guesses, the strangely perspectiveless conception of life that gave the bitterness its intensity, we should not pooh pooh the griefs of our children." I would not venture to pronounce upon the general soundness of the doctrine; in that matter we all generalise from our private experience, and are very liable to illusions; but the truth for a child of Maggie's peculiarities is undeniable and most pathetic. When she is not only snubbed by Tom, but roused to jealousy by his kindness to her cousin Lucy, "there were passions at war in her to have made a tragedy, if tragedies were made by passion only; but the essential τι μέγεθος who was present in the passion was wanting in the action; the utmost Maggie could do, with a thrust of her small brown arm, was to push poor little pink-and-white Lucy into the cow-trodden mud." The remark indicates the curious power of the book. The chief actors are children, their surroundings are of the dullest and narrowest conceivable, and yet we are spectators of a drama with really tragic interest. "Not

Leonore," we are told, "in that preternatural midnight excursion with her phantom lover, was more terrified than poor Maggie in her entirely natural ride on a short-paced donkey with a gypsy behind her, who considered that he was earning half a crown." The bray of another donkey under the setting sun becomes portentous, and the low cottages which she passes suggest a probable habitation of witches.

The *Mill on the Floss*, so far, is a singular powerful presentation, by help of her personal memories, of the theme of Andersen's "ugly duckling"; the seed of genius cast upon barren ground and yet managing to find sufficient nurture from the most unpromising materials. It is the more effective because the tragic side is not too prominent. There is none of the brutal tyranny which crushes some children in pathetic fiction. Maggie, on the whole, in spite of all her scrapes, has a good many happy hours, and is child enough to accept the unintentional stupidities of her family circle as part of the inevitable. She is not conscious of being a misunderstood genius; she only suffers because she has vague aspirations and longings, but does not feel herself to be enslaved or bound to overt revolt. The circle, forming the prose element against which her poetic impulses are to struggle, is drawn with a force and humour which, but for the author's distinct disavowal, would convince us that it was a study from the life. Indeed, though we have to admit that there was no actual counterpart of Mrs. Glegg or the Pullets, we must suppose that some of their characteristic traits were taken from real people, though more or less modified and put into different combinations. Certainly we seem to be reading a direct transcript from early recollections when we pay a visit to the Pullets with Mrs. Tulliver and her children, when Mrs. Pullet devoutly exhibits her new bonnet, and is moved by the solemnity of the occasion to thoughts of human mortality. * * * The conversation runs on with such admirable naturalness, that we can but take it as the echo of such talks as were once the staple of conversation at Chilvers-Coton. We may look out upon old farms as we are hurried past them in the railway and wonder whether they still shelter Tullivers and Dodsons, and possibly ask the more inscrutable question, whether the talk of some ladies nearer home may not in its essence resemble the remarks of Mrs. Pullet.

The precious books were meant as revelations of the romance to be found under the most commonplace exteriors. It becomes a problem whether this bit of commonplace is not too sordid. It is "irradiated by no sublime principles, no romantic visions, no active self-renouncing faith, moved by none of those wild, uncontrollable passions which create the dark shadows of misery and crime—without that primitive rough simplicity of events, that hard submissive ill-paid toil, that childlike spelling out of what nature has written which gives its poetry to peasant life." George Eliot admits that she shares the sense of oppressive narrowness, but wishes to show how it acted upon the young souls immersed in it. And, after all, she holds that it had its good results. Its religion was simply blind acceptance of tradition, and its morality adherence to established customs. The religion meant going to church on proper occasions, being baptized, because otherwise one could not be buried; and taking care that there should be the "proper pall-bearers and well-cured hams at one's funeral." Mr. Tulliver took much the same view of the services as Tennyson's immortal farmer from the same region. He considered, however, that "church was one thing and common-sense another, and he wanted nobody to tell him what common-sense was." He shows a touch worthy of the "Northern Farmer" when he orders his son to record in the Family Bible a declaration that he will not forgive his enemy, and hopes that evil may befall him. There is a strain of the old Viking blood in him after all, and it is more or less shown in the morality. The Dodsons were "a very proud race"; no one should be able to tax them with a breach of traditional duty. So, even when Mrs. Glegg, the most nagging and contradictory of them all, quarrels with her sister, she feels bound to leave their fair share of her property to her sister's children. Their pride was wholesome, as it identified honour with "perfect integrity, thoroughness of work, and faithfulness to admitted rules." Mr. Glegg, like his neighbours, was "near"; he had made money very slowly, by steady parsimony, and saving had become an end in itself. He would have thought it a "mad kind of lavishness" to give away a five-pound note to save a poor widow's furniture, but he was really sorry for her; and was as anxious to save other people's money as his own. The Tullivers had warmer hearts and more impulsive characters than their neighbours, and discharge their family duties from genuine affection as well as from a sense of traditional affection. Mr. Tulliver's kindness to his ruined sister atones for his recklessness and his perverse passion for "lawing"; and his love for his "little wench" gives her main consolation under the troubles of her childhood. Her sympathy for him under his troubles and illness is a natural stage in the development of her finer qualities.

So far, if it be true that George Eliot's fondness for the old memories had betrayed her into some disproportionate length, no one can deny the extraordinary skill and force with which the situation is prepared. We may miss at times the more idyllic elements represented by Mrs. Poyser's circle, though the charming pedlar Bob Jakin brings some of the old wit and quaint humour into the less exhilarating surroundings. At any rate, the mine is very effectually laid, and we now have to watch the explosion. Maggie, with her pathetic attempts to snatch at any floating bits of learning that may enable her intellectual wings to expand, has gone through her creator's experience in a rather more trying form. She has had to feed upon Defoe's *History of the Devil*, and made attempts to draw honey from the Latin Grammar, Euclid, and Aldrich; and now that a happy chance has introduced her to à Kempis, we can see that she is fitted to receive consolation, under the dry and barren outward life, in some form of religious mysticism. When the sensitive and artistic Philip Wakem, made eager for consolation by his deformity and his own domestic difficulties, meets the beautiful young woman, we are also not surprised that her longings for sympathy should turn to a human object. On both sides there is ample opportunity for awaking love and pity. It is natural, again, that the position should bring her into collision with her brother. He has no turn for poetry and art and mysticism, but his plunge into difficulties has called out the sturdy qualities of the Tulliver race, and we sympathise with his energy in retrieving the family fortunes. The quarrel arises inevitably when he finds that his sister is in love with a youth, not only deficient in the manly qualities, but son and heir to the enemy against whom he has inscribed a vow of vengeance. That he should take a decided course of action under the circumstances is only to be expected. Nor, perhaps, is it surprising that he behaves like a brute. There is plenty of "heredity" to account for that. But here is a first difficulty. George Eliot admitted, as I have said, that the scene between brother and sister was not quite satisfactory. The young woman, with her high-wrought enthusiasm, submits too "passively," not to say, tamely, to his imperious interference. She confesses that she has done wrong, and promises not to see her lover again in private. Tom's behaviour, I fancy, makes him simply offensive to most people, though it seems to be obvious that we are intended to retain a certain regard for him. The failure seems to me to be easily explicable. I heard once from a most intelligent lady of an elder generation that the agitation for women's rights was absurd, because as a matter of fact all women like, and always will like, to be slaves. Younger ladies, it is true, have assured me that this is a complete mistake, and that women have as strong an objection as men to be objects of tyrrany. I should be afraid to express any opinion upon a question in which women must be the best judges. Yet I am half inclined to guess that, along with other conservative tendencies, George Eliot had inherited some sympathy with this older view. Of course, she would be the last person to approve the tyranny of brothers or husbands, and is only trying to do justice to the moral code accepted in St. Ogg's circles, of which it was a part that the family should be under masculine supremacy. The true difficulty is again, as I take it, that she was too thoroughly feminine to be quite at home in the psychology of the male animal Her women are—so far as a man can judge—unerringly drawn. We are convinced at every point of the insight and fidelity of the analysis; but when she draws a man, she has not the same certainty of touch. She is, I have suggested, a little too contemptuous when the Samson yields to the Delilah; and when he asserts his privileges, his strength is apt to be too like brutality. Many rustic Tom Tullivers would, no doubt, ride roughshod over sisterly sensibilities; but if we are to retain sympathy for their better nature, they should show more twinges of conscience. Tom's profound conviction that whatever he does is therefore right, is no doubt characteristic; but he might at least feel that he is doing a painful duty, and not be represented as utterly insensible to the claims of the old childish affections.

The comparative weakness, however, of masculine portraits has a more unpleasant result. She admits that the tragedy which follows is "not adequately prepared." She will "always regret" the want of fulness in the treatment of the third volume, due, as she says, to the *epische Breite* into which she was beguiled by love of her subject in its predecessors. But she defends the position itself, which many readers have condemned. "Maggie's position towards Stephen Guest—upon which the tragedy turns—is," she says, "too vital a part of my whole conception and purpose for me to be converted to the condemnation of it. If I am wrong there—if I did not really know what my heroine would feel and do under the circumstances in which I deliberately placed her—I ought not to have written this book at all, but quite a different work, if any. If the ethics of art do not admit the truthful presentation of a character essentially noble, but liable to great error—error that is anguish to its own nobleness—then it seems to me the ethics of art are too narrow, and must be widened to correspond with a widening psychology." Without discussing the "ethics of art," we may, I should think, fully agree that the critical canon thus abjured is erroneous. I am not aware, however, that any professor of æsthetics has laid down the rule that it is wrong to represent a noble character led into fatal error, and consequent remorse, by its weaknesses. I should have supposed that nothing could be a more legitimate topic. George Eliot is unintentionally changing the issue upon which a defence is really required. We have sympathised keenly with Maggie. We understand the "strange thrill of awe" which passes through her when passages from the *Imitation of Christ* affect her like a strain of solemn music; when she infers that "the miseries of her young life had come from fixing her heart on her own pleasure"; and saw the possibility of looking at her own life as "an insignificant part of a divinely guided whole." She forms "plans of self-humiliation and entire devotedness, and fancies that renunciation will give her" the satisfaction for which she had so long been "craving in vain." "She had not perceived—how could she until she had lived longer?—the inmost truth of the old monk's outpourings that renunciation remains sorrow, though sorrow willingly borne. Maggie was still panting for happiness, and was in ecstasy because she had found the key to it." That is beautifully said, and is followed by an admirable account of her effort to attain the true spirit. When, again, Philip Wakem urges her not to stifle human affections, and persist in a "narrow asceticism," and assures her that "poetry and art and knowledge are sacred and pure," we can quite see the force of the argument, and understand why it should be the prologue to a love-scene a little later. After an appeal from Philip, Maggie at last "smiled with glistening tears, and then stooped her tall head to kiss the pale face that was full of pleading, timid love like a woman's. She had a moment of real happiness then—a moment of belief that, if there were sacrifice in this love, it was all the richer and more satisfying." The "renunciation" and the desire for happiness may be reconciled.

With Tom Tulliver in the background, we have now abundant material for tragedy. But, at the opening of the third volume, we are abruptly introduced to a new character. Maggie has become a young lady, visiting her cousin. The "fine young man," snapping a pair of scissors in the face of the "King Charles" spaniel on Miss Lucy Deane's feet, "is no other than Mr. Stephen Guest, whose diamond ring, attar of roses, and air of nonchalant leisure at twelve o'clock in the day are the graceful and odoriferous result of the largest oil-mill and the most extensive wharf in St. Ogg's." In other words, Mr. Guest is a typical provincial coxcomb, with a certain taste for music, fitted no doubt to excite the admiration of young ladies at St. Ogg's. No attempt is made to suggest that he is anything but a self-satisfied commonplace young gentleman, who has condescended to accept the hand of Miss Deane. There is no difficulty in understanding him and his manners. When he dances with Maggie at a ball soon afterwards, and takes her into a conservatory, she looks very lovely as she stretches her arm to a rose. "Who has not felt the beauty of a woman's arm?—the unspeakable suggestions of tenderness that lie in the dimpled elbow, and all the varied gently lessening curves, down to the delicate wrist with its tiniest almost imperceptible nicks in the firm softness? A woman's arm touched the soul of a great sculptor two thousand years ago, so that he wrought an image of it for the Parthenon which moves us still as it clasps lovingly the time-worn marble of a headless trunk. Maggie's was such an arm as that, and it had the warm tints of life. A mad impulse seized on Stephen; he darted towards the arm and showered kisses on it, clasping the wrist." It is curious that a little later (1864) George Eliot describes a "divine picture" by Sir F. Burton, in which a mailed knight is kissing the arm of a woman "by an uncontrollable movement." The subject, she says, is from a "Norse Legend." It "might have been made the most vulgar thing in the world—the artist has raised it to the highest pitch of refined emotion. The kiss is on the fur-lined *sleeve* that covers the arm, and the face of the knight is the face of a man to whom the kiss is a sacrament." Mr. Stephen Guest's performance does not strike one in the sacramental light. Maggie is properly angry and astonished at the time, but she soon becomes more amenable; and though she has scruples, and goes through a "fierce battle of emotions," she presently finds herself drifting to sea with him in a boat, and is only arrested by her conscience at the last moment when she is some way towards Gretna Green. Renunciation gets the better of the longing for happiness. "We can only choose," she says, "whether we will indulge ourselves in the present moment, or whether we will renounce that for the sake of obeying the divine voice within us, for the sake of being true to all the motives that sanctify our lives." To let this belief go would be to lose the only light in the darkness of life. She returns; but the knot is insoluble, and has to be finally cut by the waves of the Floss. George Eliot herself, admitting the need for more development, maintained, as we have seen, that the conclusion was right, and it has been defended upon the same ground. It is right, because the "psychology" is right. Given the character and the circumstances, that is, this was the inevitable outcome. It is, no doubt, painful and disagreeable that a young woman of so many noble qualities should be guilty of such a step: but noble young women do make slips—that, I fear, is undeniable—and Maggie behaves as might be expected from her previous history. That is where I presume to doubt. Nobody, indeed, can deny that the passion of love is apt to generate illusions. Most men would probably be able to give examples from their own experience of the truth that young women who fall in love with somebody else have a singular inability for forming a correct judgment of the truly valuable qualities of masculine character. The fact has often been noticed, and is frequently turned to account by novelists. I will not deny that even Maggie's love for Stephen is conceivable. A young woman brought up in Dorlcote Mill was no doubt liable to be imposed upon by a false appearance of gentlemanlike character. But, one thing seems to be obvious. The whole theme of the book is surely the contrast between the "beautiful soul" and the commonplace surroundings. It is the awakening of the spiritual and imaginative nature and the need of finding some room for the play of the higher faculties, whether in the direction of religious mysticism or of human affection. That such a character, with little experience of life and with narrow education, should fall into error is natural, if not inevitable. But then the error should surely correspond to some impulse which we can feel to be noble. Maggie may be wrong in attributing high qualities to her hero; but we should feel that, in her eyes, he has high qualities, and that the passion, if misdirected, is itself congenial to her better impulses. Miss Brontë's heroines fall in love with men whom the reader may dislike; but it is because they take the men to be embodiments of great masculine qualities—energy, honour, and real generosity—under rather crusty outsides. Therefore, though we may doubt the perspicacity of the hero-worship, we do not feel that the sentiment is in itself degrading. But there is this difficulty with poor Maggie. Her admiration for Mr. Guest would be natural enough in the average miller's daughter suddenly brought into a rather superior social scale and introduced to a well-dressed young man scented with "attar of roses." But as Maggie, by her very definition, as one may say, is a highly exceptional young woman, she should surely have something exceptional in her love. We can understand her sympathy with Philip Wakem who is a man of heart, and whose physical infirmity is an appeal for pity; we could have understood it if she had fallen in love with the excellent vicar of St. Ogg's, who would have been able to talk about à Kempis and religious sentimentalism; and we might even have forgiven her if, after being a little overpowered by the dandified Stephen, she had shown some power of perceiving what a very poor animal he was. The affair jars upon us, because it is not a development of her previous aspirations, but suddenly throws a fresh and unpleasant light upon her character. No one will say that the catastrophe is impossible; he, at least, who would pronounce dogmatically upon such matters must be a bolder man than I am; but neither, I think, can any one say that it was inevitable, or could have been expected, given the circumstances and the characters. The truth is, I think, different. George Eliot did not herself understand what a mere hairdresser's block she was describing in Mr. Stephen Guest. He is another instance of her incapacity for portraying the opposite sex. No man could have introduced such a character without perceiving what an impression must be made upon his readers. We cannot help regretting Maggie's fate; she is touching and attractive to the last; but I, at least, cannot help wishing that the third volume could have been suppressed. I am inclined to sympathise with the readers of *Clarissa Harlowe* when they entreated Richardson to save Lovelace's soul. Do, I mentally exclaim, save this charming Maggie from damning herself by this irrelevant and discordant degradation.

VIRGINIA WOOLF[1]

George Eliot[†]

* * * Those who fall foul of George Eliot do so, we incline to think, on account of her heroines; and good reason; for there is no doubt that they bring out the worst of her, lead her into difficult places, make her self-conscious, didactic, and occasionally vulgar. Yet if you could delete the whole sisterhood you would leave a much smaller and a much inferior world, albeit a world of greater artistic perfection and far superior jollity and comfort. In accounting for her failure, in so far as it was a failure, one recollects that she never wrote a story until she was thirty-seven, and that by the time she was thirty-seven she had come to think of herself with a mixture of pain and something like resentment. For long she preferred not to think of herself at all. Then, when the first

1. Virginia Woolf (1882–1941) was a major early twentieth-century novelist.

† From *The Common Reader* by Virginia Woolf (New York: Harcourt, Brace & World, 1925) 173–76.

flush of creative energy was exhausted and self-confidence had cor her, she wrote more and more from the personal standpoint, bu did so without the unhesitating abandonment of the young. Her self-consciousness is always marked when her heroines say what she herself would have said. She disguised them in every possible way. She granted them beauty and wealth into the bargain; she invented, more improbably, a taste for brandy. But the disconcerting and stimulating fact remained that she was compelled by the very power of her genius to step forth in person upon the quiet bucolic scene.

The noble and beautiful girl who insisted upon being born into the Mill on the Floss is the most obvious example of the ruin which a heroine can strew about her. Humour controls her and keeps her lovable so long as she is small and can be satisfied by eloping with the gipsies or hammering nails into her doll; but she develops; and before George Eliot knows what has happened she has a full-grown woman on her hands demanding what neither gipsies nor dolls, nor St. Ogg's itself is capable of giving her. First Philip Wakem is produced, and later Stephen Guest. The weakness of the one and the coarseness of the other have often been pointed out; but both, in their weakness and coarseness, illustrate not so much George Eliot's inability to draw the portrait of a man, as the uncertainty, the infirmity, and the fumbling which shook her hand when she had to conceive a fit mate for a heroine. She is in the first place driven beyond the home world she knew and loved, and forced to set foot in middle-class drawing-rooms where young men sing all the summer morning and young women sit embroidering smoking-caps for bazaars. She feels herself out of her element, as her clumsy satire of what she calls "good society" proves.

> Good society has its claret and its velvet carpets, its dinner engagements six weeks deep, its opera, and its faëry ball rooms . . . gets its science done by Faraday and its religion by the superior clergy who are to be met in the best houses; how should it have need of belief and emphasis?

There is no trace of humour or insight there, but only the vindictiveness of a grudge which we feel to be personal in its origin. But terrible as the complexity of our social system is in its demands upon the sympathy and discernment of a novelist straying across the boundaries, Maggie Tulliver did worse than drag George Eliot from her natural surroundings. She insisted upon the introduction of the great emotional scene. She must love; she must despair; she must be drowned clasping her brother in her arms. The more one examines the great emotional scenes the more nervously one anticipates the brewing and gathering and thickening of the cloud which will burst upon our heads at the moment of crisis in a shower of disillusionment and verobsity. It is partly that her hold upon dialogue, when it is not dialect, is slack; and partly that she seems to shrink with an elderly dread of fatigue from the effort of emotional concentration. She allows her heroines to talk too much. She has little verbal felicity. She lacks the unerring taste which chooses one sentence and compresses the heart of the scene within that. "Whom are you going to dance with?" asked Mr. Knightley, at the Westons' ball. "With you, if you will ask me," said Emma; and she has said enough. Mrs. Casaubon[2] would have talked for an hour and we should have looked out of the window.

Yet, dismiss the heroines without sympathy, confine George Eliot to the agricultural world of her "remotest past", and you not only diminish her greatness but lose her true flavour. That greatness is here we can have no doubt. The width of the prospect, the large strong outlines of the principal features, the ruddy light of the early books, the searching power and reflective richness of the later tempt us to linger and expatiate beyond our limits. But it is upon the heroines that we would cast a final glance. "I have always been finding out my religion since I was a little girl," says Dorothea Casaubon. "I used to pray so much—now I hardly ever pray. I try not to have desires merely for myself. . . ." She is speaking for them all. That is their problem. They cannot live without religion, and they start out on the search for one when they are little girls. Each has the deep feminine passion for goodness, which makes the place where she stands in aspiration and agony the heart of the book—still and cloistered like a place of worship, but that she no longer knows to whom to pray. In learning they seek their goal; in the ordinary tasks of womanhood; in the wider service of their kind. They do not find what they seek, and we cannot wonder. The ancient consciousness of woman, charged with suffering and sensibility, and for so many ages dumb, seems in them to have brimmed and overflowed and uttered a demand for something—they scarcely know what—for something that is perhaps incompatible with the facts of human existence. George Eliot had far too strong an intelligence to tamper with those facts, and too broad a humour to mitigate the truth because it was a stern one. Save for the supreme courage of their endeavour, the struggle ends, for her heroines, in tragedy, or in a compromise that is even more melancholy. But their story is the incomplete version of the story of George Eliot herself. For her, too, the burden and the complexity of womanhood were not enough; she must reach beyond the sanctuary and pluck for herself the strange bright fruits of art and knowledge. Clasping them as few women have ever clasped them, she would not renounce her own inheritance—the difference of view, the difference of standard—nor accept an inappropriate reward. Thus we behold her, a memorable figure, inordinately praised and shrinking from her fame, despondent, reserved, shuddering back into the arms of love as if there alone were

2. The female protagonist of *Middlemarch*, Dorothea Brooke Casaubon. [Editor]

satisfaction and, it might be, justification, at the same time reaching out with "a fastidious yet hungry ambition" for all that life could offer the free and inquiring mind and confronting her feminine aspirations with the real world of men. Triumphant was the issue for her, whatever it may have been for her creations, and as we recollect all that she dared and achieved, how with every obstacle against her—sex and health and convention—she sought more knowledge and more freedom till the body, weighted with its double burden, sank worn out, we must lay upon her grave whatever we have it in our power to bestow of laurel and rose.

F. R. LEAVIS

The Early Phase†

* * *

But of course the most striking quality of *The Mill on the Floss* is that which goes with the strong autobiographical element. It strikes us as an emotional tone. We feel an urgency, a resonance, a personal vibration, adverting us of the poignantly immediate presence of the author. Since the vividness, the penetration and the irresistible truth of the best of the book are clearly bound up with this quality, to suggest that it also entails limitations that the critic cannot ignore, since they in turn are inseparable from disastrous weaknesses in George Eliot's handling of her themes, is perhaps a delicate business. But the case is so: the emotional quality represents something, a need or hunger in George Eliot, that shows itself to be insidious company for her intelligence—apt to supplant it and take command. The acknowledged weaknesses and faults of *The Mill on the Floss*, in fact, are of a more interesting kind than the accepted view recognizes.

That Maggie Tulliver is essentially identical with the young Mary Ann Evans we all know. She has the intellectual potentiality for which the environment into which she is born doesn't provide much encouragement; she has the desperate need for affection and intimate personal relations; and above all she has the need for an emotional exaltation, a religious enthusiasm, that shall transfigure the ordinariness of daily life and sweep her up in an inspired devotion of self to some ideal purpose. There is, however, a difference between Maggie Tulliver and Mary Ann Evans: Maggie is beautiful. She is triumphantly beautiful, after having been the ugly duckling. The experience of a sensitive child in this latter rôle among insensitive adults is evoked with great poignancy: George

† From *The Great Tradition* (London: Chatto & Windus, 1948) 18–24. Reprinted by permission of the F. R. Leavis estate and the publisher.

Eliot had only to remember. The glow that comes with imagining the duckling turned swan hardly needs analysing; it can be felt in every relevant page, and it is innocent enough. But it is intimately related to things in the book that common consent finds deplorable, and it is necessary to realize this in order to realize their nature and significance and see what the weaknesses of *The Mill on the Floss* really are.

There is Stephen Guest, who is universally recognized to be a sad lapse on George Eliot's part. He is a more significant lapse, I think, than criticism commonly allows. Here is Leslie Stephen:

> George Eliot did not herself understand what a mere hairdresser's block she was describing in Mr. Stephen Guest. He is another instance of her incapacity for portraying the opposite sex. No man could have introduced such a character without perceiving what an impression must be made upon his readers. We cannot help regretting Maggie's fate; she is touching and attractive to the last; but I, at least, cannot help wishing that the third volume could have been suppressed. I am inclined to sympathize with the readers of *Clarissa Harlowe* when they entreated Richardson to save Lovelace's soul. Do, I mentally exclaim, save this charming Maggie from damning herself by this irrelevant and discordant degradation.

That the presentment of Stephen Guest is unmistakably feminine no one will be disposed to deny, but not only is the assumption of a general incapacity refuted by a whole gallery of triumphs, Stephen himself is sufficiently 'there' to give the drama a convincing force. Animus against him for his success with Maggie and exasperation with George Eliot for allowing it shouldn't lead us to dispute that plain fact—they don't really amount to a judgment of his unreality. To call him a 'mere hairdresser's block' is to express a valuation—a valuation extremely different from George Eliot's. And if we ourselves differ from her in the same way (who doesn't?), we must be careful about the implication of the adjective when we agree that her valuation is surprising. For Leslie Stephen Maggie's entanglement with Stephen Guest is an 'irrelevant and discordant degradation.'—Irrelevant to what and discordant with what?—

> The whole theme of the book is surely the contrast between the 'beautiful soul' and the commonplace surroundings. It is the awakening of the spiritual and imaginative nature and the need of finding some room for the play of the higher faculties, whether in the direction of religious mysticism or of human affection.

—It is bad enough that the girl who is distinguished not only by beauty but by intelligence should be made to fall for a provincial dandy; the scandal or incredibility (runs the argument) becomes even worse when we add that she is addicted to Thomas à Kempis and has an exalted spiritual nature. Renunciation is a main theme in her history and in her daily meditations; but—when temptation takes the form of Mr. Stephen Guest! It is incredible, or insufferable in so far as we have to accept it, for temptation at this level can have nothing to do with the theme of renunciation as we have become familiar with it in Maggie's spiritual life—it is 'irrelevant and discordant.' This is the position.

Actually, the soulful side of Maggie, her hunger for ideal exaltations, as it is given us in the earlier part of the book, is just what should make us say, in reflection, that her weakness for Stephen Guest is not so surprising after all. It is commonly accepted, this soulful side of Maggie, with what seems to me a remarkable absence of criticism. It is offered by George Eliot herself—and this of course is the main point—with a remarkable absence of criticism. There *is*, somewhere, a discordance, a discrepancy, a failure to reduce things to a due relevance: it is a characteristic and significant failure in George Eliot. It is a discordance, not between her ability to present Maggie's yearnings and her ability to present Stephen Guest as an irresistible temptation, but between her presentment of those yearnings on the one hand and her own distinction of intelligence on the other.

That part of Maggie's make-up is done convincingly enough; it is done from the inside. One's criticism is that it is done too purely from the inside. Maggie's emotional and spiritual stresses, her exaltations and renunciations, exhibit, naturally, all the marks of immaturity; they involve confusions and immature valuations; they belong to a stage of development at which the capacity to make some essential distinctions has not yet been arrived at—at which the poised impersonality that is one of the conditions of being able to make them can't be achieved. There is nothing against George Eliot's presenting this immaturity with tender sympathy; but we ask, and ought to ask, of a great novelist something more. 'Sympathy and understanding' is the common formula of praise, but understanding, in any strict sense, is just what she doesn't show. To understand immaturity would be to 'place' it, with however subtle an implication, by relating it to mature experience. But when Geoge Eliot touches on these given intensities of Maggie's inner life the vibration comes directly and simply from the novelist, precluding the presence of a maturer intelligence than Maggie's own. It is in these places that we are most likely to make with conscious critical intent the comment that in George Eliot's presentment of Maggie there is an element of self-idealization. The criticism sharpens itself when we say that with the self-idealization there goes an element of self-pity. George Eliot's attitude to her own immaturity as represented by Maggie is the reverse of a mature one.

Maggie Tulliver, in fact, represents an immaturity that George Eliot never leaves safely behind her. We have it wherever we have this note, and where it prevails her intelligence and mature judgment are out of action:

> Maggie in her brown frock, with her eyes reddened and her heavy hair pushed back, looking from the bed where her father lay, to the dull walls of this sad chamber which was the centre of her world, was a creature full of eager, passionate longings for all that was beautiful and glad; thirsty for all knowledge; with an ear straining after dreamy music that died away and would not come nearer to her; with a blind, unconscious yearning for something that would link together the wonderful impressions of this mysterious life, and give her soul a sense of home in it.

This 'blind, unconscious yearning' never, for all the intellectual contacts it makes as Maggie grows up and from which it acquires a sense of consciousness, learns to understand itself: Maggie remains quite naïve about its nature. She is quite incapable of analysing it into the varied potentialities it associates. In the earlier part of the book, from which the passage just quoted comes, the religious and idealistic aspect of the yearning is not complicated by any disconcerting insurgence from out of the depths beneath its vagueness. But with that passage compare this:

> In poor Maggie's highly-strung, hungry nature—just come away from a third-rate schoolroom, with all its jarring sounds and petty round of tasks—these apparently trivial causes had the effect of rousing and exalting her imagination in a way that was mysterious to herself. It was not that she thought distinctly of Mr. Stephen Guest, or dwelt on the indications that he looked at her with admiration; it was rather that she felt the half-remote presence of a world of love and beauty and delight, made up of vague, mingled images from all the poetry she had ever read, or had ever woven in her dreamy reveries.

The juxtaposition of the two passages makes us revert to a sentence quoted above from Leslie Stephen, and see in it a hint that he, pretty plainly, missed:

> It is the awakening of the spiritual and imaginative nature and the need of finding some room for the play of the higher faculties, whether in the direction of religious mysticism or of human affection.

—For the second alternative we need to couple with 'religious mysticism' a phrase more suggestive of emotional intensity than Leslie Stephen's. And we then can't help asking whether the 'play of the higher faculties' that is as intimately associated with a passion for Stephen Guest as the two last-quoted paragraphs together bring out can be as purely concerned with the 'higher' as Maggie and George Eliot believe (unchallenged, it seems, by Leslie Stephen).

Obviously there is a large lack of self-knowledge in Maggie—a very natural one, but shared, more remarkably, by George Eliot. Maggie, it is true, has the most painful throes of conscience and they ultimately prevail. But she has no sense that Stephen Guest (apart, of course, from the insufficient strength of moral fibre betrayed under the strain of temptation—and it is to Maggie he succumbs) is not worthy of her spiritual and idealistic nature. There is no hint that, if Fate had allowed them to come together innocently, she wouldn't have found him a pretty satisfactory soul-mate; there, for George Eliot, lies the tragedy—it is conscience opposes. Yet the ordinary nature of the fascination is made quite plain:

> And then, to have the footstool placed carefully by a too self-confident personage—not any self-confident personage, but one in particular, who suddenly looks humble and anxious, and lingers, bending still, to ask if there is not some draught in that position between the window and the fireplace, and if he may not be allowed to move the work-table for her—these things will summon a little of the too-ready, traitorous tenderness into a woman's eyes, compelled as she is in her girlish time to learn her life-lessons in very trivial language.

And it is quite plain that George Eliot shares to the full the sense of Stephen's irresistibleness—the vibration establishes it beyond a doubt:

> For hours Maggie felt as if her struggle had been in vain. For hours every other thought that she strove to summon was thrust aside by the image of Stephen waiting for the single word that would bring him to her. She did not *read* the letter: she heard him uttering it, and the voice shook her with its old strange power. . . . And yet that promise of joy in the place of sadness did not make the dire force of the temptation to Maggie. It was Stephen's tone of misery, it was the doubt in the justice of her own resolve, that made the balance tremble, and made her once start from her seat to reach the pen and paper, and write 'Come.'

There is no suggestion of any antipathy between this fascination and Maggie's 'higher faculties,' apart from the moral veto that imposes renunciation. The positive counterpart of renunciation in the 'higher' realm to which this last is supposed to belong is the exaltation, transcending all conflicts and quotidian staleness, that goes with an irresistibly ideal self-devotion. It is significant that the passages describing such an exaltation, whether as longed for or as attained—and there are many in George Eliot's works—have a close affinity in tone and feeling with this (from the chapter significantly headed, *Borne along by the tide*):

> And they went. Maggie felt that she was being led down the garden among the roses, being helped with firm tender care into the boat,

> having the cushion and cloak arranged for her feet, and her parasol opened for her (which she had forgotten)—all this by the stronger presence that seemed to bear her along without any act of her own will, like the added self which comes with the sudden exalting influence of a strong tonic—and she felt nothing else.

—The satisfaction got by George Eliot from imaginative participation in exalted enthusiasms and self-devotions would, if she could suddenly have gained the power of analysis that in these regions she lacked, have surprised her by the association of elements it represented.

The passage just quoted gives the start of the expedition with Stephen in which chance, the stream and the tide are allowed, temporarily, to decide Maggie's inner conflict. It has been remarked that George Eliot has a fondness for using boats, water and chance in this way. But there are distinctions to be made. The way in which Maggie, exhausted by the struggle, surrenders to the chance that leaves her to embark alone with Stephen, and then, with inert will, lets the boat carry her downstream until it is too late, so that the choice seems taken from her and the decision compelled—all this is admirable. *This* is insight and understanding, and comes from the psychologist who is to analyse for us Gwendolen Harleth's acceptance of Grandcourt.[1] But the end of *The Mill on the Floss* belongs to another kind of art. Some might place it under the 'art' referred to by Henry James. And it is certainly a 'dramatic' close of a kind congenial to the Victorian novel-reader. But it has for the critic more significance than this suggests: George Eliot is, emotionally, fully engaged in it. The qualifying 'emotionally' is necessary because of the criticism that has to be urged: something so like a kind of daydream indulgence we are all familiar with could not have imposed itself on the novelist as the right ending if her mature intelligence had been fully engaged, giving her full self-knowledge. The flooded river has no symbolic or metaphorical value. It is only the dreamed-of perfect accident that gives us the opportunity for the dreamed-of heroic act—the act that shall vindicate us against a harshly misjudging world, bring emotional fulfilment and (in others) changes of heart, and provide a gloriously tragic curtain. Not that the sentimental in it is embarrassingly gross, but the finality is not that of great art, and the significance is what I have suggested—a revealed immaturity.

* * *

1. Characters from George Eliot's last novel, *Daniel Deronda*. [Editor]

GEORGE LEVINE

Intelligence as Deception: *The Mill on the Floss*†

With only small exceptions, *The Mill on the Floss* can be seen as adequately representative of even the most mature of George Eliot's art—morally energetic yet unsentimentally perceptive about the meaning of experience. Like all of her works, it is thoroughly coherent and gains its coherence from a unified vision. But the vision, here as elsewhere, is, I would argue, incomplete. There were elements in experience, that is, which she was never fully able to assimilate and which, as was true of most of the major Victorian writers, she was genuinely unable to see. She pushed the boundaries of Victorian experience as far as any of her contemporaries and moved to the brink from which one can observe the modern sensibility, but inevitably she pulled back.

The point at which she stopped is the point at which *The Mill on the Floss*—which remains one of the very great novels of the period—goes wrong. The difficulty, I would suggest, is not merely George Eliot's excessive moral energy nor even, exclusively, her too close identification, criticised by F. R. Leavis, with her heroine.[1] Rather, it seems to me to result from a complex mode of self-deceit—from a combination of high intelligence with powerful moral revulsion from what that intelligence tended to reveal.

I

It is important, at the outset, to remember that George Eliot's intelligence was at home with several highly elaborated intellectual systems which, she believed, could largely—if not entirely—account for the experience being narrated. Of course, her works cannot be reduced simply to any one set of rationally coherent ideas; but it is certainly true that her empirical and rationalist biases (modified though they were by

† Reprinted by permission of the Modern Language Association of America from *PMLA* 80 (1965), 402–9.

1. See *The Great Tradition* (New York: Anchor Books, 1954), p. 58. "In George Eliot's presentment of Maggie there is an element of self-idealisation." This is obviously, but only partially, true. Indeed, the whole thematic development of the book depends on a careful rendering of Maggie's limitations. See in this connection Jerome Thale's note on Maggie in *The Novels of George Eliot* (New York, 1959), and William Steinhoff, "Intent and Fulfillment in the Ending of *The Mill on the Floss*," in *The Image and the Work* (Berkeley, Calif., 1955), pp. 235–251. Mr. Steinhoff's analysis runs parallel to my own but does not overlap. He too, however, emphasizes George Eliot's insistence on Maggie's limitations.

her total commitment to "truth of feeling")[2] demanded an explanation of experience consistent with reason, and that the explanation she accepted influenced certain crucial elements in her novels.[3] Determination is the central and dominant explanation of the facts of the experience; the moral direction of those facts is controlled largely by many ideas which might be traced to Comte and Feuerbach.[4] All of these ideas are woven inextricably into the very texture of *The Mill on the Floss*, but I shall argue that there came a recognizable point at which, especially in her use of Feuerbach, George Eliot employs them in such a way as to help her escape the implications of her own most deeply felt insights.

To begin with, then, it is necessary to clarify what the informing ideas of *The Mill on the Floss* meant to George Eliot. For her, determinism as I have explained elsewhere,[5] entailed a total commitment to the notion that every action has its causes, and only by a meticulous examination of those causes can any action be seen as comprehensible. She also argued, however, that determinism does not entail belief in inefficacy of the will. Since, that is, a man's character is always an element in his choice, he must be seen as responsible. Finally, whatever the intellectual formulation might be, to excuse a man on the basis of an abstract theory of determinism is altogether irrelevant to his evil; as Adam Bede remarks, "I see plain enough we shall never do it without a resolution, and that's enough for me."[6]

All the major themes of *The Mill on the Floss*, as well as its structure, are related to determinism. It is a commonplace that the novel develops

2. George Eliot, like the thinkers she consciously followed, recognized that feeling not thought was the major source of action and that cultivation of the intellect without cultivation of the sensibilities was morally dangerous. Her most famous statement of the notion comes in a fairly early letter: "The first impulse of a young and ingenuous mind is to withhold the slightest sanction from all that contains even a mixture of supposed error. . . . But a year or two of reflection and experience of our own miserable weakness which will ill afford to part even with the crutches of superstition must, I think, effect a change . . . and we turn to *truth of feeling* as the only universal bond of union. We find that the intellectual errors we once fancied were a mere incrustation have grown into the living body and that we cannot in the majority of cases wrench them away without destroying vitality" (*The George Eliot Letters*, ed. Gordon S. Haight, 7 vols., New Haven, 1954–56, I, 162).
3. One of the central concerns of this essay, to trace the relation of the thematic content of *The Mill on the Floss* to Feuerbach and Comte, was largely inspired by a brief essay by U. C. Knoepflmacher, "George Eliot, Feuerbach, and the Question of Criticism," *Victorian Studies*, VII (1964), 306–309. I am also greatly indebted to Bernard Paris, "George Eliot's Religion of Humanity," *ELH*, XXIX (1962), 418–443.
4. For a useful and compact survey of the relation of the ethical ideas of Comte and Feuerbach to those of George Eliot, I am indebted to the fourth chapter of Michael Wolff's unpublished doctoral dissertation, "Marian Evans to George Eliot: The Moral and Intellectual Foundation of her Career," microfilm (Princeton, 1958). It should be noted here that determinism has moral implications of its own and is an element of Positivism. John Stuart Mill goes so far as to say that "Whoever regards all events as part of a constant order, each one being the invariable consequent of some antecedent condition, or combination of conditions, accepts fully the Positive mode of thought" (*Auguste Comte and Positivism*, Ann Arbor, Mich., 1961, p. 15).
5. "Determinism and Responsibility in the Works of George Eliot," *PMLA*, LXXVII (1962), 268–279.
6. *Adam Bede*, ch. xvii. All quotations from George Eliot's works, unless otherwise noted, are from the Cabinet Edition, 24 vols. (London and Edinburgh, n.d.).

as Tom and Maggie grow: it sets them within the framework of a family and society which extensively determine what they become, shows the inevitable development of their characters according to the pressures of heredity and irrevocable events, and traces their destinies chronologically from love, to division, to unity in death. The simple narrative progression is incremental and stresses the ineluctable dependence of every act and thought on acts and thoughts which preceded them.

Both in its personal drama and in its vividly imagined description of a period of social transition the novel seems illustrative also of many of Comte's and Feuerbach's notions of social and moral growth. In a letter to John Blackwood comparing *Adam Bede* to *The Mill on the Floss*, which was then in progress, George Eliot noted that the characters in the latter "are on a lower level generally."[7] Quite deliberately, she was creating a society which has not as yet moved beyond the egoism of man's animal beginnings to the sympathy and benevolence which Feuerbach and Comte believed would grow out of egoism. Among other things, the frequency with which all the characters are compared to insects and animals makes plain that George Eliot does not see them as ready for any but the slightest advance toward the full intellectual and moral development from egoism to intelligent sympathy towards which she aspired.

Aside from working out George Eliot's characteristic theme of "the adjustment of our individual needs to the dire necessities of our lot,"[8] Maggie's story is also a dramatization of Feuerbach's religion of suffering—the "suffering, whether of martyr or victim, which belongs to every historical advance of mankind."[9] Through suffering the "obscure vitality" of the "emmetlike Dodsons and Tullivers" will be transcended, will be "swept into the same oblivion with the generations of ants and beavers," and man will move slowly towards his full humanity. The immersion in water, which in the final chapter is the form which the suffering takes, is, in Feuerbach's view, an annihilation of consciousness: it is the first step towards regeneration, but the regeneration itself must be active, not passive, the assertion of "the power of mind, of consciousness, of man."[1] Maggie's world lacks the moral guidance Comte

7. *The George Eliot Letters*, III, 133.
8. J. W. Cross, *George Eliot's Life*, Bk. III, ch. XV.
9. *The Mill on the Floss*, Bk. IV, ch. i. All quotations from this novel will be from Gordon S. Haight's careful edition (Boston: Riverside Editions, 1961). See Feuerbach's *Essence of Christianity*, transl. George Eliot (New York: Harper Torchbooks, 1957): "Man has the consciousness not only of a spring of activity, but also of a spring of suffering in himself. I feel; and I feel feeling (not merely will and thought, which are only too often in opposition to me and my feelings), as belonging to my essential being, and, though the source of all sufferings and sorrows, as a glorious divine power and perfection" (p. 63). It is, by the way, precisely the unity of thought and feeling, with feeling predominating, which Comte aspired towards. See Comte's A *General View of Positivism*, transl. J. H. Bridges (Stanford: Academic Reprints, n.d.), and Wolff, pp. 204–211.
1. Feuerbach, p. 277.

insisted was necessary for that regeneration or for the achievement of a satisfactory society: it had "no standard but hereditary custom" (Bk. IV, ch. i).

Ideas such as these form the intellectual framework of *The Mill on the Floss*. The ideas and the experience, however, are two aspects of the same thing. Here at least one feels no tension between the two halves of the almost schizophrenic (intellectual vs. emotional) George Eliot that critics have taken to creating. For all but a brief section of the book the experience itself seems a necessary and convincing source of the ideas; although the world the novel describes is entirely deterministic and largely positivistic, the "system" does not distort the experience. But since the details of the novel are so widely known, I shall concentrate on the relation between the ideas and the experience—rather than on the experience itself—in order to suggest how George Eliot's extraordinarily tough-minded and complicated analysis of personal and social experience could have concluded in a "comfortingly conventional" way, "its tone barely distinguishable from hundreds of pious and exemplary tales where salvation comes through sacrifice and love triumphs over death."[2]

II

George Eliot's "love of the childhood scenes"[3] is not likely to have carried her to such lengthy description as we have in the early books had she not felt those scenes were important, both intrinsically and for the development of the novel as a whole. They are in fact a demonstration of the idea which she found confirmed in Comte, of whom she said that "no one has more clearly seen the truth, that the past rules the present, lives in it, and that we are but the growth and outcome of the past."[4] The focus on family in the first book relates directly to the Comtean notion (shared by Feuerbach) that the family is the primary means by which man can transcend his egoism and animality.[5] These early scenes establish that the characters are, in Feuerbach's terms in a "natural" state, beneath the level of full humanity. It is no accident, for example, that the novel's first speech by an important character—Mr. Tulliver—should begin, "What I want," nor that George Eliot should pointedly repeat the clause (Bk. I, ch. ii). "The oppressive narrowness" of the Dodsons and Tullivers create a tension for both readers and characters. On the one hand, it is what must be transcended by Maggie if she is to rise above "the mental level of the generation before"

2. Miriam Allott, "George Eliot in the 1860's," *Victorian Studies*, v (1961), 105.
3. See her now famous statement: "My love of the childhood scenes made me linger over them; so that I could not develop as fully as I wished the concluding book in which the tragedy occurs, and which I had looked forward to with attentive premeditation from the beginning" (*The George Eliot Letters*, iii, 374).
4. *The George Eliot Letters*, III, 320.
5. See Wolff, pp. 214–215.

her. On the other, she is tied to that generation "by the strongest fibres of" her heart. In "the onward tendency of human things" the Dodsons and Tullivers must go, but they cannot be ignored and they must, indeed, be loved (see Bk. IV, ch. i).

The notions explicit in this view suggest how the story points towards both personal and social growth; and these notions are worked out in almost every detail of the novel. The town of St. Ogg's, to use only one example, has grown in a slow, incremental, entirely unplanned way. It has roots deep in the past, and every part of it is "familiar with forgotten years." Under the slow pressure of time the proceses of cause and effect have built it, almost as a natural growth. And George Eliot certainly means to imply a parallel between social and natural law which is central to the beliefs we have been examining:

> It is one of those old, old towns which impress one as a continuation and outgrowth of nature, as much as the nests of the bower-birds or the winding galleries of the white ants: a town which carries the traces of its long growth and history like a millennial tree, and has sprung up and developed in the same spot between the river and the low hill from the time when the Roman legions turned their backs on it from the camp on the hillside, and the long-haired sea-kings came up the river and looked with fierce eager eyes at the fatness of the land. (Bk. I, ch. xii)

Even the architecture suggests the natural connections with the primitive sea-kings; equally, the citizens of St. Ogg's are what they are because of the past: inconsistent, old-fashioned, egocentric, crude, but sympathetic because they inherit—even without being aware of it—the best (along with the worst) of what men have thought and felt. But because they lack the clarity of vision Feuerbach desiderated they are determined: they "inherited a long past without thinking of it" (Bk. I, ch. xii)

The Dodsons and Tullivers, of course, are the dramatic embodiments of the town's essential nature, and they confirm the notion that for George Eliot determinism is both dangerous and morally essential. She saw with Feuerbach that society included not merely rigid conventions but also the slowly, painfully earned developments in man's intelligence and sensibility. Maggie, then, must learn what other characters suffer by not learning—that everything must be judged on its unique merits, that no laws, habits, or traditions can apply indiscriminately in all situations. On the other hand, much of what she does learn in this way turns out to be a "relearning" of the values already implicit in social conventions. The trouble with the Dodsons and Tullivers is that they fail to establish an adequate relation to their own traditions and are therefore unable to understand their own motives derived from myriad causes out of the past. Neither they nor Maggie quite attain the "objectivity" Feuerbach requires, the ability, that is, to see "the real relation of things."[6] They cannot achieve that "right understanding" of "the unchangeable Order of the world" which Comte says "is the principal object of our actions."[7]

The predominant theme of the novel then, as George Eliot makes explicit, is the quest for unity—social, familial, and personal—that fusion of imagination and will which leads to sympathetic action. A convenient summary of Feuerbach's views will suggest the direction George Eliot wants Maggie's history to take:

> The individual who has a strongly sympathetic nature combined with profound experience and the ability to imagine the inner states of others has a moral life that is independent of traditions; he has a more highly developed conscience and a truer sense of good and evil than tradition, in its present state of development, could supply. The sympathetic tendencies can lead a person to rebel against the harsh usages of tradition, even when such rebellion involves great personal risk.[8]

But this combination of qualities, which can lead justifiably to a rebellion against convention, was more George Eliot's than Maggie's. It would not be stretching things to consider the possibility that these views of Feuerbach helped George Eliot justify to herself her decision to live with G. H. Lewes.[9] But Maggie needs yet to unify her desires with her intentions, to discipline her passions in keeping with an objective view of possibility—"knowledge of the irreversible laws within and without her, which, governing the habits, becomes morality, and developing the feelings of submission and dependence, becomes religion" (Bk. IV, ch. iii).

Socially, the quest is for unity between public opinion and individual sensibility. Comte places heavy emphasis on the value of public opinion in a way relevant to *The Mill on the Floss*. "The principal feature of the state to which we are tending," he says, "will be the increased influence which Public Opinion is destined to exercise. It is in this beneficial influence that we shall find the surest guarantee for morality. . . . Except the noblest of joys, that which springs from social sympathy when called into constant exercise, there is no reward for doing right so satisfactory as the approval of our fellow-beings."[1] Maggie's relation to public opinion seems different, but that is partially because the society in which she lives is at such a primitive stage of development. George Eliot is certainly suggesting in the final chapters both the power of public opinion

6. See Paris, p. 435:
7. Comte, p. 29.
8. Paris, p. 424.
9. This point is taken up briefly by Basil Willey in *Nineteenth Century Studies* (New York, 1949), p. 228, and Gordon Haight, *George Eliot and John Chapman* (New Haven, 1940), p. 80.
1. Comte, p. 153.

and the need to develop it more consistently to a higher level of social sympathy. The society of St. Ogg's, however, is disintegrating, as Dr. Kenn says, under the pressure of modern life, "seems tending toward the relaxation of ties—towards the substitution of wayward choice for adherence to obligation, which has its roots in the past" (Bk. VII, ch. i).

All aspects of the theme of unity are worked out in three of Maggie's moments of choice: her interview with Philip Wakem in the Red Deeps, her rowing party with Stephen Guest, and her refusal to stay with Stephen after they arrive at Mudport. The two earlier decisions show that Maggie has not achieved that personal unity which is essential to moral well-being. Philip is obviously right when, attacking her new-found asceticism, he warns her that if she persists in mere negations she will find that when she is "thrown upon the world . . . every rational satisfaction of your nature that you deny now, will assault you like a savage appetite" (Bk. V, ch. iii). Unfortunately, of course, even this sensible argument serves to weaken Maggie because it is not disinterested, but designed to keep her from leaving Philip altogether. The truth in this case is a lie, and deceit in the complicated deterministic universe of George Eliot is a form of moral disease whose dangers are far-reaching. It may be, as Maggie recognizes, that "it is other people's wrong feelings that make concealment necessary; but concealment is bad, however it may be caused" (Bk. V, ch. iii).

Nor has Maggie achieved unity by the time she meets Stephen Guest. Whatever one's objections to Stephen as a character, it is obvious that here as elsewhere George Eliot has been extremely careful to work out the reason for the action. What Maggie does with Stephen is determined by a past in which egotism and personal wilfulness keep her from moral integrity. There is no need here to list all the causes, but it is interesting to note how down to the finest details it is possible to observe kinship with the thought of Feuerbach and Comte. One of the things, for instance, which attracts Maggie to Stephen is his singing, and Maggie is deeply susceptible to music. Feuerbach argues strongly for the power of music: "What would man be without feeling?" he asks. "It is the musical power in man. But what would man be without music? Just as man has a musical faculty and feels an inward necessity to breathe out his feelings in song; so, by a like necessity, he, in religious sighs and tears, streams forth the nature of feeling as an objective, divine nature."[2] Music, George Eliot remarks, "could hardly be without some intoxicating effect on her, after years of privation." It should be noted also that Maggie's desperate need to be admired and loved, one of the causes of her fall, corresponds closely to Comte's sense of what makes people behave as they do.

Because Maggie succumbs at her second moment of choice with

2. Feuerbach, p. 63.

Stephen, she is faced with a dilemma which is, in some ways, the purest in all of George Eliot's novels. Maggie's decision now cannot be in passive accordance with the push of circumstance; it depends on her understanding of the particular situation and cannot be governed by conventions. Simply by following out the implications of her complex attitudes towards tradition and modernity, self-control and self-assertion, George Eliot here arrives at a point where tradition cannot supply an adequate answer but where her heroine's character is inadequate to the task of Feuerbach's sympathetic rebellion. Maggie cannot even decide on the basis of the likely consequences of her actions because the damage has already been done and misery will be the consequence of either choice.

Thus, in making this third choice, Maggie achieves the highest level of consciousness of which a St. Ogg's citizen is capable. She reveals an awareness of the "real relation of things" by accepting both the irrevocability of her act and the fact that it "must blot her life" and bring sorrow into lives that were "knit up with hers by trust and love." She is aware that she has broken all "the ties that had given meaning to duty, and had made herself an outlawed soul," having lost the relation to community which, in Comte's sense, provides moral guidance; she was left with "no guide but the wayward choice of her own soul" (Bk. VI, ch. xiv). Recognizing this loss and its dangers, Maggie attempts to turn to the past and inherited traditions. "If the past is not to bind us," she says to Stephen, "where can duty lie: We have not law but the inclination of the moment" (Bk. VI, ch. xiv). Through the past she attempts to overcome the persistent fragmentation of self which has hitherto left her vulnerable to the past's uncomprehended forces.

She struggles against committing herself to a "momentary triumph of my feeling," to an evil which will form a habit of surrender to impulse and fragmentation. One of George Eliot's primary insights, dramatized in the curious passivity of her characters at their moments of choice, is that "character" as it has been formed over a lifetime finally determines how one will behave in a crisis. Untrained will is unequal to the pressures of the moment; the training of the will into a habit of goodness is essential because "moral behavior is only to be found in the spontaneous exercise of moral emotion. Moral action is not the result of a decision to act morally; it is the result of moral feeling, forcing itself into practice."[3] At her present stage of development, Maggie must still labor at her choice, but she does move towards the unity of self which makes moral action a habit by recognizing that mind, memories, obligations are all part of what a man is, fully as important as natural feelings; and she

3. Wolff, p. 228. See Feuerbach, p. 321; "To the man of noble feeling, the noble action is natural: he does not place it in the scales of choice; he *must* do it. Only he who acts so is a man to be confided in." Clearly, Maggie never approaches this seemingly instinctive nobility until her last heroic act.

tries to bring her feelings into conformity with her conscious intentions. The renunciation of Stephen moves one step beyond her immature asceticism, not based on a sense of the real relation of things, which Philip had criticized in the Red Deeps.

III

In keeping with her deterministic insistence on the pressure of ordinary events, her Comtean awareness of the moral pressures of public opinion, and the deep psychological perceptions she shared with Feuerbach about the nature of human suffering and morality, George Eliot could not allow Maggie's resolution yet to be final. Resolutions must be tested moment by moment and day by day and they must establish themselves in relation not only to the complete self but to the community. Thus, all the influences so carefully prepared through the apparently leisurely movement of the early stages of the novel come into play in the last book.

The tensions between the Dodsons and the Tullivers—between the two modes of egoism represented by the forces of convention uncomprehended and rigidified and the forces of blind spontaneity of feeling—now become in a more complex way the tensions between Maggie and the town. All of Maggie's past—not understood—contributed to her fatal lapse with Stephen; so all of Maggie's past—now largely if incompletely understood—contributes to her decision to return to St. Ogg's. Equally, all the seemingly innocuous circumstances which precede Maggie's lapse help determine the rigidly conventional—that is, unimaginative and therefore unsympathetic—response of the townspeople to Maggie. In language which suggests the quite conscious influence of both Comte and Feuerbach, George Eliot describes the "ladies of St. Ogg's" as "not beguiled by any wide speculative conceptions but they had their favourite abstraction called society which seemed to make their consciences perfectly easy in doing what satisfied their egoism" (Bk. VII, ch. iv.). George Eliot's revulsion from abstractions is widely known, and in its temperamental character it is much more akin to Feuerbach than to Comte, who, though he insisted always on the positive and scientific, was himself the victim of abstractions. But this passage certainly evokes Comte, who, according to John Stuart Mill, described the "Metaphysical Stage" of human development as the stage which "accounts for phenomena by ascribing them, not to volitions either sublunary or celestial, but to realized abstractions. In this stage it is no longer a god that causes and directs each of the various agencies of nature: it is a power, or a force, or an occult quality, considered as real existence, inherent in but distinct from concrete bodies in which they reside, and which they in a manner animate."[4]

4. Mill, p. 11.

The traditions animating the kind of Dodsonian behavior which condemns Maggie are given new life and meaning by the eldest of the Dodsons, Mrs. Glegg, who is capable of dealing with new kinds of experience because she is the strongest willed and most intelligent of the clan. Her willingness to oppose public opinion and convention is certainly intended as at least in part a dramatization of the way in which family unity—recognized by both Comte and Feuerbach as the source of morality—is the first step toward community, the first means of transcending the "I" for the "Thou," for breaking away from the narrow egoism which governs the action of ordinary men. It is the source of Maggie's higher sensibility, and as it is revivified in Mrs. Glegg it helps us to understand George Eliot's commitment to the sustaining power of tradition.

Despite Mrs. Glegg's help, however, the pressures on Maggie become strong enough to make her feel again the temptation to return to Stephen. She must once again work out the relation between self-will and self-denial, and George Eliot's comment on the problem reveals the impasse at which both author and heroine have arrived: "The great problem of the shifting relation between passion and duty is clear to no man who is capable of apprehending it: the question whether the moment has come in which a man has fallen below the possibility of a renunciation that will carry any efficacy, and must accept the sway of passion against which he had struggled as a trespass, is one for which we have no master-key that will fit all cases" (Bk. VII, ch. ii). As the book has demonstrated, only in a society where egoism and self-will are not driven as in Maggie's case into excessive self-denial or, as in Tom's case, into respectability and moral brutality, does the problem of the shifting relation have a chance to be resolved. But such a positivist utopia, in which the individual and society are allied in one will, was, as George Eliot knew, a mere dream of the future,[5] and one could only move towards it through the slow increment of wasted lives, of suffering such as Maggie's and Dorothea Brooke's, from which new moral insight can be assimilated into man's consciousness. Maggie is at an impasse which everything in the book has suggested is unresolvable. And Dr. Kenn's comment that any action she might take would be "clogged with evil" is undeniably true.

5. See her famous letter to Frederic Harrison rejecting his proposal that she write a novel presenting the ideal Positivist community (*The George Eliot Letters*, IV, 300).

IV

The continuity of George Eliot's views is suggested by the similarity between Maggie's conflict as she battles temptation in the dark night preceding the flood and that of Dorothea on the night she resolves to accept Casaubon's unexplained demands. Both characters submit themselves to the higher responsibility despite the loss of the possibility of self-fulfillment. But neither character is made to face the full implications of such renunciation. Certainly, Dorothea does not achieve a fate with Ladislaw equal to her own large possibilities. Moreover, George Eliot means us to understand that her marriage to him will evoke considerable public disapprobation. But she is certainly not at such a primitive stage of development as Maggie, and Casaubon's death does save her from total and pointless frustration. This death follows almost immediately after her resolution, just as Maggie's death follows her own final renunciation.

In her first spontaneously moral action, she rushes to Tom's rescue and is swept to death in his arms, as though one were meant to see in that death her reconciliation to all those forces to which she could be temperament and action never be reconciled. Maggie's final action, however, can be seen as the last stage in the progress of her growth according to Feuerbach's principle and therefore altogether consistent with what has gone before. Beginning in mere egoism and rebellion, she moves on to the incomplete sympathy—as a result of family pressures—of her asceticism; the suffering which she endures intensifies that sympathy and produces in her a surer vision of reality so as to make her capable of a deliberate act of renunciation with Stephen; her rescue of Tom, however, is to be seen as a spontaneous moral action which suggests the real beginning of Feuerbach's genuinely noble man. But Maggie's newly earned "nobility" is once again exercised in the direction of her family, and will, moreover, never be tested in that infinitely more complicated social world which posed her moral dilemma. The escape, then, is thematically consistent, but it can be seen also as external and fortuitous, an intrusion of that "Favourable Chance" which George Eliot anathematized in *Silas Marner* (ch. ix).

One can only speculate on the reasons for such a lapse, characteristic not only of George Eliot's work but of much of the best work of the time. Perhaps Matthew Arnold's explanation of why he removed "Empedocles on Etna" from his 1853 *Poems* will throw light on the problem. Arnold, it will be remembered, asked with Schiller for an art "dedicated to Joy," since "there is no higher and more serious problem, than how to make men happy." George Eliot, for her part, during the decade following *The Mill on the Floss*, wrote that "the art which leaves the soul in despair is laming to the soul, and is denounced by the healthy sentiment of an active community."[6] She is likely to have agreed with Arnold that there were certain situations, "from the representation of which, though accurate, no poetical enjoyment can be derived. They are those in which the suffering finds no vent in action; in which a continuous state of mental distress is prolonged, unrelieved by incident, hope, or resistance; in which there is everything to be endured, nothing to be done."[7] This is Maggie's condition before the flood.

For Arnold, the solution was to abandon art for criticism; George Eliot, also too intelligent and too responsible to let need consciously dictate to art, allowed herself to flaw her art, I would suggest, by deceiving herself with her own intelligence. She could, consistently with her own view of experience, avoid the condition Arnold described by leaning on Comte and Feuerbach; and in this way she could give Maggie the heroic, tragic, but largely affirmative action with which she dies. This action is consistent not only with the details of the plot as she carefully worked them out,[8] but with the very themes which give the novel so much of its richness.

Moreover, within the system of Feuerbachian thought, the death by water makes good symbolic sense. Water, for Feuerbach, is one of the two major sacraments, the other and more important one being the bread and wine of the Lord's Supper. But although, as has been shown, much symbolic use of this sacrament occurs in *Adam Bede*[9] there is apparently no such use in *The Mill on the Floss*. The crucial dinner scene in the first book marks not harmony but the beginning of the division between the Tullivers and Dodsons. The reason seems to be that *The Mill on the Floss* concerns itself with people on "a lower level generally"—not "lower" in class but in the development of their moral perceptions—with a society not prepared for the higher sacrament. Indeed, it is likely that George Eliot sees Maggie's death by water as a preparation for the condition in which the society would be prepared.

Water, for Feuerbach, is the sacrament which symbolically asserts man's dependence on nature; the flood serves to remind man of this. Curiously, in water "the scales fall from [man's] eyes: he sees and thinks

6. Cross, III, XV.
7. "Preface" to the 1853 edition of his poems. Reprinted in *Mixed Essays, Irish Essays, and Others* (New York, 1883), p. 488.
8. An entry in her Journal for 12 Jan. 1859 records that "we went into town today and looked in the Annual Register for cases of *inundation*" (*The George Eliot Letters*, III, 33). The internal evidence that the flood was part of her conception from the first is sufficiently clear: the insistence on the Floss, the legend of St. Ogg, whose behavior foreshadows Maggie's the constant allusions to past floods and future ones.
9. Knoepflmacher, pp. 307–309. I am grateful to Gordon Haight for calling to my attention an excellent essay by George R. Creeger, "An Interpretation of 'Adam Bede'," *ELH*, XXIII (1956), 218–238, in which a similar point is made. See esp. p. 234. Creeger, who rightly refuses to regard the novel as "fictionalized philosophy," supplies in his footnotes a good many other parallels between Feuerbach's thought and the meaning of *Adam Bede*.

more clearly," and at the same time "human mental activity is nullified."[1] Both these effects of water operate in *The Mill on the Floss*. With Stephen Maggie falls into oblivion as she floats downstream; by contrast, with Tom the scales fall from her eyes as she reflects: "what quarrel, what harshness, what unbelief in each other can subsist in the presence of a great calamity, when all the artificial vesture of our life is gone, and we are all one with each other in primitive mortal needs" (Bk. VII, ch. V). Here, appropriately, Maggie not only "sees and thinks more clearly," but she is forced to these reflections by the power of Nature over the merely "artificial." And, of course, in the death which follows, consciousness is nullified, but only after, by symbolically crying "Maggie," Tom avers the love which dominated in the natural state of childhood. The death is a purification of both Maggie and Tom: "To purify oneself," as Feuerbach says, "to bathe, is the first, though the lowest of virtues."[2]

This, it seems to me, is George Eliot's attitude towards the final catastrophe; Tom and Maggie must achieve "the first, though the lowest of virtues" because even now neither they nor St. Ogg's is ready for the higher, active, creative virtues of man's full consciousness and power.

One more quotation from Feuerbach should suggest other ways in which the conclusion of *The Mill on the Floss* was firmly a part of the intellectual structure of the book: "It needs only that the ordinary course of things be interrupted in order to vindicate to common things an uncommon significance, *to life, as such, a religious import.* Therefore let bread be sacred for us, let wine be sacred, and also let water be sacred! Amen." For George Eliot, the inability to see the extraordinariness of the ordinary is an aspect of that egoism and lack of imagination which characterizes the society of St. Ogg's. She insists on the religious import, surely in Feuerbach's sense, of the ordinary, and thus follows Feuerbach by introducing into the novel the extraordinary—the flood —which is in fact only an extreme development of the ordinary and which in its extreme quality takes on the nature of a ritual. It is curious how so many of George Eliot's novels, however much the great bulk of events they include are assertively ordinary, turn on events which seem to come directly out of melodrama—Arthur Donnithorne's last-minute rescue of Hetty, the final meeting of Baldassarre and Tito, Grandcourt's drowning and Mordecai's mystical Zionist visions, the revelation of Transome's relation to the lawyer Jermyn.[3]

It is perhaps too simple to suggest that this sort of refusal to face the

1. Feuerbach, p. 276.
2. Feuerbach, p. 275.
3. See Barbara Hardy's discussion of the uses of coincidence in the novels in *The Novels of George Eliot* (London, 1959), esp. chs. vi and vii.

total implication of her own ideas and of her very temperament was the result of George Eliot's conscious effort to protect "her readers from any 'laming' effects."[4] Obviously George Eliot did seek moral order in the bleakest and most amoral elements of the world. But she was too intelligent to be satisfied with emotional need unsustained by intellectual conviction. Feuerbach, at least in *The Mill on the Floss*, seems to have supplied her with an intellectually satisfying and emotionally acceptable answer. Because we take George Eliot's perceptions to the point of the modern vision, where the only affirmation is personal, inward, and isolated, we tend to believe that in honesty she needed to do the same thing. But she turns away with characteristic Victorian strength and integrity in search of meaning, justice, and the organic community. We could do much worse.

U. C. KNOEPFLMACHER

Tragedy and the Flux: *The Mill on the Floss*[†]

The Bewildering Future: The Tragedy of Edward Tulliver

The Mill on the Floss is divided into seven books, which can be separated into two movements: in the first, Mr. Tulliver * * * vainly tries to shore his present against the impending future; in the second, where that future becomes the present of his children, Tom and Maggie vainly try to recover their childhood at Dorlcote Mill. The first movement concludes with Mr. Tulliver's death at the end of Book V; the second culminates with the drowning of Tom and Maggie. Like *Antony and Cleopatra*, the novel thus contains two related tragedies, which I shall examine individually only for the sake of making critical distinctions. In Shakespeare's play, Cleopatra's sacrifice is meant to exalt Antony's bungling death; in her tragic novel, George Eliot likewise intends Maggie's sacrifice to lend a wider meaning to the little world ignobly lost through Mr. Tulliver's recklessness. The miller's gradual ruin and self-destruction are deftly handled by a novelist sure of her control. The rash miller is in his way as convincing a tragic figure as the impetuous Antony. But George Eliot could not handle Maggie's fate with the same assurance. For reasons which I shall examine in the last section of this chapter,

4. Allott, p. 106.

† From *George Eliot's Early Novels: The Limits of Realism* (Berkeley: U of California P, 1968) 193–220. Permission granted by the Regents of the University of California and the University of California Press. Page numbers to the Norton Critical Edition of the novel have been inserted in brackets following U. C. Knoepflmacher's original citations.

George Eliot failed to convert Maggie's immolation into an action as world-stirring as that of Shakespeare's Cleopatra.[1]

Mr. Tulliver's story introduces all the basic collisions of the novel: the antithesis between the worlds of the Mill by the Ripple and of St. Ogg's-on-the-Floss, the contrast between Dodsons and Tullivers, the resulting oppositions between parents and children, brother and sister, and Maggie's consequent self-division. Yet the unit which ends with the miller's deathbed recognition that the "world's been too many" for him, possesses the tragic requisites which the remainder of the novel lacks. Like Oedipus, to whom he is compared by the narrator, Mr. Tulliver has become entangled in "the skein of life" through his own blind pride. Unlike the symbolic flood which executes Tom and Maggie, the catastrophe which marks his downfall is the direct result of the interaction of character and destiny, will and fate. Mr. Tulliver falls victim to his own faulty choices. He first selects a spouse for her presumed submissiveness and stupidity; then, betrayed by the unexpected biological "crossing o' breeds," he prefers his Tulliver daughter over his Dodson son. To prepare for Tom's future, he chooses a "gentleman's" education * * *; he adopts the advice of Mr. Riley instead of enlisting the better judgment of Mr. Deane, his brother-in-law, whom he regards as "the 'knowingest' man of his acquaintance," but whom he does not consult on family matters because of vanity and pride. Able to avoid a costly litigation, the imprudent miller opts for a lawsuit instead and thus finally places himself in the power of Chancery, that Victorian embodiment of ancient "Fortuna." Incapable of adapting to the changes taking place around him, he escapes, as Maggie will, into rebellion, fantasy, and, eventually, death. Unlike his daughter, however, he is far more the victim of his own hubris than of capricious chance.

Mr. Deane is the miller's exact counterpart. A self-made city man, he knows the ways of the world. The foolish Mr. Tulliver congratulates himself for having chosen a classicist as Tom's teacher. Always impulsive, he soon convinces himself that the boy's tutor is a "clergyman whose knowledge was so applicable to the everyday affairs of this life. Except Counsellor Wylde, whom he had heard at the last session, Mr. Tulliver thought the Rev. Mr. Stelling was the shrewdest fellow he had ever met with—not unlike Wylde, in fact: he had the same way of sticking his thumbs in the armholes of his waistcoat" (Bk. II, chap. I, p. 211) [114]. The utilitarian Mr. Deane, on the other hand, soon brands Tom's education as utterly useless. Even after the youth pathetically promises to unlearn his Latin and ancient history, Mr. Deane presses on contemptuously: "Your Latin and rigmarole may soon dry

1. These and future references to *Antony and Cleopatra* (like those to *King Lear*) are introduced for contrast only; still, the association may have a factual basis, as well: the only quotation from *Antony and Cleopatra* in all of George Eliot's letters occurs while she was writing *The Mill* (cf. GEL [*The George Eliot Letters*], III, 53).

off you, but you'll be but a bare stick after that. Besides, it's whitened your hands and taken the rough work out of you. And what do you know? Why, you know nothing about book-keeping, to begin with, and not so much of reckoning as a common shopman. You'll have to begin at the low round of the ladder, let me tell you, if you mean to get on in life. It's no use forgetting the education your father's been paying for, if you don't give yourself a new un" (Bk. III, chap. 5, pp. 361–362) [190]. Ironically, the very man whose advice Mr. Tulliver shunned, now teaches his Dodson son how to repair the father's mistakes.

Mr. Deane typifies the new ways of St. Ogg's. Like Lawyer Wakem, he plays Octavius to Mr. Tulliver's Antony. The miller who gallops incessantly around his threatened land is impulsive and sentimental; his unlanded brother-in-law exerts himself only by "taking snuff vigorously, as he always did when wishing to maintain a neutral position" (Bk. I, chap. 7, p. 105) [60]. Like Wakem, Mr. Deane remains evasive and noncommittal. Whereas Mr. Tulliver identifies his archenemy with "old Harry" himself, Mr. Deane cautiously respects Lawyer Wakem as a powerful business rival. Mr. Tulliver vows that he will not allow "anybody get hold of his whip-hand" (Bk. I, chap. 5, p. 53) [33], but when he loses control of his lands, it is his brother-in-law who asks the stricken miller to accept Wakem's demeaning offer to let him manage the property he formerly owned. Mr. Deane could easily have outbid the lawyer in order to salvage Mr. Tulliver's pride, but he does not "carry on business on sentimental grounds" (Bk. III, chap. 7, p. 383) [201]. In his unromantic world a man can succeed only by waiting patiently, as he has done, "before he got the whip in his hand" (Bk. VI, chap. 5, p. 200) [320]. If the descendant of the fiery Ralph Tulliver rides against the times, his prudent counterpart moves with the tide. Once regarded as the worst match made by the Dodson sisters, Mr. Deane has gradually risen to eminence in the Guests' "great mill-owning, ship-owning business." Progress is his motto * * *: "I don't find fault with the change, as some people do. Trade, sir, opens a man's eyes; and if population is to get thicker upon the ground, as it's doing, the world must use its wits at inventions of some sort or other" (Bk. VI, chap. 5, p. 201) [320].

While Mr. Tulliver loses control of his mill wheel by entering useless litigations over his decreasing "water-power," the self-controlled Mr. Deane steadily gains in influence by harnessing new sources of power: "It's this steam, you see, that has made the difference: it drives on every wheel double pace, and the wheel of fortune along with 'em, as our Mr. Stephen Guest said" (Bk. VI, chap. 5, p. 201) [320]. If Mr. Tulliver is the enfeebled survivor of Carlyle's "Heroical Age," Mr. Deane belongs to the new mechanical era "which, with its whole undivided might, forwards, teaches, and practices the great art of adapting means to ends."[2] Deane's sphere of action seems every bit as removed from Dorlcote Mill as Caesar's Rome is from Cleopatra's Egypt. At the mill, the relation between Luke and his master still resembles that of a vassal and his feudal lord; Luke's loyalty is not unlike the devotion of a Kent or Enobarbus. For the world soon to be lost by the miller is archaic enough to harbor what Hegel had called "romantic fidelity."[3] In it the ideal of service remains as untouched as the urge for revenge which dominates the "pagan" Mr. Tulliver and his son. Like old Adam in *As You Like It*, Luke wants to give his earnings to his master, for he feels, "after the manner of contented hard-working men whose lives have been spent in servitude, that sense of natural fitness in rank which made his master's downfall a tragedy to him" (Bk. III, chap. 8, p. 405) [213].

In St. Ogg's no such "natural fitness" exists. Luke and his master are equals despite the difference in rank; but Mr. Deane and Lawyer Wakem head a society in which mastery can be established only by competition and strife. Mr. Deane will not try to outbid Lawyer Wakem; he cannot afford to be ruled by sentiments such as Luke's. Tom, on the other hand, immediately on accepting the responsibilities of his father's position, decides to pay Luke, "if in no other way, out of his own and Maggie's money." In *As You Like It*, freed by old Adam's money, Orlando and his father's servant jointly escape into the Forest of Arden. In George Eliot's novel, there is no sanctuary. Luke's refusal to accept the payment due him cannot free either him or his young master. Tom must go to St. Ogg's to restore his father's good name. The irony is bitter. Simply by walking across the "stone bridge" that leads into the city he enters a different world. Before crossing that bridge, Tom still looked at reality with his father's eyes: "he saw the distant future before him, as he might have seen a tempting stretch of smooth sandy beach beyond a belt of flinty shingles; he was on the grassy bank then, and thought the shingles might soon be passed." But he returns as Mr. Deane's disciple: "now his feet were on the sharp stones; the belt of shingles had widened, and the stretch of sand had dwindled into narrowness" (Bk. III, chap. 5, p. 366) [192]. His vision has been adjusted. To fight Lawyer Wakem he has submitted to Wakem's oppressive world.

* * * Wakem is identified with the devil himself. Although the as-

2. "Signs of the Times," *Critical and Miscellaneous Essays*, I, *The Complete Works of Thomas Carlyle* (New York, 1901), p. 465.
3. Cf. Hegel's discussion of dramatic motivation in *Aesthetik*. Citing the swineherd's loyalty to Ulysses and Kent's loyalty to Lear, he comments: "This borders as close as possible on that which we would make clear as romantic fidelity. Fidelity at this stage is not the loyalty of slaves and churls . . . [but] the liege-service of chivalry, in which each vassal preserves his own free self-dependence as an essential element in the attitude of subordination to one of higher rank, whether lord, king, or emperor. This type of fidelity . . . forms the fundamental bond of union in a common [i.e., communal] society" (*Hegel on Tragedy*, ed. Anne and Henry Paolucci [New York, 1962], p. 204).

sociation is made by the superstitious Mr. Tulliver, there is a tinge of truth to it. * * * St. Ogg's is a modern equivalent of the "city of destruction" from which Bunyan's Christian had escaped.[4] * * * In St. Ogg's, no * * * Evangelist can rescue the modern pilgrim. Even the kindhearted Dr. Kenn must yield to the pressure of his parishioners and evict Maggie from his house. The historical past of St. Ogg's only confirms the nature of its present. Like the Rome described in *Middlemarch*, the city is merely an aggregate of historical strata, each of which has stifled and suppressed the one beneath it. * * * The narrator mercilessly uncovers all the calcified deposits of the past. The intermittent floods have only separated one age of strife from another. The present warehouses of Guest & Co. rest on the site of struggle far bloodier than those of industrial competition. Only less than two centuries ago, the town had witnessed "worse troubles even than the floods—troubles of the civil wars, when it was a continual fighting-place, where first Puritans thanked God for the blood of the Loyalists, and then Loyalists thanked God for the blood of the Puritans" (Bk. I, chap. 12, p. 181) [99]. Digging deeper, the narrator unearths further collisions: the era of the church displaced the invasion of the Norman conquerors; the Danish raiders overcame the Saxon settlers; the Vikings ended the predominance of the Roman legions. Even in the days of St. Ogg, the son of Beorl, hardhearted and indifferent men repulsed the sufferer he ferried across the river. In the city's present historical phase, where religion has given way to politics, only one superannuated inhabitant still recollects having heard * * * John Wesley * * *.

If Mr. Tulliver's latter-day agrarian existence is threatened by the industrial present of St. Ogg's, his defeat is not as inevitable as it would be in a dialectic Marxist view. For George Eliot carefully contrasts the miller's failures with the success of the Dodsons. Both families are equally archaic in their "pagan" clannishness and social orientation. Yet while Mr. Tulliver and his only sister, Mrs. Moss, find their strength depleted, the Dodsons manage to conserve their power. Once regarded as the "buck of Basset," Mr. Moss, Gritty Tulliver's husband, has become a dehumanized "machine-horse"; his farm yields diminishing returns. The husbands of the Dodson sisters, however, have all added to their wives' dowries. * * * Both the landed Mr. Pullet and the unlanded Mr. Glegg understand the value of "portable property." If Mr. Tulliver's aggressiveness is ineffectual, their defensive tactics prove to be invincible. The Gleggs have even moved into the enemy citadel, St. Ogg's itself. Financially secure as a moneylender, Mr. Glegg can * * * easily trans-

4. There are several allusions to *Pilgrim's Progress* in *The Mill.* Maggie is haunted by "images of Apollyon" on visiting the gypsy camp; after the loss of the family's property, she particularly misses "our dear old Pilgrim's Progress"; when she and Tom enter "The Valley of Humiliation" (the title of Book IV) they are, of course, entering Apollyon's domain. As a child, Maggie identifies the Floss with "the river over which there is no bridge." The analogy is ironic: Christiana will ford that river; Maggie will drown in it.

fer the country into the town. Contentedly, he follows his farming instincts by cultivating his back yard. His house affords two vistas, "two points of view." It faces the busy world of St. Ogg's and the road which leads out of the city into Tofton, the suburb where both Mr. Deane and Lawyer Wakem have built handsome houses (building materials dislodged from Tofton's wharves will kill Tom and Maggie). The back windows reveal a more idyllic scene, "the pleasant garden and orchard which stretched to the river" (Bk. I, chap. 12, p. 185) [101]. In that makeshift Eden, Mr. Glegg can relax by doing "the work of two ordinary gardeners." While his brother-in-law Mr. Deane exploits the river, Mr. Glegg enjoys its shores and remains unaffected by its motions.

Tragedy cannot touch Mr. Glegg. He picked the eldest Miss Dodson as a "handsome embodiment of female prudence and thrift." His choice of a partner is made after his own image: "being himself of a money-getting, money-keeping turn, [he] had calculated on much conjugal harmony" (Bk. I, chap. 12, p. 186) [102]. As always in George Eliot's fiction, his "calkilations" are not wholly correct. But though Mrs. Glegg is somewhat of a shrew, she does not really impede her husband's well-being. Mr. Tulliver, on the other hand, must very definitely pay for having picked a wife so unlike himself. He chose Elizabeth Dodson, he smugly informs Mr. Riley, because "she was a bit weak, like; for I wasn't agoin' to be told the rights o' things by my own fireside" (Bk. I, chap. 3, p. 24) [18]. * * * Mr. Tulliver should not have dabbled in natural selection. For not only does his choice result in the unforeseen Mendelian "crossing" which gives Maggie her father's characteristics and endows Tom with those of the Dodsons, but it also contributes directly to his own downfall.

As an "amiable hen" who usually defers to her husband, children, and sisters, Mrs. Tulliver resembles Mrs. Bennet rather than Antony's Cleopatra. Nonetheless, her husband's tragic fate is tied to the rudder of his chosen queen. Passive as she is, Mrs. Tulliver's few actions always have an effect opposite from that which she intends. Although she knows that her splenetic husband will be incensed by any opinion contrary to his own, she dutifully invites all her sisters and their husbands to discuss Tom's education—even though the miller has already made a decision. The meeting sets in motion the sequence of events which will lead to the loss of Dorlcote Mill. Angered by Mrs. Glegg's criticism, Mr. Tulliver vows to pay back the five hundred pounds she had loaned him. His wife's attempts to mediate only rankle his pride. Even though he also is in debt to Mr. Furley, the miller insists on returning the money to his sister-in-law at once. But by refusing to be indebted to Mrs. Glegg or Mrs. Pullet, this Chanticleer closes his eyes and only places himself a step closer to the fox. Against his will or better judgment, Mr. Tulliver becomes bonded to one of Lawyer Wakem's clients: " 'It must be no client of Wakem's,' he said to himself; and yet at the end of a fortnight it turned out to the contrary; not because Mr. Tulliver's will was feeble, but because external fact was stronger. Wakem's client was the only convenient person to be found. Mr. Tulliver had a destiny as well as Oedipus, and in this case he might plead, like Oedipus, that his deed was inflicted on him rather than committed by him" (Bk. I, chap. 13, p. 202) [110].

But Mr. Tulliver's mate contributes still further to his self-inflicted "destiny." After the miller loses a lawsuit in which he has foolishly supposed that he can best Lawyer Wakem on the lawyer's own terrain, his henlike wife takes up her husband's cause by making a foray into the enemy camp. But her undiplomatic efforts to dissuade Wakem from bidding for her husband's land only put a new thought into the shrewd lawyer's mind. Before her visit, he had no intention of bidding against Mr. Deane. Now, however, he decides on the very course of action she had set out to prevent. Although George Eliot probes into the lawyer's motives, she also suggests that he is only an agent for the fate brought on by the miller's own rashness. If Octavius is too cold-blooded to hate his hot-tempered rival, Wakem is no more guilty of wrath "than an ingenious machine, which performs its work with much regularity, is guilty towards the rash man who, venturing too near it, is caught up by some fly-wheel or other, and suddenly converted into unexpected mince-meat" (Bk. III, chap. 7, p. 388) [204]. After flogging one of Octavius' messengers, Antony whips himself into a frenzy and wins a land battle against the enemy who had defeated him by water. Mistaking a minor skirmish for a major triumph, Antony is soon driven to suicide. Mr. Tulliver also wins a minor engagement when he repays his creditors through the efforts of his son. Yet foolishly flushed by his success, he dies of apoplexy after flogging Wakem with his whip. The lawyer escapes with a sprained arm. Like Antony, the romantic Mr. Tulliver has even bungled his exit from life.

In an essay entitled "Tragedy and the Common Man," Arthur Miller once argued that the terror and fear of tragedy could still be evoked in a modern everyman's exposure to the pressures of social change. Defending *Death of a Salesman*, the playwright contended: "I believe that the common man is as apt a subject for tragedy in its highest sense as kings were."[5] To the reader of *The Mill on the Floss,* the statement carries a somewhat familiar ring:

> "Mr. Tulliver, you perceive, though nothing more than a superior miller and maltster, was as proud and obstinate as if he had been a very lofty personage, in whom such dispositions might be a source of that conspicuous, far-echoing tragedy, which sweeps the stage in regal robes, and makes the dullest chronicler sublime.

5. *New York Times*, 27 February 1947, Sec. II, p. 1.

> The pride and obstinacy of millers, and other insignificant people, whom you pass unnoticingly on the road every day, have their tragedy too." (Bk. III, chap. 1, p. 308) [162–63]

But George Eliot's superior miller is a much more tragic figure than Miller's Loman; there is more poetry in the loss of an ancestral mill than in an aging salesman's loss of his former "territory." Like Willy Loman, Mr. Tulliver, incapable of adjusting himself to the ways of the future, escapes into a dreamworld and ponders what might have been. But Willy's end is pathetic, whereas there is a magnificence in Mr. Tulliver's impenitent death. The miller who demands a "retributive justice" barely recognizes that he also must pay for his mistakes. Yet his nemesis does inspire us with the true terror of tragedy. The impersonal order which pushes him aside seems more fearsome than Willy's displacement by a boss who plays with a tape recorder. Willy smashes his car so that his wife and children can collect his insurance money; his death is a deliberate act by which he intends to repair the damage he has done. Mr. Tulliver's injuries to his family, however, cannot be repaired. His fall is more momentous. The indifference with which Mr. Deane and Mr. Glegg regard their brother-in-law's lost "water-power" is far closer, artistically, to the indifference which Goneril and Regan display toward Lear's regal attributes than it is to Howard's refusal to augment Willy Loman's Social Security payments. In the eyes of St. Ogg's, Mr. Tulliver is incompetent. In his archaic world, however, Maggie's fond and foolish father remains a "lofty personage." Accordingly, his fall is far more princely than that of the "hardworking, unappreciated prince" who is the father of the neurotic Biff.

Before dying, King Lear recognizes the goodness of the daughter he has so unjustly spurned; before his death, Mr. Tulliver must acknowledge his debt to the son he had tried to keep away from his own mill. He hopes that Tom will take care of the little "wench" who is the true bearer of his Tulliver blood. Yet * * * Dorlcote Mill is an heirloom that will go to no direct successors. Held by the Tullivers for "a hundred years and over," it will not be repossessed by the miller's descendants. * * * Though they * * * must go to that city, neither Tom nor Maggie really fails their father. Yet they lack his freedom. Michael asks his son to reclaim the land which otherwise would not endure another master. Mr. Tulliver, on the other hand, dimly senses that the mill is lost forever. He tells his servant: "There's a story as when the mill changes hands, the river's angry—I've heard my father say it many a time" (Bk. III, chap. 9, p. 414) [217]. His prophecy proves true. The angry river will claim his Dodson son and Tulliver daughter. Freedom of will gives way to accident and capricious forces. A different order of reality has taken over.

The Disinured Past: The Sacrifice of Maggie Tulliver

The opening books of *The Mill on the Floss* contain some of George Eliot's finest writing. Comedy and tragedy are combined through the "negative capability" which Keats recognized in Shakespeare. Ironic, tough-minded, the novelist is capable of moving our deeper emotions without ever lapsing into sentimentality. "The story of a superior miller and maltster contains analogues to the stories of Lear or Antony for the mind willing to connect the smaller to the greater. Yet though we sense Mr. Tulliver's greatness, we are never allowed to forget his limitations. High and low, heroic and mock-heroic, are held in perfect equipoise through the Victorian device of "inverse sublimity."[6] It is therefore all the more shocking to watch this equipoise break down completely in the last volume of the novel (Books VI and VII). After Mr. Tulliver's death, Maggie displaces Tom on George Eliot's stage. The tiny girl of the earlier portions of the novel is now aggrandized into a "fallen princess" who is denied her regal robes by her unheroic inferiors. Conversely, the St. Ogg's which was so terrifying to the puzzled miller becomes shrunken, exposed in its full pettiness. From Shakespeare and Wordsworth we have moved to Pope: in the opening of Book VI, Stephen Guest stands poised with a pair of scissors, ready to shear off one of Lucy's straying curls. Teacups, ratafias, a piano, have replaced the poetic Dorlcote Mill. The narrator's voice has lost its sureness, shifting uneasily between satire and sentimentalism with the same uncertainty that George Eliot had exhibited in "Amos Barton."

The narrator describes Stephen's dandified attire as "the graceful and odoriferous result of the largest oil-mill and the most extensive wharf in St. Ogg's" (Bk. VI, chap. I, p. 149) [293]. He suggests sarcastically that there is only an "apparent triviality in the action of the scissors," hinting thereby that the actions of this young man (whose appearance in the book is so sudden and unexpected) are every bit as trivial as the activities of the society to which he owes his wealth. But the attempt to typify in Stephen the society headed by his father and by Mr. Deane, his prospective father-in-law, seems heavy-handed. The satire misfires rather badly, for it has the effect of reducing the scope of the very forces that had led to Mr. Tulliver's downfall. The clear-cut, all-too-explicit picture of the "small world" that stifles Maggie with its puerilities, can hardly disturb us as deeply as the more general picture of the impersonal flywheel which had vanquished her father. The disparity between the small and the great is no longer handled ironically. In the previous portions of the book the actions of Mr. Tulliver and of little Maggie, though

6. I have borrowed this term from Max Keith Sutton, who uses it to designate the more ludicrous analogies between small and great, and the nonhuman and human in writers like Dickens, Thomas Hood, and W. S. Gilbert (" 'Inverse Sublimity' in Victorian Humor," VS, X [December 1966], 177–192).

insignificant, were prompted by the Μέγεθος[7] of true passion. But later not even so imposing an agent as a biblical flood can impress tragedy on the world of "The Rape of the Lock." The machinery of Pope's mock-epic jars with that used in earnest by such nineteenth-century imitators of Milton as John Abraham Heraud in his twelve-book epic *The Judgement of the Flood* (1834). The small and the great have become arbitrarily reversed, as well as sundered.

Even before the opening of the novel's third volume, there is a marked shift in treatment and style. If Maggie the child and Mr. Tulliver were viewed by a narrator able to maintain an aesthetic distance, the young woman's story is writ "large" whenever she makes her appearance. Whereas the commonplace miller became an Oedipus only by a stretch of our imaginations, George Eliot now tries to assist us whenever possible by likening the miller's daughter to a "tall Hamadryad" whose "queenly head" is juxtaposed to a hastily introduced backdrop of "grand Scotch firs." The ideological skeleton of the novel, so superbly enfleshed in the first half of the narrative, shows increasingly through a veneer of skin. Only by implication was Mr. Tulliver a prince falling from high to low; Maggie, however, is actually described as a regal figure without the kneeling subjects she so richly deserves. The child who wanted to be crowned as queen of the gypsies, who invented a world in which Lucy was queen, "though the queen was Maggie herself in Lucy's form" (Bk. I, chap. 7, p. 90) [52], now must escape with Lucy's Prince Charming before discovering that he too is hopelessly unworthy of her. And we are not allowed to forget the "jet crown" upon this exquisite creature's head.

Though Maggie is presumably guilty of the Tulliver pride, she is made to seem far less culpable than her willful father. Mr. Tulliver's exchanges with his wife, her relatives, or Mr. Riley always revealed his own deficiencies. The adult Maggie's exchanges with Philip or Stephen Guest seem by comparison to be hollow recitations. When Philip tells her that he has "nothing but the past to live upon," and plaintively asks her whether "the future will never join on to the past again," Maggie answers in similar abstractions: "I desire no future that will break the ties of the past" (Bk. VI, chap. 10, p. 278) [359–60]. To Stephen's entreaties that she accept the future he offers her, Maggie replies: "You feel, as I do, that the real tie lies in the feelings and expectations we have raised in other minds. Else all pledges might be broken, when there was no outward penalty. There would be no such thing as faithfulness" (Bk. VI, chap. 11, p. 287) [364]. When, drifting down the river, she suddenly awakes to Duty and Memory, she proclaims: "If the past is not to bind us, where can duty lie? We should have no law but the inclination of the moment" (Bk. VI, chap. 14, p. 329) [385]. Such speeches belong

7. Magnitude.

to a thesis-novel. They ought to come from a ventriloquist's puppet and not by the rounded human being whose growth we have observed. George Eliot has dropped all indirection. She glosses Maggie's willingness to be led by Stephen in the boat with a laconic statement, "Memory was excluded," as if an explicit stage direction could substitute for what the reader ought to feel through his own experience. Yet Maggie must be readied to play out her role as victim or martyr.

Though pitiful, Mr. Tulliver was not spared the ironic treatment accorded to his rivals in St. Ogg's; the adult Maggie, however, is untouched by the sarcasm with which the author ridicules the pretensions of a society far more sterile than Milby. Pretending to adopt the voice of "not the world, but the world's wife" (Bk. VII, chap. 2, p. 350) [397], the narrator becomes a satirist who blames society for barring its doors to an innocent victim. Maligned and defamed * * *, the "large-souled" Maggie becomes too precious for this world—even for the aunt who now surprises us by welcoming the young outcast. Life at the Ripple cannot be recovered. Rowing towards the Mill, Maggie notices a "rushing muddy current that must be the strangely altered Ripple" (Bk. VII, chap. 5, p. 396) [420]. Paradise has been washed away and soiled by the irresistible flux. Maggie must surrender. Only death can rescue the girl who demanded a higher life: in "dreadful clearness" she and Tom behold the "hurrying, threatening masses" which will engulf them in the river's current.

The concluding portions of *The Mill on the Floss* not only lack, in Professor Haight's words, "the same degree of realism" found in the earlier parts,[8] but they also betray a severe loss of artistic control. Although George Eliot spent but nine weeks on the last two books of her novel, it is highly doubtful that more time and care might have made Maggie's tragedy seem more appropriate.[9] Several reasons have been advanced for the unsatisfactory resolution of the novel.[1] Of all the explanations, that offered by George Levine comes closest to the heart of the matter. To him, the conclusion indicates the novelist's need to

8. Introduction, Riverside Edition, p. xix.
9. Barbara Hardy contends that this "cursoriness" may even be a virtue, since it makes Maggie's attraction to Stephen seem all the more rapid, violent, and superficial (*The Novels of George Eliot: A Study In Form* [London, 1959], p. 56). The observation, however plausible, does not quite account for those changes in perspective and tone which go far beyond Maggie's brief entanglement with her new lover.
1. Mr. Haight assumes that only the very ending of the novel is unsatisfactory, and he generously attributes the dissatisfaction to "George Eliot's lack of familiarity with boats and rivers" (Introduction, p. xix). F. R. Leavis advances a psychological hypothesis: it is George Eliot's "self-pity" and "self-idealization" through the adult Maggie which, in his view, determine the way in which the novelist beholds her character (*The Great Tradition* [New York, 1954], p. 58). Though shrewd, this thesis seems insufficiently developed. It does not explain how George Eliot could maintain an ironic distance with the little child whose shortcomings anticipate the "immaturity" which Mr. Leavis attributes to the adult Maggie. Indeed, the precocious little Maggie, whose eyes are so "full of unsatisfied intelligence, and unsatisfied, beseeching affection," is as much a projection of Marian Evans as the young woman who cannot turn her back on St. Ogg's provincial life.

"escape from the implications of her most deeply felt insights."[2] Pulling back from the nihilism inherent in "modern sensibility," George Eliot was able to dignify the amoral and accidental existence she distrusted only by treating Maggie's death as an extraordinary martyrdom. Mr. Levine's argument seems generally cogent, even though he almost seems to blame George Eliot for not being William Faulkner. What is more, since he advances his thesis for all of George Eliot's fiction, it is his burden to show whether his conclusions apply equally to her other works. Indeed, his statement does not adequately explain why the author who had succeeded so admirably with Mr. Tulliver's tragedy should have failed in depicting Maggie's plight.[3]

George Eliot's variation can be accounted for only if we carefully examine some of the difficulties she faced in relating Tom's and Maggie's stories to that of their father. That these difficulties had their origins in Marian Evans's need to define her own identity through her precarious relationship with both her father and brother, though undeniably true, need not concern us in this study of the novelist's more conscious intentions. (I leave it up to critics more versed in Freud to interpret the significance of the two dreams Maggie has before her "real waking" on Stephen's boat.) Both Tom and Maggie, we are told by the narrator, have evolved "above the mental level of the generation before them." In Tom, the Dodson strain has been magnified; in Maggie, the "richer blood" of the Tullivers is dominant (Bk. IV, chap. 2, p. 9) [224]. Though Tom has inherited his mother's literalism, his tenacity is even greater than that of the strongest of her sisters. Though Maggie possesses her father's faculty for perceiving that words can stand for "summat else," her greater imagination demands a more grandiose outlet for her unsatisfied intelligence and affection. Tom embraces the reality of St. Ogg's; Maggie yields to the fantasy life that was her father's destruction.

If Mr. Tulliver refused Mr. Deane's advice, Tom not only works for his uncle but also lets himself be guided by the practical Bob Jakin. Bob's strength, like Mr. Deane's, lies in his adaptability. Even as Tom's boyhood companion, he had boasted of his instinct for survival: " '*I* don't care about a flood comin',' said Bob; 'I don't mind the water, no more nor the land. I'd swim—*I* would.' " Like some of the organisms mentioned by the narrator, the amphibian Bob belongs to a species hardy enough to adapt himself to a change in environment. Aware that

2. "Intelligence as Deception," p. 402.
3. Though his artistic judgment is correct, Mr. Levine occasionally employs the wrong tools: he assumes, for example, that the waters of the Floss have regenerative qualities by referring to the symbology in *Adam Bede*; but *The Mill* is not *Adam Bede*. It is a very different "mental phase," and portrays a different historical era, belongs to a different genre, and therefore also relies on correlatives other than the Feuerbachian symbols which George Eliot gradually discarded after *Adam Bede*. The river is far less the baptismal symbol of Feuerbach (or of Milton) than it is a symbol of destruction, like the "River of Suicides" of James Thomson's "The City of Dreadful Night." It is closer to the metallic river in "The Lifted Veil" than to the water imagery in *Adam Bede*.

there is no future for him as a bargeman or rat-catcher, he chooses what to him is a less appealing profession. Bob prospers as a packman; Tom rises in his uncle's firm. Both turn their backs on a "paradisiac picture," determined to get on in the world. Yet Tom's fierce determination lacks Bob's warmth and humor. He has no time for such amenities as a wife and family. Tom's words shock even his uncle: "I want to have plenty of work. There's nothing else I care about much" (Bk. VI, chap. 5, p. 206) [323]. Transplanted to St. Ogg's, Adam Bede's doctrine of work seems grim and materialistic. In his monomaniac desire to recover Mr. Tulliver's mill Tom inherits only the miller's intolerance: "his inward criticism of his father's faults did not prevent him from adopting his father's prejudice" (Bk. VI, chap. 12, p. 299) [370]. In his desire to vindicate the past, he betrays all that was best in it by yielding uncritically to his present.

Maggie, on the other hand, cannot at all adapt herself to this changed present. As a child she fancied a world where people never got larger than the children of her own age. This fantasy sets her apart from Tom and links her to her father. The miller's incapacity to grow, his paranoid hostility toward the incomprehensible world that impinges on him, prefigures the predicament of his daughter. His maladjustment, however, is treated with an almost clinical objectivity. The novelist makes it clear that * * * Mr. Tulliver blames his own irresponsibility on the machinations of the devil. But whereas she exposes the simplicity of the miller's evasions of reality, George Eliot cannot bring herself to do the same when she depicts his daughter's plight. Instead, significantly enough, the narrator now appropriates the miller's hostility against the world at large. If Mr. Tulliver foolishly blames "old Harry" for his own inability to find fulfillment, our intelligent narrator is forced to blame a different fiction—"the world's wife." In the second chapter of the last book, "St. Ogg's Passes Judgment," the narrator pauses to satirize this imaginary figure for maligning poor Maggie. The world's wife, he tells us, has its own favorite abstraction, called "society." Yet the narrator does not hesitate to vent his own spleen on this same abstraction. As Mr. Levine suggests, intelligence can often lead to self-deception; so, obviously, can emotion.

In "The Lifted Veil," the disabled Latimer helplessly awaited the moment of his death; in *The Mill on the Floss*, Mr. Tulliver watches the auctioning of all his belongings after he has been immobilized by a stroke, and Maggie and Tom stand paralyzed in their boat as they see "death rushing on them." All four characters are equally defenseless. Yet it is Maggie, rather than her masculine brother or father, who most resembles the passive and prostrate Latimer. Like the protagonist of George Eliot's horror tale, Maggie is choiceless, the victim of her creator's apprehension over the blind chance which may determine identity and fate. To an even greater extent than Latimer (who might have been saved by Meunier), Maggie is powerless to alter her fate. While George Eliot makes Mr. Tulliver seem blameworthy for his imprudence, she comes close to pretending that Maggie's destiny is absolutely sealed because predetermined by "the irreversible laws within and without her" (Bk. IV, chap. 3, pp. 31–32) [235].

The outside forces affecting Maggie are withstood by her brother by virtue of his Dodson tenacity; the inner forces weakening her come from the characteristics she has inherited from her father. Like Mr. Tulliver, the girl possesses a "soul untrained for inevitable struggles"; like the miller, she is deeply neurotic, incapable of accepting what Freud would call the "reality principle." Maggie therefore not only succumbs to the social changes which destroy her father, but she is also victimized by a trick of heredity, by the "crossing of breeds" by the miller who had perversely chosen a wife so unlike himself. Had Maggie, and not Tom, been a man, she might have profited from Mr. Stelling's education, gone on to the university, and become a "gentleman" * * *. Had she, instead of Tom, retained her mother's characteristics, or, better still, have remained at the "mental level" of Mrs. Tulliver, she might have become an ordinary governess in a world without Byronic Rochesters or Gothic manor houses, contentedly mangling her master's sheets instead of having the world mangle her psyche. But, by a hereditary caprice, Mr. Tulliver's favorite child is a throwback to the heroic Ralph Tulliver, and hence is all the more unfitted to cope with the world than her father. She may well wish to remain insignificant, to lead the untroubled life of a child, "easy and simple, as it might have been in Paradise" (Bk. VI, chap. 11, p. 288) [364]; but in George Eliot's deterministic view of existence, such regression is not only unhealthy but also impossible. In a simpler era when Tom could have been an Adam Bede, unseduced by the ways of St. Ogg's, Maggie might have become a Dinah embracing the "reality principle." But in her stage the chasm has become too wide. The reentry into a less troubled stage of life can come only through the return to those "daisied fields" which Tom and Maggie are allowed to revisit in the flash of time which elapses before their drowning. Though treated as a greater character than her father, Maggie seems infinitely punier because she is so irrevocably determined by his genes. Character may not be destiny, as the narrator warns us, but neither are chromosomes. As Ibsen was to discover later in the century, tragedy and heredity are difficult to mix.

Like the witch in the book she shows to Mr. Riley, Maggie is condemned, regardless of her choice. Whichever way she turns lies hell. The moral which this shrewd little girl derives from her book applies to her later self:

> O, I'll tell you what that means. It's a dreadful picture, isn't it? But I can't help looking at it. That old woman in the water's a witch

> —they've put her in to find out whether she's a witch or no, and if she swims she's a witch, and if she's drowned—and killed, you know—she's innocent, and not a witch, but only a poor silly old woman. But what good would it do her then, you know, when she was drowned? (Bk. I, chap. 3, p. 21) [16]

Her question is all the more poignant in light of the answer framed by the child herself: "Only, I suppose, she'd go to heaven, and God would make it up to her." As an adult, Maggie is denied even that consolation. Her fate must be idealized in order to become bearable for her creator. For only a god-like novelist can "make it up" to choiceless victims in a Godless world.

"Choose!," thunders the six-foot Tom on finding Maggie with Philip. Yet when, pages later, she does make her single choice and dutifully returns to Tom and to St. Ogg's, she does regret it. Though innocent, she must drown. As Professor Haight points out in his preface to the novel, George Eliot's contemporaries thought Maggie's escape with Stephen was terribly "wicked"; John Ruskin (whose own sexual life was hardly exemplary) accused Maggie and Stephen of "forgetting themselves in a boat"; even the more lenient Bulwer-Lytton felt that the very "indulgence" of her temptation had violated Maggie's large Ideality. The modern reader can hardly help being amused by such reactions. Sensing Maggie's kinship to Lawrence's heroines,[4] he might easily overreact in the opposite direction and wish that Maggie had indeed "forgotten herself" with some handsome gamekeeper instead of panting like a "wounded war-goddess" after being kissed by the insipid Stephen (Bk. VI, chap. 10, p. 275) [358]. But such an enlightened view would be as far off the mark as that of Ruskin and Bulwer-Lytton. Like Philip Wakem, Stephen is merely a convenient device. Philip, whose femininity is repeatedly emphasized, acts as a spokesman for the novelist who likewise finds herself powerless to deflect Maggie from a predetermined course. Though impotent, Philip at least can chide Maggie for her nunlike mortifications ("stupefaction is not resignation"); a sufferer himself, the deformed artist foresees the far more bitter mortifications she will have to undergo. The pseudo-Byronic Mr. Guest, however, is primarily a listener * * *. He escorts Maggie down to the boat, retreats, and reappears only as the escort of the saddened, but wiser Lucy who visits her dark cousin's grave. Maggie might have escaped alone on that river * * *, but such an action would not have permitted the narrator

4. See the account, not always reliable, given by "E.T." (Lawrence's friend Jessie Chambers): "Lawrence adored *The Mill on the Floss*, but always declared that George Eliot had 'gone and spoilt it halfway through.' He could not forgive the marriage [sic] of the vital Maggie Tulliver to the cripple Philip. . . . Maggie Tulliver was his favorite heroine. He used to say that the smooth branches of the beech trees (which he especially admired) reminded him of Maggie Tulliver's arms" (*D. H. Lawrence: A Personal Record* [London, 1935], pp. 97–98).

to satirize the society which excuses Stephen but blames his female companion.

According to Professor Haight, one of George Eliot's earliest biographers, G. W. Cooke, claimed that it was not physical passion but a spiritual craving growing out of Maggie's yearning for a fuller life that led her to follow her abductor. There is at least a partial truth in this statement. Maggie's attraction to Stephen is definitely sexual * * *. If the feminine Philip proves to be an inadequate substitute for Tom, the broad-chested Stephen is quite as manly as Maggie's brother. Yet she follows him because she confuses sexual impulse with rational choice. Mistakenly, Maggie believes that Stephen can lead her into a better world. The child who was so completely hypnotized by the churning mill wheel had felt a "dim delicious awe as at the presence of an uncontrollable force" (Bk. I, chap. 4, p. 39) [26]. The adult Maggie also wants to believe that "the tide was doing it all—that she might glide along with the swift, silent stream, and not struggle any more" (Bk. VI, chap. 13, p. 313) [377]. But the forgetfulness of this Lethe is imaginary. In her childhood, fantasies of a "little world apart from her outside everyday life" were always broken by Tom. Now, daylight reveals that Stephen is not the knight she had imagined him to be. * * * George Eliot's dreamy heroine dies soon after she discovers that Stephen belongs to the same prosaic world she had tried to flee. Pain is inescapable. Philip's words come true: "there is no such escape possible except by perverting or mutilating one's nature" (Bk. VI, chap. 7, p. 229) [334]. Stephen's own appeal to Natural Law is specious: "There is nothing in the past that can annul our right to each other," he professes (Bk. VI, chap. 14, p. 331) [386]. His statement applies only to his own past, not to Maggie's. Bitterly, she discovers that she is bound by that past, even if it has been lost by her father, altered by her brother, and made irrecoverable by her own growth to adulthood.

But if Maggie bows to the past, the past lacks the authority it had possessed in *Adam Bede*. To be sure, as Thomas Pinney contends, the novel's conclusion is intended to "affirm the supreme value of the early affection of Maggie and Tom for each other.[5] But George Eliot's efforts to endow Maggie's past with a higher meaning led the novelist to inconsistencies not noted by Mr. Pinney. When Maggie and Tom become adolescents, George Eliot speaks of their having passed "the golden gates of their childhood" into a "thorny wilderness" (Bk. II, chap. 7, p. 301) [159]. This remark, like the later suggestion that Maggie's affection for Philip is "tranquil" and "tender" only because it has its roots "deep down in her childhood," seems most artificially superimposed. For Tom and Maggie's childhood had hardly been "golden"; Maggie's affection for Philip could have been just as tranquil had she met the deformed young

5. "The Authority of the Past in George Eliot's Novels," *NCF*, XXI (September 1966), 137.

artist only as an adult at the Charity Bazaar. Even in the novel's concluding remarks, there is a definite tinge of self-deception. George Eliot allows brother and sister to relive the "days when they had clasped their little hands in love, and roamed the daisied fields together." Yet there were few instances when Maggie the child was allowed to hold her brother's hand. The little girl asked by Tom to choose between two halves of a muffin found then, as later, that any choice would make her unhappy. By resorting to the Wordsworthian myth of childhood, George Eliot apparently forgot that her heroine's agonies had begun as an infant. Maggie's first memory, after all, is that of the brother who ceases to torment her only upon his death.

* * * The Victorians also longed for "an art of forgetfulness."[6] Though they made a habit of repudiating the forgetfulness of lotos-eating, they * * * fully recognized the painfulness of viewing the gaps between past and present. But the Victorian artist also derived a bittersweet satisfaction in conjuring up the lost simplicities of times past. The days when Maggie and Tom had roamed the daisied fields together may have been fictitious * * *; but it was necessary to invent that nonexistent past, to take refuge—ever so briefly—in its untroubled ways. * * *

The fiction of childhood tranquility could at least lend meaning to Maggie's death * * *. But while she is alive, as child or adult, the complex Maggie cannot link herself to any past. * * * The "Voice from the Past" which Maggie unearths in the writings of Thomas à Kempis does not speak to her own times. The author of *The Imitation of Christ* cannot really quench modern man's thirst: "She had not perceived—how could she until she had lived longer?—the inmost truth of the old monk's outpourings, that renunciation remains sorrow, though a sorrow borne willingly." (Bk. IV, chap. 3, p. 35 [237].)[7] Like Savonarola in *Romola*, this monk can at best offer a concealed kernel of truth; it is Maggie's own experience, like Romola's, which must be her teacher, even if that experience leads her to death.

Maggie must eventually bear her own crown of thorns in order to imitate Christ. But * * * she will bear her sorrow unwillingly. Her fate seems * * * unjust. * * * Maggie, on honoring the ties of the past,

6. *Idler*, No. 44.
7. George Eliot may well have been aware of Ernest Renan's influential essay on "L'Auteur de l'Imitation de Jésus Christ," in his *Etudes d'Histoire Religieuse* (1857). In his essay Renan views the author of the *Imitation* (whom he assumes to be the Benedictine Jean Gersen rather than Thomas à Kempis) much as Arnold regards the Carthusians in "Stanzas from the Grande Chartreuse." As the "last voice of monachism," the book is too simple, too reactionary and uncurious ("to increase knowledge is to increase trouble"); yet Renan holds that its incompleteness lends the work the charm of an irrecoverable simplicity: "I would not wish to exaggerate the importance of this kind of spiritual gentility, without which we can very well be useful, and even honest men. But it is certain that in losing the institution of the monastic life, the human mind has lost a great school of originality" (*Studies of Religious History* [London, 1893], pp. 231, 234, 236). George Eliot's attitude seems closer to Renan's than to Feuerbach's far harsher view of "monachism"—a view censured by Renan in another essay, "M. Feuerbach and the New Hegelian School."

finds it anachronistic, by-passed by the changes inherent in all growth, evolution, and "historical advancement." * * * The intelligent Maggie does not deserve [her fate] because of her innocence. Maggie defends Philip by saying, "He couldn't choose his father" (Bk. II, chap. 5, p. 277) [148]. Neither could she. She is born and dies as the victim of chance. Despite the adequacy of the flood as a *deus ex machina*, despite the careful foreshadowings of the flood from the very beginning of the novel, the device, like the appearance of Stephen Guest, seems extraneous and accidental. Professor Haight detects what may well be a consciously implanted parallel to *King Lear*: "Maggie's prayer, 'O God, if my life is to be long,' is answered by the waters rising about her with something of that ironic effect of the storm that follows Lear's appeal to the gods."[8] Yet Lear, it must be remembered, is not killed by the storm, whereas Maggie is sacrificed to the river.

In a tragedy like *King Lear*, the forces of circumstance are as prominent as in a "realistic" novel like *The Mill on the Floss*. The unexpected reversal of the French army, Edmund's deception, the protracted distraction of Albany and Edgar at the very moment that Cordelia is hanged contribute to the final tragedy. But it is Lear's initial act of willfulness, committed at the height of his powers, which has precipitated the ensuing concatenation of events. Maggie's one act of willfulness, itself blamed on the hypnotic influence of her seducer and on her Tulliver blood, is unrelated to the cataclysmic circumstances of her death. Had Lear not banished Cordelia, the carnage of his house would have been avoided; but had Maggie not fled with Stephen, she could still have drowned like the "helpless cattle" washed away by the Floss. Notwithstanding George Eliot's identification of the overflowing river with those deterministic "laws" within and without the girl's psyche, the drowning is not tragic. For all her queenly attributes, despite the carefully implanted parallels to figures like the drowning Ophelia, despite Maggie's own firsthand knowledge about "Shakespeare and everything," she remains a figure of pathos, the prey of circumstances that are capricious and accidental. There is no causal connection between her flight and the destiny assigned to her.

Indeed, had the flood occurred at the time of Maggie's and Stephen's escape, had it then prompted her belated return to the mill and led to her reunion in death with Tom, a logical connection between her willfulness and her denial of "irreversible laws" might have been established. But George Eliot wanted Maggie to drag her bloodied feet along the streets of St. Ogg's before her final canonization. The break, though it allowed the author to pour her sarcasm on the "world's wife," unfortunately robbed Maggie's death of the desired elevation by making her all the more a victim of chance like Latimer. Tom's military drillmaster

8. Riverside Edition, p. xix.

complains that General Wolfe did not die heroically enough: "He did nothing but die of his wound: that's a poor haction, I consider. Any other man 'ud have died o' the wounds I've had" (Bk. II, chap. 4, p. 267) [143]. The George Eliot who wept while writing about Maggie's death clearly did not consider her heroine's martyrdom to be a "poor haction." She wanted Maggie's final sojourn in St. Ogg's to be a true "Imitation of Christ."

* * *

PHILIP FISHER

[Self and Community in *The Mill on the Floss*]†

We can gauge the darkness and paradox that have entered into the relation of public and private truth in *The Mill on the Floss* by recalling the union of personal redemption and social reconciliation in the trial of Hetty[1] and contrasting it with the trial by water Maggie points out in her picture book when she is nine years old. " 'It's a dreadful picture isn't it? But I can't help looking at it. That old woman in the water's a witch—they've put her in to find out whether she's a witch or no, and if she swims she's a witch, and if she's drowned—and killed, you know—she's innocent, and not a witch, but only a poor silly old woman. But what good would it do her then, you know, when she was drowned?' " (p. 15) [16]. To come under suspicion is to be lost. If she saves herself by swimming, she is given to the fire as a witch. Only by sinking can she clear her name. Like a test of substances in chemistry, the trial by water proves and manifests the being of the old woman. But the satisfactions are those of tragedy where innocence can only be known in consenting to be sacrificed. In Hetty's trial, three aims of justice met: the truth was established, the society torn by the crime was mended and affirmed, and the criminal was brought to renounce her crime and begin to earn her way back into the community. In the trial by water, only the first goal is met. The truth is known, but only in a very dubious way. As justice, it is as wayward and mysterious as the supposed crimes of the witch herself. Like the many medieval tests it resembles, the trial by water is a proof by ordeal.

Since the old woman is lost as soon as she must be tested, the human question becomes: how did she begin to be conspicuous? Once noticed, she was thought different; once different, her substance must be known.

† Reprinted from *Making Up Society: The Novels of George Eliot* (Pittsburgh: U Pittsburgh P, 1981), pp. 66–98, by permission of the University of Pittsburgh Press. ©1981 by the University of Pittsburgh Press. Page numbers to the Norton Critical Edition of the novel have been inserted in brackets following Philip Fisher's original citations.

1. A character in George Eliot's earlier novel *Adam Bede* (1859). [Editor]

By the laws of the ordeal, she can be known only by being destroyed. The old woman is outside the community the moment she registers in its vision, the moment she is noticed. Unlike Hetty, who is exiled only to affirm through suffering her new self, the witch is in exile as soon as questions about her arise. From that point she is of no concern as a person. The trial satisfies the community's curiosity but does not rehabilitate the witch. Executed either way, she is unimportant, and the community is purified instead of healed.

The water in which the old woman is placed is more an acid that dissolves a surface that conceals her substance. Magic and chemistry at once, the water forces the truth out of the body at the moment of death. The normal medieval legal process was trial by torture. The water releases the truth because it is the executioner; the real magic is the magic of death.

The legend reported in the twelfth chapter shows that the water that tested the witch is the same water that works the Tulliver mill and flows past the town of St. Ogg's. Ogg, a boatman who lived by ferrying passengers across the Floss, was tested one stormy night by a woman, clad in rags and carrying a child, who wanted passage across the river. All other boatmen refused, but Ogg agreed. When they reached the other side, she revealed herself as the Virgin and gave Ogg the assurance that his boat would never be in peril. Both the Virgin and Ogg manifest themselves in this legend. As in magic, the gap between appearance and substance is extreme: the Virgin is in rags, and the heroic future saint is just another impoverished boatman. His ordeal over, Ogg is transformed into a magical figure over whom floods and currents have no power. At last he is St. Ogg and rules like a local divinity the town named after him.

Witch and saint are both exceptional. Both are outside humanity. The one saves the lives of men and beasts in time of flood, the other blights both with curses and potions. The water reveals substance only when the substance is miraculous. St. Ogg has the blessed Virgin in his boat. And, in Maggie's picture of the witch, there is one other figure she points out: " 'And this dreadful blacksmith with his arms akimbo, laughing—oh, isn't he ugly?—I'll tell you what he is. He's the devil *really*' " (p. 15) [16].

Maggie Tulliver is tested twice by the river. In the final flood of the book, she is the image of St. Ogg, rescuing her brother Tom. Guided on in the darkness by a mysterious protective power, she saves Tom only to be killed by the one force St. Ogg never had to overcome—machinery broken loose from the wharf. In Tom's moment of recognition, he understands that Maggie's presence has behind it "a story of almost divinely protected effort" (p. 556) [421]. The other test is the boat ride with Stephen Guest, where Maggie faces the choice of the witch: to die socially, her reputation ruined, whether she returns or elopes. Doomed either way, she takes the choice of every hero and heroine in Hanry James—to pay for everything but to get nothing for herself. By a solitary integrity, an innocence that proves itself by its willingness to stand and pay for the crimes it didn't commit, Maggie, in the act of becoming isolated and visible, has lost any chance at more than a private vindication. She dies in the flood that arrives immediately after she has learned she must leave St. Ogg's. She must be " 'a lonely wanderer, cut off from her past' " (p. 530) [415]. An exile, she has broken the continuity of place and objects and people that guarantees the continuity of experience. The word *familiar* and the word *family* have the same root. The break in continuity is the death of what is meant by the self in *The Mill on the Floss*.

In spite of the many small jokes pointing out that the mill really isn't on the Floss, we can be glad that in her title Eliot accepted the literal inaccuracy to bring the two great symbols of her book into prominence. If we think of the flood, the Tulliver mill comes to be on the Floss at last, and the title amounts to a stress on the final moment of homecoming and reconciliation, the moment, to use Proust's phrase, when the past is recaptured. Unlike Marcel, Maggie can recover the past only in the moment of losing it irrevocably. So too, Tom repays the debts and moves back to the mill, only to see the family life he has given everything to reestablish sliding away at an accelerating rate. Proust, who saw George Eliot as a forerunner, would have marked Tom's cry of "Maggsie" in the boat as one of those moments where time loops back upon itself. The past and present, pinned together by magic at certain rare moments, replace for Proust the continuity of living memory that is basic in Eliot. For Eliot, the moment of recaptured time is not made permanent by art but erased by death. The Proustian world of three experiences—in time, in memory, and in art—rests on an atomization of life into moments that could not be further from Eliot's world of permanent conditions. The moment when the mill is on the Floss is the catastrophe that joins for a moment the point from which life started and the current that carried life relentlessly away.

Speaking of Maggie late in the novel, Eliot says, "Maggie's destiny, then, is at present hidden, and we must wait for it to reveal itself like the course of an unmapped river: we only know the river is full and rapid, and that for all rivers there is the same final home" (p. 427) [325]. The image was a favorite elegiac one for Arnold, and he used it repeatedly, but its implication is obvious enough to be overlooked: the linear motion of the river is the image of a career or trajectory. Maggie's life is a sequence of acts that define and finally make visible a substance. At last there is an identity, like Tom's, that is created and willed into existence.

The river that tests substance and affirms, once the whole course is charted, the truth of a life is a metaphor of time that replaces those of space in *Adam Bede*. The arrangement of seats in the Hayslope church or around the Poyser fire embodies a truth of substance reflected everywhere in Hayslope life in modes of dress and, particularly, in the round of tasks that amounts to the occupation of one's place. To elude these marks of truth, Hetty must enter a world of fantasy and begin to seek out the solitude of bedroom or woods in order to carry out the fantasy away from the recognition that is continuous in the community life. Where everyone not only looks like but is doing "what he is," the self is legible to others and identified. The surrender to secrecy and fantasy involves shedding function, or performing it in a mechanical way that notifies those around that "this isn't really me."

When we move to the social being that opens up only in time, we reach the cluster of new images that are those of *The Mill on the Floss*. A man "on his way up" in the world, as Tom is, is not what he appears *now* to be. In fact, all men are falling, like Mr. Tulliver, or rising, like Mr. Deane. Or they are retired, like Mr. Glegg. Every man is "making his way." In the commercial language that dominates this world, life tests "what kind of stuff" you are made of. Mr. Deane is proud that Tom "appeared to be made out of such good commercial stuff" (p. 327) [251]. We speak of men "of Mr. Deane's stamp" (p. 457) [347]. And, as Mr. Deane tells Tom in his first interview, " 'If you want to slip into a round hole, you must make a ball of yourself' " (p. 245) [189].

On the public surface of life, both place and self are made. They are the final product compared to which any other good one makes is incidental. In St. Ogg's they are the only products, since money there is made in commerce and speculation, not in manufacture. The product, the self, is willed through free choice. A man can be "anything he wants to be" if only he sets his mind to it.

Since Tom Tulliver is the self-made man of the book, the man who, by will and singlemindedness, sets out to project and become what he projects, his case is, as Eliot said, of equal importance with Maggie's. To stress at once the paradox of Tom and one of the telling points of the book, it is of value to look at the phrase "Tom is not what he appears now to be." Tom is not the young clerk at Guest and Company that the conditions of his life as a boarder at Bob Jakin's imply. All men are found eventually to be men of "substance," like Mr. Deane, or "insubstantial," like Mr. Tulliver. A man like Tom, who is on his way, is nothing yet. Tom, like capitalism itself, stores up and invests. Both money and reputation are parts of the stock Tom is accumulating. Someday he will cash in by converting both money and reputation into position, and begin displaying that position through goods, through consumption. For the sake of this future of reality, the present is empty. " 'I want to have plenty of work'," Tom tells Mr. Deane. " 'There's nothing else I care about much' " (p. 424) [323]. Tom's life outside his work is described by Bob Jakin. " 'Mr. Tom 'ull sit by himself so glumpish, a-knitten his brow, an' a-lookin at the fire of a night. . . . My wife says when she goes in sometimes, an' he takes no notice of her, he sits lookin' into the fire, and frownin' as if he were watchin' folks at work in it' " (p. 414) [316].

Prominent in Tom's small parlor is one possession from the past, the large old Bible in which Tom signed his father's curse on Wakem and on which he, in turn, forces Maggie to renounce Philip. As the Bible makes clear, the future toward which Tom sells off his present is nothing but the past. First to pay off his father's debts and then to recover the mill—he has no goals but the re-creation of a past that is slipping from him at an ever increasing rate. Each partial wiping of the slate is matched, in those sour coincidences familiar from *Adam Bede,* with a resounding collapse that makes the loss of the past more definitive. When the debts are paid, Mr. Tulliver, on his way home from the celebration, strikes Wakem and dies. After Tom's three years of work, the family must leave the mill and separate. The father is dead, Maggie goes off to teach, Tom moves to lodgings, and Mrs. Tulliver circulates among her contemptuous sisters. Tom's efforts indirectly produced, as well as coincided with, this disaster. After three more years, Tom has recovered the mill, but, on the day he moves back home, Maggie elopes with Stephen Guest, disgracing the family in a final way. And when Maggie at last returns in the flood to the mill and reconciliation with Tom, they are cut off by death.

Every paradise is a paradise lost, the maxim reminds us. The motives of Tom's life suspend him halfway between old and new orders. With the techniques of will and energy, he sets out not to construct an abstract self and position (as Mr. Deane had done * * *) but to re-create his past. Tom knows that what he proposes "might not be agreeable to his uncle" (p. 422) [321]. But in a profound sense that our time has made banal (in, for example, the end of the movie *Citizen Kane*), it is only a transformed past to which we can go forward once we have to "make up" a self to become.

It is easy to notice a fall into sentimental falsity in the lines that end the final chapter. "The boat reappeared—but brother and sister had gone down in an embrace never to be parted: living through again in one supreme moment, the days when they had clasped their little hands in love, and roamed the daisied fields together" (p. 557) [422]. Alarm bells go off for any reader of Victorian novels when the words *little* and *clasped* are near enough to be in the same sentence. And "daisied fields" we find difficult to remember from the early chapters, let alone the "love" that we recall as fights and sulking pride. But the words are close to those that ended the second book after the children learned "what their father was"—a failed man. "They had entered the thorny wilderness, and the golden gates of their childhood had for ever closed behind them" (p. 266) [159]. This ideality *is* the past created through the moment of loss.

Nostalgia is the inevitable product of the discontinuity that creates the rhythm of loss and recovery. In Novalis's great phrase, memory is the one paradise from which we can never be expelled. But memory is continuity of the inner life alone. It is in terms of the need for a wider continuity, public as well as internal, that *The Mill on the Floss* must be interpreted. The continuity of memory is the wholeness of the river once its course has been charted, the wholeness of the Floss. Beyond that is the greater continuity Eliot saw as the ground of the first—and it is to this continuity that Tom sacrifices his present and future, Maggie her love for Stephen and Philip, and both their lives—the continuity of the mill.

The Continuity of Objects

To approach the continuity of the mill, the clearest path is to consider first the degraded nature of objects when they are "things." In *Adam Bede*, only Hetty is characterized by things—the box in which her treasures accumulate. Trinkets, lockets, and finally the letter from Arthur: these things were the treasures of her life. Other characters were embodied in the acts of their occupations. Even places, like the church, were defined through the use that was made of them, and they were seen in the novel only when alive through relationship to the meanings of the community life. Hetty, whose self was split into the round of life she only grudgingly carried out and the fantasy existence of her evenings alone, needed, for definition in the novel, the box of things that were the stage properties for those moments when, in front of the mirror, she came alive. Audience and actor, her two selves joined in the theater of display and appreciation. The things were tokens of a social reality not her own. In the mirror appeared the self she might someday be, and in that closed circle she was self and other—a new society.

The box with its secret society characterized the pathology of Hetty. But in *The Mill on the Floss,* the treasure chest is the hearth of every home. Hoarding replaces use as the symbolic value of "things" eclipse their actual values as "goods." The central absurdity of "things" is reached in Aunt Pullet who, in a ridiculous ceremony, tries on the hat she is afraid she will never be able to wear before Mrs. Tulliver. This little display takes place in the best room of the Pullet house, a room always kept dark and locked. "Aunt Pullet paused and unlocked a door which opened on something still more solemn than the passage: a darkened room, in which the outer light, entering feebly, showed what looked like the corpses of furniture in white shrouds. Everything that was not shrouded stood with its legs upward" (p. 94) [75–76]. The hat is wrapped in silver paper in a locked wardrobe in this graveyard of furniture. The things are being protected from people, particularly children. Instead of being items of comfort, they are tyrannical objects for which human beings are curators and guards. Upended they are of no use; covered they are of no decorative value. In a literal sense, they are dead to the human needs they were created for.

Symbolically they live, making up Aunt Pullet's hoard. The hat in the silver paper might stay there forever if relations keep dying so that Aunt Pullet is forced to stay in mourning. For one moment in the unlocked room, she is seen in it, and it is registered as part of her. "Then beginning to cry, she said, 'Sister if you should never see that bonnet again till I'm dead and gone, you'll remember I showed it to you this day' " (p. 96) [77].

Mrs. Tulliver herself has an equal hoard at home. In the first chapter we learn of her sheets: " 'I've put out sheets for the best bed. . . . They aren't the best sheets, but they're good enough for anybody to sleep in, be he who he will; for as for them best Holland sheets, I should repent buyin' them, only they'll do to lay us out in. And if you was to die tomorrow, Mr. Tulliver, they're mangled beautiful, an' all ready, an' smell of lavender as it 'ud be a pleasure to lay 'em out' " (p. 8) [10–11]. Only the dead get the best sheets, but in Mrs. Tulliver's voice one can hear how they are savored and used by the living. When Mr. Tulliver fails and the family is to be "sold up," Mrs. Tulliver is found by Tom and Maggie in the storeroom where all the precious best things are kept. "Mrs. Tulliver was seated there with all her laid-up treasures. One of the linen-chests was open: the silver teapot was unwrapped from its many folds of paper, and the best china was laid out on the top of the closed linen chest; spoons and skewers and ladles were spread in rows on the shelves; and the poor woman was shaking her head and weeping" (p. 215) [167].

Her things scattered by auction over the countryside, Mrs. Tulliver is a broken woman. Years later she speaks of the sale like a woman whose children have been lost. " 'I'm sure it was no wish o' mine, iver, as I should lie awake o' nights thinking of my best-bleached linen all over the country' " (p. 483) [366–67]. After the linen chests are gone, the family life revolves around a new box with its hoard: Mr. Tulliver's tin box, in which the money to pay off the debts is accumulating. The box was "the only sight that brought a faint beam of pleasure into the miller's eyes" (p. 295) [227].

Aunt Glegg, like the Tullivers after their fall, dispenses with goods entirely since they are bulky and must be protected, like the chairs in Aunt Pullet's locked room. Aunt Glegg's ideal of life involves having her money "out working." She wants "to have sums of interest coming in more frequently and secrete it in various corners, baffling the most ingenious of thieves" (p. 136) [107]. Finally, money is best, not inconvenient things that have to be kept upside down or in locked rooms. Money is pure symbol. Ideally compact for hoarding, it is the final abstract reduction. Far beyond the degraded goods of Aunt Pullet's locked best room—her "things"—money has pure existence in the mind of the possessor. It doesn't even have to be hidden in corners like Mrs. Glegg's but can be out on speculation as Tom's always is.

The joke Tom plays on Maggie during his school days is a perfect parable of the social theater created by these secreted hoards. Tom bribes his drill teacher to leave him the sword the old soldier has brought. He hides it under his bed, and the sword is, like Hetty's earrings, the stage property of his fantasy existence. Tom brings Maggie to his room and has her close her eyes. He belts on the sword, blackens his face with cork, and reveals himself. Maggie looks, is bewildered, then laughs, but Tom, who wants to appear ferocious, draws the sword. Maggie begins to scream and Tom, unused to its weight, drops the sword, nearly laming himself.

Like all the Dodsons, Tom hoards to surprise. Tom and his father accumulate all the money and suddenly reveal themselves, free of the disgrace of bankruptcy. The Dodson badge was to be not only rich but "richer than was supposed." Like Mrs. Tulliver's sheets, all would come out at the funeral. Tom in his lodgings is more than he appears. No one climbs, but all store up and then leap, to the amazement of the others. This social magic is the game of understatement followed by triumphant display. To this sequence is opposed the life of the Stellings, who spend more than they have in order to make a show. Mr. Tulliver before his fall is insubstantial in this way. In either direction, one is playing with the fiction of appearance. Since one is what one has, not what one does—we never learn exactly what Tom or Guest and Company do—the social surface is full of hyperbole and understatement, both purely abstract. To use Wilde's epigram, the surface is abstract because it is based on price, not value. Things have price, goods have value.

What value remains is always mediated value. René Girard in his *Desire, Deceit, and the Novel* has examined the notion of mediated desire. By extension to things, we can speak of mediated value. Aunt Pullet's hat is a very uncertain thing in her own eyes. She knows it must be right: she has spent a lot of money for it and has had it made by the right milliner. But still she is anxious. She cannot look at the hat to calm her uncertainty. Only by looking into the eyes of Mrs. Tulliver, who is looking at the hat, can she be certain of its value. In another moment the certainty is lost again. Tom with his sword must also display it and see it in Maggie's eyes. When value is mediated, the community life resolves into a series of performances in which everyone takes turns being actor and audience. Surprise is everything, and in the eyes of the others each one is being marked and placed. The notion of reputation central to both crises of the book—Mr. Tulliver's bankruptcy and Maggie's elopement—depends in its waywardness on mediated value. In this it is unlike the "good name" of the Poysers in *Adam Bede*, which could be shaken only by an actual crime, and even then could reestablish itself at once.

After Maggie's return, she walks through the streets and sees in the silence and contempt of the townspeople her "social value":

> But she had no sooner passed beyond the narrower streets which she had to thread from Bob's dwelling, than she became aware of unusual glances cast at her; and this consciousness made her hurry along nervously, afraid to look to right or left. Presently, however, she came full on Mrs. and Miss Turnbull, old acquaintances of the family; they both looked at her strangely, and turned a little aside without speaking. . . . But now she knew that she was about to pass a group of gentlemen, who were standing at the door of the billiardrooms and she could not help seeing young Torry step out a little with his glass at his eye, and bow to her with that air of nonchalance which he might have bestowed on a friendly barmaid. (P. 526) [399]

And this scandal will not lift, even in the face of testimony from Stephen, Lucy, and Philip. Rather, it spreads and contaminates anyone who tries to help her. Finally, even Dr. Kenn cannot escape the grip of rumors over Maggie's name, and he tells her she must leave St. Ogg's. The notion of reputation, crucial as an element of continuity, will be treated in detail in a later section.

To the degraded objects that are hoarded, seen in mediated value, or replaced completely by money, Eliot does not contrast objects that are simply useful. If we think for a moment of Bob Jakin's penknife, an insignificant object that appears at several points in the book, and contrast it with Tom's sword, the other pole will become clear. The knife was not bought, or rented as Tom's sword was. It was a gift to Bob from Tom, a gift given out of simple gratitude and friendship. When the two boys fight, it is the penknife that Bob throws after Tom in a moment of pique, and it is thrown because it is the mark of the friendship. So as not to waste a good knife, Bob retrieves it after Tom leaves. After the Tullivers have fallen, Bob comes to offer his help, and, when Tom seems not to recognize him, he identifies himself: " 'Why you don't remember Bob, then, as you gen the pocketknife to, Mr. Tom?' " (p. 254) [196]. And he pulls out the knife, which now has broken blades. He hasn't replaced them. " 'They might be cheatin' me an' givin' me another knife istid, for there isn't such a blade i' the country—it's got used to my hand, like. An' there was niver nobady else gen me nothin' " (p. 254) [196]. The knife is so familiar that, in Bob's striking words, "it's got used to my hand." It is not the best knife for use now that the blades are broken. But it is the only knife that is continous with Bob's own past and a concrete record of the friendship. Tom's sword, like Hetty's earrings, is part of what Eliot called the "theatre of the imagination," but Bob's knife is concrete memory, an object blessed not with symbolic fantasy meanings, like those of Tom's sword, but with the force to renew and preserve. To anyone who simply looks at it, the knife is nothing at all. For Bob himself it is not something to look at. Nor is he proud of the knife; he simply uses it.

At the other extreme, the pocketknife must be contrasted with those objects in Proust like the madeleine that, once dipped in tea, opens into the past with the suddenness of magic. In Proust, the tiny cake dipped in tea is the trigger of involuntary memory. Suddenly, an object releases the past, an object that was of no importance in itself in the past it recalls. What occurs is a moment of intense recovery, an experience of being flooded by the past called up by the object. The knife, however, is not important as a source of intense moments. Calm, continuous, living memory is held within it in a way that makes notice unnecessary. And the knife is not incidental; it is what we call a token of the intimacy. Last, it is a necessary object of use, a tool. In Proust, sensations rather than objects trigger the experience of memory; that is the key to the esthetic nature of memory in his work. Nothing could be less esthetic than the pocketknife.

Bob Jakin's knife, then, is different from the "best knife" for the job, the one he would choose if he were in a store looking over all possible knives. Equally, it is different from the knife Aunt Pullet would keep in a box and spend her time protecting and displaying. This knife is one of the world of objects that in the book are crucial to the concrete sense of continuity of the self, to legibility, and central to the reasons why bankruptcy (being "sold up") and exile, both of which take away this world of familiar objects, are forms of death.

When Maggie realizes that even her books have been sold in the auction that follows the family's bankruptcy, she describes the weight of familiar things. " 'Our dear old Pilgrim's Progress that you coloured with your little paints; and that picture of Pilgrim with a mantle on, looking just like a turtle—oh dear!' Maggie went on half sobbing as she turned over the few books. 'I thought we should never part with that while we lived—everything is going away from us—the end of our lives will have nothing in it like the beginning'!" (p. 246) [197]. As the auctioneer would say, these are items of "sentimental value only." Mrs. Tulliver tells time by "the year [she] bought the sugar tongs." In a limited way, even her linen chests record a continuity, although it is only a history of purchases.

The bankruptcy has two effects: one is on the name of the family, and this Tom sets out to repair; but the other is beyond repair, for the auction scatters their past and wipes out the chance to live continuously within the familiar. That failure kills Mr. Tulliver symbolically. He drops into a coma that is described as a "living death." He is "not himself," Maggie tells Tom. He recognizes nothing until an accident occurs that is meant to show the profound power of familiar objects. Mr. Tulliver is brought back from the dead. Tom and Mr. Glegg are searching for a note.

> Mr. Glegg had lifted out the parchments, and had fortunately drawn back a little when the iron holder gave way, and the heavy lid fell with a loud bang, that resounded over the house.
>
> Perhaps there was something in that sound more than the mere fact of the strong vibration that produced the instantaneous effect on the frame of the prostrate man; and for the time completely shook off the obstruction of paralysis. The chest had belonged to his father and his father's father, and it had always been rather a solemn business to visit it. All long-known objects, even a mere window fastening or a particular door-latch, have sounds which are a sort of recognized voice to us. . . . In the same moment when all the eyes in the room were turned upon him, he started up and looked at the chest, the parchments in Mr. Glegg's hand, and Tom holding the tin box, with a glance of perfect consciousness and recognition. (P. 236) [182]

Maggie comes and kisses him "as if her father were come back to her from the dead" (p. 237) [183]. And when Mr. Tulliver does at last revive, the family tries to explain what has taken place, but it is of no use. "The full sense of the present could only be imparted gradually by new experience—not by mere words, which must remain weaker than the impressions left by the old experiences" (p. 272) [210].

The guarantee that radiates from these objects is the continuous presence of the past, and, further, a stability against which the changes of the present can register. In the background, it is clear that the involuntary memory so magical in Proust is in fact a kind of local reprieve to the general fate of the past—it is lost, temps perdu. The premise is that the discontinuity of memory can be overcome now and then. Like the magical reappearance of people who are lost to sight as a condition of their being, the local joy is bordered by a permanent despair.

What Eliot records with an urgent force is that it is the disappearance of the world we know, the familiar world, that precipitates us into a world we choose and create. This later world is ruled by esthetics, the preference for one thing over another by the sensations it gives us, by how it looks. In one of the most important statements of the novel, she equates the two worlds.

> There is no sense of ease like the ease we felt in those scenes where we were born, where objects became dear to us before we had

> known the labour of choice, and where the outer world seemed only an extension of our own personality: we accepted and loved it as we accepted our own sense of existence and our own limbs. Very commonplace, even ugly that furniture of our early home might look if it were put up to auction: an improved taste in upholstery scorns it; and is not the striving after something better and better in our surroundings, the grand characteristic that distinguishes man from the brute? . . . But Heaven knows where that striving might lead us if our affections had not a trick of twining around those old inferior things—if the loves and sanctities of our life had no deep immovable roots in memory. One's delight in an elderberry bush, overhanging the confused leafage of a hedgerow bank, as a more gladdening sight than the finest cistus or fuchsia spreading itself on the softest undulating turf, is an entirely unjustifiable preference to a landscape gardener, or to any of those severely regulated minds who are free from the weakness of any attachment that does not rest on a demonstrable superiority of qualities. (P. 162) [127]

The demonstrable superiority of qualities is the esthetic within the "labour of choice." This choice is, of course, not limited to things. The tourist relates to place in this contrast of qualities.

One key document for the generation that followed Eliot's was Pater's conclusion to *The Renaissance* with its idea of life as a continuous choice of experiences. "Our failure is to form habits: for after all habit is relative to a stereotyped world," Pater wrote.[2] Every moment some form is perfect, and by esthetic choice we select it to be our experience for that moment. We seize that perfection, experience it, then discard it in favor of another form reaching perfection. Pater raises discontinuity to vision—the prose poem replaces the novel. Life is atomized and preserved in memory, experienced as are the discrete paintings on a museum wall. Man is a spectator, or, to speak economically, a shopper. In James's novels, he is that defective type: the collector.

The world we choose is what Maggie rejects when she leaves Stephen. When she elopes with him, she realizes "she had rent the ties that had given meaning to duty, and had made herself an outlawed soul, with no guide but the wayward choice of her own passion." (p. 504) [381]. The labor of choice that underlies estheticism sustains equally its opposite—the self-made man is one who projects what he chooses to be, then struggles to become what he has chosen. When Dr. Frankenstein creates, he first chooses every feature of the self he will make. Each feature will be the perfection of beauty. In the process of creation something goes wrong, and a monster is produced. The final thing chosen by the self-made man is the fiction of his own past. Bounderby takes

2. Walter Pater, *The Renaissance* (1873; reprint ed., New York: Mentor Books, 1960), p. 194.

that final step and chooses a new past that he, like Mr. Deane in his talks with Tom, gives out as an object lesson in social success.

Opposed to the labor of choice in Eliot's statement we find no permanent state, only the paradise of childhood. Then we did not look at the objects as one does at an auction, translating them into money, comparing them as better or worse examples of a style, or even, as with antiques, seeing those styles historically as an abstract past. They are there before we notice them. Like Bob Jakin's knife, they are "used to us"; and a diffuse memory is inseparable from the sensation we have of them, and feeling is joined to both sensation and memory. Because this is true only in childhood, the catastrophes of the novel—the auction and Maggie's exile—are melodramatic and superficially particular versions of the inevitable loss of the world of childhood and with it the world of continuity. Finally, Bob's knife will lose its blades and be replaced; finally, even the mill itself will be destroyed. The erosions of time, which we neither cause nor can prevent, are the universal part of the catastrophes of the novel.

But, in speaking of the habit of seeking for something better and better, Eliot includes the second, the willed destruction that both Maggie and Tom refuse. This destruction is at the hands of taste and mediated value. Unlike his uncle, Mr. Deane, Tom is not working for a better home in a better part of town. With prosperity, the Deanes change the things in their lives so that what they have can speak to others. These carriages and houses are those of "anyone" with so many thousands per year. They exist for envy and appreciation. Now and then they humble someone who didn't realize "who he was dealing with."

The mill that is Tom's goal is the epitome of the world of familiar objects. It is home. After his recovery, Mr. Tulliver takes the humiliating job with his enemy to keep his family in the mill he no longer owns.

> He couldn't bear to think of himself living on any other spot than this, where he knew the sound of every gate and door, and felt that the shape and colour of every roof and broken hillock was good, because his growing senses had been fed on them. Our instructed vagrancy, which has hardly time to linger by the hedgerows, but runs away early to the tropics, and is at home with palms and banyans—which is nourished on books of travel and stretches the *theatre of its imagination* to the Zambesi—can hardly get a dim notion of what an old-fashioned man like Tulliver felt for this spot, where all his memories centred, and where life seemed like a familiar smooth-handled tool that the fingers clutch with loving ease. (P. 282, emphasis added) [217]

The novelty created through choice opposes the smooth-handled tool. In the phrase the "theatre of its imagination" Eliot describes the self-alienation into roles, the community split into audience and others that is the alternative to Mr. Tulliver's painful choice. The mill is not recovered. After Tulliver strikes Wakem and dies, the family must leave, and when later Wakem sells the mill, it is to Guest and Company, who will convert it to steam and operate it with Tom as manager. At the moment of even this partial victory for Tom, Maggie elopes. Her disgrace guarantees that the family will be split forever. Tom is alone in the mill when the flood comes; what he holds is the symbol of the past, not its substance.

Beyond the mill are the more abstract loyalties and ties of which it is the emblem. Bob's knife is not only an object of continuity in his life, a unity of self; equally it is a token of intimacy bound up with the fate of his relationship to Tom. Thrown after Tom in a quarrel, produced to remind Tom of the friendship, the knife is a public mark of bonds of concern. The words *ties* and *loyalties* appear again and again in the chapters centered on Maggie. Like familiar objects, they are there before we notice them. Opposed are the ties of choice, love or friendship, where we see and compare and select. Tom is unified. He never rebels against the pattern of enemies and allies his father forces on him. The oath Tom writes in the Bible is internalized and natural to him. Maggie turns wayward and even willful in every case where she is exposed to what is fatal to her loyalties. The very qualities of impulsiveness and rebelliousness are absolutely destructive to the deeper loyalties, however delightful they appear when it is the superficial constraints of her early life she is defying. Of course, the restraints on her are unreasonable, but that means only that she wouldn't have chosen them herself. Her meetings with Philip Wakem in the Red Deeps, her equivocation with Stephen Guest that leads to the kiss in the conservatory or the walk at Aunt Moss's farm—all the breaches take place in nature, as does the most important breach of all, the flight with Guest on the river.

When Maggie begins to realize the implications of a marriage with Stephen, she thinks with a grim extremity that takes its tone from the fact that this is the first perception of what she has done. Stripped of its frantic exaggeration, the analysis holds true. It was a "breach of faith and cruel selfishness: she had rent the ties that had given meaning to duty, and had made herself an outlawed soul, with no guide but the wayward choice of her own passion. . . . Her life with Stephen could have no sacredness: she must forever sink and wander vaguely driven by uncertain impulse" (p. 504) [381–82]. It must be remembered that, for the three years between her father's death and her return to St. Ogg's as a guest at Lucy's, Maggie was a schoolteacher. But on the plane of the novel she didn't exist any more than Mr. Tulliver did for the length of his coma. Those three years are never summarized or referred to in the novel. Maggie *is* only when she is within the loyalties and resonant realities of St. Ogg's. The exile she must go into at the end is the exact equal to the death the book concludes with. Maggie's word *wanderer* is the same used in *Adam Bede* for Hetty when she was on the road, her nightmare picaresque. The word is the title of a great Anglo-Saxon complaint cataloguing the miseries of the man with no home, the man outside the law. Maggie's is an outlawed soul because she cannot identify herself with the loyalties imposed on her. Equally, she cannot free herself from them and define herself through choices.

The permanence represented by the mill or Maggie's love for Tom in their childhood might be no more than sentimental bonds, important in memory but otherwise only symbolically important for the continuity of self and existence in society. The exact society represented in the novel has a bearing on the course of loyalty and the fate of continuity and society.

Judgment and Discontinuity

The action of the novel takes place over ten years; that of *Adam Bede* took a little more than a year—if we neglect the epilogue. In the childhood chapters, Maggie is nine, at the bankruptcy she is thirteen, the affair with Philip and her father's death happen when she is sixteen, and the final third of the novel finds her nineteen. Tom, who began at thirteen, is now twenty-three. The one year of *Adam Bede* encompasses a static world tested and healed through the period of attraction, mating, pregnancy, birth, and judgment: the rural year of sowing and harvest, cycles that end where they begin. The ten years of *The Mill on the Floss* are a span of development in a situation no longer based on place. The career of a life, the chart of a river in Eliot's image, takes time to reveal substance.

A reader's comprehension of the meaning of a choice or a turn in the novel is not limited to the ten-year span. If we ask how an action is visible, how it comes to be seen for what it is, we reach one of the most complex motives for continuity, one that is built into the narrative itself. Tom's violent repudiation of Maggie after her return, unmarried, from the flight with Guest is explained by Eliot.

> There had arisen in Tom a repulsion towards Maggie that derived its very intensity from their early childish love in the time when they had clasped tiny fingers together, and their later sense of nearness in a common duty and a common sorrow: the sight of her, as he has told her, was hateful to him. In this branch of the Dodson family Aunt Glegg found a stronger nature than her own—a nature in which family feeling had lost the character of clanship, in taking on a doubly deep dye of personal pride. (Pp. 533–34) [404]

Tom's feeling is a trait transformed and inverted in time and by his circumstances, but it is continuous—as a diamond is to coal—with its source. Tom himself, we hear the aunts speculate earlier, must be either a Dodson or a Tulliver. Maggie's impetuousness is a version of her father's, and his is traced back to Ralph Tulliver, an ancestor who ruined himself. The important issue is not heredity or determination. Tom, after all, is an unpredictable variation, as different from the Dodson aunts as a lump of coal from oil. We comprehend by echoes in the novel: Tom scolding Maggie at nine, barring the gate at nineteen. The explanation of his act forces Eliot to recapitulate their entire past and allude beyond them to family traits. In heredity there is the vision of an impersonal factor in personality, a community of blood. Many of Maggie's acts are explained as well by saying "she's a Tulliver" as by any reference to her character or past. In the Tulliver blood are "elements of generous imprudence, warm affection, and hot-tempered rashness" (p. 291) [224].

Occasionally the explanation refers to the society at large or the period. Of the Glegg's hoarding, we are told the sociology, not the source in personal history. "In old-fashioned times an independence was hardly ever made without a little miserliness as a condition and you would have found that quality in every provincial district combined with characters as various as the fruits from which we can extract acid" (p. 130) [103]. What is needed of sociology or family history is supplied by the author, but the chief need for comprehension is an accurate sense of the past. When Maggie reads Thomas à Kempis, she begins a new life of renunciation. "From what you know of her, you will not be surprised that she threw some exaggeration and wilfulness, some pride and impetuosity even into her self-renunciation: her own life was still a drama for her, in which she demanded of herself that her part should be played with intensity" (p. 311) [239]. Unlike those characters in Austen who are placed with a few phrases in the first chapter and remain in focus throughout, Eliot's important characters come only gradually into register. Mr. Tulliver is the greatest accomplishment of characterization in the novel; step by step he gathers weight. What increases is not so much his complexity as the complexity of our comprehension. When Tom stands at the gate of the mill his whole life has centered on recovering, he says to Maggie: "You don't belong to me. . . . You will find no home with me." The weight of the words is a sum of our familiarity with Tom. We understand him through our knowledge of the sequence of the book. The light on the moment is nine-tenths reflected light.

One goal in Eliot continues directly the tradition of the novel of manners. It is a goal she shares with Jane Austen: the action creates situations in which we judge characters who are in the process of judging one another. Both reader and society share the same goal. Characters are exiled from the society as Lydia Bennett and Hetty Sorrel are, and the judgments of reader and society are based on the same comprehension and move in parallel.

One element of the tragedy in *The Mill on the Floss* arises from the fact that, under the new society, reputation—the judgment of society—will be as arbitrary as any mediated value, and it will no longer coincide with the judgment of art, the reader's judgment. Loss of continuity underlies the situation where only art can assemble the materials to comprehend. Only the reader is in a position to evaluate the key acts. The importance of judgment might seem weakened by the concern with sympathy. In fact, the harshness of Eliot's moral world depends on the loyalty to judgment and expiation in spite of her more prominent mentions of sympathy. She is as far as possible from that aphorism of Enlightenment psychology, *Tout comprendre, c'est tout pardonner.* Sympathy does not forgive, because that runs against the process of nemesis—Eliot's repeated assertion that evil acts have inevitable, destructive consequence both in the one who does the act and in the lives of the innocent around him. Her use of nemesis as an argument against wrongdoing amounts to an attempt to create a pragmatic, earthly replacement for the lost Christian idea of inevitable punishment after death. Where sympathy and nemesis clash, it is nemesis that is stronger. Dinah reaches a moment of perfect sympathy with Hetty in jail and then offers to ride with her to the gallows.

The divergence between the judgment of art made by the reader, with the materials assembled through the narrative, and that of society, which bases itself only on the way actions become visible, can be seen in two of the catastrophes of the book: Mr. Tulliver's fight with Wakem and Maggie's elopement. The fight never reaches public knowledge; it exists only as rumor. It has been "hushed up" and deliberately erased by all who know of it. Yet it causes the death of Mr. Tulliver, the move from the mill, and the splitting up of the rest of the family—Tom into lodgings, Maggie to a teaching post, Mrs. Tulliver to her sisters. Once hushed up, the fight disappears from explanations and makes the acts that follow cryptic. For the reader, who does know, the essence of the act depends on Tulliver's impetuosity, the depth of helplessness into which the failure threw him, and the sudden pride he felt in paying off the debts. By accident he meets Wakem, who adopts a "haughtier tone than usual" to criticize a trivial point of Tulliver's work. On the one day of his life when Tulliver's pride has returned, Wakem calls up the humiliation from which he has just surfaced. Mistaking Tulliver's excitement for the flush of drink, Wakem insults him again, and the fight begins.

In the scene both men act out of mistaken or accidentally inappropriate ideas of the other. Even worse, both act out of unconscious resentment and pride. Only the reader has the knowledge of the feelings and circumstances that ignite through the characters to produce the fight. Neither man is in focus for the other, neither is completely aware of himself. After the event, the death of Tulliver and the silence of Wakem conspire to "hush it up." Lucy Deane, two years later, speaks of it only as "some dreadful quarrel" (p. 387) [295].

The place of detail in moral judgment is argued by Eliot near the end of the novel.

> The casuists have become a byword of reproach; but their perverted spirit of minute discrimination was the shadow of a truth to which eyes and hearts are too often fatally sealed: the truth, that moral judgments must remain false and hollow, unless they are checked and enlightened by a perpetual reference to the special circumstances that mark the individual lot.
>
> All people of broad, strong sense have an instinctive repugnance to the men of maxims; because such people early discern that the mysterious complexity of our life is not to be embraced by maxims. . . . And the man of maxims is the popular representative of the minds that are guided in their moral judgment solely by general rules, thinking that these will lead them to justice by a ready-made patent method, without the trouble of exerting patience, discrimination, impartiality—without any care to assure themselves whether they have the insight that comes from a hardly-earned estimate of temptation, or from a life livid and intense enough to have created a wide fellow-feeling with all that is human. (Pp. 531–32) [403]

Maggie's highly ambiguous elopement is the central test of the gap of judgment. Those who are loyal to her are so without discrimination. Bob Jakin acts from sympathy, as does Mrs. Tulliver; both are indifferent to what she has or has not done. Mrs. Glegg calls on family loyalty in a way that makes us see it as an extended egoism driving her to protect Maggie as "one of our own." Only Dr. Kenn takes Maggie's side on the evidence of the story she tells and the letter from Stephen. Lucy and Philip, who have known Maggie longest, come closest to an intelligent judgment. At the extreme is the town, the others for whom this is that great event—a scandal.

Parallel to the magical rises and falls in economic life is the taste for moral melodrama in St. Ogg's. Reputation is the equivalent of social appearance, and both undergo the test for substance. The bankruptcy that tears the veil of Mr. Tulliver's appearance as a man of substance is one with the sudden destruction of Maggie's reputation. She is a "fallen woman" just as her father is a man who has taken a "fall." The drama of surprise and catastrophe that occurs because of the gap between appearance and substance is a drama manipulated and turned to theater on both sides. The alternative of "patience, discrimination, and impartiality" assumes a contemplative objectivity that is an exact description of a possible relationship between a reader and the characters in a novel, but a far from accurate account of social life.

Only Dr. Kenn, who is in the neutralized occupation of clergyman, acts with the objectivity Eliot describes. Behind his accuracy is a moment of intuitive understanding that marked their first meeting.

> "Oh, I *must* go," said Maggie, earnestly, looking at Dr. Kenn with an expression of reliance, as if she had told him her history in those three words. It was one of those moments of implicit revelation which will sometimes happen even between people who meet quite transiently—on a mile's journey, perhaps, or when resting by the wayside. There is always this possibility of a word or look from a stranger to keep alive the sense of human brotherhood. (P. 464) [353]

This implicit revelation between strangers becomes a substitute release. Maggie's words intimate, they do not confess. Maggie is forced by Tom to confess to her meetings with Philip Wakem. Later she volunteers the story of the elopement to Dr. Kenn. But the burden of isolation is not a set of secrets like Hetty's, or like the fight between Tulliver and Wakem that has been deliberately concealed. The real burden is an invisible and, at the extreme, unconscious level of her experience that makes of her behavior alone—and even more of the appearance of her behavior in the distortions of scandal—a half truth reversed by the missing details.

The surface of behavior is confused by more than the intimations like those in Maggie's words "I *must* go." In fact, that surface, as we see it in the relations of Maggie, Lucy, Philip, and Stephen in the sixth book, is a treacherous mixture of clues and suspicions, transferred emotion, reversal, concealment, betrayal, and even unconscious purposes. When Philip chooses a song to sing, it is "an indirect expression to Maggie of what he could not prevail on himself to say directly" (p. 444) [338]. And when Stephen talks to Maggie, he begins to stroke the ears of the dog in her lap. "It seemed to Stephen like some action in a dream that he was obliged to do, and wonder at himself all the while—to go on stroking Minny's ear. Yet is was very pleasant: he only wished he dared look at Maggie, and that she would look at him. . . . She was unable to look up, and saw nothing but Minny's black wavy coat" (p. 431) [328]. The transfer to the dog is less visible than Philip's song because it was not intended as a sign. In compensation for his growing feeling for Maggie, Stephen becomes more attentive to Lucy. "It was a subtle act of conscience in Stephen that even he was not aware of." With his growing feeling for Maggie, "there had sprung up an apparent distance between them" (p. 428) [326]. When Lucy first introduced Maggie to Stephen, the abrasiveness between them worried her, but it was a sign of their great attraction to each other.

Most of what occurs is invisible, disguised, or concealed. Experience becomes tacit and complex until an entry into a room becomes a drama.

> When Philip entered the room he was going merely to bow to Maggie, feeling that their acquaintance was a secret which he was bound not to betray; but when she advanced towards him and put out her hand, he guessed at once that Lucy had been taken into her confidence. It was a moment of some agitation to both, though Philip had spent many hours preparing it; but like all persons who have passed through life with little expectation of sympathy, he seldom lost his self-control, and shrank with the most sensitive pride from any noticeable betrayal of emotion. A little extra paleness, a little tension of the nostril when he spoke, and the voice pitched in a higher key, that to strangers would seem expressive of cold indifference, were all the signs Philip usually gave on an inward drama that was not without its fierceness. But Maggie, who had little more power of concealing the impressions made upon her than if she had been constructed of musical strings, felt her eyes getting larger with tears as they took one another's hands in silence. They were not painful tears: they had rather something of the same origin as the tears women and children shed when they have found some protection to cling to, and look back on the threatened danger. For Philip, who a little while ago was associated continually in Maggie's mind with the sense that Tom might reproach her with some justice, had now, in this short space, become a sort of outward conscience to her that she might fly to for rescue and strength. Her tranquil, tender affection for Philip, with its root deep down in her childhood, and its memories of long quiet talk confirming by distinct successive impressions the first instinctive bias—the fact that in him the appeal was more strongly to her pity and womanly devotedness than to her vanity or other egoistic excitability of her nature, seemed now to make a sacred place, a sanctuary where she could find refuge from an alluring influence the best part of herself must resist. (P. 436–37) [332]

The clues of paleness and tension are visible only to Maggie, and that Maggie now finds Philip a rescue only she and the reader understand. Maggie's new attraction to Stephen makes her display to Philip seem safe to her, but he will assume she is expressing a love we know is vanishing. Now Philip is a sanctuary. What each of the four knows and assumes about the others has passed into complete fragmentation. About himself, each stops short of the "less conscious purposes" (p. 491) [372] that are vital in the mix of the action.

Paradoxically, the details that Eliot demonstrates to be essential for moral judgment she also demonstrates to be unavailable, even to oneself. Philip begins to suspect the feeling between Stephen and Maggie when he sees Stephen anticipate her need for a footstool. "This sudden eagerness in Stephen, and the change in Maggie's face, which was painfully reflecting a beam from his . . . [was] charged with a painful meaning" (p. 446) [339]. But the attraction he sees is itself only half the truth. The mystery of this social world is one familiar from Proust and Henry James. In James or Proust, reader and character know only as much as each other. We learn of the parentage of Pansy at the same moment Isabel does. The truth she comes to learn about the circumstances of her marriage is revealed to the readers at the same time. In Proust, what is enigmatic to Marcel is equally so for us. But in *The Mill on the Floss*, it is otherwise. There is still a whole truth to which the partial versions are ironically or pathetically compared. The whole truth is that of the novel, the reader's experience. Even where unconscious motives operate, we know them, and we do not suspect others of which we have not been told. Moral judgment holds force because there is still one plane on which experience is legible, the plane of art. But within the plane of society, every self—in that terrible image used by Pater and then by T.S. Eliot in *The Waste Land*—confirms a prison. Each hears only rumors and sees only clues.

Mr. Tulliver's final word is "puzzling," and the phrase "it's a puzzling world" identifies him in a Dickensian way. The word applies with greater and greater force as we move out from the self in the novel. Unlike *Adam Bede*, *The Mill on the Floss* does not even register the life beyond the family except as a violent, inscrutable, and arbitrary set of events that can make family and personal life unstable. The two elements of that life are the law and financial speculation. Both are offstage. The verdicts that go against Tulliver bankrupt the family, but we never learn why, and the money Tom saves he makes in speculation, not from his small salary. The law is not that of *Adam Bede* but an arena for spite and foolish conflicts that get decided by craft. It is more important to have a better lawyer than a stronger case, and no one would mention the word *justice* in connection with these frivolous disputes. The social life has divided into allies and enemies, and problems of water rights that should be settled by private agreement are forced into a legal format that, with expense and hatred, can destroy all sides. Alone among the elements of public life, education is represented in the novel, and, far from bringing Tom Tulliver into life, it crushes and obscures his best traits and leads him to doubt the worth of what he can do and to respect a set of qualities that are of no point to his life.

The institutions of life have disappeared, and those that remain are dangerous and unpredictable. To the vanished society the novel can oppose only the one institution: the family. In the family itself, quarrels are the equivalent of the lawsuits of the wider life. The first book balances the quarrel with the Gleggs against the lawsuit over water rights. Both are dangerous for the same reason: Mrs. Glegg, by calling in her money, will endanger the family's financial position as much as the lawsuit will.

Family meetings are abrasive encounters where friction and resentment nearly split the group at every moment. Every encounter in the early books ends with someone walking out. Tom leaves Maggie to play with Bob Jakin, but the two quarrel and Tom walks away. Mrs. Glegg feels insulted and walks out of the Tulliver home. When Maggie, Tom, and Mrs. Tulliver visit the Pullets with Lucy Deane, Tom and Lucy abandon Maggie, who takes revenge by pushing Lucy into the mud. Then, in the most dramatic desertion, Maggie runs away to join the gypsies. In miniature, the first book acts out the destruction of every tie.

With the gypsies the novel creates the first of its symbols of those who live in the land but not in the society. Maggie runs to them because she has always been told she is like a gypsy. Everyone comments on her dark skin, and she goes to find out where she belongs. She finds she was wrong, but the gypsies represent a pole outside the social life, a pole of those who accept being outlaws and wanderers. Two of the stories mentioned in the novel suggest the extremes of those who renounce society—*Pilgrim's Progress* and the parable of prodigal son. The pilgrim and the prodigal son both renounce and depart. The novel, by balancing the one against the other, stresses the ambiguity of the act itself.

More important than the gypsies or the images of pilgrim and prodigal son are the implications of the character of Philip Wakem. An outsider by accident of birth, he is a hunchback and therefore exempt, different, someone with whom all relationships take on a special tone and set of unwritten rules. Philip is also an artist. To measure the distance between the importance of society to Eliot and its unimportance for Joyce, there is the symbol for Joyce's artist, Icarus, who soars above humanity. For Eliot, at this point, the artist is the hunchback who has fallen beneath. The story associated with Philip Wakem is that painful Greek fable of the inconvenience and yet the necessity of heroes for society, the story of Philoctetes. With his festering foot—the equal of Philip's hump—Philoctetes offends his companions in the Greek camp at the siege of Troy and is sent off to an island to complain in solitude. An omen tells the Greeks that Troy cannot be taken without Philoctetes' bow, and Ulysses is sent to bring it from the island. If the bow is taken, Philoctetes will starve; if he returns with the bow, society will be cursed with his suffering; and if neither returns, the siege will not end.

Eliot is not alone in equating the artist in modern society with Philoctetes. The title of Edmund Wilson's book of essays, *The Wound and the Bow*, describes Philoctetes, but the wound is more the Freudian one that "hurts into song." Disqualified from the world, Philip develops a compensating sense of beauty, a sensitivity that Eliot implies is part of his illness. As an outsider, he can *see* life, but being a spectator is in an inferior, degraded relationship to the world. Neither Philip nor Philoctetes chose this role. Philip's was imposed by the accident, the catastrophe, of his birth; Philoctetes' wound came from a serpent's bite. Both are exiles on an island of pain even when at home.

At certain moments in the novel, the born otherness that Philip represents seems only a more visible statement of the general condition. When talking of the Dodsons and Tullivers, Eliot suggests the inevitability of conflict.

> I share with you this sense of oppressive narrowness; but it is necessary that we should feel it, if we care to understand how it acted on the lives of Tom and Maggie—how it acted on young natures in many generations, that in the onward tendency of things have risen above the mental level of the generation before them, to which they have been nevertheless tied by the strongest fibres of their hearts. The suffering whether of martyr or victim, which belongs to every historical period, is represented in this way in every town, and by hundreds of obscure hearths. (P. 289) [222–23]

Martyrs and victims are one with Philoctetes and the witch. The wound and the hump are finally, in this current of feeling in the novel, one's uniqueness, one's self. Maggie's impetuosity is her recourse when the arbitrary rules are irreconcilable with what she is. Since her hair never will curl the way the others insist it must, Maggie cuts it off. If she must be a failure by their standards—for reasons in the nature of things—she can at least grab the side of defiance and exaggerate the difference into a distinction. And it is there that we reach the case of the witch.

What is the most necessary is the most impossible. The details that alone make judgment rational are buried in privacy or even in the unconscious. The continuity that makes life legible, even to oneself, rests on loyalties that destroy the very self that continuity was to make legible. If each person is different in substance, each is, like Philoctetes, on an island.

It is the intensity of perception on both sides of the impasse that creates the energy of the novel and creates, likewise, the stalemate. The choice is between a self more and more inscrutable within a mysterious social life of motives and concealments, or a self frustrated and resentful within an intolerable narrowness. With the loyalties and ties or without them, the novel probes to the point of impasse. None of Eliot's other novels radiates the energy of this attempt to face everything and give up nothing. The mill that cannot be lost and cannot be recovered is the emblem of the chance for continuous, visible life. Mr. Tulliver, Tom, and Maggie, the three whose interior lives dominate the book, the three who follow one another in giving direction and energy to the book—each fails to hold the mill and dies. The first third of the novel is Mr. Tulliver's; his bankruptcy is his death. Tom's energy nearly recovers the mill, but at the price of the family unity the mill stood for. And Maggie reaches the mill in the flood in a victory even more marked with defeat than Tom's.

The deaths of all three are deaths of exhaustion, life wasted in an impasse it cannot leap beyond.

MARY JACOBUS

The Question of Language: Men of Maxims and *The Mill on the Floss*†

"The first question to ask is therefore the following: how can women analyze their own exploitation, inscribe their own demands, within an order prescribed by the masculine? *Is a women's politics possible within* that order?" (Luce Irigaray)[1]

To rephrase the question: Can there be (a politics of) women's writing? What does it mean to say that women can analyze their exploitation only "within an order prescribed by the masculine"? And what theory of sexual difference can we turn to when we speak, as feminist critics are wont to do, of a specifically "feminine" practice in writing? Questions like these mark a current impasse in contemporary feminist criticism. Utopian attempts to define the specificity of women's writing—desired or hypothetical, but rarely empirically observed—either founder on the rock of essentialism (the text as body), gesture toward an avant-garde practice which turns out not to be specific to women, or, like Hélène Cixous in "The Laugh of the Medusa," do both.[2] If anatomy is not destiny, still less can it be language.

A politics of women's writing, then, if it is not to fall back on a biologically based theory of sexual difference, must address itself, as Luce Irigaray has done in "The Power of Discourse and the Subordination of the Feminine," to the position of mastery held not only by scientific discourse (Freudian theory, for instance), not only by philosophy, "the discourse of discourses," but by the logic of discourse itself. Rather than attempting to identify a specific practice, in other words, such a feminist politics would attempt to relocate sexual difference at the level of the text by undoing the repression of the "feminine" in all the systems of representation for which the Other (woman) must be

† From *Critical Inquiry* 8 (1981): 207–22. Reprinted by permission of University of Chicago Press. Page numbers to the Norton Critical Edition of the novel have been inserted in brackets following Mary Jacobus's original citations.

1. Luce Irigaray, "The Power of Discourse and the Subordination of the Feminine," *This Sex Which Is Not One*. Catherine Porter, trans., p. 81.
2. See Hélène Cixous, "The Laugh of the Medusa," Elaine Marks and Isabelle de Courtivron, eds., *New French Feminisms*, pp. 245–64 (Amherst: University of Massachusetts Press, 1980). The implications of such definitions of "*écriture feminine*" are discussed briefly in "The Difference of View," section II.1, and by Nancy K. Miller, "Emphasis Added: Plots and Plausibilities in Women's Fiction," *PMLA* (January 1981), 96(1):37; my own essay is indebted to Miller's account of *The Mill on the Floss* in the context of "women's fiction."

reduced to the economy of the Same (man). In Irigaray's terms, "masculine" systems of representation are those whose self-reflexiveness and specularity disappropriate women of their relation to themselves and to other women; as in Freud's theory of sexual difference (woman equals man-minus), difference is swiftly converted into hierarchy. Femininity comes to signify a role, an image, a value imposed on women by the narcissistic and fundamentally misogynistic logic of such masculine systems. The question then becomes for Irigaray not "What is woman?" (still less Freud's desperate "What does a woman want?") but "How is the feminine determined by discourse itself?"—determined, that is, as lack or error or as an inverted reproduction of the masculine subject.[3]

Invisible or repressed, the hidden place of the feminine in language is the hypothesis which sustains the model of the textual universe, like ether. We know it must be there because we know ourselves struggling for self-definition in other terms, elsewhere, elsehow. We need it, so we invent it. When such an article of faith doesn't manifest itself as a mere rehearsal of sexual stereotypes, it haunts contemporary feminist criticism in its quest for specificity—whether of language, or literary tradition, or women's culture. After all, why study women's writing at all unless it is "women's writing" in the first place? The answer, I believe, must be a political one, and one whose impulse also fuels that gesture toward an elusive "*écriture féminine*" or specificity. To postulate, as Irigaray does, a "work of language" which undoes the repression of the feminine constitutes in itself an attack on the dominant ideology, the very means by which we know what we know and think what we think. So too the emphasis on women's writing politicizes in a flagrant and polemical fashion the "difference" which has traditionally been elided by criticism and by the canon formations of literary history. To label a text as that of a woman, and to write about it for that reason, makes vividly legible what the critical institution has either ignored or acknowledged only under the sign of inferiority. We need the term "women's writing" if only to remind us of the social conditions under which women wrote and still write—to remind us that the conditions of their (re)production are the economic and educational disadvantages, the sexual and material organizations of society, which, rather than biology, form the crucial determinants of women's writing.

Feminist criticism, it seems to me, ultimately has to invoke as its starting point this underlying political assumption. To base its theory on a specificity of language or literary tradition or culture is already to have moved one step on in the argument, if not already to have begged the question, since by then one is confronted by what Nancy Miller, in a recent essay on women's fiction, has called "the irreducibly compli-

3. See Irigaray, *This Sex Which Is Not One*, pp. 68–85 *passim*, and her *Speculum of The Other Woman*, pp. 133–46. See also Carolyn Burke, "Introduction to Luce Irigaray's 'When Our Lips Speak Together,' " *Signs* (Autumn 1980), 6(1):71.

cated relationship women have historically had to the language of the dominant culture."[4] Perhaps that is why, baffled in their attempts to specify the feminine, feminist critics have so often turned to an analysis of this relationship as it is manifested and thematized in writing by and about women. The project is, and can't escape being, an ideological one; concerned, that is, with the functioning and reproduction of sexual ideology in particular—whether in the overtly theoretical terms of Luce Irigaray or in the fictional terms of, for instance, George Eliot. To quote Miller again, the aim would be to show that "the maxims that pass for the truth of human experience, and the encoding of that experience in literature, are organizations, when they are not fantasies, of the dominant culture."[5]

But Irigaray's "women's politics," her feminist argument, goes beyond ideology critique in its effort to recover "the place of the feminine" in discourse. The "work of language" which she envisages would undo representation altogether, even to the extent of refusing the linearity of reading. "*Après-coup*," the retroactive effect of a word ending, opens up the structure of language to reveal the repression on which meaning depends; and repression is the place of the feminine. By contrast, the "style" of women—*écriture féminine*—would privilege not the look but the tactile, the simultaneous, the fluid. Yet at the same time, we discover, such a style can't be sustained as a thesis or made the object of a position; if not exactly "nothing," it is nonetheless a kind of discursive practice that can't be thought, still less written. Like her style, woman herself is alleged by Irigaray to be an unimaginable concept within the existing order. Elaborating a theory of which woman is either the subject or the object merely reinstalls the feminine within a logic that represses, censors, or misrecognizes it. Within that logic, woman can only signify an excess or a deranging power. Woman for Irigaray is always the "something else" that points to the possibility of another language, asserts that the masculine is not all, does not have a monopoly on value, or, still less, "the abusive privilege of appropriation." She tries to strike through the theoretical machinery itself, suspending its pretension to the production of a single truth, a univocal meaning. Woman would thus find herself on the side of everything in language that is multiple, duplicitous, unreliable, and resistant to the binary oppositions on which theories of sexual difference such as Freud's depend.[6]

Irigaray's argument is seductive precisely because it puts all systems in question, leaving process and fluidity instead of fixity and form. At the same time, it necessarily concedes that women have access to language only by recourse to systems of representation that are masculine. Given the coherence of the systems at work in discourse, whether Freud-

4. Miller, "Emphasis Added," p. 38.
5. *Ibid.*, p. 46.
6. See Irigaray, *This Sex Which Is Not One*, pp. 74–80 *passim*.

ian or critical, how is the work of language of which she speaks to be undertaken at all? Her answer is "mimetism," the role historically assigned to women—that of reproduction, but deliberately assumed; an acting out or role playing within the text which allows the woman writer to know better and hence to expose what it is she mimics. Irigaray, in fact, seems to be saying that there is no "outside" of discourse, no alternative practice available to the woman writer apart from the process of undoing itself:

> To play with mimesis is thus, for a woman, to try to recover the place of her exploitation by discourse, without allowing herself to be simply reduced to it. It means to resubmit herself—inasmuch as she is on the side of the "perceptible," of "matter"—to "ideas," in particular to ideas about herself, that are elaborated in/by a masculine logic, but so as to make "visible," by an effect of playful repetition, what was supposed to remain invisible: the cover-up of a possible operation of the feminine in language. It also means "to unveil" the fact that, if women are such good mimics, it is because they are not simply resorbed in this function. *They also remain elsewhere.*[7]

Within the systems of discourse and representation which repress the feminine, woman can only resubmit herself to them; but by refusing to be reduced by them, she points to the place and manner of her exploitation. "A possible operation of the feminine in language" becomes, then, the revelation of its repression, through an effect of playful rehearsal, rather than a demonstrably feminine linguistic practice.

Irigaray's main usefulness to the feminist critic lies in this half-glimpsed possibility of undoing the ideas about women elaborated in and by masculine logic, a project at once analytic and ideological. Her attack on centrism in general, and phallocentrism in particular, allows the feminist critic to ally herself "otherwise," with the "elsewhere" to which Irigaray gestures, in a stance of dissociation and resistance which typically characterizes that of feminist criticism in its relation to the dominant culture or "order prescribed by the masculine." But like Irigaray herself in "The Power of Discourse," feminist criticism remains imbricated within the forms of intelligibility—reading and writing, the logic of discourse—against which it pushes. What makes the "difference," then? Surely, the direction from which that criticism comes—the elsewhere that it invokes, the putting in question of our social organization of gender; its wishfulness, even, in imagining alternatives. It follows that what pleases the feminist critic most (this one, at any rate) is to light on a text that seems to do her arguing, or some of it, for her—especially a text whose story is the same as hers; hence, perhaps,

7. Irigaray, *This Sex Which Is Not One*, p. 76.

the drift toward narrative in recent works of feminist criticism such as Sandra Gilbert and Susan Gubar's influential *The Madwoman in the Attic.*[8] What's usually going on in such criticism—perhaps in all feminist criticism—is a specificity of relationship that amounts to a distinctive practice. Criticism takes literature as its object, yes; but here literature in a different sense is likely to become the subject, the feminist critic, the woman writer, woman herself.

This charged and doubled relationship, an almost inescapable aspect of feminist criticism, is at once transgressive and liberating, since what it brings to light is the hidden or unspoken ideological premise of criticism itself. *Engagée* perforce, feminist criticism calls neutrality into question, like other avowedly political analyses of literature. I want now to undertake a "symptomatic" reading of a thematically relevant chapter from Eliot's *The Mill on the Floss* (1860) in the hope that this quintessentially critical activity will bring to light if not "a possible operation of the feminine in language" at least one mode of its recovery—language itself. I will return later to the final chapter of Irigaray's *This Sex Which Is Not One* in which an escape from masculine systems of representation is glimpsed through the metaphors of female desire itself.

Nancy Miller's "maxims that pass for the truth of human experience" allude to Eliot's remark near the end of *The Mill on the Floss* that "the man of maxims is the popular representative of the minds that are guided in their moral judgment solely by general rules."[9] Miller's concern is the accusation of implausibility leveled at the plots of women's novels: Eliot's concern is the "special case" of Maggie Tulliver—"to lace ourselves up in formulas" is to ignore "the special circumstances that mark the individual lot." An argument for the individual makes itself felt as an argument against generalities. For Eliot herself, as for Dr. Kenn (the repository of her knowledge at this point in the novel), "the mysterious complexity of our life is not to be embraced by maxims" (p. 628) [403]. Though the context is the making of moral, not critical, judgments, I think that Eliot, as so often at such moments, is concerned also with both the making and the reading of fiction; with the making of another kind of special case. Though Maggie may be an "exceptional" woman, the ugly duckling of St. Ogg's, her story contravenes the norm, and in that respect it could be said to be all women's story. We recall an earlier moment, that of Tom Tulliver's harsh judgment of his sister ("You have not resolution to resist a thing that you know to be wrong"), and Maggie's rebellious murmuring that her life is "a planless riddle to him" only because he's incapable of feeling the mental needs which impel her, in

8. See, for instance, Gilbert and Gubar, "Toward a Feminist Poetics," Part I of *The Madwoman in the Attic*, pp. 3–104; Gilbert and Gubar's is above all a work of literary (her)story.
9. George Eliot, *The Mill on the Floss*, A. S. Byatt, ed. (Harmondsworth: Penguin, 1979), p. 628 [403] subsequent page references in the text are to this edition. I am especially indebted to Byatt's helpful annotations.

his eyes, to wrongdoing or absurdity (pp. 504, 505) [318]. To Tom, the novel's chief upholder of general rules and patriarchal law (he makes his sister swear obedience to his prohibitions on the family Bible), the planless riddle of Maggie's life is only made sense of by a "Final Rescue" which involves her death: "In their death they were not divided" (p. 657) [423]. But the reunion of brother and sister in the floodwaters of the Ripple enacts both reconciliation and revenge, consummation and cataclysm; powerful authorial desires are at work.[1] To simplify this irreducible swirl of contradictory desire in the deluge that "rescues" Maggie as well as her brother would be to salvage a maxim as "jejune" as "*Mors omnibus est communis*" (one of the tags Maggie finds when she dips into her brother's Latin grammar) stripped of its saving Latin.[2] We might go further and say that to substitute a generality for the riddle of Maggie's life and death, or to translate Latin maxims into English commonplaces, would constitute a misreading of the novel as inept as Tom's misconstruction of his sister, or his Latin. Maggie's incomprehensible foreignness, her drift into error or impropriety on the river with Stephen Guest, is a "lapse" understood by the latitudinarian Dr. Kenn. For us, it also involves an understanding that planlessness, riddles, and impropriety—the enigmas, accidents, and incorrectness of language itself—are at odds with the closures of plot (here, the plot of incestuous reunion) and with interpretation itself, as well as with the finality of the maxims denounced by Eliot.

For all its healing of division, *The Mill on the Floss* uncovers the divide between the language or maxims of the dominant culture and the language itself which undoes them. In life, at any rate, they remain divided—indeed, death may be the price of unity—and feminist criticism might be said to install itself in the gap. A frequent move on the part of feminist criticism is to challenge the norms and aesthetic criteria of the dominant culture (as Miller does in defending Eliot), claiming, in effect, that "incorrectness" makes visible what is specific to women's writing. The culturally imposed or assumed "lapses" of women's writing are turned against the system that brings them into being—a system women writers necessarily inhabit. What surfaces in this gesture is the all-important question of women's access to knowledge and culture and to the power that goes with them. In writing by women, the question is often explicitly thematized in terms of education. Eliot's account of Tom's schooling in "School-Time," the opening chapter of Book 2,

1. See Gilbert and Gubar. *The Madwoman in the Attic*, who succinctly state that Maggie seems "at her most monstrous when she tries to turn herself into an angel of renunciation" (p. 491), and Gillian Beer, "Beyond Determinism: George Eliot and Virginia Woolf," in Mary Jacobus, ed., *Women Writing and Writing About Women*, p. 88, on an ending that "lacks bleakness, is even lubricious" in its realization of "confused and passionate needs."
2. "*Mors omnibus est communis* would have been jejune, only [Maggie] liked to know the Latin"; Eliot, *The Mill on the Floss*, pp. 217–18 [123]; see below.

provides just such a thematic treatment—a lesson in antifeminist pedagogy which goes beyond its immediate implications for women's education to raise more far-reaching questions about the functioning of both sexual ideology and language. Take Maggie's puzzlement at one of the many maxims found in the Eton Grammar, a required text for the unfortunate Tom. As often, rules and examples prove hard to tell apart:

> The astronomer who hated women generally caused [Maggie] so much puzzling speculation that she one day asked Mr. Stelling if all astronomers hated women, or whether it was only this particular astronomer. But, forestalling his answer, she said,
>
> "I suppose it's all astronomers: because you know, they live up in high towers, and if the women came there, they might talk and hinder them from looking at the stars."
>
> Mr. Stelling liked her prattle immensely. (p. 220) [125–26]

What we see here is a textbook example of the way in which individual misogyny becomes generalized—"maximized," as it were—in the form of a patriarchal put-down. Maggie may have trouble construing *"ad unam mulieres,"* or "all to a woman," but in essence she has got it right.[3] Just to prove her point, Mr. Stelling (who himself prefers the talk of women to star gazing) likes her "prattle," a term used only of the talk of women and children. Reduced to his idea of her, Maggie can only mimic man's talk.

Inappropriate as he is in other respects for Tom's future career, Mr. Stelling thus proves an excellent schoolmaster to his latent misogyny. His classroom is also an important scene of instruction for Maggie, who learns not only that all astronomers to a man hate women in general but that girls can't learn Latin; that they are quick and shallow, mere imitators ("this small apparatus of shallow quickness," Eliot playfully repeats); and that everybody hates clever women, even if they are amused by the prattle of clever little girls (pp. 214, 221, 216) [121, 125–26, 123]. It's hard not to read with one eye on her creator. Maggie, it emerges, rather fancies herself as a linguist, and Eliot too seems wishfully to imply that she has what one might call a "gift" for languages—a gift, perhaps, for ambiguity too. Women, we learn, don't just talk, they double-talk, like language itself; that's just the trouble for boys like Tom:

> "I know what Latin is very well," said Maggie, confidently. "Latin's a language. There are Latin words in the Dictionary. There's bonus, a gift."

3. "*Astronomer: ut*—'as,' *astronomus*—'an astronomer,' *exosus*—'hating,' *mulieres*—women,' *ad unum* [mulierem]—'to one' [that is, in general]. (*Eton Grammar*, 1831 edition, p. 279)"; Eliot, *The Mill on the Floss*, p. 676 *n.* 55.

> "Now, you're just wrong there, Miss Maggie!" said Tom, secretly astonished. "You think you're very wise! But 'bonus' means 'good,' as it happens—bonus, bona, bonum."
>
> "Well, that's no reason why it shouldn't mean 'gift,' " said Maggie stoutly. "It may mean several things. Almost every word does." (p. 214) [121]

And if words may mean several things, general rules or maxims may prove less universal than they claim to be and lose their authority. Perhaps only "this particular astronomer" was a woman-hater or hated only one woman in particular. Special cases or particular contexts—"the special circumstances that mark the individual lot" (p. 628) [403]—determine or render indeterminate not only judgment but meaning too. The rules of language itself make Tom's rote learning troublesome to him. How can he hope to construe his sister when her relation to language proves so treacherous—her difference so shifting a play of possibility, like the difference within language itself, destabilizing terms such as "wrong" and "good"?

Maggie, a little parody of her author's procedures in *The Mill on the Floss*, decides "to skip the rule in the syntax—the examples became so absorbing":

> These mysterious sentences snatched from an unknown context,—like strange horns of beasts and leaves of unknown plants, brought from some far-off region, gave boundless scope to her imagination, and were all the more fascinating because they were in a peculiar tongue of their own, which she could learn to interpret. It was really very interesting—the Latin Grammar that Tom had said no girls could learn: and she was proud because she found it interesting. The most fragmentary examples were her favourites. *Mors omnibus est communis* would have been jejune, only she liked to know the Latin; but the fortunate gentleman whom every one congratulated because he had a son "endowed with *such* a disposition" afforded her a great deal of pleasant conjecture, and she was quite lost in the "thick grove penetrable by no star," when Tom called out,
>
> "Now, then, Magsie, give us the Grammar!" (pp. 217–18) [123–24]

Whereas maxims lace her up in formulas, "these mysterious sentences" give boundless scope to Maggie's imagination; for her, as for her author (who makes them foretell her story), they are whole fictional worlds, alternative realities, transformations of the familiar into the exotic and strange. In their foreignness she finds herself, until roused by Tom's peremptory call, as she is later to be recalled by his voice from the Red Deeps. Here, however, it is Maggie who teaches Tom his most important lesson, that the "dead" languages had once been living: "that there had once been people upon the earth who were so fortunate as to know Latin without learning it through the medium of the Eton Grammar" (p. 221) [126]. The idea—or, rather, fantasy—of a language that is innate rather than acquired, native rather than incomprehensibly foreign, is a consoling one for the unbookish miller's son; but it holds out hope for Maggie too, and presumably also for her creator. Though Latin stands in for cultural imperialism and for the outlines of a peculiarly masculine and elitist classical education from which women have traditionally been excluded, Maggie can learn to interpret it. The "peculiar tongue" had once been spoken by women, after all—and they had not needed to learn it from Mr. Stelling or the institutions he perpetuates. Who knows, she might even become an astronomer herself, or, like Eliot, a writer who by her pen name had refused the institutionalization of sexual difference as cultural exclusion. Tom and Mr. Stelling tell Maggie that "Girls never learn such things"; "They've a great deal of superficial cleverness but they couldn't go far into anything" (pp. 214, 221) [121, 126]. But going far into things—and going far—is the author's prerogative in *The Mill on the Floss*. Though Maggie's quest for knowledge ends in death, as Virginia Woolf thought Eliot's own had ended,[4] killing off this small apparatus of shallow quickness may have been the necessary sacrifice in order for Eliot herself to become an interpreter of the exotic possibilities contained in mysterious sentences. Maggie—unassimilable, incomprehensible, "fallen"—is her text, a "dead" language which thereby gives all the greater scope to authorial imaginings, making it possible for the writer to come into being.

We recognize in "School-Time" Eliot's investment—humorous, affectionate, and rather innocently self-lovingly—in Maggie's gifts and haphazard acquisition of knowledge. In particular, we recognize a defense of the "irregular" education which until recently had been the lot of most women, if educated at all. Earlier in the same chapter, in the context of Mr. Stelling's teaching methods (that is, his unquestioning reliance on Euclid and the Eton Grammar), Eliot refers whimsically to "Mr. Broderip's amiable beaver" which "busied himself as earnestly in constructing a dam, in a room up three pairs of stairs in London, as if he had been laying his foundation in a stream or lake in Upper Canada. It was 'Binny's' function to build" (p. 206) [115]. Binny the beaver, a pet from the pages of W. J. Broderip's *Leaves from the Note Book of a Naturalist* (1852), constructed his dam with sweeping brushes and warming pans, "hand-brushes, rush-baskets, books, boots, sticks, clothes, dried turf or anything portable."[5] A domesticated *bricoleur*, Binny makes do with what he can find. A few lines later, we hear of Mr. Stelling's

4. See Virginia Woolf, "George Eliot," *Collected Essays of Virginia Woolf*, 4 vols., Leonard Woolf, ed. (London: Hogarth Press, 1966–67), 1:204: "With every obstacle against her—sex and health and convention—she sought more knowledge and more freedom till the body, weighted with its double burden, sank worn out."
5. See Eliot, *The Mill on the Floss*, pp. 675–76, *n.*44.

"educated" condescension toward "the display of various or special knowledge made by irregularly educated people" (p. 207) [115]. Mr. Broderip's beaver, it turns out, does double duty as an illustration of Mr. Stelling's "regular" (not to say "rote") mode of instruction—he can do no otherwise, conditioned as he is—and as a defense of Eliot's own display of irregularly acquired "various or special knowledge." Like Maggie's, this is knowledge drawn directly from books, without the aid of a patriarchal pedagogue. Mr. Stelling and the institutions he subscribes to (Aristotle, deaneries, prebends, Great Britain, and Protestantism—the Establishment, in fact) are lined up against the author-as-eager-beaver. Eliot's mischievous impugning of authority and authorities—specifically, cultural authority—becomes increasingly explicit until, a page or so later, culture itself comes under attack. Finding Tom's brain "peculiarly impervious to etymology and demonstration," Mr. Stelling concludes that it "was peculiarly in need of being ploughed and harrowed by these patent implements: it was his favourite metaphor, that the classics and geometry constituted that culture of the mind which prepared it for the reception of any subsequent crop." As Eliot rather wittily observes, the regimen proves "as uncomfortable for Tom Tulliver as if he had been plied with cheese in order to remedy a gastric weakness which prevented him for digesting it" (p. 208) [117]. Nor is Eliot only, or simply, being funny. The bonus or gift of language is at work here, translating dead metaphor into organic tract.

Like Maggie herself, the metaphor here is improper, disrespectful of authorities, and, as Tom later complains of his sister, not to be relied on. Developing the implications of changing her metaphor from agriculture to digestion, Eliot drastically undermines the realist illusion of her fictional world, revealing it to be no more than a blank page inscribed with a succession of arbitrary metaphoric substitutions:

> It is astonishing what a different result one gets by changing the metaphor! Once call the brain an intellectual stomach, and one's ingenious conception of the classics and geometry as ploughs and harrows seems to settle nothing. But then, it is open to some one else to follow great authorities and call the mind a sheet of white paper or a mirror, in which case one's knowledge of the digestive process becomes quite irrelevant. It was doubtless an ingenious idea to call the camel the ship of the desert, but it would hardly lead one far in training that useful beast. O Aristotle! if you had had the advantage of being "the freshest modern" instead of the greatest ancient, would you not have mingled your praise of metaphorical speech as a sign of high intelligence, with a lamentation that intelligence so rarely shows itself in speech without metaphor,—that we can seldom declare what a thing is, except by saying it is something else? (pp. 208–9) [117]

In the *Poetics* Aristotle says: "It is a great thing to make use of . . . double words and rare words . . . but by far the greatest thing is the use of metaphor. That alone cannot be learned; it is the token of genius. *For the right use of metaphor means an eye for resemblances.*"[6] Of course there's authorial self-congratulation lurking in this passage, as there is in Eliot's affectionate parade of Maggie's gifts. But an eye for resemblances (between Binny and Mr. Stelling, for instance, or brain and stomach) is also here a satiric eye. Culture as (in)digestion makes Euclid and the Eton Grammer hard to swallow; Aristotle loses his authority to the author herself. On one level, this is science calling culture into question, making empiricism the order of the day. But there's something unsettling to the mind, or, rather, stomach, in this dizzy progression from culture, digestive tract, and tabula rasa to ship of the desert (which sounds like a textbook example of metaphor). The blank page may take what imprint the author chooses to give it. But the price one pays for such freedom is the recognition that language, thus viewed, is endlessly duplicitous rather than singleminded (as Tom would have it be); that metaphor is a kind of impropriety or oxymoronic otherness; and that "we can so seldom declare what a thing is, except by saying it is something else."

Error, then, must creep in where there's a story to tell, especially a woman's story. Maggie's "wrong-doing and absurdity," as the fall of women often does, not only puts her on the side of error in Tom's scheme of things but gives her a history; "the happiest women," Eliot reminds us, "like the happiest nations, have no history" (p. 494) [311]. Impropriety and metaphor belong together on the same side as a fall from absolute truth or unitary schemes of knowledge (maxims). Knowledge in *The Mill on the Floss* is guarded by a traditional patriarchal prohibition which, by a curious slippage, makes the fruit itself as indigestible as the ban and its thick rind. The adolescent Maggie, "with her soul's hunger and her illusions of self-flattery," begins "to nibble at this thick-rinded fruit of the tree of knowledge, filling her vacant hours with Latin, geometry, and the forms of the syllogism" (p. 380) [234]. But the Latin, Euclid, and Logic, which Maggie imagines "would surely be a considerable step in masculine wisdom," leave her dissatisfied, like a thirsty traveler in a trackless desert. What does Eliot substitute for this mental diet? After Maggie's chance discovery of Thomas à Kempis, we're told that "the old books, Virgil, Euclid, and Aldrich—that wrinkled fruit of the tree of knowledge—had been all laid by" for a doctrine that announces: "And if he should attain to all knowledge, he is yet far off" (pp. 387, 383) [239, 237]. Though the fruits of patriarchal knowledge

6. Aristotle, *Poetics*, 22:16 (my italics); see Eliot, *The Mill on the Floss*, p. 676 *n*.46. J. Hillis Miller notes apropos of this passage that it "is followed almost immediately by an ostentatious and forceful metaphor [that of a shrewmouse imprisoned in a split tree (p. 209)], as if Eliot were compelled . . . to demonstrate that we cannot say what a thing is except by saying it is something else"; "The Worlds of Victorian Fiction," *Harvard English Studies* (1975), 6:145*n*.

no longer seem worth the eating, can we view Thomas à Kempis as anything more than an opiate for the hunger pains of oppression? Surely not. The morality of submission and renunciation is only a sublimated version of Tom's plainspoken patriarchal prohibition, as the satanic mocker, Philip Wakem, doesn't fail to point out. Yet in the last resort, Eliot makes her heroine live and die by this inherited morality of female suffering—as if, in the economy of the text, it was necessary for Maggie to die renouncing in order for her author to release the flood of desire that is language itself.[7] Why?

The Mill on the Floss gestures toward a largely unacted error, the elopement with Stephen Guest which would have placed Maggie finally outside the laws of St. Ogg's. Instead of this unrealized fall, we are offered a moment of attempted transcendence in the timeless death embrace which abolished the history of division between brother and sister—"living through again in one supreme moment, the days when they had clasped their little hands in love" (p. 655) [422]. What is striking about the novel's ending is its banishing not simply of division but of sexual difference as the origin of that division. The fantasy is of a world where brother and sister might roam together, "indifferently," as it were, without either conflict or hierarchy. We know that their childhood was not like that at all, and we can scarcely avoid concluding that death is a high price to pay for such imaginary union. In another sense, too, the abolition of difference marks the death of desire for Maggie; "The Last Conflict" (the title of the book's closing chapter) is resolved by her final renunciation of Guest, resolved, moreover, with the help of "the little old book that she had long ago learned by heart" (p. 648) [417]. Through Thomas à Kempis, Eliot achieves a simultaneous management of both knowledge and desire, evoking an "invisible" or "supreme teacher" within the soul, whose voice promises "entrance into that satisfaction which [Maggie] had so long been craving in vain" (p. 384) [237]. Repressing the problematic issue of book learning, this "invisible teacher" is an aspect of the self which one might call the voice of conscience or, alternatively, sublimated maxims. In "the little old book," Maggie finds the authorized version of her own and Eliot's story, "written down by a hand that waited for the heart's prompting . . . the chronicle of a solitary, hidden anguish . . . a lasting record of human needs and human consolations, the voice of a brother who, ages ago, felt and suffered and renounced" (pp. 384–85) [238].

Where might we look for an alternative version or, for that matter, for another model of difference, one that did not merely substitute unity for division and did not pay the price of death or transcendence? Back to the schoolroom, where we find Tom painfully committing to memory the Eton Grammar's "Rules for the Genders of Nouns," the names of

7. See Carol Christ, "Aggression and Providential Death in George Eliot's Fiction," *Novel* (Winter 1976), 9(2):130–40, for a somewhat different interpretation.

trees being feminine, while some birds, animals, and fish "*dicta epicoena* . . . are said to be epicene."[8] In epicene language, as distinct from language imagined as either neutral or androgynous, gender is variable at will, a mere metaphor. The rules for the genders of nouns, like prescriptions about "masculine" or "feminine" species of knowledge, are seen to be entirely arbitrary. Thus the lament of David for Saul and Jonathan can be appropriated as the epitaph of brother and sister ("In their death they were not divided"), and "the voice of a brother who, ages ago, felt and suffered and renounced" can double as the voice of a sister-author, the passionately epicene George Eliot. One answer, then, to my earlier question (why does Eliot sacrifice her heroine to the morality of renunciation?) is that Eliot saw in Thomas à Kempis a language of desire, but desire managed as knowledge is also managed—sublimated, that is, not as renunciation but as writing. In such epicene writing, the woman writer finds herself, or finds herself in metaphor.

For Irigaray, the price paid by the woman writer for attempting to inscribe the claims of women "within an order prescribed by the masculine" may ultimately be death; the problem as she sees it is this: "[How can we] disengage ourselves, *alive*, from their concepts?[9] The final, lyrical chapter of *This Sex Which Is Not One*, "When Our Lips Speak Together," is, or tries to be, the alternative she proposes. It begins boldly: "If we keep on speaking the same language together, we're going to reproduce the same history" (p.205). This would be a history of disappropriation, the record of the woman writer's self loss as, attempting to swallow or incorporate an alien language, she is swallowed up by it in turn:

> Outside, you try to conform to an alien order. Exiled from yourself, you fuse with everything you meet. You imitate whatever comes close. You become whatever touches you. In your eagerness to find yourself again, you move indefinitely far from yourself. From me. Taking one model after another, passing from master to master, changing face, form, and language with each new power that dominates you. You/we are sundered; as you allow yourself to be abused, you become an impassive travesty. (p. 210)

This, perhaps, is what Miller means by "a posture of imposture," "the uncomfortable posture of all woman writers in our culture, within and without the text."[1] Miming has become absorption into an alien order. One thinks of Maggie, a consumer who is in turn consumed by what she reads, an imitative "apparatus" who, like the alienated women imagined by Irigaray, can only speak their desire as "spoken machines, speak-

8. See Eliot, *The Mill on the Floss*, p. 676 *n*.53. [p. 124, *n*.9, in this edition. Editor.]
9. Luce Irigaray, "When Our Lips Speak Together," *This Sex Which Is Not One*, p. 212.
1. Miller, "Emphasis Added," p. 46.

ing machines." Speaking the same language, spoken in the language of the Same ("If we keep on speaking sameness, if we speak to each other as men have been doing for centuries, as we have been taught to speak, we'll miss each other, fail ourselves"), she can only be reproduced as the history of a fall or a failure (p. 205). Eliot herself, of course, never so much as gestures toward Irigaray's jubilant utopian love language between two women—a language of desire whose object ("my indifferent one") is that internal (in)difference which, in another context, Barbara Johnson calls "not a difference between . . . but a difference within. Far from constituting the text's unique identity, it is that which subverts the very idea of identity." What is destroyed, conceptually, is the "unequivocal domination of one mode of signifying over another."[2] Irigaray's experiment in "When Our Lips Speak Together" is of this kind, an attempt to release the subtext of female desire, thereby undoing repression and depriving metalanguage of its claim to truth. "The exhausting labor of copying, miming" is no longer enough (p. 207).

But for all Irigaray's experimentalism, the "difference" is not to be located at the level of the sentence, as Miller reminds us.[3] Rather, what we find in "When Our Lips Speak Together" is writing designed to indicate the cultural determinants that bound the woman writer and, for Irigaray, deprive her of her most fundamental relationship: her relationship to herself. In fact, what seems most specifically "feminine" about Irigaray's practice is not its experimentalism as such but its dialogue of one/two, its fantasy of the two-in-one: "In *life* they are not divided," to rephrase David's lament. The lips that speak together (the lips of female lovers) are here imagined as initiating a dialogue not of conflict or reunion, like Maggie and Tom's, but of mutuality, lack of boundaries, continuity. If both Irigaray and Eliot kill off the woman engulfed by masculine logic and language, both end also—and need to end—by releasing a swirl of (im)possibility:

> These rivers flow into no single, definitive sea. These streams are without fixed banks, this body without fixed boundaries. This unceasing mobility. This life—which will perhaps be called our restlessness, whims, pretenses, or lies. All this remains very strange to anyone claiming to stand on solid ground. (p. 215)

Is that, finally, why Maggie must be drowned, sacrificed as a mimetic "apparatus" (much as the solidity of St. Ogg's is swept away) to the flood whose murmuring waters swell the "low murmur" of Maggie's lips as they repeat the words of Thomas à Kempis? When the praying Maggie feels the flow of water at her knees, the literal seems to have merged with a figural flow; as Eliot writes, "the whole thing had been so

2. Johnson, *The Critical Difference*, pp. 4, 5.
3. See Miller, "Emphasis Added," p. 38.

rapid—so dream-like—that the threads of ordinary association were broken" (p. 651) [418]. It is surely at this moment in the novel that we move most clearly into the unbounded realm of desire, if not of wish fulfillment. It is at this moment of inundation, in fact, that the thematics of female desire surface most clearly.[4]

We will look in vain for a specifically feminine linguistic practice in *The Mill on the Floss*; "a possible operation of the feminine in language" is always elsewhere, not yet, not here, unless it simply reinscribes the exclusions, confines, and irregularities of Maggie's education. But what we may find in both Eliot and Irigaray is a critique which gestures beyond cultural boundaries, indicating the perimeters within which their writing is produced. For the astronomer who hates women in general, the feminist critic may wish to substitute an author who vindicates one woman in particular or, like Irigaray, inscribes the claims of all women. In part a critic of ideology, she will also want to uncover the ways in which maxims or *idées reçues* function in the service of institutionalizing and "maximizing" misogyny, or simply deny difference. But in the last resort, her practice and her theory come together in Eliot's lament about metaphor—"that we can so seldom declare what a thing is, except by saying it is something else." The necessary utopianism of feminist criticism may be the attempt to declare what is by saying something else —that "something else" which presses both Irigaray and Eliot to conclude their very different works with an imaginative reaching beyond analytic and realistic modes to the metaphors of unbounded female desire in which each finds herself as a woman writing.

JOHN KUCICH

George Eliot and Objects: Meaning as Matter in *The Mill on the Floss*[†]

It is a commonplace to observe that George Eliot's early novels cherish a world of objects. It is equally well understood that these objects are never purely natural, or "noumenal," but that they are always embedded in human centers of meaning. We have grown comfortable with the

4. Cf. Gillian Beer, "Beyond Determinism," in Jacobus, ed., *Women Writing and Writing About Women*, p. 88: "Eliot is fascinated by the unassuageable longings of her heroine. She allows them fulfillment in a form of plot which simply glides out of the channelled sequence of social growth and makes literal the expansion of desire. The river loses its form in the flood."

† From *Dickens Studies Annual: Essays on Victorian Fiction*, eds. Michael Timko, Fred Kaplan, and Edward Guilliano, 12 (1983):319–40. Reprinted by permission of AMS Press, Inc. Page numbers to the Norton Critical Edition have been inserted in brackets following John Kucich's original citations.

notion that Eliot values natural objects only insofar as they serve human knowledge, motives, and needs; that she considered an intimate relation between man and matter to be one phase of her moral program. In a representative way, Bernard Paris claims that Eliot, as a realist, may have had "a spontaneous delight in concrete reality," but only as a "starting point," since "the sophisticated realist, like the scientist, wants to add to our knowledge of the nature of things." Eliot's aim was finally to digest "concrete reality" for man's general improvement:

> like most of the other positivists, she wanted not only to describe, but also to relieve the human condition. . . . Only through positive knowledge could man adapt himself to reality and reality to his needs. Realism was thus the servant of moralism.[1]

Similarly, David Carroll claims that Eliot tries to bring psychological and physical reality into balance for her protagonists, and that those few objects that remain unmediated by the minds of her characters only become "meaningless and terrifying."[2] Even Elizabeth Ermarth, in an essay inspired by Merleau-Ponty, writes about the cultural and moral values to be gained by Eliot's version of phenomenological reduction.[3] For these readers and many others, a general extension of man into the natural world, with the satisfaction of his fundamental needs the only standard, is an Eliotic ideal.

We should not assume this principle too quickly, however. Although Eliot certainly did aspire to write "natural history," nevertheless, the conjunction of man and matter in her early novels is never an innocent one. Such conjunction always reveals the impoverished, reductive character of human efforts to appropriate the world, even while seeming to promise an idyllic harmony. In the very first chapter of *The Mill on the Floss*, for example, the narrator surveys rustic objects in what has conventionally been understood as a benign, Wordsworthian discovery of the world's symbolic plenitude: corn, ships, trees, rooftops–all can be said to take their meaning within a human act of imagination and memory; all are composed in relation to the narrator's Wordsworthian desire to unite mind with matter.[4] But what escapes notice in this scene is a more disturbing drama, one that takes its threatening qualities only in retrospect, from the pressure of the novel's later events. Following the lead of the Dutch painters she admired, in this opening Eliot has

1. *Experiments in Life: George Eliot's Quest for Values* (Detroit: Wayne State University Press, 1965), p. 3.
2. "*Middlemarch* and the Externality of Fact," in *This Particular Web: Essays on "Middlemarch,"* ed. Ian Adam (Toronto: Toronto University Press, 1975), p. 76.
3. "Incarnation: George Eliot's Conception of 'Undeviating Law,' " *Nineteenth-Century Fiction*, 29 (1974), 273–286.
4. Though such a reading is not the focal point of her argument, a good summary of this interpretation is Margaret Homans, "Eliot, Wordsworth, and the Scenes of the Sisters' Instruction," *Critical Inquiry*, 8 (1982), 223–242.

commercial objects relentlessly interpenetrate natural ones.[5] And given the novel's eventual horror over St. Ogg's commercial single-mindedness, the resulting hybridized landscape can be seen as much more ambiguous and threatening than it is usually thought to be.

> A wide plain, where the broadening Floss hurries on between its green banks to the sea, and the loving tide, rushing to meet it, checks its passage with an impetuous embrace. On this mighty tide the black ships–laden with the fresh-scented fir-planks, with rounded sacks of oil-bearing seed, or with the dark glitter of coal —are borne along to the town of St. Ogg's, which shows its aged, fluted red roofs and the broad gables of its wharves between the low wooded hill and the river brink, tinging the water with a soft purple hue under the transient glance of this February sun. Far away on each side stretch the rich pastures and the patches of dark earth, made ready for the seed of broad-leaved green crops, or touched already with the tint of the tenderbladed autumn-sown corn. There is a remnant still of the last year's golden clusters of bee-hive ricks rising at intervals beyond the hedgerows; and everywhere the hedgerows are studded with trees: the distant ships seem to be lifting their masts and stretching their red-brown sails close among the branches of the spreading ash.[6]

In this description, raw matter is never left at rest; it is always invaded by economic matter. In that sterile and, at best, amoral way (as the novel will later define provincial economy), it is actively stripped of its distance from man. "Black ships" are abruptly superimposed on a natural, watery "embrace" that had sought its own self-enclosed consummation; the wharves and roofs of St. Ogg's show between hill and river bank, "tinging" the water; the earth is "touched again" with corn; the bee hives are seen "rising at intervals" above the hedgerows; and the ships even merge visually with the ash branches. As the passage goes on, after meeting horses that must work to earn their feed, as well as a farmer who must work to earn his dinner, we are introduced to the mill and its house, "as old as the elm and chestnuts that shelter it from the northern blast." The pastoral overtones here pull our sensibilities toward approval, yet our familiarity with the novel's great, brooding theme—Maggie's inability to free herself from a world that is overly pragmatic, and overly "economic" in a number of senses—should make us wary

5. Hugh Witemeyer, *George Eliot and the Visual Arts* (New Haven: Yale University Press, 1979), p. 139, calls this scene "an anthology of motifs" from Dutch landscape painting. For a good discussion of the materialistic qualities of Dutch painting, see Roland Barthes, "The World as Object," *Critical Essays*, trans. Richard Howard (Evanston: Northwestern University Press, 1972), 3–12.

6. George Eliot, *The Mill on the Floss*, ed. A. S. Byatt (New York: Penguin, 1979), I, 1 [7]. Further references are given to book and chapter numbers in parentheses within the text.

of regarding any loss of natural independence to commercial uses too lightly.

These fusions of commercial with natural objects, which subject the entire landscape to the functional use of man, begin very subtly to suggest George Eliot's fundamental perception about material things: the perception that a world of autonomous objects does not exist, and that such a condition is inherently claustrophobic. The major symbolic objects of *The Mill on the Floss* only magnify such fusions, and such claustrophobia: the mill itself, source of Maggie's longing for origins, is rooted in nature but swamped by its commercial destiny; the boat that bears her away in romantic passion—what Stephen Guest calls "natural law" (VI, 14) [385]—is, ironically, a commercial Dutch vessel that can accommodate the two lovers only with difficulty on the poop; and even the landscape of the Red Deeps, where Maggie meets her lover, Philip Wakem, appeals to her at first because of its irregular surface, which was formed by an abandoned stone quarry—the place is described slightingly by the narrator as "mimic rock and ravine" (V, 1) [242].

Not only are there no purely natural objects in *The Mill on the Floss*, nothing antecedent to a commercialized culture, but Eliot pointedly insures that even those objects presented as symbolic alternatives to St. Ogg's are laced with economic significance. In the largest sense, all the things in this world have been imprisoned by human use, bracketed by their function. The world external to man has disappeared. And while the deceptively nostalgic tone of the opening passage may persuade us that the cohabitation of man and nature is benign, the novel very gradually reveals its ominous aspects.

Despite Eliot's humanism,[7] a novel like *The Mill on the Floss* does not merely acquiesce to man's conception of himself as the measure of all things; in part, and against the grain of its own explicitly humanistic themes, it is appalled by man's universal and irreversible amalgamation with matter. This ambiguity certainly does not undermine Eliot's humanism, but it does make humanism in her novels a much more complicated affair than it seems. For George Eliot's humanism, like that of most Victorian writers, is severely tested by her reaction against the scientific and industrial pragmatism of her age, which helped to make all human designs on the world appear to be rapacious.

What eventually makes the ambiguity in Eliot's fusions of natural and commercial objects visible, in fact, is the novel's sustained attack on the

7. Most critics accept Eliot's humanism as a close approximation of Feuerbach's *homo homini deus est*, often pointing to Eliot's own remark, very early in her career, that she agreed with Feuerbach entirely; see *The Letters of George Eliot*, ed. Gordon S. Haight, 7 vols. (New Haven: Yale University Press, 1954–55), II, 153 (hereafter referred to as *Letters*). For a good summary as well as an attack on Eliot's humanism as a disruption of her theories of realism, see U. C. Knoepflmacher, *George Eliot's Early Novels* (Berkeley: University of California Press, 1968). Interestingly, Knoepflmacher argues that in Eliot's novels the material world is always converted into a moral world.

runaway commercialism—and the related cultural narrowness—of English life. After all, *The Mill on the Floss* contains, in the Dodsons, a bitter satire on rural materialism.[8] More broadly, the novel seems to lament the destruction of Maggie's natural energies (she is often called "wild," or compared sympathetically to animals),[9] by the constricting economic and procedural preoccupations of St. Ogg's, a town that has fallen "out of keeping with the earth" (IV, 1) [222] and that has traded "the grandeur of the wild beast" for an "oppressive narrowness." In very explicit ways, Eliot regards the victory of man over matter as a blight. This blight lies not only in man's tendency to misuse or misinterpret things, his fallibility—which is how we usually qualify Eliot's faith in man[1]—but in his very belief in his right to use things at all, to make of matter a human medium. For the Tullivers and for St. Ogg's, at least, the widespread use of nature for human purposes has destroyed its romantic, creative power, and Maggie's hopeless separation from the organic world of her childhood—which has somehow become bound up in the legal and financial status of the mill—underscores the urgency of that loss. The conjunction of natural sites with functional sites haunts the very title of the novel, and Tom and Maggie are destroyed finally not just by nature and the flood but by "wooden machinery" (in a letter to her publisher, Eliot insisted on the adjective[2]). As we shall see, to, Eliot's world of enslaved objects is not just a response to her fears about industrialization or commercialism per se. An interfusion of man and matter is already present in Maggie and Tom's childhood world as a determining cultural condition for their failed emotional relations. In general, despite her widely recognized reverence for the products and worldly concerns of man, Eliot seems to tell us through Maggie that the loss of purely natural objects in nineteenth-century England has diminished human life.

From this point of view, the opening chapter's wistful conjunctions of man and matter ("I remember those large dipping willows . . . I

8. Eliot's famous disclaimer of any intention to attack the Dodsons implies only that she did not consider them personally responsible for their values.

9. See Nina Auerbach's provocative article, "The Power of Hunger: Demonism and Maggie Tulliver," *Nineteenth-Century Fiction*, 30 (1975), 150–171.

1. This qualification includes discussions of Eliot's preoccupation with egotism: most critics have written on this subject, and there are good summaries in Paris, who sees the novels as a prescription for the transcendence of egotism, and in Reva Stump, *Movement and Vision in George Eliot's Novels* (Seattle: University of Washington Press, 1959). But it also includes recent "deconstructive" approaches to Eliot. These are more fundamental qualifications of Eliot's faith in human understanding, and in our abilities to control our own destinies through it. The most widely known of these are J. Hillis Miller's "Narrative and History," *ELH*, 41 (1974), 455–473, and "Optic and Semiotic in *Middlemarch*," *Harvard English Studies*, 6: *The Worlds of Victorian Fiction*, ed. Jerome H. Buckley (Cambridge, Mass.: Harvard University Press, 1975), pp. 125–145. See also Jonathan Arac, "Rhetoric and Realism in *The Mill on the Floss*," *ELH*, 46 (1979), 673–692. My chief quarrel with such approaches, persuasive as they are, is that they assume Eliot believed any human appropriations of reality must fail unequivocally—that is, they do not take into account what I will later describe as her attempt to naturalize such appropriations.

2. *Letters*, III, 279.

remember the stone bridge . . .")—not to mention Maggie's very affection for the mill itself—seem at first to be oddly skewed. In these pastoral impulses, George Eliot does seem to desire an alternative to the debased, narrowed reality her acculturated nature often represents. But Eliot's remedy for this debasement does not finally entail any kind of redemptive return to natural objects; such a gesture seems impossible in the novels.[3]

On one level, the few instances of her characters' immersion in the material world are incomplete or distorted: Maggie, surrendering thought to the force of the tide and the objects of the river when she runs away from Stephen, is terrified by the idea of an unregulated world[4]; Hetty Sorrel, alone in nature in *Adam Bede*, is abandoned to sin. On another, even though critics often point to Eliot's desire to make human experience "particular"—that is, excessively detailed and localized—as a naturalizing narrative device, there is an insuperable doubleness here. For, as the critical tradition has long recognized, Eliot does rigorously insist on combining her "particularity" with intellectual and moral programs.

Following Ruskin, she emphasizes—more scrupulously, perhaps, than she sometimes seems aware herself—that the world can ultimately have beauty and value only through its human associations. Thus, in a famous letter written in 1866, she claimed to want "to make certain ideas thoroughly incarnate, as if they had revealed themselves first to one in the flesh and not in the spirit."[5] But the real order of generation here, masked by "as if," is important. Furthermore, in the very next sentence, Eliot proves herself to be quite clear about what use the particularizing of her ideas has; she calls it "aesthetic teaching": "I think aesthetic teaching is the highest of all teaching because it deals with life in its highest complexity." Or again, several years later, she refuses "to adopt any formula which does not get itself clothed for me in some human figure and individual experience" mainly because abstract formulas alone do not "help others to see."[6] Statements like these[7] are

3. For a good statement of this impossibility, see Ermarth, p. 276.
4. But for a more positive reading of this and other scenes of immersion in the novel, see Auerbach, who places immersion within the novel's complex of Gothic motifs, although she tends to overlook the ways in which these romantic impulses are finally frustrated.
5. *Letters*, IV, 300. Further on in this same letter, Eliot reveals another paradox in the writing of *Romola*: "I felt that the necessary idealization could only be attained by adopting the clothing of the past."
6. *Letters*, VI, 216.
7. Other key remarks on this subject occur in "The Natural History of German Life," *Essays of George Eliot*, ed. Thomas Pinney (London: Routledge & Kegan Paul, 1963), pp. 266–299 (hereafter referred to as *Essays*). But in this essay, too, Eliot does not so much reject theory as insist that it be as complex as human circumstances, that is, that science be specialized. On pp. 289–290, she writes:

> It has not been sufficiently insisted on that in the various branches of Social Science there is an advance from the general to the special, from the simple to the complex, analogous with that which is found in the series of the sciences, from Mathematics to Biology. . . . The more general science will not suffice to solve the problems of the more special.

usually cited to demonstrate Eliot's repugnance to bald appropriations of the world by the human mechanisms of theory. But if they do show her working to make theory accountable to experience, in their didactic strains they also betray an appetite for putting even the specific and seemingly discontinuous details of life in service of a complex human design, both scientific and moral.

If she is to redeem human experience from the narrowness implicit in any appropriation of the natural world, then, Eliot can only do so by discovering a "nonhuman" or material dimension within the life of man itself—not by returning us to nature. In this discovery, which anticipates a great deal of modernist and postmodernist thinking about the relation between man and nature, we may find the tenuous complexity of Eliot's humanism. For Eliot is only able to exalt man by inverting his reduction of nature to functionality. That is to say, Eliot's novels ultimately explore the functionality of things within human experience only in order to naturalize it, to make functionality itself into a kind of material world. Specifically, the novels describe both objects and human lives as intersecting in a plurality of functional relations—in a kind of static structure of human meaning—that through its size and density restores to both orders some of the monumentality of unmolested nature, without ever denying the molested status of man and his appropriated objects. So it is that the novels themselves, whatever intellectual or moral program underlies them, also strike us as somehow monumental—unfixed by whatever purposes to which we put them.

It is easiest to see this process at work in an early novel like *The Mill on the Floss* simply because Eliot had not yet abandoned material objects for that naturalized psychological world of the later works, the world in which Dorothea Brooke learns to conceive the behavior of others "with that distinctness which is no longer reflection but feeling—an idea wrought back to the directness of sense, like the solidity of objects."[8] In *The Mill on the Floss*, it is a single object—the mill itself—that forms the physical center of the novel and also becomes the ground for the various human dramas. In the first chapter, the little girl who stares at the mill wheel, "rapt in its movement" (I, 1) [8], warns us that the novel will be an investigation into the human significance of the mill. But it is also clear even at this point that the mill's importance lies partly in its ability to attain a self-completion free of the human world through

Her anxiety, in such passages, seems only that reality be adequately described by theory, rather than that theory be used to predict reality. And, of course, the use of this kind of theory is well defined in the essay: the development of a social policy. More germane, perhaps, are her remarks in "Notes on Form in Art," *Essays*, pp. 433–434, in which she arrives at a conception of artistic form as "a set of relations selected & combined in accordance with the sequence of mental states in the constructor, or with the preconception of a whole which he has inwardly evolved."

8. George Eliot, *Middlemarch*, ed. Gordon Haight, Riverside Edition (Boston: Houghton Mifflin, 1956), Ch. 21.

its very functionality, transformed now into a seemingly autonomous energy: "the rush of water and the booming of the mill bring a dreamy deafness . . . like a great curtain of sound, shutting one out from the world beyond" (I, 4) [8]. Maggie's pleasure in the mill as a child stems from this same self-completion; a man-made machine, the mill can nevertheless become a naturalized world:

> The resolute din, the unresting motion of the great stones giving her a dim delicious awe as at the presence of an uncontrollable force, the meal for ever pouring, pouring, the fine white powder softening all surfaces and making the very spider-nets look like faery lace-work, the sweet pure scent of the meal—all helped Maggie feel that the mill was a world apart from her outside everyday life.

And for the reader, the mill will finally acquire some of the nonhuman materiality Maggie finds in it as a child.

Before we explore how it does, however, it is important to see the various destructive ways in which things become humanized for the characters of the novel. For it is not just through an economic appropriation that objects like the mill are reduced to human uses, though this is, perhaps, the most obvious of man's intrusions on the world. If commercial rapacity were the only human transgression against nature here, the novel would simply have polarized the world of St. Ogg's against Maggie's moral standards. As we will see, however, this familiar polarity is only a tangential one. Rather, man and matter are fused, to the detriment of both, through a general cultural appropriation of the world—both physical and moral—in terms of use. And only by tracing the dangers of this pandemic functionality can we see how functionality itself is ultimately transformed, and exalted as a natural process.

Most importantly, characters use their control of things as a means to master each other, to aggressively assert their own identities. Tom, for example, achieves a self-righteous dominance over Maggie and over Philip Wakem through his competence with "outdoor things" (I, 3) [18]. As a child, Tom's sense of identity is crucially bound up in things—his "one point of interest" in dressing himself each day lies in transferring "the contents of his everyday pockets to those actually in wear" (I, 9) [73]—and this kind of identity never loses its relation to mastery. His superiority over Maggie comes from his knowledge of how to manipulate objects—fishing line, kites, card houses, lozenge boxes—and his early attempt to prove himself over Philip centers—almost disastrously—around a sword. As a young man, too, Tom's masterful relation to things saves him his dignity: he revenges his father's injuries by learning his way around the world's objects, by learning how to be like the fellow his Uncle Deane had praised, the fellow who "can tell you the cubic contents of anything in no time" (III, 5) [191].

Tom's aggressive use of things is not at all aberrant in his world. Mr. Tulliver attempts to conquer the world of lawyers by claiming an unimpeachable right to water. Mr. Wakem satisfies his casual vindictiveness against Tulliver through his purchase of the mill. More comically, Uncle Pullet uses his mastery of a music box to prove to the world that his character "was not of that entire nullity which might otherwise have been attributed to it" (I,9) [79]. Even a sympathetic character like Bob Jakin takes his revenge against class injuries by getting the best of Mrs. Glegg in a battle over material goods. But most striking in this context, perhaps, because it is most ineffectual, is the way the women in the novel achieve their place in the world only through their control of domestic objects: either by establishing how men are allowed to use them, as when Mrs. Glegg keeps her husband off her clean floor or dispenses his cup of tea only as a pretext for a lecture; or by impressing each other with the value, or lack of it, of things—the debate over the value of Bessy's "chany" and teapot is the most painful example of this combat, Mrs. Pullet's nearly sacerdotal bonnet the most ridiculous. Thus, too, Mr. Tulliver's injuries to his wife are entirely conceived to lie in his losing her personal possessions.

In this context, even Maggie, who is incompetent about the management of Tom's things, tries to restore the balance between herself and others through a thing, her Fetish. Yet we should note that Maggie's Fetish, an object of plural significance and use, diverts her aggression rather than being an instrument of it, and in that way avoids direct use as a means of human manipulation. And, more crucially, Maggie's refusal to be treated as a thing by her mother—to have her hair and dress and behavior regulated according to rule—is a rebellion against this aggressive confusion of mastered objects with mastered identity. After all, even Mr. Tulliver is afraid Maggie will bring "none the bigger price" (I,2) [12] because of her cleverness. Maggie's great crisis in the novel is finally provoked by Tom's attempt to control her as a thing in his battle with the Wakems. Insensitive to her human needs, Tom tries to reduce Maggie to the status of a possession of the Tulliver family, to conceive her value only as it contributes usefully to the Tullivers' goals, which are related both to economics and to identity: the recovery of financial independence and respectability.

But the human use of things in the novel is more complex than simply the conversion of things into instruments of assertion. Characters in the novel also communicate with each other through objects—in fact, they communicate more effectively through objects than they are able to without them. The Tullivers demonstrate this principle dramatically through their use of the Bible: sentiments are only considered trustworthy insofar as they become a part of the book, through writing in it or swearing upon it. Occasionally, this kind of reified communication is sympathetically presented as the only kind of understanding characters are allowed to achieve, as when Tom offers Maggie plum cake after their first fight. The reconciliation is never sealed by speech, passing only through the exchange of an object, yet Maggie hungrily prizes this kind of union, and the narrator refers to it later as a "sacrament of conciliation" (V,5). The value of Tom's gift of his pocketknife to Bob Jakin is effective in a similar way, and Wakem's restoration of the mill to the Tullivers succeeds in conveying his good intentions toward his son, if not to the Tullivers themselves. Tom's competence with money, too, comes to embody his emotional ties to his family: "I have a different way of showing my affection," he tells Maggie (V,5) [282], to which she responds, "Because you are a man, Tom, and have power, and can do something in the world."

More often, however, bound so closely to the world of objects, these reified exchanges remain frustrated, as is Mrs. Tulliver's vain attempt to display affection for Tom by intending her valuable things for him as heirlooms, or Mr. Tulliver's inadequate expression of his worries for Maggie through the money he loans to his sister. And for the most part, this kind of communication betrays the hopelessly inadequate nature of a human world devoted to objects as symbols of feeling: the imprisonment of matter in human use is in this sense the imprisonment of human nature itself. Tom, in particular, frequently misunderstands the signifying power of things in communication, reading Maggie's neglect of his rabbits and general carelessness with things as lack of affection, interpreting Bob Jakin's covetous need of his half-penny as betrayal, presuming that his own gift of a new fishing line for Maggie adequately fulfills an emotional exchange. Such inadequacy in communication is made comic when Mrs. Tulliver and Mrs. Pullet find an affinity for each other in their common preference for spots over stripes, or when Mr. Tulliver is won over by Stelling's putting his thumbs through his waistcoat in a recognizable way, or when Mr. Glegg believes that the lives of his garden vegetables display "remarkable coincidences" (I,12), [102] with events in human history. And such inadequacy in communication reaches tragic proportions when Tom assumes that Maggie's feelings for Philip or for Stephen can be understood only in terms of their use value—that is, in relation to the Tulliver's reacquisition of respectability. Even Mrs. Pullet's tears, early in the novel, have become artificial, a sign of luxury, a commodity. The lending of money to relatives at interest is a monstrous instance of this reification of human exchange; but on even the smallest level, Mr. Pullet can think of absolutely nothing to impart to his nieces and nephews but peppermints.

Despite Eliot's discomfort with the fusion of human life with humanized things, however, some of her more lyrical passages on memory share in the conjunction of human life with use-objects. Tom's pocketful of things are not just instruments of domination for him; they are also "relics of the past" (II,1) [119] through which he remembers life at the mill and Maggie when he is away at school. And Maggie's own ties to the past are also accomplished through her associations with objects that form a "home-scene" in and around the mill, that "sweet monotony where everything is known and *loved* because it is known" (I,6) [36]. Maggie's grief at being parted from her books, for example, and her fear that "the end of our lives will have nothing in it like the beginning" (III,6) [197], derives from the same general tendency to prize objects as tokens of human meaning that leads her father to litigation and that frustrates her relations to Tom. We must ask ourselves at this point: is there some difference between Maggie's investment of personal meaning and emotion in objects and, say, Tom's? Does such a difference consist only in the content of Maggie's associations with things, or is there a more fundamental difference, a methodological one?

That there is such a fundamental difference in Maggie's approach to the workings of human significance becomes clearer when we consider the other characters' persistent belief that objects always signify in some single human way. Singleness, in fact, is usually taken as the condition of an object's usability. In *The Mill on the Floss*, characters continually overestimate the direct correlation between objects and particular human use, too strictly valuing objects as complete measures of themselves or their intentions. This is apparent in Mrs. Tulliver's grief over the sale of her personal things: her sense of scandal lies in the return to public circulation of things that bear her name, things that had been singled out of the public world as unequivocal representations of her identity. The gap between public, multiple, uncontrolled significance and the private determination of an object's meaning strikes Bessy as an obscenity. Early in the novel, Bessy's literalism about things is even a source of comedy, as when she misunderstands Mr. Tulliver's hyperbole about her finding fault with moles, or when she comprehends Tom's education only through reference to laundry and meals. But Bessy is not alone in her single-mindedness. In general, the Dodson family believes that the things and procedures they have adopted as personal, their "family traditions" (IV,1) [223], take on an extraordinary, totemic value through their very singleness—so much so that things remaining in the public domain come to seem dangerous, polluted. Mrs. Glegg is afraid of draughts in strange houses, and none of the Dodsons will sample anyone else's butter or jam for fear they may have spoiled.

In many related ways, all the characters express their belief in single correspondences between objects and significance: Mr. Tulliver, through his faith in book bindings; Mr. Stelling, in his conviction that, in regard to education, there is "one remedy for all things" (II,1) [115]; Mr. Deane, in his contempt for the use value of Tom's knowledge. Mr. Glegg's confidence in the singleness of every object's function extends even to his suspicion of Bob Jakin's generosity with Laceham goods, which cannot be tied to a single, recognizable motive: "I've no opinion o' transactions where folks do things for nothing. It allays looks bad" (V,2) [256]. Mr. Tulliver so equates his entire identity with his management of the mill—the singleness of his economically useful role—that loss of the mill literally robs him of consciousness, at first, and then of life.

Over against this tendency to view things as imprisoned in single human meanings and uses, Eliot presents us, partly through Maggie, with the actual plurality of every object's human significance. The customary opposition of literal and metaphorical approaches to reality identified with the Dodsons and Tullivers is not quite accurate: for Maggie, human meaning is not synecdochic, or visionary—it is diffuse. This diffusion is implicit in Maggie's lyrical reminiscences, as when the narrator refers to the things of childhood as "a language," the "mother tongue of our imagination" (I,5) [36]. On the one hand, this comparison only confirms the tendency to appropriation that is pandemic in Maggie's world: that most human of systems, language, is here used to describe how Maggie directly transforms natural objects into signs for human meaning. On the other hand, though, the crucial fact about language, as Maggie tells Tom later, is that a word "may mean several things. Almost every word does" (II,1) [121].[9] Maggie's reading of the dictionary has taught her what she sees again, more vividly, in her encounter with the gypsies: that a single language, or a single system of knowledge—like those of geography and history, which she fails miserably to teach to those alien pupils—does not have a direct, functional relation to the world. And Maggie's version of reality, in contrast to Tom's, is often multiple. Whereas Tom is always convinced of the irrevocable justice of his actions, "Maggie was always wishing she had done something different" (I,6) [45]. Her stories about frogs and grasshoppers, which inspire in Lucy a delighted "semi-belief," are annoying to Tom because they playfully violate the singleness of things, which he demonstrates his control over by destroying Maggie's animals. The plurality of Maggie's world, in fact, is what distinguishes her at the end of the novel from other characters and their inflexible demands on her behavior. What Eliot suggests here, especially through her awareness of language's multiplicity—the famous discussion of metaphor as the undermining of human thought ("we can so seldom declare what a thing is, except by saying it is something else" [II,1] [117]) further reinforces this—is that the human use of things are not as final, fixed, and imprisoning as they appear. Though this does nothing to restore the absolute "thingness"

9. See also "The Natural History of German Life," *Essays*, p. 287:

> One word stands for many things, and many words for one thing; the subtle shades of meaning, and still subtler echoes of association, make language an instrument which scarcely anything short of genius can wield with definiteness and certainty.

of objects, it does make the human world larger, more textured—less reductive than any conviction of human efficiency would have it.[1]

Maggie's simple notion about the meaning of words as multiple is crucial in at least two ways for the novel's efforts to monumentalize human meaning. First, the notion that words have more than one meaning guarantees that human signs have a materiality apart from their function.[2] Maggie is aware of this as she pores over Tom's Latin text: she skips the rules of syntax to dwell instead on the strangeness of the Latin words themselves, which, freed of direct meaning, take on a naturalized foreignness: "these mysterious sentences snatched from an unknown context,—like strange horns of beasts and leaves of unknown plants, brought from some far-off region, gave boundless scope to her imagination" (II,1) [123]. Words, cut off from meaning, denote an entire world of their own. This delight in the Latin words as sensuous images precedes Maggie's knowledge that she could "learn to interpret them." Tom, who is too devoted to the rigidity of correspondences between signs and their signifieds, to an economy of meaning, has no appreciation of this materiality. Language for him never acquires the corporality that it has for Maggie, although even for Tom, the nonlinguistic, human objects he is more familiar with sometimes reveal a similar corporality as signs: he sees that "the pattern of the rug and the grate were 'first ideas' that it was no more possible to criticize than the solidity and extension of matter" (II,1) [127].

Second, an awareness that things may function as signs in more than one way is the beginning of a perception of meaning as a texture of possibilities, or, in the language of modern linguistics, as a semiotic structure. That is to say, by being multiple, the referents of such signs present themselves as a plane of grouped, interrelated meanings that cannot be separated from each other, but cannot be resolved into a final coherence—a logical, rational synthesis—either. The plurality of meaning is both arbitrary and fixed. And as a fixed plane of meanings, the structure of human meaning can be perceived as inefficient and idiosyncratic—not reducible to a diagram, a machine for further use. Structural signification, in this sense, thereby acquires some of the non-instrumental materiality of natural things.

In his essay, "The Eiffel Tower," Roland Barthes points out that the chief feature of the nineteenth-century's discovery of the human

1. Sensitivity to the "plurality" of meaning, it should be noted, is often invoked by post-structuralists as a more authentic approach to experience than the economic conception of the sign/signified relationship found in traditional theories of reference. See esp. Jacques Derrida, "White Mythology," *New Literary History*, 6 (1974), 5–74. In particular, Derrida writes: "Language is only language to the extent that it can analyze and master polysemie."

2. Roland Barthes, "To Write: An Intransitive Verb?" in *The Structuralist Controversy*, ed. Richard Macksey and Eugenio Donato (Baltimore: Johns Hopkins University Press, 1970), p. 136, writes that the central discovery of modern "semio-criticism" is a "new type of objectivity" that establishes "the distinctive elements of [many] levels" within signs. He then argues that this linguistic plurality can lead us to find a "homology" within the structuration of discourse that reifies language in a liberating, expansive way, grounding man in its pre-human reality.

prospect—the panorama of an urban, as opposed to a natural landscape—lies in such a perception of human but corporal structure: human objects, when viewed from above, can be grouped and composed by the observer into an arbitrary but harmonious set of relationships, just as natural objects can be, in the very act of turning them into signs for themselves, a map of their own existence that the viewer can "read."[3] Perception of structure thereby creates a tension between our purely functional understanding of human signs and our recognition that through an arbitrary multiplicity they form their own unique wholeness. Barthes defines structure, in this sense, as a "concrete abstraction": structure can be conceived not as a means to analysis but as a nonreducible end in itself, almost a physical composition, a "corpus of intelligent forms."[4]

By presenting us with the multiple significance of human objects, George Eliot provides us with a similar kind of panoramic perspective. And in terms of our perception as readers, this perspective reveals a new kind of material texture: human objects and human life in the novels take on the sprawling dimensions, the coherent but unstable randomness, of the natural.[5] The nonhuman monumentality of Eliot's work lies chiefly in this direction: dangerous tendencies to transform all matter into human functions are redeemed when they are seen to produce a pluralized texture of meanings, a living structure of composed but rationally incompatible fragments, rather than simply a one-to-one correspondence between object and function. As Barthes puts it, perception of the structural qualities of human meaning makes "the exploration of language . . . (correspond) to the exploration of the cosmos."[6] And in both these ways, then—through the materiality of signs and through that of their signifieds—appropriated objects can appear as naturalized, a world more permanent than its functionality at first indicates, an eternal dwelling place for individual men.

This process of corporalizing use-objects emerges most clearly if we look at the mill itself. A nearly invisible, enigmatic presence, sketched briefly at the beginning of the novel and then mostly forgotten by the descriptive energies of the narrator, the mill hovers in the background like a darkened stage on which all events transpire and are framed. We

3. "The Eiffel Tower," in *The Eiffel Tower and Other Essays*, trans. Richard Howard (New York: Hill & Wang, 1979), pp. 3–17. Barthes is one of the few post-structuralist critics who extensively discusses the materiality of structure. However, as with most such concepts in his work, its treatment is fragmentary and unsystematic. His discussions of structure's materiality are most traceable, though, when they coincide with his theme of the text as "body"; see in particular *S/Z*, trans. Richard Howard (New York: Hill & Wang, 1974), pp. 111, 119–120, 190–192, for good discussions of the ways in which a text's structural plurality gives it the status of a "body."
4. "The Eiffel Tower," p. 9.
5. John P. McGowan, "The Turn of George Eliot's Realism," *Nineteenth-Century Fiction*, 35 (1980), 171–192, brilliantly documents Eliot's conception of culture as a complex of fluid, structural codes, though he does not discuss how Eliot naturalizes these structures.
6. "To Write: An Intransitive Verb?" p. 144.

are always aware of the mill as the possible limits of the novel's meaning even though we seldom look at it, and even though, in the third volume, Maggie is displaced from the mill, although still psychically oriented toward it—as her return to the mill at the novel's end suggests. Our suppressed awareness of the mill thus helps magnify it as a material sign: the mill stands for everything and nothing at the same time, representing its own physical centrality in the Tullivers' lives and its ability to gather into itself endless mnemonic associations.

The mill is itself the measure of all meaning for the Tullivers. It is a cosmos. Almost everyone in the family feels the mill's tremendous emotional impact, which surpasses its economic significance: in some way, it mediates between them and their origins; it becomes a "first idea" with all the "solidity and extension of matter." Mr. Tulliver agrees to remain at the mill because it reminds him of several generations of his family. Even Tom, for the most part narrowly obsessive about money, pauses at one point to realize that he has an "old, deep-rooted affection" (V,6) [283–84] for the mill that stems from his familiarity with it. This meaning of the mill is not analogical; it precedes thought and use, or even specific memories. The mill reminds the Tullivers mainly of itself, its constancy throughout time as a human sign, and, in this sense, of the reassuring, "natural" permanence of human order.

But beyond this fundamental sign-function of the mill—which lies before reference, giving the mill an infinite kind of extension in time and space—we are also made aware that the mill has many specific kinds of significance, which are different for each character, and that these differences even reveal some of the incompatibilities between them. Mr. Tulliver sees the mill first as a symbol of his independence and unassailability—he refuses to pass it on to his son—and then, through its loss, as a sign of his dependence. Tom sees the mill in a slightly more active way, as the proof of his own strivings against the world, what the narrator calls his "ambitious resistance to misfortune" (IV,2) [225]. Maggie values the mill in yet another way, as the symbol of an impossible harmony between herself and Tom. For Mrs. Tulliver, on the other hand, the mill is more negative, a liability: "I wasn't fond o' the noise of it . . . and if I'd known as the mills had so much to do with the law, it wouldn't have been me 'ud have been the first Dodson to marry one" (III,7) [205–6].

As we move outward from the family, the mill acquires even more meanings. For Wakem, it is an indifferent means of proving his righteousness; for Lucy, the mill appears to be the one impediment to Maggie's marrying Philip. Though the mill carries all of these meanings, because of their very plurality it seems to be defined by no one of them singly. Neither does it fuse them all in a kind of symbolic coherence. These purely local uses of the mill as meaning come detached from its more enigmatic presence as a pure sign at the center of the novel, and in their variegated interdependence create a labyrinth of significance. Seeing the mill in this way as a "concrete abstraction" gives a new resonance to Eliot's conception of a "network of relations" in her work, even if that phrase is one she used primarily in an ethical context.[7]

Many other objects in the novel are similarly presented as conjunctions of divergent human meanings. The jam puff that Maggie and Tom quarrel over, for instance, is for Maggie first an object of sacrifice and for Tom an object of competition, then for Maggie a source of reverie and for Tom a symbol of Maggie's greed. Maggie's helplessness in the face of the shifting meanings of the jam puff underscores our privileged position, as observers, to sort out these changing functions, to perceive them as an intelligible texture. Similarly, Tom's pocketknife has a plural significance, being first a gift to Bob, then a symbol of Bob's defiance as well as of his boyish susceptibility to the allure of things. When Bob reminds Tom of the gift many years later, the knife is first a source of shame to Tom, then a sign of his benevolence. Bob's pack full of merchandise also has a tier of significations, which Bob manipulates in his duel of wits with Mrs. Glegg, promoting it alternately as a bargain and as a previously spoken-for collection, and profiting from it in both material and psychological terms. Tom's education, too—not a thing, certainly, but his initiation into the useful knowledge of things—has a range of meanings. For Mr. Tulliver, it is to be "a bread" (I,2) [9] to Tom, but it is also to be an instrument of gaining dignity before the lawyers, and a means of assuring that Tom will not displace his father. For Mr. Stelling, the education has an entirely different significance, connected to his own empty reverence for classical learning and his attempt to rise in his profession. For Mr. Deane, it is an object of resentment and contempt. And for poor Tom, it signifies only misery: he is left "in a state of blank unimaginativeness concerning the cause and tendency of his sufferings, as if he had been an innocent shrew-mouse imprisoned in the split trunk of an ash tree in order to cure lameness in cattle" (II,1) [117]. Many of the physical objects in *The Mill on the Floss*—the sheets of music that Stephen uses as a pretext to see Maggie and that Philip uses to sing his love; Maggie's sewing; the note marking the Moss's debts; Philip Wakem's deformed body, which

7. The structural dimension to these "networks" is suggested in several of the essays. In "Notes on Form in Art," for example, Eliot uses metaphors of the human body to describe what she calls an "interrelatedness" in aesthetic form. But it is crucial to see that the concept of interrelation in this essay is precisely what allows Eliot to make an analogy between the organic and the inorganic: form is "the limit of difference by which we discriminate one difference from another . . . this is true whether the object is a rock or a man" (*Essays*, p. 433). Through the patterning of relations, man and nature merge. It is also crucial to see that interrelation is not described as a dynamic of resolution, but as the static juxtaposition of parts, as "difference," or as "unlikeness." For a fascinating rereading of Eliot's conception of the organic, see David Carroll, " 'Janet's Repentance' and the Myth of the Organic," *Nineteenth-Century Fiction*, 35 (1980), 331–348. Carroll argues that Eliot's organic world is based in unresolvable oppositions, and he writes, p. 348, "George Eliot's view of the world is far more precarious than is usually acknowledged."

makes him an unusable thing—are charged in this way with divergent meanings.

What is more important, though, is the way that the human order itself, apart from objects, acquires monumentality through this plurality of structure. Eliot's most successful remedy for the loss of natural objects in nineteenth-century English life is to return to human events themselves, through a perception of the structural qualities of human motives, the nonhuman irreducibility of matter. These structural qualities turn time itself into a readable, material pattern.[8] Human events are overdetermined in her novels, and the process of change always leaves traces that stratify it, saving it from being lost to flux. Even the "ruined villages" along the Rhone (IV,1) [221] that signify human oblivion still endure as signs of loss—recoverable, static points in Eliot's own structure of the human meaning of duration. The much-debated relation between determinism and freedom in Eliot's work,[9] too, suggests the presence of this monumentality of structure: the "doctrine of consequences"[1] in her novels that determines events as the intersection of multiple intentions, conscious and unconscious, is, on the one hand, an instance of Eliot's own appropriation of reality—her positivistic approach to psychology—and, on the other, of the transformation of human life into an archaeology of causes and circumstances, a constellation of signs. The metaphor of the human "web" in her novels is thus a part of this renaturalizing of culture through a perception of the textural nature of meaning.

In *The Mill on the Floss*, this technique, in which human attempts to act on the world—to use it—acquire structural dimension, becoming spatialized and readable, had already been refined to great sophistication. We need think only of the process by which Tom is handed over to Mr. Stelling—a pastiche of human intentions: Mr. Tulliver's complex desires for independence, revenge, and provision for his son; Mr. Riley's desire to have an opinion; his desire also to think well of his friend's friends both as a reflection on himself and as a prospect of future back-scratching; his familiarity with Louisa Timpson's face; his general deference to classical education . This human interchange acquires a life of its own as the idiosyncratic though overdetermined conjunction of all these human motives. But the novel is prolific in examples of structural multiplicity in human purposes: Wakem's motive for buying the mill, Mrs.

8. Witemeyer, p. 43, notes that Eliot was not a practitioner of spatial form, in the modern sense, since her works do not attempt to harness flux through repeated formal motifs. Even Witemeyer, however, does concede that Eliot attempts to slow the movement of time through her contemplation of objects.
9. There are many good discussions of this issue. See esp. George Levine, "Determinism and Responsibility in the Works of George Eliot," *PMLA*, 77 (1962), 268–279; and Felicia Bonaparte, *Will and Destiny: Morality and Tragedy in George Eliot's Novels* (New York: New York University Press, 1975).
1. For a good summary of Eliot's "doctrine of consequences," see Bonaparte, *Will and Destiny*, esp. pp. 13–25.

Glegg's reasons for relenting against Maggie at the end of the novel, the characteristic hereditary impulses of Tullivers and Dodsons. It is in this sense that Eliot's work aspires to be "incarnate": that is, not by presenting human life as a series of simple, single causes and effects, but by presenting it as a complex structure of intentions so plural it acquires a massiveness of texture. Human actions, rather than being consumed in time by the uses to which they are put, are converted to palpability by their presentation as a decipherable—but not a repeatable, instrumental—pattern.

The ultimate focal point for this structural principle in the novel is the irresolution of Maggie's romantic life, and the defeat of morality as a tool for human action. The last half of the novel is devoted to a stalemating of Maggie's feelings, and, despite the tendency of critics to take sides here—to defend or condemn Maggie's actions[2]—a large part of Eliot's intention is simply the dramatization of a moral conflict in which no single human interpretation, or theory of useful practice, predominates. Instead, we are left with an "antagonism between valid claims,"[3] a nearly static vision of human conflict that is impossibly urgent in its unsolvable multiplicity. For even if we can agree with Philip, for instance, that Maggie "stupefies" (V,3) [267] herself, we also know that his interpretation of her dilemma is tainted by his own self-interest, as well as by his lack of sympathy for her very real loyalty to her father: "Maggie . . . felt there was some truth in what Philip said, yet there was a deeper consciousness that for any immediate application it had to her conduct it was not better than falsity." Similarly, while we cannot forgive Tom's lack of sympathy for Maggie, we do feel, with Maggie, the occasional justice of Tom's reproaches:

> she rebelled and was humiliated in the same moment: it seemed as if he held a glass before her to show her her own folly and

2. This aspect of the novel has, of course, drawn considerable attention. It seems appropriate here only to summarize a few of the main positions. Among those critics who defend Maggie, John Hagan, "A Re-Interpretation of *The Mill on the Floss*," *PMLA*, 87 (1972), 53–63, finds the love of Maggie and Tom genuine; Paris claims that renunication enables Maggie to attain an objectivity like that desired by science; and Felicia Bonaparte, *Will and Destiny*, argues that Maggie attains wholeness by apprehending the greatest possible context for her crisis. Among those who condemn Maggie's behavior, U. C. Knoepflmacher attacks Eliot's attempt to find through Maggie an epic teleology; and Carol Christ, "Aggression and Providential Death in George Eliot's Fiction," *Novel*, ((1976), 130–140, finds Maggie's death a similar gesture toward the numinous. Critics who dismiss Maggie's course simply as an inadequate conception on Eliot's part include F. R. Leavis, *The Great Tradition* (New York: Anchor, 1954), who finds that Maggie represents Eliot's own ill-thought-out sexuality; and Barbara Hardy, *The Novels of George Eliot* (London: Athlone Press, 1959), who sees bad faith in Eliot's avoidance of consequences of Maggie's renunciation. A more neutral reading is offered by George Levine, "Intelligence as Deception: *The Mill on the Floss*," *PMLA*, 80 (1965), 402–409; Levine argues that Maggie's renunciation is the fatal consequence of defects in the world of St. Ogg's.
3. The phrase is from "The Antigone and Its Moral," *Essays*, 261–265. For a good reading of Eliot's attitude toward unresolvable conflict in tragedy, see Sara M. Putzell, " 'An Antagonism of Valid Claims:' The Dynamics of *The Mill on the Floss*," *Studies in the Novel*, 7 (1975), 227–244.

> weakness—as if he were a prophetic voice predicting her future failures—and yet, all the while, she judged him in return. (VI,4) [318]

This undecidability, which is underscored through the sympathetic, disinterested Dr. Kenn, who vacillates in his advice as he is caught up in the conflicting, equally compelling dimensions of the problem, is a primary experience for most readers. Dr. Kenn's confusion marks the limit of our attempts to prescribe a useful course for Maggie; the narrator seizes on his predicament to claim that "the great problem of the shifting relation between passion and duty is clear to no man who is capable of apprehending it: the question, whether the moment has come in which a man has fallen below the possibility of a renunciation that will carry any efficacy, and must accept the sway of a passion against which he had struggled as a trespass, is one for which we have no master key that will fit all cases" (VII,2) [402–3]. In this sense, Maggie's earlier moral standards, her attempt to apply the formulas of Thomas à Kempis to life, appear just as narrow a form of pragmatism as the material monomania of St. Ogg's. Morality, like economics, is deadening so long as its goal is functional efficiency.[4] For Eliot, both the moral world and the world of appropriated objects become emotionally expansive only when they are corporalized, when they are given a life greater than that of individual human intentions.

It should be pointed out here that such a static, corporal vision of the human world is not incompatible with a moral program, although it does work to make Eliot's moralism passive. For George Eliot, neutralizing self-interested appropriations through a perception of the corporality of human meaning is the first step toward selfless, disinterested—and in that sense "natural"—moral response. In her later novels, in which Eliot moves further away from a concern with the human use of objects and towards a more direct naturalizing of human psychology itself, the moral consequences of such perception are made clear. Thus, in *Daniel Deronda*, Daniel's central quest is for a discovery of his rootedness in a historical context, in a complex of overdetermined racial meanings. And his discovery of that context sparks his surrender to an impersonal and abstract cause that is larger than his own ability, as a character, to define it. Similarly, *Middlemarch* provides Dorothea with a detached complexity of perception that allows her to remove herself—specifically,

4. A similar argument is made by Mary Jacobus, "The Question of Language: Men of Maxims and *The Mill on the Floss*," *Critical Inquiry*, 8 (1982), 207–222, although Jacobus defines Maggie's freedom from moral formulas more narrowly than I have, as a defiance of patriarchal hierarchies of meaning. Jacobus finds Maggie's "gift . . . for ambiguity" (p. 214) to be a characteristic of femininity in the novel—a persuasive reading, but one that ignores the tolerance for ambiguity accessible to characters like Dr. Kenn, or Philip Wakem at the end. In general, Jacobus's reading—as well as the direction set for her by Luce Irigaray's work—seeks to appropriate for feminist criticism a polemical opposition between determinate and indeterminate meaning that has its roots just as surely in the very dominant, patriarchal culture she intends to discredit, which has long been in rebellion against mimesis.

with regard to Rosamond and Lydgate—from any sphere of recognizable personal appropriations. For Eliot, and for the Victorians generally, morality is identified with an absence of appropriative, interested motives, as if a complete denial of purpose (from the point of view of the self) might guarantee one's relation to eternity.[5] But the moral use of such perception in Eliot's work does not limit its implications. In *The Mill on the Floss,* Eliot refuses to speculate on the moral use of her vision of a naturalized human order: the suppression of any final moral action in the novel is one reason the ending seems rushed, bent as it is on fusing the human order with the natural through Maggie's death. Before adapting it to moral use, George Eliot was capable of seeing structural perception as an end in itself, the conversion of a debased human reality into the apparent permanence of nonhuman matter. And to understand the peculiar qualities of her moral judgments—not merely their passivity, but their strained mixture of passion with self-repression—we must first take this naturalizing impulse into account.

It goes without saying, too, that Eliot's strategy of exploring the human order to find in it the monumental status of matter has become a widespread modern one. The formal emphasis and self-consciousness of modern literature and art, not to mention the blatant attack on the nature of structuralism and its concurrent elevation of language as an institution more permanent than man, all indicate that our search for the eternal presence and authenticity of matter now proceeds largely, paradoxically, only within the field of the human itself. Eliot's moral purposes may ultimately have prevented her from recognizing the vast implications of this shift. But its presence in her work—and, perhaps, in the fundamental assumptions of the nineteenth-century social novel—suggests a profound link between modern humanism and more nonreferential literary preoccupations that usually remains obscured.

MARGARET HOMANS

Eliot, Wordsworth, and the Scenes of the Sisters' Instruction†

Two of Wordsworth's most important lyrics about the growth of the poet's imagination, "Tintern Abbey" and "Nutting," are also the scenes

5. The genealogy of this idea is much more complex than I can suggest here. But see Gerald Graff, *Literature Against Itself* (Chicago: University of Chicago Press, 1979), p. 45, who traces the common ground linking aesthetic versions of "autonomy" from meaning with moral disinterest all the way back to Kant and to eighteenth-century aesthetic theory.

† From *Bearing the Word: Language and Female Experience in Nineteenth-Century Women's Writing* (Chicago: U of Chicago P, 1986) 122–39. Reprinted by permission of the University of Chicago Press.

of a sister's instruction.[1] Different as these two poems are, at the end of each the poet turns unexpectedly to his sister (named either as a sister or, in the case of "Nutting," as "dearest Maiden"), who enters the poem not in her own right but in answer to the poet's and the poem's needs. At the end of "Tintern Abbey," the poet exhorts the sister to "remember me" by living out the stages of youth to which he himself cannot return.[2] The last three lines of "Nutting" frame the poet's painfully earned knowledge with the address, "Then, dearest Maiden," so as to turn that knowledge into instructions:

> Then, dearest Maiden, move along these shades
> In gentleness of heart; with gentle hand
> Touch—for there is a spirit in the woods.
> (54–56)

Both sisters exist to receive the brother's wishes, to confirm for him his hope that what he has gained in the course of the poem will find a habitation in a consciousness perhaps more enduring than his own. We do not expect to learn anything from her about how she will use the gift contained in the poet's words. Her quietude verifies the power of the poet's performative words: he speaks, and for her to hear his words is, implicitly, to enact them. To ask what this listening might mean to her is a question that the text itself excludes; yet for George Eliot it is a real one, as it was also for the poet's sister. What is the female listener (or reader) to do with these words that are intended to help her avoid the painful experiences that have forged the poet's consciousness? What does it mean to follow instructions given, not for the sake of the student, but for the sake of the teacher? The poet implies that the sister he addresses will learn to follow his path if she follows his instructions, but how are they to be followed, and with what results? These are not Wordsworth's concerns, but they are Eliot's.

Mary Ann Evans's remarks on reading Wordsworth at the age of twenty suggest that while, like Wordsworth's ideal sister, her feelings are congruent with his, she also experiences some ambivalence about receiving the poet's instructions. "I have been so self-indulgent as to possess myself of Wordsworth at full length. . . . I never before met with so many of my own feelings, expressed just as I could like them."[3] She does wish to be instructed: "to possess myself of" admits to a foreign excellence that must be possessed as different, not simply recognized. Yet simply to accept the poet's words would be, like the sister in the poems, to

1. The discussion in this chapter of *The Mill on the Floss* is a revised version of an essay of the same title in *Critical Inquiry* 8 (1981): 223–41; reprinted in *Writing and Sexual Difference*, ed. Elizabeth Abel (Chicago: University of Chicago Press, 1982), pp. 223–42.
2. All quotations from Wordsworth are from the de Selincourt and Darbishire edition of *The Political Works* and from the Wordsworth, Abrams, and Gill edition of *The Prelude*. Quotations from *The Prelude* are from the 1850 version. All further references to these works will be included in the text.

remain silent. That she describes her reading as "self-indulgent" and as a recognition of her "own feelings" suggests that, even though it is done half-jokingly, she needs to diminish Wordsworth's power of suggestion and to make it clear that any act or feeling the poet describes was hers before she learned that it might seem derivative. Moreover, the phallic formulation, "possess myself . . . at full length," suggests an aggressive role reversal that puts Wordsworth in the subordinate position. This tension between the need to respect and the need to deny a powerful influence—the feeling that what she possesses herself of, she had already possessed—is representative of the attitude toward Wordsworth expressed later on in Eliot's works.

* * *

There are a number of incongruities between Wordsworth's ideas and Eliot's texts that seem more than simply differences, scenes and passages that Eliot invites her readers to find Wordsworthian while she indicates a significant pattern of divergence from his prototypes. The brotherly instructions that Eliot is most generally concerned at once to follow and to deny are contained in Wordsworth's wish, in the verse "Prospectus" to *The Recluse*, to see "Paradise, and groves / Elysian" be "A simple produce of the common day" (47–48, 55). But when she follows this wish literally, her "common day," the intensely social world of her novels, tests far more strenuously the adaptability of the paradisal vision than does anything Wordsworth wrote. The generic incompatibility between a poet's vision and the form of the novel may account for some of the obvious differences; yet, as I will try to suggest later, it may be that Eliot's choice of the realistic novel as the form for her vision is in part an effect, not a cause, of her ambivalent divergences from Wordsworth (for example, a series of her sonnets, which we will consider shortly, articulates these concerns as much as do the novels). Often seeming to intend to, Eliot neither wishes nor is able, as the good sisters invented in Wordsworth's poems are, always to carry out Wordsworthian instructions verbatim. * * * It is precisely the literalness of Eliot's transposition of Wordsworthian themes—her effort to be a docile student on the model of Wordsworth's implied sister—that constitutes her subversion of them.

The Mill on the Floss is Eliot's "most Wordsworthian novel,"[3] and it is also her novel most concerned both with female education and with the brother-sister relationship. Maggie Tulliver's experience first as a reader and then as a sister may shed light on Eliot's relation to instruction, especially to brotherly instruction. Maggie's existence in the novel is framed by scenes of her reading. She starts out as an accurate reader who distinguishes easily between elucidating a text foreign to her and inventing her own stories, the two kinds of reading that become confused

3. Donald D. Stone, *The Romantic Impulse in Victorian Fiction* (Cambridge: Harvard University Press, 1980), p. 194.

in Eliot's reading of Wordsworth. Having been reprimanded for her very perceptive reading of *The History of the Devil* as "not quite the right book for a little girl" and asked if she has "no prettier book," Maggie defends herself by opposing accurate reading to invention: "I make stories to the pictures out of my own head, you know."[4] At this point in her story, Maggie feels free both to read independently and to imagine freely, but we see her being chastized as a girl for both processes indifferently. However Maggie reads, "a woman's no business wi' being so clever; it'll turn to trouble, I doubt" (1:3).

As Maggie grows up, learning to be feminine, her way of reading changes. As an adolescent in search of spiritual food and guidance, she becomes an overly literal reader of Thomas à Kempis. The eager pupil of two guides, the author and the "quiet hand" that marked certain passages in her second-hand copy, Maggie acts out exactly the text's prescriptions and in so doing radically misreads it in at least two ways. She misconstrues renunciation, not as sorrow, but as an available form of satisfaction, and according to Philip Wakem, she misuses her own gifts: "What you call self-conquest—blinding and deafening yourself to all but one train of impression—is only the culture of monomania in a nature like yours" (5:4). The general effect of her reading Thomas à Kempis is to contribute to her education in femininity. She has turned to Thomas à Kempis in the first place because her brother Tom won't let "*my* sister" work to help pay off the family debt, depriving her of any useful (masculine) occupation. Her docility toward the text, her wish to follow its prescriptions exactly, is repeated both in the self-suppression she learns from the text's preaching and in her willingness to let her mother do with her as she pleases: "Her mother felt the change in her with a sort of puzzled wonder that Maggie should be 'growing up so good'; it was amazing that this once 'contrairy' child was become so submissive, so backward to asset her own will" (4:3). Though Maggie does not think of herself as learning how to be feminine—she sees herself as an ascetic—there is a very neat coincidence between her mother's wish for a conventionally good daughter and Thomas à Kempis's message of self-denial.

The more literal her reading, the less accurate and the more feminine. Yet when she attempts, as she used to with the pictures in *The History of the Devil,* her own imaginative departures from Scott's *The Pirate,* which she reads at about the same time, she meets with an equal lack of success that is again part of her education in femininity. Philip offers her his copy of *The Pirate* the first time they meet in the Red Deeps. "O, I began that once," she responds, "I read to where Minna is walking

4. *The Mill on the Floss,* vols. 14 and 15 of *The Works of George Eliot* (1860; Cabinet Edition, Edinburgh and London: William Blackwood and Sons, 1877), book 1, chapter 3; while I have quoted from this edition throughout, I will hereafter include in the text only book and chapter numbers, for the convenience of those using other editions.

with Cleveland, and I could never get to read the rest. I went on with it in my own head, and I made several endings; but they were all unhappy. I could never make a happy ending out of that beginning" (5:1).

Maggie is discovering here the inexorable laws of feminine plotting. It is the same discovery she makes later on when she laments that *Corinne* is merely one more repetition of the law requiring the blonde heroine to triumph over the dark heroine. Her invention of optimistic endings for a love story about a dark-haired girl is limited by the conventions both of plot and of social life. In fact, her endeavor to depart from convention only underscores for her both the heroine's and her own entrapment.[5] Her memory of trying and failing to invent happy endings for *The Pirate* is evoked by the fact that Philip has the book with him because he is studying a scene for a picture. His rationale for offering the book is, "I don't want it now. I shall make a picture of you instead—you, among the Scotch firs and the slanting shadows" (5:1). But though she refuses the book, he makes the picture anyway: whether she reads or refuses to read, she will become the static object of a man's vision, in a way that prefigures her final transformation into an object in death.

Maggie enters the novel as a reader, and in her last scene before the flood carries her toward home, Tom, and death, she is reading again, choosing this time between two texts: the letter from Stephen and the words of Thomas à Kempis that would help her resist Stephen's appeal. At this last stage in her growth, her reading is only the passive reiteration of conflicting texts for which she is simply the medium providing no original words of her own. Ironically, the two texts are really only representations of her own feelings, but she feels that they come from outside her. Stephen's writing is so vivid to her that "she did not *read* the letter: she heard him uttering it, and the voice shook her with its old strange power" (7:5). He asks her "Write me one word—say 'Come!' In two days I should be with you." Her response takes the form of writing to his dictation, a literal repetition of his word provoked by the prospect, not of her own joy, but of Stephen's sorrow and by her self-doubts, which "made her once start from her seat to reach the pen and paper, and write 'Come!' " Maggie knows that her obedient and selfless literal repetition is wrong, but she is so exhausted emotionally that she can only wait passively "for the light that would surely come again." When it comes, the corrective to the reiteration of Stephen's word is her repetition of another word: "The words that were marked by the quiet hand in the little old book that she had long ago learned by heart, rushed even to her lips, and found a vent for themselves in a low murmur that

5. I am generally indebted to the recent work of Nancy K. Miller for my understanding of the issue of feminine plotting; see especially her reading of the *Corinne* scene in "Emphasis Added: Plots and Plausibilities in Women's Fiction," *PMLA* 96 (1981): 36–48.

was quite lost in the loud driving of the rain against the window." First an unwilling copier of Stephen's word, now a ready voice for the words of Thomas à Kempis, Maggie does at last determine what her own words will be, but they "find no utterance but in a sob," and she defers writing them until the next day, which for her never comes.

Maggie's childhood capacity for original invention and for self-expression has by the end of her story quite vanished. Her adult self is a battleground for conflicting texts; when she takes up a pen or opens her mouth, the words that come forth as if they were her own are not hers. And this state of affairs results from, and in turn reinforces, the self-suppressing submissiveness that is identified throughout as feminine. To learn how to read as a repeater of others' words is feminine, and it is also fatal. Her departures from what she reads as an adolescent (her unintentional departure from Thomas à Kempis, her effort to vary the inexorable plot of *The Pirate*) are signs of her vital resistance (willful or unconscious) to feminine submissiveness, even though her efforts fail. When in the last reading scene Maggie gets her texts right, this final docility is a harbinger of her death: her complete passivity as a reader prefigures her succumbing to the flood the next morning.

When Eliot describes her own reading of Wordsworth as a process of possessing herself of what she already possesses, the ambiguous balance of originality and deference prefigures in compressed form some of the features of Maggie's development as a reader. It may be that Eliot is articulating through Maggie the stages of her own education in feminine readership, in how to be a docile or self-suppressing reader. To submit to others' words in Maggie's case is to submit to the law of cause and effect and therefore to reach the unhappy end predicted for all dark heroines. Eliot thematizes both docility and disobedience to instruction through the relation between Maggie's reading and the pattern of her life: disobedient reading is incompatible with Victorian femininity, yet complete feminine docility leads to the self's silence and ultimately to death. I would like to turn now to some instances of that dual reading in *The Mill on the Floss* and elsewhere that may suggest how the balance between docility and disobedience that Eliot thematizes in Maggie appears in her reading of Wordsworth. How is it possible to honor Wordsworth's words yet not die, as Maggie does, of the desire to be Wordsworth's sister and follow silently and involuntarily the wishes of his words? Carrying out Wordsworth's "remember me" in a way that she asks us to think of as literal (as Maggie's later readings are literal), she nonetheless departs radically from her original in passing from poetic and imaginative vision to the novelist's female vision. But the literal reading that for Maggie results in death issues for Eliot in the novelist's originality.

In calling *The Mill on the Floss* Eliot's most Wordsworthian novel, Donald Stone also locates in it "the most serious case of Wordsworthian blight on Eliot's creative imagination, "because" the heroine is paralyzed by a myth of the past and a myth of her own childhood."[6] U. C. Knoepflmacher similarly sees "George Eliot's Wordsworthian novel vainly [trying to] enlist the Romantic's power of memory."[7] As he goes on to point out, where Wordsworth restores himself in "Tintern Abbey" through his own memories and through the memory he makes visible in his sister's eyes, Maggie and Tom succumb to the realities of "evil tongues, / Rash judgments," and the "dreary intercourse of daily life" Wordsworth refers to in his poem (lines 128–29, 131). The questions that these analyses raise is why the myth of the realistic novelist's growth must diverge so radically from Wordworth's myth of the poet's growth. "Tintern Abbey" and "Nutting" have only an incidental place for the sister, whereas the poet's accounts of the growth of the imagination picture a solitary, even narcissistic relation between himself and nature's maternal presence in childhood. At its most powerful, too, the visionary imagination can shut out the ordinary, visible world, as Dorothy Wordsworth sees in the "spots of time" and the Simplon Pass passages in *The Prelude.* Eliot's myth of childhood, however, for reasons that I will explore more fully later on, necessarily includes other people and a visible world that can never be ignored. In her revision of the Wordsworthian myth, Eliot's most autobiographical characters pass through what appear to be Wordsworthian childhoods, not to become romantic poets, but to find that their ideal childhood visions are thwarted by circumstances or by social needs. This revision closely resembles the literalizations in *Wuthering Heights, Jane Eyre,* and *Frankenstein,* all of which, in different ways, distort a romantic ideal. Eliot sets her heroines' insatiable need for love, together with her own narrative commitment to realism, against the antisocial implications of what she represents as the introverting power of the imagination. Her heroines' need for love is insatiable because those who can supply it never love as unconditionally as Wordsworth's nature does, and Eliot schools her heroines to choose a love that represents a turning away from disruptive visionary power. In *The Mill on the Floss* and in the lesser-known sonnet sequence "Brother and Sister" (1869), the heroine gives up visionary aspirations (that are perhaps in any case untenable in the world of the novel) in favor of the love of a usually more practical-minded brother that makes childhood last forever and closes off the visionary world. That choice may lead to death, but the loss of vision may also be compensated for by an increase in wisdom ultimately more appropriate to the novel than to poetry.

This ambivalent relation to Wordsworth stands out in one of the moments considered most Wordsworthian in Eliot, the fishing scene in

6. Stone, *Romantic Impulse,* p. 194.
7. U. C. Knoepflmacher, *George Eliot's Early Novels: The Limits of Realism* (Berkeley: University of California Press, 1968), p. 175.

The Mill on the Floss and the narrator's subsequent reflections on the value of memories of a childhood passed in nature (1:5). A close look at these passages reveals a willful misreading of the Wordsworthian implications of the scene, and the later consequences of the scene are the opposite of Wordsworthian. Opposing one brother (Tom) to a very different one (Wordsworth, brother of silent sisters), Eliot has Maggie defend against Wordsworth's authority while retaining all the forms of a sister's deference.[8]

As Sandra Gilbert and Susan Gubar point out, Maggie and Tom spend most of their precious time together making each other miserable, and while Maggie, Tom, and their narrator cling to the idea that their idyllic fishing expedition is typical of their childhood, the reader must suspect the effort to generalize from this exceptional scene.[9] The children live in a fallen, gendered world in which they can never escape for very long the pain produced by their social condition. Fishing harmoniously together at "the old favourite spot," "Maggie thought it would make a very nice heaven to sit by the pool in that way, and never be scolded." But this heaven is brief and contingent on absolute physical and mental seclusion. That it cannot be carried over into the common day of their ordinary lives is underscored by the very precise description of its locale. The "old favourite spot" is a pool of unknown depth and mysterious origin that is literally hidden from view, being "framed in with willows and tall reeds, so that the water was only to be seen when you got close to the brink."

Tom supervises the practical business of fishing, but Maggie "had forgotten all about the fish, and was looking dreamily at the glassy water." Hearing Tom's "loud whisper," Maggie is "frightened lest she had been doing something wrong, as usual," and when it turns out instead that she has inadvertently caught a fish, she is "not conscious of unusual merit." Maggie's happiness consists in such accidental absence of wrong-doing and in listening alternately to Tom's whispers and to the "Happy whisperings" exchanged between the "light dipping sounds of the rising fish" and the gentle rustling of the willows and reeds. These illusions of reciprocity—for she and Tom communicate no more effectively than the water and the willows—encourage the children's equally illusory idea that their lives will always be like this. The narrator ends her account

8. Mary Ann Evans's beloved older brother, Isaac, seems to have provided the model for many of Eliot's fictive brothers, including their dictatorial distaste for reading and for the pleasures of the imagination. Apparently Evans was so anxious as a child to please her brother, whose only pleasures were physical, that she learned to read with difficulty and did not become an avid reader until he abandoned her to her own amusements (the story comes from her half sister, Fanny Houghton, in *George Eliot's Life as Related in Her Letters and Journals*, ed. J. W. Cross [Edinburgh and London: William Blackwood and Sons, 1885], 1:15). However, the brothers in Eliot's fiction seem to be generated not so much to immortalize him as to justify the novelist's choice of realism and of the novel, to justify her affirmation of love over the visionary imagination.

9. See Gilbert and Gubar, *The Madwoman* [*in the Attic: The Woman Writer and the Nineteenth-Century Literary Imagination* (New Haven: Yale UP, 1979)].

of Maggie and Tom by generalizing the Wordsworthian principle that the scene has apparently generated: "Life did change for Tom and Maggie; and yet they were not wrong in believing that the thoughts and loves of these first years would always make part of their lives." The narrator then turns to generalize about all human childhoods and finally speaks of her own.

It would seem at this point that "the thoughts and loves of these first years" refers primarily to the children's love for each other, with the mill and the river as setting. But as the passage continues into its larger and explicitly Wordsworthian frame of reference, the reader is given the strange impression that the foregoing scene has instead been solely concerned with the children's love for their natural surroundings.

> We could never have loved the earth so well if we had had no childhood in it,—if it were not the earth where the same flowers come up again every spring that we used to gather with our tiny fingers as we sat lisping to ourselves on the grass. . . . What novelty is worth that sweet monotony where everything is known, and *loved* because it is known?

The child's love of "rural objects" leads here, not to deeper, wider kinds of love, but simply to a renewed love of those identical objects. Even the expected reference to the endurance of Maggie's love for Tom—for which there would in any case be no place in the Wordsworthian paradigm of a solitary childhood in nature—is replaced by this love of objects. Stressing continuity over growth, the passage suggests how the Wordsworthian paradigm of a solitary childhood in nature—is replaced by this love of objects. Stressing continuity over growth, the passage suggests how the Wordsworthian features of Maggie's childhood will contribute to narrowing her consciousness, not enlarging it. When, seeing all their old possessions taken away after the bankruptcy, Maggie cries to Tom, "The end of our lives will have nothing in it like the beginning!" (3:6), Eliot is presenting us with a version of childhood far more literal than Wordsworth's.

Eliot's ambiguous expression "make part of their lives" suggests, vaguely enough so as not to appear purposely misleading, the Wordsworthian idea that the experiences of childhood seed the ground of character to bear unpredictable fruits, as when Wordsworth's "glad animal movements," remembered later, lead circuitously to the more sober pleasures of the mature poet. He recalls specific incidents from his childhood for their place in his growing awareness, first of nature's presence and then of his own mind's powers. But Maggie's yearnings later are for particular objects—this book, this mill, that river—and in this she is not altogether different from the literal-minded Tom, whose adult energies are devoted solely to repossessing his property, or even from her even more limited mother, whose worship of objects connected with her Dodson past is pathetic and un-Wordsworthian in the extreme. For Maggie, objects loved in childhood remain beloved for their own sakes, or for their place in consecrating her love for her brother, but never for what they teach her about the growth of her own mind. A literal recapitulation of childhood could hardly be further from Wordsworth's aims for himself as a poet; he does portray the danger of obsessive fixation to a particular spot, but only in characters like Margaret in *The Excursion*, never in images of himself. Within the cultural tradition that can be summarized as the symbolic order, as we have seen, daughters may view objects, or the literal, more favorably than do sons, both through training and through inclination based on early childhood; but where the transcendence of all things is valued, objects are devalued. Eliot, sharing her heroine's love of things, yet recognizing the cost of this love within the symbolic order, identifies growth with transcendence and regression and death with the literal.

The Mill on the Floss's largest plot patterns turn on Maggie's continual need to reaffirm her ties to home. Her conflicting loves for Tom and for Philip are almost equally strong, having taken root in kindnesses conferred in childhood. Among her first sensations on "waking" from "the great temptation" is the urgent need to go home, where she may affirm her identity as a child needing discipline and protection from her wilder impulses and her adult self. The feature of childhood she wishes to repeat is not its illusion of Edenic peace but its pain: "In her anguish at the injury she had inflicted—she almost desired to endure the severity of Tom's reproof, to submit in patient silence to that harsh disapproving judgment against which she had so often rebelled" (7:1). She craves and believes she can return to a pattern, established in childhood by incidents like those with Tom's rabbits or the jam puffs, of harsh judgment, confession, and forgiveness: "I will endure anything. I want to be kept from doing wrong again." Tom, refusing her home and forgiveness, refuses to let her be a child again. But her final attempt to return to the mill (on the flood) does succeed in achieving a restoration both of childhood ties and of cathartic pain. Her death in returning home is thus doubly ensured: what she wants from childhood is its pain. and her wish to turn backward to childhood is, like Cathy's in *Wuthering Heights*, a death wish.

For Wordsworth, the natural objects to which the child feels bonded are always subordinate to the bond itself and to the wider sense of connectedness and vitality engendered by that bond, but Maggie's loyalty does not shift from those primary objects themselves. Wordsworth grows past his love for his mother and even for nature's material presence, but Maggie never transcends her love for Tom. Wordsworth's memories of childhood in *The Prelude* even include "the impressive discipline of fear" (1. 603) brought by nature's "Severer interventions, ministry / More palpable" (1. 355–56). But where Wordsworth's memory transforms that pain into imaginative power, Maggie seeks a literal recapitulation of the identical pain (inflicted in the same home by the same person) in Tom's punishment. The huge fragments of machinery that overtake Maggie and Tom in the flood are literalization itself: the failure of a life's worth of experiences to transcend themselves, remaining instead an agglomeration of things—the very literalness of the novel's revision of the Wordsworthian pattern. The narrator's conclusion to the fishing episode, speaking of the "sweet monotony" of a well-known landscape and of the return of the seasons, offers a seductively beautiful version of the narrative pattern of Maggie's life. In both, what might be self-transcendent turns out to be a return to particularity. Maggie's repetitions transform the beautiful "sweet monotony" into something more dangerous, since to repeat, within the terms of the symbolic order, is to regress, and to regress is to die.

To answer the question of why neither Maggie nor her narrative can go, or even want to go, beyond the literal, it may be useful at this point to suggest the relationship between Maggie's education in feminine reading and her literalizing life. Along with her regressive wishes, her reading prefigures, if it does not actually ensure, her death. When Maggie cries out "the end of our lives will have nothing in it like the beginning," her immediate reference is to the copy of *The Pilgrim's Progress* that she interpreted so acutely for Mr. Riley in the first reading scene. " 'Our dear old Pilgrim's Progress that you coloured with your little paints; and that picture of Pilgrim with a mantle on, looking just like a turtle—oh dear!' Maggie went on, half sobbing as she turned over the few books. 'I thought we should never part with that while we lived' " (3:6). Pilgrim "looking just like a turtle" reminds us that this book symbolizes her independent way in childhood of "making stories to the pictures out of [her] own head," a way of reading that is now lost to her. When the book is sold off with all the other books, it is converted into the chief symbol, among the objects that Maggie misses, of her literalization of the Wordsworthian sense of the past and thus of the kind of literal reading into which she has now fallen. Furthermore, it is Maggie's sorrow over the loss of the book that indirectly leads her to become a more and more literal reader: it is because of witnessing her sorrow that Bob Jakin later brings Maggie the gift of assorted books among which she finds the Thomas à Kempis. Her docile feminine repetitions, first of Stephen's "Come!" and then of the memorized text of Thomas à Kempis, echo and confirm her desire to repeat her childhood by returning home to Tom and the mill, first after she has left Stephen and finally during the flood, a passive repetition that overdetermines her death. These repetitions of texts represent an abandonment of self that signals the approach of death; and that the repetition is literal prefigures the particular shape that the death will take—her being overtaken by the huge mass of machinery on the flood. This machinery recalls the "machinery of a story" into which Shelley literalizes romantic texts, with monstrous consequences that are no less fatal than those of the machinery that overtakes Maggie. Her reading acts do not themselves cause Maggie's death, but they identify the thematics of return and of love of the literal with rhetorical repetition, and they identify the thematics of death with the lack of one's own word. And a specifically feminine reading acts, they identify learned feminine behavior with return, literal repetition, death, and silence.

Maggie's docility and final silence connect her, then, to the figure Wordsworth projects of his silent, listening sister. Yet her kind of education is also linked to Wordsworth's own. The sonnet sequence "Brother and Sister" presents another version of Maggie's kind of education, one that displays some verbal similarity to a Wordsworthian scene of the poet's instruction. Drawn from the same stock of Eliot's own experience as the dreamy little sister of a practical-minded older brother, the sonnet sequence shares with the fishing scene in *The Mill on the Floss* both its general contours of plot and characterization and its ostensible aim to assert that "the thoughts and loves of these first years would always make part of their lives."[1] The sonnet sequence also revises the rowing episode from book 1 of *The Prelude*, which Eliot had reread at least two years previous to composing the sonnets and perhaps more recently than that.[2] In order to find a paradigm more suitable than that of the silent sister, Eliot considers the future poet; yet she cannot go so far as to portray herself as a brother. Remaining a sister, she makes clear the limits that gender places on what it is possible for a heroine to do or to be.

Like the round pool, the canal setting of the sonnets' fishing episode literalizes the sublime. Where the round pool is both profound and obscure, "Our brown canal was endless to my thought," and barges float into view around "a grassy hill to me sublime / With some Unknown beyond it."[3] While the brother and sister fish together in the canal, the sister tells us that "One day my brother left me in high charge, / To mind the rod while he went seeking bait" (7), with instructions to pull the line out of the way of oncoming barges. Like Maggie fishing in the round pool, the little sister's attention lapses,

1. "Brother and Sister" and *The Mill on the Floss* have always been taken to be generally autobiographical, but it is of course both impossible and unnecessary to tell how accurately they record the actual events of Eliot's early life. It is possible that these works have been taken tautologically as the source of biographical information. See Ruby Redinger, *George Eliot: The Emergent Self* (New York: Knopf, 1975), pp. 44–65, for an extensive reading of "Brother and Sister" as autobiography; see also Gordon S. Haight, *George Eliot: A Biography* (New York: Oxford University Press, 1968), pp. 5–6, 421.
2. See Thomas Pinney, "George Eliot's Reading of Wordsworth: The Record," *Victorian Newsletter* 24 (Fall 1963): 20–22.
3. Eliot, "Brother and Sister," in *The Legend of Jubal and Other Poems, Old and New* (Edinburgh and London: William Blackwood and Sons, 1874), sonnet 6, p. 202; all further references to the sonnets will be cited in the text by sonnet number. ["Brother and Sister" is reprinted here on pages 434–39. Editor]

Till sky and earth took on a strange new light
And seemed a dream-world floating on some tide—
A fair pavilioned boat for me alone
Bearing me onward through the vast unknown.
(7)

Her "dreamy peace" is broken by the arrival of a barge and by the sounds of her brother's anger, but the unhappy situation is turned around when it appears that the line she lifts out at the last minute has a fish on it, so that her "guilt that won the prey" is "Now turned to merit" (8). This scene replays very closely Maggie's fishing scene, in which she,too, felt "she had been doing something wrong, as usual," but has instead by pure chance caught a fish. Like Maggie, the little sister here, accidentally rewarded for doing wrong, learns from this event only that "luck was with glory wed." Morally ambiguous, these scenes teach Maggie and the little sister the insignificance of their actions relative to material coincidence.

Like the two fishing scenes, Wordsworth's rowing episode in book 1 of *The Prelude* concerns a child's transgression, but Wordsworth's "act of stealth / And troubled pleasure" (361–62) clearly deserves and as clearly receives punishment, unlike the ambiguous moral situations in which the two little girls find themselves. Having stolen a rowboat, Wordsworth's child enjoys a brief period of wonder that may be identified with what Coleridge and Wordsworth call "fancy." The "elfin pinnance" moves on,

Leaving behind her still, on either side,
Small circles glittering idly in the moon,
Until they melted all into one track
Of sparkling light.
(364–67)

This part of the episode corresponds to the "dreamy peace" that appears sublime for the sister in the sonnets, a remembered state that includes a vision of "The wondrous watery rings that died to soon" (6), and corresponds also to the moment of transgression before transgression is recognized as such, when "sky and earth took on a strange new light / And seemed a dream-world." The scene turns sinister for Wordsworth's child when, as he rows away from the shore, "the stars and the grey sky" beyond the ridge are replaced by "a huge peak, black and huge" that "As if with voluntary power instinct / Upreared its head" and that appears to grow larger and to stride after him as the boy tries to escape it (372, 378–80). This huge and animated peak corresponds in sonnet 8 to the "barge's pitch-black prow" appearing around the hill that—like Wordsworth's ridge, beyond which is only the sky—has previously screened a sublime vacancy.

Despite the similarity of the two situations, the moral outcome is entirely different for each child. Where Wordsworth senses that nature has arranged this spectacle for his instruction, the looming object is for Eliot an accidental occurrence, not the product of a moral design. The actual barge might be the literalization of the little girl's dream of the "fair pavilioned boat," so that its frightening arrival would be the self-inflicted punishment for daydreaming, as Wordsworth's "huge peak, black and huge" seems to embody the boy's guilt. But the barge in the sonnets is pursuing its own independent, commercial course—unknown to the girl and not therefore a product of her imagination—and does not "str[i]de after" her in the manner of the purposeful "grim shape" of Wordsworth's story. Its arrival is simply bad luck, just as the appearance of the fish on her line at the critical moment is simply good luck. Both are material accidents occurring independently of the girl's psychic growth. Significantly, Eliot's child is stationary on the canal bank, a passive spectator in a world of powerful things that are governed by chance. Of course, if we look at what actually happens in Wordsworth, the appearance of the peak on the horizon is sheer accident too. What is important is that while the girl knows that she is subject to luck, the boy never deviates from his certainty that, because nature regulates her actions according to the needs of his education, nature has in this instance acted for him.

Had the girl been punished for daydreaming, by losing the line, say, she would have received an amply ambiguous moral lesson against imaginative, rather than immoral (as for Wordsworth), actions. As it is, she is even more confusingly rewarded by not being punished for doing something that is considered wrong. Out of this confusion, if there is any lesson for her, it is that daydreaming is inefficacious and irrelevant, too trivial to be either punished or rewarded. Yet it is precisely at this point in the story that Wordsworth's child's imagination is made to grow. One of nature's "severer interventions" on his behalf issues first and almost incidentally in a moral lesson that is both clear and just, a lesson that is, however, subordinate to the deep and troubling indeterminacy he feels in response to his discovery of nature's ministrations:

> my brain
> Worked with a dim and undetermined sense
> Of unknown modes of being; o'er my thoughts
> There hung a darkness, call it solitude
> Or blank desertion.
>
> (391–95)

This "blank desertion" suspends and restructures the boy's total relation to the world around him. Lacking nature's active ministry, Eliot's child learns both to fear and to discount her imagination.

Following the fishing episode, the little sister completes her conversion from dreaming by entering into her brother's exclusively physical pleasures, such as knocking apples out of trees and playing with marbles and tops.

> Grasped by such fellowship my vagrant thought
> Ceased with dream-fruit dream-wishes to fulfill
> My aëry-picturing fantasy was taught
>
> Subjection to the harder, truer skill
> That seeks with deeds to grave a thought-tracked line
> And by "What is," "What will be" to define.
>
> (10)

This conversion to the principles of linear plot and realism is presented as good, supported by and reinforcing the myth of George Eliot as a contentedly realistic novelist, even though the examples of realistic behavior she adduces are not very persuasive. The next (and final) sonnet's sketch of the two children's futures confirms the realist's patterning of "What will be" on "What is," when "the dire years whose awful name is Change" "pitiless" shapes their souls "in two forms that range / Two elements which sever their life's course" (11). Eliot is formulating here in terms that seem applicable to herself as a realistic novelist the same discovery that Maggie makes when she tries to invent alternate endings for the heroine in *The Pirate.* "I could never make a happy ending out of that beginning" is Maggie's recognition that, like Minna, she will succumb to the inexorable laws of cause and effect of realistic plotting.

The sonnets' commitment to linear plotting reverses Wordsworth's conclusion to the rowing scene. Moving from the actual "huge peak, black and huge" to the "huge and mighty forms" of the mind, Wordsworth concludes with a disruption between the familiar past and any possible future, a cleavage that is the signature of the imagination:

> No familiar shapes
> Remained, no pleasant images of trees,
> Of sea or sky, no colours of green fields;
> But huge and mighty forms, that do not live
> Like living men, moved slowly through the mind
> By day, and were a trouble to my dreams.
>
> (395–400)

Wordsworth does value familiar shapes and rural images, but ultimately because they aid in forming and sustaining the affections of the heart, which then can survive independently of shapes and images. The imagination casts off, if painfully, precisely those things that both Maggie and the narrator of *The Mill on the Floss* cling to and affirm to be of highest value in themselves. While Wordsworth moves from actual sight to figurative vision, Eliot moves in the opposite direction, from figure (Wordsworth's text) to thing. The sonnets' turn to realism and the asserted determination of the future by the present reiterates both Maggie's suffocating repetitions of the past and the way in which the novel's narrator, moving at the close of the fishing scene, like Maggie, not from the finite to the sublime but from particular to particular, recalls and celebrates the literal repetition of exactly those "familiar shapes," those "pleasant images of trees, / Of sea or sky," those "colours of green fields" that Wordsworth's young imagination in its most powerful activity discards. For the narrator, love of a natural scene leads beautifully but statically to love of the same natural scene:

> These familiar flowers, these well-remembered bird-notes, this sky, with its fitful brightness, these furrowed and grassy fields, each with a sort of personality given to it by the capricious hedgerows—such things as these are the mother tongue of our imagination, the language that is laden with all the subtle inextricable associations the fleeting hours of our childhood left behind them. Our delight in the sunshine on the deep-bladed grass to-day, might be no more than the faint perception of wearied souls, if it were not for the sunshine and the grass in the far-off years which still live in us, and transform our perception into love. (1:5)

The allusion to the imagination is problematic here, since this love, rich as it is, is not what Wordsworth, whose presence is so clearly invoked, would call the imagination. Human relatedness stands in the place of Wordsworth's solitary perception of nature as the central formative influence on the growing child. Prefatory to the series of related incidents that culminates in the rowing episode, Wordsworth writes: "Fair seed-time had my soul, and I grew up / Fostered alike by beauty and by fear" (301–2). In a comparable position prefatory to the fishing incident, Eliot recalls Wordsworth's lines, but with a crucial difference:

> Thus rambling we were schooled in deepest lore,
> And learned the meanings that give words a soul,
> The fear, the love, the primal passionate store,
>
> . . . .
>
> Those hours were seed to all my after good.
>
> (5)

Wordsworth's beauty and fear are nature's ministries, devoted gratuitously and unconditionally to the growing boy, while for Eliot "the fear, the love" are purely human. The love is between the sister and the brother, and the fear is merely of its loss (and also of a gypsy glimpsed in the sonnet preceding these lines). Just as throughout *The Mill on the Floss* Maggie's "ned of love had triumphed over her pride, . . . it is a wonderful subduer, this need of love" (1:5), the little sister's allegiance to realism results from a kind of emotional blackmail through which her other needs as an individual are subordinated to the one overwhelming craving to be loved. The sister purchases love through acknowledging the preeminence of the objects that the brother loves. The transformation of perception into love defines the imagination as a binding love (of things and of the brother inextricably) that for Maggie will become obsessive and constricting and that for Wordsworth is antithetical to the imagination.

That "things" should have so privileged a relation to the imagination is troubling, but that things should be "the mother tongue of our imagination" is more problematic still, as the phrase ironically illuminates one source of Eliot's heroines' exclusive need to choose love over the world of imagination. A "mother tongue" in Wordsworth might signify feminized nature's fostering of imaginative growth in passages such as the rowing episode, a fostering made possible by the myth of the mother's early disappearance and replacement by figurative substitutes. But the nature for which Eliot's narrator expresses her enduring love is not at all Wordsworth's maternal nature but rather the nature of objects that signify the brother's realism and the sister's devotion to it. Because of the girl's differing place in and experience of the family configuration, it would be impossible for any female character in Eliot ever to imagine herself in the same relation to the idea of maternal nature that Wordsworth is privileged to feel. As in *Jane Eyre* and Wuthering Heights, the mother in Eliot would repeal, not encourage, her daughter's entry into the symbolic order, an entry about which Eliot appears to feel some ambivalence. Mrs. Tulliver's restrictiveness toward Maggie, her partiality to Tom, and her preoccupation with domestic objects reappear in the mother in "Brother and Sister," whose loving overprotectiveness the children try to escape: "Our mother bade us keep the trodden ways," while "the benediction of her gaze / Clung to us lessening, and pursued us still" (3). In a social world in which mothers are not "presences" but socially conditioned beings, these little sisters are unable to assume nature's figuratively maternal love and guidance in the way that Wordsworth's young self can, and no other, more specifically female, relation to the mother can be valued instead.

Wordsworth's introduction to the rowing episode, "One summer evening (led by her)" (357), emphasizes the theme of nature's purposive moral instruction. Introducing her comparable story in "Brother and Sister," Eliot writes, "One day my brother left me in high charge." It is under the brother's responsibility that the girl experiences the moral confusion of luck. The brother can hardly regulate circumstances as nature can, and he cannot be expected to direct the event toward his sister's moral growth. His love, like almost any human love after the myth of maternal love, is conditional, almost as accidental as the motions of barges and fish, and can never be taken for granted by his sister.

Lacking the unconditional devotion of the reinvented mother, daughters in Eliot seek for the imagination a *brother* tongue. But because of the brother's fixation on objects that seal him, together with the sister who accepts his values, away from the imagination, that tongue is unobtainable. The transformation of perception into love prevents the transformation of perception into the Wordsworthian, visionary imagination.

In the rowing episode, the boy must violate the law in order to learn of nature's ceaseless attention to his actions, just as in "Nutting" the boy must ravage the virgin bower before he can discover that "there is a spirit in the woods." Such experiences are necessary to the boy's moral and imaginative education, and they are never final because maternal nature always forgives. It is these experiences from which Wordsworth as a brother would protect his sister. Eliot's young sisters are just as much protected from experiencing such enlarging transgressions by their fear of losing the brother's love. The two kinds of brothers (Wordsworth, on the one hand and Tom and the brother of the sonnets on the other) share this trait of mediating, or attempting to, between their younger sisters and the sublime. They are linked only in this regard, standing otherwise for opposing values, but this connection suggests the significance of their opposition in Eliot's alignment of them.

Eliot's comments about reading Wordsworth, we have seen, like the change in Maggie's reading, reflect an ambivalent response to the authority of a text that seems both to foster and to subvert her originality. The temptation to silence or rote repetition is an especially feminine one, a temptation to docility and self-suppression. Thus though Eliot might like to write in congruence with a revered male authority, conforming as Wordsworth's silent sister might do, or as Maggie does in devoutly repeating the words of Thomas à Kempis, she cannot and does not want to do so in these gendered matters. To defend against being Wordsworth's sister (and perhaps in part also because Mary Ann Evans had such a brother), Eliot represents her heroines as sisters of explicitly anti-Wordsworthian brothers, so that to follow the authority of one is necessarily to contravene that of the other. Excluded from the Wordsworthian paradigm for continuity between a childhood spent with a guiding maternal nature and visionary imagination, Eliot and her female characters seek approval in brothers. But they find that the brother's approval is earned only by turning away from what the other brother, Wordsworth, would approve, the solitary world of the imagination, toward a world governed by the law of cause and effect. When Eliot's heroines are torn between the imaginary world of Wordsworth and the practical world of the other brothers, they thematize the tension between Eliot's desire to listen silently to or repeat Wordsworth and her desire to show that what she reads in his authoritative texts was originally her own. To have the heroine enter fully into the world of imagination would be to concur that there are no truths beyond Wordsworth's, while to have her wholly allied with the brother would be, for Eliot, to deny altogether the values she shares with Wordsworth. Defending herself from one powerful male authority by inventing (or trusting) another, Eliot finds a way to be at once original and deferential.

To repeat Wordsworth literally would in any case be a contradiction in terms. Eliot exploits this contradiction fully: to pay proper homage to Wordsworth would be to have him speak through her, as Maggie lets Thomas à Kempis speak through her; but to do so is necessarily to get Wordsworth wrong and thus to fail to pay proper homage. The more literally Maggie repeats the texts authoritative for her, and the more literally Eliot has her live out what seem to be Wordsworthian notions (in her repetitions of childhood experiences and in her desire for the home objects), the closer she comes both to perfect femininity and to death. But the more literal the repetition, the more divergent from, and subversive of, Wordsworth's aims, for to read Wordsworth literally in a female context is to become a realist. Where the Wordsworthian imagination interrupts or would interrupt between "What is" and "What will be," between material cause and effect, and between the introduction of a dark heroine and the certainty that her end will be unhappy, Eliot's heroines, in submitting to these laws, define a realistic fictional world. The literalizing that characterizes Maggie's adult feelings and actions (her love of the home objects, her desire for literal repetitions of her early life, and her repetitions of texts) is paralleled by Eliot's general turn toward what she persuades us is realism. For Maggie, literalization leads to her death, but it leads for Eliot to something definitively her own—her identity as a novelist of real life and of female experience, an identity that she establishes under cover of seeming to be a docile, feminine reader of her beloved Wordsworth. It is in fact Maggie's death that consolidates Eliot's vital independence from Wordsworth: Maggie dies of choosing social bonds over the self's needs. The scenes of Maggie's reading and instruction are also the scenes of Eliot's reading and instruction; but while Maggie fatally learns the lesson of feminine readership, Eliot fortunately fails.

* * *

DEIRDRE DAVID

Maggie Tulliver's Desire†

Veiled by an anonymity which may have concealed his identity but certainly not his magisterial male confidence, Henry James declared that 'the discursive portions of *Middlemarch* are, as we may say, too clever by half. The author wishes to say too many things, and to say them too well'.[1] The female character in Eliot's fiction who may be charged with a desire 'to say too many things, and to say them too well' is, of course, Maggie Tulliver. But where George Eliot lived on to write *Daniel Deronda* (if only to have it greeted by James as possessing an 'over-cultivated' sense of the 'universal'), Maggie's immodest presentation of her mind is tempered by her experience. As she grows up she restrains her desire to say 'too many things' and understands that saying them 'too well' earns male scorn rather than approbation.

I began my discussion of George Eliot with a scene in *The Mill on the Floss* which the anonymous reviewer for the *Dublin University Magazine* declared to be one where 'the woman's hand is unmistakably shown, and the lack of true perspective becomes most palpable'.[2] Eliot does indeed betray her 'woman's hand' by having Maggie Tulliver desire to possess as many books as the Rev. Walter Stelling, and by deploying strategies of containment to manage the conflict between female mind and male authority in a particularly intense and difficult way. I want now to return to *The Mill on the Floss* and to suggest that in this novel the conflict is at its most intense and the strategy of containment at its most problematical. Because the conflict in *The Mill on the Floss* also stems from Eliot's ambivalent views of past and present as well as from Maggie Tulliver's desire to say a lot of things and say them very well, I shall argue that strategies of containment are deployed by Eliot not only to manage the conflict between woman's mind and male authority: Eliot must confront her own ambiguous attitudes towards past and present. Figuring Maggie Tulliver as a metaphor, these strategies relegate past, present, ideology, and politics to the definitively ahistorical topos of death. In the drowning of Maggie Tulliver we see the destruction of all that constrains her.

Eliot's enigmatic assessment of her own historical time is signalled

† From *Intellectual Women and Victorian Patriarchy: Harriet Martineau, Elizabeth Barrett Browning, George Eliot* (Ithaca: Cornell UP, 1987) 209–24.

1. Quoted in David Carroll, ed. *George Eliot: The Critical Heritage* (London: Routledge and Kegan Paul, 1971) 359. [Editor]
2. Carroll 148. [Editor]

most clearly by her enduring preoccupation with the past which she sustained until setting her last novel a mere five years or so back in time from its composition. That she situates almost all her fiction in the historical past is interpreted by Steven Marcus as evidence of a desire to control the present. Order imposed on irregular, disjunctive events by narrative is the means to mastery of the present: 'By possessing the past we assert our possession of the present as well; by defining the past in a certain way we control the possibilities of the present.'[3] Elaborating Marcus's point, one might add that the slim hope of a better present is also implied by narrative closure: the finality of narrative ending we encounter at least up until *Daniel Deronda* shuts off the possibility of positive social or political change occurring in the present, for if the irrecoverable world is the superior one, then the feasibility of useful political action in the present seems uncertain. In Eliot's fiction, concentration upon the past also functions as reassurance for a society troubled at unsettling moments in history. By evoking in 1866 political turbulence and its stable resolution in the Reform Bill of 1832, *Felix Holt*, for example, offers implicit reassurance that history *will* repeat itself, not as tragedy or farce but as dramatic triumph of social order.

At the close of her *Westminster* article on Riehl, Eliot draws attention to certain aspects of his conservative social thought which she finds ideal: 'Riehl's conservatism is not in the least tinged with the partisanship of a class, with a poetic fanaticism for the past, or with the prejudices of a mind incapable of discerning the grander evolution of things to which all social forms are but temporarily subservient.'[4] If Eliot is affectionately partisan to any social class in her fiction, it is certainly not the one which encouraged and authorised her intellectual production: worthy as they are, the rural lower-middle-class ambitions of Caleb Garth to remain solvent, honest, hard-working, and surrounded by his happy family, are not those which directed Mary Ann Evans's transformation from intelligent, provincial girl to sibylline metropolitan intellectual. The interests of the class to which she is emotionally bound are not the interests which govern her career. Eliot does, however, return with some fanaticism to the past in her fiction, indeed with 'a poetic fanaticism' if one thinks of *Adam Bede* where, as Philip Fisher aptly observes, Mrs. Poyser's dairy 'is described with an intensity beyond realism.'[5] But that 'grander evolution of things to which all social forms are but temporarily subservient' is surely Eliot's secularised, and particularly Comtean, vision of a world unfolding according to a divine plan. *The*

3. "Literature and Social Theory: Starting in with George Eliot," *Representations: Essays on Literature and Society* (New York: Random House, 1975) 190. [Editor]
4. *Essays of George Eliot*, ed. Thomas Pinney (New York: Columbia University Press, 1963) 298–99. [Editor]
5. *Making Up Society: The Novels of George Eliot* (Pittsburgh: University of Pittsburgh Press, 1981) 64. [Editor]

Mill on the Floss reveals significant attitudes towards past and present, towards the social class which dominates St. Ogg's, and towards the sacrifice of an intellectually ambitious young woman to 'the grander evolution of things to which all social forms are but temporarily subservient'.

The elegaic discourse of *Adam Bede* implies that the world celebrated in that novel can never be recovered: the vital involvement of individuals with their community, the values embodied in Adam's fidelity to his family, in Dinah's power of sympathetic identification, in Mrs Poyser's spotless kitchen—all of this is part of what Peter Laslett terms the world we have lost.[6] Eliot's first narrator, in unfolding the sad story of Amos Barton, scoffs at the 'well-regulated mind' which rejoices in the 'New Police, the Tithe Commutation Act, the penny post, and all guarantees of human advancement'. Eliot fully develops this rejection of modern progress in her evocation of the lost world through the personification of 'Leisure' in *Adam Bede,* the most consciously pastoral of her novels. Because the joys of 'Old Leisure' partially express Eliot's implicit desire for a world unmolested by disruptive historical change, I shall quote the passage at length:

> Leisure is gone—gone where the spinning-wheels are gone, and the pack-horses, and the slow waggons, and the pedlars, who brought bargains to the door on sunny afternoons. Ingenious philosophers tell you, perhaps, that the great work of the steam-engine is to create leisure for mankind. Do not believe them: it only creates a vacuum for eager thought to rush in. Even idleness is eager now—eager for amusement: prone to excursion-trains, art-museums, periodical literature, and exciting novels: prone even to scientific theorising, and cursory peeps through microscopes. Old Leisure was quite a different personage: he only read one newspaper, innocent of leaders, and was free from that periodicity of sensations which we call post-time. He was a contemplative, rather stout gentleman, of excellent digestion,—of quiet perceptions, undiseased by hypothesis: happy in his inability to know the causes of things, preferring the things themselves. He lived chiefly in the country, among pleasant country seats and homesteads, and was fond of sauntering by the fruit-tree wall, and scenting the apricots when they were warmed by the morning sunshine, or of sheltering himself under the orchard boughs at noon, when the summer pears were falling. (*A.B.*, Ch. 52)

6. Laslett argues that the source of our 'feeling that there is a world which once we all possessed, a world now passed away, is the fact of the transformation of the family life of everyone which industrialism brought with it (*The World We Have Lost* [(New York: Charles Scribners Sons, 1973)], p. 19). His perception is born out by Eliot's invitation to the Victorian reader to peep in at the windows of the Hall Farm as it looked in 1799 and to witness the strong familial and communal ties that bind the Poysers to each other and to their community of farmhands.

In this hymn to pastoral serenity, the slowness of the waggon never caused interminable journeys in bad weather for hard-pressed agricultural labourers, the pedlar was never a surly character who haggled with weary housewives on a stormy day, and modern invention never the source of an improved way of life. The technological advances celebrated by Harriet Martineau are the direct object of Eliot's criticism: the railway, which for Martineau brought previously estranged social classes together and enabled town dwellers to see the seaside and dairy products and vegetables to be brought efficiently to the town, is, for Eliot, the means to gratify idleness. The museums, the technological developments in publishing, which are for Martineau a sign of an increasingly better educated and more rational-minded populace, are for Eliot a sign of cultural degeneration. Leaders similar to those written by Harriet Martineau for the London *Daily News* were, in Eliot's view, happily unavailable to 'Old Leisure'. The narrator disdains modern speed, modern eagerness for new ideas and new amusements, disdains all that Martineau celebrated in her ratifications of the achievements of the English middle class.[7]

To prefer newspapers free of political bias is to reject ideology; to prefer perceptions 'undiseased by hypotheses' is to perceive ideology itself as a symptom of diseased culture and society. The phrase 'undiseased by hypothesis' clearly echoes Carlyle's controlling image in the 'Characteristics' essay: in fact, those objects of the narrator's scorn in *Adam Bede*—periodical literature, exciting novels, concern with first causes—are Carlylean symptoms of a society sick with the disease of self-consciousness, and also the object of Elizabeth Barrett Browning's social criticism. 'Old Leisure' possesses an unusually relaxed cast of mind, tuned not to 'post-time', but to natural time measured by the rhythms of a mythologised country topos. In this ideal place untainted by ideology, a place somewhat reminiscent of Mr Boythorn's rustic paradise in *Bleak House*, time is so fixed that it becomes atemporal: it is always a sunny summer morning and the fruit is always fragrantly ripe. Relegating disruptive historical change to the space outside the mythologised country topos, keeping it, so to speak, on the other side of the 'fruit-tree wall', Eliot virtually literalises her strategy of containment.

In itself, Eliot's employment of pastoral idyll as Victorian social criticism is hardly remarkable; as the towns became dirtier, the urban populace more pressing, the demands for social justice more urgent, the mythological attractions of the country became that much more ap-

7. Martineau, *History of England* [(Philadelphia: Porter and Coates, 1864)] 4: 450. Eliot's attitudes towards the railway altered somewhat and by the time of *Middlemarch* she has Caleb Garth articulate a more accommodating view of technological progress in his mollification of the farm labourers who attack the railway surveyors with their pitchforks: 'Now my lads, you can't hinder the railroad: it will be made whether you like it or not. . . . Somebody told you the railroad was a bad thing. That was a lie. It may do a bit of harm here and there, to this and to that, and so does the sun in heaven. But the railway's a good thing' (p. 408).

pealing. Eliot adds her elegaic voice to a nineteenth-century chorus that began with Wordsworth's strong critique in the Preface to the *Lyrical Ballads*, which traces a 'multitude of causes, unknown to former times, [that] are now acting with a combined force to blunt the discriminatory powers of the mind, and, unfitting it for all voluntary exertion'. Wordsworth laments 'the increasing accumulation of men in cities, where the uniformity of their occupations produces a craving for extraordinary incident, which the rapid communication of intelligence hourly gratifies', and he roundly condemns a 'degrading thirst after outrageous stimulation'.[8] What is remarkable is that Eliot's deployment of the pastoral topos as the place where intolerable history is shut out aligns itself with her self-mythologisation as a traditional intellectual resistant to rupturing political change. Here it is only the slow history of *otium* that continues unmolested by alteration.

Where the passage from *Adam Bede* describing 'Old Leisure' argues that negative social and cultural change has taken place, that the self-conscious, self-interested present has destroyed the gentle, ideologically untainted, harmony of a mythical country life, the Proem of *Romola* postulates an unchanging, eternal 'human lot'. The tone, too, is markedly different, not merely by virtue of what is usually characterised as a maturity of novelistic and intellectual imagination, to say nothing of the difference between late eighteenth-century England and late fifteenth-century Florence. Where the narrator of *Adam Bede* is ruefully nostalgic, eventually if reluctantly reconciled to a changed social order, the narrator of *Romola* is majestically judgemental; where the narrator of *Adam Bede* speaks in a wryly resigned tone about social and cultural change, the narrator of *Romola* addresses the reader in the sibylline voice of a maturing 'George Eliot'. Philosophical and sagacious, the narrator speaks about history, culture, and society from above and beyond its determinants.

This narrator evokes a Renaissance 'spirit' of 1492 embodied in a student pondering the eternal mystery of human existence: he has been

> questioning the stars or the sages, or his own soul, for that hidden knowledge which would break through the barrier of man's brief life, and show its dark path, that seemed to bend no whither, to be an arc in an immeasurable circle of light and glory. The great river-courses which have shaped the lives of men have hardly changed; and those other streams, the life-currents that ebb and flow in human hearts, pulsate to the same great needs, the same great loves and terrors. As our thought follows close in the slow wake of the dawn, we are impressed with the broad sameness of the human lot, which never alters in the main headings of its

8. William Wordsworth, *Selected Poems and Prefaces* [ed. Jack Stillinger (Boston: Houghton Mifflin, 1965)], p. 449.

> history—hunger and labour, seed-time and harvest, love and death. (*R.*, p. 43).

This student displays that ambitious curiosity which impels Lydgate's research in *Middlemarch*: like Lydgate, he wants to penetrate the code of human genesis itself, to illuminate the 'dark path' of man's life which *seems* to have no direction, so that it may be seen as a curve in that 'immeasurable circle of light and glory', an image of coherent, radiant enclosure. In contrast to the pervasive insistence in *Adam Bede* upon a social and cultural degeneration, the narrator of *Romola* asserts that the human 'lot' remains unchanged. Eliot's image works to evoke immutable likeness between the 'streams' of natural and human existence; the flow of great rivers is evoked as a shaper of human life, a metaphor for what gives form to man's existence, and the flow of human blood in man's heart (literally and metaphorically) pulsates to unchanging feelings. 'Hunger, and labour, seed-time and harvest, love and death' are eternal 'headings' in the metaphorical text of man's life.

If we attempt to reconcile the 'Leisure' passage from *Adam Bede* and the Proem passage from *Romola* in Eliot's discourse of past and present, it would seem that what changes for the worse is the way in which man *chooses* to do his hungering and his labouring. However, the discourse of past and present becomes more complex when we read on in the Proem to *Romola*. The 'resuscitated spirit' of Florence in 1492 is not only a man hungering, labouring, and so on, but a man whose culture bears a more than passing resemblance to that of Eliot's own Victorian time. Our 'Spirit' turns out to have been

> not a pagan philosopher, nor a philosophising pagan poet, but a man of the fifteenth century, inheriting its strange web of belief and unbelief; of Epicurean levity and fetichistic dread; of pedantic impossible ethics uttered by rote, and crude passions acted out with childish impulsiveness; of inclination towards a self-indulgent paganism, and inevitable subjection to that human conscience which, in the unrest of a new growth, was filling the air with strange prophecies and presentiments. (*R.*, p. 48)

The contending values and manners of fifteenth-century Florence resemble those of nineteenth-century England; they imply the paradigms of conflict Victorians constructed for themselves as a means of giving order to the disturbing effects of rapid social change and unrest upon their lives. Creating such antinomic relationships is one way of understanding what was, perhaps, in actuality not so neatly assignable to such antithetical categories as 'belief and unbelief', 'levity' and 'dread', rigid 'ethics' and 'crude passions', and, in the dualistic assignment most suggestive of Eliot's participation in Comtean discourse, 'inclination' and 'subjection', the former suggesting egoistical choice and the latter acceptance of immutable laws of social progress.

Analysis of these passages from *Adam Bede* and *Romola* suggests that Eliot is saying at least three things: society and culture have changed irrevocably for the worse; despite these changes the human condition remains essentially the same; fifteenth-century culture is not unlike nineteenth-century culture and is probably no worse or better. Moreover, as further complication of Eliot's discourse of past and present, the nostalgic celebrations of the past are also sometimes disrupted by traces of attraction to the ideology very much present, so to speak, in the Victorian period: this is the ideology of self-advancement whose constitutive characteristic of disciplined work was not disdained by Eliot in her struggle to establish herself as a self-supporting woman intellectual in a male-dominated culture.

* * *

If there is one character in Eliot's fiction who bears the burden of this ideological conflict more than any other, it is Maggie Tulliver. In her, the past is symbolically the place of poetry, imagination, feeling; and in her, too, the present is both the place of an ambition born of aggressive intelligence and, by association, a sterile wasteland of facts and petit-bourgeois stocktaking. The struggle and eventual destruction of Maggie Tulliver may, in part, be read as a political metaphor, her social and cultural status as an intellectually ambitious, passionately imaginative young woman making her a figure who embodies and suffers ideological contradiction. Maggie Tulliver's provocative death cancels the immutable autonomy of the contending political views she metaphorically embodies, and, what's more, liberates her from a form in which she seems to have no home. Eliot's most problematic strategy of containment reveals itself in the relegation of Maggie Tulliver and all she metaphorically represents to the realm of death. Maggie dies in part because she bears the intolerable weight of contending ideas.

Eliot opens Book 4 of *The Mill on the Floss* with the narrator's assumption that the reader has journeyed down the Rhône and noted the dreary villages that stud the banks, the dismal sign of a lost but unlamented world:

> Strange contrast, you may have thought, between the effect produced on us by these dismal remnants of commonplace houses, which in their best days were but the sign of a sordid life, belonging in all its details to our own vulgar era; and the effect produced by those ruins on the castled Rhine, which have crumbled and mellowed into such harmony, the green and rocky steeps, that they seem to have a natural fitness, like the mountain pine: nay, even in the day when they were built they must have had this fitness, as if

> they had been raised by an earth-born race, who had inherited from their mighty parent a sublime instinct of form. (*M.F.*, p. 237) [221]

Eliot immerses us in river gloom and river glory.

The antinomy between Rhône and Rhine is that between disjunctive fragment and coherent unity. The ruins of Rhône village houses are 'dismal remnants', the ruins of Rhine castles have 'crumbled and mellowed' into such harmony with nature that they seem like trees. The castles were built by people who 'inherited' a 'sublime instinct of form', even if, as the narrator acknowledges, those people were robber-barons. Associating the fragmented ruins of the Rhône with contemporary Victorian communities, the former at best a 'sign of a sordid life' similar to that conducted by inhabitants of the present vulgar era, the passage shows that medieval France and the Victorian Midlands are governed by the rules of commonplace materialism. The people of St Ogg's, while not utterly condemned to river gloom, are certainly less than glorious. Although set back in time from the narrator's vulgar present and inhabiting a town pleasingly remarkable for its organic relationship to the landscape, they live a life whose values destroy Maggie Tulliver, the radiant antithesis of all that is connected with Rhône villages. Maggie Tulliver ambiguously belongs with the epic builders of Rhine castles. She possesses the qualities absent in St Ogg's, a place 'irradiated by no sublime principles, no romantic visions, no active, self-renouncing faith—moved by none of those wild, uncontrollable passions which create the dark shadows of misery and crime—without that primitive rough simplicity of wants, that hard submissive ill-paid toil, that childlike spelling-out of what nature has written, which gives its poetry to peasant life' (*M.F.*, p. 238) [222].

What the Dodsons, the Pullets and the Gleggs lack is to be found in Maggie Tulliver—she signifies an active and vital transcendence of St Ogg's materialism in the way her life *is* governed by sublime principles, romantic visions and self-renouncing faith. And she, too, possesses the seemingly less heroic qualities which the narrator delineates in the above description, yet in her they are transfigured by virtue of her heroic subjugation by the debasing worldliness of her community. Her passion is wild and uncontrolled, leading her most certainly to misery and to a social 'crime' as she transgresses the sexual code; in her childhood her wants are primitive and rough, and her tragedy is that she must continue to 'spell-out' as an adult what 'nature'—in the form that her community understands as the correct expression of a 'naturally' fine intelligence—has inscribed for her. She brings poetry, if not to a peasant life, then certainly to the petit-bourgeois world of perennial stock-taking, whether it be in terms of the linens and 'chiny' cherished by her mother and her aunts or the land fiercely possessed by her father and her uncles.

The worldly lives of Maggie Tulliver's relations are, as we can see, defined in negative terms: not enlightened, not sublime, not romantic, lacking principles and visions. It is Maggie Tulliver's unhappy fate to possess qualities aligning her with the vital pre-industrial era, with the robber barons who rode away 'to die before the infidel strongholds in the sacred East', an era eradicated, in the largest historical sense, by the aggressive mercantilism of the class to which her relations belong. This is the respectable, rural, petit-bourgeoisie, whose values the narrator summarises in these terms: 'Obedience to parents, faithfulness to kindred, industry, rigid honesty, thrift, the thorough scouring of wooden and copper utensils, the hoarding of coins likely to disappear from the currency, the production of first-rate commodities for the market, and the general preference for whatever was home-made' (*M.F.*, p. 239) [223]. The positive meaning of such attributes as obedience, faithfulness, honesty, and thrift is syntactically undermined by a taxonomy that makes domestic cleanliness semantically equivalent to fidelity to one's family; such an arrangement can, of course, raise cleanliness to a high virtue, but it can also reduce all the virtues of the Dodsons to mere commodities. If one considers that St Ogg's tends to commodify everything that passes along the Floss, the latter possibility is more likely. Eliot concludes that the 'vices and virtues' of the Dodson character are 'phases of a proud, honest egoism, which had a hearty dislike to whatever made against its own credit and interest'. Refusing the moral demand that she establish moral credit by marriage to Stephen Guest, Maggie Tulliver is destroyed by values expressed in mercantile language. 'Credit' and 'interest' do indeed 'make' life along the Floss and, if accumulated against the merchants of St Ogg's, would destroy their power and reputation.

Maggie Tulliver has no such power, she 'discredits' herself in the Stephen Guest episode, loses credibility in her community, and can earn no 'interest' upon herself. Her strength is in her intellect and in her aggressiveness, and her weakness is in her sex and gender. If she had been a man, if, indeed, she were Tom rather than Maggie, the intelligence would have found a place and function in the community. St Ogg's culture and society would have licensed the direction of that intelligence to social renovation, would have appropriated potentially disruptive moral interrogation for improvement of the community. Maggie's intellectual vitality, therefore, may be aligned with the male drive for self-advancement which built St Ogg's. Unhappily for her, then, she is not only associated with the epic past, but is also implicated in the aggressive, mercantile present whose values she subverts with that intelligence embodied in her stunning female form. Maggie Tulliver must eventually be destroyed by Eliot for she bears the weight of irreconcilable ideologies, so powerful in their individual autonomy that they can only lead to a self-cancellation. She is poetry, feeling, epic grandeur, aggressive intelligence, the best of the past and the hope of the future. It is her present which remains highly problematical.

What's more, Maggie Tulliver is not only the highly charged metaphor for historical, cultural and political contradiction, she is also a character in a novel, possessing all the individual yearning in conflict with social authority we connect with fictive characterisation. In her association with those Rhine Castles which 'thrill' the narrator with a 'sense of poetry', those ruins which 'belong to the grand historic life of humanity', Maggie may be read as a metaphor for 'high culture' trapped in the form of the novel. She is doomed to a form of Lukácsian homelessness: in literal exile from her childhood home, in moral exile from her community, she possesses a kind of epic grandeur making her unfit for survival in the prosaic realism and historical contingency associated with the novel as a genre. As the adolescent Maggie sits by the bed of her paralysed father, looking at the 'dull walls' of the room that is the 'centre of her world', Eliot describes her as a 'creature full of eager, passionate longings . . . yearning for something that would link together the wonderful impressions of this mysterious life and give her soul a sense of home in it' (*M.F.*, p. 205) [194]. Her yearning intensified by her sex and gender, like so many of Eliot's women characters, she longs to make connections, to discover a pattern that will explain her universe, to find gratifying expression of her woman's intelligence.

That female intelligence is a burden is made clear to Maggie at the age of nine when the St Ogg's auctioneer and appraiser, Mr Riley, is appalled by the vivid acuity she displays in interpreting illustrations for Defoe's *The History of the Devil*. Her retreat from humiliation is the attic of the mill where she keeps a 'fetish', the trunk of a large wooden doll, whose most significant part is its head. Driving nails into it, grinding and beating it against the brick chimneys, the humiliated and enraged child Maggie punishes the head of the doll as she is punished for her own 'head', for her own acute intelligence. Maggie's head becomes a compelling image of female intelligence in the novel. She cuts off her luxuriant dark hair as a child, hoping that her cleverness will shine more clearly: as she stands cropped before a dazed Tom she feels 'a sense of clearness and freedom, as if she had emerged from a wood into the open plain' (*M.F.*, p. 56) [55]. Wanting to punish her own intellect and also to display it, wanting to be thought feminine by her provincial culture and also to free herself from reification into a mere object of womanly attractiveness, she is trapped in and by her conflicting desires. Cropping the extraordinary hair which is the sign of her gender, she aggressively displays her intelligence. In giving herself the appearance of being a boy, she symbolically punishes herself for being an intelligent girl, almost as if she fictively repeats Mary Ann Evans's cropping of her female identity so that she may 'appear' as 'George Eliot'.

At the end of Book 2, their father's financial failure behind them, Tom and Maggie enter 'the thorny wilderness, and the golden gates of their childhood had for ever closed behind them'. Her vibrant pleasures mixed with painful humiliation, tormented by her longing for Tom's love and for familial acceptance of her acuteness, Maggie can hardly be said to have had a 'golden' childhood. Here, the Edenic image suggests that Maggie falls into a painful, developed form of the knowledge she possessed as a child: she passes into a thorny wilderness of the conflict between a desire to use her mind and the restraints of her provincial culture. Exiled at the significant age of thirteen from Eliot's ambiguously mythologised prelapsarian childhood, Maggie falls into full knowledge of the limitations imposed upon intelligent women in early nineteenth-century England. She passes through those 'golden gates' into a society where the one thing she possesses that might enable her to survive that passage, her moral intelligence, is the source of her eventual defeat.

Some feminist critics have tried to redeem Maggie's grief and destruction; they see the melodramatic drowning less as instance of Eliot writing herself into a corner, than as a tonic instance of the woman novelist emerging victorious through subversion in the battle for control of sexual and aesthetic ideology. A serious problem with these readings is that they tend to rehearse the Victorian dualisms of man equals rational thought and woman equals passionate feeling.

Exploring the problematic of whether the 'female self' can only be conceived in terms of resistance to plot, Gillian Beer concludes that Eliot 'rescues Maggie from the grim, cramped future that the social determinism of the plot has seemed to make inescapable'. Nancy Miller believes that as Maggie refuses Stephen Guest, so Eliot refuses plausibility: dominant ideology in the form of male fictions, in expected resolutions according to male form, is rejected for 'the peculiar shape of a heroine's destiny in novels by women'. Mary Jacobus believes that the novel's notorious ending signifies subversion of dominant discourse, a reaching beyond the analytic and realistic modes to 'metaphors of unbounded desire'.[9] Where in Miller's view dominant ideology is refused by rejection of plausibility, in Jacobus's formulations dominant ideology is refused by rejection of rational discourse. While these two readings offer suggestively fresh interpretations of Eliot's fiction, they have nagging implications: Eliot rejects plausibility and stable discourse for skittishness, flux, instability, and wanton metaphor. She may emerge as triumphant over dominant ideologies of form and imagery, but her victory is achieved through methods conventionally and negatively associated with female thought and practice.

9. See Gillian Beer, 'Beyond Determinism: George Eliot and Virginia Woolf' [in *Women Writing and Writing about Women*, ed. Mary Jacobus (New York: Barnes and Noble, 1979)]; Nancy K. Miller, Emphasis Added: Plots and Plausibilities in Women's Fiction [*PMLA* 96 (1981): 36–47]; Mary Jacobus, 'The Question of Language: Men of Maxims and *The Mill on the Floss*' [printed in this volume, pages 543–57]. William Myers interprets the ending as a conflict between 'meliorist' and 'realistic' perspectives. His study, in general, insists that we always comprehend what Eliot 'intends' in her fiction. Nowhere, however, does he refer to what Eliot may have 'intended' about Maggie's problems with sex and gender (*The Teaching of George Eliot* [Leicester: Leicester UP, 1984]).

A more particularised political reading of Maggie Tulliver is less compatible with an opposition between the female dissatisfaction of women novelists and male orders of representation. Such a reading shifts the ground from subversion of conventional modes of fictional representation to subversion of the structures of society that both produce, and are produced by, ideologies of form. Plot and metaphor, fiction itself, are elements of a discursive formation that is, in its turn, an element of a larger order of social discipline—the ideologies of the dominant middle class that constitute and are constituted by a number of modes of discourse, the novel among them. Miller and Jacobus confine their readings to what Frederic Jameson terms an 'ideologeme': as he defines it, 'the smallest intelligible unit of the essentially antagonistic collective discourses of social classes'[1]—or, to cast this in terms of feminist criticism, we can see the 'ideologeme' as 'the essentially antagonistic collective discourses' of women novelists and male-dominated ideologies of form.

If we argue that through the destruction of her heroine Eliot expresses her antagonism to conventional modes of fictional representation, then we must also allow that she expresses her antagonism to the social classes which authorise, by their patronage, those conventional modes. Through the destruction of Maggie, Eliot may be said to express her antagonism to two related institutions: one, the petit-bourgeois social class which has both created and rejected Maggie; and two, the form of the popular novel which as well as dictating logical resolutions of erotic confusion and female dissatisfaction, is also the favoured form of the petit-bourgeoisie. It is important to remember here that Eliot did not consider herself an 'ordinary' novelist. She worked on *The Mill on the Floss* from April to "December 1859 and in the following June, before she had started *Silas Marner* and with the reception of *The Mill* fresh in her mind, she wrote to an old Swiss friend to correct Continental confusions between Dinah Mulock and herself: 'The most ignorant journalist in England would hardly think of calling me a rival of Miss Mulock, a writer who is read only by novel readers, pure and simple, never by people of high culture. A very excellent woman she is, I believe, but we belong to an entirely different order of writers'.[2] If Eliot writes for people of 'high culture', then St Ogg's is a community of 'novel readers, pure and simple'.

Writing from an earlier critical perspective, Leslie Stephen also noted disjunction in Eliot's plot: Stephen Guest is a 'provincial narcissist' and Maggie's attraction to him 'jars upon us, because it is not a development of her previous aspirations, but suddenly throws a fresh and unpleasant light upon her character' (*George Eliot*, p. 103). Stephen does not de-

1. *The Political Unconscious: Narrative as Socially Symbolic Act* (Ithaca: Cornell UP, 1981) 76. [Editor]
2. *The George Eliot Letters*, ed. Gordon S. Haight, 9 vols. (New Haven: Yale University Press, 1954–78) 3: 302. [Editor]

velop a definition of this unpleasant light, but what he objects to, perhaps, is the pleasure Maggie derives from the attentions of a physically attractive and socially powerful figure. The appeal of Stephen Guest lies in his status as the provincial and pampered narcissist Leslie Stephen perceives him to be. The relationship between Maggie and Stephen is a struggle for sexual power: he masters her reluctance to get in the boat and so compromises her that, in the view of all concerned, she must elope with him. But she refuses in her own exercise of power, in fact in the only means of power available to her, that of a moral superiority expressed in Eliot's discourse of past and present: 'If the past is not to bind us, where can duty lie? We should have no law but the inclination of the moment' (*M.F.*, p. 417) [385]. Maggie's unhappy, even existentialist, freedom comes from realising that she is powerless to escape the determinants of her past life in the form of familial ties to Tom, her cousin Lucy, and of moral ties to her community. The dilemma in which she finds herself leads, in effect, to a privileged, and tragic, form of consciousness. Her bitter recognition is that the only power and freedom to be achieved comes from understanding that neither woman nor man is free from the contingencies of history. In this recognition she accepts the restrictions and suffering that history places upon her and she acknowledges her burdensome intelligence as enabling such a bittersweet understanding. The woman intellectual who created this character in all likelihood experienced another, related understanding: Eliot's acute intelligence surely made her painfully conscious of how history both limited other intellectual women and permitted her own dazzling eminence.

And what Maggie understands, too, is the power of her own will and the miserably restricted opportunities she has to exercise it. Throughout her life, she has struggled to renounce that will, has spent two years of her life from the age of 17 to 19 with the mirror turned to the wall, has slept on the floor (a form of punitive self-enlightenment adopted by Dorothea Brooke after she sees Rosamund Lydgate and Will Ladislaw together), has agonised about whether she should forego the indulgent pleasure of walking in the Red Deeps. What Eliot seems to articulate through Maggie Tulliver's experience is that in the provincial society which she, as Mary Ann Evans, left behind in her journey to metropolitan celebrity, the *only* expression for an intelligent female self is renunciation of that self. Maggie's intellectual being is relegated by this strategy of containment to a topos of *moral choice*, a territory patrolled by women in the Victorian period. Actively renouncing the self, showing that renunciation is the only means of expression for a self denied any other form of activity, Maggie seems to possess an ironic understanding of what is happening to her. When she refuses Stephen's wrenching appeal, Eliot says of her, 'She had made up her mind to suffer' (*M.F.*, p. 416) [384]. What distinguishes Maggie Tulliver from all of Eliot's other women characters who experience a conflict between the drive of their own minds and the punitive governance of their fathers, husbands, brothers, indeed of their male culture, is that she consciously makes a choice—even if it is the choice to suffer.

Sadly and powerfully, then, the primary contradiction embodied in Maggie Tulliver is that between her vital intelligence and her confining gender. Because she is so splendid in so many ways, because she can symbolise that intellectual and moral progress involved in the struggle of young people 'to rise above the mental level of the generation before them', because she can metaphorically bear the weight of so much (the grand poetic past, the driving, fertile present, a morally better future) she can only die. All remains autonomous, locked in ideological contention in this character, and all seems to deny reconciliation, to demand only one strategy of containment—the relegation of Maggie to a place where intolerable history has no meaning. As Maggie Tulliver drowns in the Floss, she makes an end to ideology and she is the end of ideology. She ends ideology in her death and her death is the result of ideological conflict.

I suggested earlier that in identifying narrative paradigms or in analysing rhetorical figures, it is essential also that we identify and analyse those larger systems of signification producing the paradigms and the larger systems of social relationships reproduced in rhetorical figures. If we do that, if we identify these broader systems, we must confront, of course, the androcentric culture which enabled Eliot's success as a woman intellectual. Maggie Tulliver, then, along with all her other ideological burdens, carries the weight of Eliot's own dilemma: how to reconcile her complicity with and her resistance to patriarchal attitudes?

Eliot, as we know, does not reconcile her conservative sexual politics (primarily expressed in her letters and essays) with the desires of her female characters for cultural and social autonomy and to believe that she should have is to bring to her work those unfair expectations I spoke of at the beginning of my discussion. I submitted that Eliot's success leads us to ask more from her than we do from other Victorian women intellectuals and that we sometimes unfairly expect Eliot's intelligence, learning, and fame to have made her more strongly resistant to a male-dominated culture. I have aimed to work against such unfair expectations and have tried to elucidate in Eliot's work the conflict *inherent* in her position as iconised woman intellectual in Victorian patriarchy. Eliot's own conflicts, of course, do not give us the primary hermeneutic key to *The Mill on the Floss*. Maggie Tulliver's death is radically overdetermined and Eliot's most intelligent and unhappy female character is vanquished on a number of ideological fronts. In the death that unites sister and brother, she is destroyed as an intellectually ambitious young woman and as a metaphorical representation of a way of life eradicated by the materialism of St Ogg's; she is also destroyed as a character whose consciousness is produced *by* the historical forces of St Ogg's and whose epic grandeur dislocates her from the contingent social realism of the popular novel. And, lastly, she dies, perhaps, as an emblem of irresolvable contention between the Victorian containment of woman to an undeveloped intellectual life and the elevation of one woman intellectual to iconic sagehood. For me, Maggie Tulliver embodies more movingly than any other character in Eliot's fiction the conflict felt by an intelligent woman living in an androcentric world. Feeling the sadness of *The Mill on the Floss* is tonic antidote to immersion in the myth of 'George Eliot', iconic sage. To defend itself against the anomalous conjunction of rigorous mind and female body, Victorian patriarchy created this myth, but it was also created by Mary Ann Evans—an intellectual woman who lived with the painful knowledge that to be 'George Eliot' was to *be* an anomaly.

Chronology

1819	Mary Anne Evans born in Warwickshire, November 22.
1844–46	Translates Strauss's *Das Leben Jesu.*
1852–54	Serves as assistant editor of *The Westminster Review.*
1854	Translates Feuerbach's *Das Wesen des Christenthums.* Goes to Germany as the common-law wife of G. H. Lewes.
1855–56	Translates Spinoza's *Ethics.*
1857	Publishes her first fiction, *Scenes from Clerical Life*, in *Blackwood's Magazine* under the pseudonym George Eliot.
1859	*Adam Bede*
1860	*The Mill on the Floss*
1861	*Silas Marner*
1862–63	Publishes *Romola* in *Cornhill Magazine.*
1866	*Felix Holt, the Radical*
1868	*The Spanish Gypsy*
1871–72	*Middlemarch*
1876	*Daniel Deronda*
1878	G. H. Lewes dies.
1879	*Impressions of Theophrastus Such*
1880	Marries John Walter Cross. Dies in London.

Selected Bibliography

This bibliography does not include those works from which the excerpts above have been taken.

Arac, Jonathan, "Rhetoric and Realism in Nineteenth-Century Fiction: Hyperbole in *The Mill on the Floss*." *ELH* 46 (1979): 673–92.

Auerbach, Nina. "The Power of Hunger: Demonism and Maggie Tulliver." *Nineteenth-Century Fiction* 30 (1975): 150–71.

Beer, Gillian. *George Eliot*. Bloomington: Indiana UP, 1986.

Bennett, Joan. *George Eliot: Her Mind and Art*. Cambridge: Cambridge UP, 1948.

Carroll, David, ed. *George Eliot: The Critical Heritage*. London: Routledge & Kegan Paul, 1971.

Christ, Carol. "Aggression and Providential Death in George Eliot's Fiction." *Novel* 9 (1976): 130–40.

Ermarth, Elizabeth. "Maggie Tulliver's Long Suicide." *Studies in English Literature* 14 (1974): 587–601.

Fraiman, Susan. "*The Mill on the Floss*, the Critics, and the *Bildungsroman*." PMLA 108 (1993): 136–50.

Gilbert, Sandra M. and Susan Gubar. *The Madwoman in the Attic: The Woman Writer and the Nineteenth-Century Literary Imagination*. New Haven: Yale UP, 1979.

Graver, Suzanne. *George Eliot and Community: A Study in Social Theory and Fictional Form*. Berkeley: University of California Press, 1984.

Haight, Gordon S. *George Eliot: A Biography*. New York: Oxford UP, 1968.

Haight, Gordon S., and Rosemary T. VanArsdel, eds. *George Eliot: A Centenary Tribute*. Totowa: Barnes and Noble, 1982.

Hardy, Barbara. *The Novels of George Eliot: A Study in Form*. London: Athlone, 1959.

———. *Particularities: Readings in George Eliot*. Athens: Ohio UP, 1983.

Harvey, William John. *The Art of George Eliot*. New York: Oxford UP, 1962.

Kucich, John. *Repression in Victorian Fiction: Charlotte Brontë, George Eliot, and Charles Dickens*. Berkeley: U of California P, 1987.

McGowan, John P. "The Turn of George Eliot's Realism." *Nineteenth-Century Fiction* 35 (1980): 171–92.

Miller, Nancy K. "Emphasis Added: Plots and Plausibilities in Women's Fiction." *PMLA* 96 (1981): 36–48.

Newton, Judith Lowder. *Women, Power, and Subversion: Social Strategies in British Fiction, 1778–1860*. Athens: U of Georgia P, 1981.

Pinney, Thomas, ed. *The Essays of George Eliot*. New York: Columbia UP, 1963.

Redinger, Ruby V. *George Eliot: The Emergent Self*. New York: Knopf, 1975.

Sadoff, Dianne F. *Monsters of Affection: Dickens, Eliot, and Brontë on Fatherhood*. Baltimore: The Johns Hopkins UP, 1982.

Showalter, Elaine. *A Literature of Their Own: British Women Novelists from Brontë to Lessing*. Princeton: Princeton UP, 1977.

Shuttleworth, Sally. *George Eliot and Nineteenth-Century Science: The Make-believe of a Beginning*. Cambridge: Cambridge UP, 1984.

Stump, Reva. *Movement and Vision in George Eliot's Novels*. Seattle: U of Washington P, 1959.

Welsh, Alexander. *George Eliot and Blackmail*. Cambridge: Harvard UP, 1985.

Wilt, Judith. *Ghosts of the Gothic: Austen, Eliot, and Lawrence*. Princeton: Princeton UP, 1980.